W9-BQJ-515

DATE DUE

JAN 1 0 2005		
GAYLORD		PRINTED IN U.S.A.

introduction
to
the
old
testament

JAMES KING WEST

CATAWBA COLLEGE

Introduction to the

old

testament

second edition

Macmillan Publishing Co., Inc.
New York

Collier Macmillan Publishers
London

Copyright © 1981, James King West.

Printed in the United States of America

Earlier edition copyright © 1971 by Macmillan Publishing Co., Inc.

This book and its companion, *Introduction to the New Testament: "The Word Became Flesh,"* by Donald J. Selby, are available in a one-volume edition entitled *Introduction to the Bible,* by Donald J. Selby and James King West, copyright © 1971 by Macmillan Publishing Co., Inc.

The Scripture quotations in this publication are from the Revised Standard Version of the Bible, copyrighted 1946 and 1952, by the Division of Christian Education, National Council of Churches, and used by permission.

Selections from *Ancient Near Eastern Texts Relating to the Old Testament,* ed., James B. Pritchard (3rd edition, with Supplement, copyright © 1969 by Princeton University Press) reprinted by permission of Princeton University Press.

Macmillan Publishing Company
113 Sylvan Avenue, Englewood Cliffs, NJ 07632

Library of Congress Cataloging in Publication Data

West, James King (date)
   Introduction to the Old Testament.

   Bibliography: p.
   Includes indexes.
   1. Bible.   O.T.—Introductions.   I. Title.
BS1140.2.W478   1981   221.6'1   80-15139
ISBN 0-02-425920-9

PRINTING   12 13 14 15   YEAR   4 5

ISBN   0-02-425920-9

Dedication

To my mother and late father,
Pearl C. and Charles T. West,
whose love for the Bible
prompted my early curiosity
as to its meaning.

preface

to the Second Edition

In the decade since the first edition of this book was written, scholarly study of the Old Testament has proceeded at a rapid pace and has undergone significant changes of direction. Some of the "assured results" of the past are being opened to question, neglected dimensions of the literature are being rediscovered, and new interpretive methods are being applied. If a consensus on many items of literary, historical, and theological import is accordingly more difficult to discover, the new developments bring nevertheless a fresh and stimulating atmosphere to the exploration of the Old Testament's multi-faceted message. It is to take account of these changes that *Introduction to the Old Testament* has been extensively revised, expanded, and brought up to date in this second edition.

Since many of the new studies relate to methods of interpreting and utilizing the Old Testament, the introductory chapter, which treats these concerns, has been largely rewritten. The renewal of interest in these books as canon, i.e., their appropriation as the normative expression of the Judaeo-Christian faith, is reflected in the expanded discussion of the canon's formative history in Judaism, Catholicism, and Protestantism. A review of recently developed exegetical techniques has been added, along with further evaluation of the results of the older methods. For convenient reference, charts and lists showing the extent and order of the Judaic and Christian canons, the growth of the Old Testament literature, and the variety of its literary forms are included.

Substantial revision of Israel's early history prior to the Davidic monarchy (see chapters 1, 2, and 3) has been necessitated by a steadily growing body of archaeological material, new appraisals of the social and economic patterns of tribal and pastoral societies, and reexaminations of the biblical record itself. The current questioning of older reconstructions of the periods of the patriarchs, Exodus, conquest, and tribal league, and the appearance of provocative new historical models, make it imperative that students of the Old Testament be apprised of the viable alternatives and the evidence upon which they are built. Thus, the strengths and weaknesses of the major proposals are evaluated and the as-yet-unanswered questions are kept before the reader.

The new edition reflects the awakened interest in the wisdom literature: the efforts to determine its genre, its social and intellectual setting in Israel, and its extent and limits within the Old Testament corpus. Not only has the section on wisdom (see chapter 8) been recast, but portions of the Old Testament only recently included in some wisdom classifications are examined with the wisdom question in view.

Readers familiar with the first edition of the book will note considerable expansion in other areas also, including new theories of Pentateuchal composition, forms of prophetic address, redactional elements in the prophetic books, and recent archaeological finds relating to the period of the Hebrew monarchy. In addition, attention is directed to numerous new studies through footnotes and notations in the text, as well as up-dated bibliographies at the end of each chapter and the general bibliography in the appendix. Finally, the new edition includes a table locating the literary sources in the Pentateuch, a revised chart of Pentateuchal development, and some fresh photographs and drawings.

Notwithstanding these changes, the aim of *Introduction to the Old Testament* remains the same, namely, to provide a clear yet thorough text for introducing the literary, historical, and theological dimensions of the Old Testament in a manner consistent with the best standards of contemporary scholarship. The book's wide adoption as a text at colleges, universities, and theological schools of varying style, size, and religious or secular affiliation, appears to bear out its practical versatility as a teaching tool. It is hoped that in its revised and expanded form it will better serve the continuing needs of classroom instructors, students, and other readers.

Acknowledgments

The author extends his gratitude to all those professors, students, colleagues, and others who have passed along their helpful comments and suggestions, many of which have influenced the changes incorporated in the new edition. He wishes to thank especially Kenneth J. Scott, College and Professional editor at the Macmillan Company, and Hurd Hutchins, production editor, for their technical assistance and counsel with the project; Old Testament scholars Dr. James L. Crenshaw, Dr. Alan J. Hauser, and Dr. James L. Pace, and colleagues Dr. Donald J. Selby, Dr. Martha H. Morehead, Dr. J. Daniel Brown, and Dr. James L. Gillespie, for the benefit of their seasoned and balanced judgments on questions concerning the content and format of the book; typist Nancy Trexler and student assistants Debbie Potter, Charles Sigler, and Keith Valencourt for outstanding service; and, finally, his wife, Dr. Martha Kirkland West, for sharing in both the labor and joy of this, another mutual undertaking.

J.K.W.

preface

————•◦•————

to the First Edition

This book is offered as a basic introduction to the collection of religious writings known to Catholics as the Old Testament (Proto- and Deutero-canons), to Protestants as the Old Testament with Apocrypha, and to Jews as the Tanak plus other major pre-Talmudic works. It is designed for the reader, of whatever religious or theological persuasion, who seeks to understand how these books originated, the history and culture of the people who produced them, and the characteristic ideas which they contain.

Considering the number of Old Testament introductions already available, it is pertinent to ask, "Why another one?" The answer is not that some pioneering methodology or totally new set of interpretations is here being tested. Rather, the purpose of this book is to make available to as wide a range of readers as possible the accumulated results of modern Old Testament scholarship, and to do so in a manner that combines the advantages of both the familiar literary and historical organizational methods. It has arisen out of the practical needs of classroom teaching, in which the weakness of either of these approaches alone have become increasingly apparent. The finest of the literary introductions leave historical and cultural backgrounds all but untouched, whereas in the recent spate of books employing the historical approach crucially significant literary units are unavoidably split apart or otherwise bypassed altogether.

The organizational pattern adopted for this work follows the broad divisions of the Hebrew canon. Such an approach allows the reader to see the Law, Prophets, and Writings in the framework created for them by the same Hebrew tradition which produced the books. It also avoids, on the one hand, undue rearrangement of the literature for the sake of debatable chronological or theological schemes, and, on the other hand, the ill-advised neglect of important literary units and categories (*e.g.*, Pentateuch, legal codes, prophecy, psalmody, wisdom, apocalyptic) that results from efforts to compress the entire Old Testament into a strict historical framework. To follow the canon, moreover, is to begin with the Torah and Former Prophets, and thus to lay the necessary historical background without which the remainder of the Old Testament is largely unintelligible. At only one point is it felt advisable to compromise our method and deviate from the canonical arrangement, namely, in the books of the Latter Prophets. These books, though beset with problems as to the dates of their final editions, are far more intelligible when treated in the historical order of appearance of the prophetic figures themselves—a sequence which, for the most part, can be established with reasonable confidence.

Since there is no substitute for reading the Old Testament first-hand, the reader is advised to keep a copy of the Bible close at hand for use with this book. To lessen the labor of constant referral, however, Biblical passages crucial to the discussion are often quoted. The English translation employed throughout, unless otherwise indicated, is the Revised Standard Version. In discussions involving extrabiblical texts, care has been taken to provide sufficient detail for the benefit of the reader without access to the primary sources. James Pritchard's *Ancient Near Eastern Texts Relating to the Old Testament* and its abridged paperback edition, *Ancient Near East*, contain most of these sources, and provide handy references for further readings in this area.

Acknowledgments

This book was written as a companion volume to *Introduction to the New Testament* by my colleague, Dr. Donald J. Selby. Consequently, there has been extensive collaboration between us in an effort to produce volumes suitable for use in courses following an Old Testament–New Testament sequence. I am indebted to him for countless insights incorporated into the design and detail of my work, and most especially for extensive assistance with the final chapter.

Special acknowledgments are also due a number of other persons. Dr. J. L. Crenshaw of Vanderbilt University, Dr. Harry E. Jenkins, Jr. of Oklahoma City, and Dr. A. J. Mattill, Jr. of Winebrenner Theological Seminary have painstakingly read the manuscript and made invaluable suggestions. Also, Rabbi Jack Bemporad, Director of the Commission on Worship, Central Conference of American Rabbis, has read much of the material and offered helpful counsel. My colleague Dr. Richard Schiemann has not only provided several of the photographs that appear here, but has borne some of the burden of my teaching load, thereby allowing me additional time for this project. Dr. Martin L. Shotzberger, President of Catawba College, Dr. Charles Turney, Academic Dean, and Dr. Daniel Kirk, former Dean, have been equally understanding of the time demands. Mr. Charles E. Smith, Editor of the College and Professional Division of The Macmillan Company, has provided the editorial guidance, encouragement, and no small degree of patience that have seen this work through to completion. For technical assistance I have depended heavily upon Professors Martha Kirkland and Martha Morehead and Dr. Hans Roemer of the Catawba faculty, the staff of the Catawba Library, my students George Fouts and Gary Hauze, and typists Allene Selby, Margaret Handfield, Velma Booth, and Sandra Reitz.

My indebtedness to teachers in the fields of Old Testament and Judaism under whom I have studied includes especially Drs. J. Philip Hyatt, Lou H. Silberman, Walter Harrelson, Eric Rust, Solon Cousins, and Vernon S. McCasland.

J.K.W.

contents

————•I•————

1
O, HOW I LOVE THY LAW

CONTENTS

II

ALL HIS SERVANTS THE PROPHETS

III

THE OTHER BOOKS OF OUR FATHERS

Lists

Maps

Drawings

Photographs

Abbreviations

ANE	James Pritchard, *The Ancient Near East*
ANET	———, *Ancient Near Eastern Texts Relating to the Old Testament*
BA	*Biblical Archaeologist*
BA Reader	*The Biblical Archaeologist Reader* (3 vols.)
BAR	*Biblical Archaeology Review*
BASOR	*Bulletin of the American Schools of Oriental Research*
BHT	Beiträg zur historischen Theologie
BJRL	*Bulletin of the John Rylands Library*
BTB	*Biblical Theology Bulletin*
BWANT	Beiträg zur Wissenschaft vom Alten und Neuen Testament
BWAT	Beiträg zur Wissenschaft vom Alten Testament
BZAW	Beihefte zur *Zeitschrift für die Alttestamentliche Wissenschaft*
CBQ	*Catholic Biblical Quarterly*
CBQMS	*Catholic Biblical Quarterly* Monograph Series
DOTT	D. Winton Thomas, *Documents of Old Testament Times*
HTR	*Harvard Theological Review*
IB	*The Interpreter's Bible*
ICC	The International Critical Commentary
IDB	*The Interpreter's Dictionary of the Bible* (vols. 1–4)
IDBS	*The Interpreter's Dictionary of the Bible, Supplementary Volume*
Int	*Interpretation*
IOVCB	*The Interpreter's One-Volume Commentary on the Bible*
JAAR	*Journal of the American Academy of Religion*
JBC	*The Jerome Biblical Commentary*
JBL	*Journal of Biblical Literature*

JBR	*Journal of Bible and Religion*
JNES	*Journal of Near Eastern Studies*
JSOT	*Journal for the Study of the Old Testament*
JTC	*Journal for Theology and the Church*
JTS	*Journal of Theological Studies*
KJV	The King James Version of the Bible
LXX	The Septuagint (Greek) Version of the Bible
MT	The Masoretic (Hebrew) Text of the Old Testament
NEB	The New English Bible
RB	*Revue biblique*
RE	*Review and Expositor*
RL	*Religion in Life*
RSV	The Revised Standard Version of the Bible
ST	*Studia Theologica*
TSTS	*Toronto Semitic Texts and Studies*
VT	*Vetus Testamentum*
VTS	Supplements to *Vetus Testamentum*
WMANT	Wissenschaftliche Monographien zum Alten und Neuen Testament
ZAW	*Zeitschrift für die Alttestamentlische Wissenschaft*
ZTK	*Zeitschrift für Theologie und Kirche*

Introduction

The Old Testament is in many respects the most remarkable collection of books ever written. It has been sacred to Jews and Christians for the past two thousand years,[1] and its influence has probably exceeded that of any other single literary work. So basic and pervasive has been its effect on Western culture, that even persons who have never read its books are affected daily by the cultural patterns which derive from them.

The Old Testament's archetypal themes of creation, fall, judgment, exodus, exile, and restoration are basic to much of our modern literature, drama, music, and art, reflecting a powerful if sometimes subtle influence on the way we view ourselves and our world.[2] Such familiar book titles as Steinbeck's *East of Eden* and Camus' *The Fall* and such productions of the American stage as McLeish's *J.B.* and Chayefsky's *Gideon*, attest this widespread presence in modern fiction and theater. Blake's Job etchings and Chagall's Jerusalem windows contemporize through art the ancient Israelite's struggle toward faith, even as Mendelssohn's oratorio *Elijah* confronts its hearer with the power of the Hebrew prophet, and the contemporary folk song *Turn, Turn, Turn* renews Ecclesiastes' reflections on "a time for every matter under heaven."

In innumerable ways our Western governmental and legal systems are undergirded by principles of social justice and personal worth which derive in part from the Old Testament books of the Law and the Prophets. The recent impetus toward civil rights, particularly for black persons in American society, finds its most effective symbols in the Hebrew Exodus from Egyptian bondage and the prophets' protest against political and economic oppression. Even the current struggle for women's rights is not unrelated to the same basic principles of individual worth and freedom.[3]

---

[1] Islam also recognizes portions of the Old Testament as divinely revealed, but regards Jewish and Christian versions as lacking the authenticity that is supplied only by the Koran.

[2] The treatment of Old Testament themes in some of the classic art, poetry, music, and fiction of the past may be seen in the anthology of Cynthia Pearl Maus, *The Old Testament and the Fine Arts* (New York: Harper & Row, Publishers, 1954).

[3] This is not to ignore the separate status and inequality of women in many aspects of ancient Hebrew religion. It is, however, to agree with Phyllis Trible that "the intentionality of

1

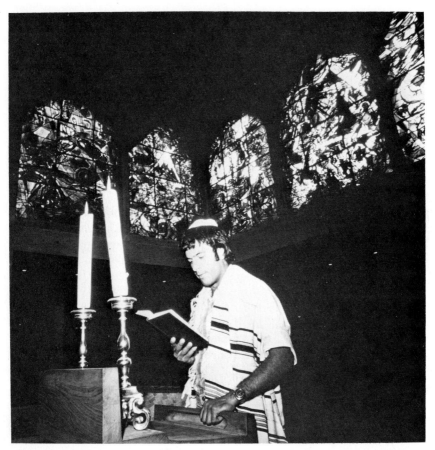

Synagogue of the Hadassah Hospital, Jerusalem. Since the late Old Testament period, synagogues have served in Judaism as centers for the reading and study of the biblical books. The Hadassah synagogue contains twelve stained glass windows depicting the twelve tribes of Israel—painted by Marc Chagall. (Courtesy of the Israel Government Tourist Office.)

No one who is concerned with human history can afford to ignore the Old Testament, because more than a thousand years of the Near Eastern past is recorded within its pages. There is no other source to which one can go for a record of the origins and early history of the Jewish people. The Old Testament preserves, as well, a rich body of information concerning other early Middle Eastern cultures and religions, some of which, such as the Philistine, Moabite, and Edomite, left behind few records of their

biblical faith, as distinguished from a general description of biblical religion, is neither to create nor to perpetuate patriarchy but rather to function as salvation for both women and men." ("Depatriarchalizing in Biblical Interpretation," *JAAR*, XLI [1973], p. 31).

own. A clear understanding of Christian history, moreover, would be impossible without these earlier books, which are basic to its heritage.

The Old Testament is remarkable also because the Hebrew people who are central to its narrative continue as a living cultural and national entity in our time, embodying in their corporate life many of the ancient motifs and aspirations of these books. The recent history of the Jews, notably the grim episode of the Nazi holocaust and the emergence of the modern state of Israel, activate a host of ancient images from the turbulent biblical history, from bondage and conquest to exile and restoration, and thereby renew the timeless paradigm of the Jew as the inordinate sufferer and the inveterate believer.

In all these respects and many more, the Old Testament appeals to a broad spectrum of cultural, historical, literary, artistic, and ethical interests, assuring its continuing study by persons of all faiths who seek a better understanding of themselves and their world. But, without doubt, these books have their strongest appeal for those persons who approach them as a canon, i.e., as a guide for religious faith and practice. For the Old Testament is first and foremost a collection of religious books, created by faith and addressed to persons who share that faith. Its basic premise is the reality of the living God of creation and history, and its primary aim is to expose the active purpose of God at work within the world. We shall begin this study of the Old Testament, therefore, by examining the peculiar authority of these books within the communities of faith which have preserved and revered them, giving particular attention to the processes by which they attained this special status.

1. THE OLD TESTAMENT CANON

Canon is the technical term used to describe the Bible in its peculiar role as authoritative literature, having been first employed in this sense by the fourth-century Church Father Athanasius.[4] The transliteration of a Greek word, derived in turn from an old Babylonian term meaning "reed" or "papyrus rod," canon expresses the concept of a measure, standard, or norm. In its original sense it referred literally to a long, straight reed, used as a measuring stick or ruler. As such, it designates those writings accepted as the standard for belief and conduct—the divinely given rule or guide.

Since the Church inherited these books from the older Judaism, and since it also possessed its own peculiarly Christian books based on the witness of the apostles and early Church, there developed separate designations for the two-part Christian canon, i.e., the "Old Testament" (Old

---

[4] *De decretis Nicaenae synodi*, 18.3. Athanasius used the term in reference to the books of the New Testament; later it came to be used for both testaments.

Covenant) and "New Testament" (New Covenant).[5] *Testament* or *covenant* expresses the function of the literature as the written conditions governing the relationship between God and his people, and thus, like *canon*, denotes the unique authority of the books. Much the same meaning is implied by the earlier names employed in the New Testament and among the early Church Fathers, such as "the scripture(s)," "the sacred writings," "the book of Moses," and the like.[6] It was the sense of a distinct written collection set apart from all other books that led eventually to the designation *"the* books" (Greek: *ta biblia*), or "Bible," by which name most persons know the canon to this day.[7]

The Talmud and other early Jewish writings likewise employ designations suggestive of a written norm, for example, "the holy scriptures," "what is written," "the book," or "the twenty-four books."[8] To the rabbis who produced the Talmud these were books that "defile the hands" because of their superlative holiness.[9] Whereas "Old Testament" is a distinctively Christian title, a characteristically Jewish name is the acronym "Tanak," formed from the initial consonants of the Hebrew titles for the three broad divisions of the Jewish canon: *Torah* (Law), *Nebi'im* (Prophets), and *Kethubim* (Writings). Not infrequently the word Torah, which designates the books of Genesis through Deuteronomy, is used in reference to the entire canon.

THE THREE CANONS. The Old Testament is not the same in all Bibles, as a glance at the accompanying canonical lists will reveal. In the course of canonization, i.e., the process by which canonical authority was attained, there developed differing traditions as to the books which properly belong in the collection, their titles, arrangement, and enumeration. The small community of Samaritans of northern Palestine, for example, accept as canonical only the five books of the Torah. Among the larger Judaeo-Christian communions, however, there are three major Old Testament canons: (1) the Jewish, (2) the Roman Catholic (and Eastern Orthodox), and (3) the Protestant.

The most notable contrast among these three canons concerns the larger number of books included in the Roman Catholic and Orthodox collections.

---

[5] The earliest known usage of the title "Old Testament" in reference to the Hebrew Bible was by Melito, Bishop of Sardis, c. A.D. 180. "New Testament" was used as a designation for the Christian writings by Tertullian c. A.D. 200. For the biblical background of this usage, cf. Jer. 31:31–34, Luke 22:20, I Cor. 11:25, and Heb. 8–10.

[6] Cf. Mark 12:24, 26; Luke 24:32; John 2:22; Acts 8:32; Rom. 1:2; I Cor. 15:3–4; Gal. 3:22; II Tim. 3:15–16; I Clement 43:1, 45:2, 53:1.

[7] The earliest known usage of *ta biblia* as a canonical designation is in II Clement 14:2, written toward the middle of the second century A.D.

[8] Cf. Philo, *The Life of Moses* I, 23; II, 290, etc.; Josephus, *Antiquities of the Jews* I, iii, 13; X, iv, 210, etc.; Mishnah: *Yadaim* 3.2, 5; 4.6; *Shab.* 16.1; *Er.* 10.3, etc.

[9] Cf. Mishnah: *Yadaim* 3,5.

4

1. THE OLD TESTAMENT CANON

In respect to formal titles, there are twenty-four books in the Jewish Old Testament, thirty-nine in the Protestant, forty-five in the Orthodox, and forty-six in the Roman Catholic. The difference between the Jewish and Protestant enumerations is purely formal, however, and is easily explained: the twelve books of the Minor Prophets in Christian Bibles (Hosea through Malachi) are counted as a single book in Hebrew tradition ("The Book of the Twelve"); so too are I and II Samuel, I and II Kings, I and II Chronicles, and Ezra-Nehemiah. The Christian enumeration follows the pattern of the Septuagint, the Greek translation of the Hebrew Old Testament which was produced by Jews in Egypt before the time of Christ and served as the early Church's Bible. Thus, the books of the Jewish and Protestant Old Testaments are identical, differing only in their titles and arrangements within the collection.

The Roman Catholic and Orthodox canons include additional books known to Catholics as the Deuterocanon and to Protestants as the Apocrypha. These additions appear both in the form of separate books and as supplements to the books of Esther and Daniel. Written by Jewish authors toward the end of the biblical period, they circulated in both Palestine and Egypt and were included among the books of the Septuagint. Judaism does not extend canonical status to these books and Protestants either omit them altogether or set them apart as a secondary collection. Catholicism accepts them as fully canonical, but distinguishes them from the rest of the Old Testament ("Protocanon") as "Deuterocanon" ("second canon," i.e., books accepted as canonical at a later date). The churches of Eastern Orthodoxy have, in large part, followed a canonical tradition differing only slightly from that of the Roman Church.[10]

The different arrangement of the books in the Jewish and Christian canons is also associated with the early Church's use of the Septuagint. Whereas the Jewish canon's division into Law, Prophets, and Writings corresponds to the three stages of Hebrew canonical development, the Septuagint (and hence Christian) order resulted from a combination of factors, including a concern for chronology, subject matter, and reputed authorship. In both traditions practical considerations, such as the size of a book, were sometimes determinative of the sequence.

The Torah (or Pentateuch, i.e., "five books") stands at the beginning of both Jewish and Christian Bibles. Containing the narrative and legal traditions associated with Israel's great founder and lawgiver Moses, as well as stories of universal and pre-Mosaic beginnings, it is basic to all that follows. Not only does the Torah provide the traditional account of Israel's origins, but—of primary significance—it preserves the conditions of the covenant that is to bind the nation to its God, Yahweh.[11]

[10] See below, pp. 19–20 and fn. 40.
[11] On the divine name "Yahweh"—familiar to readers of some English Bibles as "Jehovah"—see below, p. 62, fn. 8.

THE BOOKS OF THE OLD TESTAMENT

JEWISH CANON	ROMAN CATHOLIC AND ORTHODOX CANONS	PROTESTANT CANON
The Law (Torah)	*The Pentateuch*	*The Pentateuch*
1. Bereshith (Genesis)	1. Genesis	1. Genesis
2. Shemoth (Exodus)	2. Exodus	2. Exodus
3. Wayiqra (Leviticus)	3. Leviticus	3. Leviticus
4. Bemidbar (Numbers)	4. Numbers	4. Numbers
5. Debarim (Deuteronomy)	5. Deuteronomy	5. Deuteronomy
The Prophets (Nebi'im):		
The Former Prophets	*The Historical Books*	*The Historical Books*
6. Yehoshua (Joshua)	6. Joshua	6. Joshua
7. Shophetim (Judges)	7. Judges	7. Judges
	8. Ruth	8. Ruth
8. Shemuel (Samuel)	9–10. I–II Samuel	9–10. I–II Samuel
9. Melakim (Kings)	11–12. I–II Kings	11–12. I–II Kings
	13–14. I–II Chronicles	13–14. I–II Chronicles
	15. Ezra	15. Ezra
	16. Nehemiah	16. Nehemiah
	17. Tobit*	
	18. Judith*	
	19. Esther‡	17. Esther
The Latter Prophets		
10. Yeshayahu (Isaiah)		
11. Yirmeyahu (Jeremiah)		
12. Yehezqel (Ezekiel)		
13. Tere Asar (The Twelve)		
	The Poetical and Wisdom Books	*The Poetical and Wisdom Books*
The Writings (Kethubim)	20. Job	18. Job
	21. Psalms	19. Psalms
14. Tehillim (Psalms)	22. Proverbs	20. Proverbs
15. Mishle (Proverbs)		
16. Iyyob (Job)	23. Ecclesiastes	21. Ecclesiastes
	24. Song of Solomon	22. Song of Solomon
17. Shir Hashirim (Song of Songs)		
	25. Wisdom of Solomon*	
	26. Ecclesiasticus* (Wisdom of Ben Sirach)	
18. Ruth		
19. Ekah (Lamentations)		
20. Qoheleth (Ecclesiastes)		
21. Ester (Esther)		
22. Daniel		
23. Ezra-Nehemyah (Ezra-Nehemiah)		
24. Dibre Hayamim (Chronicles)		
	The Prophetic Books	*The Prophetic Books*
	27. Isaiah	23. Isaiah
	28. Jeremiah	24. Jeremiah
	29. Lamentations	25. Lamentations

THE BOOKS OF THE OLD TESTAMENT

JEWISH CANON	ROMAN CATHOLIC AND ORTHODOX CANONS	PROTESTANT CANON
	30. Baruch †	
	31. Ezekiel	26. Ezekiel
	32. Daniel ‡	27. Daniel
	33. Hosea	28. Hosea
	34. Joel	29. Joel
	35. Amos	30. Amos
	36. Obadiah	31. Obadiah
	37. Jonah	32. Jonah
	38. Micah	33. Micah
	39. Nahum	34. Nahum
	40. Habakkuk	35. Habakkuk
	41. Zephaniah	36. Zephaniah
	42. Hagaai	37. Haggai
	43. Zechariah	38. Zechariah
	44. Malachi	39. Malachi
	45. I Maccabees *	
	46. II Maccabees *	

*Deuterocanonical (Apocryphal) book; included as fully canonical only in Roman Catholic and Orthodox canons.
†Book included as fully canonical (Deuterocanon) only in the Roman Catholic canon.
‡Book that includes supplements in Roman Catholic and Orthodox canons. This supplementary material appears in the Protestant Apocrypha as Additions to Esther and Additions to Daniel (The Story of Susanna, The Song of the Three Young Men, and The Story of Bel and the Dragon).

The books known in Jewish tradition as the Former Prophets (Joshua, Judges, Samuel, and Kings) continue the Torah's narrative by tracing the Hebrew history from Moses' death to the Babylonian Exile—some six or more crucial centuries of the Israelite past (c. thirteenth to sixth centuries B.C.). The use of the name "Prophets" for these books of history reflects either a tradition of their prophetic authorship or the fact that they contain stories about some of Israel's earliest prophets. The Christian canons emphasize the historical character of the books by joining them not with the Latter Prophets, as in the Jewish canon, but with several historical books of the Writings and (in Catholic Bibles) the Deuterocanon. Ruth takes a position following Judges, reflecting the setting of its story in the period of the Judges (c. 1200–1000 B.C.), and the books of I–II Chronicles, Ezra–Nehemiah, and Esther extend the Israelite history into the Persian period (539–333 B.C.). In the Catholic canon, the Deuterocanonical Tobit, Judith, additions to Esther, and I–II Maccabees trace Israel's fortunes yet further into the Maccabean era (2nd century, B.C.). The effect of this arrangement for Protestant and Catholic canons is to bring together in a nearly consistent sequence the entirety of the early Hebrew history from its beginnings to the period of post-Exilic restoration and beyond.[12]

The Jewish books of the Latter Prophets are distinguished from the Former Prophets in that they contain oracle collections of Israel's great "writing prophets." Three of the collections i.e., Isaiah, Jeremiah, and Ezekiel, were sufficiently lengthy to require an entire scroll for each book, and thus are known as the Major Prophets. The brevity of the collections in the Book of the Twelve (the Minor Prophets) allowed them to be copied together on a single scroll in Jewish Bibles. Thus the sequence of the prophetic books, which is the same in both Jewish and Christian canons, was determined in part by the practical consideration of size. Although the books of the Major Prophets appear in the chronological sequence of the spokesmen whose names they bear and the same principle appears to have guided the order of the Minor Prophets, by a modern reckoning at least three of the latter group are chronologically misplaced, i.e., Amos, who prophesied slightly before the time of Hosea, and Joel and Obadiah, who very likely are the latest of the entire group. Christian canons situate the book of Daniel, the hero of which is traditionally regarded as a prophet, immediately following the Major Prophets; and Lamentations is made to follow Jeremiah, reflecting a tradition of Jeremianic authorship. In Catholic Bibles, Lamentations is followed by yet another work traditionally associated with Jeremiah, i.e., the book of Baruch. The Orthodox canon omits the latter book.

The *Kethubim* or "Writings" is a catch-all title given the remainder of the books of the Jewish Bible. Representing a variety of literary genres (hymnody, wisdom, short stories, history, and apocalyptic) and religious concerns (worship, instruction for living, hope amidst persecution, etc.), these eleven books attained a fixed order in Hebrew Bibles only after the invention of the printing press. Since that time they have been traditionally grouped as poetical books (Psalms, Job, and Proverbs); festal scrolls, i.e., books to be read on the occasion of religious festivals (Song of Songs, Ruth, Lamentations, Ecclesiastes, and Esther); and history (Daniel, Ezra-Nehemiah, and Chronicles).[13] As we have just seen, Christian Bibles distributed some of these books among the works of history and prophecy, largely in the interest of chronology. Several nonhistorical books of poetry and wisdom remained apart, however, and were placed between the historical and the prophetical collections. Each of these books was associated with a prestigious figure of the biblical past: Job, David (Psalms), Solomon (Proverbs, Ecclesiastes, Song of Solomon, and Wisdom of Solomon), and Ben Sirah (Ecclesiasticus).

---

[12] The historical sequence in the Christian canon involves some repetition in I and II Chronicles and slight backtracking in Tobit, Judith, and Esther.

[13] Cf. the Talmud, *Baba Bathra* 14b, where the order is Ruth, Pss., Job, Prov., Eccles., Song of Sol., Lam., Dan., Esther, Ezra–Neh., and Chron.

1. THE OLD TESTAMENT CANON

The titles of the books in Jewish Bibles are in the Hebrew language, in which all but a few parts of the Old Testament are written.[14] Often they consist of the opening word (e.g., *Bereshith*, "In the beginning") or a key word (e.g., *Bemidbar*, "In the wilderness") from the book.[15] Christian titles derive from the Septuagint's Greek titles and purport to describe the book's contents, author, or central personality. Until recently, Roman Catholic Bibles in English, such as the Douay–Rheims Version, followed the Latin Vulgate spellings; but with the recent publication of the Catholic Confraternity Bible (NAB)[16] the spellings current in Protestant Bibles have been adopted for Catholic Bibles as well.

The Formation of the Old Testament Canon

Basic to a consideration of the canon is the question of how the Old Testament books achieved their special status. Why did these specific books, and not others, become the revered scriptures? The question, of course, recognizes the production and circulation of other Hebrew books during and shortly after the biblical period. The earliest of these books, which included works of poetry, history, and prophecy, no longer survive except in the allusions, quotations, and data derived from them now preserved in the canonical books. We read, for example, of a lost Book of Jashar, a Book of the Acts of Solomon, Chronicles of the Kings of Israel and Judah, and books by various prophets, such as Samuel, Nathan, Gad, and others.[17] Some of the later and extant noncanonical works have long been grouped together in a collection known to Protestants as the Pseudepigrapha and to Catholics as the Apocrypha (not to be confused with the Protestant Apocrypha, i.e., Deuterocanon).[18] Other books have more recently come to light in the discovery of the Dead Sea Scrolls, which include the writings of an Essene Jewish sect[19] that lived near the Dead Sea from the mid-second century B.C. until A.D. 68. We may safely assume that yet other writings were produced in early Israel, about which we know nothing at all because they have long since perished and are without mention in any of the surviving literature.

The concept of a canon implies a termination point and thus a final decision that no more books would be admitted to the normative collection.

---

[14] The following portions of the Jewish Bible are written in Aramaic, a sister Semitic tongue which came into common use among Jews of the late biblical period: Dan. 2:4b–7:38; Ezra 4:8–6:18, 7:12–26; Jer. 10:11; and one phrase in Gen. 31:47.

[15] *Biblia Hebraica*, however, one of the most widely used scholarly editions of the Hebrew Bible, employs the Septuagint titles for the books.

[16] *The New American Bible* (New York: P. J. Kenedy & Sons, 1970).

[17] Cf. Josh. 10:13; II Sam. 1:18; I Kings 11:41; 14:19, 29; I Chron. 29:29; II Chron. 9:29; 12:15; 13:22; 20:34; 32:32, etc.

[18] Cf. R. H. Charles, ed., *The Apocrypha and Pseudepigrapha of the Old Testament* (Oxford: Clarendon Press, 1913), 2 vols.

[19] Cf. below, pp. 501–504.

Two columns of a Qumran (Dead Sea) manuscript. Although many of the Dead Sea manuscripts are Old Testament books, some are sectarian works. Shown here is a portion of a nonbiblical scroll, known as the Manual of Discipline or Community Rule. (Courtesy of the Israel Department of Antiquities and Museums.)

For Judaism this came by the end of the first Christian century or shortly thereafter; but the Church deferred a final pronouncement on its Old Testament canon until the period of the Protestant Reformation (16th cen. A.D). It is necessary to recognize, however, that no Rabbinic or Church council acting on behalf of Judaism, Catholicism, or the Protestant churches could possibly have established these books by formal decree had they not already enjoyed a long history of use within the respective worshiping communities. That is to say, canonization was the result of a centuries-long development, whereby only those writings which proved useful for faith and worship were elevated to such a decisive role. One writer describes the process as follows:

> Like the growth of a tree, which passes imperceptibly from the stage of a sapling that might be transplanted, to the stage where it is impossible to remove it, save by felling, canonicity grew imperceptibly.[20]

[20] H. H. Rowley, *The Growth of the Old Testament* (New York: Harper Torchbooks, 1963), p. 173.

1. THE OLD TESTAMENT CANON

CANONIZATION IN JUDAISM. In a real sense, the beginning of canonization in Israel did not await the completion of any one of the three divisions of the Hebrew Bible. Rather, it began during the very time when the books were being produced, since their production typically involved a process of selecting, combining, and reformulating older oral and written traditions from the Hebrew past. As the Old Testament was thus put together bit by bit over its long literary history, we may assume that judgments were repeatedly being made as to which traditions voiced the authentic faith of Israel. Such decisions did not belong solely or primarily to the literary figures or schools that produced the canonical books but to the community of faith that provided the oral tradition from which the writers drew, and, once the traditions were put to writing, accepted, preserved, and used the books for the inspiration and instruction they offered.[21]

Modern scholars have attempted to distinguish within the canonical history an original, authoritative, and motivating category or function that directed Old Testament development and thereby guided the canonical process.[22] Some perceive such a criterion in the concept of law. The Old Testament, of course, portrays Moses as a lawgiver, and, as a part of the Torah, the law codes occupy a pre-eminent place in Judaic faith. The earliest record of the promulgation of an authoritative book to guide Israel's corporate life, moreover, refers to a book of law, generally identified as an early edition of Deuteronomy, established by King Josiah's 622 B.C. reform movement in Judah (II Kings 22–23). Two centuries later, in the period of restoration following Judah's exile in Babylon, the reformer Ezra (c. 428–?) read to the people of Jerusalem from a book of law (Neh. 8), perhaps the entire Torah, which is believed to have been compiled by a priestly circle in Babylonian exile (587 B.C. and following). That the Torah attained to full canonical status in Israel prior to the other portions of the Old Testament, there can be no doubt, and by one way of reckoning, the books of the Prophets and Writings were received into the canon as interpretation and commentary on the Torah. Thus, it is held, did Israel build its authoritative traditions around the concept of God's legal requirements for his people.

Another theory, however, consistent with postbiblical Judaism's stress on prophetic inspiration as scripture's distinguishing feature, conceives prophecy or inspired utterance as the definitive criterion of Old Testament canonization. Only those traditions were accepted which had some claim to containing utterances of divinely inspired spokesmen, whether prophets, priests, or sages. The prime example is the great spokesman, Moses, whose traditional reputation as Israel's foremost prophet was invoked for the authority of the Torah.

---

[21] On this broad interpretation of canonization, cf. James A. Sanders, *Torah and Canon* (Philadelphia: Fortress Press, 1972).

[22] For a brief review of the theories resulting from these efforts, cf. Lou Silberman, "The Making of the Old Testament Canon," *IOVCB*, pp. 1213–1215.

Yet a third position stresses the function of cultic recital as explanation of the canon's growth. The Old Testament is approached as a confessional literature which extols the mighty actions of God in guiding the history of the Israelite people and in entering into covenant with them. The canon's development is thus explained as the growth of those traditions which originated in worship settings, as Israel recited its faith or renewed its covenant with God. Such an approach takes into account the importance of the Old Testament narrative—the story of Israel's history of salvation—as a unifying element in the canon. The Torah, itself, consists not simply of a set of laws, but relates as well the story of Israel's deliverance from Egyptian bondage, which establishes the basis for God's claims to the nation's obedience. Likewise, the prophets' summons to faith draw heavily upon the story of God's gracious dealings with his people.

Although each of these approaches sheds important light on the Hebrew canon, it is impossible to explain the complex history of canonization by means of a single concept, category, or function. In point of fact, not all of the Old Testament will fit into the pattern of law, nor prophecy, nor recital of history. Indeed, some parts of the canon, notably the wisdom books (Proverbs, Job, Ecclesiastes), resist all these categories. It seems best, therefore, to allow for a variety of patterns that guided Old Testament canonization, all of which attested to Israel's conviction that God had a claim on the life of nation and individual and had revealed himself through the manifold witness of Law, Prophets, and Writings.

Since early in this century it has been widely held that the three divisions of the Hebrew Bible correspond with a three-staged history of canonization, whereby the collections achieved canonical status by the following approximate dates: the Law by c. 400 B.C., the Prophets by c. 200 B.C., and the Writings by A.D. 90 or 100.[23] The last of these stages has been traditionally associated with the so-called council of Jamnia, where the final deliberations about the Jewish canon are assumed to have occurred. It is now apparent that this portrayal of events is in need of qualifications at a number of points.[24]

The Law. It has already been noted that by Ezra's time, near the end of the fifth century B.C., the post-Exilic Jewish community possessed a book of the law which may have been an early edition of the Torah. It is clear

[23] A full statement of this traditional portrayal of canonization may be found in R. H. Pfeiffer, *Introduction to the Old Testament* (New York: Harper & Row, Publishers, 1941), pp. 50–70, or idem, "Canon of the Old Testament," *IDB*, A-D, pp. 498–520.

[24] Two important technical studies advocating revisions of aspects of the traditional version of canonization are Jack Lewis, "What Do We Mean by Jabne?" *JBR*, XXXII (1964), pp. 125–132, and Albert Sundberg, *The Old Testament of the Early Church* (Cambridge, Mass.: Harvard University Press, 1964). Recent summary articles incorporating the newer insights are Raymond E. Brown, "The Canon of the Old Testament," *JBC*, pp. 518–524, and John H. Hayes, *An Introduction to Old Testament Study* (Nashville, TN: Abingdon Press, 1979), pp. 15–44.

Reading the Torah at the Wailing Wall. The ancient practice of recording the Torah on scrolls is still maintained in Judaism. The Sabbath Torah reading shown here takes place in Jerusalem—at the western wall of the huge platform upon which the Jewish temple once stood. (Courtesy of the Israel Government Tourist Office.)

that Ezra established this book as the authoritative guide for Judah's corporate life and found in it the program for the reforms which he instituted (Neh. 8–10). What is not so clear, however, is whether Ezra's lawbook included the entire Torah as we know it today. At least one argument long used for the canonization of the Torah by this time (c. 400 B.C.) no longer appears valid, i.e., the traditional fourth century date for the separation of the Samaritan sect from the main body of Judaism. As the Samaritans possessed a version of the Torah (the Samaritan Pentateuch) and accepted these five books, and no others, as scripture, it follows that the Torah had already achieved canonical status in Judaism prior to the Samaritan schism. Recent evidence indicates, however, that the Samaritan schism may have occurred as late as the second century B.C., thus rendering this datum useless as proof for a fourth century Torah-canon in Israel. The earliest indisputable evidence for the independent existence and scriptural status of the Torah as a whole is the translation of these books into Greek in the third and second centuries B.C. and the custom of Sabbath Torah readings in the synagogues, which are attested by that time. To many scholars, nevertheless, there appears no conclusive reason for doubting what is probably the viewpoint of the author of the Ezra account (Neh. 8–10), that the Torah in something like its present form became Judaism's scripture by Ezra's time.

Although the Torah contains some (originally oral) traditions as old or older than the Mosaic era (c. 13th century B.C.), in its final form it is a product of the exiled Jewish community in Babylon. Presumably, it was from there that Ezra brought it to Judah. The motives which prompted its compilation and establishment as the authoritative guide of the post-Exilic Jewish community are not difficult to conceive. In the Babylonian destruction of Judah, Jewish faith was dealt a shattering blow. Following four centuries of self-rule, Judaism was suddenly bereft of its land, temple, and political independence. The exiled Jews perceived that they were reliving the plight of their homeless ancestry who had wandered the Sinai desert in the Exodus era. They were convinced, nevertheless, that God's covenant with Israel, under which Moses had led his followers to the land of promise, availed for the current generation of exiles. Thus, by putting the covenant narrative and legal obligations into a fixed and definitive form, a program for Israel's future restoration was assured.[25]

The Prophets. The experience of exile and the subsequent hope for restoration also account for the growth in authority of the books of the prophets. Such information as we possess about the pre-Exilic prophets suggests that their warnings of national disaster were given a deaf ear by many if not most of their contemporaries.[26] Judah's fall and exile, however, vindicated the worst of their predictions and thereby added stature to the surviving collections of their oracles. Nor was it overlooked that the prophets' messages reflected the same element of hope inherent in the Torah. In thus assisting the exiles to perceive that Judah's fall was no defeat of God's purpose, but, rather, an inevitable consequence of the nation's folly, the prophetic books offered encouragement for a new beginning beyond the disaster.

[25] A perceptive analysis of the Exile's effect on the formation of the canon is offered by James A. Sanders in *Torah and Canon.*

[26] This point receives particular emphasis in James L. Crenshaw, *Prophetic Conflict* (Berlin/New York: Walter de Gruyter, 1971), ch. 5.

1. THE OLD TESTAMENT CANON

Post-Exilic prophets continued to appear for a time following the return of exiles to Judah, but more and more the living witness of the prophet gave way to the written word of Torah and the scholar or rabbi who served as its interpreter. In time, the rabbis came to believe that prophecy had ended with Ezra. This being the case, it was imperative to assure the preservation of the great prophetic collections in which Judaism rediscovered its unique identity as the chastened nation of promise.

The earliest indication of the existence of a collection of prophetic books is found in the book of Ecclesiasticus. Its author, Ben Sirah, who wrote about 180 B.C., alludes to a succession of persons and events as they appear in the books of the Former and Latter Prophets.[27] Whether he knew these books as scripture is impossible to say; but by the time of his grandson, who translated his work from Hebrew to Greek in 132 B.C., they clearly had gained scriptural status. In his prologue to Ecclesiasticus the grandson refers to "the law and the prophets and the other books of our fathers," revealing that the prophets had attained to a position alongside the Torah. Also there are references to the law and prophets in portions of the Dead Sea Scrolls which appear to date from the latter part of the second century B.C.[28] Further evidence appears in the fact that the book of Daniel (written c. 165 B.C.) was not included among the prophets in the final Hebrew canon, as it most likely would have been had not the prophetic collection already reached its limits before the book was either written or well known. We must be careful to note, however, that the exact titles and number of books in this second-century B.C. collection cannot be determined.[29]

The Writings. The books mentioned in the vague reference of Ben Sirah's grandson as "the other books of our fathers" without doubt included some of the books later given the nondescript title *Kethubim.* Thus, as early as the second century B.C., the stage was being set for the expansion of the Jewish canon by its third and final collection. It is unclear, however, precisely how this development took place. According to one long-held theory, two distinctly different canonical traditions prevailed in Judaism until the end of the first century A.D. Palestinian Jews, it is said, accepted a smaller number of books than did Greek-speaking Jews in Alexandria, who produced the Septuagint version with its additional books.[30] Recently, however, it has been argued that prior to the closing of the canon both Palestinian and Alexandrian Jews envisioned a fluid or open-ended scripture, without fixed limits of any sort.[31] Beyond the books of the Torah

[27] Ecclus. 46–49.

[28] *The Manual of Discipline (Community Rule)*, col. 8; *The Damascus Document (Damascus Rule)*, col. 7 (Geza Vermes, *The Dead Sea Scrolls in English* [New York: Penguin Books, 1962], pp. 86, 104).

[29] The indirect evidence of Ecclus. 44–49 allows no basis for certainty on this matter.

[30] Cf. R. H. Pfeiffer, *Introduction to the Old Testament*, pp. 65–70.

[31] Cf. Albert Sundberg, *The Old Testament of the Early Church.*

and Prophets, whose special status was acknowledged by all, there existed a yet larger number of books which were in wide use throughout Judaism and for which no apparent boundaries had been determined. The Dead Sea Scrolls may be cited as evidence of the fluidity of the tradition in Palestine, since that collection contains not only copies of all the books of the Hebrew Bible except Esther, but also certain books of the Apocrypha and Pseudepigrapha, as well as a number of sectarian works as yet found nowhere outside the Dead Sea community.[32]

Not until the late first century A.D. and, quite possibly, the second century, were problems concerning the authority of the disputed books debated and the broad limits of the canon finally established. The assumption that all these decisions were made c. A.D. 90 by a rabbinic council at Jamnia, a town near the Palestinian coast and a center of Jewish religious life after A.D. 70, lacks sufficient evidence for its support.[33] Not only is it uncertain whether disputes concerning the more controversial books were settled by that time, but the notion of a formal council issuing authoritative decrees is reflected nowhere in the sources available to us. Nevertheless, references to a fixed collection of books by Jewish writers of the late first and early second centuries,[34] as well as Judaism's second-century proscription of the Septuagint and adoption of Aquilla's Greek version of the Hebrew Bible (the contents of which correspond to the Jewish canon), argue for a stabilization of the Jewish canon by the second century.

The factors which precipitated the closing of the Hebrew canon are reminiscent of the earlier conditions which prompted the establishment of the books of Torah. In A.D. 70, as reprisal against zealot revolts, the Roman army destroyed the city of Jerusalem and the Jewish temple, both of which had been rebuilt by the struggling Jewish community following the Babylonian Exile. Once again, dispossessed Jews sought a common identity in their sacred writings. Only now there existed a large and growing number of books on the authority of which there was no common agreement. Apocalyptic books posed a particularly vexing problem. Claiming a special authority respecting the course of future events and typically written under famous pseudonymns, these writings grew progressively more bizarre in their portrayals of expected world cataclysms. By the end of the first century, moreover, the rapidly expanding Church had produced a sizable liter-

---

[32] In respect to the Apocrypha or Deuterocanon, the Qumran manuscripts include copies of The Letter of Jeremiah (= Baruch, ch. 6), Tobit, and Ecclesiasticus; among the Pseudepigraphal books, there are copies of Jubilees, Enoch, and The Damascus Document (the latter now generally believed to have originated in some branch of the Essene sect). Cf. Frank Cross, *The Ancient Library of Qumran*, rev. ed. (Garden City, NY: Doubleday Anchor, 1961), pp. 1–47.

[33] Cf. Jack Lewis, "What Do We Mean by Jabne?"

[34] Josephus, in *Contra Apionem* I, 37–43 (written c. A.D. 90–95), refers to a collection of twenty-two books, which some scholars believe to be the canonical twenty-four, according to a different arrangement. II Esdras 14 (probably from the first half of the second century A.D.) contains the oldest certain reference to a canon of twenty-four books.

ature that offered its own unique interpretations of Judaism and Jewish scripture. For these very practical reasons, questions concerning the authority of disputed books demanded a resolution.

By this time no questions remained concerning the Torah's status; and among the prophets only Ezekiel still gave rise to some doubts. The story is told that one scholar labored day and night, burning three hundred jars of oil, before resolving to his satisfaction the conflicts between Ezekiel and the Torah.[35] The most serious objections centered upon the Writings, notably, Song of Songs, Ecclesiastes, and Esther. Song of Songs consists entirely of romantic love poems and Ecclesiastes voices a decided skepticism, unique within Jewish circles. Both works, however, were believed to have been written by Solomon; and by means of allegorization Songs of Songs was received as an expression of God's boundless love for Israel. Notwithstanding the fact that Esther does not once mention the name of God, the book was favored for its association with the Purim festival and the example it offers of Judaism's survival in the face of dire persecution.

Canonization affords a clear example of the vital human element in Judaeo-Christian religion. The deliberations over the sacred books obviously included some mistaken premises. Solomon, for example, wrote neither the Song of Songs nor Ecclesiastes—nor, for that matter, did he compose the book of Proverbs, as popularly believed. Although these books, and several others, did not reach their eventual forms earlier than the Greek period (late fourth century B.C. and following), inspiration was assumed to have ceased with Ezra, and no work known to be of later origin was approved. Daniel, written about 165 B.C., and most likely the latest book in the Hebrew canon, was received as the work of the sixth-century Jewish exile whose name it bears. Other works, equal or superior to some canonical selections, were denied a place because of the unquestionably late dates of their composition. All told, however, the rabbis did their work thoroughly and well; and few would argue with the claim that the books upon which they settled disclose to us the true character of Judaism.

THE FORMATION OF THE CHRISTIAN OLD TESTAMENT. For Christians, of course, there is yet a further stage in the history of Old Testament canonization, consisting of the Church's use and formal adoption of these books as a part of its canon. As already noted, final pronouncements on the Christian canon did not come until the period of the Reformation, at which time Catholics and Protestants chose the different courses which they have followed ever since.

Naturally enough, both Catholics and Protestants have sought to discover the position of Jesus and the early Church on the question of the canon, but agreement is made difficult by the obscurity of the New Tes-

---

[35] Talmud: Shabboth 13b; Hagigath 13a; Menahoth 45a.

tament evidence. Although it is clear that Jesus knew and treated as authoritative a significant number of Hebrew Old Testament books, the New Testament records no pronouncement by him as to the extent or limits of the canon. A typical New Testament formula for authoritative books is "the law and the prophets" or "Moses and the prophets," expressions which occur fourteen times in the New Testament. But since the New Testament writers could use the word "prophets" in a loose sense of authoritative books lying outside the Torah, the formula provides no gauge as to the extent of such books.[36] Nowhere in the New Testament is there a clear reference to the tripartite Hebrew canon, unless one so construes the allusion in Luke 24:44 to "the law of Moses and the prophets and the psalms." The New Testament authors, writing during the latter half of the first century and the early years of the second, used the Septuagint version of the Old Testament;[37] and in some instances they quote from or allude to books of the Apocrypha and Pseudepigrapha, as well as to works otherwise unknown to us.[38] They leave no clear impression, however, as to the degree of authority or sanctity assigned to these books. The same would have to be said of their references to some books of the Hebrew canon, not to speak of the canonical books to which there are no allusions at all.

In short, the New Testament evidence lends itself to varying interpretations, some of them supporting the Catholic canon, some the Protestant. One current position is that the New Testament lacks the notion of a fixed or "closed" canon of any sort.[39] If one takes seriously the evidence for a flexible or open-ended canon in Judaism prior to the second century, then the New Testament, having been written largely before the end of the first century, might be expected to reflect that same perspective.

After the New Testament period, Christians continued to use the Septuagint, but lacked official guidelines as to the limits of the Christian Old Testament. A variety of the Deuterocanonical books were treated as scripture by the Apostolic Fathers and their popularity increased in the Church. By the mid-second century, however, Church theologians such as Justin Martyr (c. A.D. 100–163?) and Origen (c. A.D. 185–252) were sensitive to the differences between the Jewish and Christian collections and, when in-

[36] This usage is demonstrated in the practice of citing quotations from the Psalms as prophecies fulfilled in Jesus' life, e.g., Matt. 13:35; Heb. 1:1–13.

[37] It is estimated that about 80 per cent of the New Testament writers' citations and allusions to the Old Testament are taken from the Septuagint (R. H. Pfeiffer, "Canon of the Old Testament" p. 511).

[38] Scholars disagree as to the extent of the New Testament usage of such books (compare Albert Sundberg, *The Old Testament of the Early Church*, pp. 54–55; S. Z. Leiman, *The Canonization of Hebrew Scripture: The Talmudic and Midrashic Evidence* [Garden City, NY: Doubleday Anchor 1976], pp. 40–41; and R. H. Pfeiffer, "Canon of the Old Testament" p. 512). The clearest examples appear in the book of Jude (vv. 9, 14–15), where the author alludes to an account from the Assumption of Moses and quotes from I Enoch.

[39] The evidence for this position is detailed in Albert Sundberg, *The Old Testament of the Early Church*.

volved in debates with Judaism, could restrict themselves to the Hebrew canon. In time, therefore, a few Christian voices—notably that of Jerome (c. A.D. 340–420)—were heard in favor of limiting the Christian Old Testament to the Jewish collection. Jerome was less than consistent in his position, however, and at the request of the bishop of Rome, included in his Latin Vulgate translations of the disputed books. In the meantime, the Church in North Africa took definite action at the Synods of Hippo (A.D. 393) and Carthage (A.D. 397 and 418) to establish the larger canon.

Although the matter continued to be debated throughout the Church, the prevailing opinion, particularly in the West, was in favor of the larger canon. In the sixteenth century the issue came to a head. In Martin Luther's debates with John Eck at Leipzig in 1519, the reformer argued against the Catholic doctrine of purgatory and the text from II Maccabees 12:46 which supported it, by declaring the disputed books to be less than fully canonical. Thus, in his German translation of the Bible (1534) he collected the latter books and set them apart from the rest of the Old Testament with the heading, "Apocrypha: these books are not held to be equal to the sacred scriptures, and yet are useful and good for reading." At the Council of Trent in 1546 the Roman Church responded to Luther's challenge by establishing the books of Jerome's Vulgate, and thus the larger canon, as Catholicism's official Old Testament.

Luther's action set the pattern for the Protestant churches of the Reformed tradition, whose Bibles continued to include the Apocrypha, but in a separate position at the end of the Bible or between the two Testaments. The King James Bible of 1611, for example, included them in this manner, i.e., printed between the Testaments. More pronounced opposition to the books among confessional and Calvinistic Protestant bodies resulted in their removal from some Bibles altogether. The Presbyterian Westminster Confession of 1648 stipulated: "The books commonly called Apocrypha, not being of divine inspiration, are no part of the canon of Scripture; and therefore of no authority to the church of God, not to be otherwise approved, or made use of, than any other human writings." Following opposition to the books in England, the British and Foreign Bible Society in 1827 dropped the Apocrypha from all its publications except pulpit Bibles. The Anglican Church, however, has consistently retained the books in its lectionary for morning and evening prayer, in keeping with Article 6 of the Thirty-nine Articles of 1562, which established them as books "which the Church doth read for example of life and instruction in manners; but yet doth it not apply them to establish any doctrine."

Within the churches of Eastern Orthodoxy the larger canon has had a long though not altogether consistent history. Its books have not corresponded entirely with those of the Roman Church, and in some Eastern churches, e.g., the nineteenth-century Russian Orthodox Church, the shorter canon prevailed. The important Synod of Jerusalem in 1672, how-

19

ever, established a canonical list varying only slightly from that of Trent.[40]

In today's Church, with the advance of modern biblical science and a growing ecumenicity in theological dialogue, many of the old arguments over the limits of the canon seem far less important than they once did. According to the assessment of one well-known Protestant: "If the debates about marginal books in antiquity should all be resolved today in favor of the marginal, little would be different."[41] One observes an increasing use of common editions of the Bible by Catholics and Protestants; and some Protestants are making new appraisals of the Apocrypha in view of recently revised theories of canonical history.[42]

2. THE BIBLICAL TEXT AND TEXTUAL CRITICISM

Modern editions of the Bible are the end products of a long and complex textual history. As none of the authors' original manuscripts (autographs) of biblical books has survived, the oldest manuscripts in our possession are copies, which in turn were copied by hand from yet other copies, and so on back to the originals. From the time of Ezra the task of copying biblical manuscripts and thus keeping the books in circulation fell to the lot of professional scribes known as Sopherim ("men of the book"). They originally wrote in a consonantal Hebrew script on scrolls of papyrus or leather (the codex or book form did not appear until the third century A.D.), with no system of punctuation, versification, or chapter divisions.[43] Notwithstanding the reverence in which these copyists held the biblical text, the primitive conditions under which they worked made common errors of the eye and ear unavoidable.

Some of these "textual corruptions" are readily apparent, even in modern editions of the Bible,[44] and include such confusions as dittography, the repetition of letters or words;[45] haplography, copying a letter, word, or line once when it should occur twice; and homoioteleuton, the omission of

---

[40] The Synod expressly designated as canonical the books of Wis. of Sol. Judith, Tobit, I–II Macc., Ecclus., and the additions to Dan. (Bel and the Dragon and Susanna).

[41] G. Ernest Wright, *The Old Testament and Theology* (New York: Harper & Row, Publishers, 1969), p. 168.

[42] Albert Sundberg, "The Protestant Old Testament Canon: Should It Be Re-examined?" *CBQ*, XXVII (1966), pp. 194–203.

[43] Verse and chapter divisions were not employed by copyists before the Christian era. Those currently used were developed in medieval Jewish and Christian Bibles.

[44] In I Sam. 13:1 the RSV literally renders the Hebrew text with its missing material, i.e., Saul's age upon taking the throne and the length of his reign.

[45] Compare Lev. 20:10 in the KJV and the RSV. The KJV preserves the dittography of four words in the Hebrew text (cf. the textual footnote to the verse in RSV).

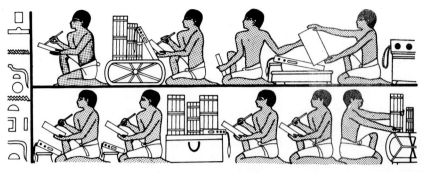

Ancient scribes at work

material intervening between two occurrences of the same word.[46] Letters that look alike, such as the Hebrew *nun* ("n") and *resh* ("r"), gave trouble, as in the name of the Babylonian king Nebuchadrezzar, which often appears in the Old Testament as "Nebuchadnezzar." Since the scribes sometimes copied from oral dictation, words with similar sounds could just as easily be confused. The difference between the rendering of Psalms 100:3 in the KJV and more recent translations (e.g., RSV, JB, NEB) turns on a single Hebrew word, recorded in the manuscripts as the negative, "not" (*lō'*). The verse makes much better sense, however, if one reads it with the recent translators as *lô*, pronounced like the negative, but an altogether different word, meaning "for him" or "his." Although most scribal errors were of this inadvertent variety, copyists on occasion deliberately altered a text in order to make it conform with a theological or ethical judgment. We have an instance of this in the change of the name of Saul's son Ishbaal ("man of Baal") to Ishbosheth ("man of shame"), resulting from a scribe's embarrassment that the son of Israel's first king should have borne the name of a pagan deity.[47] Such alterations, once having entered the text, were often recopied without correction, thus giving rise to variant "families" of texts circulating in different localities.

The effort to recover as nearly as possible the authoritative text of the Bible is the aim of the discipline known as "lower (or textual) criticism." Since the books of the Jewish canon were written almost entirely in Hebrew[48] the Old Testament text critic works in the first instance with a standard Hebrew text, known as the Masoretic Text (or MT). By the second

[46] In I Sam. 14:41 Hebrew manuscripts lack that portion of Saul's speech found between the two occurrences of the word "Israel," a scribe's eye having skipped over it and the error having been transmitted in subsequent manuscript copies. The error in this case was revealed by the Septuagint, which preserved the full reading.

[47] II Sam. 2:8ff.; the older form of the name is preserved in I Chron. 8:33, 9:39.

[48] See footnote 13 above. Most of the books of the Deuterocanon (Apocrypha) were written in Hebrew or Aramaic; at least two were written in Greek. See ch. 9.

century A.D., it would appear, the Sopherim had virtually established a standard consonantal text of the Hebrew Bible. The job was not complete, however, until the Masoretes, medieval scholars (c. A.D. 600–1000) who continued the work of the Sopherim, supplied the Hebrew text with vowels and thus produced a more definitive edition of the Old Testament. [49]

For comparisons with the MT the text critic depends on ancient manuscripts and versions which antedate the MT. Until the discovery of the Dead Sea (Qumran) Scrolls in 1947 and succeeding years, our oldest known manuscripts of substantial portions of the Hebrew Bible were no earlier than the ninth century A.D. Only one tiny fragment, consisting of a few verses from Exodus 20 and Deuteronomy 5 and 6, known as the Nash Papyrus, could be dated as early as the first century A.D. The Dead Sea finds, however, described by W. F. Albright as "the greatest manuscript discovery of modern times,"[50] have made available a wealth of Hebrew manuscripts dating from the first and second centuries B.C. and the first century A.D. Included are fragmentary portions of every Old Testmant book except Esther, and relatively complete copies of Isaiah, Leviticus, and Psalms. The Dead Sea text of Isaiah has been employed by the RSV and other recent translators, and in thirteen minor instances is favored over the MT readings. Each of the thirteen changes is marked in the RSV textual footnotes by the notation "one ancient manuscript."[51]

Early translations of the Old Testament into other languages (versions) also provide a major tool for textual criticism. The most important of these, by far, is the Greek Septuagint (LXX), a production of Greek-speaking Jews in Egypt in the years between 250 B.C. and the first century A.D. Named for the seventy (or seventy-two) scholars to whom legend attributed the translation,[52] it included all the books of the Apocrypha (Deuterocanon) except II Esdras and, as we have seen, served as the "Bible" of the early Christians. It is significant that the Dead Sea manuscripts agree in some passages with the MT and at other points with the LXX.

The Aramaic Targums developed as oral paraphrases to scripture readings in the post-Exilic synagogues when Hebrew had ceased to be the spoken language of the Jews. Early in the Christian era these translations were committed to writing, the two of greatest significance being the Targum of

---

[49] The oldest extant Hebrew manuscript of the entire Old Testament (MT) is the Leningrad Bible, which dates from A.D. 1008. It was this manuscript that supplied the text for the most widely used critical edition of the Old Testament, Rudolph Kittel's *Biblia Hebraica*, which was first published in 1937. An even older manuscript (from c. A.D. 930), now incomplete following a partial mutilation three decades ago, is the Aleppo Codex. An edition of the Hebrew scriptures is currently being produced from the latter manuscript by the Hebrew University Bible Project. Cf. M. H. Goshen-Gottstein, "The Aleppo Codex and the Rise of the Massoretic Bible Text," *BA*, 42 (1979), pp. 145–163.

[50] Millar Burrows, *The Dead Sea Scrolls* (New York: The Viking Press, Inc., 1955), p. 15.

[51] Cf. ibid., ch. XIV.

[52] Cf. The Letter of Aristeas in the Pseudepigrapha.

A cave in the Judean desert. The Dead Sea Scrolls were discovered in eleven caves scattered throughout the rocky hillsides of the Wilderness of Judah. (Courtesy of the Consulate General of Israel in New York.)

Onkelos (Torah) and the Targum of Jonathan (Prophets). The most notable of the early Christian versions of the Old Testament are the Syriac Peshitta, produced in the late first or second century to facilitate Christian missions in the Syrian interior, and the more famous Latin Vulgate, commissioned by Pope Damasus in A.D. 382 and translated by Jerome. After meeting with considerable opposition at first, the Vulgate became by the seventh century the official Bible of the Roman Catholic Church, and until the translation of William Tyndale in 1529, all English versions were based upon it.

The versions, of course, do not always clarify the problematical passages in the Hebrew text; and when a versional reading differs from the MT the more authentic text must be determined on the basis of contextual meaning. Agreement between two or more versions against an MT reading

Pottery jars from the Dead Sea Caves. Prior to storage in the caves, some of the Dead Sea Scrolls were carefully wrapped in linen, sealed with wax, and placed in jars like those shown here. (Courtesy of the Israel Department of Antiquities and Museums.)

strengthens the case for an emendation of the MT, but only if it results in improving the sense of the text. RSV textual footnotes indicate each instance in which a versional reading was preferred to that of the MT by the RSV translators.[53]

English Versions

It was not until the fourteenth century (c. 1384) that a translation of the entire Bible into English was produced by the followers of John Wyclif,

---

[53] In reference to Gen. 4:8, for example, footnote "h" tells us that the words of Cain, "Let us go out to the field," do not appear in the Hebrew text (MT); but the Samaritan Pentateuch, Septuagint, Peshitta, and—in an altered form—the Vulgate include them.

Dead Sea Scrolls, on display at the Shrine of the Book, Jerusalem. The Dead Sea Scroll collection includes a complete scroll of the Book of Isaiah, twenty-four feet long, and a scroll containing the text of the first two chapters of Habakkuk with running commentary and interpretation. (Courtesy of the Consulate General of Israel in New York.)

"the father of English prose, the morning star of the Reformation, and the flower of Oxford scholarship." Like earlier English paraphrases and partial translations of the Bible, Wyclif's version was based on the Vulgate. The revival of interest in Hebrew and Greek occasioned by the Renaissance, the invention of printing, and the development of English into a form suitable for literary expression stimulated the translations of the sixteenth century, beginning with the work of William Tyndale (1529). Tyndale's Bible, the first English version to be made by direct translation from the original languages, was followed in rapid succession by eight English versions, culminating in the King James Version of 1611. Among these were Cover-

25

dale's Bible (1535), "Matthew's" Bible (1537), the Great Bible (1539), and the Geneva Bible (1560). At the same time, Roman Catholic seminarians at Douai and Rheims, France, produced a translation from the Latin for English-speaking Catholics, called the Rheims-Douai Version (1610).

The Authorized or King James Version had its beginnings in 1604, when James I ordained "that a translation be made of the whole Bible, as consonant as can be to the original Hebrew and Greek . . . , and only to be used in all churches of England in time of divine service." The forty-seven scholars and learned clergymen appointed to the translation committee labored seven years on the project. Although it was a half-century or more before the KJV superseded the Geneva Bible in common usage, once accepted, it took a firm hold. No other English version before or since has had so great an influence on so many readers for so long a time. As a noble monument of English prose, it has evoked the highest praise of the literary critics. Sir Frederic Kenyon thus wrote of it:

> It is the simple truth that, as literature, the English Authorized Version is superior to the original Greek. It was the good fortune of the English nation that its Bible was produced at a time when the genius of the language for noble prose was at its height, and when a natural sense of style was not infected by self-conscious scholarship.[54]

The music of its cadences made it an ideal version for oral readings and use in worship. Some portions of the KJV, however, do not match the literary merit of other parts. Throughout the past three and a half centuries it has undergone several revisions, noteworthy among them, the English Revised Version of 1885, the American Standard Version of 1901, the Revised Standard Version of 1952, and the New American Standard Version of 1971.

The twentieth century, especially in the past three decades, has seen the production of a number of important English translations, both by committees and individuals, and as interfaith and intrafaith undertakings. The first Jewish Bible in English was published in the United States just before the turn of the century (1884); and in 1917 the Jewish Publication Society made available *The Holy Scriptures According to the Masoretic Text*. A new Jewish version is currently in production, the first part of which appeared in 1963 as *The Torah: the Five Books of Moses*.[55] Roman Catholic scholars have been particularly active in the production of new translations since the papal encyclical of Pope Pius XII in 1943 encouraging the study of the Bible. The highly readable translation of Ronald Knox (1950) is based largely on the Vulgate; the Old Testament portion of the New American Bible (1970), however, is translated directly from the Hebrew. Although

---

[54] Frederic Kenyon, *The Story of the Bible* (New York: E. P. Dutton, & Co., Inc. 1937), pp. 53–54.

[55] Other installments, published by the Jewish Publication Society of America (Philadelphia), are *The Five Megilloth and Jonah* (1969), *The Book of Isaiah* (1973), *The Book of Psalms* (1973), and *The Book of Jeremiah* (1974).

the KJV remained in standard use within Anglican and Protestant circles throughout the first half of the century, the works of individual scholars, aimed at updating its English, were well received. Among them the translations of Moffatt and Smith-Goodspeed are notable.

Four current translations that promise to be in wide use for some time are the Revised Standard Version, the Jerusalem Bible, the Anchor Bible, and the New English Bible. The Revised Standard Version, completed in 1957 (1952 without Apocrypha), has already taken its place as a basic Bible in American churches and classrooms. It was commissioned in 1937 by the International Council of Religious Education, a cooperative organization of forty Protestant denominations in the United States and Canada, and was produced by an international committee of thirty-seven members. Designed as a modern revision of the KJV, the RSV reflects an updating of the King James English in the light of the best manuscripts in the original languages. The Jerusalem Bible (1966), produced by French Catholic scholars, and the New English Bible (1970), a version sponsored by several denominations in England and Scotland, offer fresh and dynamic translations. Unlike the RSV committee, the latter translators made no attempts to remain within the tradition of the KJV. The Anchor Bible is a work of Protestant, Catholic, and Jewish scholars from many countries, being made available in fifty separate volumes, with introductions and notes. The translation of each biblical book represents the work of a single scholar; thus diversity of viewpoint and the latest judgments of specialists on the separate books mark this work.

COMPARATIVE TRANSLATIONS OF GENESIS 1:1–3 IN FOUR MODERN ENGLISH VERSIONS

REVISED STANDARD VERSION	JERUSALEM BIBLE	ANCHOR BIBLE	NEW ENGLISH BIBLE
In the beginning God created the heavens and the earth. The earth was without form and void, and darkness was upon the face of the deep; and the Spirit of God was moving over the face of the waters. And God said, "Let there be light"; and there was light.	In the beginning God created the heavens and the earth. Now the earth was a formless void, there was darkness over the deep, and God's spirit hovered over the water. God said, "Let there be light," and there was light.	When God set about to create heaven and earth —the world being then a formless waste, with darkness over the seas and only an awesome wind sweeping over the water —God said, "Let there be light." And there was light.	In the beginning of creation, when God made heaven and earth, the earth was without form and void, with darkness over the face of the abyss, and a mighty wind that swept over the surface of the waters. God said, "Let there be light," and there was light . . .

27

Among the growing list of popular translations and paraphrases for which ease of reading in colloquial English is the primary aim, the most effective is undoubtedly The Bible in Today's English Version. Commissioned by the American Bible Society and completed in 1976, its most popular edition appears under the title The Good News Bible.

3. THE OLD TESTAMENT LITERATURE: EXEGETICAL METHODS

Textual criticism, which makes possible more accurate translations of the Bible, lays the necessary groundwork for the larger enterprise of biblical exegesis.[56] Exegesis concerns "the process by which one comes to understand a text,"[57] and, properly conceived, requires both systematic analysis and imaginative insight. Since the latter half of the eighteenth century and the path-finding studies of the French scholar Jean Astruc, the same rigorous methodology employed in the study of other ancient literature has been applied to the books of the Bible.[58] "Historical criticism," as most modern biblical study is known, is guided by the principle that exegesis must be as informed as possible about the circumstances surrounding the origins of the books. Scholars attempt to determine the authorship or processes by which the books were composed, their historical, cultural, and religious settings, the sources employed in their composition, the audiences for which they were intended, and the purposes which they were designed to serve.[59]

The demands thus placed upon the biblical exegete are formidable. Few of the Old Testament books originated at a single time or place or as the production of a single author, and fewer than half of them identify their authors by name. The titles given the books in modern editions of the Bible, moreover, are secondary and traditional and cannot in themselves settle the questions of authorship. In view of the complexities of the Old Testament literature, it is understandable that historical criticism has developed more than a single method for exploring its origins.

---

[56] The designations "lower criticism" and "higher criticism," although not so widely employed as in the past, distinguish between textual (i.e., lower) criticism, which establishes the text, and exegesis (i.e., higher criticism), which interprets the text thus established. The distinction, however, is not always so neatly drawn, since textual criticism normally utilizes the data of the other critical disciplines and is itself a form of exegesis.

[57] Leander E. Keck and Gene M. Tucker, "Exegesis," IDBS, p. 296.

[58] For a survey of the history of modern Old Testament criticism, see the works of Anderson (1979), Clements, Hahn, Kraeling, Krentz, Rowley, or Terrien, listed under "Biblical Criticism; Its Methodology and Recent History" in the General Bibliography.

[59] For a more detailed definition and description of historical criticism, see Edgar Krentz, The Historical-Critical Method, Guides to Biblical Scholarship (Philadelphia: Fortress Press, 1975).

3. THE OLD TESTAMENT LITERATURE

Source Criticism

The oldest of the historical-critical methods is known as source criticism or, in a restrictive use of the term, literary criticism. This technique focuses primarily on questions of authorship and the formation of the books as *written* documents. Based almost solely on such internal clues as literary style, vocabulary, and allusions to known persons, events, or cultural features, source criticism seeks to establish when, where, why, and by whom the books were composed. Since older sources underlie the final editions of many of the Old Testament books, a major aim is to distinguish such units or strands (i.e., as written sources) and to suggest the circumstances of their incorporation into the larger works by the authors or redactors.

Source criticism dominated the historical-critical scholarship of the nineteenth and early twentieth centuries and, notwithstanding its limitations, established a framework for comprehending some of the most universally acknowledged features of Old Testament literary development. It was discovered that the earliest written portions of the Old Testament appeared in about the tenth century B.C., or the time of David and Solomon, and included anonymous strands of the Pentateuch (the so-called J source) and the historical books (II Sam. 9–20; I Kings 1–2). The Pentateuch was found to be a composite work of four major sources, dating from different eras of Israelite history and brought together as a final edition in the period of the Exile. Similarly, stages of editing were recognized in the prophetic books, with portions of some books (e.g., Isaiah) separated from other portions of the same works by as much as two or more centuries. Equally lengthy and complex editorial histories were evident in the collections of sacred songs and wisdom sayings compiled in the books of Psalms and Proverbs— processes which encompassed several centuries and engaged the talents of multiple psalmists and sages. It was determined that by the second century B.C. the last of the books of the Jewish canon (probably Daniel or Esther) had been written; and within another two centuries all the books of the Catholic Deuterocanon were complete. Thus the actual writing of the Old Testament encompassed a period of approximately a thousand years.[60]

Form and Tradition Criticism

Although source criticism has taught us much about the literary origins of the Old Testament, it has remained for other methods to reveal the importance of oral patterns and the long preliterary stages in the formation of Israel's traditions. Like few other books, the Bible is the production of

---

[60] For an up-to-date description of source or literary criticism, see Norman C. Habel, *Literary Criticism of the Old Testament*, Guides to Biblical Scholarship (Philadelphia: Fortress Press, 1971). For examples of works written in source criticism's heyday, see S. R. Driver, *Introduction to the Literature of the Old Testament*, rev. ed. (New York: Charles Scribner's Sons, 1913) or R. H. Pfeiffer, *Introduction to the Old Testament*.

The Growth of the Old Testament Literature

	BEFORE THE 10TH CENTURY B.C.	10TH CENTURY B.C.	9TH CENTURY B.C.	8TH CENTURY B.C.
Law	–Early oral traditions of the Patriarchs and Moses –Early laws –Early poems (e.g., Ex. 15)	–J Tradition (earliest of 4 tradition strands in Pentateuch) achieves written form		–E Tradition (2nd of Pentateuchal strands) achieves written form
Former Prophets	–Oral accounts underlying Joshua, Judges, and I Samuel –Early poems (e.g., Judg. 5)	–"Court History of David" (II Sam. 9–20; I Kings 1–2) –Other stories of David	–Royal records underlying I–II Kings, I–II Chronicles ————→ –Elijah and Elisha stories (I Kings 17– II Kings 13)	
Latter Prophets			–Amos * –Hosea * –Micah * –Isaiah (core of chs. 1–39) *	
Writings		–Early Psalms used in temple worship ————————→ –Early proverbs —————————→		–Collection of some proverbs in Hezekiah's time (Prov. 25–29)
Apocrypha (Deuterocanon)				

* Books expanded or edited at a later time.

THE GROWTH OF THE OLD TESTAMENT LITERATURE (Continued)

7TH CENTURY B.C.	6TH CENTURY B.C.	5TH CENTURY B.C.	4TH–3RD CENTURIES B.C.	2ND CENTURY B.C.	1ST CENTURY B.C.–1ST CENTURY A.D.
–J and E traditions combined to form JE. –D Tradition (Nucleus of 3rd Pentateuchal strand) achieves written form.	–P Tradition (last of Pentateuchal strands) achieves written form	–Completion of Pentateuch: JEDP combined			
	–"Deuteronomic History" → (Josh.–II Kings) completed				
–Zephaniah * –Nahum –Habakkuk –Jeremiah *	–Jeremiah * –Ezekiel * –Deutero-Isaiah (Isa. 40–55) –Editing of Pre-Exilic Prophets –Haggai –Zechariah 1–8	–Malachi –Trito-Isaiah (Isa. 56–66) –Obadiah (?)	–Joel (?) –Jonah (?) –Deutero-Zechariah (Zech. 9–14) (?)		
——————————————————————————→			–Psalms (final collection)	–Esther (?) –Daniel	
——————————————————————————→			–Proverbs (final collection)		
	–Lamentations –Job (?)	–Memoirs of Ezra and → Nehemiah –Song of Songs (?)	–Chronicler's History (I–II Chron., Ez., Neh.) –Ecclesiastes		
				–Ecclesiasticus –Baruch –Tobit –Judith –Additions to Esther –Additions to Daniel –I Maccabees	–II Maccabees –Wisdom of Solomon

(?) Books of uncertain date.

the people whose origins and history it records. Long before any portion of the Old Testament reached written form, oral tradition, passed down through generations of Israel's ancestors, circulated in story, song, sayings, and sacred recital. Written Hebrew documents have not been attested earlier than Iron Age I (1200–900 B.C.); and even after that time widespread illiteracy and scarcity of writing materials, together with the phenomenally retentive memory of the ancient Eastern mind, assured the continuation of the mouth-to-ear method of transmission.

In the years since Herman Gunkel's (1862–1932) studies in the Pentateuch and Psalter, the schools of form criticism (*Formsgeschichte*) and tradition criticism (*Traditiongeschichte*) have carried source criticism a step further through exploration of the oral stages of textual transmission. Form criticism strives to isolate the primitive oral traditions which underlie the written text, classify them according to their typical forms, and reconstruct the life situations (*Sitzen-im-Leben*) in which they arose.[61] To trace the processes by which such oral units passed from their original settings to their present positions in the biblical text is the specific concern of tradition criticism.[62] The form and tradition critics have marshaled persuasive evidence for the crucial role of the cult or worship rites as the locale for the formation and preservation of many Old Testament accounts. Brief cultic confessions of faith are viewed by Gerhard von Rad as the oral nucleus around which the Pentateuchal traditions gathered; and Martin Noth assigns the same function to broad confessional themes which were celebrated at early Israelite shrines.[63]

The specific characteristic that has given form criticism its name is its concern with the peculiar forms or genres in which persons of the biblical world typically expressed their thought. As in the study of any literature, the genre in which a saying is expressed or a work composed is a prime consideration for its right interpretation. One does not, for example, impose upon a poem the literal categories of a legal code; nor is a parable treated in the same manner as a work of history. Since no one literary form has a monopoly on truth, the Old Testament is the richer for the broad diversity which characterizes its books. Most of the classical literary types, with the exception of drama and epic poetry of the Homeric type, are

---

[61] On form criticism, see Gene M. Tucker, *Form Criticism of the Old Testament*, Guides to Biblical Scholarship (Philadelphia: Fortress Press, 1971). For more detailed treatments, see John H. Hayes, ed., *Old Testament Form Criticism* (San Antonio, TX: Trinity University Press, 1974) or Klaus Koch, *The Growth of the Biblical Tradition: the Form Critical Method*, S. M. Cupitt, trans. (New York: Charles Scribner's Sons, 1969; paperback, 1971). For a classic example of form criticism, see Hermann Gunkel, *The Legends of Genesis*, W. H. Carruth, trans. (New York: Schochen Books, Inc., 1964).

[62] On tradition criticism, see Walter E. Rast, *Tradition History and the Old Testament*, Guides to Biblical Scholarship (Philadelphia: Fortress Press, 1972). For an example of tradition criticism in a major work, see Martin Noth, *A History of Pentateuchal Traditions*, Bernhard W. Anderson, trans. (Englewood Cliffs, N.J.: Prentice-Hall, Inc., 1972).

[63] See below, pp. 73–74.

found here; and, in addition, the unique mind and faith of Israel created forms—or modified forms—in a way peculiarly their own.

Form criticism has gone far toward distinguishing some of the earliest oral units in the Old Testament, for example, the victory songs of Miriam and Deborah,[64] etiological ("origins") stories relating to specific sites, customs, life patterns, etc.,[65] and folk tales concerning early Israelite heroes.[66] The brevity and rhythm of songs and poetic sayings made them easy to memorize and thus most suitable to the earliest stages of oral transmission. In its analysis of genres, however, form criticism cannot be restricted solely to the primitive and oral, since distinctions between early/late and unwritten/written are not always evident. Accordingly, the Old Testament literature in its entirety has been systematically classified according to type and subtype. That no two classification systems entirely agree or that the proposed categories are frequently a mixture of types is to be expected for so vast and complex a literature. Prose and poetry are basic in distinguishing form, since the Old Testament is approximately two thirds prose and one third poetry. But important content categories such as prophecy and wisdom appear in the form of both poetry and prose. Thus categories of content or subject matter may cut across purely formal patterns in the classification of the genres.

In a number of prominent classification systems three broad categories of the literature are recognized as Songs, Sayings, and Prose.[67] Songs originated both within and outside formal worship contexts and, although the distinction is often blurred, can with some justification be designated as "secular" and "sacred." The book of Psalms, which is the largest collection of religious songs in the Old Testament, nevertheless contains some song types which apparently arose within political and secular settings, i.e., royal and wisdom songs, and were only later adapted to cultic use. Sayings occupy a midpoint between poetry and prose, being found in both forms, but typically appearing as brief, poetic units, such as oracles and proverbs. Prose consists in the main of narrative types in which the lines of distinction, e.g., between history, legend, myth, and parable, are not at all sharply defined and are thus subject to the criteria of the individual in-

---

[64] Ex. 15; Judg. 5.

[65] Gen. 3; 19; 28:10–22; 32:13–32; etc.

[66] Gen. 12–15; Exod. 1–14; Judg. 13–16, etc.

[67] Cf. the classifications of Otto Eissfeldt, *The Old Testament; An Introduction*, P. R. Ackroyd, trans. (New York: Harper & Row, Publishers, 1965), pp. 9–153; Artur Weiser, *The Old Testament: Its Formation and Development*, Dorothea M. Barton, trans. (New York: Association Press, 1961), pp. 21–68; Aage Bentzen, *Introduction to the Old Testament*, 2nd ed., (Copenhagen: G. E. C. Gad, 1952), pp. 102–264; George Fohrer (initiated by Ernst Sellin), *Introduction to the Old Testament*, David E. Green, trans. (Nashville, TN: Abingdon Press, 1968), pp. 36–102; Robert H. Pfeiffer, *Introduction to the Old Testament* (New York: Harper & Row, Publishers, 1941), pp. 20–40; Norman K. Gottwald, *A Light to the Nations* (New York: Harper & Row, Publishers, 1959), pp. 21–29. For the more detailed subtypes, see John H. Hayes, ed., *Old Testament Form Criticism*.

terpreter. "Myth," in particular, can be a misleading label, but in respect to Old Testament usage is generally restricted to stories of the origins of the world and mankind and passes no judgment on the truth of the accounts. By most classifications, legend is distinguished from myth in that its stories occupy a fixed geographical locale outside a primeval setting; and both forms differ from history in that data exist (no matter how slight) for checking the credibility of the latter. The accompanying classification of Old Testament literary forms demonstrates one manner of comprehending the diversity of the literature under these broad categories and offers one or more prominent examples of each type.

Other Methods

Among other methods of biblical criticism that have appeared in recent years, some aim at refining or supplementing the older techniques. Two of these are redaction criticism and rhetorical criticism. Redaction criticism focuses on the final stage in the formation of a biblical unit or book, and involves the theological perspectives and intentions of the writer or redactor as perceived in the manner in which he arranged, edited, and expanded upon the traditional material that was available to him. As an example, one may note how the historian responsible for the book of Judges brought together stories of early tribal heros, supplied them with an editorial framework, and made them yield a meaning consistent with the theme of the book. The technique is employed as a logical extension of tradition criticism in the Pentateuchal exegesis of Gerhard von Rad and H. W. Wolff. The latter, in particular, attempts to discover the *kerygma* (theological proclamation) of the biblical redactors as responses to cultural changes which influenced their shaping of the older traditions.[68]

A corrective to form criticism is claimed for rhetorical criticism, a method advocated by the American scholar James Muilenburg and his students. Rhetorical criticism strives to expose the literary structures and techniques employed in fashioning a unit of scripture through a study of such devices as parallelism of thought, repetition of words or refrains, and the like. As contrasted with form criticism, which stresses the typical and representative features of literary forms, rhetorical criticism centers greater attention on the distinctive and unique style of a given author or speaker.[69]

In some quarters, interest in the biblical text as a finished product has resulted in an abandonment of historical-critical methodology and its search

---

[68] On redaction criticism, see Norman Perrin, *What Is Redaction Criticism?* Guides to Biblical Scholarship (Philadelphia: Fortress Press, 1969) and Walter E. Rast, *Tradition History and the Old Testament*, Guides to Biblical Scholarship (Philadelphia: Fortress Press, 1972).

[69] On rhetorical criticism, see James Muilenburg, "Form Criticism and Beyond," *JBL*, LXXXVIII (1969), pp. 1–18, and Jared J. Jackson and Martin Kessler, eds., *Rhetorical Criticism: Essays in Honor of James Muilenburg* (Pittsburgh, PA: Pickwick Press, 1974). Further applications of the method may be seen in Phyllis Trible, *God and the Rhetoric of Sexuality*, Overtures to Biblical Theology (Philadelphia: Fortress Press, 1978).

OLD TESTAMENT LITERARY FORMS

I. *Songs*
- A. "Secular" (Noncultic) Songs
  1. Work Songs (Num. 21:17–18)
  2. Feast and Drinking Songs (Isa. 22:13; 56:12)
  3. Songs of Battle (Num. 10:35–36) and Victory (Exod. 15:1–18; Judg. 5)
  4. Songs of Love and Marriage (Song of Songs)
  5. Funeral Songs (II Sam. 1:19–27; 3:33–34)
  6. Taunt Songs (Isa. 23:16; Num. 21:27)
  7. Royal Songs* (Pss. 45, 72)
  8. Wisdom Songs* (Ps. 49; Prov. 31:10–31)
- B. Sacred (Cultic) Songs
  1. Hymns (Pss. 8, 46)
  2. Thanksgivings: Corporate (Pss. 67, 107) and Individual (Pss. 9, 18)
  3. Laments: Corporate (Pss. 60, 74) and Individual (Pss. 3–7)
  4. Royal Psalms* (Pss. 2, 110)
  5. Wisdom Psalms* (Pss. 1, 37)

II. *Sayings*
- A. Prophetic Oracles (Amos 1–2; Isa. 1)
- B. Proverbs (Prov.; Ecclus.; Wis. of Sol.)
- C. Priestly Oracles (Gen. 25:23)
- D. Blessings and Curses (Gen. 49; Num. 6:24–26; Deut. 27:11–26)
- E. Taunts and Boasts (Gen. 4:23–24; I Sam. 17:43–47)
- F. Laws in Absolute Form (Exod. 20:1–17)

III. *Prose*
  1. History (I–II Kings; I–II Chron.; I–II Macc.)
  2. Legends or Folk Stories (Gen. 12–50; Judg.)
  3. Myths or Primeval Accounts (Gen. 1–11)
  4. Didactic Stories (Dan. 1–6; Tobit) and Parables (Jonah)
  5. Fables (Judg. 9:8–15)
  6. Apocalyptic (Isa. 24–27; Dan. 7–12)
  7. Records: Contracts (Gen. 21:22–32; 23:17–20); Edicts (Ezra 1:1–4); Letters (Jer. 29:1–23); Lists and Genealogies (Gen. 10; II Sam. 8:16–18; Num. 31:32–40)
  8. Laws in Casuistic Form (Exod. 21:1–11)
  9. Speeches and Sermons (I Sam. 12; Jer. 7)
  10. Prayers (I Kings 3:6–9; Dan. 9:4–19)

---

*Forms subject to more than a single category.

---

for the historical settings, origins, and development of texts. On the assumption that appearances do not constitute reality, modern structuralism probes the Bible for the "deep structures," i.e., structures of the mind, which are believed to be coded into the surface structures of the text.[70]

---

[70] On structuralism as a method of biblical interpretation, see the special issue of *Int.* XXVIII, 2 (1974) and Robert M. Polzin, *Biblical Structuralism*, Semeia Supplement (Philadelphia: Fortress Press, 1977).

And the so-called "new literary criticism" or "Bible as literature" method disavows interest in the Bible as either historical or theological literature in order to consider it exclusively as a literary document.[71] "The decisive clues for interpreting any piece of literature," says one spokesman for this method, "come from other works of literature;" therefore, to consider the Bible as literature "means to incorporate it within the vast body of literature as a whole and study its relationship with other parts of that body."[72] Particularly in the nonhistorical portions of the Old Testament the latter approach has produced some provocative exegesis.

Whereas advocates of structuralism so define the exegetical task as to preclude other more traditional methods, the new literary criticism generally allows for the validity of other techniques, without itself applying them. Both methods, however, adhere to a *synchronic* rather than a *diachronic* approach, i.e., confront the biblical books in the forms in which we now possess them and as totalities, rather than as products of tradition history or source redaction. One positive effect of these new schools may be to turn criticism from an almost exclusive concern with textual prehistory toward a healthy balance that allows as well for "a free encounter with a writing in its final form."[73]

Affirmation of the biblical text as it stands, though not necessarily without the assistance of historical criticism, is characteristic also of the recent "canonical criticism" advocated by the American scholars Brevard Childs and James Sanders. Childs urges interpreting the Bible with its canonical function clearly in view, i.e., as a literature designed for and utilized by the historical community of faith. And this, in Childs' view, argues for the priority of the text in its final form, since "it alone bears witness to the full history of revelation."[74] Childs places a high value upon the many tools and methods provided by the history of the exegetical tradition which relate the biblical writings to each other and to the life of today's community of faith. Accordingly, the New Testament's use of Old Testament passages is given a special prominence; and Augustine or Luther may speak with as much validity concerning the meaning of a text as a modern critical scholar.[75] With

---

[71] On the "Bible as literature" method, see David Robertson, *The Old Testament and the Literary Critic*, Guides to Biblical Scholarship (Philadelphia: Fortress Press, 1977); idem, "Literature, the Bible as," *IDBS*, pp. 547–551; Kenneth R. R., Gros Louis et al., eds., *Literary Interpretations of Biblical Narratives* (Nashville, TN: Abingdon Press, 1974); and Rene Wellek and Austin Warren, *Theory of Literature* (New York: Penguin Books, 1973).

[72] David Robertson, *The Old Testament and the Literary Critic*, p. 9.

[73] Amos N. Wilder, "Norman Perrin, What Is Redaction Criticism?" in *Christology* (Claremont, CA: The New Testament Colloquium, 1971), p. 153.

[74] Brevard S. Childs, *Introduction to the Old Testament as Scripture* (Philadelphia: Fortress Press, 1979), p. 76.

[75] Brevard S. Childs, *Biblical Theology in Crisis* (Philadelphia: The Westminster Press, 1970), pp. 61–87. See also the exegetical application of Childs' method in *The Book of Exodus* (Philadelphia: The Westminster Press, 1974) and *Introduction to the Old Testament as Scripture*.

interests similar to Childs', Sanders advocates projecting canonical concerns back into the formative stages of Old Testament development. Alongside source analysis, form criticism, and tradition history, one would also apply canonical criticism by considering at every appropriate point the canonical function or authority which a unit of scripture was designed to serve. [76]

This by no means exhausts the methodological options available to the interpreter of the Old Testament. There are yet other approaches that employ the expertise of such disciplines as sociology, anthropology, or psychology to shed significant light on aspects of the Bible. Also new theological approaches utilizing the categories of "theology as story," "realistic narrative," and the like, are striving to overcome many of the limitations of the traditional historical-critical methodology. The perspective adopted here is that no method which assists toward a better understanding of the Bible should be ignored, although obviously not all of them can be employed concurrently in the same work. Our own indebtedness to more than a single method will be readily apparent in the pages which follow.

4. ISRAELITE HISTORY

When one opens a Hebrew Bible at Genesis and begins reading, he finds that he is following a narrative which does not finally end until he has completed the book of Kings. In Christian Bibles the historical sequence remains uninterrupted to the end of Nehemiah, except for a retracing in I and II Chronicles of the ground already covered in the preceding books. Together, these books—the Torah, Former Prophets, and Chronicler's History (I–II Chronicles, Ezra, Nehemiah) [77] comprise roughly one half of the Old Testament and preserve the only extant record of the origins and early history of the Hebrew people.

From early clan migrations in the Near East, usually dated to the early or mid-second millennium B.C., Israel's ancestry is traced through a stage of rural, village, and pastoral culture, leading eventually to a period of enslavement in Egypt (Genesis). With the Exodus from Egypt under Moses' leadership and a generation spent under his guidance in the Sinai desert (thirteenth century B.C.?), the former slaves are consolidated around a set of common aims, beliefs, and cultic patterns—and the nucleus of the later Israel is formed (Exodus–Deuteronomy). The settlement in Canaan gives the newly formed people possession of the land of their forefathers (Joshua), where they exist for a time either as independent clans or in a

[76] James A. Sanders, *Torah and Canon* and "Reopening Old Questions About Scripture," *Int.*, XXVII (1974), pp. 321–330.

[77] The evidence for treating Chronicles–Ezra–Nehemiah as a single work is discussed below, pp. 484–487.

loosely structured confederation of tribes (Judges). Finally, owing chiefly to David's ingenuity, an experiment with monarchy, begun under Saul, is successful and Israel becomes a small but significant kingdom, including all Palestine, Transjordan, and sizable territories north and south (c. 1000–922 B.C.) (I–II Samuel, I Kings 1–11). At the death of Solomon, David's son, tensions between the northern and southern halves of the kingdom lead to a schism, resulting in the divided monarchies of Israel (north) and Judah (south), the former ruled by a succession of dynasties until its capital, Samaria, is destroyed by the Assyrians in 722 B.C., and the latter governed by Davidic kings until Jerusalem's fall to the Babylonians in 587 B.C. (I Kings 12–II Kings; I–II Chronicles). The dark period of Babylonian Exile (597/587–538 B.C.) is lifted for some Jews when Persia's conquest of Babylon results in a decree allowing groups of exiles to return home, rebuild Jerusalem, and restore the Jewish temple and cult (Ezra-Nehemiah). This they do under the leadership of a succession of governors and religious leaders, the most notable of whom are Nehemiah (445–? B.C.) and Ezra (428–? B.C.).

This portion of the Old Testament provides the historical settings for most of the remainder of the books of the Jewish-Protestant canon, i.e., the Latter Prophets and several of the Writings. These books are not works of history, as such, though they offer valuable and firsthand insights into the periods in which they were written and must be studied alongside the history if either is to be properly understood. For the settings of the books of the Deuterocanon and those portions of the Writings which are later than the Chronicler's History, one must go to the records provided by I–II Maccabees and such noncanonical sources as Josephus' works, which record the course of Jewish history during the Persian (539–333 B.C.), Greek (333–165 B.C.), and Hasmonean (165–63 B.C.) periods.[78] Other ancient records, once known and used in Israelite circles, have long since disappeared.

During the course of the last century our knowledge of Israel's history has been considerably expanded by significant archaeological discoveries throughout the Near East. Some of these, like the initial Dead Sea Scroll finds, have come quite unexpectedly and accidentally. Many others must be credited to the precise, scientific methods of modern archaeology. Since Sir Flinders Petrie's work at Tell el-Hesi (probably the biblical Eglon) in 1890, numerous excavations of Palestinian tells (mounds containing the remains of past occupations), employing the techniques of stratigraphy (layer-by-layer removal) and pottery dating, have enabled biblical historians to piece together a much more detailed picture of ancient Israel's cul-

---

[78] For English translations of the Greek text of Josephus' works, see Henry St. John Thackeray et al., eds. and trans., *Josephus*, Loeb Classical Library, vols. I–IX (Cambridge, MA: Harvard University Press, 1961–1968), or William Whiston, trans., *The Life and Works of Flavius Josephus* (New York: Holt, Rinehart and Winston, 1957).

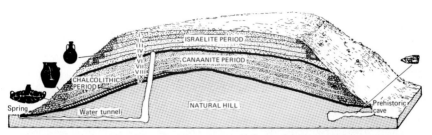

Stratification of a tell. A pottery chronology, developed from the study of chang-ing ceramic styles, enables archaeologists to assign broad dates to the separate stages in the life of an ancient town. (Redrawn from Macmillan Bible Atlas by Y. Aharoni and Michael Avi-Yonah. Copyright © 1968 Carta, Jerusalem. © Copyright 1964 by Carta, Jerusalem. © Copyright 1966 by Carta, Jerusalem.)

tural development than would have been otherwise possible. Moreover, other regions of the Near East, namely Syria, Mesopotamia, Egypt, and eastern Asia Minor, have produced large numbers of written texts and inscriptions that relate to the early phases of the Old Testament period.[79] Outstanding examples of such texts are the royal chronicles from ancient Assyria and Babylon. By providing a means of cross-checking events and persons mentioned in the Old Testament, these records have made possi-ble a relatively precise chronology for the period of the Hebrew monarchy.

The illumination afforded by extrabiblical sources notwithstanding, it is impossible to reconstruct from the Old Testament a precise and all-inclusive history of early Israel such as would be written by a modern histo-rian. This is owing primarily to the unique theological purpose and princi-ple of selectivity which motivated the Old Testament writers. They recorded history not for its own sake, but in order to expose the underlying and controlling designs which move the course of human affairs and pro-voke the response of faith. This unique viewing of history—this perspective of faith—is, of course, what gives to the books their special appeal as religious literature. It explains, as well, why questions asked by the mod-ern historian do not always find their answers in the Old Testament faith history. Items of major concern to the secular historian, whether involving the specific date of a given event or the full range of political, social, and cultural realities associated with it, are often incidental or irrelevant to the religious interests addressed by the Old Testament writers. Thus, the theo-

---

[79] The most notable of the Palestinian epigraphical materials, such as the Gezer Calendar, Siloam inscription, Lachish Ostraca, and Dead Sea Scrolls, are described at the appropriate points throughout this text. In recent years, about two hundred ostraca (inscribed potsherds), dating from the period of the Hebrew monarchy, were discovered at Arad, in southern Israel; and caves in the vicinity of Samaria have yielded a collection of papyrus documents written in the fourth century B.C. The oldest known Hebrew inscription is a listing of the letters of the alphabet on a single clay sherd found recently at Izbet Sartah (possibly biblical Ebenezer) and dating from the period of the Judges (c. 1200–1000 B.C.).

Stratified remains at ancient Gezer, shown in a cross section of the tell. (Courtesy of Dr. Richard Schiemann.)

logically rich narratives of the pre-Davidic era, i.e., the accounts of the patriarchs, Exodus, and settlement, are sufficiently vague respecting historical setting as to have resulted in long-standing scholarly debates concerning the date and circumstances of the events which they describe.

The emphasis which Hebrew religion places upon its history, therefore, must be seen for what it is: a history comprehended by faith and written to inspire faith in the God of history and his mighty deeds on behalf of his people. Much more than simply a record of the historical epochs of Israel's past, the books of Old Testament history depict a divine participation in the pivotal events affecting Israel's destiny. Repeatedly one perceives God's hand at work: in the early migrations of the Hebrew fathers, the covenant-making events of the deliverance from Egypt and the gift of Torah, the arrival in crisis of mighty leaders endowed with God's charisma, the bestowal of land and kingdom, the grave confrontations between the nation and its prophets, and the new faith ventures provoked by national catastrophe.

The significance of history for Hebrew religion has been so often remarked, that it is important not to overstate the point. The Hebrews were not the only people of the ancient world to conceive of divine activity within historical events. Although the ancient polytheistic religions characteristically emphasized the seasonal cycles of the natural order and the cultic rites designed to sustain them, they were not inattentive to a deity's action in causing the defeat of an enemy or in punishing his own devotees through historical means.[80] For example, Mesha, ancient king of Moab, could account for his nation's subjection by the Israelites as owing to nothing other than the god Chemosh's displeasure with his people.[81] By the same token, Hebrew religion is not lacking a theology of creation and a sensitivity to the divine designs written into the natural order. That the Hebrews, nevertheless, gave a distinctive emphasis to history and so interpreted events with respect to the one God, Yahweh, as to create a unique and enduring phenomenon in the history of world religion—of that there can be no doubt.

5. THE OLD TESTAMENT WORLD

The larger stage upon which the Old Testament drama unfolds is the world of the ancient Near East, the meeting place of three continents (Asia, Africa, and Europe) and the territory of the modern states of Turkey, Syria, Lebanon, Israel, Jordan, Egypt, Saudi Arabia, Iraq, and Iran. An area of widely contrasting terrain, climate, and culture, it includes the rugged mountains of Armenia, the great Arabian Desert, and, in between, the long, crescent-shaped strip of land known as the Fertile Crescent. The latter territory stretches from Egypt on the southwest, up the Mediterranean coast through Palestine and Syria, and down the Tigris-Euphrates Valley to the Persian Gulf. In contrast to the surrounding mountains and desert, the Fertile Crescent is capable of supporting agriculture and settled life, and here the earliest civilizations developed.

At the center of this stage, insofar as Hebrew history is concerned, is the

[80] Bertil Albrektson, *History and the Gods* (Lund, Sweden: CWK Gleerup, 1967) documents the problems associated with an overemphasis on the historical feature of Hebrew religion at the expense of the historical consciousness of other ancient religions. Although something of an overstatement of the case, this study provides a needed corrective to G. Ernest Wright's *The Old Testament Against Its Environment*, Studies in Biblical Theology, No. 2 (London: S.C.M. Press, 1950) and idem, *The God Who Acts, Studies in Biblical Theology*, No. 8 (London: S.C.M. Press, 1952).

[81] *ANET*, p. 320 (*ANE*, p. 209).

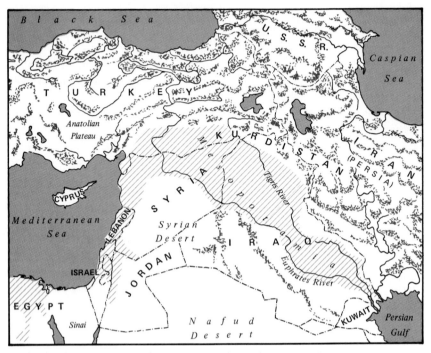

The Fertile Crescent—modern states. (Redrawn from Macmillan Bible Atlas *by Y. Aharoni and Michael Avi-Yonah. Copyright © 1968 Carta, Jerusalem. © Copyright 1964 by Carta, Jerusalem. © Copyright 1966 by Carta, Jerusalem.)*

land of Palestine, a narrow corridor between the Mediterranean Sea and the Arabian Desert, the southern extension of Syria and Egypt's closest neighbor to the north. A small land, measuring only about 150 miles "from Dan to Beersheba," the biblical idiom for its north-south extremities (Judg. 20:1, etc.), it played nevertheless a significant role in the political, economic, and cultural life of the ancient world. Situated astride the major highways joining Egypt and Mesopotamia, centers of power in the ancient Near East, Palestine commanded a strategic location for commercial and military affairs. At some periods in her history, notably during Solomon's reign, Israel managed to capitalize on the heavy commercial traffic that moved through the land. More often than not, however, one or another of the larger nations, Assyria, Babylon, Persia, or Egypt, was on her soil as an invading army or an exactor of tribute. But, whether as bane or blessing, few significant international developments in the larger Near East left Palestine unaffected.

Palestinian topography is characterized by four major longitudinal zones, extending southward from Syria and running the length of the land. From west to east, these consist of (1) the Coastal Plain, (2) Central Highlands,

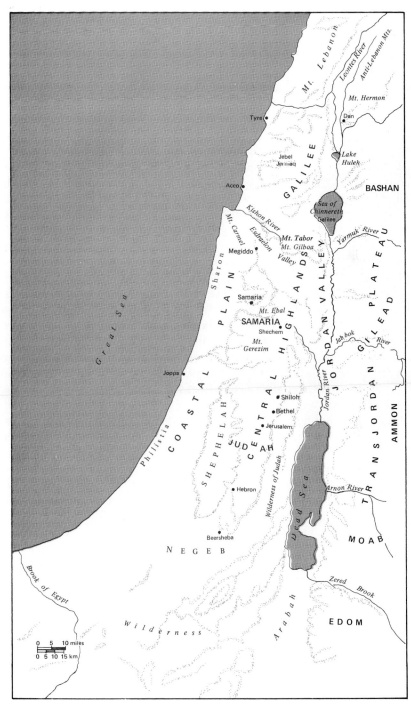

Topography of Palestine

(3) Jordan Valley, and (4) Transjordan Plateau. The unbroken coastline south of Mount Carmel provides no natural harbors and accounts for the fact that Israel, unlike neighboring Phoenicia, did not develop as a maritime power. When the enterprising Solomon built a fleet of ships and launched the nation on a brief experiment in sea trade, he was forced to use the Gulf of Aqabah on the Red Sea as an outlet. For many years the broad, southern portion of the Coastal Plain (the Plain of Philistia) was controlled by the Philistines, a foreign people who settled there near the beginning of the eleventh century B.C., and from whose name the word Palestine derives. One of the more fertile regions in the land, it was densely populated in biblical days and given over to grain fields and gently rolling hills. To the north, between Joppa and Mount Carmel, lies the narrow and marshy Plain of Sharon, once thickly covered with oak forests. One of the important overland routes from Egypt, known as "the Way of the Land of the Philistines," followed the coast to a point near Megiddo, then veered northeastward to Damascus and connected with points east and west.

It was the Central Highlands, Palestine's long backbone of mountains, hills, and valleys, that provided the setting for most of the Old Testament history. Its ridges form the watershed of the land, sloping westward toward the Mediterranean and eastward into the Jordan rift. The most lofty elevations are Jebel Jermaq (3,962 ft.) in northern Galilee and a point near Hebron in the south (3,370 ft.). Notwithstanding the rugged character of the land, the moisture-laden winds from the Mediterranean and the long season of winter rains nourish olive, fig, and other fruit trees on many of the hill slopes and fields of grain and vineyards in the intervening valleys. The Central Highlands have been divided historically into the three regions of Galilee, Samaria (or Ephraim), and Judah (or Judea). Galilee, in the north, is separated from the central heartland of Samaria by the important east-west Valley of Esdraelon (or Jezreel), through which passed the major trade route linking the Palestinian coast and Syria. The Esdraelon is a fertile plain drained by the Kishon River and across from which Mount Tabor (1,843 ft.) and Mount Gilboa (1,698 ft.) face each other. At the southern entrance to the pass stood the city of Megiddo, site of numerous decisive battles, by reason of which its name became synonymous with the final world struggle anticipated in apocalyptic tradition.[82]

Mount Ebal (3,085 ft.) and Mount Gerizim (2,849 ft.), the highest peaks in the region of Samaria, overlook the site of ancient Shechem, another important mountain pass and, along with Shiloh, Bethel, and Samaria (the city), one of the historically significant towns in Palestine's midsection. Although no well-defined geographical feature separates Samaria from Judah,

[82] The "Armageddon" of Revelation 16:16 is a Greek transliteration of the Hebrew *Har Megiddo*, "Mountain of Megiddo."

Palestinian coast at Ashkelon. Named for the escallot (scallion) which grew there, Ashkelon was one of the five chief Philistine cities. (Courtesy of Dr. Richard Schiemann.)

to the south, one has to travel but a few miles south or east of Jerusalem or Bethlehem before entering upon the forbidding Wilderness of Judah, where the stony, gray hills support no vegetation throughout most of the year. Between the Judean hill country and the Philistine plain is the Shephelah, a region of foothills and valleys, in which many of the clashes between Hebrews and Philistines took place. South of Beersheba, the Judean hills flatten out into the barren southern steppe, the Negeb, which merges with the Sinai Desert.

Palestine's most distinctive geographical feature is the Jordan Valley. A part of the great geological rift which extends through Syria and continues southward as the Wadi Arabah, it parts the country lengthwise from north to south, and through it the Jordan River descends in its serpentine course. The Jordan's waters are supplied by springs at the foot of Mount Hermon and empty finally into the Dead Sea, which, because it has no outlet, is so heavy in saline deposits that it is unable to support life. The rapid descent of the Jordan's waters may be seen in the contrasting surface levels of its

Lower Galilee. Shown here are the saddle-shaped hills known as the Horns of Hittin, where Saladin defeated the Crusaders in 1187. (Courtesy of Israel Government Tourist Office.)

lakes: the former Lake Huleh (230 ft. above sea level[83]); the Sea of Galilee or Chinnereth (686 ft. below sea level); and the Dead Sea (1,284 ft. below sea level). Comparative figures likewise reveal the river's meandering course between the Sea of Galilee and the Dead Sea, only 65 miles as the crow flies, but three times that distance as the river flows. Though shallow enough for fording at a number of places, the Jordan is set in dense thickets of thorn scrub and tamarisk, which, together with the precipitous heights of the surrounding cliffs, provide a natural boundary between Cis-Jordan (west) and Transjordan (east).

Israel's control of Transjordan during the biblical period was sporadic and often limited to the central sector. A high tableland which rises impos-

---

[83] In recent years, the waters of Lake Huleh were drained into canals and made to serve agricultural purposes. Consequently, there is no longer a Lake Huleh such as that shown on biblical maps.

The Wilderness of Judah. On the road from Jerusalem to the Dead Sea one enters the Wilderness of Judah and descends almost 4000 feet in less than 35 miles.

ingly out of the Jordan Valley and slopes off into the great Arabian Desert, Transjordan's several regions are set apart by four tributaries of the Jordan: the Yarmuk, Jabbok, and Arnon Rivers, and the Zered Brook. The fertile belt is widest in Bashan, north of the Yarmuk, a region famous for its grain and sleek cattle, as reflected in the proverbial figure, "cows of Bashan" (Amos 4:1; Ps. 22:12). Between the Yarmuk and Jabbok was Gilead, a well-forested territory, good for growing grapes and olives, and noted in biblical times for its medicinal balm (Jer. 8:22; 46:11). South of Gilead, the Arnon River separated Ammon from Moab; and the Zered Brook marked the division between Moab and Edom. Modest agriculture and sheepherding are possible in the former territories. South of the Zered, however, the land becomes so arid as to have forced the ancient Edomites to live chiefly off the revenues from the trade routes which traversed their region and the mining of copper ore in the hills bordering the Arabah. An important East Jordan artery was "the King's Highway," which joined Damascus and Ezion-geber on the Gulf of Aqabah.

Palestine's climate is dominated by two seasons. From October to April is the rainy season, at the end of which comes the harvest of the winter grain crops. The rest of the year is dry, except at the highest elevations, and provides the growing season for grapes, figs, and olives. On the average, rainfall tends to decrease from north to south and from west to

47

The Jordan near its source in Upper Galilee.(Courtesy of the Consulate General of Israel in New York.)

east, and increases on the seaward slopes of hills and mountains. The average rainfall at Jerusalem, in the central hills, is about 22 inches per year. The autumnal equinox marks the beginning of the agricultural year and, quite understandably, came to be observed as the Israelite New Year. Palestinian temperatures, as varied as the terrain and seasons, are affected particularly by elevation and prevailing winds. Jerusalem's average temperature is about 48° F. in midwinter and about 74° F. in midsummer; in winter there may be frost or, less frequently, snow. At Jericho, only a few miles distant but set in the deep depression of the lower Jordan Valley, a subtropical climate prevails; and in the wilderness of southern Judah the midsummer heat is almost unbearable. Just as the monsoon or sea winds off the Mediterranean bring life-giving moisture and cool temperatures to Palestine's western slopes, so the Sirocco or dry wind from the eastern desert, felt particularly in early autumn and late spring, has a withering effect on man, beast, and vegetation, and it became in the Old Testament a symbol

Sea of Galilee at Tiberias. (Courtesy of the Israel Government Tourist Office.)

of God's wrath (Isa. 27:8; Jer. 4:11). If something less than a "land of milk and honey" by Western standards—though the employment of modern technology and irrigation appear destined to make it so—Palestine offered unusual opportunities to the ancient Hebrew and influenced his cultural patterns, his literature, and even his faith in innumerable ways that will become apparent in the pages that follow.

6. DISCOVERING THE OLD TESTAMENT'S MESSAGE

Anyone who would discover the message of the Old Testament must be prepared to encounter the books on their own terms. In the experience of many readers, this involves a confrontation with "the strange new world of

49

The Jordan Valley. The Jordan River descends in a contorted, serpentine pattern between the Sea of Galilee and the Dead Sea. (Courtesy of the Consulate General of Israel in New York.)

the Bible,"[84] where contemporary patterns of thought and logic are challenged by the unique categories in which ancient Israel expressed its faith. Especially do the rational, abstract, and individualistic traits of Western thought require accommodation to the poetic, concrete, and corporate patterns of the early Hebrew psychology. If one successfully resists the urge toward eisegesis, i.e., misrepresentation of meanings for the sake of preserving one's own preconceptions, then one is likely to experience a degree of confusion, surprise, perhaps even shock, at some of the things discovered. Certainly, to open oneself to the Old Testament's message is to run the risk of changing rather drastically one's previously held views of what constitutes religion, morality, or the sacred.

This is not to say that a proper understanding of the Bible necessarily sidetracks the reader into patterns unrelated to his original interests. Each new generation, as Wheeler Robinson candidly observed, "will interpret the past in its own characteristic way," according to its own theological needs.[85] This is both inevitable and necessary, so long as the Bible continues to speak to the existential issues confronting the changing human so-

[84] This apt and striking phrase was made famous by Karl Barth in *The Word of God and the Word of Man*, Douglas Horton, trans. (New York: Harper & Row, Publishers, 1957), pp. 28–50.

[85] H. Wheeler Robinson, *Inspiration and Revelation in the Old Testament* (Oxford: Clarendon Press, Oxford Paperbacks, 1962), p. 282.

Salt-coated driftwood on the Dead Sea. (Courtesy of the Israel Government Tourist Office.)

ciety. In taking our questions to the scriptures, however, we must be prepared for the sort of fruitful dialectic wherein the current thought patterns and vocabulary interact with those of the biblical writers in a constant process of rethinking, rephrasing, and readjustment of the questions, the more deeply we delve into the minds of the writers. The result is what has often been called "the hermeneutical circle." One writer observes:

> We read the text with a question in mind—and reading the text, we have to adjust our question to the intention of the text. And having done this, we must start anew.[86]

To capture the essence of the Old Testament is to hear all the voices within it: the absolutes of the lawgiver and the searchings of the sage; the narrator's sense of a guidance in history and the psalmist's delight in the created order; the prophet's demand for present change and the apocalyptist's promise of future deliverance.[87] The reader is unavoidably drawn into

---

[86] Erich Dinkler, "The Historical and the Eschatological Israel in Romans chaps. 9–11: A Contribution to the Problem of Predestination and Individual Responsibility," *JR*, XXXVI (1956), p. 109.

[87] Two recent books which set forth clearly the major issues in current Old Testament theology are Gerhard Hasel, *Old Testament Theology: Basic Issues in the Current Debate*, rev. ed. (Grand Rapids, MI: Eerdmans, 1975) and Brevard S. Childs, *Biblical Theology in Crisis*.

living dialogue with the books and must resolve for himself how the points of difference are to be bridged or the normative position is to be determined. For those who approach the Bible as a canon such decisions are not undertaken in isolation but involve the confessing community of faith in which one shares membership.

Although the Old Testament's message cannot, then, be reduced to a single, one-dimensional formula, a dynamic, unifying element is to be seen in the one God who is recognized by all its spokesmen. It is this central focus that underlies the most prominent of the Old Testament themes and motifs. Much of the Old Testament moves along a historical axis and is informed by the theme of God's covenant with Israel. Repeated emphasis falls upon God's direction of Israel's fortunes—especially his deliverance in the Exodus—and the nation's obligations as a responsible covenant partner. A more inclusive perspective, however, is provided by those Old Testament strands in which God's creation of the world or his universal lordship over both nature and all of earth's creatures is in view. This creation theme is developed yet further in the wisdom books where the proper response to God takes the form of human discovery, creativity, and responsibility for one's own destiny. At their best, the Old Testament books envision the God of creation and history as far enough in advance of human calculations to encourage hope for the new and unexpected thing, the next encounter, the new kingdom.

SELECTED READINGS

Titles of journals and reference works indicated here in abbreviated form are cited in full in the table of abbreviations that are placed at the end of the contents.

History and Authority of the Canon

Anderson, George W., "The Old Testament: Canonical and Non-Canonical," *The Cambridge History of the Bible*, Vol. I: From the Beginnings to Jerome, P. R. Ackroyd and C. F. Evans, eds. (Cambridge, England: Cambridge University Press, 1970), pp. 113–159.

Bright, John, *The Authority of the Old Testament* (Grand Rapids, Mich.: Baker Book House, 1975). Paperback.

Childs, Brevard, *Biblical Theology in Crisis* (Philadelphia: Westminster Press, 1970). An advocacy of canonical criticism as the method for a new biblical theology. An original and path-finding proposal.

————, *Introduction to the Old Testament as Scripture* (Philadelphia: Fortress Press, 1979). An application of canonical criticism as a method of interpreting the Old Testament books.

Filson, Floyd, *Which Books Belong in the Bible?* (Philadelphia: The Westminster Press, 1957).

Hayes, John H., "The Canon of the Old Testament," *An Introduction to Old Testament Study* (Nashville, TN: Abingdon Press, 1979), pp. 16–44. A succinct and up-to-date summary of Old Testament canonization.

Lewis, Jack, "What Do We Mean by Jabne?" *JBR*, XXXII (1964), pp. 125–132.

Leiman, S. Z., *The Canonization of Hebrew Scripture: The Talmudic and Midrashic Evidence* (Hamden, CT: Doubleday Anchor, 1976).

Murphy, Roland E., Albert C. Sundberg, Jr., and Samuel Sandmel, "A symposium on the Canon of Scripture," *CBQ*, XXVIII (1966), pp. 189–207. Incisive reflections on the Old Testament canon from Judaic, Catholic, and Protestant perspectives.

Sanders, James A., "Cave 11 Surprises and the Question of Canon," *New Directions in Biblical Archaeology*, David N. Freedman and Jonas C. Greenfield, eds. (Garden City, NY: Doubleday & Company, Inc., 1969), pp. 101–116. Also available in paperback (Doubleday Anchor, 1971). A discussion of the most recent Dead Sea Scroll finds in respect to the growth of the Old Testament canon.

————, *Torah and Canon* (Philadelphia: Fortress Press, 1972). A fresh treatment of canonicity as the process by which the Old Testament was formed.

Silberman, Lou, "The Making of the Old Testament Canon," *IOVCB*, pp. 1214–1215.

Smith, Moody, "The Use of the Old Testament in the New," *The Old Testament in the New and Other Essays*, James M. Efird, ed. (Durham, NC: Duke University Press, 1972), pp. 3–65.

Sundberg, Albert C., *The Old Testament of the Early Church*, Harvard Theological Studies, XX (Cambridge, MA: Harvard University Press, 1964). Argues for an open-ended scripture in the New Testament Church and first-century Judaism.

Torro, James C., and Raymond E. Brown, "Canonicity," *JBC*, pp. 513–534. An informative and up-to-date survey article on the history and meaning of the canonization of the Bible within Judaism and the Church.

West, James King, "Rethinking the Old Testament Canon," *RL*, XLV (1976), pp. 22–32. A review of current issues and views on the canon's development and use.

Wright, G. Ernest, "The Canon as Theological Problem," *The Old Testament and Theology* (New York: Harper & Row, Publishers, 1969), ch. 7.

Old Testament Text and Versions

Ap-Thomas, D. R., *A Primer of Old Testament Text Criticism*, 2nd ed. (Oxford: Basil Blackwell, 1964). Available in paperback (Philadelphia: Fortress Press, 1966). A succinct, clearly written introduction to text criticism.

Barthélemy, Dominique, "Text, Hebrew, History of," *IDBS*, pp. 878–884.

Cross, Frank M., Jr., *The Ancient Library of Qumran and Modern Biblical Studies*, rev. ed. (Garden City, NY: Doubleday Anchor, 1961). Paperback. Ch. 4. A discussion of the Old Testament textual tradition reflected in the Qumran manuscripts.

————, and Shemaryahu Talmon, eds., *Qumran and the History of the Biblical Text* (Cambridge, MA: Harvard University Press, 1975). Paperback. Essays, both technical and introductory, relating the Dead Sea Scrolls to the textual study of the Bible.

Hayes, John H., "The Textual Criticism of the Old Testament," *An Introduction to Old Testament Study* (Nashville, TN: Abingdon Press, 1979), pp. 46–81. An up-to-date summary description of the materials and methods of textual criticism.

Kenyon, Sir Frederick, *Our Bible and the Ancient Manuscripts*, rev. by A. W. Adams (New York: Harper & Row, Publishers, 1958).

Klein, Ralph W., *Textual Criticism of the Old Testament* (Philadelphia: Fortress Press, 1974). An introductory treatment that focuses primarily on the role of the Septuagint in textual criticism.

Orlinsky, Harry M., "The Textual Criticism of the Old Testament," *The Bible and the Ancient Near East*, G. Ernest Wright, ed. (Garden City, NY: Doubleday & Company, Inc., 1961), ch. 5. Also available in paperback (Doubleday Anchor, 1965).

Roberts, Bleddyn J., *The Old Testament Texts and Versions: The Hebrew Texts in Transmission and the History of the Ancient Versions* (Cardiff: University of Wales Press, 1951).

Skehan, Patrick W., "The Scrolls and the Old Testament Text," *New Directions in Biblical Archaeology*, David N. Freedman and Jonas C. Greenfield, eds. (Garden City, NY: Doubleday & Company, Inc., 1969), pp. 89–100.

Würthwein, Ernst, *The Text of the Old Testament*, Peter R. Ackroyd, trans. (Grand Rapids, MI: Eerdmans, 1980). A standard treatment of the most important problems concerning the Old Testament text and the procedures of textual criticism.

The English Bible

An Introduction to the Revised Standard Version of the Old Testament by members of the Revision Committee (New York: Thomas Nelson Inc., 1952).

Bailey, Lloyd R., ed., "Recent English Versions of the Bible," *The Duke Divinity School Review*, 44 (1979), pp. 67–195. Evaluations by leading scholars and translators of the major English versions of the Bible which have appeared since the publication of the R.S.V.

Bruce, F. F., *History of the Bible in English*, 3rd ed. (New York: Oxford University Press, 1978). Paperback. One of the most readable, comprehensive, and up-to-date accounts of the history of the English Bible.

Hinson, E. Glenn, ed., "Recent Study Bibles and Translations," *RE*, 76 (1979), pp. 297–416. Evaluations of recent Bible versions comparable to those in Bailey, above.

May, H. G., *Our English Bible in the Making* (Philadelphia: The Westminster Press, 1952).

Orlinsky, Harry M., "The New Version of the Torah," *JBL*, LXXXII (1963), pp. 249–264.

Price, I. M., *The Ancestry of Our English Bible*, 2nd ed., rev. by W. A. Irwin and A. P. Wikgren (New York: Harper & Row, Publishers, 1949).

Sanders, James A., "The New English Bible: A Comparison," *CC*, LXXXVII, 11 (Mar. 18, 1970), pp. 326–328.

Wikgren, Allen, "The English Bible," *IB*, Vol. I, pp. 84–105.

Biblical Criticism

See the works listed under this category in the General Bibliography.

Israelite History

See the works cited in the General Bibliography.

Geography of Palestine and the Near East

Aharoni, Yohanan, *The Land of the Bible; A Historical Geography,* A. F. Rainey, trans. (Philadelphia: The Westminster Press, 1967). An important work by a respected Israeli scholar that treats Palestinian geography in the context of biblical history.

Baly, Denis, *Geographical Companion to the Bible* (London: Lutterworth Press, 1963).

————, *The Geography of the Bible,* rev. ed. (New York: Harper & Row, Publishers, 1974). A standard reference work, clearly written and illustrated with photographs, maps and charts.

————, *Palestine and the Bible* (London: Lutterworth Press, 1960). Paperback.

See the atlases cited in the General Bibliography.

I

o
how
I
love
thy
law

O, how I love thy law! It is my meditation all the day.
—Psalms 119:97

1

these aRe the GeneRations

These are the generations of the sons of Noah, Shem, Ham, and Japheth; sons were born to them after the flood.
—Genesis 10:1

No other portion of the Hebrew canon equals in importance the first five books known as the Torah. From the fourth century B.C., or soon thereafter, they have served as Judaism's Bible *par excellence*, alongside which the rest of the Old Testament is viewed as commentary. The word *torah*, commonly translated "law," derives from a Hebrew verb meaning "to give direction" or "to point the way" and is more accurately rendered "guidance" or "instruction." This describes precisely the role accorded these books by Judaism and the Church. Composed of both narrative and law, they not only set forth God's demands for his people, but demonstrate his works on their behalf and reveal his promises for the future.

1. THE STRUCTURE AND COMPOSITION OF THE PENTATEUCH

The Torah's composition, as we shall see, was far more complex than the division into five books would indicate. With the exception of Deuteronomy, the book divisions were not original, but arose as a practical means of transmitting the Torah on scrolls of manageable proportions. The five-fold division was customary, however, as early as the Septuagint translation; and by the second century A.D., the Torah was known to Greek-speaking readers as *he pentateuchos biblos* ("the book of the five scrolls"),[1] whence the current name Pentateuch.

Recent studies of the Old Testament attest the difficulty of separating the Pentateuch from the books which follow it in the canon. The Former Prophets depend upon its narrative, even as the Pentateuch itself contains a thread of promise which remains unfulfilled apart from the later history. When scholars of the last century discovered literary patterns common to the Pentateuch and Joshua, it became popular to speak of a "Hexateuch" (six books) or, if the patterns were traced beyond Joshua, of an "Octateuch" (Genesis–Samuel) or an "Enneateuch" (Genesis–Kings). In more recent years Martin Noth has won wide acceptance for the view that Deuteronomy is an integral part of the Former Prophets, thus grouping these books together as a "Deuteronomic History," in separation from Genesis–Numbers (which becomes a "Tetrateuch").[2] This is an attractive theory in view of the common Deuteronomic themes evident throughout the books of the Former Prophets and absent from the Tetrateuch. It allows for an independent composition of Deuteronomy and explains how that work was appropriated by a later "Deuteronomist" as a beginning for the Former Prophets, although admitting to its use by yet other redactors who joined it with the Mosaic traditions of Genesis–Numbers.

Notwithstanding the complex literary relationships reflected in these several approaches, it was with good reason that Judaism treated the Torah as a unity, for it is in these five books that we possess the crucially significant traditions concerning Moses and the religious faith of which he is believed to be the founder. The book of Exodus begins with the story of his birth in Egypt, and Deuteronomy concludes with his death in Moab. Situated in the midst of this long narrative and complicating its sequence somewhat are the several legal codes which tradition attributed to Moses. Although most of these laws actually derive from later periods of Israel's history, the close relationship between law and covenant in Hebrew tradition is vividly depicted by this arrangement. The universal and broader Semitic setting for the Mosaic narrative is contributed by Genesis, with its ancient stories of primeval beginnings and patriarchal backgrounds. The following outline distinguishes the Pentateuch's major narrative and legal units.

---

[1] Attested first in the writings of Tertullian, the Latin Church father (c. A.D. 160–230).

[2] *Überlieferungsgeschichtliche Studien*, I (Halle, East Germany: Niemeyer, 1943). See below, pp. 66, 186.

1. THE STRUCTURE OF THE PENTATEUCH

	NARRATIVE	LAW CODES
Gen. 1–11	Primeval beginnings	
Gen. 12–50	Patriarchs	
Ex. 1–15	Egyptian oppression and Exodus	
Ex. 16–18	Guidance in the wilderness (I): Egypt to Sinai	
Ex. 19 and 24	Sinai covenant	Decalogue: Ex. 20:1–17 (Deut. 5:6–21)
		Covenant Code: Ex. 20:22–23:33
		Cultic Law (interwoven with narrative): Ex. 25–Num. 10:10
		Ritual Decalogue: Ex. 34
Num. 10:11–36:13	Guidance in the wilderness (II): Sinai to Moab	Holiness Code: Lev. 17–26
Deut. 1–4; 29–33	Covenant renewal	Deuteronomic Law (interwoven with narrative): Deut. 5–28
Deut. 34	Moses' death	

Literary Analysis of the Pentateuch

Moses being the central figure in these books and the stamp of his personality resting so heavily upon them, it is easy enough to understand why tradition came to regard him as their author. References to "the law of Moses," "the book of Moses," and the like, appear in the late books of the Old Testament and Apocrypha[3]; and the New Testament speaks of "Moses and the Prophets" in reference to the first two divisions of the Hebrew canon.[4] In the Pentateuch itself, however, references to Moses are in the third person and claims of Mosaic authorship extend only to specific portions, namely, the Decalogue (Exod. 24:4; 34:28), the curses upon Amalek (Exod. 17:14), the wilderness itinerary (Num. 33:2), and the Deuteronomic injunctions (Deut. 31:9, 24).

Although the full complexity of Pentateuchal composition has been recognized only in the course of the last century, difficulties with the traditional view of Mosaic authorship have long been apparent. Early rabbinical sources, for example, pointed out that Moses did not write his own death account (Deut. 34:5–12)[5]; and the medieval Jewish scholar, Ibn Ezra (d. 1167), puzzled over such improbable Mosaic phrasings as "beyond the Jordan" (Deut. 1:1) or "at that time the Canaanites were in the land" (Gen.

[3] II Chron. 23:18; 25:4; 30:16; 35:12; Ezra 6:18; 7:6; Dan. 9:11, 13; Eccus. 24:23.
[4] Luke 24:27, 44; cf. Matt. 19:8; Mark 12:26; John 7:19, 23.
[5] Baba Bathra 14b (c. A.D. 500). Joshua was held to have written these verses.

12:6). The first reference was written from the perspective of Cis-Jordan, looking east, but Moses, according to the record, never crossed the Jordan into the west. The latter reference reflects a time at least as late as the monarchy (David) when the Canaanite population in Palestine had so amalgamated with the Hebrews that one would no longer speak of Canaanites apart from some indication of their disappearance as a separate people ("at that time").

Scholars today recognize numerous such anachronisms throughout the Pentateuch, among them names of peoples and places unknown in Moses' time (e.g., Philistia, Dan, Hebron),[6] references to the later monarchy,[7] and laws designed for the settled, agricultural society of later Israel but inappropriate to the nomadic life attributed to Moses. In addition, the Pentateuch's composite character is evident in a variety of literary styles, duplicate and triplicate accounts of the same event, and other inconsistencies of detail. The narrative of Genesis 1, to cite a prime example, is related in a formal, poetic, and liturgical style, marked by a deliberate outline, stylized refrains, and majestic rhythm. Genesis 2, on the other hand, is narrated in the spontaneous, warm, and personal manner of the folklorist. Similar contrasts distinguish the highly personalized stories of the patriarchs (Gen. 12–50) from the dry, genealogical framework that surrounds them (Gen. 11:10–32; 25:7–19; 36). Likewise, the long, tedious catalogues of cultic and priestly law that begin in the latter half of Exodus and continue through the first third of Numbers contrast with the vivid, hortatory style of Deuteronomy.

With these distinctive styles one can associate corresponding vocabularies. The best example, perhaps, is seen in the different names for God. Associated with the colorful style of chapter 2 of Genesis is a preference for the personal name for God, YHWH (probably to be vocalized, "Yahweh") or Lord.[8] Throughout the book of Genesis this divine name appears only in passages where the corresponding style is evident. Elsewhere in Genesis the preferred name is the impersonal "Elohim," meaning simply "God." One strand of Pentateuchal tradition (Exod. 6:3), in fact, views God's personal name as unknown before the time of Moses. To cite another example, the formal or priestly hand can be identified wherever the word *toledoth*, "generations" or "families," appears. This term, and especially the phrase, "These are the generations of . . . ," are peculiarly characteristic of the priestly style.

Among the doublets in the Pentateuch are the two versions of the

---

[6] Gen. 21:32, 34; 26:1, 8, 14, 15, 18; Ex. 13:17; Gen. 14:14 (cf. Judg. 18:29); 13:18; 23:2, 19; 35:27; 37:14; Num. 13:22.

[7] Gen. 36:31.

[8] The familiar "Jehovah" is a hybrid name formed of the consonants of Yahweh (Jahveh) plus the vowels of "Adonai," the Hebrew word for "Lord." In Jewish tradition Adonai is substituted for the ineffably personal Yahweh in oral readings of the Scriptures.

Decalogue (Exod. 20, Deut. 5) and dual accounts of Hagar's ejection from Abraham's household (Gen. 16, 21), the gift of manna and quail (Exod. 16; Num. 11), and the namings of Beersheba (Gen. 21, 26), Bethel (Gen. 28, 35), Esau (Gen. 25:25, 30), and Israel (Gen. 32, 35). There are no fewer than three separate stories of a patriarch passing off his wife as his sister while sojourning in a foreign land (Gen. 12:10–20; 20; 26:6–11). Some accounts display a close interweaving of originally separate versions, as in the flood story (Gen. 6–9), where there are inconsistencies regarding the flood's duration and the number of animals taken aboard the ark. The story of Joseph's sale into Egypt (Gen. 37) affords another instance of a conflated account. The confusions involving the brother who came to Joseph's defense (was it Reuben or Judah?) and the people to whom Joseph was sold (were they Midianites or Ishmaelites?) witness a redactor's interest in retaining both versions of the story. One of the more striking discrepancies within the legal codes concerns the legitimacy of altars; Exodus 20:24–26 permits a number of altars, whereas Deuteronomy 12 insists there shall be only one.

In some instances theological interests may be associated with distinguishable literary traits. Thus the exalted style of Genesis 1 proves to be consistent with an unusually profound sense of God's transcendence, whereas the anthropomorphic (manlike) speech of Genesis 2 conveys more vivid images of a personal deity's entry into intimate relationships with humankind. Or, again, the different accounts of a patriarch's misrepresentation of his wife exhibit contrasts in ethical sensitivity. The one account (Gen. 12) indicates no sense of embarrassment concerning either the patriarch's lie or the possible violation of the wife, but the other (Gen. 20) offers an explanation for both (vss. 4, 6, 12). Though they are in no sense mutually exclusive, one might also contrast the Priestly concerns of Leviticus with the moral and prophetic tone of Deuteronomy.

It was not until the eighteenth century that any serious attempts were made to differentiate the component parts of the Pentateuch according to a theory of multiple sources or documents.[9] The first step in this direction was taken in 1711 by a German pastor, H. B. Witter, who recognized in Genesis 1:1–2:4a and 2:4b–3:24 parallel accounts of the Creation, distinguished by the different names for God, Elohim and Yahweh. Somewhat later, in 1753, the French physician Jean Astruc arrived at the same con-

[9] A thorough presentation in English of the history of Pentateuchal source analysis is Joseph E. Carpenter and G. Harford-Battersby, *The Hexateuch According to the Revised Version*, 2 vols. (New York: Longmans, Green, and Company [now Longman, Inc.], 1900). More concise treatments appear in the following Old Testament introductions: Aage Bentzen, *Introduction to the Old Testament*, 2nd ed. (Copenhagen: G. E. C. Gad, 1952); S. R. Driver, *Introduction to the Literature of the Old Testament*, 9th ed. (Edinburgh: T. Clarke, 1913); Otto Eissfeldt, *The Old Testament, An Introduction*, P. R. Ackroyd, trans. (New York: Harper & Row, Publishers, 1965); and R. H. Pfeiffer, *Introduction to the Old Testament*, rev. ed. (New York: Harper & Row, Publishers, 1948).

clusion independently. On the basis of the alternation of the divine names, Astruc posited an Elohim source and a Yahweh source from which he concluded the book of Genesis had been compiled. This beginning was significantly advanced by J. G. Eichhorn, who in 1780 utilized the evidence of doublets, diversities of style, and characteristic words and phrases to define further and characterize the two sources. When, in 1798, K. D. Ilgen theorized that the Elohim source should be subdivided into two distinct parts, a three-document theory was born.

By the early nineteenth century, not simply Genesis, but the entire Pentateuch was being probed in the light of this documentary hypothesis. As a result of Hermann Hupfield's studies (1853), it became clear that the characteristic traits of three documents or literary traditions (somewhat differently conceived from those of Ilgen) could be found in varying degrees in the books of Genesis, Exodus, Leviticus, and Numbers. These consisted of (1) a Yahweh document (eventually abbreviated J after the German spelling of Yahweh), (2) an Elohim document (E), and (3) a second Elohim document, characterized by priestly interests and thus designated P. A redactor, it was concluded, had skillfully combined the originally independent documents into an organic whole. Deuteronomy was recognized as a work basically distinct from anything found in Genesis–Numbers and took its place as a fourth Pentateuchal source (D). This rudimentary form of the documentary hypothesis lacked only a clear conception of the dating sequence of the four sources in order to assume the broad outline by which it has been known for more than a century.

The two German scholars who correlated the earlier findings and proposed the classic chronology of J, E, D, P were Karl H. Graf (1815–1869) and Julius Wellhausen (1844–1918). Their dating of the documents was made possible by W. M. L. de Wette's significant studies in Deuteronomy, the book which became the key element in the hypothesis. As early as 1805, de Wette had reached the conclusion that Deuteronomy was the book found in the Jerusalem temple and made the basis of Josiah's reforms in the last quarter of the seventh century B.C. (cf. II Kings 22). He further concluded that Deuteronomy contained laws written long after Moses' time and was itself a product of the seventh century. Graf and Wellhausen were able to establish that the Deuteronomist was familiar with the Yahwistic material (J) and one of the Elohistic strands (E), but not with the Priestly material (P). P, therefore, was the most recent of the sources; and J and E were older than D. This can be illustrated from the legal materials. J and E know nothing of the Deuteronomic law of the one altar (Deut. 12); Priestly legislation, however, simply assumes it, thereby reflecting a time by which the Deuteronomic principle was already well established. Likewise, neither J nor E recognizes any restriction as to who may offer sacrifice; in D such functions are reserved for the tribe of Levi, but without distinction between priest and Levite (Deut. 18:1–8); P restricts full priestly prerogatives to the descendants of Aaron, to whom the other Levites minister as temple associates (Num. 3:5–10). Since J was marked by features slightly more primitive than E, the chronological order of the documents was shown to be: J (c. 850 B.C.); E (c. 700 B.C.); D (c. 650 B.C.), and P (c. 500–450 B.C.).

According to Wellhausen,[10] the documents underwent three broad stages of redaction. The Deuteronomist, it was concluded, knew J and E in a combined form; thus, the redaction JE was created prior to 650 B.C. The Deuteronomic Code was added by a D redactor about 550 B.C., forming JED. The addition of the Priestly document in about 400 B.C. resulted in the redaction JEDP and the Pentateuch as we know it today. There has never been, of course, unanimous agreement by the proponents of the hypothesis as to the assignment of every chapter and verse to one or the other of the sources. A comparison of the standard Old Testament introductions and commentaries, however, reveals a broad consensus on the major units.[11]

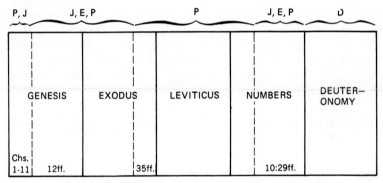

Broad locations of the JEDP sources in the Pentateuch

Since Wellhausen's generation the original documentary hypothesis has undergone considerable modification. Scholars no longer contend, for example, that the sources originated as written "documents," after the fashion of works produced in the private study of a modern author. The tendency is to view them, rather, as living, growing streams of tradition that developed, in large part, alongside each other, and in close association with the religious life of the community (the cult). Each is assumed to contain a core of very old traditions, originally transmitted in oral form; and for this

---

[10] Cf. Julius Wellhausen, *Prolegomena to the History of Ancient Israel* (Cleveland, OH: Meridian Books, 1957), an English edition of the original German work of 1883, *Prolegomena zur Geschichte Israels.*

[11] Cf. Norman Gottwald, *A Light to the Nations,* pp. 215–218; 248–249; 450–453; Walter Harrelson, *Interpreting the Old Testament* (New York: Holt, Rinehart and Winston, 1964), pp. 487–492; and "Source Analysis of the Pentateuch," below, pp. 564–566.

reason some portions of D or P may be fully as old as or older than parts of J or E. The dates proposed by Wellhausen continue to be useful, but only as the terminal points at which the respective source traditions took their fixed—and probably written—forms. The date suggested for J has been moved backward by roughly a century, to c. 950 B.C.[12]

The JED stage envisioned in the older source theories has been largely abandoned in current schemes. The point has been persuasively made by Martin Noth and others that since the D source is largely or entirely confined to the book of Deuteronomy, the books of Genesis through Numbers constitute a JEP Tetrateuch or Priestly Work. By this manner of reckoning, the final stage in the Pentateuch's formation was effected by a postexilic redactor who combined D with the JEP Tetrateuch. According to Noth, an early edition of D (essentially, Deut. 5–26; 28) was appropriated by a Deuteronomistic historian of the sixth century B.C. and made to serve as an introduction to the long historical work Joshua through Kings. The edition of Deuteronomy eventually included in the Pentateuch contains the editorial additions of the Deuteronomist, significantly the introductory chapters 1–3 or 1–4. The current four-source hypothesis, revised along these lines, is depicted in the accompanying diagram.

A working knowledge of the literary strata and their locations within the biblical text is indispensable for an intelligent discussion of the Pentateuch. The following summaries of their salient features will be considerably expanded by the more detailed analyses of the separate Pentateuchal books.

THE YAHWISTIC SOURCE. The Yahwistic source (J) designates the stratum in which the divine name "Yahweh" predominates or in which the peculiar characteristics associated with this pattern are evident. It alone among the sources preserves the tradition that the personal name for God was used before the time of Moses (Gen. 4:26). It is marked by the colorful folk narrative and the human and personal manner of describing the actions of God noted in our earlier observations. Chapters 2 and 3 of Genesis, wherein God forms man from the dust, breathes into his nostrils, walks in the garden, and the like, are typical of J. The account of Abraham's misrepresentation of Sarah which is free of explicit ethical judgments (Gen. 12) belongs to this source and is characteristic of its manner of allowing vivid descriptions of events to speak for themselves, without interpretive comment.

The version of the Joseph story which depicts Joseph's sale to Ishmaelites and credits Judah with saving Joseph's life is from the J narrative.

---

[12] Major departures from the commonly accepted JEDP sequence and dating may be seen in Yehezkel Kaufmann's effort to show that P is earlier than D (*The Religion of Israel*, Moshe Greenberg, trans. [Chicago: The University of Chicago Press, 1960], pp. 175–200) and John Van Seters' contention for an exilic J, a post-Exilic P, and a fragmentary E, which antedated J (*Abraham in History and Tradition* [New Haven, CT: Yale University Press, 1975]).

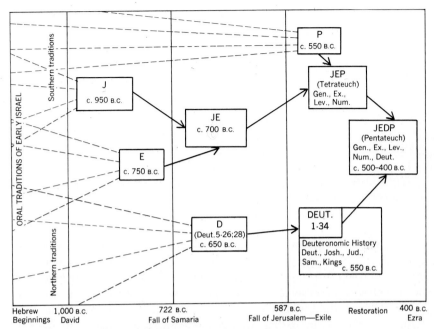

Pentateuchal development according to source analysis.

The prominence of Judah here is consistent with the attention given south-ern personalities, localities, and shrines, all of which point to an origin in the south. The abbreviation "J," therefore, may stand conveniently for both Jahveh (Yahweh) and Judah. The tenth century dating, which is now com-mon for J, allows it a significant role in Israel's transformation from tribal confederacy to dynastic state. As the record of Yahweh's covenant with Israel, his providential guidance of the fathers, and his promises for the na-tion's future, the J epic witnessed mightily to an unbroken religious tradi-tion in a critical period of change.

J constitutes the basic narrative core of the books of Genesis, Exodus, and Numbers. Even with Elohistic additions and its final Priestly dress, the essential shape of the Yahwistic narrative shows through, giving to the Pen-tateuch much of its epic and dramatic character. Through a pattern of promise and fulfillment, it contributes a continuity and mood of antici-pation to these books. Its stories of the garden, the flood, and the tower of Babel revolve around the theme of man's repeated failures and God's inter-ventions for judgment and renewal. This implicit chain of promise becomes explicit in the patriarchal covenants and moves toward its fulfillment in the Exodus and entry into the land of promise.

Although the J material is less than uniform in all its parts, it bears, in the main, the unmistakable stamp of a creative individual of considerable talent, called for convenience the Yahwist. The Yahwist's perspective is always the human one. This applies not alone to his personal conception of God, but to an existential rapport with all humanity and a characteristic manner of exposing universal human emotions in his narratives. His accounts are charged with a dramatic suspense centering in a series of crises. Again and again God's promise is threatened with defeat, and the tension mounts for the participants in the drama as well as for the reader, until at the crucial moment God's intervention asserts once again his claim over human history and vindicates his intention of keeping his word.[13]

THE ELOHISTIC SOURCE. The Elohistic source derives its name from the consistent use of "Elohim" as the name for God throughout the book of Genesis. Its account of Moses' call (Exod. 3:9–14) indicates its agreement with the Priestly source (Exod. 6:3) that the personal name "Yahweh" was disclosed first to Moses. The source is frequently so closely interwoven with J as to resist separate identification; and according to one view the two depended upon a common body of tradition.[14] E has been distinguished, nevertheless, on a basis of several notable contrasts with the Yahwist, only one of which is the tradition concerning the divine name. It is the Elohist, for example, who—unlike the Yahwist—deemed it necessary to protect the moral tone of the Abraham-Sarah narrative by explaining that Abraham did not lie in representing Sarah as his sister (she was his half-sister); nor did the foreign king violate Sarah. A similar attention to detail is evident in the avoidance of anthropomorphic descriptions of God through the characteristic employment of angels and dreams as the media of divine revelation.[15]

[13] A classic theory of the Yahwist's theology is offered by Gerhard von Rad in *Genesis*, J. H. Marks, trans. (Philadelphia: Westminster Press, 1961); idem, *The Problem of the Hexateuch and Other Essays*, E. W. T. Dicken, trans. (New York: McGraw-Hill Book Company, 1966); and idem, *Old Testament Theology*, Vol. I, D. M. G. Stalker, trans. (New York: Harper & Row, Publishers 1962). Hans Walter Wolff and Walter Brueggeman propose a Yahwistic *kerygma* (faith proclamation) centering in the divine purpose for Israel as a blessing for all nations and aimed specifically at the opportunities and dangers implicit in the Davidic-Solomonic state (Hans Walter Wolff, "The Kerygma of the Yahwist," *Int.* 20 [1966], pp. 131–158; reprinted in Walter Brueggemann and Hans Walter Wolff, *The Vitality of Old Testament Traditions* [Atlanta, GA: John Knox Press, 1975], pp. 41–66; Walter Brueggemann, "Yahwist," *IDBS*, pp. 971–975). A cautious skepticism, however, regarding the possibility of tracing a detailed Yahwistic theology based on specific historical provocations is voiced by an increasing number of scholars (e.g., Rolf Rendtorff, *Das uberlieferungs-geschichtliche Problem des Pentateuch*, BZAW 147 [1977]). For a survey of some recent positions, see Peter E. Ellis, *The Yahwist: the Bible's First Theologian* (Notre Dame, IN: Fides Publishers, 1968).

[14] Martin Noth, *A History of Pentateuchal Traditions*, Bernhard W. Anderson, trans., (Englewood Cliffs, NJ: Prentice-Hall, Inc., 1972). Noth leaves open the question whether or not this common tradition, which he designates by the siglum G (*Grundlage*), was in oral or written form.

[15] Gen. 15:1; 20:3, 6; 21:17; 22:11; 28:12; 31:11, 24; 46:2; Num. 22:9, 20. Moses is a notable exception; for according to Ex. 31:18 (E), God spoke with him directly and wrote with his very finger upon the tablets of stone brought down from the mountain by Moses. Perhaps, then, this characteristic of E is not so much an example of advanced theological sensitivity as an in-

It is no coincidence that much of the Joseph cycle derives from this source, nor that Reuben is portrayed as the protector of Joseph; for the Joseph tribes, Ephraim and Manasseh, along with Reuben, are northern tribes, and the Elohist betrays an allegiance to the north. Northern localities such as Bethel and Shechem are prominent. A commonly proposed date for E is the mid-eighth century, at which time the northern kingdom was the stronger of the two divided states and doubtless had produced a corpus of traditions which were distinctively northern in character. About half a century later, following the fall of the northern kingdom, the Elohistic traditions were combined with J in a manner which resulted essentially in an accommodation of E to J.

Elohistic material does not appear at all in the first eleven chapters of Genesis, but alternates with J in the patriarchal accounts and in portions of the books of Exodus and Numbers. Since E in its extant form largely supplements J, the latter providing the common base, it is quite impossible to trace a continuous Elohistic narrative as one can do with J; and it is frequently necessary to speak of the two together as JE. Perhaps the finest narrative account to derive solely from E is the dramatic and sensitive description of Abraham's near sacrifice of his son Isaac (Gen. 22:1–19).[16]

THE DEUTERONOMIC SOURCE. "The Deuteronomist(s)" is the name given the traditioner or school which produced both the book of Deuteronomy and, according to the view of many contemporary scholars, the final edition of the Former Prophets. For the present our interests concern only the Pentateuch, and thus the book of Deuteronomy, to which—among the Pentateuchal books—this source is almost, if not exclusively, limited.[17]

Although itself a composite work, Deuteronomy bears throughout the characteristic marks of a distinctive literary style, vocabulary, and theology. The book consists largely of laws couched in sermonic form and marked by such hortatory phrases as "Hear, O Israel," "remember," "take heed to yourselves," "with all your heart and soul," "that you may live," "keep all the commandments," and the like.

Israel's fidelity to God's law, the uppermost concern of the Deu-

terest in setting Moses apart from all other persons in his unique relationship to God (R. H. Pfeiffer, *Introduction to the Old Testament*, p. 174).

[16] On the Elohist, see T. E. Fretheim, "Elohist," *IDBS*, pp. 259–263; Alan W. Jenks, *The Elohist and North Israelite Traditions* (Missoula, MT: Scholars Press, 1977), The Society of Biblical Literature Monograph Series, no. 22; and Hans Walter Wolff, "The Elohistic Fragments in the Pentateuch," *Int.*, XXVI (1972), pp. 158–173. The last of these is reprinted in Walter Brueggemann and Hans Walter Wolff, *The Vitality of the Old Testament Traditions*, pp. 67–82. Wolff's kerygmatic interpretation conceives E's message as "the fear of God," which encouraged Israelite resistance to the threat of Canaanite syncretism in the ninth and eighth centuries B.C.

[17] Evidence of Deuteronomic phrasing in Genesis-Numbers is restricted to a few brief passages: Gen. 15:13–16; Ex. 12:24–27; 13:1–16; 15:25b–26; 32:7–14.

teronomist, is set forth as the only sure guarantee of the people's corporate well-being. Moses thus assures the people:

> And if you obey the voice of the Lord your God, being careful to do all his commandments which I command you this day, the Lord your God will set you high above all the nations of earth.
>
> Deut. 28:1

Israel's disobedience, however, will surely issue in dire expressions of God's displeasure:

> But if you will not obey the voice of the Lord your God or be careful to do all his commandments and his statutes which I command you this day, then all these curses shall come upon you and overtake you.
>
> Deut. 28:15

This theological formula—obedience to God's law brings its sure rewards and disobedience effects certain adversity—is a consistent mark of the Deuteronomic school and appears in a variety of forms throughout the books of the Former Prophets.

Other characteristic theological features are the insistence on confining the cult to one central shrine (presumed by later generations to be Jerusalem) and the ascription of Israel's election to nothing short of God's inscrutable love. "It was not because you were more in number than any other people," Moses reminds Israel, "but it is because the Lord loves you . . ." (Deut. 7:7–8). Divine love is thus the rationale for the strict obedience enjoined in the Mosaic speeches (4:37–40).

The legal code which constituted the original edition of Deuteronomy (chs. 12–26 or 5–26, 28) was probably written during the early seventh century B.C., not long before the incident recorded in II Kings 22. It may have originated and circulated in the north before being used in King Josiah's reform movement in the south. Thus established as the official guidebook for life in Judah, it provided the perspective for the Deuteronomist(s), who added the introduction (chs. 1–3 [4]) and epilogues (27; 29–34) and utilized the edited work as an introduction to the longer history (Joshua–Kings).[18]

THE PRIESTLY SOURCE. The Priestly source, as its name implies, is distinguished by the unmistakable interests of priesthood and cult and by the method and precision associated with the priestly mind. A concern with ritual origins and laws and the genealogical and chronological details of

[18] On Deuteronomy, see E. W. Nicholson, *Deuteronomy and Tradition* (Philadelphia: Fortress Press, 1967) and G. Ernest Wright, "Introduction and Exegesis to Deuteronomy," *IB.*, Vol. II, pp. 311–537. On the Deuteronomist and Deuteronomic History, see Martin Noth, *A History of Pentateuchal Traditions,* and Hans Walter Wolff, "The Kerygma of the Deuteronomic Historical Work," in Walter Brueggmann and Hans Walter Wolff, *The Vitality of Old Testament Traditions,* pp. 83–100.

Israel's past is manifest in a uniform style, marked by such stereotyped phrases as "these are the generations," "after its kind," and "be fruitful and multiply."[19]

The detailed attention given institutions of the cult in the latter half of the book of Exodus, the prescriptions governing sacrifice, festivals, and purity that constitute the whole of Leviticus, and the miscellaneous ritual laws and traditions in Numbers may with assurance be ascribed to this source. The accounts in Genesis involving altars—the offerings of Noah and the Patriarchs—cannot belong to the Priestly source, however, for P conceived of the legitimate sacrificial cultus as having begun later, with Moses and the Sinai covenant. Elsewhere in Genesis there appear the exhaustive genealogical tables, chronological data, and precise, orderly accounts which are P's stock in trade. Chapter 1 of Genesis provides a good example of the formal priestly style in the service of cultic interests, that is to say, the six days of Creation and the seventh day of rest as the prototype for the law of the Sabbath.

A comparison with the Yahwistic creation account reveals, furthermore, the greater reserve with which P describes the acts of God. This is achieved not simply by the avoidance of anthropomorphic expressions, but by the use of simple speech forms; human encounters with God are cited without elaboration. It is enough to say that "God called," "God said," or the like, thus leaving details to the imagination and protecting the divine holiness.[20] Likewise typical of the differences between P and J is the centrality of God as the sovereign subject of chapter 1 of Genesis, his wholly otherness and his glorification in the created order, as compared with chapters 2 and 3 where greater attention focuses upon man, his problem with evil, and his destiny.

The P source has contributed much less of the Pentateuchal narrative than has JE. Apart from the long record of ritual and legal data in Exodus 25 through Numbers 10, P appears chiefly in the form of genealogical lists and narrative glosses. The latter, nevertheless, prove to be more than a "dressing" for the JE traditions, for thereby the Priestly writer managed to give to the Pentateuch an outline consistent with his view of Israel's history. It consists of four broad eras: (1) the primeval (Adam to Noah), (2) the postdiluvian (Noah to Abraham), (3) the patriarchal (Abraham to Moses), and (4) the Mosaic (Moses and following). Marking the transitions of the ages are the three covenants with Noah (Gen. 9:1–17), Abraham (Gen. 17), and Moses (Ex. 19ff.).[21]

---

[19] E.g., Gen. 1:3ff.; 1:11ff.; 1:28; 2:4a; 5:1; 6:9, 20; 7:14; 8:17; 9:1; Levit. 11:14ff.; etc.

[20] E.g., Gen. 1:3ff.; 6:13; 8:15; 9:8, 17; 17:1. God may be said to "appear" to men (Gen. 17:1; 35:9:13; 48:3; Ex. 6:3), but only in the Sinai theophany is the manner of his appearance described (Ex. 24:1ff.; 34:29; 40:34ff.).

[21] On the Priestly source, see B. A. Levine, "Priestly Writers," *IDBS*, pp. 683–687. Compare Frank M. Cross, *Canaanite Myth and Hebrew Epic* (Cambridge, MA: Harvard University Press, 1973), pp. 293–325, where P is treated as a redaction rather than a source.

The failure of JEDP to account for more than the very broad patterns in the literature has long been apparent. At mid-century one could conclude: ". . . as matters now stand, the history of any one of the 'documents' may well be as complicated as the history of the whole Pentateuch was conceived to be only thirty years ago.'[22] Efforts to account for these complexities have led in some quarters to a multiplication of subsources. J, in particular, can be shown to encompass more than a single, clear-cut stream of tradition and has therefore been subjected to further delineations, often labeled J[1] and J[2]. Alternative proposals for a separate narrative strand composed of J material have been assigned names appropriate to the milieu in which the source purportedly originated: L ("Lay source"),[23] N ("Nomadic source"),[24] S ("Seir source"),[25] or K ("Kenite source").[26] Efforts to dissect P into continuous and independent threads have been more limited, but its composite character is likewise apparent.[27] And even Deuteronomy is a composite work in the sense that its introductory and concluding chapters, at least, and perhaps other portions as well, are secondary to the original work. Overly presumptuous tendencies, however, to posit scores of such substrata on the basis of minute and obscure textual details have been rather generally discredited, and in some quarters there have even been attempts to eliminate one or more of the major sources, notably the Elohist. These efforts have not, however, met with very wide acceptance.

BEHIND THE WRITTEN SOURCES. The provocative studies of Hermann Gunkel and Hugo Gressman shortly after the turn of the century revealed one of the major shortcomings of the older source criticism, namely, its failure to depict the organic growth of the Old Testament traditions within the history of the people, and hence its failure to capture the vital religious experience which they embody.[28] This could best be done, it was felt, through a recovery of the preliterary forms back of the Pentateuch and the living situations in which they arose. Form criticism and tradition criticism, pursuing these objectives, have succeeded in correcting and complementing source analysis in a number of ways, one of which has already been

[22] C. R. North, "Pentateuchal Criticism," *The Old Testament and Modern Study*, H. H. Rowley, ed., (Oxford: Clarendon Press, 1951), p. 81.

[23] Otto Eissfeldt, *Hexateuch-Synopse*, 2nd ed. (Darmstadt, West Germany: Wissenschaftliche Buchgemeinschaft, 1962). For a summary description in English, see his *The Old Testament; An Introduction*, pp. 194–199.

[24] Georg Fohrer, *Introduction to the Old Testament*, pp. 159–165.

[25] R. H. Pfeiffer, "A Non-Israelitic Source of the Book of Genesis," ZAW, XLVIII (1930), pp. 66–73; *Introduction to the Old Testament*, pp. 159–167.

[26] Julian Morgenstern, "The Oldest Document in the Hexateuch," *Hebrew Union College Annual*, IV (1927), pp. 1–138.

[27] Gerhard von Rad divided P into two parallel strands ("*Die Priesterschrift im Hexateuch*," BWAT, IV, 13, 1934).

[28] The opening section of Hermann Gunkel's monumental *Commentary on Genesis* (*Die Genesis*, 1901) is available in English translation as *The Legends of Genesis*, W. H. Carruth, trans.

noted—by calling attention to the long and creative oral backgrounds of the sources.

Form criticism, however, has not yet produced a systematic and generally accepted theory of Pentateuchal development after the manner of the older source critical consensus. It is inhibited by the nature of early saga, which as Gunkel recognized, "has woven a poetic veil about the historical memories," thereby obscuring the circumstances of time and place.[29] But in analyzing the forms and distinguishing their relative age sequence, certain developmental patterns are proposed. The more primitive of the "memory units" thus isolated include rhythmic and colorful aphorisms, songs, liturgical confessions, and a variety of etiological stories—traditions purporting to explain the origin of some familiar object or phenomenon, such as a custom, a personal or place name, a natural pattern, a national or racial characteristic, a geographical or geological feature, or the sanctity of a shrine. Many such tiny units exhibit signs of having circulated independently before being combined with other small units or becoming the nucleus of a longer account. When the insights of literary, form, and tradition criticism are combined, J, E, D, and P are viewed as the end processes of such long and complex oral histories.

Gerhard von Rad conceived the oral beginnings of Pentateuchal development in brief, pithy confessions of faith such as appear in Deuteronomy 6:20–24, 26:5–9, and Joshua 24:2–13. These credos, he believed, were carried in the oral memory at a very early time and were employed in a manner akin to the Church's use of the Apostle's Creed, namely, as affirmations of the basic elements of the faith, recited to the accompaniment of specific worship rites. Deuteronomy 26:5–9, for example, was repeated with the offering of First Fruits.

> A wandering Aramean was my father; and he went down into Egypt and sojourned there, few in number; and there he became a nation, great, mighty, and populous. And the Egyptians treated us harshly, and afflicted us, and laid upon us hard bondage. Then we cried to the Lord the God of our fathers, and the Lord heard our voice, and saw our affliction, our toil, and our oppression; and the Lord brought us out of Egypt with a mighty hand and an outstretched arm, with great terror, and gave us this land, a land flowing with milk and honey.

Upon analysis, the items of faith here are seen to include God's deliverance of the Hebrews out of Egyptian bondage and the gift of Canaan as a homeland, along with allusions to the patriarchal fathers. All these elements prove to be basic to the Pentateuch's overarching structure.

From such confessional beginnings, von Rad concluded, the larger framework of the Pentateuch developed. He assigned a major, creative role to the Yahwist as the one who collected early sagas associated with separate

---

[29] *The Legends of Genesis*, p. 22.

Palestinian cult centers and combined them into an outline consistent with the central claims of the early confessions.[30] Noting that the brief credos make no mention of the primeval history or the giving of the law at Sinai, von Rad theorized that neither of these elements belonged to the earliest oral tradition, but were first introduced into the Israelite epic by the Yahwist.

Proceeding along similar lines, Martin Noth proposed five basic themes around which the Pentateuchal narrative gathered: (1) the Exodus from Egypt, (2) the entrance into the Promised Land, (3) guidance in the wilderness, (4) the promise to the patriarchs, and (5) the primeval history. According to Noth, these themes derived from diverse cultic backgrounds but were combined and expanded in a common tradition which underlies the J and E sources. Noth designated this tradition as "G" or *Grundlage* (German for "basis") and dated it to the period of the Judges, when Israel supposedly existed as a twelve-tribe league or confederacy.[31]

The creative role of the cult figures prominently in the proposals of other tradition critics, for example, Johannes Pedersen's interpretation of the Exodus narrative (Exod. 1–15) as a cult legend for the Passover festival[32] and Sigmund Mowinckel's approach to the Sinai account (Exod. 19ff.) as a cultic drama enacted in celebrations of the New Year.[33] Albrecht Alt (1883–1956) likewise posited a stage of cultic transmission for some of Israel's earliest laws, notably the Decalogue. Applying the principles of form and tradition Criticism, Alt distinguished two main forms of law: case law, which is well represented in the Covenant Code of Exodus 20:22–23:33, and apodictic (absolute) law, which is best exemplified in the Decalogue of Exodus 20:2–17 and Deuteronomy 5. The latter takes the form of direct speech from God and, according to Alt, was originally transmitted orally within the cult.[34]

CURRENT ISSUES IN PENTATEUCHAL RESEARCH. Some form of the classic source analysis, combined with an awareness of the complex oral tradition underlying the sources, continues to provide the working hypothesis for most studies of the Pentateuch. Von Rad and Noth, whose influence has dominated Pentateuchal scholarship for a generation, accepted the basic

[30] "The Form Critical Problem of the Hexateuch," *The Problem of the Hexateuch and Other Essays*, pp. 1–78. For a brief summary of his position see the introductory chapter of his *Genesis*.

[31] *A History of Pentateuchal Traditions*.

[32] "Passahfest und Passahlegende," ZAW, LII (1934), pp. 161–175. Cf. his *Israel, Its Life and Culture* (New York: The Oxford University Press, Inc., 1926, 1948), Vol. II, pp. 726–737.

[33] *Le decalogue* (Paris: F. Alcan, 1927), pp. 114–130.

[34] "The Origins of Israelite Law," *Essays on Old Testament History and Religion*, R. A. Wilson, trans. (Garden City, NY: Doubleday & Company, Inc., 1967), pp. 101–171. For the more recent analysis of apodictic law by Erhard Gerstenberger, see below pp. 174, 180, and 181, footnotes 54 and 64.

premise of written sources, even while pioneering tradition-critical theories of the preliterary stages of transmission. Recently, however, there have arisen serious challenges to the manner in which both the written sources and the patterns of oral tradition have been envisioned, as well as questions concerning the compatibility of the methods of source and tradition criticism. In the opinion of some scholars, Pentateuchal scholarship has entered a new and revolutionary phase, the eventual outcome of which is not yet apparent. According to one writer, "Pentateuchal studies may now be described as in a state of anxious disarray or as on the move, but in a new and fruitful direction, depending on one's perspective."[35]

In respect to source criticism, it has been charged that the criteria by which scholars of the past distinguished sources, particularly J, have never been adequately defined. Thus, Rolf Rendtorff proposes a radical revision of the source hypothesis which denies that either the Yahwist or the Priestly writer produced a continuous account or a "source" in the commonly accepted sense.[36] Similarly, Frank Cross views the Priestly work as a redaction of the older JE tradition, rather than as a pre-existing, independent source.[37] In Rendtorff's view, only the Deuteronomist provided a continuous account of the Pentateuchal tradition, which would mean that the basic outline of the Pentateuchal narrative was very late in developing. A radical departure from the commonly accepted JEDP dating sequence is set forth in John Van Seter's contention for an Exilic J, a post-Exilic P, and a fragmentary E which antedated J. According to Van Seters, the sources developed not in parallel, but according to a pattern whereby each source built upon and supplemented earlier tradition.[38]

As to tradition criticism, serious doubts have been raised concerning von Rad's assumption that the structural outline of the Pentateuch developed from ancient confessional credos. In their present form in the text, it is unclear whether the credos antedated the Yahwist or, as some scholars believe, originated at a time after the formal design of the Pentateuch was a reality. Yet greater dissatisfaction surrounds von Rad's contention that the Sinai theme was not a part of Israel's earliest epic tradition.[39] More basic than the questioning of these specific hypotheses, however, are the current debates concerning the social, cultic, and theological institutions of Israel's pre-monarchical era. Tradition-critical theories of the recent past, notably

---

[35] John H. Hayes, *An Introduction to Old Testament Study*, p. 195.

[36] "The 'Yahwist' as Theologian? The Dilemma of Pentateuchal Criticism," *JSOT*, III (1977), pp. 2–9; *Das uberlieferungsgeschichtliche Problem des Pentateuch*, BZAW 147 (Berlin/New York: Walter de Gruyter, 1977).

[37] *Canaanite Myth and Hebrew Epic*, pp. 293–325.

[38] *Abraham in History and Tradition*, pp. 125–313.

[39] See J. Philip Hyatt, "Were There an Ancient Historical Credo in Israel and an Independent Sinai Tradition?" *Translating and Understanding the Old Testament*, Harry T. Frank and William L. Reed, eds. (Nashville, TN: Abingdon Press, 1970), pp. 152–170, and the sources cited there.

those of Martin Noth, have perceived the early setting of the Pentateuch's formation in a twelve-tribe Israelite league of the Judges period, a covenant between deity and people, and a covenant renewal ceremony which instilled a sense of pantribal identity and loyalty. Some recent studies have questioned the existence of all these institutions, i.e., tribal league, covenant, and covenant ceremony, prior to the monarchical period.[40] Although these challenges have not yet proved conclusive, particularly in respect to the covenant concept, they have succeeded in demonstrating the complexity of the issues involved and the limitations of our knowledge of premonarchical Israel. At the very least, they are reminders of the caution with which tradition criticism must proceed in its efforts to reconstruct the social and religious contexts of early Israelite tradition.

The following examination of the pentateuchal books assumes the validity of the broad literary patterns identified by the JEDP source theory. It also accepts as a working hypothesis the traditional dating of the sources, but avoids unduly speculative characterizations of the sources as theological statements directed toward identifiable historical crises.

2. IN THE BEGINNING: GENESIS 1–11

Genesis is characterized by its Greek title as a book about origins—of the world and humankind, of natural and behavioral patterns, and of cultures and the distribution of peoples. More significantly, it is a commentary on the eternal values through which all things exist and in conformity with which they realize their highest purposes. The book also serves as the prologue to Israel's unique faith-history. It is, however, no more a work of history in the strict sense than is the book of Revelation, which provides the epilogue of Christian Bibles. Even as the latter book includes visions of the future which project beyond the historical plane, Genesis treats phases of the distant past for which there can be no formal documentation, and is properly a prehistory.

Attempts at selecting a more precise classification for the Genesis narratives have called forth a variety of proposed labels, such as "myth," "saga," "legend," "poetic narratives," "parables," and "symbolical stories." Although often confused in the popular mind with fairy stories and fanciful notions, "myth" refers in its broadest sense to a characteristic manner of viewing the world and one's existence within it. The term is particularly apt when used of stories of primeval beginnings and the world-views which they embody.[41] Thus, to categorize the Genesis accounts as myth is not to represent them as untrue, but to recognize that certain truths resist the

---

[40] See below, pp. 170–175, 212–213.

[41] For a helpful survey of different definitions of myth and their applicability to Old Testament literature, see J. W. Rogerson, *Myth in Old Testament Interpretation* (Berlin/New York: Walter de Gruyter, 1974) and the bibliography cited.

strict categories of history and science, and find as a vehicle of expression the parablelike stories derived from a peculiar folk culture. In this sense, the term has been widely employed by biblical scholars, particularly as a designation for chapters 1–11 of Genesis.

More narrowly defined, myth exists in the Old Testament only in a significantly altered form. A common literary usage restricts the term to stories of gods and goddesses in their relationships with each other—a pattern altogether alien to the monotheism of the Bible.[42] Or, again, a phenomenological definition treats as its characteristic element the conception of a primeval event which determines present reality through continuous re-enactment in cultic rites.[43] The latter usage accords with common patterns found in primitive nature religions and in the well-known epic poetry of the ancient Near East. In Babylonian religion, for example, cultic dramatization of the creation myth at New Year's, with its enactment of the creator god's victorious struggle against opposing deities, was believed to effect an annual renewal of the natural order. Accordingly, the New Year's festival was the central rite of the Babylonian cult. Whether early Israel observed a similar New Year's rite is a debated issue within Old Testament scholarship. The so-called "myth and ritual school" contends for such a festival, whereas proponents of the "history-of-salvation school" conceive of an annual ceremony of covenant renewal, celebrating historical events of divine deliverance upon which Israel's national life was founded and continually sustained.[44] Although this question is far from settled, it is clear that Israel's religious faith included the awareness of both God's creation of the world[45] and his guidance of the nation's history. Occasionally these two themes are joined in Old Testament texts.

> But now thus says the Lord,
>   he who created you, O Jacob,
>   he who formed you, O Israel:

[42] Cf. Otto Eissfeldt, *The Old Testament: An Introduction*, pp. 34–37.

[43] Brevard Childs, *Myth and Reality in the Old Testament*, Studies in Biblical Theology, No. 27 (London: S.C.M. Press, 1962), pp. 13–30.

[44] The case for an Israelite New Year's festival of the "myth and ritual" type is set forth by Sigmund Mowinckel in *The Psalms in Israel's Worship*, D. R. Ap-Thomas, trans. (Nashville, TN: Abingdon Press, 1962), pp. 106–192. A covenant renewal festival, stressing historical and national themes, is advocated by Gerhard von Rad, *The Problem of the Hexateuch and Other Essays*, pp. 1ff., and Martin Noth, *The Laws in the Pentateuch and Other Studies*, D. R. Ap-Thomas, trans. (Philadelphia: Fortress Press, 1967), pp. 28ff. A position that argues for the institution of an Israelite New Year's festival during David's reign, but envisions it differently from observances of the non-Israelite cults, is offered by Walter Harrelson, *From Fertility Cult to Worship* (Missoula, MT: Scholars Press, 1980), pp. 49–64. See also Frank Moore Cross, *Canaanite Myth and Hebrew Epic*, pp. 79–90, where it is held that "in Israel myth and history always stood in strong tension, myth serving primarily to give a cosmic dimension and transcendent meaning to the historical, rarely functioning to dissolve history" (p. 90).

[45] The full creation faith, however, was slow in arising. See Gerhard von Rad, "The Theological Problem of the Old Testament Doctrine of Creation," *The Problem of the Hexateuch and Other Essays*, pp. 131–143.

> "Fear not, for I have redeemed you;
> I have called you by name, You
> are mine."
>
> Isa. 43:1

As to the polytheistic motif of a struggle between opposing deities and the assurance of fertility through its cultic reenactment, one hears nothing in the Old Testament, except as faint and fleeting echoes.[46] When Israel employed the older mythologies in her own recitals of faith, as in the creation story of Genesis, the foreign accounts were brought into conformity with the uncompromising conviction that Yahweh's designs are neither contested by other gods nor controlled by the rituals of his worshipers. For this reason, it is sometimes said that the Old Testament includes no pure mythology, but only remnants and adaptations of common Near Eastern mythological themes, i.e., "broken" or "transformed" myth.

Thomas Mann commented concerning the truth of myth: "It is, it always is, however much we may say, it was."[47] Genesis displays such a concern with present reality. Particularly of chapters 1–11 it must be said that the subjects are not so much the persons and events of the distant past as the universal human experiences at any given moment of time. These chapters have enjoyed a timeless appeal for the reason that the reader senses his own personal involvement in the stories. They are more nearly a pithy theological treatise on human nature than is any other portion of the Old Testament, speaking as they do to the existential questions: "Who am I?" "In what kind of world do I live?" "To whom am I responsible?" "What is my destiny?" As a penetrating exposure of the possibilities and limitations of the human race and of the universal and constant tension between the two, they are without an equal.

Creation

Throughout the Bible there are allusions to God's creation of the world and man.[48] For sheer epic grandeur and dramatic effect, however, none equals the Priestly account which begins the Book of Genesis. In brief compass (1:1–2:4a) this classic liturgy of the seven days of creation surveys the natural order as a manifestation of God's marvelous designs and celebrates man's unique position within it.

The compact and poetic character of the story results largely from its deliberate outline and stately refrains. God creates the world in six days, each

---

[46] Cf. Job 3:8; 26:10–13; Ps. 74:13–14; 89:9–10; Isa. 27:1; II Esd. 6:49–52. Leviathan or Rahab is the sea monster against whom the creation god does battle in some early Near Eastern mythology.

[47] *Joseph and His Brothers*, H. T. Lowe-Porter, trans. (New York: Alfred A. Knopf, Inc., 1948), p. 33.

[48] Some of the more significant passages are Gen. 1–2; Prov. 8:22–31; Ps. 74:12–17; 89:10–12; 104; Job 26; 38:4–11; Isa. 40:12–31.

of which is distinguished by the same beginning and concluding formulas: "And God said, 'Let (there be) . . .' "; "And there was evening and there was morning . . . ." On each day, and twice on the third and sixth days, God utters his command and a new and distinct act of creation begins. On all but the first and third days the divine fiat is followed with a further statement of its execution through God's direct action ("And God made . . ."); and, with one exception (the fifth day), each act is climaxed with the words, "And it was so," or the like (cf. 1:3; "And there was . . ."). On the first three days the act of creating involves naming the created work ("God called . . ."). Its function within the broader natural order is in some instances specified (the second, third, fourth, and sixth days); and where God's design for the reproduction of life is concerned (the third, fifth, and sixth days) there appears the descriptive phrase, "according to its kind," or the direct command, "Be fruitful and multiply." The latter directive is associated with a blessing which God twice bestows upon his creation (fifth and sixth days). Finally, on all but the second day, God's approval of his work is stated: "And God saw that it was good."

The component elements of the story and the patterns of their appearance may be outlined as follows:

	DAYS	NUMBER OF OCCURRENCES
God's command ("Let there be . . .")	All 6	8
Execution of command ("And God made . . .")	2, 4, 5, 6	6
Naming the work ("God called . . .")	1, 2, 3	3
God's approval of the work ("it was good")	1, 3, 4, 5, 6	7
Words of fulfillment ("and it was so"; "and there was . . .")	1, 2, 3, 4, 6	7
Function of the work	2, 4, 6	3
Provision for reproduction ("according to its kind"; "Be fruitful and multiply")	3, 5, 6	5
Blessing	5, 6	2
Conclusion of the day ("And there was evening and there was morning . . .")	All 6	6

There are thus six days of work, eight separate creative acts, and altogether ten created works (the seas and the heavens are treated together in the account, as are also the sea creatures and bird life). This, together with the lack of uniformity in the employment of the refrains, indicates the long oral history behind the account. Perhaps there existed an older story of a ten-day creation and possibly versions consistent in describing the mode of creation—either by divine fiat or direct action. The Priestly version, however, has with symmetrical artistry compressed the older traditions into a pattern of three pairs of days, whereby the works of the first three days establish the conditions for the last three, as follows:

First day:	Light
Fourth day:	Luminaries
Second day:	Sea and heavens
Fifth day:	Fish and fowl
Third day:	Earth and vegetation
Sixth day:	Land creatures and man

The light of the first day is given the form of luminaries on the fourth day; the seas and sky (second day) provide the domains for fish and fowl (fifth day); and earth and plants (third day) sustain man and beast (sixth day).[49]

The cosmology (i.e. conception of the universe) here is not unlike that depicted in the literature and art of other ancient Near Eastern peoples. A "three-story" universe of heavens above, earth below, and waters underneath (and above) the earth was the common early view of the world, for example, in Mesopotamia and Egypt. Such a view finds clear expression elsewhere in the Bible:

> You shall not make for yourself a graven image, or any likeness of anything that is in heaven above, or that is in the earth beneath, or that is in the water under the earth . . .
>
> Ex. 20:4

This is the primitive conception of nature as viewed by the naked eye: a flat earth spanned by a solid and dome-shaped sky. Waters above the earth account for the rain, which appears to fall from openings in the sky,[50] and waters beneath the earth supply the springs, streams, and rivers.[51] The sun, moon, and stars move as on a frame across the sky, performing the service of lighting the earth and marking the seasons. A range of mountains encircles the earth at its outermost limits and serves as a support for the sky. The earth, in turn, rests upon great pillars; and in the heart of the earth is *Sheol*, the Hebrew counterpart of the underworld, the gloomy pit where the "shades" of the dead abide.[52]

The account speaks of darkness and the primeval waters, the great "deep" (*tehom*), prior to God's first creative work. Sumerian texts, dated to the beginning of the second millennium B.C. and reflecting traditions more ancient still, trace the origins of all things, including the gods and goddesses, back to primordial waters. Personified as the goddess Nammu, the

[49] For a more detailed explanation, see Umberto Cassuto, *A Commentary on the Book of Genesis*, Israel Abrahams, trans. (Jerusalem: Magnes Press, 1961).

[50] Job 38:22–30.

[51] Gen. 7:11; Ps. 104:10.

[52] Num. 16:30; Job 26:7; Jonah 2:6.

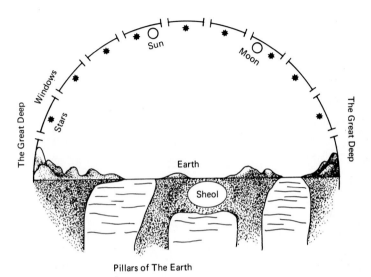

Heaven, Dwelling of God

Waters Above the Firmament

Sun

Moon

Windows

Stars

The Great Deep

The Great Deep

Earth

Sheol

Pillars of The Earth

Waters Under the Earth

HEBREW CONCEPTION OF THE UNIVERSE

waters give birth to heaven and earth, the latter conceived both as deities and as solid elements.[53] A similar mythology underlies the more famous Babylonian epic *Enuma Elish*.[54] Recorded in cuneiform on seven clay tablets, *Enuma Elish* takes its name from the words with which the poem begins, "When above. . . ." The earliest extant copies date to approximately 1000 B.C., but its composition is much earlier and probably belongs to the first Babylonian Dynasty (c.1830–1530 B.C.), when under the energetic king Hammurabi, Babylon rose to political supremacy and Marduk became the national god. The epic begins with the primeval sweet- and salt-water oceans and the hosts of deities to which they give birth, then proceeds to describe the creation of the world itself out of the body of Tiamat (cf. *tehom*), the chaotic salt-water ocean. This is dramatically depicted as the issue of a terrible battle among the gods wherein Marduk, the powerful storm god, slays the goddess Tiamat and from her carcass fashions the heavens and the earth. The description of the placing of the firmament

[53] Samuel Noah Kramer, *Sumerian Mythology*, rev. ed. (New York: Harper Torchbooks, 1961), p. 39.
[54] *ANET*, pp. 60–72, 501–503 (*ANE*, pp. 31–39; *ANE*, II, pp. 1–5). Cf. Alexander Heidel, *The Babylonian Genesis* (Chicago: University of Chicago Phoenix Books, 1963) and W. G. Lambert, "A New Look at the Babylonian Background of Genesis," *JTS*, 16 (1965), pp. 287–300.

*Egyptian conception of the universe. Nut, the sky goddess, is supported by Shu,
the air god, who stands on Geb, the earth god.*

and its function in retaining the waters above the earth is reminiscent of
the second work of creation in Genesis.

> Then the lord Marduk paused to view
>   her dead body,
> That he might divide the monster and do
>   artful works.
> He split her like a shellfish into two
>   parts:
> Half of her he set up and ceiled it as sky,
> Pulled down the bar and posted guards,
> He bade them to allow not her waters to
>   escape.
>
> *Enuma Elish*, IV, 135–140[55]

And God made the firmament and separated the waters which were under
the firmament from the waters which were above the firmament. And it was
so.

Gen. 1:7

The sequence of the works of creation in *Enuma Elish* is consistent with
the Genesis account, but abbreviated: (1) heaven and earth, (2) luminaries,
(3) man. Interestingly, both accounts assume the existence of light and the
alternation of day and night before the creation of the heavenly bodies.
This should remind one of the futility of trying to press the biblical cosmogony (i.e. origin of the world) into a modern scientific mold. The latter,
of course, would call for long stages of evolutionary development and the
sun as the precondition for both light and growing plants.

[55] *ANET*, p. 67 (*ANE*, p. 35).

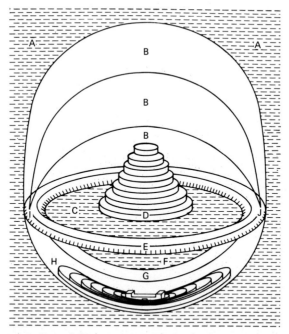

Babylonian conception of the universe. A. Heavenly ocean. B. Three heavens. C. Sea surrounding the earth. D. Earth mountain. E. Mountains confining the sea. F. Bottom of the ocean. G. Underworld. H. Palace of the underworld. I. Mountain of the rising sun. J. Mountain of the setting sun. (After Meissner.)

As revealing as the features which Genesis and the Babylonian cosmogony share in common are the striking contrasts between the two. These center in the fundamental difference between the ancient Near Eastern polytheism and the Hebrew concept of one sovereign God of purposive will. *Enuma Elish* describes the generation of multiple deities from the parent gods, each identified with a facet of the natural world. A dominant motif of the epic is the constant strife and clash of wills within the divine ranks. Creation of the world is merely a final episode in the warfare waged between the two hostile camps of gods; and the creation account, as such, occupies less than two of the seven tablets of the epic. Man, a virtual afterthought, is formed of the blood drained from one of Tiamat's fallen supporters and owes his creation to the service he can render in freeing the gods of their menial labors. Creation is thus accorded little of the significance that marks the Hebrew account.

The Hebrew God, by contrast, has no family tree. He is "in the beginning"—prior to all else. Although there is no apparent speculation here concerning the origin of the great deep which exists prior to the first day of creation, and thus no explicit statement of *creatio ex nihilo* (the view that

God creates all that exists out of nothing),[56] clearly God is independent of the matter which he orders and, by implication, the source of the entire natural order as man knows it. The total creation is shaped to conform with his consistent and uncontested designs; and the order, purpose, and harmony which he has placed within the world are given succinct affirmation: "God saw that it was good."

Man is the pinnacle of God's work, just as the Psalmist declares:

> Yet thou hast made him little less
>   than God,
>   and dost crown him with glory
>   and honor.
> Thou has given him dominion over
>   the works of thy hands;
>   thou hast put all things under his
>   feet.
>   Ps. 8:5–6

Last in the order of creation, man is made in God's own image, given dominion over the earth, and entrusted with the propagation of the race. Not until the appearance of man is it said of the creation, "it was *very* good."

It exceeds our ability to trace the precise historical connections between the Hebrew story and the older Mesopotamian mythologies. It appears beyond question, however, that the old traditions were known in some form to the Hebrews, possibly through an early link with Mesopotamia as depicted in the Terah-Abraham story (Gen. 11:27–32).[57] Israel's familiarity with the old epics makes all the more significant the divergencies between the two traditions. The older stories are demythologized, as it were, through "the deliberate, quiet utterances of Scripture, which sets the opposing views at naught by silence or by subtle hint."[58] For example, the only trace remaining in Genesis of a battle with the primordial waters is the similarity between the names *tehom* and Tiamat. There is no conflict with the dragonlike sea monster (the apparent form of Tiamat in *Enuma Elish*), though some Old Testament poetry alludes perhaps to the myth.[59] Rather, in the Priestly story, the great sea monsters are specifically named as the creation of God (1:21). Neither chaos nor order threatens the existence of God, since nothing exists apart from his direct or permissive will.

The first account of creation is concluded with the Priestly colophon of

---

[56] The doctrine of *creatio ex nihilo* comes to expression in II Macc. 7:28. Cf. also Rom. 4:17 and Heb. 11:3.

[57] William F. Albright, *From the Stone Age to Christianity* (Garden City, NY: Doubleday Anchor, 1957), p. 238.

[58] Umberto Cassuto, *A Commentary on the Book of Genesis*, p. 7.

[59] Cf. Job 3:8; 7:12; 9:13; 26:12–13; Ps. 74:13–15; 89:10; 104:25–26; Isa. 27:1; 30:7; 51:9–10; Hab. 3:8. For a different interpretation of these passages, see Alexander Heidel, *The Babylonian Genesis*, pp. 102–114.

Cuneiform tablets containing an early Assyrian version of the creation. (Courtesy of the Trustees of the British Museum.)

Genesis 2:4a: "These are the generations of the heavens and the earth when they were created." That the account which follows is from a separate Israelite tradition (J) is attested by the folk narrative style, the use of the personal name of God (Yahweh), and the different manner of describing the creation. Here the sequence of the creative works is (1) man, (2) the garden with its trees and rivers, (3) beasts, (4) woman. Man (male, as distinguished from female), the first rather than the last of God's creatures, is formed "when no plant of the field was yet in the earth and no herb of the field had yet sprung up." One is transported here from the Priestly writer's transcendent vista of the whole cosmic order to the Yahwist's world of human experience. Not the vast primordial deep, but the crusty earth, the sphere of man's future labors, is the Yahwist's point of departure.

Little is to be gained by extended comparisons of the conflicting features in our two accounts. It is of greater importance to recognize the dissimilar purposes served by each in the broader scriptural context. The aim of the Priestly story is to extol the purpose and precision with which the divine will governs all that exists—the cosmic order, man, animate and inanimate life, space, and time. In this tradition God's ordering of time is especially significant, for the six days of labor and the seventh day of rest provide the *imitatio Dei* model whereby man can affirm God's designs in the created order and share in the very creative process itself.[60]

[60] The law of the Sabbath, as such, is not enjoined here; but in the E Decalogue (Exod. 20:8–11) God's pattern in the creation is established as the rationale for Sabbath observance.

85

The Yahwist's account, on the other hand, is not a self-contained creation story, but only the beginning of the longer Yahwistic narrative of the fall of man and the loss of paradise (2:4a–4:26). This version displays little interest in the precise sequence of the creative acts or in cosmogony as such. Attention centers, rather, upon man and the microcosmic environment (the garden) in which his nature and his struggle with moral decision are exposed. Interest lies in the claim of God to the conscious will and in the effects of the human response upon the entire created order, including the community of men and women.

If we may presume, then, to explain the Priestly redactor's decision to follow the creation story of chapter 1 with another tradition differing from it, we must consider the separate functions served by the two accounts. Chapters 2 through 4 add a new dimension to the creation account of chapter 1 by portraying the Hebrew consciousness of a history of sin and forgiveness. Creation is not static or once for all, but is perceived through historic experiences which are here given graphic form in the disobedience of Adam and Eve, Cain's fratricide, and God's provision for new beginnings.

Paradise Lost

The Adam and Eve stories (2:4b–4:26) must be read and interpreted in the continuous sequence which the Yahwist intended for them. They lend themselves, nevertheless, to separation into shorter and more primitive units. With the garden as a setting, the Yahwist develops the classic outline of his epic: (1) creation, (2) fall (including temptation, sin, confrontation with Yahweh, penalties, and expulsion),[61] (3) Cain's murder of Abel, (4) the Cainite genealogy, and (5) the birth of Seth. That a long oral tradition stands behind the stories is as apparent here as in the Priestly creation account. Easily isolated are primitive etiological motifs purporting to explain such diverse patterns as sexual desire (2:21–24), the crawling serpent (3:14), human aversion to snakes (3:15), woman's pain in childbearing (3:16), the frustrations of earning a livelihood (3:17–19), the use of clothing (3:21), and human mortality (3:19, 22–24).

Some of the central figures in these stories belong to the common stock of ancient mythological themes. The idyllic land of Dilmun in early Sumerian mythology depicts a state of innocence and bliss similar to that portrayed in the biblical Eden,[62] and variant traditions of a garden of God are reflected in allusions elsewhere in the Old Testament itself.[63] Two Baby-

---

[61] Claus Westermann (*Creation*, John J. Scullion, trans. [Philadelphia: Fortress Press, 1974], pp. 108–109) objects to "The Fall" as a title for the Genesis 3 account, finding in it the misleading suggestion that Adam was "an historical individual whose 'Fall' was passed on through him to his descendants." This traditional title need not carry such a meaning, however, and its usage here should not be so construed.

[62] *ANET*, pp. 37–38, 44, 119, 297, 343–344.

[63] Ezek. 28:11–19; 31:8–9, 16–18.

lonian epics which had wide currency in the ancient world, the stories of Adapa[64] and Gilgamesh,[65] tell of man's squandered chance for attaining immortality. The loss in both cases derives from failure to consume a life-giving element—for Adapa, the bread and water offered by the god Anu, and for Gilgamesh a magical plant which is stolen away from him by a serpent. The Yahwist can speak without further introduction of "the" tree of life, "the" tree of the knowledge of good and evil, "the" cherubim, and the like, for the apparent reason that these were familiar subjects in the traditions common to his cultural milieu.[66] Such motifs appear in his stories, however, basically free of mythological and magical features. They are, moreover, subordinate or incidental to J's broader themes, for which there are no close parallels in extrabiblical mythology;[67] and for the most part they are thoroughly integrated into the aims of the longer narrative. A notable exception is the tree of life (2:9; 3:22, 24), which has no place in the temptation story as such and complicates the otherwise clear figure of the forbidden tree—the tree of the knowledge of good and evil.

For the Yahwist, it would appear, the garden stories were grounded in actual space and time. He is at pains to include a tradition localizing Eden and its four rivers in the east (2:8, 10–14), though the exact site intended remains an enigma.[68] It is in the universal applications of these stories, nevertheless, that they find the profound meanings intended by the Yahwist. Adam (Hebrew: 'adham, "man") is mankind; Eve, "the mother of all living," is woman ('ishshah; from 'ish, "man"); Eden ("delight") is the state of a full and free fellowship between God and his creation; and that which happens in the garden is a parable of human history.

J is at one with P in conceiving the goodness of God reflected in his creation. This is affirmed not in pronouncements of God, but in the bounty and beauty of the garden, the sparing of no effort to find the most suitable companion for man, and the initial childlike innocence in the relationship between man and woman. The serpent is not so much a demonic evil lurking in the shadows, corrupting the garden's beauty, as the alter-ego of man through which his pride and doubt are voiced. There is surely no suggestion that the serpent is Satan—a view which developed long after the time of our story. He is said to be more wise, not necessarily more evil, than all

---

[64] ANET, pp. 101–103 (ANE, pp. 76–80).

[65] ANET, pp. 72–98 (ANE, pp. 40–75).

[66] Thus far no parallel to the tree of knowledge has been found; but cf. the mural from Mari (Gaalyah Cornfeld, Adam to Daniel [New York: Macmillan Publishing Co., Inc., 1962], pp. 1, 19).

[67] Adapa's chance for immortality is forfeited, not as a result of disobedience, but through faithfulness to his patron god's counsel. Similarly, Gilgamesh's loss of the plant of perpetual youth is through inadvertence rather than overt disobedience. Nor does the role of the snake—which consumes the plant in the latter story—correspond to the tempter's role of the Genesis serpent.

[68] For a review of the theories, see John Skinner, A Critical and Exegetical Commentary on Genesis, ICC (New York: Charles Scribner's Sons, 1910), pp. 62–66.

the other wild creatures, and like man he is held accountable for his deed. He becomes a "snake in the grass" only after the curse (3:14–15). If a symbol of the evil external to man is in some sense intended, it is nevertheless man's decision and not the serpent's nature that captures the attention of the story.

Man appears here as a unique creation of God, molded of dust from the ground (*'adhamah*) and infused with God's life-giving breath. Dual dimensions of human nature are thus portrayed: man's unity with the material world, the ground from which he is taken and to which he returns, and his vital life processes which are set in motion when God breathes into his nostrils. No dichotomy of body and soul such as may be associated with Greek thought, however, is intended. The Hebrew anthropology, as the rest of the Old Testament makes clear, conceives man as a psychophysical unity or, stated differently, an animated body.[69] And, what is particularly noteworthy in this context, no evil stigma attaches to his physical being as such. Whether in obedience or disobedience, he functions as a *whole* man—body and soul acting together, as it were. Good and evil are conceived not as static substance, but in dynamic categories of moral decision and choice. This is the point of the story of the fall: that man is responsibly involved in the creation as he now experiences it, that it is man's sin which separates him from Eden. The story speaks of the organic unity of the whole creation, thus tying man's guilt to the askew order of things reflected in the old etiologies (3:14–19): enmity, violence, pain, fruitless toil, and death.

Common patterns of man's disobedience are poignantly dramatized. Here is the familiar pattern of chain reaction whereby sin compounds itself: distortions of God's words ("You shall not eat of *any* tree. . ."; ". . . neither shall you touch it.")[70] provoke distrust of their truth ("You will *not* die.") and the motive behind them ("For God knows that when you eat of it your eyes will be opened . . ."), which in turn looses powerful sensual ("good for food"), esthetic ("a delight to the eyes"), and egotistical ("to make one wise") longings for the forbidden thing. Paralleling this is a graphic demonstration of sin as a social contagion: the serpent persuades the woman; and the woman, seeking an accomplice to share her guilt, effortlessly involves the man, whose boldness is made easy by the prior and manifestly safe venture of the woman. The effect, nevertheless, is immediate and involves them both. They do not drop dead; rather, consistent with sin's normative consequences, it is the relationship between them—and

[69] H. Wheeler Robinson, *Inspiration and Revelation in the Old Testament*, pp. 69–77.

[70] Both the serpent and the woman misrepresent God's command. The serpent's opening remark is designed to arouse skepticism, and stands midway between a question and a reflective exclamation, "Ay, and so God has said . . ." (John Skinner, *Genesis*, p. 73). The woman's reply adds to and intensifies God's actual words. "It is as though she wanted to set a law for herself by means of this exaggeration" (Gerhard von Rad, *Genesis*, p. 86).

between themselves and God—that is affected. The prior innocence gives way to shame, fear, and withdrawal. God now stands before his creatures in a new role—as judge.

The Yahwist's command of his materials is nowhere more evident in these stories than in the structural pattern whereby the tension mounts toward a climax—God's confrontation with the guilty pair—then unwinds via the common "buck-passing" routine: the man shoves the blame onto the woman, and the woman points the finger at the serpent. Thus the sequence by which the temptation proceeds is serpent–woman–man. The inquest reverses the order: man–woman–serpent. Then follow the judgments of God (3:14–19) which befall the entire garden—serpent, woman, man, and the very earth—reflecting the unity of creation in guilt as in innocence.

In the figure of the forbidden tree the Yahwist conceives the bounds of man's freedom. The eating of the fruit—the sin—is man's attempt to take what he does not rightfully possess, what belongs to God alone, and what only he can control. It is not knowledge in the academic sense that the tree represents; nor is it the "good and evil" used in distinguishing right from wrong, since God would not withhold that which moral responsibility presupposes. Still less is one specific kind of knowledge in question, namely, sexual awareness, as woman was created expressly to be a partner to man. Rather, "knowledge" (da'ath) in Old Testament usage has a range of meaning encompassing our English term "experience." And the phrase, "good and evil" in the Hebrew idiom may carry the sense of "everything," "all that there is to be known," or the like. By "the tree of the knowledge of good and evil" the Yahwist intends the urge "to experience everything," or better, "to have it all." In insisting on the forbidden tree, man demonstrates a lust for unqualified command—experience of everything.[71]

The couple, it is true, as a consequence of their transgression become ashamed of their sexual differences. This, however, is most probably the Yahwist's manner of illustrating, with poignant example, their awareness of an infinitely broader alienation now separating them, a consequence of their corporate guilt. This would be in accord with the broad fragmentation of the "fallen" order recognized in God's judgments and with the biblical principle whereby the penalty for the crime is innate within the deed itself.[72] Whatever might have been the role of the forbidden tree in traditions known to the Yahwist, he has emptied the figure of its magical features and shifted the full weight of the account upon its deeper and pervasive meaning. To man, he contends, is given all save one prerogative:

---

[71] For a different interpretation, cf. W. Malcom Clark, "A Legal Background to the Yahwist's Use of 'Good and Evil' in Genesis 2–3," *JBL*, LXXXVIII (1969), pp. 266–278.

[72] Cf. Klaus Koch, "Gibt es ein Vergeltungsdogma im Alten Testament?" *ZTK*, LII (1955), pp. 1–42; Johannes Pedersen, *Israel*, I–II (London: Oxford University Press, Inc., 1954), p. 361.

ultimate lordship over all. This belongs to God alone; and man assumes it at his own peril.

The loss of access to the tree of life (3:22, 24), a subordinate and secondary element in the story, adds an irrevocable note to that which man's rebellion and God's consequent judgments ("to dust you shall return") have already assured: man shall not live forever. This is but a part, nevertheless, of the broader fulfillment of God's initial warning, "in the day that you eat of it you shall die." The death of which God warns is more than the loss of physical immortality. It is the loss of the authentic kind of life in communion with God and his creation which Eden symbolizes. Man's effort to take the place of God is by its very nature the beginning of death. As Bonhoeffer puts it, "man's becoming like God, promised by the serpent, can be nothing but what the Creator calls death."[73]

That life shall indeed go on east of Eden is the point of both the penalties pronounced by God and the account which follows them. Standing guilty and ashamed before God, the couple is yet respected by God and clothed with garments which he himself fashions for them (3:21). The woman is given the name "Eve" (associated with "life") and will become "the mother of all living" (3:20). The flesh and blood fulfillment of these expectations comes with the births of Cain and Abel (4:1–2).

CAIN AND ABEL. The Cain and Abel story (4:1–16) reflects both the basis on which life will continue and the further consequences of sin's prolific tendency to reproduce itself within the race. The story had a history independent of its present setting which presupposed the existence of other people on the earth besides the first family, for Cain takes a wife and fears those who will set upon him in his wanderings about the earth. His jealousy and murder of Abel have often been interpreted as symbolic of a tension between farmer (Cain) and shepherd (Abel) in early Near Eastern society. Recent studies have revealed, however, that the lines of ancient conflict were drawn not so much between agriculturalists and pastoralists as between urban-dominated societies, on the one hand, and marginal populations of the rural, hill, and steppe zones, on the other.[74] More often than not, pastoralism and agriculture co-existed as interdependent facets of the same tribal society. A careful reading of the account, moreover, reveals that the Yahwist regards Cain not simply as the ancestor of farmers, but as a city-builder whose descendants include craftsmen, musicians, and even shepherds (4:17–22). Rather than a single branch of ancient society,

---

[73] Dietrich Bonhoeffer, *Creation and Fall* (New York: Macmillan Publishing Co., Inc., 1959), p. 70.

[74] Cf. Norman K. Gottwald, "Were the Early Israelites Pastoral Nomads?" *Rhetorical Criticism: Essays in Honor of James Muilenburg*, J. J. Jackson and M. Kessler, eds. (Pittsburg, PA: The Pickwick Press, 1974), pp. 223–255, or the author's shorter article of the same name in *BAR*, IV, 2 (June, 1978), pp. 2–7.

Cain is best viewed as propagator and representative of all mankind.[75]

Why Cain's cereal offering is less pleasing to God than Abel's animal sacrifice is not explained. It is clear, nevertheless, that Cain has the same freedom to do God's bidding and master predatory drives as did his parents (4:7). The consequences of his failure to do so add a new chapter to the history of the human problem: the estrangement of persons, which had its beginning with the first couple's transgression, here takes the form of murder. Otherwise, Cain's sin is a close parallel to that of the parents. The provocation is again to possess that which God withholds, in this case a status superior to that of the brother; and the deed is an open rebellion against God's express will. Once again God confronts the guilty party with his crime, and as before there is the futile effort toward self-justification, this time coupled with a more blatant lie. Even the penalties are alike: an alienation from the earth, expulsion from God's immediate presence, and further estrangement, violence, and fear among men. Finally, just as the first couple is not left hopeless but is clothed by God, so does Cain receive the assurance of God's protection and a visible mark of his grace.

Paralleling the advance of culture among Cain's descendants (4:17–24) goes an increase in violence. The ancient song of Lamech, with its exultation in blood vengeance, is cited by the Yahwist as gory evidence (4:23–24).

> I have slain a man for wounding me,
>   a young man for striking me.
> If Cain is avenged sevenfold,
>   truly Lamech seventy-sevenfold.

With the birth of Seth, Adam's third son, the Yahwist perceives a replacement for the slain Abel and injects the hopeful note: "At that time men began to call upon the name of the Lord (Yahweh)" (4:26).

THE FLOOD. The flood epic (6:5–9:17) is framed by two J traditions (the sons of God and the daughters of men, 6:1–4; and the cursing of Canaan, 9:18–27), which in turn are set within the genealogies of Adam and Noah, respectively. The Sethite genealogy (ch. 5) is Priestly and is the only link between the creation and flood stories from that source. The generations from Adam through Noah are recorded in a formalized pattern that is unmistakably P:

> When ____ had lived ____ years, he became the father of ____. ____ lived after the birth of ____ ____ years, and had other sons and daughters. Thus all the days of ____ were ____ years; and he died.

The flood is here removed from creation by 1656 years, yet by only ten generations. The exaggerated life spans of the antediluvian fathers, averag-

---

[75] Cf. H. C. Brichto, "Cain and Abel," *IDBS*, pp. 121–122.

ing better than 850 years each, are typical of ancient conceptions of the longevity of the earliest men. An ancient Sumerian king list, compiled in the late third millennium B.C., contains the names and reigns of eight rulers who reigned prior to a disastrous flood, from the time "when kingship was lowered from heaven" until "the flood swept over." Their combined reigns total 241,200 years, an average for each king of more than 30,000 years. In a later version of this same list, compiled by the Babylonian priest Berossos in the early third century B.C., there are ten rulers (as in Genesis), and the length of their reigns is more exaggerated still: 432,000 years, or an average of 43,200 years![76] Following the flood the biblical genealogies depict a gradual decrease in life spans. For the generations from Shem through Terah the average is 333 years; from Abraham through Moses, 147 years. By the time of David, 70 years is considered "a good old age, full of days" (I Chron. 29:28).

Our extant Priestly material is totally lacking any reference to the garden or the Cain and Abel traditions. Nor does the Sethite genealogy contain any hint of the moral decline conceived by the Yahwist in the Cainite lineage. Rather, through Seth the "likeness of God" in which Adam was created is passed on (5:1b,3).

> When God created man, he made him in the likeness of God. . . . When Adam had lived a hundred and thirty years, he became the father of a son in his own likeness, after his image, and named him Seth.

For the immediate flood generation, nevertheless, the Priestly tradition conceives the same prevailing corruption as that described by J (6:11–13).

The flood story provides the first example in Genesis of a close interweaving of the Yahwistic and Priestly sources into a single narrative.[77] On the basis of the different names for God and the characteristic vocabularies and styles, two separate and nearly complete accounts may be distinguished. The two versions virtually duplicate the basic features of the familiar Noah story. In both accounts God beholds the prevailing wickedness of man and decides to destroy the life which he has created. Noah, because of his righteousness, is excepted from the decree. God reveals to him that he and his family shall escape in an ark—a boxlike boat—and instructs him to take on board male and female specimens of all animate life. Noah responds dutifully to God's instructions. The great deluge begins, and the waters increase on the earth until all life outside the ark is destroyed. The waters prevail upon the earth for a period, then gradually recede. When the land is finally dry, the company ventures forth from the ark and activity

---

[76] *ANET*, pp. 265–267; Jack Finegan, *Light from the Ancient Past*, 2nd ed., (Princeton, NJ: Princeton University Press, 1959), pp. 29–31; George A. Barton, *Archaeology and the Bible*, 7th ed. (Philadelphia: American Sunday-School Union, 1949), p. 320.

[77] For an analysis that perceives the unifying design in the final form of the flood account, notwithstanding its composition from two tradition strands, see Bernhard Anderson, "From Analysis to Synthesis: The Interpretation of Genesis 1–11," *JBL*, 97 (1978), pp. 23–39.

upon the earth is renewed. God promises never again to repeat the flood.

Some of the more striking differences between the two accounts reflect characteristics of the Yahwistic and Priestly traditions. Only the Priestly version of God's instructions for building the ark is retained (6:14–16), and typical of Priestly interests, the description is precise and detailed. The ark is a three-storied houseboat, its dimensions roughly 450 by 75 by 45 feet. The Yahwist includes the instructions for taking animal specimens on board (7:2–3), seven pairs of all clean animals and fowl and a pair each of all unclean species. The Priestly instructions call for only one pair of every beast, bird, and insect. This difference reflects the Yahwistic assumption that distinctions between pure and impure applied from the very beginning, whereas from the Priestly point of view such Levitical categories were unknown prior to Moses. Likewise, only the Yahwist records Noah's sacrificial offering following the flood, since in Priestly terms sacrifice, too, was initially established by Mosaic legislation. Altogether characteristic of the Yahwist's colorful and personal manner of describing God's relations with men in his notation that after Noah had entered the ark, "Yahweh shut him in" (7:16b).

J FLOOD ACCOUNT	P FLOOD ACCOUNT
6:5–8	6:9–22
7:1–5, 7–10, 12, 16^b–17, 22–23	7:6, 11, 13–16^a, 18–21, 24
8:2^b, 3^a, 6–12, 13^b, 20–22	8:1–2^a, 3^b–5, 13^a, 14–19
	9:1–17

In J the flood appears as a forty-day rain, followed by a period of three weeks in which the waters recede from the earth. Birds are released to test the abatement of the waters, first a raven, then a dove. The suspense which the Yahwist brings to his narrative is evident here in the initial return of the dove, there being no dry land on which to settle, then the second and third trials, bringing signs of life and a recession of the waters. P conceives the flood as a breaking forth of waters from above and beneath the earth ("all the fountains of the great deep burst forth, and the windows of heaven were opened"), virtually restoring the watery abyss which prevailed prior to the creation. In this account the deluge lasts 150 days, and at the end of five months the ark comes to rest on a mountaintop. The waters recede for another seven months and ten days, making the entire duration of the flood more than a year.

In the brief epilogue with which the Yahwist concludes his version of the flood (8:20–22), Yahweh smells the pleasing odor of Noah's sacrifice and is moved to pity the human dilemma whereby "the imagination of man's heart is evil from his youth." The flood having revealed God's impatience with wickedness, its aftermath evokes his forbearance and the reaffirmation of his initial creation. The patterns intended for the earth are restored and serve as a sign that life shall go on.

> While the earth remains, seedtime and harvest, cold and heat, summer and winter, day and night, shall not cease.

The Priestly tradition (9:1–17) conceives this as a covenant made with Noah and his descendants. They receive God's blessing and are charged with the role first assigned Adam: to populate the earth and subdue it. But a new privilege is extended; man shall have animals as well as plants for his food (cf. 1:29). As an anticipation of Levitical law, however, the permission to take life necessitates immediate restrictions. Man is not to eat the blood, for the potency of life resides in the blood and God declares it sacred. Neither shall a man take the life of another man since God's own image is in man. The elementary principle of the *lex talionis* receives its first expression in the Old Testament: "Whoever sheds the blood of man, by man shall his blood be shed." The bow in the clouds—perhaps the death weapon which God now sets aside—is established as a covenant witness.

> When the bow is in the clouds, I will look upon it and remember the everlasting covenant between God and every living creature of all flesh that is upon the earth.

The significance of the covenant with Noah lies in its conception of the inclusiveness of God's designs. His pact is with all mankind, indeed with the entire creation, and not simply with Israel alone. As such, it reconfirms God's plans for man as in the beginning, man's wickedness notwithstanding. And, quite logically, it marks a new era in the history of God's tireless search for communion with man.

Evidence points to an original Mesopotamian provenance for the Hebrew flood story. The high elevation and dry climate of Palestine assure an absence of such inundations as have been known to occur in the flat plain between the lower Tigris and Euphrates. At the sites of ancient Ur, Kish, Uruk, Shuruppak, Lagash, and Nineveh flood strata of varying depths and periods have been uncovered.[78] Although the localized character of these deposits offers no support for the historicity of a universal flood, they doubtless explain the popularity of such accounts in this part of the world.[79] An early Sumerian deluge tradition had its origin here and became the prototype for later versions found in Mesopotamia and elsewhere. Since George Smith's discovery of an Akkadian cuneiform version of the story in 1872, its remarkable similarities with the Hebrew account have been broadly publicized.[80]

---

[78] Charles Leonard Woolley, *Ur of the Chaldees* (London: E. Benn, 1929), pp. 22–29.

[79] André Parrot, *The Flood and Noah's Ark* (London: SCM Press, 1955), pp. 51ff.

[80] James B. Pritchard, *Archaeology and the Old Testament* (Princeton, NJ: Princeton University Press, 1958), pp. 160ff.

A fragmentary tablet found at Nippur in southern Mesopotamia preserves the partial text of the oldest Sumerian version of the story presently known.[81] The tablet dates from about the time of Hammurabi (c. 1728–1686 B.C.), but the story itself is much older. Only about one third of the text survives. It tells of a seven-day flood decreed by an assembly of the gods, from which Ziusudra ("Life-day Prolonged"), king of Shuruppak, escapes in a boat. He appears to have been warned in a dream of the impending disaster designed "to destroy the seed of mankind." Following his deliverance, the king prostrates himself before the gods and offers an animal sacrifice. Enlil, at this time the supreme god in the Sumerian pantheon, then bestowing upon him "life like that of a god," and he takes up his immortal abode in the mythical land of Dilmun. Berossus, a Babylonian priest of the third century B.C., recorded a version of the story, two excerpts of which are preserved in the quotations of later Greek writers.[82] The hero is here called Xisuthros (or Sisithros), a Grecized form of the name Ziusudra. Fragments of another Babylonian and Assyrian version are known in which the hero's name is Atrahasis, and in which the flood is decreed by Enlil to silence the noisy tumult of man.[83]

By far the most complete and best known of the Mesopotamian flood stories is the version recounted in the eleventh tablet of the Gilgamesh epic.[84] It was a cuneiform fragment of this account, discovered in excavations of Ashurbanipal's seventh century B.C. palace at Nineveh, which Smith revealed to the Society of Biblical Archaeology in 1872, a development described by one scholar as "the beginning of a new epoch in our understanding of the early stories in Genesis." Based on the older Sumerian tradition, the account is known to have circulated widely in the ancient world. Since the initial discovery of the cuneiform copies at Nineveh, other translations have been found as far away as Hattusa (modern Bogazkoy) in Asia Minor and Megiddo in Palestine.

The longer epic in which the flood narrative is incorporated is a collection of stories concerning Gilgamesh, legendary king of Uruk. The latter's quest for immortality takes him to Utnapishtim ("Day of Life"), the flood hero who had survived the great deluge and attained eternal life. Relating

---

[81] *ANET*, pp. 42–44 (*ANE*, pp. 28–30); Alexander Heidel, *The Gilgamesh Epic and Old Testament Parallels* (Chicago: University of Chicago Phoenix Books, 1963), pp. 102–105.

[82] Alexander Heidel, *The Gilgamesh Epic and Old Testament Parallels*, pp. 116–119.

[83] Ibid., pp. 106–116, and the more complete text of the epic in W. G. Lambert and A. R. Millard, *Atrahasis: the Babylonian Story of the Flood* (New York: Oxford University Press, Inc., 1969). Cf. Tikva Frymer-Kensky," The Atrahasis Epic and Its Significance for Our Understanding of Genesis 1–9," *BA*, 40 (1977), pp. 147–155, where it is held that the Atrahasis epic provides the most fruitful comparisons with the Genesis account, since in both versions the flood is set within the context of a longer primeval history, including a creation account. Thus, the Atrahasis epic is felt to support the organic unity between the creation and flood stories in Genesis.

[84] *ANET*, pp. 92–97 (*ANE*, pp. 65–75); Alexander Heidel, *The Gilgamesh Epic and Old Testament Parallels*, pp. 80–93.

his story to Gilgamesh, Utnapishtim tells of a decision of the great gods at Shuruppak to bring on a flood. Ea, Utnapishtim's patron, warns him of the approaching danger:

> Man of Shuruppak, son of Ubar-Tutu,
> Tear down (this) house, build a ship!
> Give up possessions, seek thou life.
> Forswear (worldly) goods and keep the soul alive!
> Aboard the ship take thou the seed of all
>   living things.[85]

Following Ea's instructions, he builds a cube-shaped boat, seals it with pitch, and loads on it silver and gold, one of each kind of animal, craftsmen, and all his family and kin. When he has entered the boat and closed the door a storm of such fierce proportions breaks forth that even the gods are terror stricken and "cower like dogs," lamenting their decision to unleash the violence. On the seventh day the storm ceases and, looking from the window of his boat, Utnapishtim discovers that "all mankind has turned to clay."

The ship comes to rest on Mount Nisir. After seven days have passed, birds are sent out to test the water's recession: a dove, a swallow, and a raven, in that order. With the drying of the earth, Utnapishtim offers a sacrifice to the gods.

> The gods smelled the savor,
> The gods smelled the sweet savor,
> The gods crowded like flies about the sacrifice.[86]

Enlil, the war-prone god, is filled with anger upon discovering that some mortals have escaped death. But, when rebuked by Ea for having prompted the ill-advised destruction, he grants immortality to Utnapishtim and his spouse. Hence forth they dwell as gods at the far end of the earth.

The common elements in the Hebrew and Mesopotamian flood accounts are sufficiently impressive to assure a Mesopotamian background for the Genesis story. In each version the deluge is the result of a divine decree, one man and his family are selected to survive, and the means of escape is a houseboat. In the Utnapishtim version, especially, the similarity of details—the provision for preserving species of life, the mountaintop landing, the release of birds, and the sacrifice offered the gods—is striking.

As with the creation stories, nevertheless, in items of religious significance the differences far outweigh the similarities and thus assist our understanding of the truly unique features of the Hebrew account. Once again, it is the contrasting conception of deity that is the revealing factor.

---

[85] *ANET*, p. 93 (*ANE*, p. 66).
[86] *ANET*, p. 95 (*ANE*, p. 70).

The eleventh clay tablet from the Gilgamesh epic, containing an Assyrian version of the Babylonian flood story. The tablet shown was found at Ashurbanipal's (seventh century B.C.) library at Nineveh. (Courtesy of the Trustees of the British Museum.)

In the Mesopotamian polytheism the gods dispute among themselves the wisdom of the deluge, and the motive for it is not in every case apparent. They display their human foibles, cringing in fear before forces which they cannot control and crowding like flies about the sacrifice upon which their lives depend. There is no one omnipotent will directing events toward purposeful and moral ends. The immortality granted the flood hero is incidental, since, as Gilgamesh discovers, it is not made available for the common lot of mankind.

Yahweh, by contrast, is undivided in his decision to use the flood as a punishment for wickedness and to provide a fresh beginning with a faithful remnant. It is human corruption and not divine caprice that brings on the flood in the Hebrew account. The underlying principle is, as one writer puts it, "that man cannot undermine the moral basis of society without endangering the very existence of civilization."[87] Noah puts himself completely at God's disposal, assured that he commands the means necessary for fulfilling his good and well-laid plans. God's purpose, furthermore, is a universally significant one: a binding covenant with the newly purged race for all ages to come.[88]

NOAH'S DESCENDANTS. The Yahwistic story of Noah's drunkenness and his pronouncement of the curse on Canaan (9:20–27) is hardly intended as a moral aspersion on the character of Noah. His role as the first husbandman, notwithstanding his experimentation with wine, is extolled as a source of relief from the cursed soil (5:29). The account is, first of all, an etiology of the depravity of the Canaanites as depicted in their eponymous ancestor, Canaan, and of their subjugation by Israel (Shem). In our text an earlier form of the story has been accommodated to the prevailing Shem-Ham-Japheth tradition. In the original account Noah's youngest was not Ham, but Canaan (cf. verses 24–25); and Canaan, of course, is the actual recipient of the curse. The intoxication and sexual offense quite possibly reflect Hebrew antipathy to the inordinate role of wine and sex in the Canaanite culture and cultus. In any event, the recipients of the curse are not, as such, the black peoples of earth, who constitute only a part of the Hamites, according to chapter 10. The chief service of the story at this point in the narrative is to set the scene for further alienation and divisions among the postdiluvian generations.

The "Table of Nations," chapter 10, is a composite of J and P material, set within a framework that is basically from a Priestly "generations" source. It conceives the entire population of the ancient world as descended from the three sons of Noah: Shem, Ham, and Japheth. As strict ethnographical or linguistic classifications, the lists are of little import, and some of the names defy precise identification. Very broadly speaking, however, Japheth represents the Indo-Europeans or, geographically, peoples of the north and west: Asia Minor, the territories surrounding the Black and Caspian seas, southern Spain, and portions of Greece and Italy. The Hamites are associated with lands in the Egyptian orbit, including Libya,

[87] Nahum M. Sarna, *Understanding Genesis* (New York: McGraw-Hill Book Company, 1966), p. 52.
[88] Tikva Frymer-Kensky ("The Atrahasis Epic and Its Significance for Our Understanding of Genesis 1–9"), on the basis of a comparison with the Atrahasis epic, concludes that the motive of the Genesis flood was the cleansing of the earth from the pollution of bloodshed (4:10–12, 23). The laws given to Noah after the flood (9:1–17) were intended to prevent the future pollution of the earth.

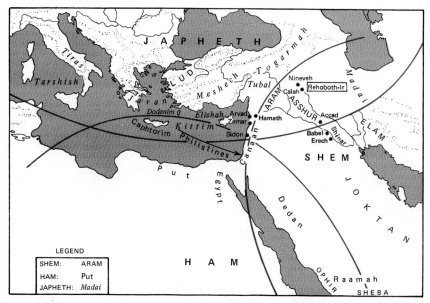

The families of the nations according to Genesis 10. (Adapted with permission of Macmillan Publishing Co., Inc., from Macmillan Bible Atlas *by Y. Aharoni and Michael Avi-Yonah. Copyright © 1968 Carta, Jerusalem. © Copyright 1964 by Carta, Jerusalem. © Copyright 1966 by Carta, Jerusalem.)*

Ethiopia, and Canaan, together with southeastern Arabia and a portion of southern Mesopotamia (Nimrod). Shem's descendants (Semites) are the peoples of Arabia, Mesopotamia, Elam, and southern Asia Minor, representing the strain from which the ancestry of Israel derives. Modern technical usage employs the term "Semite" as a classification for ancient Near Eastern peoples or their descendants who used one of a common family of inflectional languages, such as Akkadian, Aramaic, Hebrew, or the like. The Canaanites, who were related to the Hamites by neither blood nor language, were thus Semites, whereas the Elamites actually were not.

The normal pattern of naming the first-born at the head of such genealogical tables has been reversed here in order that the underlying theme of the patriarchal narrative might be served, namely, that from the great number of the nations of earth God's choice of a peculiar people might be seen as narrowing down to Israel.

THE TOWER OF BABEL. The last of the major narrative units in the primeval history (11:1–9) tells of man's thwarted effort to build on the Babylonian plain a city with a tower scaling the heavens. The account (from J) fits its context awkwardly, since the phenomenon which it purports to explain—the multiplication of nations and tongues—has already been de-

The remains of the Ziggurat of ancient Ur, built c. 2100 B.C. (Courtesy of the Trustees of the British Museum.)

veloped in the preceding chapter. It is here, nevertheless, to supply insights such as lie outside the scope of genealogical tables.

The story answers a number of etiological questions. In addition to explaining the distribution of peoples and languages, it accounts for the origin of the city of Babylon, its name,[89] and an unfinished or fallen Babylonian ziggurat.[90] Ziggurats, known from Akkadian sources and the reports of Herodotus,[91] as well as from actual remains found in lower Mesopotamia, were massive sacred towers, built of tiered brick, and located in or near a temple complex. They first appeared, it would seem, as men from the north, where the gods were associated with mountains, moved down into the flat Mesopotamian plain and there proceeded to erect substitute promontories for their gods. The great ziggurat at Babylon, called *Etemenanki* ("house of the foundation of heaven and earth"), was begun by Hammurabi and finished by Nebuchadrezzar. It once towered to a height of almost 300 feet and consisted of six square terraces, covered with plants and crowned at the top with a temple. Perhaps our story arose in a period when this huge monument was in ruins between two rebuildings.

The theological point which the Yahwist intended for the story is none too clearly drawn. What was there about this enterprise that was so displeasing to Yahweh? It might have been man's resistance to God's com-

---

[89] The Hebrew name *bābel*, derived from the Akkadian *bab-ilu* ("gate of the gods"), is here (vs. 9) interpreted by the similar sounding but unrelated Hebrew verb *balal* ("confuse").

[90] It has been proposed that the Yahwist has actually combined two stories here: one concerned with Babel and the confusion of tongues, the other with the memory of some ruined tower and the dispersion of the race. Cf. John Skinner, *Genesis*, pp. 223ff.

[91] *The History of Herodotus*, Everyman's Library (New York: E. P. Dutton & Co., Inc., 1916), Vol. I, Bk. I, 181–183, pp. 92–93.

mand to spread abroad and fill the earth ("lest we be scattered abroad upon the face of the whole earth"), though that specific injunction is from the Priestly rather than the Yahwistic tradition (1:28; 8:17). The express purpose of the builders ("let us make a name for ourselves") and the disquieting reflection of Yahweh ("this is only the beginning of what they will do") suggest a broader interpretation, namely, man's rebellious and prideful effort to build, without benefit of God, a culture of his own making and a monument dedicated to his own self-aggrandizement. The episode speaks of the fact that "man is constantly tempted to forget the finiteness of his cultures and civilization and to pretend a finality for them which they do not have."[92] It thus provides a fitting climax to the primeval history and its broader theme wherein the human problem is consistently depicted as man's futile urge to assume the place of God.

As von Rad has noted,[93] the usual word of grace—the redemptive note which concluded the stories of the fall, Cain's evil, and the flood—is lacking in the Babel story. The effect thus achieved is to end the primeval history on a note of judgment and tension which will be resolved only in the patriarchal narrative. In this manner the patriarchs are shown to be God's word of grace to man's predicament. God sets about preparing for himself a peculiar people through whom he will reestablish a hope for his creation.

3. A WANDERING ARAMEAN WAS MY FATHER: GENESIS 12–50

The reader of Genesis has little difficulty recognizing the unity which inheres in the remainder of the book, chapters 12–50. Even though it is none too easy finding the precise literary classification with which to distinguish these chapters from chapters 1–11 ("saga" and "legend" are commonly applied labels),[94] in respect to subject matter the differences are apparent. In these chapters we find longer, sustained accounts, centering around the four major patriarchs: Abraham, Isaac, Jacob, and Joseph. The brief and highly compact stories of Genesis 1–11, with their universal themes of human beginnings, here give way to cycles of stories associated with the several Semitic fathers and their families. In the real sense, the chief actor in the drama continues to be God, but there is less anthropomorphism in describing his actions and more of the localized saga concern-

[92] Reinhold Niebuhr, *Beyond Tragedy* (New York: Charles Scribner's Sons, 1937), p. 28.
[93] *Genesis*, pp. 148–150.
[94] When Herman Gunkel wrote his famous *Commentary on Genesis* at the turn of the century (cf. *The Legends of Genesis*) he treated Genesis in its entirety under the classification of *Sagen* (saga). His criteria for distinguishing these accounts from history in the strict sense are still valid, but other approaches have been more sensitive to the relevance of legend to historical concerns, e.g., John Skinner, *Genesis*, pp. iii ff. and John M. Holt, *The Patriarchs of Israel* (Nashville, TN: Vanderbilt University Press, 1964), pp. 29–35.

ing specific tribes and their movements, particularly as these are associated with well-known sacred sites. Through every episode, there runs like a red thread the theme of God's election of Israel. The pattern of promise and fulfillment, which gives theological substance to the entire biblical history, is here portrayed as having its beginning in God's call of Abraham. From this point onward, the tracing of the promise, its renewal with Abraham's successive offspring, and the anticipation of its eventual fulfillment in the Israelite successes in Canaan are the chief concerns of the patriarchal narrative.

Hebrew Origins

Since history, as such, is not the purpose of these stories, the ethnic origins of the patriarchs and their connections with known peoples of the Near East are depicted only in the most general and schematic fashion. The J element in the Table of Nations introduces Eber, the eponym for "Hebrew," as the great grandson of Shem through the latter's son Arpachshad (10:21–24). Arpachshad resists geographical location [95]; but Eber's sons, Peleg and Joktan, can be identified as the northern "Arameans" and the southern branch of Semites in Arabia, respectively. It is from Peleg, the Semites of northwest Mesopotamia and Syria, that the Priestly genealogical list of 11:10–26 traces the lineage of Abraham. The names of some of these patriarchal ancestors—Peleg, Serug, Nahor, and Terah—correspond to the names of towns in that region; and the Hebrew spelling of Haran, here named as Abraham's brother, varies only slightly from that of the north Syrian town with which the patriarchs are closely associated (11:31ff.; 27:43ff.). [96]

No fact concerning the ancestry of the Hebrews seems more firmly established than their associations with Syria and northwest Mesopotamia. Although the biblical tradition records a migration of Abraham's father, Terah, and his tribe from Ur, in southern Mesopotamia, [97] it is Haran rather than Ur that occupies the more central position in the patriarchal narratives. [98] It is at Haran that Abraham receives his call (12:1ff.), that a wife is

[95] Cf. John Skinner, Genesis p. 205; John M. Holt, The Patriarchs of Israel, pp. 38–39.

[96] The difference is that the brother's name is spelled with a soft "h" (the Hebrew he), the town's with a hard "h" or "ch" (ḥēth).

[97] Gen. 11:31–32; cf. 11:28; 15:7.

[98] "Ur of the Chaldeans" is explained by most scholars who date Abraham to the early second millenium B.C. as an anachronistic designation for Sumerian Ur, since "Chaldeans" normally refers to the Neo-Babylonians of the late seventh and sixth centuries B.C. (cf. Roland de Vaux, The Early History of Israel, David Smith, trans., [Philadelphia: Westminster Press, 1978], pp. 187–192). Some efforts have been made to identify the Ur of Abraham's origins with a smaller town of that name in Upper Mesopotamia (cf. C. H. Gordon, "Abraham and the Merchants of Ura," JNES, 17 [1958], pp. 28–31; "Where Is Abraham's Ur?", BAR, III, 2 [June 1977], pp. 20–21, 52), and it is reported that an "Ur in Haran" is mentioned in an as-yet-unpublished tablet from the recently discovered Ebla archives (cf. BAR, II, 4 [Dec. 1976], p. 42).

secured for Isaac (ch. 24), and that Jacob puts in long years of service for his father-in-law, Laban (chs. 28–31). Something akin to a Hebrew reverence for that region as the ancestral homeland is suggested in the fathers' insistence that Isaac and Jacob bypass the Canaanite women and take their wives from there.

It was in this area that the Semitic Arameans settled in force, as reflected in names given the region: Aram,[99] Paddan-Aram ("the Plain of Aram"),[100] and Aram Naharaim ("Aram of the Two Rivers").[101] The tradition linking Hebrew history with the Arameans is reflected in the credo repeated in the festival of First Fruits: "A wandering Aramean was my father" (Deut. 26:5); and the patriarchal kinsmen in the Haran area are repeatedly called Arameans in the Genesis accounts.[102] Scholars who date the Hebrew patriarchs in the early second millennium B.C., however, regard these biblical references to Aram and Arameans as anachronistic, since the names do not appear in other ancient sources as designations for the Syrian region and its people before late in the second millennium B.C.[103]

In any event, the patriarchal association with the Arameans is at best a partial identification. In the Table of Nations, as we have seen, the Hebrews are traced not through Aram, but through the enigmatic Arpachshad (10:22). Perhaps, as John Holt suggests, "the author of P was unable to find a geographical niche for the line of Arpachshad."[104] At any rate, we are unable to do so; and the fact that the name is non-Semitic further complicates the problem. A categorical assertion of the composite origins of the Hebrews appears in Ezekiel 16:3, in words addressed to Jerusalem:

> Your origin and your birth are of the land of the Canaanites; your father was an Amorite, and your mother a Hittite.

The Amorites, indicated here, are regarded in the Old Testament accounts as one of the pre-Israelitic peoples of Palestine, and are not to be equated as such with the earlier Amorites or Amurru mentioned in nonbiblical texts from the late third and early second millennia B.C.[105] The early Amorites, nevertheless, were a Semitic people and, in the opinion of some Old Testament scholars, constituted the broader strain from which both Arameans and Hebrews derived.[106] The Canaanites and Hittites were by Hebrew reckoning Hamitic. The biblical evidence as a whole, then, suggests the complexity of Hebrew origins and the involvement in their ancestry of non-

---

[99] Gen. 22:21; Num. 23:7.

[100] Gen. 25:20; 28:2ff.; 31:18; 33:18; 35:9, 26; 46:15; 48:7.

[101] Ps. 60.

[102] 25:20; 28:1ff.; 31:20, 24.

[103] Cf. Roland de Vaux, *The Early History of Israel*, pp. 200–205.

[104] John M. Holt, *The Patriarchs of Israel*, p. 39.

[105] Cf. Roland de Vaux, *The Early History of Israel*, pp. 132–133, 200ff., and H. B. Huffmon, "Amorites," *IDBS*, pp. 20–21.

[106] Roland de Vaux, *The Early History of Israel*, pp. 200–209.

Babylonian world map as depicted on a sixth-century B.C. clay tablet. (Courtesy of the Trustees of the British Museum.)

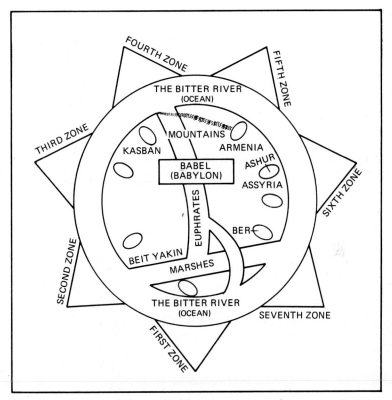

Babylonian world map reconstructed.

Semitic as well as Semitic strains. In the opinion of W. F. Albright, "the genetic affiliations of the early Hebrews were probably so mixed that all the theories reflected in later Israelite tradition have some justification."[107]

The Patriarchal World

To write a formal history of the patriarchs is impossible, notwithstanding the significant role attributed to them in Hebrew tradition as the ancestors of the later Israel. Our only indisputable sources of information concerning the Hebrew fathers are confined to the book of Genesis and the passing references found elsewhere in the Bible. Not a single one of the specific individuals or events mentioned in these accounts can with certainty be identified with persons or events described in the ancient extrabiblical records provided by Near Eastern archaeology. The Genesis narratives, moreover, are marked by evident theological interests, embellishment with layers of interpretive tradition, and a vagueness as to historical setting.

[107] *From the Stone Age to Christianity*, p. 239.

Until recently, most of the evidence for dating the patriarchs appeared to converge on the Middle Bronze Age (c. 2200–1550 B.C.); and even scholars who differed widely in their assessments of the historicity of the accounts, more often than not favored that period or one of its phases as the "patriarchal age." Current re-evaluations of the evidence, however, including the steady accumulation of new archaeological data, have opened the question anew. It is probably fair to say that most of Old Testament scholarship is now in a state of suspended judgment on the issue. At the very least, one must be aware of the major options and the evidence offered in their support. But this requires, first of all, some background knowledge of the Middle East—its cultural, political, and social patterns—during the third and second millennia B.C.

EARLY MESOPOTAMIA. At whatever precise point the Hebrews appeared on the stage of history, they were relative latecomers. As John Bright has noted, "it is quite as far if not farther from the beginnings of civilization in the Near East to the age of Israel's origins as it is from the latter to our own!"[108] Permanent villages existed as early as the eighth millennium in Palestine (Jericho) and by the seventh millennium in Anatolia (Catal Huyuk).[109] By the third millennium a flowering of culture, including cuneiform writing, a system of city-states, refinement of the arts and crafts, and a highly developed religious cult, had been brought to southern Mesopotamia by the Sumerians. This period, known as the Classical Sumerian Age (2800–2360 B.C.), saw the production of the famous mythological epics which became the prototypes for much of the later Assyrian, Babylonian, and Canaanite mythology. The age ended when the Semitic Akkadians, under Sargon the Great, subdued Sumer and all Mesopotamia and founded one of the earliest true empires in world history (2360–2180 B.C.).

The Akkadians essentially took over the Sumerian culture, including its gods, and adapted the cuneiform script as a vehicle for their Semitic tongue. Thus established, cuneiform Akkadian became the *lingua franca* throughout much of the Near East for centuries to come. The collapse of the Empire of Akkad before an onslaught of barbaric Caucasian peoples, the Gutians, marked a period of decline, which was followed by a brief but dramatic revival of Sumerian culture under the Third Dynasty of Ur (c. 2060–1950 B.C.). Ur-nammu, the founder of Ur III, promulgated the first known code of laws and erected the massive ziggurat at Ur which was excavated by Sir Leonard Woolley in 1922–1934.[110] Ur, in this period of its

---

[108] *A History of Israel* (Philadelphia: The Westminster Press, 1959), p. 18.

[109] For the prehistorical and pre-Israelitic archaeology of Palestine, see Kathleen Kenyon, *Archaeology in the Holy Land*, 3rd ed. (New York: Praeger Publishers, Inc., 1970), pp. 17–161.

[110] Charles Leonard Woolley, *Ur of the Chaldees; Excavations at Ur* (New York: Barnes & Noble Books, 1954). For the Ur-nammu code of law, see below, pp. 178ff.

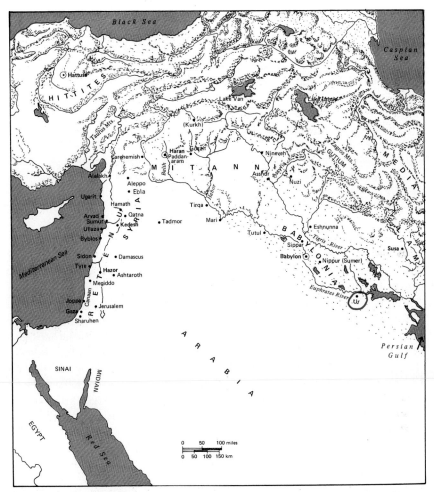

The Near East in the third and second millennia B.C. (Adapted with permission of Macmillan Publishing Co., Inc., from Macmillan Bible Atlas by Y. Aharoni and Michael Avi-Yonah. Copyright © 1968 Carta, Jerusalem. © Copyright 1964 by Carta, Jerusalem. © Copyright 1966 by Carta, Jerusalem.)

prosperity, has been described as "the greatest commercial capital that the world had yet seen.[111] That claim may require revision, however, in view of the impressive remains of the ancient city of Ebla, recently discovered in Syria.

EARLY EGYPT. History began in Egypt at approximately the same time as the cultural flowering of ancient Sumer. Near the beginning of the third

[111] William F. Albright, "Abram the Hebrew: A New Archaeological Interpretation," *BASOR*, 163 (1961), p. 44.

millennium, Upper and Lower Egypt united in the First Dynasty, which soon developed into the grandeur known as the Old Kingdom (c. 2700–2200 B.C.). The production of a classicial Egyptian literature, religion, and architecture, including the building of the great pyramids, was made possible by a stable government under the Old Kingdom's pharaohs. During this period Egypt exercised considerable influence over the city-states of Syria and Palestine. When the Old Kingdom finally lapsed into anarchy, there followed a period of two centuries (the First Intermediate Period) before the Middle Kingdom brought a resurgence under the pharaohs of the Twelfth Dynasty (c. 1991–1786). Once again, Egypt experienced an era of political, economic, and cultural advance that lasted until the mid-eighteenth century, when the decline during the Second Intermediate Period (mid-eighteenth to mid-sixteenth century) led to the takeover of the government by the foreigners known as "Hyksos."

EBLA. From 1964 to the present, Italian archaeologists have uncovered at Tell Mardikh, in northern Syria, the palace and archives of a hitherto unknown empire as large as that of Sargon the Great.[112] Previously known only as a name in ancient Mesopotamian records, Ebla is now recognized to have been a major cultural, commercial, and political center during the latest phase of the Early Bronze Age, c. 2400–2250 B.C., or perhaps earlier.[113] Its commercial and political significance was apparent to Sargon, who conquered it and placed on its throne a certain King Ebrum (or Ebrium). The third and strongest of six successive rulers of Ebla, Ebrum succeeded in turning the tables on Akkad following Sargon's death and made tribute-paying vassals of its cities. At its height, Ebla's sphere of influence included Palestine, Phoenicia, Cyprus, and Mesopotamia, as well as Syria. Not until 2250 B.C. was Sargon's grandson, Narum-Sin, able to escape Ebla's yoke by conquering the city and putting *it* to the torch.

Among the remains thus far uncovered at Tell Mardikh are massive city walls fortified with a sloping rampart or *glacis*, a royal palace, and a large tripartite temple (the earliest known of this design) dedicated to the goddess Ishtar.[114] Between 1974 and 1977 there were discovered within the palace ruins more than 17,000 inscribed clay tablets, representing a

---

[112] Cf. Giovanni Pettinato, "The Royal Archives of Tell-Mardikh-Ebla, *BA*, 39 (1976), pp. 44–52; Paolo Matthiae, "Ebla in the Late Early Syrian Period: The Royal Palace and the State Archives," *BA*, 39 (1976), pp. 94–113; Paul C. Maloney, "Assessing Ebla," *BAR*, IV, 1 (Mar. 1978), pp. 4–10.

[113] Disagreement exists as to the exact dates of the empire of Ebla. The excavator, Paolo Matthiae, on the basis of archaeological and stratigraphical evidence, dates the remains to 2400–2250 B.C. The epigrapher, Giovanni Pettinato, interprets the style and format of the tablets, together with their contents, as pointing to the period 2580–2450 B.C.

[114] For examples of tripartite or three-chambered temples of the ancient Middle East, see below, pp. 245–249.

Ebla. The mound of Tell Mardikh, in northwest Syria, is now known to contain the remains of ancient Ebla. (Courtesy of Dr. Lawrence Geraty.)

portion of the state archives. It is believed that some 30,000 to 40,000 tablets may eventually be recovered. Written in the Cuneiform script common to the earliest Mesopotamian texts, the language of an estimated 80 per cent of the tablets is Sumerian. The remaining 20 per cent are composed in a previously unknown Semitic dialect, which has been given the name "Eblaite" or "Paleo-Canaanite." Giovanni Pettinato, The Tell Mardikh epigrapher, regards the latter language as a direct ancestor of Hebrew and other West Semitic languages.[115]

The majority of the Ebla tablets consist of administrative and economic documents, many pertaining to Ebla's international commerce in textiles, timber, copper, and precious stones. Of historical and geographical importance are records of royal edicts, state correspondence, international treaties, and lists of subject cities. Also included are bilingual dictionaries or vocabularies, scientific lists of animals, fish, birds, and geographical sites, as well as mythological texts concerning Mesopotamian deities well-known from the Sumerian and Babylonian epics. The mythological sources are reputed to contain accounts of the creation and primeval deluge, and thus promise to be significant in future studies of Near Eastern mythology. To date, however, only a fraction of the materials have been closely studied, and it appears that their publication will be slow in coming.

[115] "The Royal Archives of Tell-Mardikh-Ebla," pp. 50–52.

AMORITES. There began near the close of the third millennium a disruption of life throughout the Middle East which effected major social, cultural, and political changes. Ur, weakened for lack of a strong, centralized government, fell before an attack of Elamites. This ushered in a period of confusion and conflict lasting two centuries, when rival states in upper and lower Mesopotamia struggled for power. Elam, Isin, Larsa, and Babylon vied for control in the south: Assyria (Asshur), then Mari, held the balance of strength in the north. The most striking feature of this turbulent era was the seizure of powerful city-states by a people speaking northwest Semitic dialects and known in southern Mesopotamia as MAR.TU (Sumerian) or Amurru (Akkadian: "Westerners"), which is to say, Amorites. Although the name suggests an association with the Syrian region, it encompasses a variety of people and is best not interpreted in a geographic or ethnic sense. According to one analysis, "the designation is largely socioeconomic, i.e., peoples who are 'foreigners' to the fully urbanized way of life in the Mesopotamian city-states."[116]

Mentioned in Mesopotamian sources from the time of Sargon, the Amorites are depicted as a primitive, barbarous people, who ate raw meat, neither lived in houses nor buried their dead, and only slowly adapted to sedentary life. Such descriptions, however, were written from the perspective of urbanists and doubtless depict a biased view. Recent research suggests that these people were not so much nomadic invaders, seeking escape from the desert, as partly settled village, rural, and steppe-zone pastoralists, who came increasingly into contact with urban life.[117] At any rate, by the eighteenth or seventeenth century B.C. the most important city-states in Mesopotamia were ruled by Amorites or persons bearing their West-Semitic type names.[118] Many scholars believe that they are to be connected, as well, with the broad cultural transitions archaeologically documented in Syria and Palestine which ushered in the Middle Bronze Age (c. 2200–1550 B.C.). One long-popular theory, now subject to much debate, conceives the Hebrew patriarchs as one phase of Amorite migrations from Mesopotamia and/or Syria into the Palestinian region during that period.[119]

MARI. One of the most impressive of the Amorite city-states was Mari, located at modern Tell Hariri, on the upper Euphrates.[120] The latter half of

---

[116] William G. Dever, "Palestine in the Second Millennium B.C.E.; The Archaeological Picture," in *Israelite and Judean History*, John H. Hayes and J. Maxwell Miller, eds. (Philadelphia: The Westminster Press, 1977), p. 110.

[117] Reference is to the studies of M. B. Rowton, J. T. Luke, and M. Liverani. For a summary discussion and detailed bibliography, cf. William G. Dever, pp. 102–111.

[118] Thomas L. Thompson, *The Historicity of the Patriarchal Narratives* (Berlin/New York: Walter de Gruyter, 1974), pp. 67–75, discusses the problem of identifying the Amorites on the evidence of the names.

[119] See below, pp. 119–120.

[120] On Mari and the Mari texts, see Abraham Malamat, "Mari," *BA*, 34 (1971), pp. 2–22, and the bibliography cited there.

"The main route" and the "King's Highway" in the ancient Near East. (Adapted with permission of Macmillan Publishing Co., Inc., from Macmillan Bible Atlas *by Y. Aharoni and Michael Avi-Yonah. Copyright © 1968 Carta, Jerusalem. © Copyright 1964 by Carta, Jerusalem. © Copyright 1966 by Carta, Jerusalem.)*

the eighteenth century (c. 1750–1697 B.C.) is sometimes designated "the Mari Age," in recognition of Mari's replacement of Assyria as the dominant power in upper Mesopotamia. The French excavations at the site of the ancient city, conducted since the 1930s, have revealed an impressive Amorite culture, including the remains of a royal palace covering more than 15 acres and with nearly three hundred rooms, halls, and courts. Of greatest significance was the discovery of the royal archives—some 25,000 cuneiform tablets, consisting chiefly of diplomatic correspondence and business records. Many of these were letters written to Mari's king, Zimri-Lim, from other eastern kings and officials, some of them from no less a figure than King Hammurabi of Babylon.

Of interest to biblical scholars are the personal names in the Mari texts,

111

some of which are similar to or identical with patriarchal names, for example, Abi-ram (Abraham), Laban, and Iahqub-el (Jacob). To be sure, there are no grounds for identifying any of these names with the specific persons of the same name in Genesis. Nor do they prove a Middle Bronze date for the patriarchs, since the names are not exclusive to the era.[121] The Mari texts are significant for biblical study, nevertheless, in illuminating a type of society that shared institutions similar to those of the early Hebrews, including a dimorphic pattern of partly settled pastoralists and entrenched city-dwellers.[122]

BABYLON. With the fall of Mari to Hammurabi's armies in 1697 B.C., Babylon reached the zenith of its glory under the First Dynasty (1830–1530 B.C.) and became for a while the strongest power in Mesopotamia.[123] Under the brilliant Hammurabi (c. 1728–1686 B.C.), there was erected on the base of the older Sumerian culture a flourishing civilization which saw the advancement of knowledge in various fields, a codification of law, and the elevation of Marduk to the supreme position in the hierarchy of the gods. Babylon's strength was not sufficient, however, to bring lasting stability to the Fertile Crescent. Movements of non-Semitic peoples, notably the Hurrians and Hittites, along with a people—at least partially Semitic—called Hyksos by the Egyptians, kept the Near East in an unsettled state well to the end of the First Dynasty.

HURRIANS. In the early seventeenth century, by which time the Hyksos had taken over Egypt, increasing numbers of Hurrians and peoples with Indo-European names began pushing into Mesopotamia from the northern regions. In the course of the next several centuries their presence was felt in every part of western Asia, including Syria and Palestine. They appear as a Palestinian people in Old Testament references under the name of Horites or Hivites, and to some Egyptians all Palestine was known as "Hurru" (Hurrian country). Their greatest concentration was in northern Mesopotamia, where they built a political kingdom known as Mitanni (c. 1500–1370 B.C., extending from east of the upper Tigris to the coast of northern Syria. Excavations at the site of Nuzi, a solidly Hurrian city in that region, unearthed approximately five thousand cuneiform documents which shed much valuable light on Hurrian legal practices, social customs, and family life. These texts are also useful for comparisons with Hebrew cultural patterns, although they fail to establish a direct connection between Nuzi and the Hebrew patriarchs.[124]

---

[121] See below, pp. 120–121.

[122] See below, pp. 123ff.

[123] Dates cited here follow the so-called "low chronology" of W. F. Albright.

[124] On Nuzi, see C. J. Mullo Weir, "Nuzi," in *Archaeology and Old Testament Study*, D. Winton Thomas, ed., (Oxford: Clarendon Press, 1967), pp. 73–83. For examples of the Nuzi texts, see the selections in *ANET*, pp. 219–220 (*ANE*, pp. 167–70).

Life-size head of Hammurabi, as depicted in a Babylonian diorite sculpture (c. 1700 B.C.). (Courtesy of the Nelson Gallery–Atkins Museum [Nelson Fund], Kansas City, Missouri.)

HITTITES. The rise of Mitanni halted temporarily the expansion of the Hittite kingdom. The Hittites were an Indo-European people who became a prominent power in central and eastern Anatolia by early in the second millennium. As revealed in some ancient business texts from Anatolia, they carried on commercial relations from an early time with Assyrian traders who encamped around the Hittite towns. Under King Suppiluliumas I (c. 1386–1356 B.C.), the Hittites conquered northern and central Syria and made a protectorate of Mitanni, thus establishing an empire that lasted until c. 1200 B.C., when it was overthrown by the "Sea Peoples."[125] Following the fall of the empire, migrations of Hittites into northern Syria and the Taurus region resulted in the so-called Neo-Hittite states, and explain the references to Syria as "Hatti" (i.e., Hittite land) in Assyrian inscriptions from the late twelfth century B.C. onward. Later Assyrian texts also include

---

[125] On the Sea Peoples, see below, pp. 151 and 220.

113

Business tablets from ancient Nuzi (fourteenth century B.C.) listing the sale of sheep and goats. (Courtesy of the Trustees of the British Museum.)

Palestine within the designation "Hatti." As the Hittite conquests never reached Palestine, Old Testament references to Hittites or "Sons of Heth" as early residents in Canaan[126] can be understood in terms of this later Assyrian usage of the name. There is no evidence that these persons were Hittites in the ethnic sense.[127]

HYKSOS. The people called Hyksos (i.e., "foreign rulers") by the Egyptians were an ethnic amalgam of northwest Semites and others who infiltrated and eventually took control of Egypt shortly after the end of the Middle Kingdom. Whatever the origins of these people, they entered the Nile delta apparently from Palestine, and by the late eighteenth century (perhaps c. 1720 B.C.) became the ruling element in Lower Egypt. Abetted by the weakness of the native Egyptian leadership, they subsequently extended their control to Upper Egypt, thus beginning a foreign administration of the entire land that lasted a century (c. 1650–1550 B.C.). The capital was moved from Thebes, on the southern Nile, to Avaris, in the delta, allowing ready access to the small Syro-Palestinian city-states, with which they maintained commercial, cultural, and political relations.

Such a bitter embarrassment was this era of foreign domination to native Egyptians that little is recorded in early Egyptian annals about it. Centuries later, the Egyptian historian Manetho employed exaggerated descriptions of Hyksos ferocity in recording that "a blast of God smote us."[128]

[126] E.g., Gen. 23:3; 26:34; 27:46.

[127] On the Hittites, see O. R. Gurney, *The Hittites* (London: Penguin Books, 1952); Roland de Vaux, *The Early History of Israel*, pp. 134–136; and Aharon Kempinski, "Hittites in the Bible; What Does Archaeology Say?" *BAR*, V, 4 (Sept./Oct., 1979), pp. 20–45.

[128] *Manetho*, W. G. Waddell, trans., Loeb Classical Library (London: William Heinemann Limited, 1940), pp. 79–81.

Their expulsion from Egypt was gradual, but was brought to its climax by Ahmose I (1552–1527 B.C.), founder of the eighteenth dynasty. He destroyed their capital at Avaris and pursued them into Palestine, where the destructive remains of several towns bear evidence of the campaigns.[129]

HABIRU. One other Near Eastern people, or class of people, who have centered in discussions of Hebrew origins are the Habiru (or 'Apiru). References to them appear in second millennium sources from all over the Near East. The texts from Mari, Nuzi, and Anatolia mention them, as do Canaanite (Ras Shamra) and Egyptian (Amarna) documents. They can be identified with no one ethnic or national group but apparently represent a social status and mode of life.[130] In the Mari and Amarna texts they appear as persons of vagrant status who raided towns and pestered settled populations, particularly in Palestine during the Amarna age (fourteenth century B.C.). In other contexts they are described less as troublemakers than as a class of indigent persons who sold their services as mercenary soldiers or migrant workers and on occasion entered into voluntary servitude. They are characteristically portrayed as a rootless and foreign element within whatever society they happen to appear.

The resemblance of the names Habiru and Hebrew, though they cannot be simply equated etymologically, raises the question of some connection between the Habiru and the Hebrew fathers. An interesting feature of the name Hebrew in Old Testament usage is that it appears quite infrequently and then only in connection with the earliest phase of Israel's past—chiefly in the patriarchal and Exodus accounts.[131] The common name by which Israel referred to itself was *bene Yisrael*, "children of Israel." When the name Hebrew is used in the Old Testament it appears, with few exceptions, either in the speech of foreigners or in contexts in which foreigners are being addressed. Since, then, both the names Habiru and Hebrew bear in their respective contexts the connotation of outsiders—in a social, if not an ethnic sense—and since they are used of people who possibly shared a common historical era (the second millennium) and, to a degree, a similar style of life, some relation between the two appears likely. If the connection were primarily or exclusively one of social class, then the Hebrew patriarchs would have belonged to that broader stratum of Near Eastern society known widely as "Habiru." Since the Habiru appear in some contexts far removed from the biblical Hebrews, a closer identification than this appears doubtful.

---

[129] On the Hyksos, see Roland de Vaux, *The Early History of Israel*, pp. 75–81, and John Van Seters, *The Hyksos; A New Investigation* (New Haven, CT: Yale University Press, 1966).

[130] Moshe Greenberg, *The Hab/piru* (New Haven, CT: American Oriental Society, 1955).

[131] Gen. 14:13; 39:14, 17; 40:15; 41:12; 43:32; Ex. 1:15, 16, 19, 22; 2:6, 7, 9, 11; 3:18; 5:3; 7:16; 9:1, 13; 10:3; 21:2; Deut. 15:12; I Sam. 4:6, 9; 13:3, 19; 14:11, 21; 29:3; Jer. 34:9, 14.

EARLY PALESTINE. Unlike Mesopotamia, Egypt, Anatolia, and northern Syria, the land of Palestine gave birth to no large kingdoms or empires prior to the time of David (tenth century B.C.). Geographical location, however, assured Palestinian involvement in the political fortunes of neighboring powers, particularly those of Syria and Egypt. Ebla appears to have laid claim to the region during its period of empire (c. 2400–2250 B.C.), and Egypt exercised control of the Palestinian city-states during eras of Egyptian strength. Throughout most of the third and second millennia B.C., Palestine remained a land of numerous small and largely independent city-states, surrounded by villages and rural areas which supported an agricultural-pastoral economy.

It is impossible to find a satisfactory name with which to describe the pre-Israelitic inhabitants of Palestine, since the population was ethnically and socially diverse and known by different names in the ancient records. The Old Testament includes a variety of names, such as Canaanites, Amorites, and Hittites, derived for the most part from first-millennium usage. If we must employ a single label, then "Canaanites" is to be preferred. "Canaan" means perhaps "land of the purple," so-named after the red-purple dye produced from the murex shellfish on the northern Mediterranean coast. It first appears in Syrian and Egyptian inscriptions from the fifteenth century B.C., referring initially to a single group or area within the larger Syro-Palestinian sphere. It may have developed into an ethnic term for the inhabitants of the Phoenician coast, where a class of merchants were widely known for their trade in purple dye. In Old Testament usage, it can denote the whole of Palestine west of the Jordan, the limited area of the coast and plains, or, infrequently, Phoenicia.[132] As employed by modern scholars, "Canaanite" is a convenient designation for the pre-Israelitic people of both Palestine and Syria, who to a large degree shared a common early culture and history.[133]

The city-state culture which prevailed in Palestine throughout most of the third millennium (i.e., the Early Bronze Age, c. 3000–2200 B.C.) underwent a major disruption in the period known as Middle Bronze I (c. 2200–2000 B.C.).[134] This was a time of large-scale collapse and abandonment of towns, until the only significant distribution of small settlements existed on the fringes of the country, in the Negeb and Transjordan. As we have seen, this era brought changes throughout much of the Middle East, associated in Mesopotamia with the emergence of the Amorites. Many scholars attribute this interval in Palestinian history to the same people,

[132] E.g., Gen. 12:5–6; 50:11; Num. 33:51; Josh. 7:9 (designating all of Palestine west of the Jordan); Num. 13:29; 14:25; Josh. 11:3 (coast and plains); Neh. 9:8; Isa. 23:11; Obad. 20 (Phoenicia).

[133] Cf. Alfred Haldar, "Canaanites," IDB, Vol. I, pp. 494–498.

[134] For an explanation of the varied nomenclature and dates employed for Middle Bronze I, see William G. Dever, "The Patriarchal Traditions," pp. 82–84.

Canaanite altar at Megiddo. An open-air shrine of the Early Bronze Age (third millennium B.C.) included this circular altar, approximately twenty-five feet in diameter and five feet high. (Photo by the author.)

theorizing an Amorite migration or invasion from the North, replacing the former urban centers with a pastoral, seminomadic pattern of life.[135] Others are dubious of the Amorite theory and assign the changes not to newcomers, but to events within Palestine itself.[136] It is noted, for example, that the MBI pottery forms display a clear continuity with the EB pottery, rather than new forms which one would expect from newcomers.[137]

This disruptive interval, however it is to be explained, was relatively short-lived for most of Palestine. At the turn of the millennium, in the period known as Middle Bronze II A (c. 2000–1800 B.C.), there occurred a revival of urban life and the beginnings of a new pottery, characterized by innovative forms, a burnished red finish, and manufacture on a fast wheel.[138] Corresponding to the name given the period, there is evidence of a limited use of bronze weapons. These new cultural features are consistent with contemporaneous patterns in Syrian remains and suggest that at

[135] See Kathleen M. Kenyon, *Archaeology in the Holy Land*, pp. 135–161, and Roland de Vaux, *The Early History of Israel*, pp. 58–64.

[136] Cf. Thomas L. Thompson, *The Historicity of the Patriarchal Narratives* (Berlin/New York: Walter de Gruyter, 1974), pp. 144–171.

[137] Cf. William G. Dever, "The EB IV-MB I Horizon in Transjordan and Southern Palestine," *BASOR*, CCXXVI (1974), pp. 31–52.

[138] Kathleen Kenyon, *Archaeology in the Holy Land*, pp. 162–194.

least some of the MB II A settlers came from that region. Whether the new element is to be identified with a second infusion of Amorites, as some believe—perhaps a group which had been partially or wholly urbanized in Syria—is once again a matter of debate.[139] At any rate, the type of Palestinian society instituted at this time was to prevail for the remainder of the Middle Bronze Age (MB II B and C; c. 1800–1550 B.C.) and came to full flower in the powerful and prosperous city-states of the mid-second millennium (c. 1600 B.C.). It was a society marked by a free flow of international trade, cities fortified with a three-way entry gate and a sloping earthen embankment or *glacis,* and by a continuation of cultural links with Syria. Even Transjordan, long regarded as abandoned during the MB II and Late Bronze periods except for seminomadic tribes, is now recognized to have supported a settled population in some areas.[140]

Palestine experienced further turbulence at the end of the Middle Bronze Age, when numerous cities suffered partial or total destruction. If the Egyptian documents are to be believed, the violence resulted from punitive campaigns of the Egyptians, as they pursued the Hyksos into Palestine and went on to reassert a stronger hand in Palestinian affairs. This was not, however, the end of the Canaanite urban society. Although some of the fallen towns, such as Jericho, lay in ruins for many years, others, such as Megiddo, were reoccupied almost immediately. The Late Bronze Age (1550–1200 B.C.) brought no substantial changes in the cultural life of the country. Pottery imports bear evidence of an increase in trade contacts with the rest of the eastern Mediterranean; but there is no break in the styles and forms of the native wares, only the addition of new elements.[141] Although the second phase of the Late Bronze Age (LB II A–B; c. 1400–1200 B.C.) witnessed the troublesome attacks of Habiru and the revolt of prominent city-states against Egyptian control, it was not until the end of the period that the arrival of foreign elements began to change once-for-all the Canaanite cultural patterns which had persisted for so long.

The Date and Setting of the Patriarchs: Current Views

Is it possible to place the Hebrew patriarchs somewhere within the known history of the ancient Middle East? The search for the patriarchal age has led to several major proposals, which we shall consider now in the sequence of the historical periods favored by their respective advocates.

THE EARLY BRONZE AGE. The most recent entry among the competing theories, and the one representing the earliest dating, is a bold hypothesis provoked by the discovery of the Ebla tablets and set forth by David N.

---

[139] William G. Dever, "The Patriarchal Traditions," pp. 84–86.
[140] Cf. Thomas L. Thompson, *The Historicity of the Patriarchal Narratives,* pp. 192–194.
[141] Kathleen Kenyon, *Archaeology in the Holy Land,* pp. 195–220.

Freedman.[142] It conceives the period of the Early Bronze (EB) empire of Ebla, or approximately the twenty-fifth century B.C. (i.e., EB III, based on an early dating of the Eblaite empire, c. 2580–2450 B.C.), as the age of Abraham. The proposal is based on the alleged identity of Ebla's King Ebrum and Abraham's biblical ancestor Eber (Gen. 10:24–25) and a correlation of the number, order, and names of the biblical "cities of the plain" (i.e., Sodom, Gomorrah, Admah, Zeboiim, and Bela; Genesis 14) with towns mentioned in the Ebla tablets. It further identifies these sites, which according to the Genesis account were destroyed in Abraham's day, with recently excavated EB sites on the eastern perimeter of the Dead Sea. The most serious problem with Freedman's proposal, at least at the time of this writing, is the unavailability in published form of the Ebla texts, which has resulted in conflicting reports on their contents. Thus, only at such time as the texts are made available for broad scholarly study, can Freedman's proposal receive serious consideration. Lacking such evidence, the crucial question is whether a mid-third millennium date does not set the patriarchs too far apart chronologically from the periods of the Exodus and settlement of Canaan. As it is unlikely that the latter episodes can be dated before the thirteenth century B.C., at the earliest, one would have to reckon a full millennium between Abraham and Moses.

THE MIDDLE BRONZE AGE. Mention has been made of the popularity of a Middle Bronze Age (MB) dating for the patriarchs. For a time it appeared that all that remained to be determined was the specific phase of the Middle Bronze, i.e., whether MB I (c. 2200–2000 B.C.), one of the phases of MB II (c. 2000–1550), or MB II generally. W. F. Albright and Nelson Glueck, largely on the basis of data which are no longer viable, argued for the disruptive interval, MB I (dated by Albright as 2100–1900/1800 B.C.), which they identified with the arrival in Palestine of the earliest contingent of Amorites.[143] Abraham and his clan were viewed as seminomadic Amorites who migrated from Mesopotamia to Syria, then to Canaan, as described in Genesis 11 and 12. Also, Glueck's conviction that surface explorations in Trans-Jordan proved a cessation of settled life there between the nineteenth and the thirteenth centuries B.C. was related to the Genesis 14 account of Abraham's battles with the eastern kings in the Transjordan region and the subsequent destruction of the cities of the plain. According to the latest version of Albright's proposal, Abraham is viewed as an itinerant donkey caravaneer or Amorite merchant, who traveled the trade routes from Syria to the Palestinian Negeb and Egypt. The major objection to an MB I date for the patriarchs is the evidence gathered since Albright and

---

[142] "The Real Story of the Ebla Tablets," *BA*, 41 (1978), pp. 143–164.

[143] Cf. William F. Albright, "From the Patriarchs to Moses," BA, 36, (1973), pp. 5–33; and Nelson Glueck, *Rivers in the Desert; A History of the Negev* (New York: Grove Press, Inc., 1960), pp. 60–110.

Glueck's time, revealing that the most important Palestinian town sites mentioned in the patriarchal stories (i.e., Shechem, Bethel, Hebron, and Beersheba) contain few if any traces of MB I occupation.[144] Furthermore, Glueck's conclusions concerning the absence of Transjordanian settlements during the MB and early LB periods have been corrected by recent archaeological finds in Jordan.[145]

Most scholars who subscribe to a Middle Bronze setting for the patriarchs place them in MB II. Sometimes a preference is expressed for a specific MB II phase. For example, some interpreters cite the nineteenth to eighteenth centuries B.C. on the basis of the form of patriarchal names and the fact that the Canaanite god Baal, who later supplanted the god El in the Canaanite pantheon, is not mentioned in the patriarchal accounts. Kathleen Kenyon favors the seventeenth or sixteenth century in order to reduce the length of time in which the traditions had to survive.[146] More typical, however, is the choice of MB II in general, i.e., the first half of the second millennium. Among the many well-known exponents of this approach, Roland de Vaux has produced the most detailed and impressive synthesis of archaeological and biblical data for its support.[147] Accepting the identification of patriarchs and Amorites, he associates the Hebrew fathers with a second influx of Amorites, believed to have arrived in Canaan in the nineteenth century B.C. and to have established the Middle Bronze II urban culture which prevailed for the remainder of the period. The patriarchs are viewed as a pastoral, seminomadic people, who moved on the edges of this urban culture, and were even then in the process of settling down. The frequent allusions in the patriarchal accounts to Palestinian kings and cities would, in general, suit the conditions of the time as revealed by archaeological excavation. The exceptions would be the areas of southern Transjordan and the Negeb (notably Beersheba), where evidence of MB II occupation is lacking.

Proponents of the MB II dating have offered a large collection of cultural parallels to the patriarchal accounts drawn from contemporaneous extrabiblical documents, such as the Mari, Nuzi, and Hittite texts.[148] These parallels concern such matters as personal, ethnographic, and geographic names; socioeconomic patterns; and a broad array of customs, laws, and religious forms. Typically, these common elements have been used to support two claims: (1) that the patriarchal accounts are compatible with the culture of the MB age, but not with that of other periods, thus establishing

[144] Cf. William G. Dever, "The Patriarchal Traditions" pp. 99–101.
[145] Cf. footnote 140 above.
[146] Kathleen Kenyon, *The Bible and Recent Archaeology* (London: Colonnade Books, 1978), p. 10.
[147] *The Early History of Israel*, pp. 55–120.
[148] Cf. G. Ernest Wright, *Biblical Archaeology*, rev. ed. (Philadelphia: The Westminster Press, 1962), pp. 40–58.

the time of the patriarchs as the MB age; and (2) that such harmonization enhances the historical reliability of the patriarchal stories. Recently there have appeared strong rebuttals to this line of argumentation.[149] Some of the alleged parallels have been shown to be dubious, if not erroneous; others have proven real, particularly in the case of common names (e.g., those from Mari), but are not restricted solely to the Middle Bronze Age. It must be said to the credit of Father de Vaux, that in his latest work he identified and corrected the more excessive of these claims.[150]

THE LATE BRONZE AGE. A Late Bronze Age date (1550–1200 B.C.) for the patriarchs is favored by some scholars. Archaeology has supplied fewer epigraphical remains from this period than for the Middle Bronze Age; but the social and legal customs found in the Nuzi and Ras Shamra texts (fifteenth to thirteenth centuries B.C.) have been utilized. C. H. Gordon, who is doubtless the chief proponent of LB dating, points to such patterns at fifteenth-century Nuzi as adoptions of heirs by childless couples, the use of slave women as bearers of children on behalf of barren wives, birthrights, death-bed blessings, and other examples drawn from Hurrian family customs. Supporters of MB dating have cited the same data, on the assumption that such customs must have prevailed in the MB period as well. In either case, the uniqueness of many of the parallels has been challenged by de Vaux, and more strongly by Thomas L. Thompson and John Van Seters,[151] the latter two of whom feel that more convincing correspondences appear in later Iron Age texts. Looking primarily to the biblical rather than archaeological evidence, Otto Eissfeldt regards the LB date as fitting best with the genealogies which place Abraham only four generations prior to the Israelites' settlement in Canaan.[152] The difficulty of settling the issue on the basis of biblical genealogies, however, has often been remarked.

THE IRON AGE. That the patriarchal stories contain certain elements belonging to the Iron Age (c. 1200–300 B.C.), such as ethnic and place names (e.g., Philistines, Arameans, "Ur of the Chaldeans"), socioeconomic institutions (e.g., domestication of camels), and the like, is recognized by practically all interpreters of the accounts. Until recently, however, few questioned that the presence of such elements was due to anything other than anachronistic usage, i.e., the current nomenclature or some other familiar feature of the writers' day imposing itself upon the older tradi-

---

[149] Thomas L. Thompson, *The Historicity of the Patriarchal Narratives* and John Van Seters, *Abraham in History and Tradition.*

[150] *The Early History of Israel*, esp. pp. 241–256.

[151] See footnotes 149 and 150, above.

[152] "Palestine in the Time of the Nineteenth Dynasty," *Cambridge Ancient History*, Vol. II, Pt. 2 (London: Cambridge University Press, 1975), pp. 312–314.

tions.[153] Such anachronisms have ordinarily been regarded as posing no serious challenge to the antiquity of the patriarchs themselves. Just such a claim, however, has now appeared in the analyses of Thompson and Van Seters.[154] The latter scholars' rejection of the arguments advanced for a Bronze Age dating, as noted above, is coupled with a detailed set of data adducing an Iron Age provenance for the patriarchs, i.e., basically the period of the Israelite monarchy and later. Much of this evidence consists of those very elements regarded by other interpreters as anachronisms. In essence, Thompson and Van Seters perceive in the patriarchal accounts' only such cultural and political patterns as are compatible with the first millennium B.C.: a sedentary society, the presence of the Arameans and Philistines, and a host of sociolegal institutions and customs which are viewed as consistent with those depicted in Iron Age texts. The most serious problem raised by this approach is at once apparent: if the patriarchs cannot be dated earlier than the Iron Age, then the biblical conception of early Hebrew history prior to the establishment of the monarchy is hopelessly confused. There is, then, no "patriarchal age," or at least none about which we can learn from the Genesis accounts. The patriarchal figures themselves can only be viewed as literary and theological constructs which serve as "the means by which the biblical tradition has expressed Israel's political, sociological, and geographical ties with the world surrounding it."[155] The historicity of these persons thus becomes, in Thompson's words, "hardly possible and totally improbable."[156]

THE CONTINUING QUEST. With the question of the patriarchal age far from settled and the promise of new data on the horizon, any evaluations of the currently proposed solutions must of necessity be tentative. The Iron Age thesis, as just noted, suffers from its negative estimate of the Israelite nation's awareness of its past. That the biblical writers were capable of filling in a dimly remembered ancestral era with details drawn partially or largely from their own historical milieu is not difficult to conceive. But to conclude that no such era ever existed would require more conclusive evidence than is currently being offered. The undeniable service of Thompson's and Van Seters' studies, nevertheless, is to demolish the "assured proofs" of the popular Middle Bronze Age dating. It can no longer be maintained—given the evidence currently available—that the cultural patterns reflected in the patriarchal accounts are compatible *only* with the Middle

---

[153] It should be noted, however, that a much earlier generation of Old Testament scholarship, i.e., that of Julius Wellhausen (see above, pp. 64ff.), viewed the Iron Age elements in the patriarchal traditions as proof of their non-historical character (see Wellhausen's *Prolegomena to the History of Israel*, pp. 318–319).

[154] Thomas L. Thompson, *The Historicity of the Patriarchal Narratives* and Van Seters, *Abraham in History and Tradition*.

[155] Thomas L. Thompson, *The Historicity of the Patriarchal Narratives*, p. 298.

[156] Ibid., p. 328.

Bronze Age. By the same token, it is by no means certain that the accounts are not anchored somewhere within the MB II phases of that era. In fact, a new sociological understanding of pastoralism and the dimorphic society, i.e., the coexistence of urban and agricultural-pastoral elements within a single society, such as that at Middle Bronze Mari, could possibly provide a cultural pattern applicable to both the patriarchs and Middle Bronze Amorites.[157] With the diminishing of the evidence marshaled for a Middle Bronze provenance, however, the possibility of a Late Bronze date for the patriarchs will undoubtedly receive increased consideration. As matters now stand, either an MB II or an LB date would not be grossly incompatible with archaeological evidence and would at the same time maintain the basic integrity of the biblical traditions as regards the existence of a pre-settlement patriarchal age.

Patriarchal Life and Customs

Assessments of the socioeconomic patterns of early Hebrew society, along with those of the larger Near East, have undergone considerable revision in recent years. The long-popular notions that agricultural and village societies invariably evolved later than pastoral-nomadic life and that invasions of the settled zones by desert nomads caused the major disruptions of civilizations in the ancient Fertile Crescent, are now perceived to be inaccurate. Recent ethnological and ecological studies of pastoral nomadism, by revealing the coalescence of pastoral and agricultural elements within many of the self-same societies, have created an entirely new model for comprehending the pattern of life reflected in the patriarchal narratives.[158]

THE PATRIARCHS AND PASTORALISM. The changed perspective affects the familiar portrayal of Abraham, Isaac, and Jacob as seminomads, newly arrived from the desert steppe, moving about the interior of Syria and Palestine with their flocks and herds, and sharply distinguished from the settled farmers and villagers. This view assumes a type of self-sufficient pastoralism that never existed, i.e., one that could maintain itself without the products of agriculture or access to the pasturage and water supply of the settled regions during the long, dry Palestinian summers. In contrast, pastoral nomadism is now recognized as existing in diverse combinations with agricultural and sedentary patterns, and frequently is so thoroughly

---

[157] William G. Dever, "The Patriarchal Traditions, pp. 112–117.

[158] Cf. M. B. Rowton, "Enclosed Nomadism," *JESHO*, XVII (1974), pp. 1–30; J. T. Luke, "Pastoralism and Politics in the Mari Period" (Ph. D. Dissertation, University of Michigan; Ann Arbor: University Microfilms, 1965); and Norman Gottwald, "Were the Early Israelites Pastoral Nomads?" *Rhetorical Criticism: Essays in Honor of James Muilenburg*, Jared J. Jackson and Martin Kessler, eds., pp. 223–255. A good summary of the new studies as they pertain to the Middle Bronze Age and the question of patriarchal society is provided by William G. Dever, "The Patriarchal Traditions," pp. 102–117.

A Palestinian herdsman. Pastoralism is combined with agriculture in many areas of modern Israel and Jordan. (Courtesy of The Israeli Government Tourist Office.)

integrated with life in the settled zones as to be indistinguishable as a separate phenomenon.

That pastoral nomadism, with its transhumance seasonal treks, represented *one* element in the early Hebrews' socioeconomic mode of life, is altogether probable. The patriarchs are represented as living in tents, and there is frequent mention of their holdings in sheep, goats, and donkeys—the staple elements of nomadic pastoralism. But there is considerable evidence that they also had attachments to the land and engaged in diversified and intensive agriculture. Both Abraham and Jacob are represented as purchasing land; and Isaac is depicted as sowing and reaping in the vicinity of Gerar.[159] Among the agricultural products associated with the patriarchal households are grain, meal, lentils, nuts, mandrakes, honey, and wine.[160] Furthermore, the possession of cattle and oxen reported of Abraham, Lot, Isaac, and Jacob, indicates a pattern of heavy-stock breeding characteristic of the settled zones.[161] As for the patriarchal movements across the Fertile Crescent, most such journeys are described with reference to famines, the securing of wives, intergroup conflicts, and—theologically explained—response to divine summons, i.e., concerns other than the shepherding of animals. Thus, strictly speaking, such movements are best understood as migrations rather than pastoral-nomadic treks.[162]

Recently, Norman Gottwald has suggested that some of the patriarchal groups may have practiced transhumance pastoralism of the sort associated with the mountains of Spain and Switzerland. According to such a pattern, we can visualize early Hebrew shepherds grazing their flocks and herds on the vegetation available in the Palestinian steppe zones during the rainy, winter season. Then, with the coming of spring and summer, pasturage would have been sought on the seaward side of the coastal mountains. But, more significantly, Gottwald concludes:

> However, it is completely clear that all of the pastoralists of the area were fully familiar with agriculture and that most of them are to be viewed as engaging in some form of agriculture. While there was some transhumance pastoralism, there is no evidence that entire communities engaged in this practice.[163]

PATRIARCHAL FAMILIES. The one and only distinguishable unit of patriarchal society is the family. The patriarchs, that is to say, are depicted as owing allegiance to no kingdom or empire; and even the possibility of larger clan or tribal associations is uncertain.[164] Patriarchal families were large, however, consisting not only of the patriarch, his wives, and children, but also of such adult sons and daughters-in-law as had not formed separate households, the children of such unions, and family slaves. Absolute authority was exercised by the patriarch, though in some instances responsibilities may have been shared with the sons (e.g., Gen. 34). Rights of inheritance were determined by descent on the father's side.

Wives filled a none too romantic but essential role as household laborers and bearers of children. At the same time, the strong personalities of

---

[159] Gen. 23; 33:19; 26:12–14.
[160] Gen. 25:29–34; 27:25–29; 37:5–8; 43:11.
[161] Gen. 12:16; 13:5; 15:8; 18:7–8; 20:14; 21:27; 24:35; 26:14; 32:5, 7, 15.
[162] See the description of pastoralism in Norman Gottwald's recent works, i.e., "Were the Early Israelites Pastoral Nomads?" and *The Tribes of Yahweh* (Maryknoll, NY: Orbis Books, 1979).
[163] "Were the Early Israelites Pastoral Nomads?" *BAR*, IV, 2 (June 1978), p. 5.
[164] Cf. Roland de Vaux, *The Early History of Israel*, pp. 238–240.

Sarah, Rebekah, and Rachel are clearly and colorfully depicted in the Genesis accounts, and on occasion their influence is determinative in decisions of the husband. The high prestige and economic advantage that came with large families made concubinage, if not polygamy, the norm, and failure to bear children, particularly sons, was a source of shame to the barren wife. Thus, our accounts tell of Sarah, Rachel, and Leah providing their husbands with slave maidens that the wives might have children through the slaves. The practice of having the slave woman give birth on the knees of her mistress and the latter's naming of the newborn child, doubtless indicate ancient adoption rites.[165] Although adoptions of sons from outside the patriarchal families have often been alleged, there are no clear examples for such a practice in Genesis. Had no sons been born to Abraham, the household slave Eliezar would have become the patriarch's heir (Gen. 15:2–4). The account makes no mention, however, of an adoption of the slave.

The limiting of adoption to children born within the family is indicative of an interest in maintaining the purity of the bloodline, which was the basic bond of tribal life. The same concern underlies the parents' efforts to assure that the sons did not marry foreign wives, but chose rather their own blood relatives.

Marriages. Hebrew marriages, like those in surrounding cultures, were arranged either by the parents or by the bridegroom and his future father-in-law. Sometimes a brother of the bride might negotiate for the dowry, as in the case of Laban's barter with Isaac's servant over the hand of Laban's sister Rebekah (24:28–61). The gift of the dowry—which in Jacob's case was rendered in service to his father-in-law—recognized the bride's anticipated usefulness to the family of her husband and the consequent loss of her services to her father's clan. Henceforth, her labor and offspring were, in a real sense, the property of her father-in-law's family, so long as she and her husband lived in their midst. Should the husband die prematurely, by the principle of levirate marriage it became the responsibility of his family to provide the widow with another husband—normally, the eldest living brother of the deceased.[166] Onan's reluctance to perform this service for Tamar, the widow of his brother Er (38:7–9), was prompted by the fact that the first male offspring of such unions belonged legally to the dead man and not to the real father.

Birthrights and Blessings. Written wills appear to have been virtually unknown in the ancient Near East. But two principles of inheritance remained constant among the Hebrews and have their parallels in the neighboring societies.[167] One is the principle that only sons had a right to in-

---

[165] Cf. ibid., p. 236.

[166] Deut. 25:5–10.

[167] Cf. Ignatius Hunt, *The World of the Patriarchs* (Englewood Cliffs, NJ: Prentice-Hall, Inc., 1967), p. 60.

herit, unless there was no male heir. The other is the custom of primogeniture or birthright, which assured the eldest son a double share of the family wealth. Quite clearly, however, the birthright could be forfeited, either because of some fault, as in the case of Reuben (Gen. 35:22; 49:3–4), or owing to deliberate renunciation, as in Esau's barter with Jacob (Gen. 25:29–34).

Esau, of course, also lost to Jacob's trickery the paternal blessing of Isaac (ch. 27). The tangible value assumed for these oral pronouncements of the father is apparent in the seriousness with which they are taken both in the Old Testament and in some of the extrabiblical documents. The legal validity of the deathbed blessing at Nuzi was such that judgments in contested cases might be rendered on that basis alone.[168] In Hebrew society they appear to be distinguished from the primogeniture principle, in that the latter concerned particularly the inheritance of property, whereas the blessing had to do with "destiny, fertility, prosperity, and the bestowal of the father's life, strength, and authority on his son."[169] There is some evidence, moreover, that in the oral blessing the father's ultimate control over the birthright—his ability to confirm or reverse it—was recognized.[170] The blessing, once pronounced, however, was irrevocable. Once Isaac had bestowed Esau's blessing on Jacob, neither the revelation of Jacob's deceit, nor the pleading of Esau, nor even Isaac's own anguish could effect a retraction.

Patriarchal Religion

Our chief interest in the patriarchs concerns their role in Israelite religion. Throughout the Pentateuch and elsewhere in the Bible their continuity with Mosaic religious history is a basic assumption. In Yahwistic tradition (J) they call on the very name of Yahweh; and even those sources (E and P) which deny to them knowledge of the personal name of God consistently represent them as the authentic ancestry of Yahweh faith. Thus, when God reveals his name to Moses, it is as "Yahweh, the God of your fathers, the God of Abraham, the God of Isaac, and the God of Jacob" (Exod. 3:15, E). By whatever names the fathers worshiped their deity or deities, later Israel was confident that the God who directed their ways was none other than Yahweh himself. There are many unanswered questions about the specific nature of patriarchal religion, however, largely owing to this very fact. So thoroughly have our sources integrated the religion of the fathers into the broader concerns of the later Israelite faith, that the unique features of their era as distinctive phenomena in the origin and development of early religion are often obscured.

[168] C. H. Gordon, "Biblical Customs and the Nuzu Texts," *BA*, III (1940), p. 8 (reprinted in the *BA Reader*, 2, p. 28). Cf. *ANET*, p. 220.
[169] Ignatius Hunt, *The World of the Patriarchs*, p. 61.
[170] Ibid. Cf. Gen. 48:17–20; 49:8–12; Chron. 26:10.

THE PATRIARCHAL GOD(S). We are unable to determine at what precise position the patriarchs are to be placed between the polytheism of their forebears "beyond the river" (i.e., in Mesopotamia; Joshua 24:15) and the developed monotheism of the later Old Testament writers. The northwest Semitic culture with which they have the most in common was clearly polytheistic. The Arameans and Hurrians knew and worshiped many of the same deities prominent in the Babylonian and Assyrian pantheons. Haran, like Ur, was a cult center of the moon god Sin; and, interestingly, the names Terah, Sarah, Milcah, and Laban can all be associated with names common in moon worship.

There are within the patriarchal accounts a variety of divine names and epithets. The name *El* occurs, frequently in combination with some qualifying attribute: *El Elyon*, "God Most High"; *El Shaddai*, "God Almighty"; *El Bethel*, "God of Bethel"; *El Roi*, "God of Seeing"; and *El Olam*, "Everlasting God." According to the Priestly source, it was by the name of *El Shaddai* that Yahweh made himself known before the time of Moses (Ex. 6:3).[171]

As a generic name for deity, widely used among Semitic peoples, *El* could designate "the numinous divine power that fills men with awe and dread."[172] In Canaanite religious texts from Ugarit the name is abundantly evident as the chief deity and father of the gods. It has been suggested that the various *El* names represent manifestations of the supreme god *El* as venerated at different Canaanite shrines, such as Shechem, Bethel, Mamre, and Beersheba—cult centers that were adopted by the Israelites as their own.[173] *El Shaddai*, however, is not so easily associated with a specific geographical site. This name appears, rather, in covenant-making contexts, and apparently was regarded in Priestly tradition as God in his peculiar covenanting relationship with Abraham and his descendants.[174]

The covenant aspect of patriarchal religion is also apparent in certain epithets that recognize a close personal relationship between each clan father and his god. As God renews his covenant with Isaac and Jacob, he reveals himself as "the God of Abraham, your father" (26:24) or "the God of Abraham your father and the God of Isaac" (28:13); and there appear such euphemisms for deity as "Shield of Abraham" (15:1), "Mighty One of Jacob" (49:24), and "Fear (or Kinsman) of Isaac" (31:42, 53).

As Albrecht Alt has demonstrated, patriarchal religion was patterned largely around the patron deity of the clan—the "god of the fathers."[175]

[171] For the proposal that the proper name Yahweh arose as an epithet of El, cf. below, p. 158.
[172] Bernhard W. Anderson, "God, Names of," *IDB*, E–J, p. 411. Cf. also Frank M. Cross, *Canaanite Myth and Hebrew Epic*, pp. 13–75.
[173] Roland de Vaux, *Ancient Israel*, pp. 289–294.
[174] John M. Holt, *The Patriarchs of Israel*, pp. 131–132.
[175] "The God of the Fathers," *Essays on Old Testament History and Religion*, R. A. Wilson, trans., pp. 1–100. Cf. the informative appraisals and modifications of Alt's positions in

Sufficient parallels have been adduced to show that such a pattern existed among other Near Eastern peoples wherein the clan father would choose as his personal god the family deity, with whom he would then enter into a special contractual relationship. Such a god was bound to no one locality or shrine, but as the patron of the family maintained a close association with them wherever they might go.

In the view of Alt the patriarchs were the founders of originally *separate* cults; and Herbert May carefully distinguishes between an early "god of the father" in which the god is identified with the name of a single patriarch in any given instance, and a later "god of Abraham, Isaac, and Jacob" wherein the same god is clearly the god of all three.[176] Frank Cross denies that these patriarchal gods were typically nameless, and views them as high gods who were also known by cultic or clan epithets, i.e., the names of the clan fathers. Once brought to Canaan by the Hebrew fathers, he feels, they were quickly identified by common traits or by cognate names with gods of the local pantheon.[177] By stressing the personal and clan aspects of the "god of the fathers," the patriarchal accounts emphasize the compatibility of patriarchal religion with the patterns of promise and covenant typical of the later Old Testament faith. Thus, for all its differences from the developed Yahweh faith, patriarchal religion most likely provided the basic elements out of which the latter was built.

WORSHIP AND RITUAL. There is much truth in S. H. Hooke's contention that religion in the early Near East consisted not so much in certain beliefs as in common patterns of ritual enactment.[178] This observation is much more easily documented for non-Hebraic religions, however, than for the patriarchs themselves. The worship and rites of patriarchal religion were apparently quite simple and centered around the clan father. Nothing is heard of an organized cult, calendar, priesthood, or the like; but there is frequent mention of altars and stone pillars (*masseboth*), at which the fathers "called on the name of the Lord" and performed spontaneous rites of sacrifice, votive offerings, and libations.[179] Such traditions served to establish Israelite claims to ancient and sacred histories for these sites, although studiously avoiding any reference to Canaanite shrines which existed in the same localities. We cannot, therefore, determine the degree to which there was participation in the Canaanite cultus, other than in the sharing of the *El* names. We can only note that few of the characteristic Canaanite fertility motifs left a lasting impression on Hebrew religion.

Roland de Vaux, *The Early History of Israel*, pp. 267–282, and Frank Cross, *Canaanite Myth and Hebrew Epic*, pp. 3–75.
[176] "The God of My Father—A Study of Patriarchal Religion," *JBR*, IX (1941), pp. 155–158, 200.
[177] *Canaanite Myth and Hebrew Epic*, pp. 3–12.
[178] *In the Beginning* (Oxford: Clarendon Press, 1947), p. 132.
[179] Gen. 12:7; 13:18; 22:13; 26:25; 31:54; 35:14; 46:1.

There is scarcely any detail regarding the specific conduct of patriarchal sacrifices. One may assume that they did not differ materially from Canaanite offerings, except perhaps in the case of child sacrifice, which is known to have been practiced in the Canaanite and certain other Near Eastern cults. The story of Isaac's near death on the altar (ch. 22) is sometimes offered as evidence for an ancient practice of sacrificing the first-born, which was later rejected in favor of an animal substitute. That is not, however, the point of the surviving version of the story. When Abraham, at Yahweh's direction, offers the ram instead of Isaac, he burns it on the altar as an act of obedience and loyalty. Elsewhere, sacrifice accompanies invocations of the paternal deity's blessing (46:1) and oaths sworn in ratifying a covenant (31:54).

The most detailed account of a patriarchal ritual is the J version of the covenant ceremony between Yahweh and Abraham (ch. 15). Even so, there is not enough detail for a clear understanding of the rite apart from a further reference in Jeremiah 34:18–19 and the parallels afforded by extrabiblical documents. It bears the marks of an ancient covenant tradition whereby animals were cut in half and laid in parallel rows, thus forming a corridor through which two covenant parties would pass. The rite apparently included a curse upon either party who failed to observe his part of the agreement. Should he fail to keep his word, he would suffer the same fate as that of the slain animals. Also, it would appear, as the parties passed between the bloody pieces, they were thereby united with the victims and, through this unifying force, were bound with each other in a covenant relationship.

Circumcision, according to Priestly tradition (17:9–14), originated as a covenant rite with Abraham. The practice existed among Egyptians and other peoples as early as the third millennium;[180] and the use of flint knives, mentioned in some Old Testament accounts (Ex. 4:25; Josh. 5:2–9), suggests the antiquity of the custom in Hebrew circles. Its observance on the eighth day of birth represents a departure from the common Near Eastern pattern whereby it was performed as a puberty rite.

THEOPHANIES. Theophanies—visual or auditory manifestations of deity—are a prominent feature of our accounts. In some of the more dramatic instances, God comes as an unexpected ally to the distraught Hagar in the wilderness (16:7–14; 21:15–21), as the dinner guest of Abraham at Mamre (ch. 18), and even as a nocturnal wrestler with Jacob at Peniel (32:22–32). The strange shifts of subject that occur in these stories, whereby in one verse God himself appears, and in the next it is an angel, a man, or a group of men, are indicative of the age of the traditions and their

---

[180] Roland de Vaux, *Ancient Israel*, pp. 46–48, and idem, *The Early History of Israel*, pp. 286–287.

revision by later hands. The immediate, direct appearances of the deity, related in the earliest versions, were tempered, but not altogether removed, by the introduction of messengers or mediators in the later revisions. Jacob's night vision at Peniel may derive from an ancient pre-Israelitic legend of a nocturnal spirit associated with that spot—one that supposedly lurked at the ford of the Jabbok, contested those who crossed over, and vanished before the dawn.

Similar visits of deity to men are to be seen in early Canaanite mythology, wherein El and an entire company of gods visit King Keret, and the god Kothar is entertained in the home of the proverbial wise man Danel.[181]

The Patriarchs and Covenant Faith

ABRAHAM. Many years ago, John Skinner observed of the patriarch Abraham:

> He moves before us on the page of Scripture as the man through whom faith, the living principle of true religion, first became a force in human affairs.[182]

It should be apparent in what has been said thus far, however, that for the essential faith ingredient of patriarchal religion we are dependent upon the interpretations offered by our sources. In fact, a legitimate theological interpretation of the patriarchal accounts must concern itself especially with the faith which inherited these traditions, heard in them the word of the living God, and gave to them their classic literary forms.

That Abraham was a singular figure of faith is witnessed by all three of the Genesis sources. The narrative of his faith pilgrimage, however, is chiefly the work of the Yahwist. Other than the revealing story of the barely averted sacrifice of Isaac (ch. 22), recognizable E material is confined to variants of the J stories of the patriarch's foreign sojourn (20:1–17) and Hagar's ejection (21:8–21), plus the etiological record of the naming of Beersheba (21:22–34). Only two major items are from P: a variant account of the covenant (ch. 17) and the purchase of the Machpelah cave (ch. 23).

The theology of promise and fulfillment which controls the various elements in these stories receives its finest expression in Abraham's call.

> Go from your country and your kindred and your father's house to the land that I will show you. And I will make of you a great nation. And I will bless you, and make your name great, so that you will be a blessing. I will bless those who bless you, and him who curses you I will curse; and by you all the families of the earth shall bless themselves [or: shall be blessed].
>
> 12:1–3

---

[181] *ANET*, pp. 146–147.
[182] *Genesis*, p. xxvii.

Panel from the mosaic floor of the Beth Alpha (Israel) Synagogue (sixth century A.D.), depicting the binding of Isaac. Shown at the top center is the hand of God with the words "lay not," the initial words in God's command to halt the sacrifice. (Courtesy of the Institute of Archaeology, The Hebrew University of Jerusalem.)

Here is foretold the election of a people who shall not only attain stature among the nations of earth, but shall set the pattern by which the destinies of all nations shall be determined. The "name" which the would-be builders of Babel tried so unsuccessfully to gain for themselves is destined for humankind as the free gift of God.

The two covenant accounts (ch. 15, J; ch. 17, P) repeat the theme of promise and fulfillment. In the ancient ceremony described by the Yahwist, God himself takes the initiative and enters into a contractual relationship with the patriarch, thereby obligating himself to fulfill his promise. In the later account, viewed by the priests as instituting a new epoch in human affairs, God likewise binds himself by solemn oath to an everlasting covenant and institutes circumcision as the sign and seal of his promise.

Abraham's role is to believe in God's faithfulness to keep his word. He must leave the security of his ancestral homeland and go forth to an unknown land, armed solely with the promise God has made him. In the classic words of the older covenant account:

> He believed the Lord; and he reckoned it to him as righteousness.
> 15:6

The Yahwist's narratives excel in the depth of understanding with which they portray the trials that beset man's best efforts to believe. As we have seen, it is in the tension between threats to the promise and their resolution through God's intervention on behalf of his covenant bond, that the drama of these accounts unfolds.[183] The promise depends upon offspring; yet Sarah's barrenness is a recognized fact even before the call of Abraham. No sooner does the family reach the Negeb than a famine forces them into Egypt, where Sarah is taken temporarily into the pharaoh's harem. Upon the return to Canaan, disputes over grazing rights threaten the unity of the clan and necessitate the separation of Abraham and Lot. The conception of a child by the handmaiden Hagar has an unhappy outcome, as friction develops between herself and Sarah, leading finally to Hagar's flight to the wilderness. Abraham and Sarah's difficulty in believing the promise of a child in their old age poses an even more serious threat.[184]

The story of the patriarch's supreme test of faith (ch. 22) is Elohistic, but it could hardly have been better situated for its climactic effect had the Yahwist himself designed it.[185] Nothing short of a literary masterpiece, it describes the most intense emotions in restrained, simple, and direct language and has understandably aroused the theological interests of interpreters such as Kierkegaard, who treated it as the classic parable on the radical meaning of faith. After Sarah gives birth to Isaac and it appears finally that an heir to the covenant is assured, there comes God's inscrutable command that the child be sacrificed as a burnt offering. Once more, the patriarch surrenders himself to God's will and makes the terrible journey of faith. And, once again, it is in losing his life that he finds it. As Kierkegaard put it, "only he who draws the knife gets Isaac."[186]

In the resolution of crisis after crisis, these traditions perceive God's sovereign command of history and his long-suffering faithfulness in directing events toward his covenant goals. Again and again, the promise is reaffirmed in the conviction that neither adverse fate, nor even the faithlessness of the fathers, for long delays its fulfillment. But, comparable to the later apostolic Church, which began with its own "rock of faith," St. Peter, Hebrew tradition depicts God's covenant as premised on the ability of his people to believe its promise and entrust themselves to its risky demands. In the stories of Abraham, Israel saw the entire course of its crisis-ridden, and often faithless, covenant history, whose unsteady pattern did not cease with the Davidic kingdom but became even more pronounced between the days of the Yahwist and the post-Exilic priests. Of greater significance, however, is the covenant people's sense of identity with the patriarch's indomitable faith. For, whatever else may be said of Abraham the man, he is in these accounts and in the minds of those who preserved them the prototype of believing Israel.

[183] See above, pp. 67-68.

[184] In the J source only Sarah's faith is in question (18:9-15); but cf. 17:15-21 (P).

[185] E. A. Speiser goes so far as to ascribe the episode to J rather than E (*Genesis*, The Anchor Bible [Garden City, NY: Doubleday & Company, Inc., 1964], p. 166).

[186] Soren Kierkegaard, *Fear and Trembling* (Garden City, NY: Doubleday & Company, Inc., 1954), p. 38.

The stories of Lot (chs. 13, 14, 18, 19) embody several prominent etiologies, the most notable of which supplies a reason for Sodom and Gomorrah's untimely destruction. Some interpreters theorize that the conflagration which gave rise to our metaphor "fire and brimstone," and which is here attributed to the great wickedness of these cities, preserves the memory of an earthquake, accompanied by lightning and the ignition of natural gases in the area of the lower Jordan Valley.[187] If so, the remains of the ancient towns might be expected to lie beneath the Dead Sea waters south of the Lisan peninsula, in what was once the fertile Vale of Siddim. No evidence of any such underwater remains has yet appeared, however, and more likely theories look to sites in the land areas bordering the Dead Sea.[188] The salt mountain known as Jebel Usdum (Mount Sodom), situated immediately to the west, is marked by conspicuous salt masses, long connected with the legend of Lot's wife. The incestuous union between Lot and his daughters, coming as it does after the annihilation of the cities of the plain and their male populations, is not necessarily an effort to stigmatize the origins of Moab and Ammon, the offspring of the affair and the eponymous ancestors of the Moabites and Ammonites. The story does, however, purport to explain the locale of the Moabite and Ammonite homelands in the eastern Dead Sea region.

The inevitable comparison of the characters of Lot and Abraham is hardly unintended by our accounts. Alongside Lot's selfish choice of the better land and his consequent vulnerability to both human foes and divine retribution, Abraham's magnanimous courage and selfless intervention on the weaker man's behalf stand out in bold relief. Nowhere is the spirit of Abraham more effectively portrayed than in his willingness to put the promise in jeopardy by deigning to approach God and plead for the sparing of Lot. His appeal is reminiscent of the prophets:

> Wilt thou indeed destroy the righteous with the wicked? . . . Shall not the
> Judge of all the earth do right (justice)?
> 18:23, 25

Once assured by God that for the sake of so few as ten innocent persons he will not destroy the entire population of Sodom, Abraham rests his case.

ISAAC. The space devoted to Isaac in the Genesis narrative is so slight that to some he appears as little more than a genealogical link between Abraham and Jacob. In the most memorable of the Isaac traditions, as the near victim of child sacrifice (ch. 22) and the aged victim of Jacob's decep-

---

[187] J. Penrose Harland, "The Location of the Cities of the Plain," *BA*, V (1952), pp. 17–32; "The Destruction of the Cities of the Plain," *BA*, VI (1943), pp. 41–52 (both reprinted in *BA Reader*, I, pp. 41–75).

[188] Cf. William G. Dever, "The Patriarchal Traditions," p. 101; David N. Freedman, "The Real Story of the Ebla Tablets," pp. 152–153.

tion (ch. 27), he is overshadowed by father and son. Even the wooing of his wife Rebekah (ch. 24), which von Rad calls "the most pleasant and charming of all the patriarchal stories,"[189] is conducted for him by his father's servant. In only one chapter (26;E) is he the subject in his own right of the accounts in which he appears. In view of the sparseness of traditions concerning him, his inclusion as an essential link in the chain of promise is all the more remarkable. So intent were the Priestly redactors on assuring for him a formal place within the tradition that they subsumed the entire cycle of Jacob stories (25:19–35:29) under the heading, "These are the generations of Isaac" (25:19), reserving his obituary for the conclusion of the unit (35:27–29).

A more detailed presentation of Isaac's career might have revealed him as a much less passive figure. We can hardly assume, at any rate, that he lacked either the natural energies or the zealous urge for a share of destiny that moved Abraham and Jacob. The more obvious fact is that his role within the tradition simply did not depend as such upon these characteristics. Unlike the pioneering Abraham, he is by his very birth a child of promise. And, unlike his own son Jacob, he has no elder brother whom he must outwit and supplant in order to win a place for himself. The promise is his; he has but to affirm it. That he did so, in full obedience to God's will, is never in question. Thus, his quiet, submissive character makes him an apt symbol of the covenant's dependence, not so much upon human ingenuity as upon the willingness to conform human life to the good designs which God has pledged himself to support.

JACOB. The Jacob narratives are composed chiefly of a fusion of J and E traditions,[190] organized around two major sequences involving (a) Jacob and Esau (25:19–28:22; 32–33) and (b) Jacob and Laban (29–31). Among the more significant shorter segments are those concerning important cult centers, such as the "ladder" dream at Bethel (28:10–22),[191] the wrestling at Peniel (32:24–32), and the destruction of Shechem (ch. 34).

The elements of crisis and suspense, which had not been lacking in the Isaac stories, are particularly evident in the conflicts surrounding the patriarch who "wrestled with God and with man and prevailed." The struggle with Esau is poignantly dramatized from the very womb of Rebekah (25:22–23) and in the birth itself (25:24–26), with Jacob's determined hold on the first-born's heel. In the memorable accounts telling of Esau's loss of the birthright and blessing to Jacob's ingenious plots, the rivalry develops to such a point that, in order to escape Esau's reprisals, Jacob is forced to

[189] *Genesis*, p. 248.
[190] For a precise delineation of the J, E, and P elements, see "Source Analysis of the Pentateuch" in the Appendix.
[191] The Hebrew term which our versions translate "ladder" (*sullam*) occurs only here in the Old Testament. It hardly refers to a ladder in the familiar sense, but to a ramp or stairway, such as was built onto the Mesopotamian ziggurats.

flee to Aram. Along the way, at Bethel, Yahweh renews with him the promise made to Abraham and Isaac.

The tradition spends no time reflecting on the question of how such deception on Jacob's part could ethically allow him a pivotal role in covenant history. One may speculate that it was his compelling and uncompromising zeal, as compared with Esau's callousness, that entitled him to it. But our accounts are not at all concerned with such rationalizations. Though we may be sure that Israel did not fail to perceive the sinister side of Jacob's character, it was enough, apparently, that his actions be allowed so speak for themselves and that Yahweh's oracle, declaring that "the elder shall serve the younger" (25:23), be understood as a divine suspension of the normal rights of the first-born. Thus, perhaps even more than the Abraham and Isaac accounts, the stories of Jacob demonstrate that God uses whomever he pleases to effect his purposes and in no sense does his election rest upon human merit.

Jacob's flight from Esau is but the beginning of another series of struggles, described in the colorful and entertaining Laban stories. Finally, after twenty years of matching wits with his father-in-law, and enriched with wives, children, and possessions, Jacob returns to Canaan for the inevitable confrontation with Esau. At this climactic point, on the eve of the reunion, there takes place the wrestling episode at Peniel. This latter account, as we have seen, has undergone a transformation of meaning in reaching its present form. No longer is the night demon at the Jabbok or the etiology of the hollow in man's hip of major concern, but rather the new name which God grants Jacob. He is no longer Jacob the cheat, but *Israel*, ancestor of the people of God and father of the twelve tribes. As such, his struggle for God's blessing is Israel's own. Indeed, "Israel has here presented its entire history with God almost prophetically as such a struggle until the breaking of the day." [192]

There is a substratum of international history as well in these accounts. Esau is the ancestor of the Edomites (25:30), just as Jacob is also Israel. Laban is in a real sense Aram. Thus, Israel's long history of conflict with Edom to the south and Aram to the north is depicted here in the sort of colorful, personalized saga in which folk tradition delights. Viewed in this light, one can easily imagine the gusto with which these stories were told in ancient Israelite circles. In Jacob's facile displacement of the dimwitted Esau and his outmaneuvering the equally crafty Laban, Israel perceived Yahweh's designs for the opponents of the covenant people.

JOSEPH. Joseph is a transition figure in covenant history. The story of his sale into Egypt, his rise to fame in the pharaoh's court, and the settlement of his family in the Egyptian delta (chs. 37–50) is the manner in which

[192] Von Rad, *Genesis*, p. 320.

Traditional Cave of Macpelah at Hebron. Walls of Herodian and Mameluke construction surround a mosque built over a cave traditionally identified as the burial site of the patriarchs. (Courtesy of the Israel Government Tourist Office.)

Hebrew tradition accounts for the passing of the patriarchal era and the presence of a colony of Hebrews in Egypt at the time of Moses' birth.

The local color which marks the Joseph story differs significantly from the story cycles of Abraham, Isaac, and Jacob. It is characteristically and authentically Egyptian in such details as personal names and official titles, geographical and climatic features, the conception of the ideal life span (110 years; 50:26), and customs involving dream interpretation (40–41), embalming (50:2–3, 26), and table separation from foreigners (43:31–34). Also, the account of Joseph's temptation by Potiphar's wife is closely paralleled by the Egyptian *Tale of the Two Brothers*,[193] though the theme of the two stories is too common to prove dependence. A close scrutiny of other cultural and geographical details, however, reveals the Palestinian vantage point of the Hebrew writer and argues against a composition of the Joseph story in its present form before the time of David or Solomon.[194]

The sale of Joseph into Egyptian slavery is not difficult to conceive as there are known to have been Asian and Semitic slaves in Egypt as early as the Middle Bronze Age.[195] The migration of Asians to Egypt in time of famine, moreover, is well attested in native records and pictures. Because of the normally dependable Nile inundations, Egypt was less vulnerable to

---

[193] *ANET*, pp. 23–25 (*ANE*, pp. 12–16).
[194] See Roland de Vaux, *The Early History of Israel*, pp. 295–303.
[195] *ANET*, p. 229.

drought than her neighbors. Famine there was not unknown, however, and there are recorded instances of distribution of food to the needy in such crises, just as we find in the Joseph story. There is even one Egyptian document which includes a tradition of seven lean years followed by years of plenty.[196]

Just as the Abraham, Isaac, and Jacob stories simplify and telescope the Palestinian patriarchal era, in like manner the Joseph story rests upon a much more complex and obscure history of Israel's Egyptian backgrounds. As neither the pharaoh who elevated Joseph nor any other official known from extrabiblical documents is named personally, the date of the settlement in Egypt has never been conclusively determined. Some scholars have concluded that the Hyksos period affords the most plausible conditions under which a northwest Semite could conceivably have reached the high administrative office claimed for Joseph. The Hyksos, themselves largely Semitic in background, might be expected to have welcomed both Joseph's family and his own superior administrative leadership. Also, the settlement of the Jacob clan in Goshen (the northeast sector of Lower Egypt), presumably in close proximity to Joseph's own residence, suits the conditions of the Hyksos period, when the capitol was situated in the delta. The nationalization of land and other property, recorded of Joseph's administration, is known to have prevailed in Egypt just following the expulsion of the Hyksos and conceivably could have replaced the older feudal system during the rule of the Hyksos themselves. If one accepts a thirteenth-century B.C. setting for the Exodus, moreover, a Hyksos date would not be inconsistent with a biblical tradition which places the Exodus four hundred years after the entry into Egypt (Gen. 15:13).[197] None of this is decisive, however, and alternative proposals include the Amarna period (see below), when Pharaoh Akhenaton (c. 1370–1353 B.C.) is known to have used non-Egyptians as functionaries, and a time toward the end of the second millennium B.C., when a Bedouin people known to the Egyptians as Shasu migrated from the northeast into Egypt.[198] The most that one can conclude is that the Joseph story likely telescopes separate movements of Semites into the Egyptian delta, thus representing a long period of tribal history.[199]

[196] ANET, pp. 31–32 (ANE, pp. 24–27).
[197] Cf. also Ex. 12:40, where the period in Egypt is cited as 430 years.
[198] The case for an Amarna dating is argued by Cyrus H. Gordon, "Hebrew Origins in the Light of Recent Discoveries," Biblical and Other Studies, A. Altmann, ed. (Cambridge, MA: Harvard University Press, 1963), pp. 3–14, and H. H. Rowley, From Joseph to Joshua (New York: Oxford University Press, Inc., 1950), note 109, pp. 116–120. Evidence for an identification of the Hebrews in Egypt with the Shasu is presented by Siegfried Hermann, A History of Israel in Old Testament Times, John Bowden, trans. (Philadelphia: Fortress Press, 1975), pp. 56–61.
[199] Among the many supporters of such a position are Roland de Vaux, The Early History of Israel, pp. 291–320 (esp. p. 320), and Kathleen M. Kenyon, The Bible and Recent Archaeology, pp. 30–31.

The contrasts between the Joseph story and the other patriarchal accounts go beyond the difference of geographical locale. Whereas the story cycles of Abraham, Isaac, and Jacob are formed of originally independent and disconnected narratives, the Joseph material has been integrated into a single and connected novella. Gunkel regarded it as "the highest level of composition attained in Genesis."[200] Around the central character there unfolds a sustained, dramatic plot, unbroken except for the interludes involving Judah and Tamar (ch. 38) and Jacob's farewell blessing (ch. 49).[201]

The narrative has been formed from parallel J and E versions, which can be more easily identified by the alternating names "Israel" (J) and "Jacob" (E) than by variation in the divine name.[202] Priestly additions are slight and scattered. The amount of E material exceeds that found in the other portions of Genesis; and, for the most part, it is smoothly and harmoniously fused with J. Chapter 37 offers an exception. Here variant accounts of Joseph's sale into Egypt are recognizable: one in which Reuben saves Joseph's life by persuading his brothers to place Joseph in a pit from which he is then stolen by Midianite traders (E); the other, in which Judah is Joseph's protector and the one who convinces the brothers to sell him to a caravan of Ishmaelites en route to Egypt (J).

Another marked difference between the Joseph story and the rest of the patriarchal material is to be seen in the human plane on which the narrative moves. Unlike the other accounts, in which God continually intervenes in human affairs, here he is seldom mentioned except as the remote, overruling providence, whose mysterious and unseen guidance moves the course of events toward purposeful ends. Never does he appear to Joseph or make him a recipient of the covenant promise.

According to von Rad the story originally served a wisdom function.[203] If so, it was less concerned with covenant and tribal history, cult-center theophanies, and the like, than with the individual model which Joseph affords

---

[200] Quoted in S. H. Hooke, *In the Beginning*, p. 115.

[201] Cf. George W. Coats, "From Canaan to Egypt: Structural and Theological Context for the Joseph Story," *CBQMS*, 4 (1975), where the inherent structural unity of the Joseph novella is maintained; and Dorothy Irvin, "The Joseph and Moses Stories as Narratives in the Light of Ancient Near Eastern Narrative," in John H. Hayes and J. Maxwell Miller, eds., *Israelite and Judaean History*, pp. 180–191, which offers comparisons with the plot motifs found in ancient Near Eastern folk tales.

[202] For an identification of the source strands, see "Source Analysis of the Pentateuch" in the Appendix.

[203] "The Joseph Narrative and Ancient Wisdom," in *The Problem of the Hexateuch and Other Essays*, E. W. Truman Dicken, trans. (London: Oliver & Boyd, 1966), pp. 292–300 (reprinted in James L. Crenshaw, ed., *Studies in Ancient Israelite Wisdom* [New York: KTAV Publishing House, 1976], pp. 439–447). The wisdom interpretation enjoys wide support, e.g., George W. Coats, "From Canaan to Egypt: Structural and Theological Context for the Joseph Story," but is subjected to serious criticism by James L. Crenshaw, "Method in Determining Wisdom Influence Upon 'Historical' Literature," *JBL*, LXXXVIII (1969), pp. 129–142 (reprinted in James L. Crenshaw, ed., *Studies in Ancient Israelite Wisdom*, pp. 481–494), and Thomas L. Thompson, "The Joseph and Moses Narratives," in John H. Hayes and J. Maxwell Miller, eds., *Israelite and Judaean History*, pp. 178–180.

as the ideal son, brother, servant, and administrator. The story thus incorporates many of the virtues in which Israel's wisdom teachers instructed the young: self-control and discipline, propriety in speech and outward demeanor, fear of God, family loyalty, and high standards of sexual morality.

The incorporation of the Joseph story into the composition of the patriarchal narrative, however, brought to it a further dimension of meaning. Once joined with the Abraham, Isaac, and Jacob accounts, it, too, became a vital chapter in the covenant history, sharing its characteristic pattern of promise and fulfillment. Near the conclusion of the story, in two speeches of Joseph to the brothers (45:5–7; 50:20f.), the theological significance of the account for the longer patriarchal narrative is disclosed:

> And now do not be distressed, or angry with yourselves, because you sold me here; for God sent me before you to preserve life.
>
> 45:5

> As for you, you meant evil against me; but God meant it for good, to bring it about that many people should be kept alive, as they are today.
>
> 50:20

Here, then, is the implicit principle underlying all the patriarchal stories.

> Both texts point to God's saving rule, which is concealed in profound worldliness. This rule of God for the salvation of men continuously permeates all realms of life and includes even man's evil by making the plans of the human heart serve divine purposes, without hindering them or excusing them.[204]

SELECTED READINGS

Pentateuchal Composition

Anderson, George W., "Some Aspects of the Uppsala School of Old Testament Study," *HTR*, 43 (1950), pp. 239–256. A clear presentation of the Scandinavian school's positions on Pentateuchal criticism.

Bright, John, "Modern Study of the Old Testament Literature," *The Bible and the Ancient Near East*, G. Ernest Wright, ed. (Garden City, NY: Doubleday/Anchor, 1965), pp. 1–26. Paperback. A helpful review article.

Brueggemann, Walter, "Yahwist," *IDBS*, pp. 971–975.

——— and Hans Walter Wolff, *The Vitality of Old Testament Tradtions* (Atlanta, GA: John Knox Press, 1975). Paperback. Essays aimed at exposing the *kerygma* (theological proclamation) of the J, E, D, and P Pentateuchal sources.

Carpenter, Joseph E., G. Harford-Battersby, *The Hexateuch According to the Revised Version*, 2 vols. (New York: Longmans, Green, 1900). A detailed explanation of the documentary hypothesis.

Cassuto, Umberto, *The Documentary Hypothesis and the Composition of the Pentateuch*, Israel Abrahams, trans. (Jerusalem: Magnes Press, 1961). A rebuttal of the documentary hypothesis of Pentateuchal origins by a conservative Jewish scholar.

[204] Gerhard Von Rad, *Genesis*, p. 433.

Clements, Ronald E., *One Hundred Years of Old Testament Interpretation* (Philadelphia: The Westminster Press, 1976), pp. 7–30. A succinct review of Pentateuchal interpretation during the past century.

——, "Pentateuchal Problems," *Tradition and Interpretation*, G. W. Anderson, ed. (Oxford: Clarendon Press, 1979), pp. 96–124. An up-dating of C. R. North's survey of the recent history of Pentateuchal criticism.

Cross, Frank Moore, *Canaanite Myth and Hebrew Epic* (Cambridge, MA: Harvard University Press, 1973), pp. 293–325. A new interpretation of the Priestly source (P) in the Pentateuch.

Durham, John I., "Credo, Ancient Israelite," *IDBS*, 197–199.

Ellis, Peter E., *The Yahwist: the Bible's First Theologian* (Notre Dame, IN: Fides Publishers, 1968).

Engnell, Ivan, "The Pentateuch," *A Rigid Scrutiny: Critical Essays on the Old Testament*, John T. Willis, trans. (Nashville, TN: Vanderbilt University Press, 1969). An outstanding Scandinavian scholar's traditio-historical analysis of Pentateuchal origins.

Fohrer, Georg, *Introduction to the Old Testament*, initiated by Ernst Sellin; David E. Green, trans. (Nashville, TN: Abingdon Press, 1968), pp. 103–195. A solid discussion of the concerns of Pentateuchal composition and the character of the sources.

Freedman, David N., "Pentateuch," *IDB*, K–Q, pp. 711–727. An insightful summary article of the Pentateuch's structure and theories regarding its composition up to the time of the article's publication.

Fretheim, Terence E., "Elohist," *IDBS*, pp. 259–263.

Hayes, John H., *An Introduction to Old Testament Study* (Nashville, TN: Abingdon Press, 1979), pp. 155–197. A brief survey of modern theories of Pentateuchal composition.

Journal for the Study of the Old Testament, 3 (1977). The entire issue is devoted to Rolf Rendtorff's recent theories of Pentateuchal composition and the critiques of other prominent Pentateuchal scholars.

Levine, Baruch A., "Priestly Writers," *IDBS*, pp. 683–687.

Montgomery, Robert M., *An Introduction to Source Analysis of the Pentateuch* (Nashville, TN: Abingdon Press, 1971). Paperback. A programmed-learning approach to the identification and analysis of source-critical strands in the Pentateuch.

North, C. R., "Pentateuchal Criticism," *The Old Testament and Modern Study*, H. H. Rowley, ed. (New York: Oxford University Press, Inc., 1951). Paperback. A helpful review of the state of Pentateuchal composition studies at mid-century. Now supplemented by the more recent article of R. E. Clements.

Noth, Martin, *A History of Pentateuchal Tradition*, Bernhard W. Anderson, trans. (Englewood Cliffs, NJ: Prentice-Hall, Inc., 1972). A highly influential work by one of the foremost form- and tradition-critical scholars of this century.

——, *Uberlieferungs-geschichtliche Studien*, I (Halle, Belgium: Niemeyer, 1943). Contains an explication of Noth's theory of the Deuteronomistic history and its implications for pentateuchal composition.

Rad, Gerhard von, "The Form-Critical Problem of the Hexateuch," *The Problem of the Hexateuch and Other Essays*, E. W. T. Dicken, trans. (London: Oliver & Boyd, 1966), pp. 1–78. A form- and tradition-critical theory of Pentateuchal origins that has provided a model for much of the Pentateuchal criticism of the recent past.

Rendtorff, Rolf, *Das überlieferungsgeschichtliche Problem des Pentateuch*, BZAW, 147 (1977). A provocative proposal for a new manner of viewing the traditional J, E, D, and P sources in the Pentateuch.

Sandmel, Samuel, "The Haggada within Scripture," *JBL*, LXXX (1961), pp. 105–122. An approach to the growth of Pentateuchal tradition utilizing the analogy of Jewish haggada, i.e., the retelling of stories.

Soggin, J. Alberto, *Introduction to the Old Testament*, John Bowden, trans., The Old Testament Library (Philadelphia: The Westminster Press, 1976), pp. 79–184. A balanced and generally up-to-date review of Pentateuchal composition and the individual sources.

Thompson, R. J., *Moses and the Law in a Century of Criticism since Graf*, VTS, 19 (Leiden, Netherlands: E. J. Brill, 1970). A valuable history of modern Pentateuchal criticism.

Van Seters, John, *Abraham in History and Tradition* (New Haven, CT: Yale University Press, 1975), Part II, pp. 123–313. A proposal for a new literary analysis of the Pentateuch deviating widely from the traditional dating and delineation of the sources.

Weiser, Artur, *The Old Testament: Its Formation and Development*, Dorothea M. Barton, trans. (New York: Association Press, 1961), pp. 69–142. An excellent analysis of the problem of Pentateuchal composition as perceived at mid-century.

Wellhausen, Julius, *Prolegomena to the History of Ancient Israel*, Allan Menzies and J. Sutherland Black, trans. (New York: Meridian Books, 1957). Paperback. An English translation of the definitive formulation of the documentary hypothesis, first published in German in 1883.

Genesis

Gunkel, Hermann, *The Legends of Genesis, The Biblical Saga and History*, W. H. Carruth, trans. (New York: Schocken Books, Inc., 1964). Paperback. The opening section of Hermann Gunkel's monumental commentary on Genesis, first published in German in 1901. A path-finding application of the form-critical technique to the Old Testament.

Hooke, S. H., *In the Beginning* (New York: Oxford University Press, Inc., 1947).

Rad, Gerhard von, *Genesis*, J. H. Marks, trans., The Old Testament Library (Philadelphia: The Westminster Press, 1961). The best commentary on Genesis available in English. Von Rad works within the framework of the JEP source theory, but displays a profound feeling for the smaller units of material.

Richardson, Alan, *Genesis I–XI*, The Torch Bible Commentaries (London: S.C.M. Press, 1959).

Sarna, Nahum M., *Understanding Genesis* (New York: McGraw-Hill Book Company, 1966). Also in paperback (New York: Schocken Books, Inc., 1970).

Skinner, John, *A Critical and Exegetical Commentary on Genesis*, The International Critical Commentary (New York: Charles Scribner's Sons, 1910). Many of the insights of this technical work remain fresh.

Speiser, E. A., *Genesis*, The Anchor Bible (New York: Doubleday & Company, Inc., 1964). A helpful translation with insightful notes.

Vawter, Bruce, *On Genesis: A New Reading* (Garden City, NY: Doubleday & Company, Inc., 1977). A very readable commentary on Genesis, treating literary historical, and theological concerns.

Westermann, Claus, *Creation,* by John J. Scullion, trans. (Philadelphia: Fortress Press, 1974). An English translation of the first installment (covering Genesis 1–3) of a monumental commentary on Genesis, written in German.

Peoples and Cultures of the Ancient Near East

De Vaux, Roland, *The Early History of Israel,* David Smith, trans. (Philadelphia: The Westminster Press, 1978). One of the best sources available for comprehending the peoples, cultures, and history of the Middle East during the period of Hebrew origins.

Gottwald, Norman K., "Were the Early Israelites Pastoral Nomads?" *Rhetorical Criticism: Essays in Honor of James Muilenburg,* Jared J. Jackson and Martin Kessler, eds. (Pittsburgh, PA: The Pickwick Press, 1974), pp. 223–255. A pathfinding sociological analysis of pastoral societies and the implications for an understanding of early Hebrew culture. A summary article by the same author and bearing the same title appears in the *BAR,* IV, 2 (June 1978), pp. 2–7.

Greenberg, Moshe, *The Hab/piru* (New Haven, CT: American Oriental Society, 1955).

Gurney, O. R., *The Hittites,* 2nd edition (New York: Penguin Books, 1954). Paperback.

Kramer, S. N., *The Sumerians: Their History, Culture, and Character* (Chicago: University of Chicago Press, 1963). Available in paperback. (Phoenix Books, 1971).

Luke, J. T., "Pastoralism and Politics in the Mari Period" (Ph.D. Dissertation, University of Michigan; Ann Arbor: University Microfilms, 1965). An important study revising long-held theories concerning early Middle Eastern society, with special attention to Mari.

Matthiae, Paolo, "Ebla in the Late Early Syrian Period: The Royal Palace and the State Archives," *BA,* 39 (1976), pp. 94–113. A description of the Ebla discoveries by the archaeologist who directed the excavations.

Pettinato, Giovanni, "The Royal Archives of Tell-Mardikh-Ebla," *BA,* 39 (1976), pp. 44–52. A description of the Ebla texts by the epigrapher who participated in the discoveries.

Rowton, M. B., "Enclosed Nomadism," *JESHO,* XVII (1974), pp. 1–30. A new appraisal of nomadism in early Middle Eastern society.

Van Seters, John, *The Hyksos: A New Investigation* (New Haven, CT: Yale University Press, 1966).

Woolley, Sir Leonard, *Ur of the Chaldees* (London: Ernest Benn Ltd., 1929). Available in paperback (New York: Penguin Books, 1950).

Mythology and Legend

Anderson, Bernhard W., *Creation versus Chaos: The Reinterpretation of Mythical Symbolism in the Bible* (New York: Association Press, 1967).

Barr, James, "The Meaning of 'Mythology' in Relation to the Old Testament," *VT,* IX (1959), pp. 1–10.

Brandon, S. G. F., *Creation Legends of the Ancient Near East* (London: Hodder & Stoughton Ltd., 1963).

Childs, Brevard S., *Myth and Reality in the Old Testament*, Studies in Biblical Theology, no. 27 (London: S.C.M. Press, 1960).

Eliade, Mircea, *Cosmos and History; The Myth of the Eternal Return*, W. R. Trask, trans. (New York: Harper Torchbooks, 1959). Paperback.

————, *The Sacred and the Profane*, W. R. Trask, trans. (New York: Harcourt Brace Jovanovich, Inc., 1959). Also available in paperback (Harper Torchbooks, 1961).

Frankfort, H., H. A. Frankfort, et al., *The Intellectual Adventure of Ancient Man* (Chicago: University of Chicago Press, 1946). Reprinted in paperback as *Before Philosophy* (Penguin Books, 1949).

Gaster, Theodor H., *Myth, Legend, and Custom in the Old Testament* (New York: Harper & Row Publishers, 1969). Also available in paperback (Harper Torchbooks, 2 vols., 1975). Brings the findings of comparative folklore and mythology to bear on the Old Testament.

————, *Thespis; Ritual, Myth, and Drama in the Ancient Near East* (New York: Abelard Schuman, 1950). Also available in paperback (Doubleday & Company, Inc., 1961).

Heidel, Alexander, *The Babylonian Genesis*, 2nd ed. (Chicago: University of Chicago Press, 1951). Also available in paperback (Phoenix Books, 1963).

————, *The Gilgamesh Epic and Old Testament Parallels* (Chicago: University of Chicago Press, 1946). Also available in paperback (Phoenix Books, 1963).

Hooke, S. H., *Myth, Ritual, and Kingship* (Oxford: Clarendon Press, 1958).

————, *Middle Eastern Mythology* (New York: Penguin Books, 1963). Paperback.

Kraemer, S. N., ed., *Mythologies of the Ancient World* (Chicago: Quadrangle Press, 1961). Also available in paperback (Doubleday Anchor, 1961).

Loew, Cornelius, *Myth, Sacred History and Philosophy* (New York: Harcourt Brace Jovanovich, Inc., 1967).

Lord, Albert, *The Singer of Tales* (Cambridge, Mass.: Harvard University Press, 1964.). Also available in paperback (Atheneum Publishers, 1973.)

McKenzie, John L., "Myth and the Old Testament," *CBQ*, XXI (1959), pp. 265–282.

Rogerson, J. W., *Myth in Old Testament Interpretation* (Berlin/New York: Walter de Gruyter, 1974).

The Patriarchs and Patriarchal Backgrounds

Albright, William F., "From the Patriarchs to Moses, I. From Abraham to Joseph," *BA*, 36 (1973), pp. 5–33. A summary of the author's views on the patriarchal age, written shortly before his death.

Alt, Albrecht, "The God of the Fathers," *Essays on Old Testament History and Religion*, R. A. Wilson, trans. (Garden City, NY: Doubleday & Company, Inc., 1967), pp. 1–100.

Bright, John, *Early Israel in Recent History Writing*, Studies in Biblical Theology, No. 19 (London: S.C.M. Press, 1956).

————, *A History of Israel*, 2nd ed. (Philadelphia: The Westminster Press, 1972), pp. 67–102. A defense of patriarchal historicity and Middle Bronze Age dating, based on archaeological data. Compare the critiques of Thompson and Van Seters.

Cross, Frank Moore, *Canaanite Myth and Hebrew Epic* (Cambridge, MA: Harvard University Press, 1973), pp. 3–75. Provocative essays on early Hebraic concepts of God: El, Yahweh, and the "gods of the fathers."

De Vaux, Roland, *The Early History of Israel,* David Smith, trans. (Philadelphia: The Westminster Press, 1978), pp. 161–287. The most comprehensive treatment of the patriarchal accounts and Near Eastern history, culture, and religion during the Middle Bronze Age.

———, "Method in the Study of Early Hebrew History," and the responses of G. E. Mendenhall and M. Greenberg, *The Bible in Modern Scholarship*, J. Philip Hyatt, ed. (Nashville, TN: Abingdon Press, 1965).

Dever, William G., and W. Malcolm Clark, "The Patriarchal Traditions," *Israelite and Judaean History,* John H. Hayes and J. Maxwell Miller, eds. (Philadelphia: The Westminster Press, 1977). A valuable summary of current scholarly approaches to the patriarchs, including a judicious appraisal of archaeological data.

Gordon, Cyrus H., "The Patriarchal Age," *JBR,* 21 (1953), pp. 238–243.

Gottwald, Norman K., "Were the Early Israelites Pastoral Nomads?" *Rhetorical Criticism,* Jared J. Jackson and Martin Kessler, eds., (Pittsburgh, PA: Pickwick Press, 1974), pp. 223–255. See above listing under "Peoples and Cultures of the Ancient Near East."

Holt, John, *The Patriarchs of Israel* (Nashville, TN: Vanderbilt University Press, 1964).

Hunt, Ignatius, *The World of the Patriarchs* (Englewood Cliffs, NJ: Prentice-Hall, Inc., 1967).

Luke, John Tracy, "Abraham and the Iron Age: Reflections on the New Patriarchal Studies," *JSOT,* 4 (1977), pp. 35–47. A critique of Thomas L. Thompson's and John Van Seter's contention for an Iron Age provenance of the Patriarchs.

Rad, Gerhard, von, "History and the Patriarchs," *ET,* 72 (Apr. 1961), pp. 213–216. A reply to the article of Wright cited below.

Redford, Donald B., *A Study of the Biblical Story of Joseph, VTS,* 20 (Leiden, Netherlands: E. J. Brill, 1970).

Thompson, Thomas L., *The Historicity of the Patriarchal Narratives* (Berlin/New York: Walter de Gruyter, 1974). A detailed argument against a second-millennium B.C. patriarchal age, as well as the historicity of the patriarchal accounts.

Van Seters, John, *Abraham in History and Tradition* (New Haven, CT: Yale University Press, 1975). A study that challenges many of the widely held views concerning the patriarchs and pentateuchal composition. Takes a position similar to that of Thompson.

Vergote J., *Joseph en Egypte* (Louvain, Belgium: University of Louvain Press, 1959).

Warner, S. M., "The Patriarchs and Extra-Biblical Sources," *JSOT,* 2 (1977), pp. 50–61. See also the response to this article by J. Maxwell Miller in the same issue, pp. 62–66.

Wright, G. Ernest, "History and the Patriarchs," *ET,* 71 (July 1960), pp. 292–296. Argues the value of archaeology in assessing the historicity of the patriarchal accounts.

145

2

and the lord brought us out of egypt

Then we cried to the Lord the God of our fathers, and the Lord heard our voice, and saw our affliction, our toil, and our oppression; and the Lord brought us out of Egypt with a mighty hand and an outstretched arm, with great terror, with signs and wonders.
—Deuteronomy 26:7–8

"Now there arose a new king over Egypt, who did not know Joseph" (Exod. 1:8). This terse declaration of the Yahwist[1] tells all, and yet not nearly enough, about the turn of affairs in Egypt which brought on the enslavement of the Hebrews. At some point, we are informed, when the accomplishments of Joseph were forgotten, the Hebrews in Egypt were made slaves of the state and forced to build the cities of Pithom and Rameses (1:11). The failure to mention the pharaoh's name has opened the door to the same sort of speculation that surrounds the question of the Hebrew entry into Egypt. The Priestly notation that Israel's descendants were fruitful and "filled the land" (1:7), though equally vague, implies a long and peaceful Egyptian domicile prior to the era of bondage. It is widely held

---

[1] Exodus I includes J, E, and P material: vss. 1–7, P; vss. 8–12, 22, J: vss. 15–21, E.

146

that the unnamed king was either Seti I (1309–1290 B.C.) or Rameses II (1290–1224 B.C.), early pharaohs of the Nineteenth Dynasty under whom the cities of Pithom and Rameses were built. If so, the Hebrew bondage coincided with a period of political expansion and economic growth in Egyptian history.[2]

1. THE EXODUS SETTING

During the Eighteenth Dynasty (1570–1310 B.C.) Egypt became the dominant power in the Near East. Repeatedly her armies penetrated Palestine and Syria until by the time of Thutmose III (c. 1490–1435 B.C.) her northern frontier extended all the way to the Euphrates.[3] Only the strength of the Kingdom of Mitanni, which at this time controlled all of Upper Mesopotamia, blocked further Egyptian expansion. After an initial clash between these two powers, an alliance was formed offering mutual security against the rising power of the Hittites in Asia Minor.

THE AMARNA PERIOD. The most serious revolution in Egyptian affairs since the days of the Hyksos occurred in the fourteenth century, during the reign of Amenhotep IV (c. 1370–1353 B.C.). In a dramatic break with the powerful priests of Amon, high god of Egypt, the young pharaoh devoted himself solely to the worship of Aton, the sun disk, and attempted to make his "solar monotheism" the official religion of the empire. He took the name of Akhenaton ("Splendor of Aton") and moved his capital from Thebes to a site near modern Tell el Amarna, to which he gave the name Akhetaton ("Horizon of Aton").

Akhenaton's revolution deserves recognition for its far-reaching, though brief, innovations in Egypt's traditional patterns of life. All aspects of Egyptian culture—politics, art, and literature, as well as religion—were affected. Whether or not he was "history's first monotheist," as often alleged, his Aton faith embraced the universality and beneficence of the god, his creation of all things, and his incomparable place in the cosmos. The descriptive phrases in the Hymn to Aton, preserved in a wall relief at Tell el Amarna, are strikingly similar to those praising Yahweh in Psalm 104.[4]

Akhenaton's theological genius could not compensate, however, for his weakness as a ruler. He had little support among his subjects; and his preoccupation with internal reforms had disastrous results for Egypt's Asian

---

[2] Brevard Childs (*The Book of Exodus* pp. 14–15) cautions against an undue historicizing of the vague reference in 1:8, and points to "the biblical style which makes use of stereotyped idioms in order to highlight the beginning of a new epoch in Israel's life."

[3] Cf. Thutmoses's account of his victory at Megiddo in ANET, pp. 234–238 (ANE, pp. 175–182).

[4] ANET, pp. 369–371. (ANE, pp. 226–230).

King Akhenaton and Queen Nefertiti standing with offerings for the sun god Aton; from Tell el Amarna, Egypt. (Courtesy of the Metropolitan Museum of Art.)

empire, as evidenced in a collection of letters found at Tell el Amarna.[5] Addressed to the king from Egyptian vassals in Palestine and Syria, they show these lands in a state of chaos, as local princes struggle to control their towns against invasion by rival dynasts and a powerful Habiru ('Apiru) element. Rulers of towns such as Accho, Megiddo, Shechem, Pella, Gezer, and Jerusalem accuse each other of treachery and disloyalty and appeal to the pharaoh to send armies to protect them against the despised Habiru. 'Abdu-Heba, prince of Jerusalem, complains that if aid is not forthcoming he shall be forced to submit, even as Lab'ayu of Shechem who "gave the land of Shechem to the 'Apiru."[6] Divided and weakened by internal dissension, Egypt was in no condition to intervene. Consequently, she retained little more than nominal control of Canaan and lost her Syrian and Phoenician territories to the Hittites, now at the peak of their strength under the great Shuppiluliuma (c. 1375–1340 B.C.).

THE NINETEENTH DYNASTY. Atonism as a religious force had a negligible effect on Egypt's masses and, following Akhnaton's death, was soon replaced by the former Amon faith. By the beginning of the Nineteenth Dynasty (c. 1310–1200 B.C.) all vestiges of the "heretical" revolution were removed and peace and prosperity returned to the troubled land. The two strong pharaohs, Seti I (c. 1309–1290 B.C.) and his son Rameses II (1290–1224 B.C.), were unable to recapture the Syrian lands lost to the Hittites, but apparently succeeded in recouping Egypt's losses in Canaan. A victory stele discovered at Beth-shan contains the account of one such campaign waged by Seti in northern Palestine.[7]

Both Seti and Rameses, particularly the latter, carried on extensive building programs in which Habiru worked as state slaves. Avaris, the former Hyksos capital, was rebuilt and once more made the capital, presumably to allow for better control of Egypt's Asian empire. Named "House of Rameses" in honor of Rameses II, it is the same city mentioned in Exodus 1:11 as the one on which the Hebrews labored.

The last noteworthy king of the Nineteenth Dynasty was Merneptah (c. 1224–1216 B.C.), son of Rameses II. On a stele erected in the fifth year of his reign (c. 1220 B.C.), he celebrated a victorious campaign in Canaan and, in the hyperbolic style typical of royal inscriptions, claimed to have annihilated the Israelites.[8]

---

[5] ANET, pp. 483–490 (ANE, pp. 262–277).

[6] ANET, p. 489 (ANE, p. 274).

[7] ANET, pp. 253–254 (ANE, pp. 182–183).

[8] Bertil Albrektson has recently proposed that much of what appears to be arrogant boasting in royal inscriptions from the ancient Near East is in fact communication from the king to his god, recorded not so much to enhance the ruler's stature among his people as to praise the god who has acted through him (History and the Gods, pp. 42ff.). See also H. M. Dion, "Le genre littéraire sumerian de l' hymne à soi-même et quelques passages du Deutéro-Isaie," RB, LXXIV (1967), pp. 215–234.

Tablets from Tell el Amarna, Egypt, including letters addressed to the pharaoh from a Palestinian prince (c. fourteenth century B.C.). (Courtesy of the Trustees of the British Museum.)

1. THE EXODUS SETTING

Israel is laid waste, his seed is not; Hurru is become a widow for Egypt![9]

This is the earliest known reference to Israel outside the Bible and, notwithstanding the exaggerated military claim, is especially significant as evidence that the Israelites were in the land of Canaan by that date. Of the conquered foes named in the inscription, Israel is the only one whose name is written with the determinative of a people rather than a land, suggesting to some interpreters that they were not yet in possession of a territory.

During Merneptah's reign Egypt faced the first in a series of invasions by the so-called Sea People, displaced hordes from the Aegean Islands, before whom the Hittite Kingdom collapsed. Together with the Libyans, they moved upon Egypt from the west, and although Merneptah was able to repel them, his victory offered no more than a temporary respite. A generation later Rameses III confronted them in yet greater numbers.

The Exodus As Historical Event

Within this historical framework we must attempt to set the familiar narratives of Moses and the Exodus. To assess the historicity, date, and circumstances of the events described in these accounts poses numerous and formidable problems, which in the opinion of many scholars can lead only to inconclusive results.[10] Neither Moses nor the flight of the Hebrew slaves is mentioned in any extant Egyptian text; and the biblical accounts themselves are cast in a confessional, liturgical, and poetic form, embellished with the colorful elements of folklore, and are often obscure as to historical detail. The Exodus narrative alone, moreover, could scarcely account for the history of all the diverse components of the later Israel. As we shall see, the process by which the nation achieved its ultimate form was exceedingly complex; and apparently what we have in these stories are the early experiences of but one of the several strains within Israel's ancestry.

Notwithstanding the many questions that remain unanswered, there is reason to believe that the Exodus is grounded in historical fact. God's deliverance of the Hebrews from Egyptian bondage is a fundamental premise of Israel's covenant faith and the formative event from which Hebrew tradition traces its origins as a nation. As we have seen, prominent confessional liturgies in the Old Testament (Deut. 6:20–24; 26:5–9; Josh. 24:2–13) celebrate it, as well as the ancient Song of Miriam (Exod. 15:21).

---

[9] ANET, p. 378 (ANE, p. 231).

[10] Compare the different approaches of Martin Noth, *The History of Israel*, rev. ed., S. Godman, trans. rev. by P. R. Ackroyd (New York: Harper & Row Publishers, 1960), pp. 110–138, and John Bright, *A History of Israel*, pp. 97–127. See further the analyses of Thomas L. Thompson and Dorothy Irvin ("The Joseph and Moses Narratives," *Israelite and Judaean History*, John H. Hayes and J. Maxwell Miller, eds., pp. 149–212, esp. 210–212), in which the Exodus accounts are viewed as ahistorical folk tales, linked by a narrative framework that is essentially secondary to the originally independent tales.

It is one of the primary themes of the Hebrew Bible, and more than half of the books make reference to it. The event, in turn, demands its human counterpart. As has often been remarked, if the Bible did not tell us of Moses, we should be forced to presuppose someone quite like him to account for the mobilization and leadership of the Hebrew slaves in their successful bid for freedom.

THE DATE OF THE EXODUS. Although there can be no certainty regarding the exact date of the Exodus, the evidence accumulated in recent years converges upon the first three quarters of the thirteenth century—perhaps early in the reign of Rameses II—as the most suitable period. Some of the relevant data have already been mentioned. As Hebrew slave labor was enlisted in the building of Pithom and Rameses,[11] which we are now convinced were built by Seti I and Rameses II, the Exodus could not have occurred before the reign of Seti at the earliest—unless, of course, the names of the Egyptian cities in Exodus 1:11 are anachronistic. By the same token, Merneptah's stele shows the Israelites as a people already in Palestine by about 1220 B.C. Therefore, if the entry into Canaan of the Exodus contingent of Hebrews is envisioned at a point prior to 1220 B.C., and the traditional generation in the wilderness of Sinai is allowed, we arrive at the approximate period 1290–1250 B.C., or the reign of Rameses II, as providing a plausible setting for the escape from Egypt.

At first glance this appears to contradict the one explicit mention of the date in I Kings 6:1, where the initial work on the temple in the fourth year of Solomon's reign (c. 958 B.C.) is put at 480 years after the Israelites came out of Egypt. If taken literally, this would place the Exodus in the second half of the fifteenth century and allow for a connection between the settlement and the turmoil in Palestine during the Amarna era. Few today hold to this view, however, because the archaeological data bearing on the settlement lend it no support. Probably the 480 years is no more than a round figure for twelve generations, arrived at by employing the traditional forty years for a generation. If we assume that a generation is actually nearer to twenty-five years, as some suggest,[12] then we are carried back to the period of Rameses II. We must hasten to note, nevertheless, that harmonizations of this kind involving biblical chronologies are of limited value and run the risk of confusing the flexible approach to genealogy in ancient literature with the strict chronologies of modern historiography.

---

[11] The city of Rameses, built on the site of the ancient Hyksos capital Avaris, is usually identified with Tanis or perhaps Qantir, a few miles to the south (cf. John Van Seters, *The Hyksos*, pp. 127–151). Pithom was probably at Tell er-Retabeh, where excavations reveal ambitious building in the thirteenth century B.C. Both sites were situated in the Egyptian delta.

[12] John Bright, *A History of Israel*, 2nd ed., p. 121.

2. I BORE YOU ON EAGLE'S WINGS: THE PENTATEUCHAL NARRATIVE, EXODUS–DEUTERONOMY

As we have seen, the narrative element in Exodus–Deuteronomy is found chiefly in the first half of the Book of Exodus (Exod. 1–19) and the latter two thirds of Numbers (Num. 10:11–36:13). These sections consist largely of closely woven J and E traditions, the notable exceptions being Numbers 15–20 and 25–36, which contain large amounts of legal, cultic, and genealogical materials ascribed to P. The Priestly element in Exodus 1–19 is most conspicuous in one of two versions of Moses' call (6:2–7:13), strands of the plague traditions, the Passover narrative (ch. 12), and the manna and quail stories (ch. 16).

Martin Noth has distinguished in Exodus–Deutonomy four central themes: (1) exodus from Egypt, (2) covenant at Sinai, (3) guidance in the wilderness, and (4) entry into the Promised Land.[13] The wilderness motif serves to tie together the other three themes and takes the form of two journeys, from Egypt to Sinai and Sinai to Transjordan. The last of the themes is traced in the Pentateuch only so far as the entry into Transjordan, which nevertheless anticipates the subsequent conquest of the land west of Jordan as described in the book of Joshua.

A comparison with the short credos of Deuteronomy 6:20–25, 26:5–11 and Joshua 24:1–13 reveals how closely the Pentateuchal themes correspond to those celebrated in Israel's devotional life—its liturgies and catechisms.

> We were Pharaoh's slaves in Egypt; and the Lord brought us out of Egypt with a mighty hand; and the Lord showed signs and wonders, great and grievous, against Egypt and against Pharaoh and all his household before our eyes; and he brought us out from there, that he might bring us in and give us the land which he swore to give to our fathers. And the Lord commanded us to do all these statutes, to fear the Lord our God, for our good always, that he might preserve us alive, as at this day. And it will be righteousness for us, if we are careful to do all this commandment before the Lord our God as he has commanded us.
>
> Deut. 6:21–25

Indeed, the narratives themselves are shaped largely to conform to the needs of a confessional faith. Their end is to give glory to Yahweh for the marvelously designed and executed deliverance of his people, his provi-

[13] Cf. Martin Noth, *A History of Pentateuchal Traditions*, and idem, *Exodus: A Commentary*, J. S. Bowden, trans. (Philadelphia: The Westminster Press, 1962), pp. 9–12.

dential guidance through each dangerous stage of their pilgrimage, and his gifts of covenant, law, and land.[14]

The Deliverance from Egypt

The first of the four themes finds expression in chapters 1–15 of Exodus, which is composed of the following episodes: (a) enslavement of the Hebrews (1:1–14), (b) threat against the Hebrew children (1:15–22), (c) birth of Moses (2:1–10), (d) Moses' flight to Midian (2:11–25), (e) call of Moses (chs. 3–4, 6), (f) plagues (5:1–11:10), (g) Passover (12:1–13:16), and (h) escape at the Sea of Reeds (13:17–15:21)

MOSES' BIRTH. Viewed from the perspective of Hebrew faith, the Exodus is Yahweh's mighty deed whereby he took the initiative and revealed himself once for all as Israel's God. Yahweh himself, properly speaking, is the subject of all that we read in these accounts. On its human side, however, the Exodus is the story of the genius, courage, and faith of the man Moses. So crucial is his role both as leader and interpreter that his very name becomes synonymous with the deeper meaning of the event.

> He made known his ways to Moses,
> his acts to the people of Israel.
> Ps. 103:7

Moses' lineage is traced to the tribe of Levi and a family whose members bear good Hebrew names: Amram, Jochebed, Miriam, and Aaron (Ex. 6:20; Num. 26:59). His own name, notwithstanding the effort to derive it from the Hebrew verb *masha* ("to draw out"; Ex. 2:10), is authentically Egyptian (compare Ah-mose, Thut-mose) and comes from the verb meaning "to beget a child." The familiar story of his deliverance from death as an infant (Ex. 2:1–10)—the only incident concerning his youth that survives— bears the marks of popular folklore. Its themes are well known in the legends of the ancient world. Sargon of Akkad (c. 2300 B.C.), for example, claimed to have been placed by his mother in a reed basket, set afloat on the Euphrates, rescued and adopted by a peasant, and finally made king by the goddess Ishtar.

---

[14] Brevard Childs finds the theological or canonical shape of the book of Exodus not so much in its broad divisions, which are less than distinct, as in the forms of certain smaller units, such as the legal corpus of chapters 19–24, the narratives of the broken and restored covenant (chs. 32–34), and the descriptions of the ordering and building of the tabernacle (chs. 25–31, 35–40). Thus, the structural focus of the book, he concludes, falls on certain specific moments within the Exodus history, rather than on broad narrative sequence as such. See his *Introduction to the Old Testament as Scripture* pp. 170–179; and compare the more detailed exegesis in idem, *The Book of Exodus; A Critical, Theological Commentary.*

Wall painting from Thebes (XVIII Dynasty, c. 1450 B.C.), showing brickmakers. (Courtesy of the Metropolitan Museum of Art, Egyptian Expedition, Rogers Fund, 1930.)

> My changeling mother conceived me, in secret
> she bore me,
> She set me in a basket of rushes, with bitumen
> she sealed my lid.
> She cast me into the river which rose not over me.
> The river bore me up and carried me to Akki,
> the drawer of water.
> Akki, the drawer of water, lifted me out
> as he dipped in his ewer.
> Akki, the drawer of water, took me as his
> son and reared me.[15]

Other heroes of the East, including Cyrus the Great,[16] are subjects of legends involving the same motifs: a brush with death as a child, providen-

---

[15] *ANET*, p. 119 (*ANE*, pp. 85–86). See further Dorothy Irvin, "The Joseph and Moses stories as Narrative in the Light of Ancient Near Eastern Narrative," pp. 191–193; Otto Rank, *The Myth of the Birth of the Hero* (New York: Vintage Books, 1959); and Brevard S. Childs, "The Birth of Moses," *JBL*, LXXIV (1965), pp. 109–122.

[16] Herodotus I, 108ff.

155

tial escape, and a subsequent rise to leadership and prominence. The object of such accounts was to demonstrate the providence which had guided the hero safely to his appointed role as deliverer of his people, as well as to reflect the troubled history out of which the people themselves had emerged. In the case at hand the threat against the infant Moses bespeaks the near annihilation of the Hebrew people as a whole. But, the account is saying, Yahweh had other plans.

THE CALL OF MOSES. Moses' identity with his people is demonstrated in the first action recorded of him (2:11ff.). Seeing an Egyptian taskmaster beating a Hebrew slave, he intervenes on the slave's behalf and kills the Egyptian. Then, fearing for his life, he flees to the land of Midian, where he finds a home with a sheepherding clan of Kenites headed by a priest variously called Jethro, Reuel, and Hobab.[17] Here he remains for an indefinite period of time, but long enough to take Jethro's daughter Zipporah as his wife and become the father of a son (2:21–22).[18] Whether the locale of Moses' exile was Midian proper, located east of the Gulf of Aqabah on the western side of the Arabian desert, or the Sinai Peninsula, into which such Bedouin clans doubtless migrated, is a point of debate.[19] The question involves the uncertain location of Mount Sinai (Horeb), since "the mountain of God" is indicated as the site of Moses' call (3:1) while tending his father-in-law's flocks.[20]

The account of the call (Ex. 3:1–4:17) is composed of J and E traditions; the portion containing the revelation of the name Yahweh (3.9–15) is Elohistic. Although the story is replete with the theophanic elements of a bush that burns without being consumed, an angel, and a voice from the bush, the reader is also apprised of the peculiar psychological factors impinging upon the exiled Hebrew, influences powerful enough—from the human standpoint—to have provoked such a vision. The notation which prefaces the account (2:23–25) explains that the pharaoh under whom Moses fled Egypt is now dead, but that the plight of the Hebrews has not improved; they continue to groan under their bondage and cry out for help. The most plausible date for these conditions, according to some interpreters, is the year 1290 B.C., just following the death of Seti I and at the beginning of Rameses II's reign.

The narrative is chiefly concerned with Yahweh's intervention on the Hebrews' behalf: he *sees* their afflictions, *hears* their cry under the Egyp-

[17] Cf. Ex. 2:18; 3:1; 4:18; 18:1–2, 5–6, 12; Num. 10:29; Judg. 4:11. For a detailed examination of the Midianite/Kenite elements in the Moses story, cf. Roland de Vaux, *The Early History of Israel*, pp. 330–338.

[18] The implication of 4:25 (J) is that Moses' son is quite young (of circumcision age) at the time of the return to Egypt, suggesting a sojourn in Midian of a few years at most; in Priestly tradition (7:7) Moses was assumed to have reached the ripe old age of eighty.

[19] Cf. Roland de Vaux, *The Early History of Israel*, pp. 332–333.

[20] See below, p. 168.

tian taskmasters, *knows* their sufferings, and *comes down* to deliver them (3:7). His plan, however, calls for the enlistment of Moses: "Come, I will send you to Pharaoh" (3:10). When Moses withdraws from such a demanding commission, protesting his inadequacy (3:11), Yahweh pledges his support, which will more than compensate for the Hebrew's weakness: "But I will be with you" (3:12). What is more, God offers a sign—not some extraordinary wonder adduced as proof of his words, but a promise dependent on faith: Moses will bring the people of Israel back to the very spot where he now stands, and here they will engage in the service of God.[21]

It is at this point in the dialogue that the Elohist records a second protestation of Moses, and one which leads to the revelation of God's personal name "Yahweh." As we have seen, the Yahwist had already employed the name, conceiving of its use since the days of Enosh (Gen. 4:26). But in Elohistic (and Priestly) tradition it is used here for the first time. Moses contends that his people will question him concerning the deity whom he represents and thus asks for God's name (3:13). The reply which God gives him is threefold: (a) *"ehyeh 'asher 'ehyeh,"* usually translated "I am who I am," or "I will be what I will be"; (b) "Say this to the people of Israel, *'ehyeh* (I am) has sent me to you' "; (c) "Say this to the people of Israel, 'Yahweh, the God of your fathers, the God of Abraham, the God of Isaac, and the God of Jacob, has sent me to you'." The first two phases of God's response are highly enigmatic, as the endless number of interpretive treatises on the subject readily attests.[22] Apparently the Elohist intends to show the connection between the name Yahweh, and the Hebrew verb *hayah* ("to be"), of which *'ehyeh* is the first-person singular and Yahweh (or *Yih*ᵉ*yeh*, or *yih*ᵉ*weh;* the Hebrew was written without vowels) the third-person singular. By one interpretation, God is presenting himself to Moses as the one who is ever present with his people, a real and ready ally in their cause. This would fit well with God's pledge *to be with* Moses as he returns to Egypt to take up the cause of his enslaved people (3:11). Others would prefer to alter the text slightly so as to cast God's words in a causative form: "I cause to be what I cause to be" (or, what occurs).[23] This rendering captures the dynamic element in the Hebrew descriptions of Yahweh, who is in no case a god of static being but ever the Lord of historical process, who acts creatively and providentially in the whole realm of human experience. The response thus becomes an assertion of his creative lordship.

Yet another approach to this provocative passage understands Yahweh's response as intentionally evasive and cryptic and tantamount to a refusal to

[21] Martin Buber, *Moses* (New York: Harper Torchbooks, 1958), pp. 46–47.

[22] On the revelation of the divine name, see Roland de Vaux, *The Early History of Israel*, pp. 338–357, and the bibliography cited there.

[23] Cf. W. F. Albright, *From the Stone Age to Christianity*, pp. 258–261, and Frank M. Cross, "Yahweh and the God of the Patriarchs," *HTR*, LV (1962), p. 253.

give his name.[24] In Semitic thought a name was not simply a convenient label, but an expression of a person's inmost being. Parents chose the names for their children with utmost care so as to express their individually distinctive character—real or imagined; and, as we have seen in the examples of Abraham and Jacob, radical change in a man's character might result in his receiving a new name to express it. To know the name, moreover, was to possess a degree of power over its bearer. Thus Jacob in his wrestling bout with the divine being at the Jabbok (Gen. 32:22–32) seeks to learn his assailant's name that he might use it against him. Yahweh's words to Moses, perhaps, rebuke him for attempting to get a similar hold upon deity. God is the possessor and not the possessed. He refuses therefore to give his name to be used as a magic formula with which to call down miracles. He shows himself to be free to act wherever and through whomever he will; and he prefers to be known by the mighty deed that he is about to enact for Israel. Martin Buber suggests an apt paraphrase for Yahweh's enigmatic words which does justice to both their revelatory and reticent aspects:

> If the first part of the statement ["I am"] states: "I do not need to be conjured for I am always with you," the second ["Who I am"] adds: "but it is impossible to conjure me."[25]

Quite apart from the interpretation of the call story is the question of the etymological origins of the name Yahweh. The tradition (E and P) that depicts Moses as first introducing the name to the Hebrews in Egypt is supported by the fact that Hebrew personal names compounded with abbreviations of the name Yahweh (e.g., Joshua, which means "Yahweh is salvation"; Elijah, "Yahweh is my God") are not attested earlier than Moses's day.[26] Frank Cross traces the name to an ancient sentence-name for the Canaanite high god El, whereby the biblical *Yahweh Sebaoth* ("Yahweh of Hosts") is taken as meaning, originally, "(El who) creates the hosts."[27] According to the so-called Kenite hypothesis, Yahweh was originally the tribal god of the clan of Kenites headed by Moses' father-in-law Jethro. From them Moses allegedly first learned of the name and worship of Yahweh.[28] Jethro, it is noted, was a priest and officiated as such over a sacrifice and

[24] Martin Buber, *Moses*, pp. 52ff.

[25] Ibid., pp. 52–53. Compare other interpretations discussed in Brevard Childs *The Book of Exodus; A Critical, Theological Commentary*, pp. 47–89.

[26] The etymology of "Jochebed" is uncertain. If it is a Yahweh name (e.g., "Yahweh is glory") and authentic, it would point to worship of Yahweh by Moses' family before his birth.

[27] *Canaanite Myth and Hebrew Epic: Essays in the History of the Religion of Israel*, pp. 60–75.

[28] First proposed by R. Ghillany in 1862, the theory was popularized by Karl Budde in *Religion of Israel to the Exile* (New York: G. P. Putnam's Sons, 1899). For a more recent defense of the view see H. H. Rowley, *From Joseph to Joshua* (London: Oxford University Press, 1951), pp. 149–160. Roland de Vaux, *The Early History of Israel*, pp. 333–338, provides an insightful critique.

common meal in which all the elders of Israel were participants (Exod. 18). This, according to the hypothesis, was the rite whereby the Hebrews were initiated into the Yahweh cult. That some of the Kenites actually accompanied the Israelites into Canaan (Judg. 1:16; 4:11, 17; I Sam. 15:6) is offered as further evidence. The zealous Yahweh-worshipping Rechabites (II Kings 10:15–17, 23; I Chron. 2:55; Jer. 35:1–19) were among their descendants.

The Kenite hypothesis obviously has its strengths and should not be rejected out of hand as diminishing the significance of Moses. Proponents of the view, in fact, see in Moses' act of choosing the Yahweh religion— and, conversely, Yahweh's choice of the Hebrew people—a mark of the high ethical character of the Hebrew religion. According to Karl Budde, one of the early advocates of the theory, "Israel's religion became ethical because it was a religion of choice and not of nature, because it rested on voluntary decision which established an ethical relation between the people and its god for all time." [29] The weakness of the theory is its failure to account for the strong and ancient tradition (J) that Yahweh had been known by the Hebrew fathers prior to Moses and the difficulty of understanding how Moses could have induced his people to leave Egypt under the guidance of a god of whom they knew absolutely nothing. [30] In view of the evidence that the later Israel was constituted of not one, but a number of tribal groups, some of whom were not involved in the Egyptian Bondage and Exodus, it seems best to suppose that among Israel's pre-Mosaic precursors there had been at least one Yahweh-worshiping group. Theophile Meek makes a strong case for identifying that element with the southern Palestinian tribe of Judah. [31] The geographical proximity of the Judahites and Kenites, furthermore, makes it easy to conceive of a Yahweh kinship between the two.

If this be correct, then Moses (as claimed by E and P) brought to the Hebrews in Egypt the revelation of a god in whose name they had not personally worshiped, but (consistent with J) one who was not totally unknown to them. The compelling power of Moses and the faith which he espoused is seen in his ability to persuade the enslaved Hebrews that Yahweh had truly chosen them. His appeal was that he brought no "new god," but the god of the fathers. Like the patriarchal god, Yahweh comes to the people on his own initiative and promises to go with them on the paths into which he sends them. [32] Only the event of the Exodus itself, however, was powerful enough to vindicate and sustain Moses' claim.

The JE account of the call includes, in all, four protests of Moses against his commission. In addition to his pleas of inadequacy (3:11) and lack of

---

[29] *Religion of Israel to the Exile*, p. 38.
[30] Theophile J. Meek, *Hebrew Origins* (New York: Harper Torchbooks, 1960), p. 96.
[31] Ibid., pp. 111–118.
[32] Cf. Martin Buber, *Moses*, pp. 43–44.

Statue of Rameses II (1290–1224 B.C.), probable pharaoh of the Exodus. (Courtesy of Alinari/Editorial Photocolor Archives.)

God's name (3:13), he complains that the people will not believe him (4:1) and that he lacks the necessary eloquence (4:10). The granting of the miraculous signs (4:1–9) is written from the perspective of the plague miracles which follow and bears the marks of an interpolation; the "sign" which Yahweh offers in 3:12 is of an entirely different sort.[33] When Moses cites his poor manner of speech, Yahweh appoints Aaron his brother to be his "mouth" (4:10–17). "You shall be to him as God," says Yahweh, which is to say that Aaron is related to Moses as his spokesman in the same way as Moses himself speaks at Yahweh's direction (cf. 7:1).

[33] Ibid., pp. 46–47.

The narrative of the return to Egypt is beset with difficulties that manifest the patchwork fashion in which it was pieced together from different traditions. On the one hand, Moses is accompanied by his wife Zipporah and "his sons" (4:20); elsewhere there is mention of only one son (2:22; 4:25; but cf. 18:3–4) and an otherwise unexplained tradition that Moses at some point sent his wife and children back to Midian (18:2–3). Aaron joins Moses, moreover, "at the mountain of God" after the party has already departed Midian (4:27). The strange and eerie story of Yahweh's unprovoked attack upon Moses (4:24–26), which Zipporah wards off by circumcising their son, makes little sense in its context. The episode is but a fragment of an account which possibly concerned a demon of the particular "lodging place" where Moses and his family spend the night. Fused with it, presumably, is a legend of Zipporah's circumcision of Moses on the occasion of their marriage or betrothal, conceived as a rite efficacious for deterring the demon which according to folklore claimed the bride on her wedding night (cf. Tobit 3:8, 6:13–8:17). Among the possible explanations for the incorporation of the primitive account at this point in the Exodus narrative is that suggested by Martin Buber: as an indication of the sudden collapse of the newly won certainty experienced by Moses, and Yahweh's impression upon him of the fullness of devotion required for his task.[34] Johannes Pedersen, who stresses the cultic orientation of the Exodus narratives, views it, however, as an emphasis upon circumcision as the prerequisite for participation in the Passover (Exod. 12).[35]

THE PLAGUES. Exodus 5–15 presents Moses' dramatic confrontations with the Pharaoh and the consequences to which they lead. From the initial petition for the release of the Hebrew slaves that they might worship Yahweh in the wilderness (ch. 5) to their ultimate escape from Egypt (chs. 14–15), the drama focuses upon the two strong-willed antagonists. The real contest, however, to which all else is subordinated, is the conflict between the Pharaoh and Moses' god. Not only is the freedom of the Hebrews at stake, but the crucial question of who controls history: the Pharaoh, incarnation of the sun god, or Yahweh, Lord of the slaves.

The element of suspense is heightened in these accounts through the insurmountable obstacles which have to be overcome before the oppressor can be made to yield. Moses' first audience with the Pharaoh (5:1–5) results only in a worsening of the lot of the hapless slaves (5:6–21). Refusing to recognize the unknown Yahweh and his claims, the Pharaoh imposes upon them the added burden of gathering their own straw for making the

---

[34] Ibid., p. 58.

[35] *Israel*, Vols. III–IV, p. 736. Dorothy Irvin also perceives the necessity of circumcision as the intent of the story, but explains it against the background of an ancient Egyptian folk tale ("The Joseph and Moses stories as narrative in the light of ancient Near Eastern narrative," pp. 193–194).

bricks with which to build his cities. The morale of the Hebrews reaches such a low level that Moses can evoke in them no response of faith (6:9); and reassurances are necessary for assuaging his own doubts (5:22–6:1). The stage is thus set for Yahweh's action, which alone can break the Pharaoh's stubborn will.

The deliverance does not come at once, but is preceded by an extended narrative recounting ten scourges brought by Yahweh, only with the last of which does the Pharaoh finally yield. The plague narrative (7:8–11:10) is composed of elements attributed to each of the J, E, P traditions.[36] None of the three sources, however, reports all ten scourges. According to the usual reckoning, the Yahwist recorded seven (numbers 1, 2, 4, 5, 7, 8, and 10; the identical ones mentioned in Ps. 78:43–57); the Elohist, five (numbers 1, 7, 8, 9, and 10); and the Priestly writer, five (numbers 1, 2, 3, 6, and 10). Only the first and the last plagues, the pollution of the Nile and the death of the first-born, are mentioned in all three sources. The flies and the diseased cattle are exclusive to J; gnats and boils appear only in P; darkness, only in E (see chart).

The descriptions of the plagues are marked by a variety of forms; no two of them are related in exactly the same manner. One can detect, nevertheless, a pattern basic to the oldest stratum (J), which is seen in its full form in the first, fourth, seventh, and eighth scourges. It begins with Yahweh's directions to Moses to go before the Pharaoh ("Go to Pharaoh and say to him") and petition for the release of the slaves ("Let my people go"), warning the king of what will befall if he refuses ("Else if you will not let my people go, behold I will . . ."). Moses does as he is bidden; and, though in only one instance (the eighth plague) are the negotiations actually recounted, the Pharaoh's rejection is in each case understood. Thus Yahweh brings on the scourge of which he has warned ("And Yahweh did so"). Only then does the frightened monarch summon Moses and agree to Yahweh's terms ("The Pharaoh called Moses and said, 'Entreat Yahweh to remove . . .' "). Accordingly, Moses petitions Yahweh to remove the plague ("So Moses went out from the Pharaoh and prayed to Yahweh."). Once freed from the scourge, however, the Pharaoh breaks his agreement and refuses to let the Hebrews go ("But Pharaoh hardened his heart, and did not let the people go.").

The pattern is somewhat different in the Priestly versions, as seen most clearly in the plagues unique to that source: the gnats and boils. The preliminary negotiations with the Pharaoh are in each instance omitted. Yahweh simply calls for the scourge, which is brought on by Aaron's rod ("Say to Aaron, 'stretch out your rod . . .' "; "Aaron stretched out his hand . . ."), after which the court magicians attempt to match the feat with their

---

[36] Scholarly opinion has differed on the question of the E material in Ex. 7–12; cf. J. L. Mihelic and G. E. Wright, "Plagues in Exodus," *IDB*, K–Q, pp. 822–824.

THE PLAGUES *	
1. Nile to blood	J—7:14–15ª, 16–17ª, 17ᶜ–18, 20ᶜ–21ª E—7:15ᵇ, 17ᵇ, 20ᵇ, 23–25 P—7:19–20ª, 21ᵇ–22
2. Frogs	J—8:1–4, 8–15ª P—8:5–7, 15ᵇ
3. Gnats	P—8:16–19
4. Flies	J—8:20–32
5. Cattle disease	J—9:1–7
6. Boils	P—8:8–12
7. Hail	J—9:13–21, 23ᵇ, 24ᵇ, 25ᵇ, 34 E—9:22–23ª, 24ª, 25ª, 35
8. Locusts	J—10:1–11, 13ᵇ, 14ᵇ–15ª, 15ᶜ–19, 24–26, 28–29 E—10:12–13ª, 14ª, 15ᵇ, 20
9. Darkness	E—10:21–23, 27
10. Death of first-born	J—11:4–8; 12:21–27, 29–36 E—11:1–3 P—11:9–10; 12:1–20, 28

* According to S. R. Driver, *Introduction to the Literature of the Old Testament*, rev. ed., pp. 24–29.

own magic ("the magicians tried by their secret arts . . ."). Only in the first two plagues are they successful; but the Pharaoh remains unmoved ("But the Pharaoh's heart was hardened . . ."). Aaron plays a much more prominent role here than in JE; he, and not Moses, wields the marvelous rod. What is wrought, moreover, is not simply a scourge to bring more pressure on the Pharaoh, but a sign and wonder reflective of Yahweh's unmatched control of the world.

The stereotyped features and high drama of these accounts do not, of course, rule out the possibility of a series of historic events as a nucleus around which they grew. The plagues have often been interpreted according to the natural phenomena common to Egypt. Some would even reconstruct the causal relationships by which one plague followed the other.[37] The Nile, as it crests in late summer, often takes on a reddish color owing to a large number of tiny organisms. Scourges of frogs are not unknown, particularly in early autumn, and might be expected to follow upon a pollution of the Nile waters. Large numbers of dead frogs could account for gnats and flies, in turn, spreading the plague to cattle and human beings. Hail storms in Egypt are rare, but not unknown; and locusts and spring

[37] G. Ernest Wright, *Biblical Archaeology*, rev. ed. (Philadelphia: The Westminster Press, 1962), p. 54.

dust storms, sometimes severe enough to darken the skies, are familiar enough.

No amount of rationalizing of this sort, however, can fully account for the wonder element in these stories. They were recited by the faithful in Israel precisely because the events which they describe were viewed as something more than natural happenings. The providential timing with which they occur and the exemption of the Hebrews themselves from the afflictions suffered by the Egyptians are essential to the stories' meanings. Convinced that the Exodus had happened by Yahweh's designs, Israel interpreted the events leading to it as an integral part of his overall plan, paving the way for what was to come. That Israel's faith encouraged a broad freedom in the handling of history in these stories is owing to nothing else so much as a passion for conveying the wonder of the Exodus itself. Methodically and purposefully, each episode sustains the tension as it builds to its climax. At every turn, action is blocked by the Pharaoh's "hardening" of his heart. Yet the reader is never in doubt as to what the outcome will be; for, viewed from the faith perspective, Yahweh is moving all toward the imminent deliverance which he has determined. He it is who hardens the Pharaoh's heart that he might show his signs and wonders through him.

One must bear in mind, of course, that the ancient Hebrew did not view nature as governed by natural laws in the way that we do today. The world, as he conceived it, was altogether and constantly open to God's personal designs. In one sense, all that happened day by day was at his direction. Such common phenomena as the rising of the sun and the falling of the rain were nothing short of divine actions. In the crucial events depicted in the Exodus stories, however, Hebrew faith sensed Yahweh's special intervention for his people's deliverance; hence the interest in depicting the unusual—in our terms, miraculous—pattern by which he made nature serve his purpose. In only one other portion of the Old Testament, the Elijah and Elisha stories (I Kings 17–II Kings 13), do we find as large a number of wonders concentrated in a single unit of scripture.

THE PASSOVER. The tenth plague, the death of the Egyptian first-born, occupies a special role in the Exodus narrative. It is the climactic scourge which breaks the Pharaoh's stubborn will, giving the Hebrews their chance at freedom. It also provides an interpretation—though after the fact—of Israel's most prominent and probably its oldest religious festival: the Passover (Hebrew: *pesah*). The feast actually developed independently of the Exodus tradition, having originated as a pastoral celebration of the birth of new lambs at the first full moon of spring. The original meaning of the name is unknown, but it came to be explained in terms of the "passing over," and hence the sparing, of the Hebrew households by the destroying angel in Egypt. By connecting the ancient *pesah* rites with the Exodus events (12:1–20; 12:40–13:2, P; 12:21–27, 29, J), Israel gave to them a new set of meanings which converted them into a commemoration of her historic deliverance. The smearing of the entrance to the tents with lambs' blood, originally designed to protect the flocks from evil spirits, became the identifying mark by which the Hebrews escaped the final scourge visited upon the Egyptians (12:21–27). The *pesaḥ* meal, with its traditional elements of roasted lamb, bitter herbs, and unleavened bread (a shepherd's fare), now memorialized the final preparations for Israel's hasty departure. Together with the prescriptions for the Passover, there are also incorporated here the rites for the Feast of Unleavened Bread (12:14–20, P; 13:3–10, J), an agricultural festival, and the dedication of the first-born (13:1–2, P; 13:11–16, J).

THE SEA OF REEDS. The number of the Hebrew slaves and other Habiru ("a mixed multitude"; 12:38) that fled Egypt is unknown. The 600,000 males (men of fighting age) mentioned in Exodus 12:37 is much too large a figure and appears to be based on a later census list.[38] By such reckoning we should have to imagine some two to three million persons in all, more than the desert of Sinai could have possibly supported. Three to five thousand has been suggested as a reasonable figure.[39] Even so, all such estimates remain little more than guesses, and serve as a further reminder that the essential message of these accounts lies in the wonder with which later Israel viewed the experiences of their Exodus forebears.

From the very beginning, the Hebrews' successful escape is providentially engineered by Yahweh. It is he who charts their course, going before them by day in a pillar of cloud and by night in a pillar of fire (13:21). The coastal route that went most directly from the Egyptian delta to Canaan, the "Way of the Land of the Philistines," is avoided with good reason (13:17). This much traveled commercial and military highway was tightly guarded by a line of Egyptian fortifications. The chosen route went first to Succoth, some 32 miles to the southeast of Avaris, and from there followed "the way of the wilderness by the Reed Sea" (13:18). The familiar translation of the Hebrew name *yam suph* as Red Sea can hardly be correct. The words literally mean sea of reeds or papyrus marsh; and reeds do not grow in the vicinity of the Red Sea or its northern extension, the Gulf of Suez.[40] It is furthermore unthinkable that the fleeing Hebrews could have gotten as far as the Red Sea without having been overtaken by the Egyptians, not to mention the feat of crossing such a mighty body of water, once having

---

[38] Num. 1 and 26, which are doubtless based on still later lists, record the number of males as slightly over 600,000.

[39] G. Ernest Wright, *Biblical Archaeology*, p. 66.

[40] The confusion of *yam suph* with Red Sea is probably due to the Septuagint, where the Hebrew is so translated. This rendering passed into English translations by way of the Vulgate.

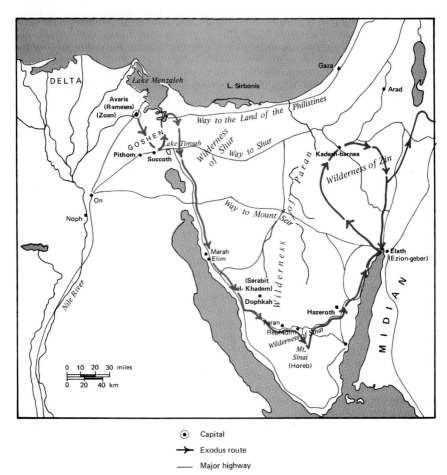

○ Capital

→ Exodus route

—— Major highway

Traditional route of the Exodus. (Adapted with permission of Macmillan Publishing Co., Inc., from Macmillan Bible Atlas *by Y. Aharoni and Michael Avi-Yonah. Copyright © 1968 Carta, Jerusalem. © Copyright 1964 by Carta, Jerusalem. © Copyright 1966 by Carta, Jerusalem.)*

arrived there. Papyrus marshes are attested, however, in the region of the modern Suez canal, between Lake Menzaleh and the Suez Gulf. It was most probably in this region, perhaps at the southern extension of Lake Menzaleh, that our accounts envision the Hebrews, after backtracking from Succoth (14:2), being overtaken by the Pharaoh's army.

Viewed through the eyes of Israel's faith, the event at the Sea of Reeds is more than simply the climactic moment for the Exodus narrative. It is the crucial turning point, prior to which there was only a heterogeneous collection of frightened, disorganized slaves, and after which there existed a people whose corporate experience of deliverance bore the potential of a nation's birth. The oldest record of the event is the poetic couplet ascribed to Miriam (15:21; E).

> Sing to the Lord, for he has triumphed
> gloriously;
> The horse and his rider he has thrown
> into the sea.

The vivid, primitive character of these lines is such as to suggest an origin not far removed in time from the event which it celebrates. That the longer poem contained in 15:1–18 is a later expansion of the shorter couplet may be deduced from its quotation of the latter verse at its beginning, as well as its allusions to later events (vss. 13–17).[41]

The narrative record of the Reed Sea crossing (ch. 14) consists of a blending of Yahwistic and Priestly versions. The following excerpts account for the major contrasts between the two.

J	P
(21b) . . . and the Lord drove the sea back by a strong east wind all night, and made the sea dry land . . .	(21a, c) Then Moses stretched out his hand over the sea . . . and the waters were divided.
(24) And in the morning watch the Lord . . . looked down upon the host of the Egyptians . . .	(22) And the people of Israel went into the midst of the sea on dry ground, the waters becoming a wall to them on their right hand and on their left.
(25) clogging their chariot wheels so that they drove heavily; and the Egyptians said, "Let us flee from before Israel; for the Lord fights for them against the Egyptians."	(23) The Egyptians pursued, and went after them into the midst of the sea, all Pharaoh's horses, his chariots, and his horsemen.
(27) . . . and the sea returned to its wonted flow when the morning appeared . . . and the Lord routed the Egyptians in the midst of the sea.	(26) Then the Lord said to Moses, "Stretch out your hand over the sea that the water may come back upon the Egyptians . . ."
	(27a) So Moses stretched forth his hand over the sea . . .
	(28a) The waters returned and covered the chariots and all the host of Pharaoh . . .

In the older (J) account the waters of the marshy lake are swept back by a nocturnal east wind, a phenomenon none too difficult to conceive. Obscured by a cloudy darkness from the enemy encamped at their rear, the Hebrews cross over during the night. With the dawn the Egyptians pursue the same path, but with disastrous results; the abating of the wind and the

[41] Cf. Frank M. Cross and David N. Freedman, "The Song of Miriam," JNES, 14 (1955), pp. 237–250; Frank M. Cross, Canaanite Myth and Hebrew Epic, pp. 112–144; Brevard S. Childs, The Book of Exodus, pp. 240–253.

immobility of the heavy chariots in the muddy lake lead to their destruction. Thus through the providential ordering of the natural elements of wind and water, the Hebrews are saved. A comparison with the P account reveals the manner in which the wonder element grew through repeated retellings. Here, the miracle is brought on by the waving of Moses' rod, and the waters stand up like walls to allow the Hebrews passage. Though the versions differ, the faith element in all three—J, E, and P—is essentially the same; the victory is Yahweh's. In the moment of crisis he vindicates Moses' claims, revealing himself as the defender of the Hebrews' cause and setting into motion his plans for Israel's future as the people of God.[42]

Guidance in the Wilderness: Reed Sea to Sinai

Archaeology has been of little help in efforts to determine the route taken by the Hebrews after departing the Sea of Reeds. The immediate destination was Mount Sinai, the site of Moses' call. But neither the mountain itself nor the oases along the route can be located with certainty. Some see evidence of volcanic activity in the description of the Sinai theophany (Exod. 19), and accordingly locate the holy mountain east of the Gulf of Aqabah in Midian, a volcanic region. It is doubtful, however, that the references to the quaking mountain are to be taken so literally. Awesome natural phenomena constitute a familiar feature of Old Testament theophanies; and in this instance storm activity has supplied some of the imagery. Another theory locates the mountain somewhere in the vicinity of Kadesh, an oasis which figures prominently in the wilderness accounts, and in a region (Seir, Paran) linked poetically with Sinai (Deut. 33:2; Judg. 5:4, 5; Hab. 3:3). Yet, according to Deuteronomy 1:2, the journey from Mount Horeb (Sinai) to Kadesh took eleven days. Such a distance is consistent with the traditional identification of the holy mountain with *Jebel Musa* (Arabic for "Mount of Moses"), a 7,500 foot granite outcropping in the southern apex of the Sinai Peninsula. Since the fifth century A.D. Christian tradition has accepted the latter site; the Monastery of Saint Catherine, erected in the sixth century, stands today on its northwest slope. All told, it remains the most likely choice. As G. Ernest Wright comments:

> it is extremely difficult to understand why the early Church would have located the sacred spot in the most inaccessible and dangerous area imaginable for pilgrims . . . unless the tradition was so old and firmly fixed that no debate was permitted about it.[43]

[42] For an interpretation of the Reed Sea event as a military clash between Egyptians and Hebrews, see Lewis S. Hay, "What Really Happened at the Sea of Reeds?" *JBL*, LXXXIII (1964), pp. 397–403.

[43] *Biblical Archaeology*, p. 64. For other alternatives, cf. Menahem Haran, "Exodus, the," *IDBS*, pp. 304–310.

Traditional Mount Sinai (Jebel Musa), showing St. Catherine's Monastery at its base. (Courtesy of the Consulate General of Israel in New York.)

Of infinitely greater significance than the wilderness itinerary as such are the events connected with it, their corporate effect upon the nascent Israel, and the meaning that faith attached to them.[44] Though idealized by some of Israel's prophets as Yahweh's "honeymoon" with his newly acquired people,[45] the wilderness era is depicted in these accounts as a period of hardship, testing, and rebellion. Notwithstanding all that Yahweh had done in their deliverance, the emancipated slaves, once confronted with the rigors of desert life, complain of their precarious freedom and long for the safety of Egyptian bondage. It is this very murmuring, nevertheless, that lends to the narrative its most acute sense of Yahweh's providential control over his

[44] On the wilderness traditions, see especially Brevard Childs, *The Book of Exodus*, pp. 254–264, where the murmuring element is viewed as a part of the oldest tradition. For other interpretations, cf. George W. Coats, *Rebellion in the Wilderness* (Nashville TN: Abingdon Press, 1968), and Simon J. De Vries, "The Origins of the Murmuring Tradition," *JBL*, LXXXVII (1968), pp. 51–58.

[45] Hos. 2:17; Jer. 2:2; but cf. Ezek. 20:10f.

people's destiny. Even in the face of their stubborn resistance, he does not abandon them. Another prophetic metaphor grasps the wilderness theme perfectly:

> When Israel was a child, I loved him,
> and out of Egypt, I called my son.
> Hos. 11:1

The desert sojourn is viewed as Israel's childhood, when under the most austere conditions Yahweh taught his fledglings the necessity of discipline and trust for fulfilling their mission as the people of God.

The major threats posed by the desert were lack of food and water and attack by hostile tribes. Moses, as Yahweh's gifted representative, provided the needed leadership in the utilization of such resources as were to be had, the discovery of hidden desert springs and the challenge to courageous faith in clashes with the enemy. His ability to inspire his followers is dramatically depicted in the account of the battle against the Amalekites (17:8–13). While Joshua led the attack, Moses stood on a hill in full view of his men, arms outstretched to heaven. The effect on the Hebrews was decisive.

> And Joshua mowed down Amalek and his people with the edge of the sword.
> Exod. 17:13

Israel recalled especially the manna and quail as indications of Yahweh's miraculous provisions for his hungry people. These stories are related to actual phenomena which may be observed in the Sinai Peninsula today. Manna can be identified with the small honeydew pellets produced by excretions of scale insects that suck the sap of the tamarisk plant.[46] In some localities it appears in abundance in the morning hours of early summer, before being carried off by ants. Although it was hardly sufficient to have supplied the daily fare for the Israelites, its tasty sweetness could have provided a welcome supplement to a scanty Bedouin diet. Flocks of quail from the Mediterranean area cross the Sinai on their autumn migrations to Africa and Arabia, and again in flights northward in the spring. When alighting en route to refresh themselves, the birds are exhausted and thus easily caught.

The Covenant at Sinai

Exodus 19 is a transition chapter. It brings the narrative of the wilderness period to the locale of Mount Sinai-Horeb (in J and P, Sinai; in E, Horeb) and introduces the setting for the great block of legal material which follows (Exod. 20—Num. 10:10). The narrative does not actually end at this point; rather, the codes of law are woven together by means of a

---

[46] Cf. F. S. Bodenheimer, "The Manna of Sinai," *BA*, X (1947), pp. 2–6. Reprinted in *BA Reader*, I, pp. 76–80.

contrived narrative framework, whereby Yahweh instructs Moses and he in turn either informs the people or else (as in the case of the regulations governing the tabernacle and ark) carries out the prescriptions on the spot. For the sake of clarity, we shall withhold consideration of the law codes for the moment, in order to follow the narrative.

The covenant ceremony at the holy mountain is described in chapters 19 and 24. Though separated by the insertion of the Decalogue (20:1–17) and The Covenant Code (20:22–23:33), both chapters describe the same event: chapter 19, the preparations for it, and chapter 24, the ceremony itself. In the account of the preparations God apprises Moses of the terms of the covenant: if the Hebrews will but acknowledge that it is Yahweh who delivered them from Egypt and, as a consequence of that fact, will obey his voice and keep the law which he is about to reveal, they will be his people—a kingdom of priests and a holy nation. Moses delivers this word to the people, and the people respond: "All that Yahweh has spoken we will do." Thus, Yahweh instructs Moses to prepare for a meeting between himself and the people. They are to wash their garments and consecrate themselves for three days. On the third day the mountain is wrapped in smoke because, we are told, the Lord descended upon it in fire.

The two accounts are each constituted of J and E elements, which relate two different versions of the covenant ceremony itself. In the Yahwistic version (24:1–2, 9–11) the ceremony is on top of the mountain. There Moses, Aaron, Aaron's sons, and seventy elders meet with Yahweh and, as representatives of the people, bind the covenant by eating a sacred meal in God's presence. In the Elohistic account (24:3–8, 12–14) the whole assembly of the people meet God at the foot of the mountain and make a vow to keep his law: "All the words which the Lord has spoken we will do." Moses erects an altar there along with twelve pillars to represent the twelve tribes. Animal sacrifices are offered from which the blood is drained and dashed in equal portions against the altar and the people.

In recent years considerable new light has been shed on ancient Near Eastern covenant forms. The blood of the slain animal as a binding factor between covenanting members finds its parallel in the Mari texts, where "to slay an ass" means nothing other than "to make a covenant."[47] As a result of G. E. Mendenhall's and Klaus Baltzer's studies of Hittite treaties, two distinctive covenant forms are now widely acknowledged: (a) parity and (b) suzerainty treaties.[48] The parity or bilateral treaty is one in which the

[47] Martin Noth, *The Laws in the Pentateuch and Other Studies* (Philadelphia: Fortress Press, 1967), pp. 108–117.

[48] George E. Mendenhall, *Law and Covenant in Israel and the Near East*, and "Covenant," *IDB*, A-D, pp. 714–723; Klaus Baltzer, *The Covenant Formulary in Old Testament, Jewish and Early Christian Writings*, David E. Green, trans. (Philadelphia: Fortress Press, 1971). Cf. also Walter Beyerlin, *Origins and History of the Oldest Sinaitic Traditions*, Stanley Rodman, trans. (Oxford: Basil Blackwell, 1965), pp. 50ff., and Delbert R. Hillers, *Covenant: The History of a Biblical Idea* (Baltimore, MD: The Johns Hopkins University Press, 1969).

covenant partners are equals, at least insofar as the treaty is concerned. Each member needs the cooperation or support of the other, as, for example, in the covenants between Abraham and other Canaanite princes who enter into mutual pacts respecting pasture and water rights. In some instances stones or altars might be set up as witnesses to each man's pledge, as in the covenant between Jacob and Laban (Gen. 31:44–50). The suzerainty treaty, on the other hand, is arrived at unilaterally; one party to the covenant is more powerful than the other and grants the treaty largely as an act of benevolence. Among the Hittites, such treaties were bestowed by strong kings (suzerains) upon their less powerful vassals. The vassal was thereby promised the protection of the powerful suzerain, offering in return his compliance with such stipulations as his patron should require.

The Sinai covenant is cast in the second of these two forms. Yahweh strikes no bargain here with Israel after the manner of the trading of favors between men. He acts rather as the powerful Lord of history who grants the covenant as a gift to the people of his own free choosing. Having proved his lordship in the Exodus, he now offers a lasting alliance, requiring in return that Israel accept its role as his covenant people and respond in faithfulness to the instruction he offers. It is thus not a favor to be earned, but a grateful response to a love already demonstrated.

Although the Near Eastern suzerainty treaties thus enlighten the broad relationship of law and covenant in ancient Israel, their relevance to the specific form and age of the Sinai tradition is much less certain. It has been alleged, for example, that the formal features of Israel's most famous code of laws, the Decalogue (Exod. 20:1–17; Deut. 5:6–21), were adapted directly from the suzerainty treaty form. In the Hittite treaties six elements have been distinguished: (1) preamble, (2) historical prologue, (3) stipulations, (4) deposit and public reading, (5) lists of witnesses, and (6) curses and blessings.[49] The preamble serves to introduce the "great king" who gives the treaty:

> These are the words of Sun Mursilis, the great king, the king of the Hatti land, the valiant, the favorite of the storm god, the son of Suppiluliumas, the great king, the king of the Hatti land, the valiant.[50]

Similarly, the Decalogue begins, "I am Yahweh your God . . ." (Ex. 20:2a). The historical prologue describes the past history of the suzerain's benevolent deeds on behalf of the vassal, frequently couched in the "I-Thou" form of address. Just so does the preface to the Decalogue include Yahweh's reminder of what he has done for his people: ". . . who brought you out of the land of Egypt, out of the house of bondage" (Exod. 20:2b). The treaty stipulations set forth the vassal's obligations, which without ex-

---

[49] Cf. George E. Mendenhall, *Law and Covenant in Israel and the Near East.*
[50] *ANET*, p. 203.

ception include the promise of undivided allegiance to the great king. The first condition of Israel's covenant with Yahweh is "You shall have no other gods before (or, beside) me" (Exod. 20:3).

A close examination of the Decalogue's wording, however, reveals basic differences from the typical formulas of the Hittite treaties,[51] and the last three elements of the treaty form are missing entirely. The treaties typically contained a clause requiring that a written record of the pact be deposited in the temple of the vassal's city and periodically read to the people. Although Moses is reported to have written down the words of the covenant (Exod. 24:4; 34:27–28), deposited them in the ark (Exod. 25:21; Deut. 10:5), and provided for their public reading at the end of every seven years (Deut. 31:10–11), these elements do not appear in the Decalogue itself. Further, the witnesses required for binding the suzerainty treaties were the gods of the respective parties. Such a pattern could hardly be duplicated in Israel's covenant, since Israel's sovereign Lord was himself a party to the pact. In other Old Testament contexts, it is true, the people themselves are addressed as witnesses (Josh. 24:22); and in a poetic vein the heaven and earth might be so addressed:

> [God] calls to the heavens above,
>   and to the earth, that he may judge
>   his people:
> "Gather to me my faithful ones,
>   who made a covenant with me by
>   sacrifice!"
>
> Ps. 50:4–5

Finally, the Hittite treaties conclude with lists of blessings and curses which set forth the consequences of faithfulness or disloyalty to the covenant oath. The only suggestion of such rewards and sanctions in the Decalogue comes in the explanatory comments of the second and fifth commands; but lengthy hortatory injunctions appear as the concluding portions of other Hebrew codes (Exod. 23:20–33; Lev. 26; Deut. 27, 28; Josh. 8:34).

Even as the influence of the Hittite treaties upon specific Hebrew legal forms is debatable, just as tenuous are the efforts to use such comparisons as proof of the Mosaic origins of Israel's covenant and law. The Late Bronze Age provenance of the Hittite treaties, which corresponds with the Mosaic era, would argue for such a conclusion only if the alleged influences could be demonstrated more persuasively. Although Moses' role as covenant mediator and lawgiver is sufficiently attested in Hebrew tradition as to caution against dismissing it too lightly, the origins of Israelite law and

---

[51] Dennis J. McCarthy, *Treaty and Covenant: A Study in Form in the Ancient Oriental Documents and in the Old Testament,* Analecta Biblica 21 (Rome: Pontifical Biblical Institute, 1963), and *Old Testament Covenant: A Survey of Current Opinions* (Atlanta, GA: John Knox Press, 1973), pp. 33–52.

covenant were undeniably complex and involved a long development of legal and religious tradition which is at best only partially understood. Some modern interpreters trace the beginnings of the law, e.g., the Decalogue, to a covenant tradition reaching all the way back to Sinai,[52] but others regard the period of settlement in Canaan (cf. Josh. 24) as the formative era for both the covenant ceremony and the earliest laws associated with it.[53] In either case, many scholars envision an ongoing cultic institution of covenant renewal extending back into Israel's premonarchical period as the vehicle by which the earliest legal traditions were transmitted. In recent years, however, some have sought the origins of the Decalogue and other apodictic laws (see below) in the traditional instruction of early Israelite family circles, rather than in cultic or ceremonial settings.[54] Also, one notes a current trend to attribute an increasingly greater role to the Deuteronomic authors (seventh century B.C. and later) in the development of the Old Testament covenant theme.[55] It is, therefore, unlikely that we shall arrive at any consensus within the forseeable future on either the age or setting of Israel's earliest covenant and legal traditions.

An issue that has engendered much debate in the recent past concerns the question of whether the Exodus and Sinai episodes were originally united in a single tradition, as depicted in the pentateuchal narrative, or derived from separate Israelite circles, only to be combined at a later time.[56] Von Rad has argued forcefully for the separate origins of the traditions, on the grounds that the Sinai episode is not mentioned in the brief creedal confessions of faith found in the Pentateuch and the Book of Joshua.[57] Artur Weiser, however, has offered a reasonable explanation for the omission, in that the Sinai event is not the same type of event as those celebrated in the credos. The confessions, such as Deuteronomy 26:5–10, recall the redemptive acts performed by Yahweh on Israel's behalf, as in the Exodus and the military victories in Canaan; whereas the Sinai event concerns the encounter between Yahweh and his people, in which Israel

---

[52] E.g., George E. Mendenhall, *Law and Covenant in Israel and the Near East;* Walter Beyerlin, *Origins and History of the Oldest Sinaitic Traditions.* Stanley Rodman, trans. (Oxford: Basil Blackwell, 1965), pp. 50ff.,

[53] E.g., Martin Noth, *The Laws in the Pentateuch and Other Studies,* pp. 12–60; idem, *The History of Israel,* pp. 127–138.

[54] Erhard Gerstenberger, *Wesen und Herkunft des sogenannten apodiktischen Rechts im Alten Testament* (Neukirchen, West Germany: Neukirchener Verlag, 1965), and "Covenant and Commandment," *JBL,* 84 (1965), pp. 38–51. His position is discussed in J. J. Stamm and M. E. Andrew, *The Ten Commandments in Recent Research,* Studies in Biblical Theology, series 2, no. 2 (Naperville, IL: Alec R. Allenson, 1967), pp. 45–54, 68–75, and Eduard Nielsen, *The Ten Commandments in New Perspective,* Studies in Biblical Theology, series 2, no. 7 (Naperville, IL: Alec R. Allenson, 1968), pp. 72–78.

[55] Cf. E. W. Nicholson, *Exodus and Sinai in History and Tradition,* pp. 53–84.

[56] The various positions on this issue, along with a fresh analysis, are discussed in Nicholson, ibid.

[57] Gerhard von Rad, "The Form-Critical Problem of the Hexateuch," in *The Problem of the Hexateuch and Other Essays,* pp. 1–78.

An oasis in the Sinai wilderness. (Courtesy of the Israel Government Tourist Office.)

accepts the commandments of the God who has thus delivered. There appears, then, no definitive reason for concluding that the Sinai tradition originated independently of the Exodus tradition in early Israel.[58]

The J and E accounts of the Sinai covenant have no parallel in the P source. Priestly interest centered rather in the giving of the law. According to this source (24:15–18), Moses spent forty days alone on the mountaintop, receiving the specifications for the building of the ark and the tabernacle (chs. 25–31), all of which he carried out to the letter (chs. 35–40). Sandwiched between these Priestly units are the JE accounts of the apostasy of the golden calf (ch. 32), Moses' continual intercession for the people (33:1–16), and his request to see Yahweh's glory, only to be shown his back (33:17–23). The story of the smashing of the original tablets of law as a result of the people's rebellion (32:19) allows for the introduction of yet another set of laws (ch. 34; J). Then follows the long collection of cultic, legal, and genealogical material (P) which includes the entire book of Leviticus and the early chapters of Numbers.

Guidance in the Wilderness: Sinai to Kadesh

According to Priestly chronology the Hebrews spent nearly a year at Mount Sinai (Exod. 19:1; Num. 10:11) before finally breaking camp and

---

[58] Artur Weiser, *The Old Testament: Its Formation and Development*, Dorothea M. Barton, trans. (New York: Association Press, 1961), p. 86.

setting out toward the Wilderness of Paran. Taking with them the portable ark and tabernacle as evidences of Yahweh's presence and accompanied by Hobab the Kenite, they journey to the vicinity of Kadesh, where the remainder of the traditional forty years in the wilderness is spent (Num. 10:11–20:21). Among the miscellaneous episodes that have their setting here are those that repeat the themes of Exodus 15–18: further murmuring and rebellion, some of it led by Aaron and Miriam; Moses' persistent intercession for the people; and Yahweh's faithful provision of water, manna, and quail.

An abortive effort to enter Palestine by way of the Negeb is related in Numbers 13 and 14. It begins with the dispatching of a scouting party to spy out the southern hill country in the vicinity of Hebron. The spies return with a reconnaissance report describing a fertile land ("flowing with milk and honey"), but one in which there are strongly fortified towns and a giant aboriginal people (13:26^b–31). Consequently, differences of opinion arise among the Israelites as to whether or not they should go up against the land. Caleb and Joshua, members of the reconnaissance force, favor making the attack in spite of the unfavorable odds. A majority are against it, however, and their protest takes the form of a rebellion against Moses. Not even Moses' intercessions in their behalf can prevent Yahweh's decision that none of their number shall see the Land of Promise. The attack upon southern Palestine is launched, but without Yahweh's sanction or the visible presence of Moses and the ark. As a consequence, the Hebrews are soundly defeated and driven back to the desert by the Amorites and Canaanites.

Entry into Transjordan

Having failed in the effort to enter Canaan from the south, Israel, we are told, journeyed eastward and sought access to the King's Highway, a major north-south route joining Damascus and Ezion-geber. When passage through the territories of Edom and Moab was denied, a circuitous detour around the two kingdoms was taken, leading into central Transjordan north of Moab. Israel's earliest military victories in the new land came with the successive defeats of the Amorites in central Transjordan, under their king Sihon (Num. 21:21–32; Deut. 2:26–37; Josh. 24:12), and the kingdom of Og in Bashan (Num. 21:33–35; Deut. 3:1–11). The territory thus conquered included the "Plains of Moab," a region extending some eight miles north of the Dead Sea, formerly controlled by Moab. Here Israel encamped until ready to launch her assault upon the land across the Jordan.

BALAAM. The Balaam episode (chs. 22–24; JE) provides a delightful interlude in the Numbers narrative. Though it adds little of substance to the history of Israel's fortunes in Transjordan, it offers interesting examples of early divining techniques and oracle (curse and blessing) forms. Hired by

Mount Nebo. Located in Transjordan, Mt. Nebo provides a panoramic view of the Jordan Valley and the land to the west. From this peak, we are told, Moses viewed the Land of Promise prior to his death on the Plains of Moab (Deut. 34: 1–4). (Courtesy of the Jordan Ministry of Education.)

Balak of Moab to curse the Israelite camp, Balaam employs the ritual typical of a Mesopotamian *baru* priest, including the search for omens (23:3, 15; 24:1), the early morning hour favored for divining (22:41), and the three (a magical number) thwarted efforts to pronounce the curse (23:7–10, 18–24; 24:3–9).[59] The talking ass lends a note of intentional humor; the dumb beast is more enlightened than his master! Speaking animals are none too unusual in the literature of antiquity (e.g., Achilles' horse Xanathus in the Iliad); but the only other Old Testament parallel is the serpent in the Garden of Eden (Gen. 3). The episode belongs to a version of the story (J) in which Balaam's trip to Moab is treated as an act of disobedience. According to the E version God authorized the journey, providing that, having arrived, Balaam should speak only at God's direction (22:20).

The four oracles in their extant form probably date from the time of the early Israelite monarchy (cf. the allusion to royal symbols in 24:17). They may rest on oracular models, however, as ancient as the thirteenth or twelfth centuries. As in the deathbed blessings of Jacob (Gen. 49) and Moses (Deut. 33), the pre-eminence of Israel is extolled. The insistence here that an oracle is efficacious only when it conforms to Yahweh's will anticipates the later prophetic conception of the divine word.[60] The only foreigner in the Old Testament represented as a conscious agent of Yahweh, Balaam is made to acknowledge:

[59] G. Ernest Wright, *Biblical Archaeology*, p. 73.
[60] See below, pp. 266ff.

> Behold I received a command to
> bless:
> he has blessed, and I cannot
> revoke it.
> 23:20

The story of Moses' last days and death on the Plains of Moab is supplied by the book of Deuteronomy. Following three long farewell speeches, he commissions Joshua as his successor (31:14ff.), gives his final blessing to the Israelite tribes (ch. 33), and climbs to the top of Mount Nebo (Pisgah) for a last look at the Land of Promise. Here, according to the record, he died without ever setting foot in the land across the Jordan.

3. NOW, THEREFORE, IF YOU WILL OBEY MY VOICE: THE LAWS IN THE PENTATEUCH

Set within the context of the mosaic covenant are the several codes of Israelite law, representing a variety of legal tradition and forms and developed over a broad span of Hebrew history. These codes, taken together, comprise the second component of the Torah, combining with the recital of Yahweh's creative and saving deeds the corresponding imperatives through which God's people are themselves to fulfill the divine purpose in creation and redemption. Grounded in the divine-human relationship affirmed by covenant faith, they point the way toward a full expression of that relationship in a divinely ordered community life. As such, there are no conscious distinctions between civil and criminal law, on the one hand, and religious and cultic prescriptions, on the other. Both appear side by side in these collections. In the eyes of faith, Yahweh's claims rest equally on all of life. From the general to the most minute provisions, Israel's law was an attempt at ordering her corporate life according to the purposeful designs of Yahweh's kingship.

Pre-Mosaic Law

As we have observed in connection with the Genesis accounts, a system of legal procedures based on custom was observed by Israel's pre-Mosaic ancestors and other early Near Eastern peoples. The earliest written codes of law thus far discovered are those promulgated by Mesopotamian kings near the beginning of the second millennium B.C.: the codes of Ur-Nammu of Ur (c. 2050 B.C.), Bilalama of Eshnunna (c. 2000 B.C.), Lipit-Ishtar of Isin (c. 2000 B.C.), and Hammurabi of Babylon (c. 1700 B.C.).[61] The best known and preserved of these is the code of Hammurabi, inscribed on a

---

[61] Cf. *ANET*, pp. 161–177 (*ANE*, pp. 133–167).

The Hammurabi stele, found at Susa. The laws are inscribed around the stele; at its top Hammurabi is shown receiving instructions from the god Shamash. (© Arch. Phot., Paris/S.P.A.D.E.M./V.A.G.A., 1981).

black diorite stele more than 7 feet high and consisting of about 250 stipulations. A bas-relief at the top of the monument shows the king being commissioned to write the laws by the god of justice, Shamash. In a prologue to the collection Hammurabi describes himself as a "god-fearing prince," and cites as his reasons for establishing the laws,

> To promote the welfare of the people . . . to cause justice to prevail in the land, to destroy the wicked and the evil, that the strong might not oppress the weak . . .[62]

Actually, the stipulations here were no more the creation of the king himself than were the long collections of Deuteronomic and Priestly law in the Pentateuch the personal words of Moses. What we have, rather, is a codification of a select number of existing laws, published under the king's name and designed "more for the reassurance of the common man than as a source of reference for judges in deciding cases of law."[63] By contrast, if Israel's earliest law existed before the monarchy's establishment, then it received its authority not from a king, but solely from Yahweh himself.

In the Babylonian codes and other Near Eastern legal traditions the laws were formulated in conditional form: "If a man . . . (description of the crime), then . . . (specification of penalty)." This form of stipulation is known as casuistic law (cf. Latin *casus*), because it builds on a history of specific cases of conduct and sets forth the judgment which shall be rendered in each separate instance. The social, civil, and criminal laws in the Pentateuch are cast in this form. The subjects covered include the various facets of a complex society, but, as compared with Hebrew law, the extrabiblical codes exhibit a greater concern with property rights, a less rigorous attention to persons, and scarcely any regulation at all of religion and cult. Though an elementary sense of justice pervades the Babylonian codes, class distinctions are presupposed and the separate provisions for noblemen, the middle class, and slaves scrupulously defined.

That Israel's debt to the older law is evident at many points should occasion no great surprise. The maintenance of life in community involves similar problems in every culture, and the principles applied toward their solution are basic to all legal systems, including our own. Israel, however, gave prominence to a distinctive legal form, peculiarly adapted to the absolute character of Yahweh's covenant demands. This apodictic law, unlike the casuistic form, is cast in the second person imperative, "Thou shalt . . ." or "Thou shalt not . . . ," and includes no conditional "ifs" and "buts." It is seen at its best in the unconditional covenant requirements of the Decalogue.[64]

---

[62] James B. Pritchard, *Archaeology and the Old Testament*, p. 210.

[63] Ibid., p. 211.

[64] For other series of apodictic laws in the Pentateuch, cf. Deut, 27; Exod. 21:12, 15–17; 22:18–19; 31:14ff.; Lev. 20:2, 9–13, 15–16, 27; 24:16; 27:29; Lev. 18:7–18; Exod. 22:17, 20,

3. THE LAWS IN THE PENTATEUCH

The Decalogue

The Decalogue or Ten Commandments (Hebrew: "Ten Words") is preserved in two Old Testament versions: Exod. 20:1–17 (E) and Deut. 5:6–21 (D). Its terse, absolute demands, so basic to the Judaeo-Christian ethic, adapted easily to oral transmission, each word recited on one of the ten fingers. As originally formulated, the stipulations were probably free of all explanatory comment and may have been phrased somewhat as follows: [65]

1. You shall have no other gods before me.
2. You shall not make for me any graven image or any likeness.
3. You shall not invoke the name of Yahweh your God in vain.
4. Remember the Sabbath day to keep it holy.
5. Honor your father and mother.
6. You shall not commit murder.
7. You shall not commit adultery.
8. You shall not steal.
9. You shall not bear false witness against your neighbor.
10. You shall not covet your neighbor's house.

The Decalogue is unique among the Pentateuchal legal codes in expressing what is most fundamental and essential in the maintenance of man's relationship to God and society. The negative phrasing of all but two of the commands (vss. 8 and 12) allows for the broadest possible exercise of human freedom within the covenant relationship, because only those actions and intentions are prohibited that specifically violate the bond established between God and his people. The first four stipulations concern especially the worship of God; the remainder govern the life of the human community. This distinction, however, can be overstated. Covenant presuppositions admit to no cleavage between ethical duty and service to God. Couched in the "I-Thou" form, each command speaks directly to a people already committed by ties of faith and gratitude to the divine author of their freedom.

In this light, the first command should not be forced into an abstract as-

21, 27; 23:1–3, 6–9 (Lev. 19:15ff.). Erhard Gerstenberger has shown that apodictic law encompasses a variety of styles and that it was not unique to Israel. He regards as the original basis of the apodictic form a "prohibitive" style, which he traces to early clan settings and finds reflected in wisdom literature (cf. footnote 54, above). According to this theory, the Decalogue's covenant setting was not original.

[65] The specific wording is that of James Muilenburg, "The History of the Religion of Israel," *IB*, Vol. 1, p. 303. For other attempts at reconstructing the primitive Decalogue see Eduard Nielsen, *The Ten Commandments in New Perspective*, Studies in Biblical Theology, series 2, no. 7 (London: S.C.M. Press, 1968), pp. 78–93. The striking features of Nielsen's formulation are that all commandments are phrased as prohibitions (e.g., "Thou shalt not do any work on the Sabbath day"; "Thou shalt not despise thy father or thy mother") and refer to concrete objects (e.g., "Thou shalt not bow down before any other god"; "Thou shalt not commit adultery with thy neighbor's wife"; "Thou shalt not pour out the blood of thy neighbor"; "Thou shalt not steal any man from thy neighbor").

sertion of the principle of monotheism. Whether or not the command originally denied the existence of other gods is open to question, but is in any event irrelevant to its meaning. For Israel, there can be no other god beside Yahweh. This is what the command is about. The full implications of that claim were long in coming to expression; but its meaning for Israel's faith, as well as that of other religions which learned from her experience, appears to have had its beginnings in the contemplation of the Exodus. In the same vein as Yahweh's demand for total allegiance is the prohibition of images—not simply of other gods, but representations of Yahweh himself. An image, by the ancient way of thinking, embodied power given it by the being whom it portrayed. Yahweh will have no image because he gives no means by which he can be controlled.[66] As we have seen, he does give Israel his name, likewise a source of power, but he does so only with the stipulation that it be used guardedly and for no evil purpose ("in vain").

One of the few deviations between the Decalogue of Exodus 20 and that of Deuteronomy 5 concerns the rationale for Sabbath observance. In language strongly reminiscent of the Priestly creation account (Gen. 2:2–3), the Exodus Decalogue (20:11) views the Sabbath as a memorial to God's creation of the world; one should rest as God rested. In Deuteronomy the Sabbath is virtually a weekly Passover, since the Israelite is enjoined to remember the deliverance from Egypt each time that he observes the Sabbath (5:15). In either event, the Sabbath observance antedated the efforts to explain it.[67]

The command to honor parents has been described as a "bridge" between the two parts of the Decalogue, for although it actually belongs to the sphere of human relations, the Israelite's obligation to his parents is a deeply religious one and analogous to the community's relation to God.[68] Through the parental relationship God establishes his claim on all life. Because every man's life is God-given, it is not at man's disposal to take life. Though Israel made exceptions for capital punishment and holy war, it is a conception of the sacredness of human life that underlies the effort manifest in the Decalogue to maintain the integrity of life at every level. Adultery is prohibited as a violation of the unity Yahweh intends for man and woman, and thus an abuse of personality at its deepest level. Likewise the prohibitions against theft, false witness, and covetousness are crimes against the person: his property, reputation, and status.[69] Originally, the

---

[66] Martin Noth, *Exodus*, J. S. Bowden, trans. (Philadelphia: The Westminster Press, 1962), pp. 162–163.

[67] Cf. J. J. Stamm and M. E. Andrew, *The Ten Commandments in Recent Research*, IL, pp. 90f.

[68] Walter Harrelson, "Ten Commandments," *IDB*, R–Z, pp. 569ff.

[69] The eighth command, correspondingly, is sometimes interpreted as concerning the theft of a man (illegal enslavement) rather than theft of property. Cf. Albrecht Alt, "Das Verbot des Diebstahls im Dekalog," *Klein Schriften zur Geschichte des Volkes Israel*, I (Munich : Beck'sche Verlag, 1953), pp. 333–340.

tenth command had to do not only with the mental desire for persons and things that belong to another, but the objective actions taken to secure them for oneself.

The account of the rewriting of the Ten Commandments in Exodus 34 (usually assigned to J) contains a decalogue quite different from that of Exodus 20 and Deuteronomy 5. Known as the "Ritual Decalogue" (as distinct from the "Ethical Decalogue") because of its predominantly cultic character, it embodies only three of the stipulations of the Ethical Decalogue (vss. 14, 17, 21), and some of its laws have their parallels in the Covenant Code (Exod. 20:22–23:33). Though resting perhaps on an ancient version of the Decalogue, in its extant form it is little more than a conglomerate of heterogeneous cultic regulations.[70]

The Covenant Code

Immediately following the Decalogue in Exodus is a collection of laws generally designated the Covenant Code or Book of the Covenant (Exod. 20:22–23:33; E)—the name derived from Exodus 24:7. The collection contains both pronouncements of the apodictic type (20:23–26; 22:18–23:19) and casuistic ordinances (21:1–22:17), the latter stipulating the precise penalty that will follow upon each specified violation. The laws cover a wide range of personal and property rights, as well as cultic requirements, many of which presuppose a settled agricultural society. Generally dated to the period after the settlement in Canaan and ascribed in part to Canaanite influence, some of the laws nevertheless may rest on traditions brought to Palestine by the earliest Hebrew ancestors.[71] The fact that not even the latest of these laws reflect the principle of cultic centralization required by the seventh-century Deuteronomic Code, argues for their compilation earlier than that time.

Similarities to the early Mesopotamian legal codes are remarkable, as the following example from the Eshnunna Code illustrates:

> *Eshnunna:* If an ox gores an (other) ox and causes (its) death, both owners shall divide (among themselves) the price of the live ox and also the equivalent of the dead ox.[72]
>
> *Ex. 21:35:* When one man's ox hurts another's so that it dies, then they shall sell the live ox and divide the price of it; and the dead beast also they shall divide.

One notes in both instances the case-law form, "If (or when) . . . then . . . ," as well as the identical subject matter and judgment.

The ancient principle of equal retaliation or *lex talionis* ("eye for an eye") finds expression in the Hammurabi Code, and also here.

[70] Artur Weiser, *The Old Testament: Its Formation and Development*, p. 105.
[71] Walter Harrelson, "Law in the Old Testament," *IDB*, K–Q, p. 83.
[72] *ANET*, p. 163 (*ANE*, p. 138).

Hammurabi: If a seignior [noble] has destroyed the eye of a member of the aristocracy, they shall destroy his eye.

If he has broken a (nother) seignior's bone, they shall break his bone.[73]

Ex. 21:22–25: When men strive together, and hurt a woman with child . . . If any harm follows, then you shall give life for life, eye for eye, tooth for tooth, hand for hand, foot for foot, burn for burn, wound for wound, stripe for stripe.

The principle aimed at making the penalty commensurate with the crime so as to prevent unrestrained blood vengeance. Furthermore, a humane tendency is evident in both traditions wherein a willful violation is distinguished from the accidental or unpremeditated offense (21:12–14, 18–19). Exodus 21:12–14 provides for appointed places to which one accused of murder might flee and receive asylum until justice is done (cf. the "cities of refuge"; Num. 35:9–34; Deut. 19:1–13; Josh. 20). In both the Hammurabi and Covenant codes there is no penalty if a man's ox gores another man to death, providing the ox has not been an habitual gorer or the owner has not been warned (Ham. 250; Ex. 21:28); but in both traditions the owner is liable if the ox is a known gorer and warning has been duly issued (Ham. 251; Exod. 21:29). A "lie-detector test," wherein accused parties take an oath in the presence of the god, appears to have been standard procedure in Hebrew (Exod. 22:7–9) and Babylonian (Esh. 36–37; Ham. 23) circles.

The penalties for property violations are more humane in the Hebrew code. Restitution for the theft of an animal by Hammurabi's standards was ten- to thirtyfold; by Covenant Code stipulations, two-, four-, or fivefold (22:1, 4). Housebreaking carried the death penalty in the Babylonian law (Ham. 6:22). According to Hebrew procedure (22:2–3) the thief might be slain with impunity by the householder only if caught in the act at night. The high value placed on persons in Hebrew law, however, led to more stringent penalties for personal violations. The owner of the killer ox, once warned, is put to death if the ox kills a man (Exod. 21:29); according to the Hammurabi Code, the owner is fined (Ham. 251). For striking one's father, the son loses his hand by Hammurabi's standards (Ham. 195); by Hebrew principles, his life (Exod. 21:15). Hebrew law lacks the class distinctions of Babylonian law (cf. the three classes: seigniors [nobles], middle class, and slaves), though separate provisions cover offenses against slaves. A slave was both person and property; as a person, his master was bound to respect his rights. According to the Covenant Code (21:1–11), Hebrew slaves were eligible for their freedom after six years' service; at a later time (Lev. 25:39–42) the enslavement of Israelites was prohibited altogether. The rationale for the humane treatment of the slave is explicitly and emphatically stated in the later codes:

---

[73] *ANET,* p. 175 (*ANE,* p. 161).

3. THE LAWS IN THE PENTATEUCH

> You shall remember that you were a slave in the land of Egypt, and the Lord
> your God redeemed you; therefore, I command you this day.
> Deut. 15:15; cf. Lev. 25:42

Grateful acknowledgment of Yahweh's election of Israel is never far
from the surface in Hebrew law. The Covenant Code enjoins compassion
for weak and defenseless persons, as well as strangers, on the basis of the
divine compassion demonstrated in Israel's deliverance (22:21–27; 23:9).
No one of God's people shall benefit at the expense of another's ill fortune;
hence the prohibition of usury (22:25–27). The Sabbatical Year for the land,
wherein the fields shall lie fallow one year in seven, served the needs of
the poor (23:10–11). Not even enmity between Israelites should prevent
the offer of assistance in time of trouble (23:4–5).

The Covenant Code stipulates as the three annual feasts when all male
Israelites shall "appear before the Lord God," that is, assemble at the local
sanctuaries for their observance, the festivals of (a) Unleavened Bread, (b)
First Fruits, and (c) Ingathering (23:14–17). Each of these was originally an
agricultural feast and possibly had its origins in Canaan. Unleavened Bread,
as we have seen (Exod. 12:14–20), came to be associated with the Exodus
and the Passover rite. Initially, however, it marked the season of barley
harvest in the spring month of Nisan (March–April). A seven-day festival, it
was observed by eating only bread made from the new crop of grain, hence
without the leaven of the old grain. First Fruits or Pentecost came at the
beginning of wheat harvest in early summer, fifty days or seven weeks after
the first day of Unleavened Bread. The Feast of Ingathering or Booths
(Sukkoth) was an autumn festival, coming at the time of the grape vintage
and final harvest of olives and fruits. It, too, came to be connected with the
Exodus and wilderness history. The booths from which the vineyard
owners guarded the ripening grape crop suggested the tents in which the
fathers lived in the wilderness, and the festival was celebrated by families
tenting in such rude shelters.

Deuteronomy

The book of Deuteronomy is a law book and belongs as such among the
other legal collections of the Old Testament. References within the book itself designate it "this book of the law" (29:21; 30:10; 31:26) or "this law"
(1:5; 4:8; 17:8–19, etc.). It differs from the typical legal code, however, in
consisting not simply of an itemized list of rules but of sustained exhortation to covenant faithfulness. It is law put into the form of Mosaic speeches.
Old laws, many of which are found in some form within the Covenant
Code, make up the core of the book (chs. 12–26; 28). Affinities with Hosea's oracles and the Elohistic work,[74] both associated with northern Israel,

---

[74] Deuteronomy shares with the Elohist such common terminology as Horeb (for Sinai) and
Amorites (for Canaanites), in addition to the laws of the Covenant Code.

as well as the prominence of Shechem (cf. 11:26–32; 27), suggest to many scholars that we are dealing here with northern legislation, once taught and preserved within either Levitical or prophetic circles in the north.[75] With the fall of the northern kingdom, presumably, the traditions were brought to Judah, where they were reworked and expanded, perhaps during the reign of Hezekiah (c. 715–687 B.C.). According to other interpretations, the Deuteronomic legislation originated in Judah, either in Jerusalem or among the Levites of the Judaean countryside.[76] In either event, King Josiah used the work as the basis for his sweeping reforms in 622 B.C, at which time the stipulation concerning the place of worship chosen by Yahweh (12:5, 11, 14) was interpreted in reference to Jerusalem. Still later, the book was made the starting point for the Deuteronomic History (Deut.–II Kings), and chapters 1–3 were added as introduction.[77] It was through such stages that the book finally achieved the form in which we know it. The following outline indicates its basic divisions:

1. First address: 1:1–4:43
    a. Historical summary, Sinai to Transjordan: chs. 1–3
    b. Exhortation: 4:1–43
2. Second address: 4:44–26:19; 28
    a. Exhortation: 4:44–11:32
    b. Deuteronomic Law Code: 12–26; 28
3. Third address: 29–30
4. Supplements
    a. Covenant ceremony: 27
    b. Last words of Moses: 31–33
    c. Moses' death: 34

Although the words of Deuteronomy are not actually those of Moses, the spirit that pervades the work is true to the traditional portrait of the famous lawgiver. Consequently, the timeless and contemporary character of the Israelite covenant receives here its most emphatic expression. Each new generation is made to stand before the God of Sinai, hear the words of the lawgiver, and renew the covenant made with the forefathers.

> Hear, O Israel, the statutes and the ordinances which I speak in your hearing this day, and you shall learn them and be careful to do them. The Lord our

[75] E.g., Artur Weiser, *Introduction to the Old Testament*, p. 132, and John Bright, *A History of Israel*, pp. 320ff. For a full discussion and bibliography, see E. W. Nicholson, *Deuteronomy and Tradition* (Philadelphia: Fortress Press, 1967), pp. 58–82.

[76] Gerhard von Rad proposes a seventh-century B.C. provenance among the Judaean Levites (*Studies in Deuteronomy* [London: S.C.M. Press, 1956]); R. E. Clements ("Deuteronomy and the Jerusalem Cult-Tradition," *VT*, 15 [1965], pp. 300–315) and Norbert Lohfink ("Deuteronomy," *IDBS*, pp. 229–232) regard Jerusalem as the place of origin. For a detailed discussion and bibliography, cf. E. W. Nicholson, *Deuteronomy and Tradition*, pp. 83–106.

[77] See pp. 66, 69–70, 199ff.

3. THE LAWS IN THE PENTATEUCH

> God made a covenant with us in Horeb. Not with our fathers did the Lord
> make this covenant, but with us, who are all of us here alive this day.
> 5:1–3

The urgent and persuasive tone of the book most likely reflects the grave crises that came with the Assyrian period. In a manner reminiscent of the early prophets, it warns of the dire consequences of turning away from Yahweh to go after other gods. The first commandment is of central importance, as seen in the *Shema'* (6:4–9, the first word of which is *shema'*, meaning "Hear").

> Hear, O Israel: the Lord our God is one Lord; and you shall love the Lord
> your God with all your heart, and with all your soul, and with all your might.
> 6:4–5

Faithfulness by Deuteronomic standards involves the elimination of all paganizing influences. The holy war which Moses envisions on the plains of Moab is to be translated into an all-out assault against the idolatrous syncretism which infiltrated the Israelite high places during the years of the monarchy. Whether the original (northern) legislation called for centralization of all worship at one shrine (Shechem?) is no longer clear. It is a widely held view that the law of the one sanctuary (12:5ff.) was added by the Deuteronomic circle in Judah, under Josiah's auspices. Be that as it may, it was this feature of the code as emphasized in Josiah's reforms that had the most far-reaching and immediate effects upon the Israelite cultus. To comply with the principle, all altars outside Jerusalem were closed.

The obedience demanded by Yahweh calls for strict adherence to Israel's covenant obligations, including the ethical demands of the Decalogue, established civil and criminal procedure, cultic and festal regulations, and exclusive loyalty of the mind and heart. Repeatedly, the covenant society is reminded of the rewards of obedience and the pitfalls of unfaithfulness (ch. 28). "Walk in all the way which the Lord your God has commanded," Israel is exhorted, "that you may live, and that it may go well with you" (5:33). All Israel's striving would avail for nothing, however, had not Yahweh as an act of sheer grace chosen Israel and set his love upon her. Notwithstanding Deuteronomy's stress upon the rewards of obedience, the motive of right behavior lies in nothing else than a willing response to God's goodness. Any ultimate grounds for self-sufficiency or self-righteousness are ruled out. The resulting ethic is one that issues from love of God and involves the total response of the person—heart, soul, and might.

The Priestly Code

It would be difficult to exaggerate the significance of the priesthood for Israel's religious life. To the priests was entrusted the conduct of the covenant people's worship, including the offering of the sacrifices at the altar. In addition, they had custody of the sacred oracle (the Urim and Thum-

Howland-Garber model of the ark. The top of the ark is depicted here as a hinged lid; the carrying staves on either side were removable. (Courtesy of Paul L. Garber and Southeastern Films, Atlanta.)

mim), attended to the study and teaching of the law, rendered judgments in legal cases, pronounced blessing and curse, and in general served as the intermediaries between Yahweh and his people. As we have seen,[78] it was not until the Exile and following (the sixth or fifth centuries B.C.) that the large body of priestly tradition, the accumulation of centuries, was finally brought together and given its definitive form. It is from the priestly records themselves that our accounts of the origin and program of the Israelite priesthood derives.

The priestly law in the latter half of Exodus (chs. 25–31; 35–40) accounts for the establishment of Israel's earliest cultic institutions—the ark and tabernacle—and the appointment of a special order of priests as their custodians. We are told that Aaron (descendant of Levi) and his sons were set apart to serve as Israel's duly ordained priesthood, and the remainder of the tribe of Levi designated as their assistants. Although much of the priestly legislation presupposes the later Jerusalem temple and its cultus, there is no reason to doubt the existence of a wilderness cult which served as its forerunner.[79] The ark was the sacred object of chief significance and appears to have been no more than an oblong wooden box with four rings into which carrying staves were inserted. A portable throne for the invisible Yahweh, it accompanied the Israelites wherever they went, and whether wandering or in battle, served as a constant reminder of the Lord in their midst.

> Whenever the ark set out, Moses said, "Arise, O Yahweh, and let thy enemies be scattered; and let them that hate thee flee before thee." And when it rested, he said, "Return, O Yahweh, to the ten thousands of Israel."
> Num. 10:35–36

When not in transit, the ark was housed within the tabernacle or tent of meeting, the desert shrine where Moses met with Yahweh and proclaimed his words to the assembled people. Notwithstanding the highly idealized

---

[78] See above, pp. 61ff.

[79] Cf. Frank Cross, Jr., "The Priestly Tabernacle," *BA*, VII. (1944), pp. 1–20. Reprinted in *BA Reader*, I, pp. 201–228.

descriptions of the tabernacle, such portable sanctuaries are among "the oldest motifs of Semitic religion."[80]

LEVITICUS. More than any other book in the canon, Leviticus is the ritual handbook of the Jerusalem priests of the post-Exilic era. Only, it is not to be thought of as a separate book, but a continuation of the great block of priestly legislation that begins with Exodus 25. Consisting of the bare rubrics of worship, it needs to be studied alongside the Psalter in order that the vital content of its ritual forms might be better understood and appreciated. For what we find here is little more than the formal skeleton of Israel's colorful and exciting worship, celebrated to the accompaniment of prayer, praise, and sacred dance. The subjects covered include (a) sacrifices (chs. 1–7), (b) consecration of priests (8–10), (c) ritual purity (11–15), (d) the Day of Atonement (16), (e) holiness (the Holiness Code) (17–26), and (f) religious vows (27).

Modern efforts to understand Israel's ancient sacrificial system are inhibited by the absence from the Old Testament of anything akin to a theology of sacrifice.[81] The motives for sacrificing appear to have varied with the different types of offerings that were made. The most common sacrifice was the peace offering (shelem or zebaḥ; Lev. 3:1–17; 7:11–21) in which the blood of the slain animal, the fat, and the internal parts were burned on the altar and the remainder eaten by the sacrificer, his family, and friends as a communion meal in Yahweh's presence. The peace offering might be made in fulfillment of a vow, as a free will offering of praise, or as a thank offering.[82] The burnt offering ('olah, kalil; Lev. 1:1–17, 6:8–13), on the other hand, consisted of the sacrifice of the whole animal and was effective as an atonement, reconciling man with God. In the ritual of the burnt offering the offerer first placed his hands upon the head of the unblemished animal, thus identifying with the victim; then the smoke from the sacrifice went up as "a pleasing odor to the Lord."

Either the peace offering or the burnt offering might be accompanied by a cereal offering (minhah; Lev. 2:1–16; 6:14–23) of grain or cakes, as well as libations of wine or oil. The sin offering (ḥaṭṭa'th; Lev. 4:1–5; 13; 6:24–30) and guilt offering ('asham; Lev. 5:14–6:7; 7:1–10) constituted special categories of expiatory sacrifices in which only the priests—and then only under certain conditions—might consume portions of the offerings. In the latter rites the significance of the blood of the slain victim received greater emphasis. The blood, being the seat of life ("the life of the flesh is in the blood"; Lev. 17:11), was a potent and sacred substance, forbidden to human consumption (17:12). Its efficacy as a sin offering, however, was due to no intrinsic or magical power of blood-letting, but only to

---

[80] BA Reader, I, p. 219.
[81] Nathaniel Micklem, "The Book of Leviticus," IB, Vol. II, p. 11.
[82] Ibid., p. 22.

the fact that Yahweh had ordained the rite as an acceptable means of healing the breach between himself and the violater.[83] Such sacrifices availed only for unintended or inadvertent offences, and not at all for sins committed willfully or "with a high hand."

Properly understood, the Hebrew's sacrifice was neither a *do ut des* contract with God, nor a magical means of escaping guilt, nor yet a provision of food for a hungry deity.[84] The acceptable motives for sacrifice were, rather, a profound awareness of Yahweh's holiness and a compelling need to relate to it through traditional and established worship rites. Through his offering the Israelite sought (a) to acknowledge God's ownership of all life by giving back to him a portion of his flocks and crops, (b) to establish communion with him, and (c) to repair the covenant relationship, broken by inadvertent transgressions. Although the temptation to make the external rite an end in itself was real, the priestly legislation presupposes sincerity of motive as the indispensable qualification for any effectual offering. It is especially important to remember that the external act at the altar was accompanied by prayers, confessions, and psalms expressive of the mood of worship. Father de Vaux's description of sacrifice as "acted prayer" is apt.

> Sacrifice is the essential act of external worship. It is a prayer which is acted, a symbolic action which expresses both the interior feelings of the person offering it, and God's response to this prayer. It is rather like the symbolic actions of the prophets. By sacrificial rites, the gift made to God *is* accepted, union with God *is* achieved, and the guilt of man *is* taken away. But these effects are not achieved by magic: it is essential that the external action should express the true inward feelings of man, and that it should be favorably received by God. Failing this, sacrifice is no longer a religious act.[85]

Priestly distinctions between clean and unclean things (Lev. 11–15) cover a broad variety of animals, diseases, bodily functions, and the like, the rationale for which has long since passed into obscurity. Uncleanness apparently connoted neither the unhygienic nor the sinful, as such, but rather customary improprieties which one either avoided or removed by undergoing the necessary purificatory rites.[86] If such customs have little meaning today, one can nevertheless respect the zeal with which Israel strove to order her entire corporate life in a manner pleasing to Yahweh.

Along with the annual feasts stipulated in the Covenant Code, Levitical law added the Day of Atonement (*Yom Kippur*), the most solemn of all Hebrew fasts. Observed on the tenth day of Tishri (September–October), it marked the culmination of ten days of penitence at the beginning of the New Year, when forgiveness was sought for the sins of the past year. Al-

---

[83] Ibid., p. 25.
[84] Roland de Vaux, *Ancient Israel*, pp. 447–450.
[85] Ibid., p. 451.
[86] Nathaniel Micklem, "The Book of Leviticus," *IB*, Vol. II, pp. 52–56.

though it was not until the post-Exilic period that it received a fixed place, in the liturgical calendar, its rituals appear to be quite old. Sin offerings were made by the high priest for himself, his family, and "for all the assembly of Israel," after which the nation's sins were symbolically laid upon the scapegoat ("goat for Azazel"), which was driven into the wilderness to die. The Day of Atonement was the one day in the year when the high priest entered into the Holy of Holies, the inner shrine of the temple.

THE HOLINESS CODE. Leviticus 17–26, although contained in the P source, constitutes a unit unto itself, with a formal beginning and conclusion. Known as the "Holiness Code" (or H) because of a marked concern for the holiness of the Israelite nation, it contains laws of a mixed character, some of them older than the Deuteronomic Code.[87] In its present form the collection dates from the period of Exile (sixth century) and shares characteristics in common with Ezekiel, the early Exilic prophet. The holiness which these laws are designed to preserve is conceived as a quality of life befitting Yahweh's elect nation as a people set apart for his service. The whole range of Hebrew law, cultic, civil, and ethical, receives here its deepest interpretation in terms of God's very character.

> You shall be holy to me; for I Yahweh am holy, and have separated you from the peoples, that you should be mine.
>
> 20:26

Israel shall be set apart as a separate people even as Yahweh himself exists in his unique character as the divine "Other." "I am the Lord" is a refrain that occurs almost fifty times at the conclusion of separate commandments or series of commandments. Chapter 19 has been regarded as the highest development of ethics in the Old Testament.

SELECTED READINGS

Egyptian Backgrounds

Morenz, Siegfried, *Egyptian Religion*, Ann E. Keep, trans. (Ithaca, NY: Cornell University Press, 1973).

Pfeiffer, Charles F., *Tell el Amarna and the Bible*, Baker Studies in Biblical Archaeology (Grand Rapids MI: Baker Book House, 1963). Paperback.

Steindorff, George, and Keith C. Seele, *When Egypt Ruled the East*, 2nd ed. (Chicago: University of Chicago Press, 1957). Also available in paperback (Phoenix Books, 1963).

Wilson, John A., *The Burden of Egypt* (Chicago: University of Chicago Press, 1951). Also available in paperback as *The Culture of Ancient Egypt* (Phoenix Books, 1951).

---

[87] Cf. 17:1–7, which requires that all animals be slaughtered at the sanctuary. This would have been manifestly impossible after the Deuteronomic reforms had closed all the local sanctuaries.

Moses and Hebrew Origins

Beegle, Dewey M., *Moses, Servant of Yahweh* (Grand Rapids, MI: Eerdmans, 1972). A historical and literary study that defends the historicity of Moses.

Buber, Martin, *Moses* (London: East and West Library, 1946). An outstanding study of the life of Moses. Also available in paperback (New York: Harper Torchbooks, 1958).

Coats, George W., "History and Theology in the Sea Tradition," *ST*, 29 (1975), pp. 53–62.

———, *Rebellion in the Wilderness* (Nashville, TN: Abingdon Press, 1968). A study of the murmuring motif in the Pentateuchal wilderness traditions.

De Vaux, Roland, *The Early History of Israel*, David Smith, trans. (Philadelphia: The Westminister Press, 1978), pp. 321–472. A detailed and balanced appraisal of the Moses and Exodus accounts in the light of historical questions.

Engnell, Ivan, "The Wilderness Wandering" in *A Rigid Scrutiny: Critical Essays on the Old Testament*, John T. Willis, trans. (Nashville, TN: Vanderbilt University Press, 1969).

Fackenheim, Emil L., *God's Presence in History: Jewish Affirmations and Philosophical Reflections* (New York: Harper & Row, Publishers, 1970). Paperback.

Haran, Menahem, "Exodus, the," *IDBS*, pp. 304–310. A concise summary of the evidence regarding historical and geographical aspects of the Exodus.

Hay, Lewis S., "What Really Happened at the Sea of Reeds?" *JBL*, 83 (1964), pp. 397–403.

Hermann, Siegfried, *A History of Israel in Old Testament Times*, John Bowden, trans. (Philadelphia: Fortress Press, 1975), pp. 56–68. Connects the early Hebrews of the Exodus accounts with the Shasu tribes from Edom and the northern Sinai.

Meek, Theophile, *Hebrew Origins*, rev. ed. (New York: Harper & Row, Publishers, 1950). Provocative proposals concerning the origins of the Hebrew people, law, Yahwism, priesthood, prophecy, and monotheism. Also available in paperback (New York: Harper Torchbooks, 1960).

Rad, Gerhard, von, *Moses*, World Christian Books (London: Lutterworth Press, 1960).

Rowley, Harold H., *From Joseph to Joshua* (London: The British Academy, 1950). Although dated, this study of early Hebrew origins still has value.

Thompson, Thomas L., and Dorothy Irvin, "The Joseph and Moses Narratives," *Israelite and Judaean History*, John H. Hayes and J. Maxwell Miller, eds. (Philadelphia: The Westminster Press, 1977), pp. 149–212. An interpretation of the Exodus traditions as historical folk tales within secondary narrative settings.

Voeglin, Eric, *Israel and Revelation* (Baton Rouge, LA: Louisiana State University Press, 1956).

Covenant

Baltzer, Klaus, *The Covenant Formulary in Old Testament, Jewish and Early Christian Writings*, David E. Green, trans. (Philadelphia: Fortress Press, 1971). A pioneering study of ancient Near Eastern treaty forms and their implications for the biblical covenants.

Beyerlin, Walter, *Origins and History of the Oldest Sinaitic Traditions,* Stanley Rudman, trans. (Oxford: Basil Blackwell, 1965). A rebuttal to the theory that the Exodus and Sinai traditions were originally unrelated.

Hillers, Delbert R., *Covenant: The History of a Biblical Idea* (Baltimore, MD: The Johns Hopkins University Press, 1969). Paperback.

Huffmon, Herbert B., "The Exodus, Sinai, and the Credo," *CBQ,* XXVII (1965), pp. 101–113.

McCarthy, Dennis J., *Old Testament Covenant* (Atlanta, GA: John Knox Press, 1972). Paperback. A helpful summary of current scholarly opinions concerning the covenant in ancient Israel.

———, *Treaty and Covenant, A Study in Form in the Ancient Oriental Documents and in the Old Testament,* Analecta Biblica 21 (Rome: Pontifical Biblical Institute, 1963).

Mendenhall, George E., *Law and Covenant in Israel and the Ancient Near East* (Pittsburgh, PA: Biblical Colloquium, 1955), Reprinted from *BA,* XVII (1954), pp. 26–46, 49–76. A pathfinding study of the Hebrew covenant form in the light of Hittite treaties.

———, "Covenant," *IDB,* A–D, pp. 714–723.

Muilenburg, James, "The Form and Structure of the Covenantal Formulations," *VT,* IX (1959), pp. 347–365.

Newman, Murray L., Jr., *The People of the Covenant: A Study of Israel from Moses to the Monarchy* (Nashville, TN: Abingdon Press, 1962).

Law

Alt, Albrecht, "The Origins of Israelite Law," in idem, *Essays on Old Testament History and Religion,* R. A. Wilson, trans. (Garden City, NY: Doubleday & Company, Inc., 1967), pp. 101–171. Also available in paperback (Doubleday Anchor, 1967).

DeVaux, Roland, *Ancient Israel: Its Life and Institutions,* J. McHugh, trans. (New York: McGraw-Hill Book Company, 1961), Part II, ch. 10. Also available in paperback (McGraw-Hill, 1965).

Harrelson, Walter, "Law in the Old Testament," *IDB,* K–Q, pp. 77–89.

———, "Ten Commandments," *IDB,* R–Z, pp. 569–573.

Nielson, Eduard, *The Ten Commandments in New Perspective,* D. J. Bourke, trans., Studies in Biblical Theology, series 2, no. 7 (Naperville, IL: Alec R. Allenson, 1968). A traditio-historical approach to the Decalogue.

Noth, Martin, "The Laws in the Pentateuch: Their Assumptions and Meanings," in idem, *The Laws in the Pentateuch and Other Studies,* D. R. Ap-Thomas, trans. (Philadelphia: Fortress Press, 1967), pp. 1–107.

Rowley, Harold H., "Moses and the Decalogue," *BJRL,* 34 (1951–1952), pp. 81–118.

Stamm, J. J., and M. E. Andrew, *The Ten Commandments in Recent Research,* Studies in Biblical Theology, series 2, no. 2 (Naperville, IL: Alec R. Allenson, 1967). Includes an explication of Gerstenberger's thesis that elements of Israelite law originated in family settings.

Williams, Jay G., *Ten Words of Freedom* (Philadelphia: Fortress Press, 1971). Paperback. Analysis of the Decalogue for contemporary meaning.

Wright, G. Ernest, "The Lawsuit of God: A Form-Critical Study of Deuteronomy

32," in *Israel's Prophetic Heritage*, Bernhard W. Anderson and Walter Harrelson, eds. (New York: Harper & Row, Publishers, 1962), pp. 26–67.

Exodus

Cassuto, Umberto, *A Commentary on the Book of Exodus*, Israel Abrahams, trans. (Jerusalem: Magnes Press, 1967).

Childs, Brevard S., *The Book of Exodus: A Critical, Theological Commentary*, The Old Testament Library (Philadelphia: The Westminster Press, 1974). A fresh and provocative approach to the book, focusing on its canonical role.

Knight, George A. F., *Theology as Narration; a Commentary on the Book of Exodus* (Grand Rapids, MI: William B. Eerdmans, 1976). Approaches the Book of Exodus as theological essay.

Nicholson, E. W., *Exodus and Sinai in History and Tradition* (Atlanta, GA: John Knox Press, 1973). An assessment of current conflicting views on the relationship between the Exodus and Sinai themes in Israelite tradition.

Leviticus and the Israelite Cult

Clements, R. E., *God and Temple* (Philadelphia: Fortress Press, 1965).

De Vaux, Roland, *Ancient Israel: Its Life and Institutions*, J. McHugh, trans. (New York: McGraw-Hill Book Company, 1961), Part IV. Also available in paperback (McGraw-Hill, 1965).

—————, *Studies in Old Testament Sacrifice* (Cardiff: University of Wales Press, 1964).

Harrelson, Walter, *From Fertility Cult to Worship* (Garden City, NY: Doubleday Anchor, 1970). Paperback. A judicious appraisal of fertility elements in the Israelite cult.

Kapelrud, Arvid S., "The Role of the Cult in Old Israel," and the responses of B. Vawter and H. G. May, *The Bible in Modern Scholarship*, J. Philip Hyatt, ed. (Nashville, TN: Abingdon Press, 1965), pp. 44–73.

Kraus, Hans Joachim, *Worship in Israel*, Geoffrey Buswell, trans. (Atlanta, GA: John Knox Press, 1965).

Micklem, Nathaniel, "Introduction and Exegesis to the Book of Leviticus," *IB*, Vol. II. A sensitive treatment of early Israel's worship.

Noth, Martin, *Leviticus*, Old Testament Library, J. E. Anderson, trans. (Philadelphia: The Westminster Press, 1965).

Ringgren, Helmer, *Sacrifice in the Bible*, World Christian Books (New York: Association Press, 1962).

Rowley, Harold H., *Worship in Ancient Israel: Its Forms and Meaning* (Philadelphia: Fortress Press, 1967).

Numbers

Levine, Baruch A., "Numbers, Book of," *IDBS*, pp. 631–635.

Marsh, John, "Introduction and Exegesis to Numbers," *IB*, Vol. II, pp. 137–308.

Noth, Martin, *Numbers: A Commentary*, James D. Martin, trans., The Old Testament Library (Philadelphia: The Westminster Press, 1968).

Deuteronomy

Clements, R. E., *God's Chosen People: A Theological Interpretation of the Book of Deuteronomy* (London: S.C.M. Press, 1968).

Cross, Frank M., "The Themes of the Book of Kings and the Structure of the Deuteronomistic History," in idem, *Canaanite Myth and Hebrew Epic* (Cambridge, MA: Harvard University Press, 1973), pp. 274–289.

Nicholson, E. W., *Deuteronomy and Tradition* (Philadelphia: Fortress Press, 1967). A concise coverage of the modern literary and historical research on Deuteronomy.

Rad, Gerhard, von, *Deuteronomy: A Commentary* (Philadelphia: The Westminster Press, 1966).

————, *Studies in Deuteronomy*, Studies in Biblical Theology, no. 9 (London: S.C.M. Press, 1953).

Weinfeld, Moshe, *Deuteronomy and the Deuteronomic School* (New York: Oxford University Press, Inc., 1972). Relates the Deuteronomic literature to the wisdom movement.

Welch, A. C., *The Code of Deuteronomy* (London: J. Clarke and Company, 1924) and idem, *Deuteronomy: The Framework of the Code* (New York: Oxford University Press, Inc., 1932).

Wright, G. Ernest, "Introduction and Exegesis to Deuteronomy," *IB*, Vol. II, pp. 311–537.

II

—◆—

all
his
servants
the
prophets

You have neither listened nor inclined your ears to hear, although the Lord persistently sent to you all his servants the prophets.

—Jeremiah 25:4

3

afteR the death of moses

After the death of Moses the servant of the Lord, the Lord said to
Joshua the son of Nun, Moses' minister, "Moses my servant is dead;
now therefore arise, go over this Jordan, you and all this people,
into the land which I am giving to them, to the people of Israel.
—Joshua 1:1–2

The books of the Former Prophets (Joshua, Judges, Samuel, and Kings)
provide the historical record of Israel's fortunes in Palestine from the Hebrew settlement to the fall of Jerusalem in 587 B.C. For the period of the
monarchy (tenth-sixth centuries) we also possess the parallel record of the
Chronicler (I–II Chron.), but the latter work is largely dependent upon the
Former Prophets, its coverage of the history much less complete, and its
theological bias more pronounced. For these reasons, the Former Prophets
are the primary source for any survey of Israel's history. They contain
much excellent historical material which can be fully appreciated only
when one compares them with other ancient literature of comparable age
and considers the research conditions of the time.

No less than the books of Torah, the Former Prophets offer a theological
approach to history. Their concern is not to report the "bare facts" of national and international happenings, but to penetrate the meanings of the
events and expose their religious significance. It is precisely at this level
that the unity inherent in these books is most apparent. Utilizing a variety
of older sources, a historian (or historians) of the Deuteronomic school

combined the traditions pertaining to the several historical eras—
Conquest, Judges, United and Divided Monarchies—into a framework
consistent with the philosophy set forth in the book of Deuteronomy. Regardless of the unique patterns which characterize the separate books, the
basic theological perspective remains unchanged: Israel's fortunes rise or
fall depending upon her faithfulness to the covenant with Yahweh. A comparison with Deuteronomy is enough to convince the reader that in style
and vocabulary, as well as viewpoint, these books are closely related.[1]

1. WHAT DO THESE STONES MEAN?
JOSHUA

The book of Joshua records the Israelite occupation of Canaan, the ap-
portionment of the land among the tribes, and the renewal of the covenant.
The broad divisions of the book are as follows:

1. Conquest of Palestine: chs. 1–12
2. Division of the Land: chs. 13–22
3. Concluding events
    a. Joshua's farewell address: ch. 23
    b. Covenant ceremony; Joshua's death: ch. 24

That the Deuteronomic historian worked with older sources is evident in
certain inconsistencies and duplications within the narrative. Beside the
Deuteronomist's own sweeping claims of Joshua's subjugation of the whole
of Canaan (e.g., 11:16–20) stand the more modest admissions of his sources
that some areas remained in the hands of the Canaanites (13:13; 15:13–19,
63; 16:10; 17:11–13, 16–18). One finds duplicate accounts of the crossing of
the Jordan (3:17; 4:11), the capture of Hebron (10:36–37; 15:13–14), the
death of its king (10:26; 10:37), the gift of the town to Caleb (14:13–15;
15:13–14), and the farewell address of Joshua (chs. 23 and 24). Most likely,
the non-Deuteronomic material in chapters 1–12 was provided by a JE
conquest narrative, and the data concerning tribal allocations in chapters
13–22 were based on old lists of tribal borders and towns.[2] The Deuteronomist's own style and viewpoint are particularly evident in chapter 1;

---

[1] Compare Deut., chs. 4, 6, 8, 28, and 30 with Josh., chs. 1 and 23; Judg. 2:6–23; I Sam.,
ch. 12; II Sam., ch. 7; I Kings 8:1–9: 9; II Kings 17:7–23.
[2] Martin Noth presents the evidence for the material in chs. 13–22 (*Das Buch Joshua*, 2nd
ed., Handbuch zum Alten Testament, I. 7 [Tübingen, West Germany: Mohr, 1953]) but
vigorously denies the presence of the JEP sources in the Deuteronomistic History. See, however, John Bright, "The Book of Joshua," *IB*, Vol. 2, pp. 543–544. Bright is in basic agreement with Noth in denying the identification of chs. 13–22 with the P source.

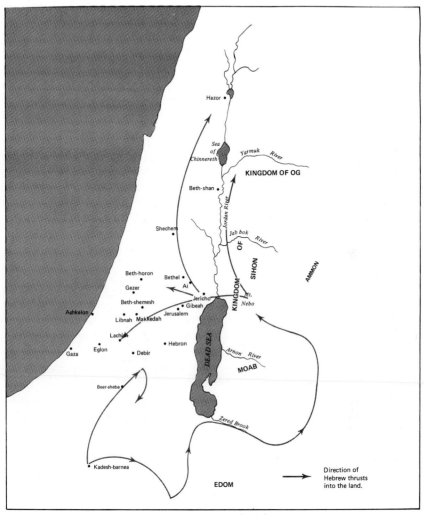

Conquest of Canaan according to Numbers and Joshua.

11:15–12:24; and chapter 23. In some places his skillful editing of his sources consists of no more than brief expansions of the text; in other instances, the older material has been thoroughly rewritten.[3]

The Deuteronomist's version of the conquest in chapters 1–12 is told with all the color, solemnity, and ceremony of a religious rite. The invasion of Canaan, with Joshua in command, proceeds by three swift and decisive campaigns to bring the whole land into the Israelites' hands. The first cam-

[3] Cf. John Bright, "The Book of Joshua," *IB*, Vol. 2, pp. 542–546.

paign establishes their hold in the region of Jericho and the central hills. Upon receiving a favorable reconnaissance report from spies dispatched to Jericho (ch. 2), the people set out from the Plains of Moab in the direction of the Jordan, the priests bearing the ark in the lead. Miraculously, the Jordan waters stop their flow, allowing them passage (ch. 3)—a phenomenon otherwise observed in modern times as a result of earthquakes and landslides from the high clay bluffs beside the river. Reminiscent of the Reed Sea crossing, the incident betokens Yahweh's intervention on his people's behalf, and memorial stones are set up to mark the spot.

> When your children ask their fathers in time to come, "What do these stones mean?" then you shall let your children know, "Israel passed over this Jordan on dry ground." For the Lord your God dried up the waters of the Jordan for you until you passed over, as the Lord your God did to the Red Sea, which he dried up until we passed over, so that all the peoples of the earth may know that the hand of the Lord is mighty; that you may fear the Lord your God forever.
>
> 4:21–24

After a brief encampment at Gilgal, where the new generation of males is circumcised and the Passover is kept (ch. 5), the assault on Jericho begins. Ritual-like, the Israelites march around the city, the priests carrying the ark and blowing trumpets. On the seventh day, after seven circuits of the city, a mighty shout by the Israelites is enough to topple Jericho's walls (ch. 6). The point of the famous story is clear: Israel's victory is due not to the superior strength of her armies but to Yahweh's mighty presence in her midst. The city is accordingly placed under the ban or *herem*, a practice of holy warfare whereby a conquered town, along with all its inhabitants and wealth, is totally destroyed as a sacrifice to the deity.

A lesson in the necessity of obedience is enforced when Israel's expedition against Ai meets with defeat as a result of Achan's taking forbidden booty from Jericho (ch. 7). The extension of the culprit's guilt to the whole people is characteristic of the solidarity between individual and group in Hebrew psychology. Consequently, his annihilation along with family and livestock purges the nation, and the second assault on Ai is rewarded with victory. Apparently encountering no further resistance in the central hills, Joshua builds an altar at Shechem, in the very center of the land, and offers thank offerings to Yahweh (ch. 8).

The second phase of the Hebrew invasion, according to the Deuteronomist, takes the invaders deep into the Shephelah and southern hill country. After being tricked into a peace pact with the sly Gibeonites (ch. 9), Joshua's forces rescue them from an attack by a coalition of Canaanite kings (10:1–27). The battle is the occasion of the famous "standing still of the sun," a prosaic literalizing of a poetic petition quoted from the lost Book of Jasher:

1. WHAT DO THESE STONES MEAN? JOSHUA

> Sun, stand thou still at Gibeon,
> And thou Moon in the valley of Aijalon.
> 10:12

Bypassing the strongly fortified towns of Jerusalem, Gezer, and Bethshemesh, the Israelites move against the city-states of Makkedah, Libnah, Lachish, Eglon, Hebron, and Debir. It takes but a bare twelve verses to rehearse—like a liturgy—the fall of each city and its utter destruction as a victim of the ḥerem (10:28–39).

The last campaign is fought with a coalition of kings in the far north in the region of the Sea of Chinnereth (Galilee). Hazor, whose king Jabin heads the opposition, also meets the fate of the southern cities; the surrounding towns, though withheld from the ḥerem, are likewise put to the sword (11:1–15). The Deuteronomist sums up the victories:

> So Joshua took all that land, the hill country and all the Negeb and all the land of Goshen and the lowland and the Arabah and the hill country of Israel and its lowland from Mount Halak that rises toward Seir, as far as Baal-gad in the valley of Lebanon below Mount Hermon.
> 11:16–17

This portrayal of the conquest as a sudden and complete military takeover has long been recognized as an oversimplification. We have already noted the evidence of the older sources scattered throughout the latter half of the book of Joshua which indicates a less thoroughgoing victory. The contrasting account in chapter 1 of Judges is even more striking. There the first question raised by the Israelites following Joshua's death is, "Who shall go up first for us against the Canaanites, to fight against them?" Clearly, many parts of the land still remained outside Israel's control; and the occupation of numerous sites involved individual efforts by the separate tribes, as well as a gradual amalgamation with the indigenous Canaanite population.

Conquest, Immigration, or Revolt?

Modern historical reconstructions of the Hebrew occupation of Canaan reflect the tensions within the biblical accounts and posit conflicting models to explain what some scholars have called "the most difficult problem in the whole history of Israel."[4] While the theories are many and complex, the major proposals may be reduced to the three models of peaceful immigration, military conquest, and internal revolt.[5]

The immigration model, favored by the German scholars Albrecht Alt,

---

[4] Roland de Vaux, *The Early History of Israel*, p. 475.
[5] Summaries of the primary models are provided by J. Maxwell Miller, "The Israelite Occupation of Canaan," *Israelite and Judaean History*, John H. Hayes and J. Maxwell Miller, eds., pp. 262–279; Norman K. Gottwald, *The Tribes of Yahweh*, pp. 191–219; and Roland de Vaux, *The Early History of Israel*, pp. 475–487.

Martin Noth, and Manifred Weippert,[6] conceives of a long and primarily peaceful infiltration of Palestine by diverse groups, rather than the pan-Israelite military assault described in the book of Joshua. The theory takes its cue from such details in the biblical accounts as the alliance with the Gibeonites, the absence of fighting in the Shechem area, the indications that not all of Israel participated in the Exodus, and the notations that some parts of the land were slow in coming under Israel's domination. The arrival of the groups that eventually merged into the nation Israel is envisioned as migrations of seminomadic herdsmen in search of pastures. Settling in unoccupied areas, apart from the Canaanite cities and city-states, their transition from a seminomadic to an agrarian life was initially uneventful. Only much later, toward the end of the Judges period, did sporadic fighting erupt between the immigrants and the Canaanites, as the newcomers extended their territory at the expense of the city-states. According to Alt and Noth, Joshua occupied nothing like the central role attributed to him in the battle stories of the book of Joshua. Noth regards it as likely, however, that he played an important part in uniting the tribes into a common alliance as described in the covenant ceremony of Joshua 24. It was at this point, and not before, that Israel came into being as a distinct people. Thus, according to Noth, the settlement of Canaan was a development involving some two hundred years, from the late fourteenth to the late twelfth century B.C. In time, as folk tradition created etiological stories to explain the ruins of former Palestinian cities, the process of peaceful settlement was converted into a swift and spectacular military victory by a united Israel.

Some elements of the immigration model have won wide approval, even from scholars who otherwise oppose its major thesis. For example, many proponents of the conquest and revolt models regard it as undeniable that Israel derived from more than a single group, or that means other than military encounter alone explain aspects of the occupation. The latter interpreters are unconvinced, however, by efforts to reduce the element of conflict to so negligible a role, and in particular reject the emphasis placed on the etiological factor. Weippert has, in fact, modified the immigration theory to include the arrival of the Joshua group (i.e., the Rachel tribes) as the impetus for the period of armed occupation which followed the initially peaceful migrations.[7] Perhaps the most serious flaw in the immigration model lies in its assumptions concerning the role of nomadism in ancient Near Eastern political affairs. Implicit within the model is the familiar but

[6] Albrecht Alt, "The Settlement of the Israelites in Palestine," *Essays on Old Testament History and Religion*, R. A. Wilson, trans. (Garden City, NY: Doubleday & Company, Inc., 1967), pp. 173–221; Martin Noth, *The History of Israel*, pp. 53–109, 141–163; Manifred Weippert, *The Settlement of the Israelite Tribes in Palestine*, James D. Martin, trans. (London: S.C.M. Press, 1971).

[7] *The Settlement of the Israelite Tribes in Palestine*, p. 146.

Jericho. Excavations at Jericho directed by Kathleen Kenyon revealed a walled city and a great stone tower (the top of which is shown here), dating from the Neolithic period (eighth millennium B.C.). (Courtesy of the Israel Government Tourist Office.)

now discredited notion that the changing political fortunes in the fertile lands were characteristically due to the encroachment of nomads upon settled populations.

The American scholar W. F. Albright and many of his former students, including G. Ernest Wright and John Bright, defend the basic integrity of the biblical account in its depiction of military successes under Joshua's leadership.[8] The battles are dated to the latter half of the thirteenth century B.C. or the last phase of the Late Bronze Age, at which time archaeology reveals widespread cultural changes in Palestine and the destruction or abandonment of a number of cities, such as Hazor, Megiddo, Beth-shan, Bethel, Gezer, Tell Beit Mirsim, and Lachish. With the beginning of the Iron Age (Iron I, 1200–900 B.C.), moreover, there sprung up numerous small villages in the rural countryside and on the sites of the former cities, characterized by a material culture noticeably inferior in technique and sophistication to the earlier LB culture. Such patterns are thought to fit the manner of life of a people fresh from the desert. The late thirteenth-century date, furthermore, coincides with an Exodus from Egypt during the reign of Rameses II, followed by the traditional generation in the wilderness of Sinai. It would also allow for Israel's presence in Canaan by about 1220 B.C., as attested by Merneptah's stele.

Objections to the conquest model center particularly on its interpretation of archaeological data. Archaeology, of course, provides a tangible means of assessing the culture of a given period at specific sites, and as such is a valuable tool for reconstructing biblical history. Unwritten artifacts, however, are frequently subject to a variety of interpretations; and this is surely the case with the question at hand. Notwithstanding the impressive evidence of cultural change that marks the transition from the Late Bronze to the Early Iron Age in Palestine, there is no data that connects these developments specifically with the Israelites. Other peoples, notably the Philistines, also entered Canaan during this period (c. 1175 B.C.); and the desperate attempts of Egypt to maintain an influence in the unruly land resulted in military actions such as those reported by Pharaoh Merneptah. Archaeological finds at some sites, moreover, present more of a problem than a support to the conquest model. Notably, Jericho appears to have been either a small settlement or virtually unoccupied during the thirteenth century,[9] and Ai was a ruin (the name means "ruin") between about 2000 and 1200 B.C.[10] Also Gibeon, with whose occupants the Israelites are said to have entered into an alliance, has thus far offered little

---

[8] W. F. Albright, "The Israelite Conquest of Canaan in the Light of Archaeology," *BASOR*, 74 (1939), pp. 11–23, and *The Biblical Period from Abraham to Ezra* (New York: Harper Torchbooks, 1963), pp. 24–34; G. Ernest Wright, *Biblical Archaeology*, pp. 69–84; John Bright, *A History of Israel*, 2nd ed., pp. 126–139. Bright's reconstruction combines the conquest and revolt models.

[9] Cf. Kathleen Kenyon, *Digging Up Jericho* (New York: Frederick A. Praeger, 1957), pp. 256–265; idem, *Archaeology in the Holy Land*, ch. 8, esp. pp. 211–212; idem, *The Bible and Recent Archaeology*, ch. 3. Serious erosion of the LB level of the mound at Jericho has caused some to theorize the existence of a thirteenth-century city of which no remnant has survived. Kenyon, however, who excavated the site, disputes this theory (*The Bible and Recent Archaeology*, pp. 42–43).

[10] Cf. J. A. Callaway, "New Evidence on the Conquest of 'Ai'," *JBL*, LXXXVII (1968), pp. 312–320. Albright's theory that the fall of Bethel, located near Ai, was confused with the lat-

sign of habitation during the last phase of the LB Age.[11] As for southern Transjordan and the Negeb, contrary to Nelson Glueck's earlier conclusions, sedentary patterns began later than the thirteenth century. In Moab and Edom generally and at the sites of Arad, Hormah, and Heshbon, invaders coming from the Sinai would not likely have met with the resistance reportedly encountered by the Hebrews in their earliest penetrations of the land.[12]

As with the immigration theory, supporters of the conquest model have modified the proposal in recent years in response to some of these problems. Most proponents readily acknowledge the impossibility of fitting all the evidence into either a literal interpretation of the Joshua account or a single pattern of military action. Typically, a long and complex period of settlement is envisioned as following the initial victories, which included peaceful alliances with some segments of the population, as well as further military clashes. De Vaux, for example, assigns the major role in the conquest of central Palestine to an invading force under Joshua's command, but ascribes the occupation of the northern and southern sectors of the land to other groups, some settling peaceably and others using force. J. A. Callaway, the excavator of Ai and a supporter of the conquest model, conceives it in terms of minor-scale raids on small villages, which he dates to Iron Age I, i.e., the twelfth rather than the thirteenth century.

The third major alternative, the revolt model, was first formulated by G. E. Mendenhall and recently adopted by Norman Gottwald and others.[13] It portrays the settlement of Canaan as—in the main—neither a peaceful immigration nor a sweeping invasion from outside, but as a sociopolitical upheaval by the peasantry within Canaan, as they sought relief from the oppressive feudal system imposed by the Canaanite city-states. As early as the Amarna period (fourteenth century B.C.), it is felt, the disaffection of some Palestinian elements was manifest in the socially disturbing actions of the *Habiru*. Mendenhall conceives the *Habiru* as revolutionary groups, whether of rebellious serfs, restive free farmers, or anyone occupying the lower levels of Canaanite society who threatened the established order. The catalyst for a broad egalitarian revolution came in the thirteenth century with the arrival in Canaan of the Israelites led by Joshua. The new-

---

ter site, has been adopted by some (cf. G. Ernest Wright, *Biblical Archaeology*, pp. 80–81 and John Bright, *A History of Israel*, 2nd ed., pp. 128) and criticized by others (cf. J. Maxwell Miller, "The Israelite Occupation of Canaan," pp. 272–273).

[11] Cf. James B. Pritchard, *The Bronze Age Cemetery at Gibeon*, Museum Monographs (Philadelphia: University of Pennsylvania Press, 1963), p. 72; idem, *Gibeon, Where the Sun Stood Still* (Princeton, NJ: Princeton University Press, 1962), pp. 157–158.

[12] Cf. Num. 14:25, 39–45; 21:1–3; Josh. 12:14; Judg. 1:16ff. On the archaeological finds in the Negeb and Transjordan, see J. Maxwell Miller, "The Israelite Occupation of Canaan," pp. 258–260, and the bibliography cited there.

[13] Cf. George E. Mendenhall, "The Hebrew Conquest of Palestine," BA XXV (1962), pp. 66–87, reprinted in *BA Reader*, 3, pp. 100–120; and Norman K. Gottwald, *The Tribes of Yahweh*, esp. pp. 210–219.

comers shared with the restive serfs and peasants both a common lower-class identity and a history of servitude under their former Egyptian task-masters. In the Israelite religion, moreover, was the new and appealing element of Yahwism, which celebrated a deliverance from past bondage and the promise of Yahweh's continuing protection for his followers. The two groups joined forces in a mutual covenant with Yahweh, the results of which are described by Gottwald:

> In the highlands, wherever they were strong enough, the combined exodus tribes and converted Canaanite lower classes threw off their overlords and formed "tribal" rule by elders in deliberate rejection of centralized political rule by imperial-feudal "kings." Taxation and corvée to support a large royal establishment were obliterated at one stroke wherever Israel prevailed. The Canaanite overlords in the plains were too weak to contest the revolt effectively in the hill country, and the symbiotic exodus Israelite/Canaanite lower class "conquest" went forward with measureable success.[14]

Proponents of the revolt model point to the correctives which it brings to the older schemes of immigration and conquest. Similar to the conquest model, it attributes a critical role to the Joshua group, who came from outside; but, like the immigration theory, it posits no sharp distinction between Canaanites and Hebrews and views the later Israel as an amalgam of different ethnic elements. It corrects the erroneous conception of the ancestry of Israel as nomads or seminomads and avoids the common stereotype of invading nomads pitted against a settled population. In the process, it offers an explanation for the sociopolitical matrix in which the central Exodus or deliverance theme of Yahwism was nurtured. Also, it is able to deal more flexibly with the archaeological evidence, since "destruction of cities by any of several agencies could easily fit within the model."[15]

The revolt model has weaknesses of its own, however, the most serious being the absence of a single clear statement in the biblical account itself giving expression to the egalitarian objectives claimed by the model or the revolution which these purported grievances called forth. The treatment of *Habiru*, "Hebrew," and "Israelite" as virtually synonymous terms, moreover, has been criticized as an oversimplification. Further, some critics of the model suspect an imposition upon the ancient accounts of contemporary ideologies of social and political revolution or principles of modern liberation theology.[16]

As with the other major issues in early Hebrew history—the patriarchal

---

[14] Norman K. Gottwald, *The Tribes of Yahweh*, p. 214.

[15] Ibid., p. 217.

[16] Cf. Alan J. Hauser, "Israel's Conquest of Palestine: A Peasants' Rebellion?" *JSOT* 7 (May 1978), pp. 2–19, and the responses in the same issue by Thomas L. Thompson (pp. 20–27) and Norman K. Gottwald (pp. 37–52). Cf. also J. Maxwell Miller, "The Israelite Occupation of Canaan," pp. 278–279.

age and the Exodus from Egypt—so too is the question of the occupation of Canaan likely to remain a subject of debate for some time to come. For all their differences, however, the competing models are not totally inconsistent; and, as expressed in some recent modifications, their common elements become all the more evident. Representatives are to be found in each camp who can agree on the involvement of more than a single group in the settlement of the land; on ascribing a significant, if not crucial, role to the Joshua or Exodus group; on a pattern of initial occupation of the Palestinian hill country, leaving for a later time the more entrenched cities of the plains and valleys; and on the importance of an alliance or covenant among the merging groups, whereby the Yahwism of the Exodus group served as a basic, uniting element.

The Covenant at Shechem

The absence of any references to military conflict in the vicinity of Shechem, together with the account of the tribal convocation there (Josh. 24), argues for the presence in that area of persons of Hebrew ancestry or otherwise friendly Habiru with whom the Exodus group had to fight no battle, but only to establish or renew its ties through treaty. Otherwise, so strategic a site, commanding the major north-south highway through central Palestine, could hardly have escaped becoming a crucial battle area. Archaeological evidence at Shechem reveals no signs of military conflict for the period in question; and the Amarna Letters, as we have seen, mention Habiru control of the area at least a century earlier than Joshua's time.

Ancient traditions relate that Jacob purchased land at Shechem and built an altar there to "El, God of Israel" (Gen. 33:18–20); and the account of Genesis 34 reflects conflict between the Shechemites and the Leah tribes (Reuben and Simeon, who staged the attack on Shechem, were two of Jacob's sons by Leah; the others were Levi, Judah, Issachar, and Zebulun). Such allusions fit well with the theory of an early settlement of the area by Leah tribes, who accordingly either did not experience the Egyptian bondage or else left Egypt considerably earlier than the group under Moses. If this be so, then Joshua's followers—consisting of the Rachel tribes, Joseph (Ephraim and Manasseh) and Benjamin—had but to ally themselves with the Leah clans and initiate them into the faith of Yahwism. Although hypothetical, this could explain the covenant ceremony of Joshua 24. More than simply a rite of covenant renewal for the Joshua group—though it was this too—it was the occasion whereby those who had not themselves shared in the Mosaic deliverance from Egypt, now through personal choice made the Exodus experience their own. Joshua's words, "choose this day," thus challenged them to separate from the Canaanite element in the land and take their stand with the god who had revealed himself so mightily in Egypt.

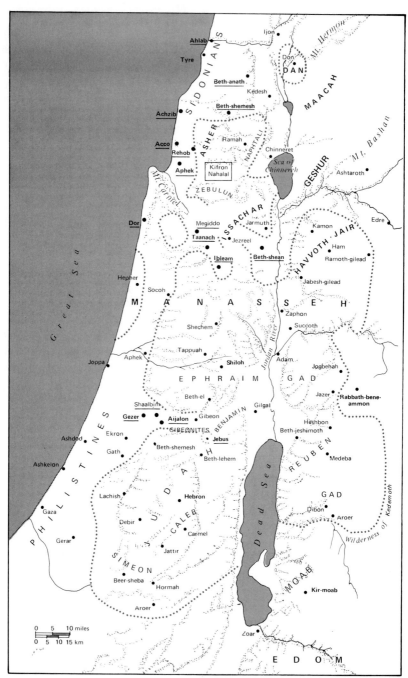

The limits of Israelite control of Palestine in the twelfth century B.C., according to traditional locations of the tribes (Cf. Josh. 15:63; 16:10; 17:11–18; Judg. 1:21–35). (Adapted with permission of Macmillan Publishing Co., Inc., from Macmillan Bible Atlas by Y. Aharoni and Michael Avi-Yonah. Copyright © 1968 Carta, Jerusalem. © Copyright 1964 by Carta, Jerusalem. © Copyright 1966 by Carta, Jerusalem.)

The Shechem ceremony, although presented here as a singular event, most likely reflects a recurring ritual whereby the Israelite tribes reaffirmed and renewed the covenant, perhaps on a regular basis. We cannot, assume that we have here the original form of the ceremony, however, as the language is largely Deuteronomic and appears to reflect the conditions of the Israelite monarchy or the Exile.[17] Also, attempts to find in the account the specific form of the suzerainty treaty have not been entirely successful. The several elements in the ceremony, nevertheless, are instructive: a convocation of the people in Yahweh's presence; a recitation of the Lord's mighty deeds in Israel's history; the challenge to put away other gods and to render sincere and faithful service to Yahweh alone; the inclusion of statutes and ordinances; and the erection of covenant stones as witnesses.

Holy War and Covenant Faith

The modern reader of the book of Joshua is likely to experience a sense of moral uneasiness with the scenes of aggressive warfare depicted there. Of course, one's choice of an explanatory historical model will determine the estimate of how bloody or how defensible the occupation of the land actually was. According to the immigration hypothesis, the episode was not nearly so violent as it appears on the surface. Or, should the revolt model be correct, the goal of liberation from the tyrannical control of the city-states puts the conflict in a different light. Be that as it may, Israel obviously distinguished between the battle for Canaan, which she conceived as a holy war, and other aggressive and barbaric forms of warfare which are denounced elsewhere in the Old Testament.[18] In thus making a place for holy war, the Hebrews were neither better nor worse than other peoples of the ancient world. The practice of the *herem* finds its counterpart in an inscription of Mesha, king of Moab, on the famous Moabite Stone.

> And Chemosh [the Moabite god] said to me, "Go, take Nebo from Israel!" So I went by night and fought against it from the break of dawn until noon, taking it and slaying all, seven thousand men, boys, women, girls and maid-servants, for I had devoted them to destruction for Ashtar-Chemosh.[19]

In Israel's eyes, Canaan was the land to which her ancestors had long ago laid claim, as related in the patriarchal legends. Yahweh, moreover, had promised the land as a gift for her faithfulness. Never did she claim to deserve it, nor even to own it. The land was Yahweh's; only his doing battle on Israel's behalf had assured her possession of it. It was within his designs, so Israel reasoned, that her warfare was conducted.

[17] Cf. Dennis J. McCarthy, *Old Testament Covenant, A Survey of Current Opinions* (Atlanta, GA: John Knox Press, 1972) p. 75.
[18] E.g., Hos. 1:4; Amos 1:3ff.; Hab. 1:17; Nah. 3:19.
[19] *ANET*, p. 320 (*ANE*, p. 210).

The Tribes of Yahweh

The boundary lists found in chapters 13–19 of Joshua describe the location of the Israelite tribes after the settlement in Canaan. As we have seen, Hebrew tradition traced each tribe back to one of the twelve sons of Jacob. Notwithstanding Judah's absorption of the tribe of Simeon nor the omission of the Levites from territorial allotments because of their special priestly status, the number twelve was maintained. Simeon continued to be reckoned as a full-fledged tribe; and the bifurcation of the Joseph tribe into Ephraim and Manasseh balanced the loss of Levi. While there is general agreement among Old Testament scholars that the twelve-tribe system did not originate before the time of the events described in the book of Joshua, opinion is divided as to precisely when and in what manner the traditional tribal allocations become a reality. It has been recently proposed by Gottwald that the full number of twelve tribes was not attained until just prior to the establishment of the monarchy.[20]

The more vexing question is whether there was a broader social organization of the tribes between the time of the settlement and the formation of the monarchy (c. 1250–1000 B.C.) and, if so, what it was like. An epochal study of this problem was conducted in the 1930s by Martin Noth, who concluded that early Israel was organized in a sacred league, comparable to the amphictyonies that existed in the Mediterranean world among the Greeks, Old Latins, and Etruscans.[21] All of the essential characteristics of the Graeco-Roman amphictyonies, Noth contended, were present in the tribal alliance of early Israel: an association of autonomous groups in twelve or six-member confederations; the worship of a common deity at a central shrine; the acceptance of a sacred law that was binding on all members; and a body of amphictyonic officers delegated by the member group.

According to Noth, the earliest Israelite amphictyony consisted of the six Leah tribes and existed before the arrival in Canaan of Joshua and "the house of Joseph." With the coming of the latter group and the covenant ceremony at Shechem (Josh. 24), the alliance expanded to include the full twelve members. It is believed that Shechem served as the first amphictyonic center. But, since the site is not mentioned further in connection with the cult, it is thought to have been replaced by a succession of shrines, such as Shiloh, Bethel, and Gilgal, or wherever the holy ark was housed. There the tribes gathered regularly to hear the reading of the divine law, to proclaim Yahweh's deeds, and to reaffirm a common identity through the renewal of covenant vows.

No matter how ingenious this correlation of the Israelite tribes with the

---

[20] *The Tribes of Yahweh*, pp. 362–363.
[21] *Das System der Zwölf Stämme Israels*, IV–1 (Stuttgart, West Germany: Kohlhammer, 1930). See also Noth, *The History of Israel*, pp. 85–109.

Graeco-Roman amphictyonies, it is now evident that Noth failed to reckon adequately with either the ambiguity of the biblical evidence or the inherent differences between the Hebrew and Graeco-Roman societies.[22] In respect to an Israelite amphictyonic shrine, not only is Noth forced to posit its transfer from place to place, but nowhere does the Old Testament refer to a single shrine or series of shrines during the tribal era. A more natural reading of the biblical record suggests the existence of multiple shrines. Further, there is no recognizable reference in the accounts to amphictyonic delegates analogous to the representatives of the city-states in the Greek alliances. And, as we have just noted, it is far from clear that the full twelvefold tribal system was a reality until the time of the monarchy. The Song of Deborah (Judg. 5), which likely dates from the twelfth or eleventh century B.C., mentions only ten tribes. Nor does this ancient poem refer to a central shrine as a rallying point for the tribes. Thus, one is forced to conclude that Noth has failed to make a convincing case for the existence of an Israelite amphictyony analogous to the Graeco-Roman alliances.

This does not mean, however, that there was no cooperative alliance through which the Israelite (or "proto-Israelite") tribes—whatever their number and however many their cultic shrines—expressed their common allegiance to Yahwism and united in concerted efforts to overthrow tribal enemies. The Song of Deborah, which includes the summons to ten tribes to come forth and confront the Canaanite enemy, clearly assumes pantribal obligations. The formation of the monarchy would be difficult to envision, moreover, without some such preliminary tribal association to prepare its way. It thus seems reasonable to posit the existence of a loosely structured tribal confederation or league, which allowed the fullest possible autonomy to the separate tribes, but nurtured a pantribal identity, centered in devotion to the common deity.[23]

Canaanite Culture

Israel confronted among her Canaanite neighbors a set of cultural patterns in many respects more highly advanced than her own. As we have seen, Canaan's predominantly agricultural economy had given rise to a

[22] For criticisms of the amphictyony model, cf. Harry M. Orlinsky, "The Tribal System of Israel and Related Groups in the Period of the Judges," *Studies and Essays in Honor of Abraham A. Newman* (Leiden, Netherlands: E. J. Brill, 1962), pp. 375–387; George W. Anderson, "Israel: Amphictyony: ʿAm; *Kāhāl; ʿEdâh*," *Translating and Understanding the Old Testament*, Harry Thomas Frank and William L. Reed, eds. (Nashville, TN: Abingdon Press, 1970), pp. 135–151; Roland de Vaux, *The Early History of Israel*, pp. 695–749; Dennis J. McCarthy, *Old Testament Covenant*, pp. 61–65; and Norman K. Gottwald, *The Tribes of Yahweh*, pp. 345–386.

[23] Norman K. Gottwald's detailed analysis of pre-Davidic Israelite society assumes an intertribal confederacy, but one that differed from the Graeco-Roman amphictyonies and lacked a twelve-tribal form (*The Tribes of Yahweh*). Cf., however, Alan J. Hauser, "Unity and Diversity in Early Israel before Samuel," *JETS*, 22 (1979), pp. 239–303, for a provocative reconstruction of the pre-monarchical era which reckons without a tribal league.

feudal society of small city-states, each with its strongly fortified town and surrounding lands. The local prince or king owned a large share of the land, and guilds of merchants, craftsmen, soldiers, and priests functioned under his patronage. The excavated remains of Canaanite sites reveal richly cosmopolitan cities, including large temples and elegantly furnished palaces. In language, art, and music, as well as architecture, the Israelites were to learn much from the neighboring Canaanites, Phoenicians, and Syrians. Inscriptions show that by the time of the Israelite settlement both Egyptian hieroglyphics and a native cuneiform alphabetic script were in use in these lands. So advanced were their art forms over those of the Hebrews, that as late as the time of Solomon Phoenician artisans were hired to execute the designs in the Jerusalem Temple.

THE FERTILITY CULT. Just as the Amarna letters portray the political conditions in Canaan before the conquest, a collection of clay tablets discovered in 1929 at Ras Shamra (ancient Ugarit) on the north Syrian coast, provide a firsthand picture of Canaanite religion. The collection, which is about one half the volume of the Hebrew book of Psalms, is written largely in the alphabetic cuneiform now known as Ugaritic and dates from the fourteenth century B.C. Most of the tablets consist of an epic poetry which relates the mythology of the chief gods and goddesses of the Canaanite pantheon.[24] Revealing parallels to the structure and vocabulary of the poems appear in some of the earliest parts of the Old Testament, including the Song of Miriam (exod. 15) and the Oracles of Balaam (Num. 23–24).

Being first and foremost a fertility religion, the Canaanite polytheism made much of the sexual pairing of the major gods and goddesses, as follows:

El. Chief god of the pantheon; sky god; father of the gods and ruler over the heavenly assembly; symbolized by the bull.

Ashirat (or *Ashirat of the Sea;* in the Old Testament, *Asherah*). El's consort and mother of the gods; symbolized by a wooden pole.

Baal. "Lord of the Earth"; one of the 70 offspring of El and Ashirat; active god of storm and fertility; creator of mankind; appears, like El, in the form of the bull (symbol of strength and fertility); active in the fertilizing powers of springtime.

Anath (Ashtart). Consort-sister of Baal; warrior goddess; sadistic and brutal; given to violent sexual passion; yet capable of tender love for Baal and his deliverer from death.

[24] Cf., *ANET*, pp. 129–142 (*ANE*, pp. 92–132).

The Canaanite fertility and storm god, Baal, depicted with club and lance. On his helmet are the horns of the bull, symbolizing fertility. The upper part of the lance may symbolize lightning. This relief was discovered in a sanctuary at Ras Shamra, Syria. (© ARCH. PHOT., Paris/S.P.A.D.E.M./V.A.G.A., 1981.)

Other gods that figure prominently in the Ugaritic mythology are these:

Yam (or *Lothan;* Biblical *Le-viathan*). God of the sea; seven-headed monster, whom Baal battles and defeats.

Mot. God of death; active in summer drought and destructive powers that bring sterility and death to field, flock, and family; dreaded enemy of Baal.

Baal, the most active god of the Canaanite pantheon, is mentioned often in the Old Testament. In some instances his name appears in the plural (*Baalim* or Baals), indicative of the god's association with numerous localities and towns. The myth of Baal's death and resurrection is the Canaanite counterpart of the Mesopotamian Tammuz-Ishtar mythology. Baal is killed by Mot and carried to the underworld, whereupon all life on earth languishes. Then Anath finds Mot and kills him in a terrible struggle, after which Baal is restored to life. The god's resurrection is accompanied by a corresponding renewal of the energizing forces of nature. Fertility of field, flock, and family was thought to depend upon sexual relations between Baal and Anath; their mating caused the new life of spring to come out of the barrenness of winter. The mythology was enacted by devotees of the cult in orgiastic rites at the temples. According to a pattern of sympathetic or imitative magic, whereby the worshiper imitates the actions he desires the gods to perform, male and female worshipers engaged in sacred prostitution, supposing thereby to assure the rhythmic cycle of nature.

Such in brief was Baalism. Contrasting in many basic respects with Yahwism, it nevertheless held a powerful attraction for the Israelites. Undeniably, Canaanite religious elements were assimilated into Hebrew faith and culture, as witnessed by the Baal names given prominent Israelites (e.g., Jerubbaal, Ishbaal, Meribbaal), the Palestinian agricultural festivals common to both religions, and the presence of fertility altars and figurines in some Israelite households (e.g., Judg. 6:25). Some Hebrews, perhaps without consciously abandoning Yahweh, became active participants in the fertility cult.

The threat to Hebrew religion presented by such syncretism was due to no incompatibility between Yahwism and the natural world as such. Notwithstanding the centrality of history for Hebrew faith, Yahweh was properly conceived as Lord of both nature *and* history. It made no sense, declared Israel's great prophets, for the Hebrew farmer to turn to Baal for success in agriculture, when Yahweh himself was the giver of the grain,

An ivory representation of a fertility goddess feeding goats, from a tomb near Ras Shamra, Syria. (© ARCH. PHOT., Paris/S.P.A.D.E.M./V.A.G.A., 1981.)

wine, and oil (Hos. 2:8). The same delivering God of the Exodus and the Sinai wilderness was the very source of the natural energies upon which the life of man depends. In contrast to the fertility deities, however, Yahweh was not himself subject to the death and resurrection of the natural world. Nor was his direction of nature attributed to sexual union with a female consort. (Biblical Hebrew even lacks a word for "goddess.") Thus there was no proper place in the worship of Yahweh for sexual rites designed to coerce fertility. As we have seen, the very name Yahweh means that he is the uncontrollable God, who is not manipulated through magical or mechanical means, but whose actions result from his own good intentions for humankind. The loss of these unique principles through syncretism with the Baal cult would surely have spelled the death of Yahwism. Time and again, Israel would be called back from such a course to a renewed commitment to the God of her origins. For, as declared by Joshua in his address at Shechem (Josh. 24), Israel's future depended upon nothing so much as a clear-cut choice concerning her ultimate loyalties.

Canaanite cult figure of a mother goddess, from a grove near "Rachel's tomb," Bethlehem (eighth–sixth century B.C.). (Courtesy of the Trustees of the British Museum.)

2. THE LORD RAISED UP JUDGES: JUDGES

The book of Judges, as generally interpreted, provides the only record of Israel's first two centuries in the land of Canaan, from the death of Joshua to Saul's reign as the first Hebrew king (c. 1200–1020 B.C.). These were crucial years of testing for the newly formed tribal alliance. Sporadic fighting for the control of Canaanite towns continued for some time, as both the biblical accounts (Judg. 1) and archaeological findings attest. Excavations at Bethel reveal no fewer than four destructions by fire during these two centuries.[25] At the beginning of the period the Canaanites were

[25] G. Ernest Wright, *Biblical Archaeology*, p. 88.

Terracotta lid of a Philistine coffin from Tell Yahudiyeh, Egypt (twelfth century B.C.). (Courtesy of the Trustees of the British Museum.)

firmly entrenched on the coastal plain and in the all-important valleys, and still maintained pockets of resistance in the central highlands. The important southern cities of Gezer and Jerusalem were in Canaanite hands, as were the fortresses of Megiddo, Taanach, and Bethshan in the Esdraelon valley. Consolidation of the Israelite holdings was thus far from realized, with enemy-held territory separating the Galilean tribes from their fellows to the south, and the Transjordan clans largely isolated by the great Jordan cleft. Nor were the Canaanites the only enemy with whom the tribes had to deal. Lacking any centralized authority or standing army, they were constantly exposed to attacks of neighboring Moabites, Ammonites, Midianites, and Philistines.

The Philistines were a part of the great migration of Sea Peoples who, once repelled from Egypt by Pharaoh Merneptah, mounted further attacks early in the reign of Rameses III (c. 1175–1144 B.C.). Moving upon Egypt in successive waves and from three directions—from Asia, Libya, and by sea—they were driven back once more, but only after Rameses had exhausted the country's last reserves of manpower and finances. Too weak to pursue them in retreat, Egypt was helpless to prevent some of their number from settling on the southern Palestinian coast. Thus coming perhaps a generation after Joshua and his followers, they were to remain a formidable part of the Canaanite scene for the next two centuries. A characteristic feature of their exotic Mycenaean type culture was a fine, highly decorative pottery which has appeared in excavations at various Palestinian sites. Although restricted for the most part to a small strip of coastal territory, Philistia's strength was concentrated in an effective Pentapolis (military league of five cities): Gaza, Gath, Ashkelon, Ashdod, and Ekron (Josh. 13:3). The well-watered plain supported an abundant supply of agricultural products; and the secret of iron manufacture, derived from the Hittites, provided a powerful economic and military monopoly that remained unbroken until the time of David (I Sam. 13:19–22). This period, in fact, marks the beginning of the Iron Age in Palestine (c. 1200–300 B.C.).

Charismatic Heroes

The Book of Judges is composed of three distinct parts, as follows:

1. Settlement of the tribes in Canaan: 1:1–2:5
2. The "Major" and "Minor" Judges (plus the story of Abimelech): 2:6–16:31
3. Appendices: chs. 17–21
   a. Migration of the Danites: chs. 17–18
   b. Crime of the Benjamites: chs. 19–21

The hand of the Deuteronomic editor is as evident here as in the Book of Joshua. Once again, older sources have been reworked and fitted into a pattern consistent with the Deuteronomic understanding of history. The subject matter concerns, for the most part, tribal heroes who served as unofficial leaders of the tribes during the twelfth and eleventh centuries B.C. Six of these figures received a more detailed treatment and are commonly referred to as the Major Judges: Othniel (3:7–11), Ehud (3:12–30), Deborah (and Barak) (chs. 4–5), Gideon (chs. 6–8). Jephthah (10:6–12:7), and Samson (chs. 13–16). The so-called Minor Judges (Shamgar, 3:31, Tola, Jair, 10:1–5; Ibzan, Elon, and Abdon, 12:8–15) have received such scant attention as to be little more than names. Abimelech (ch. 9), the leader of an early and abortive effort to become Israel's first king, is the subject of a critical account which avoids referring to him as judge. The two appendices to the book (17–18 and 19–21) may not be so old as the stories of the judges. When and how they became attached to the book, whether by the Deuteronomic historian or a later editor, are impossible to determine. They reflect none of the characteristic marks of the Deuteronomic style.[26]

Our English word "judge" fails to bring out the breadth of meaning encompassed in the Hebrew term *shophet* (from the verb *shaphat*, to "judge," "justify," or "deliver"). The *shophet*, as the title is used in the Old Testament, is not in the first instance an arbitrator of legal disputes, though he (or she) might serve in that capacity (Judg. 4:4–5). He is, rather, one who defends the right or just cause, whether in the capacity of a juridical official who hears cases and renders judgments or as a military leader who throws off the oppressor of a victimized people. In either case, the results are the same: the punishment of the offender, the vindication of the innocent party, and the restoration of the right (just) order of things. The heroes of the Judges stories are chiefly military leaders or tribal champions who arose in hours of crisis to deliver their people from the hands of enemy oppressors. Their sole authority appears to have resided in their "charismatic" (spirit-directed) personality, rather than in any hereditary or elected office.[27] Powerfully courageous and zealous for the independence and well-being of the tribes, they rallied the necessary support to combat the recurring harassment and open attacks of nearby enemies: Canaanites, Moabites, Midianites, and Ammonites.

This is the essential nature of the stories which the Deuteronomist received from Israelite tradition and to which he attached his editorial framework. By means of a moralizing introduction to the accounts as a whole (2:6–3:6) plus the brief introductory and concluding formulas which frame each of the separate episodes, he gave to the book its peculiar theological stamp: a cyclical pattern of apostasy-oppression-repentance-deliverance, expressed in stereotyped phrases.

> And the people of Israel did what was evil in the sight of the Lord and served the Baals. . . . So the anger of the Lord was kindled against Israel and he gave them over to plunderers. . . . Then the Lord raised up judges who saved them out of the power of those who plundered them . . . for the Lord

---

[26] Martin Noth contends that chs. 17–18 originated in the circle of the royal Israelite sanctuary of Dan which was established by Jeroboam I (922–901 B.C.) ("The Background of Judges 17–18," *Israel's Prophetic Heritage*, Bernhard W. Anderson and Walter Harrelson, eds. [New York: Harper & Row, Publishers, 1962], pp. 68–85).

[27] Efforts to depict the Judges as pantribal officials or administrators have thus far proved less than convincing. For the different proposals, cf. Roland de Vaux, *The Early History of Israel*, pp. 751–773 and the bibliography cited there. Martin Noth's contention that the Minor Judges, as distinguished from the military deliverers or Major Judges, filled a legal and administrative office in the tribal league ("Das Amt des 'Richters Israels,'" *Festchrift A. Bertholet* [Tübingen, West Germany: J.C.B. Mohr, 1950], pp. 404–417; *The History of Israel*, pp. 101ff.) creates an artificial distinction between the Major and Minor Judges and is soundly criticized by Alan J. Hauser ("The 'Minor Judges'—A Reevaluation," *JBL*, 94 [1975], pp. 190–200).

was moved to pity by their groaning. . . . But whenever the judge died, they turned back and behaved worse than their fathers, going after other gods. . . .

Judg. 2:11–19

Thus, in a typically Deuteronomic vein, the problems of the tribes are traced in each case to their disloyalty to Yahweh. Only the oppression by an enemy people can bring them to a state of repentance.[28] Then it is that Yahweh responds to their change of heart and raises up a judge for their deliverance. Once peace is restored, however, the people turn back to idols, and the cycle repeats itself.

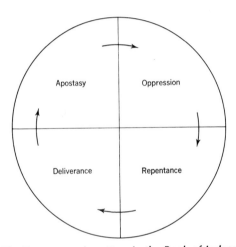

The Deuteronomic pattern in the Book of Judges.

One may be quick to observe the oversimplification that results from the Deuteronomic editor's theological framework. Deeds originally relating to only one or a few of the tribes are made to appear as crises involving them all, when in fact, the largest muster of tribes for any single battle is the six-clan coalition led by Deborah and Barak (chs. 4–5). Samson's battles with the Philistines are neither tribal nor national in scope, but of a purely personal sort. We cannot be certain, furthermore, that this arrangement of the stories is according to strict chronological sequence; nor can the round figures cited for the periods of the Major Judges—in 20s, 40s, and 80s—be taken at face value.[29] By a literal reckoning, the Deuteronomic chronology

---

[28] The conception of repentance reflected in the Old Testament is not simply that of a state of mind, but an active change in behavior—a reversal of a characteristic life-pattern. See below, p. 300.

[29] Jephthah (6 yrs.; 12:7) is the exception.

for the entire period of the judges totals some 410 years, which is roughly twice the length of the period from Joshua to Saul.

The Deuteronomist, it should be noted, has seldom allowed his editorial additions to obscure the content of the stories themselves. As a result, we have here authentic accounts from the judges period, some of them—notably the Song of Deborah—possibly going back to the very events recorded. About the first judge, Othniel (3:7–11), and the oppression of a Mesopotamian king, there is little that can be said. The appearance of a Mesopotamian invader in Palestine at this date is hard to conceive; and the absence of any further description beyond the Deuteronomic formulas arouses further suspicion. The Ehud episode (3:12–30), on the other hand, bears the color and detail of an authentic folk account. The scene in which the left-handed Benjamite delivers "a message from God" to the fat king of Moab in the form of a well-concealed dagger has suffered no loss of dramatic effect in its Deuteronomic setting. The clever ruse by which he turned the tables on the Moabites doubtless inaugurated a successful campaign by which Benjamin and Ephraim (vs. 27) united to drive the invaders out of the West Jordan territory.

The Deborah story is told in two versions, the song of Deborah (ch. 5), the oldest poem of its length in the Old Testament, and a later prose account (ch. 4). Barak, the Israelite military commander who is spurred into action by Deborah, might have been the original hero of the story. The enemy in this instance is the northern coalition of Canaanite city-states that continued to control the important trade route through the Esdraelon Valley and thereby to throttle Israelite commerce.

> In the days of Shamgar, son of
>   Anath,
>   in the days of Jael, caravans
>   ceased
> and travelers kept to the byways.
> 5:6

According to the prose account, King Jabin of Hazor headed the Canaanite coalition. Hazor, depicted as an earlier victim of the Israelite invasion (Josh. 11:1–15), would by this reckoning have fallen once again into Canaanite hands and regained its status as a leading northern city. Excavations at Hazor, however, reveal that no city of size existed there in the twelfth and eleventh centuries.[30] The Song of Deborah mentions only Sisera (5:20) as the leader of the enemy forces and does not identify his city. The ancient

---

[30] Yigael Yadin, *Hazor: The Rediscovery of a Great Citadel of the Bible* (New York: Random House, Inc., 1975), pp. 249–257. Yadin discusses the proposed solutions for dealing with the apparent discrepancy between Josh. 11 and Judg. 4. The problem is heightened by the reference to the death of King Jabin in both accounts.

and firsthand report of the poem must be accepted as the more authentic of the two accounts.

There are yet other differences between the prose and poetical accounts. In the prose story Deborah is identified as a prophetess living in the central hills of Ephraim (4:5); in the poem she appears to belong to the tribe of Issachar in Galilee (5:15). The only two tribes that oppose the Canaanites in the prose version are the Galilean clans of Naphtali and Zebulun; in Deborah's Song six tribes respond to the summons to arms and are forthrightly commended (Ephraim, Benjamin, Manasseh, Zebulun, Issachar, and Naphtali), whereas those who fail to respond are the recipients of bitter scorn (5:14–18). Also, the battle appears to take place in the region of Mount Tabor according to the prose (4:12–16), but "at Taanach, by the waters of Megiddo" (in Esdraelon) according to the poem (5:19).[31] Finally, there are two versions of Sisera's death scene. The Canaanite commander, fleeing for his life after the defeat of his forces, seeks shelter in Heber the Kenite's tent. According to the prose account (4:21), Jael, wife of Heber, puts a tent peg through Sisera's temple as he sleeps; in the poem, Jael strikes him as he stands, drinking "curds in a lordly bowl" (5:25–27).

The Song of Deborah is a masterpiece of ancient poetry. Stylistic parallels with the Ras Shamra poems are evident and lend further support to its early date. To read it, even in English translation, is to experience through the power of its verse the throbbing heat of battle and the joining of human and cosmic hosts:

> From heaven fought the stars,
> from their courses they fought
> against Sisera.
> The torrent Kishon swept them
> away,
> the onrushing torrent, the
> torrent Kishon.
> March on, my soul, with might!
> 5:20–21

The waters of the Kishon River, flowing through the Esdraelon Valley, were apparently at a swollen stage from heavy rains. With his chariots bogged in the mud, Sisera lost a prime military advantage over the Hebrew

---

[31] Excavations reveal an occupational gap at Megiddo, between 1150 and 1075 B.C. This period (c. 1150 or 1125 B.C.) is viewed by W. F. Albright and others as a logical time for the victory described in Judg. 5:19 under the name of Taanach, an otherwise insignificant site nearby (W. F. Albright, "The Song of Deborah in the Light of Archaeology," *BASOR*, 62 [1936], pp. 26–31; *The Biblical Period from Abraham to Ezra*, pp. 39ff. and note 82; *Yahweh and the Gods of Canaan* [Garden City, NY: Doubleday Anchor, 1969] p. 13, note 35). For a criticism of this reasoning, cf. Roland de Vaux, *The Early History of Israel*, pp. 794–796 and A. D. H. Mayes, "The Period of the Judges and the Rise of the Monarchy," *Israelite and Judaean History*, John H. Hayes and J. Maxwell Miller, eds., pp. 314–315. De Vaux, on other grounds, accepts a mid-twelfth century B.C. date for the battle.

army. The Israelites' decisive ally, however, is shown to be Yahweh himself, who figuratively marched from Sinai to enter the fray on behalf of his people (vss. 4–5). His saving actions (vs. 11; RSV "triumphs"; plural of *tsedakah*, "righteousness") are to be told every place that Israelites gather and provide the actual subject for Deborah's victory song. The unforgettable picture of Sisera's mother awaiting her dead son (vss. 28–30) is, for all its pathos, primarily a word of encouragement to the people of Israel that their would-be attackers shall surely have to answer Israel's God.

> So perish all thine enemies,
> O Lord!
> But thy friends be like the sun as
> he rises in his might.
> 5:31

The days of Gideon and Jephthah witnessed further encroachment upon the tribal territories at the hands of neighboring Transjordan peoples. The stories that gathered about Gideon (chs. 6–8) show him to have been one of the most popular of the tribal heroes. He is credited with leading the men of his own tribe, Manasseh, together with recruits from Asher, Zebulun, and Naphtali in a successful repulsion of camel-riding Midianite raiders who were plundering the Palestinian heartland as far north as the Esdraelon. The colorful account of the reduction of his army from thousands to only three hundred brave warriors proclaims Israel's continuing dependence upon Yahweh's favor. The stories also reveal the alarming pace of Baal syncretism within Israelite circles: Gideon has a Baal name (Jerubbaal, "Baal contends"); his father maintains a fertility shrine (6:25); and Gideon himself fashions an idolatrous ephod, after which "Israel played the harlot" (8:24–28). Jephthah, a Transjordanian hero, delivers the Gileadites from absorption by the adjoining Ammonites (chs. 11–12). The tragedy of Jephthah's daughter, resulting from his rash vow before the battle, is probably not, as sometimes supposed, indicative of a fixed custom of human sacrifice in early Israel.[32] The extraordinary story may have originated to explain an annual ceremony of mourning at the time of summer drought (11:39–40), thus historicizing a nature rite adopted from Canaanite fertility religion.[33] Whatever its background, the story's simplicity of detail and appeal to the imagination are, as in the other stories in Judges, a reminder that "the Hebrew story tellers were among the best of all time."[34]

The Samson tales (chs. 13–16) add considerably to our understanding of the relations between Israelites and Philistines during the late twelfth and early eleventh centuries. The hero's exploits as such are hardly other than those of a Hebrew Paul Bunyan, in whose extraordinary feats of strength

---

[32] Cf. Roland de Vaux, *Ancient Israel*, p. 442.
[33] Walter Harrelson, *Interpreting the Old Testament*, p. 146.
[34] Jacob M. Myers, "The Book of Judges," *IB*, Vol. 2, p. 772.

the Israelite folk mind delighted. Not even the inclusion of the stories within the broader Deuteronomic framework can disguise their almost total lack of a religious or moral tone. Their delightful quality, in fact, is due precisely to the rugged, lusty, and mischievous character of the hero's private feuds and romantic escapades.[35] It is historically significant that the stories indicate no hostilities between the Philistines and Hebrews at this time except those of a purely personal and local sort. The Danite tribe, to which Samson belonged, still maintained its position in the Shephelah, adjacent to Philistia (cf. ch. 18). By the end of the eleventh century, however, the picture had so changed that the Philistines were the major threat confronting the Israelite tribes.

AN EXPERIMENT WITH KINGSHIP. The closing chapters of the Book of Judges depict the growing internal problems faced by the Israelite confederacy. The bloody battle between the Benjamites and the rest of the tribes provoked by the outrage at Gibeah (chs. 19–21) served as a warning of what could continue to happen so long as there was no centralized authority in Israel. The summarizing comment of the editor of Judges 17–21 attests the near anarchy of the times.

> In those days there was no king in Israel; every man did what was right in his own eyes.
>
> 17:6; 21:25

At the same time, Abimelech's short-lived reign as king over Shechem and the surrounding territory (Judg. 9) witnesses Israel's reluctance to submit to monarchical rule. Gideon, Abimelech's father, had purportedly rejected the proffered role of king. Only his son's indomitable ambition for a kingdom and the extreme measures he took to get it allowed him his brief three years' reign. Even Shechem, whose initial support had brought Abimelech to power, soon rebelled against his brutality. The antimonarchical note of Jotham's fable, with its warning against a bramblebush king, useless for shade and likely tinder for fire (Judg. 9:7–21), was to be heard once again, even as the resistance to monarchy gave way before the mounting tide of Philistine aggression.

The transition period which brought Israel's change of heart was the generation of Samuel, a singular Israelite leader and, in a real sense, the last of Israel's judges. So powerful was his influence among the tribes that when the first Israelite king was chosen, no one other than he could have possibly made the selection. It is with the story of his birth that the Book of Samuel begins.

---

[35] A perceptive literary and theological analysis of the Samson stories is provided by James L. Crenshaw, *Samson: A Secret Betrayed, A Vow Ignored* (Atlanta, GA: John Knox Press, 1978).

3. THE LORD HAS SET A KING OVER YOU: I–II SAMUEL

The books of I–II Samuel are best studied as one continuous narrative, even as they form a single book in Hebrew manuscripts. They treat the period from the appearance of Samuel (c. 1070 B.C.) to the closing years of David's reign (c. 961 B.C.) and can be outlined around the careers of their three principal characters: Samuel, Saul, and David.

1. Samuel: I Sam. 1–8
   a. Birth and call: chs. 1–3
   b. History of the ark: chs. 4–6
   c. Samuel as judge: chs. 7–8
2. Samuel and Saul: I Sam. 9–16
3. Saul and David: I Sam. 17–II Sam. 1
4. David: II Sam. 2–24
   a. King over Judah: chs. 2–4
   b. King of all Israel: chs. 5–8
   c. David's court history: chs. 9–20 (Completed in I Kings 1–2)
   d. Appendices: chs. 21–24

That the Samuel work rests on older sources is evident in its parallel narratives, contrasting appraisals of the monarchy, and different portrayals of Saul and Samuel. There are no fewer than three separate accounts of Saul's elevation to the kingship, in only one of which Samuel takes the initiative in anointing Saul as king (9:15–10:8). Elsewhere (10:17–27) Samuel yields reluctantly to the demands of the people, anointing Saul only after warning that selection of a king is tantamount to rejection of Yahweh. In the third account (ch. 11) it is Saul's display of charismatic leadership in delivering Jabesh-gilead from the Ammonites that leads to his coronation through popular acclaim. According to one tradition Samuel is a local seer sought out by Saul on account of his clairvoyant powers (ch. 9); in another, he appears as a prominent magistrate who travels a circuit in the Ephraimite hill country (7:15–17). There are likewise parallel accounts of Samuel's rejection of Saul (I Sam. 13:8–15; 15), David's introduction into Saul's court (16:14–23; 17:55–58), his flight from Saul (19:11–18; 20), and his sparing of Saul's life in the wilderness (24; 26).

Efforts have been made to reduce the older sources in Samuel to two: (1) an early promonarchical source from the period of the United Monarchy, which is somewhat more favorably disposed toward Saul; and (2) a late antimonarchical source from the period of the later Monarchy (c. 750–650

B.C.), which centers most of its attention on Samuel.[36] That we have in Samuel a compilation of promonarchical and antimonarchical traditions is not to be doubted, but that these two criteria can be made the basis for a simple duality of sources running the length of the work is far from certain. To regard the sources as continuations of the J and E strands of the Pentateuch is even less defensible. It is more likely that the compiler utilized a number of independent sources, of which—in addition to the (1) promonarchical and (2) antimonarchical traditions—we can distinguish (3) a Samuel infancy narrative (I Sam. 1–3), (4) a history of the ark (I Sam. 4–6; II Sam. 6), and (5) the so-called "Court History of David" or "Throne Succession Narrative" (II Sam. 9–20 and I Kings 1–2). The Deuteronomist's role in the production of the work is not as easily determined as in the other books of the Former Prophets. His unmistakable style and theology are evident, however, in passages such as I Samuel 8 and 12, where he appears to have reworked the older antimonarchical traditions, giving them a peculiarly Deuteronomic point of view.

The End of the Tribal Era

Because of the Samuel records we are better informed about the period of the early monarchy than any comparable era in Israel's history. To begin with, we are left in little doubt as to why in the latter half of the eleventh century a monarchical form of government became imperative for Israel. By that time the Philistine menace had reached proportions far exceeding the local threats posed by Israel's previous foes. The tribal rally which had proved effective in throwing off the enemy in earlier days was no match for the disciplined Philistine soldiers, with their horse-drawn chariots and iron weapons. Border skirmishes and mounting Philistine pressure in the Shephelah eventually gave way to crucial battles in which the control of all Palestine was at stake. The first such contest appears to have been at Aphek, at the edge of the coastal plain (I Sam. 4). Here the Israelites, in a desperate bid for victory, carried the ark onto the field. But not even this vessel of Yahweh's presence could avail for the unorganized troops; they were put to rout, and the ark was taken as a Philistine trophy. With the way thus opened to the Israelite hill country and the Valley of Esdraelon, the Philistines were well on their way toward conquest of the entire land. Archaeological and biblical evidence suggests that Shiloh, seat of an important Israelite shrine, was destroyed at about this time.[37]

Such were the perilous times into which Samuel was born. Placed under

---

[36] The Early Source is generally held to have included I Sam. 4–6; 9:1–10:16; 11:1–11; 24 (or 26); 25; 27–31; II Sam. 2–7; 9–21. To the Late Source is assigned I Sam. 1–3; 7–8; 10:17–27; 12; 26 (or 24); 28; II Sam. 1. Cf. George B. Caird, "The First and Second Books of Samuel," *IB*, Vol. 2, pp. 855–861.

[37] G. Ernest Wright, *Biblical Archeology*, p. 89. Cf. Jer. 7:12ff.; 26:6ff.

the Nazirite vow[38] from birth and reared under the tutelage of Eli at the Shiloh shrine, his charismatic qualities brought him to the fore as Israel's most able leader following Eli's death. Owing in part to the separate source traditions, but also apparently to his peculiar versatility, Samuel fills multiple roles in these accounts: charismatic judge, magistrate, priest, prophet, seer, and king-maker. After the fall of Shiloh, he appears to have divided his time between his home village of Ramah and other towns in the Ephraimite hill country: Bethel, Gilgal, and Mizpah. Perhaps for a time he led the clans in efforts to resist the Philistines (I Sam. 7:7–14), possibly even succeeding in slowing their infiltration of the central highlands. By Samuel's later years, however, Philistine fortresses existed at strategic sites throughout the land (I Sam. 10:5; 13:3f., 23).

The United Monarchy (c. 1020–922 B.C.)

As we have seen, both the promonarchical and antimonarchical sources in I Samuel agree that Samuel anointed Saul as Israel's first king, though they disagree as to his attitude toward the action. There is no way of determining which of the two traditions is closer to Samuel's actual position, although it is often assumed that the antimonarchical version reflects the coloration of Israel's later disappointments with the monarchy's failures. There is no reason that the latter account has to be the later of the two versions, however, nor is it unlikely that Samuel actually entertained misgivings about the monarchy. His later break with Saul, which seems authentic enough, is less than adequately explained by either of the stories concerning improprieties in sacrificing before battle (13:9–15) and failure to implement the *herem* (ch. 15). Nowhere else in the Saul stories—lest it be in his patronage of a sorceress in his last, desperate hours—is his scrupulous observance of religious duties called into question. If Samuel had reservations about the monarchy from the very beginning, however, the final rift with Saul is much more easily understood. The antimonarchical passages, on the other hand, lent themselves to the larger embellishments of the Deuteronomic historian; Samuel's lecture on the evils of kingship in I Samuel 8:10–18 is similar in tone to Deuteronomy 17:14–17 and reflects a bitter resentment against the absolutist policies of Solomon and his successors.

> These will be the ways of the King who will reign over you: he will take your sons and appoint them to be his horsemen, and to run before his chariots. . . . He will take your daughters to be perfumers and cooks and bakers. He will take the best of your fields and vineyards . . . and in that day you will cry out because of your king, whom you have chosen for yourselves; but the Lord will not answer in that day.
>
> 8:10–18

[38] The Nazirite vow was a dedication to holiness that included absention from wine, refusal to cut the hair, and strict observance of purity laws. The vow might be taken for life or as a temporary observance.

Beth-shan. Situated at the junction of the Jezreel and Jordan valleys, Beth-shan was an important caravan station and fortress-city. It was controlled by Egypt during the Late Bronze Age and by the Philistines during the time of King Saul. (Courtesy of the Consulate General of Israel in New York.)

SAUL (c. 1020–1000 B.C.). In most respects Saul bears a closer resemblance to the judges who preceded him than to the succession of kings who followed his reign. Tall and handsome, the son of a well-to-do Benjamite named Kish, he might well have attracted the attention of Samuel as described in the promonarchical tradition (ch. 9). His courageous defense of Jabesh-gilead (ch. 11), particularly the manner in which he mustered the tribes for battle, leaves little doubt as to his charismatic endowments and military ability. After the manner of the judges, he served his people primarily as a warrior-leader. One of the source traditions, in fact, calls him a "prince" (*nagid*), rather than "king" (*melek*).

Under Saul's administration the tribal organization was left essentially unchanged. There was no reorganization of the land into administrative districts, no court bureaucracy, no levy of taxes, and no formal military conscription. His army was composed of volunteers plus any strong and courageous man who came to the king's attention (14:52). The only military officer of whom we are informed was his commander, Abner, a cousin. In short, Saul's reign was marked by few of the trappings of the typical eastern monarchies. He had no harem or splendid court. His palace at Gibeah, in

230

Benjamin, is revealed by archaeology as a simple, rustic fortress, with none of the finery of the Canaanite or later Israelite royal palaces.

Together with his stalwart son Jonathan, Saul must be credited with checking for a time the Philistine advance into central Palestine. An early and important engagement at the pass of Michmash in the central hills turned the tide in Israel's favor (chs. 13–14). Following Jonathan's daring attack upon the enemy camp, Saul's army drove the occupation forces all the way back to the coastal plain. The Philistine threat was by no means ended, but the central highlands were once more under Israel's control and open to freedom of movement. Saul was also successful in driving Amalekite raiders out of the Negeb (ch. 15), a campaign that brought Samuel's criticism for his failure to institute the *herem*. From the perspective of the antimonarchical tradition, Samuel was justified in his denunciation of Saul; the new king had failed in a religious duty. Samuel, however, hardly increases in stature—at least for the modern reader of the account—in his gory dissevering of the Amalekite king:

> And Samuel hewed Agag in pieces before the Lord in Gilgal.
> 15:33

Saul has probably not received his due in Israelite tradition as a result of the antimonarchical bias of some of his biographers, on the one hand, and the strong pro-Davidic sentiment of others. So endeared to the later tradition was the figure of David, that it was inevitable that his strengths should be compared with Saul's weaknesses. One can hardly fail to note that once David appears in the accounts Saul's personality deterioration begins (I Sam. 16). It is not to be assumed, however, that this was altogether the creation of the later tradition. Saul's later years were marked by manic states of fitful depression and paranoia, described in the language of the times as "an evil spirit from the Lord" (16:14). Perhaps the loss of Samuel's favor, together with the popularity that young David enjoyed with the masses, was too much of a strain for the aging Saul. As his jealousy of David increased, apparently so too did his irrational behavior. The several attempts on David's life and the latter's magnanimous refusal to retaliate in kind may reflect the pro-Davidic slant of the sources. The bloody massacre of the eighty-five priests at Nob (ch. 22), however, reads like a deed of the sick man that Saul had become.

To add to Saul's problems, the Philistines mounted renewed attacks in central Palestine. On the eve of the fateful battle at Mount Gilboa, on the edge of the Valley of Jezreel, Saul is depicted as seeking through necromancy the counsel of the dead Samuel (ch. 28). When the medium of Endor brings up the shade of Samuel, his prophecy spells out the bitter fate in store for Saul. The following day the Philistines successfully storm the Israelite position on the summit of Mount Gilboa, scatter Saul's army to the winds, and slaughter the brave defenders who stand their ground. Among the slain bodies are those of Saul and Jonathan. David's beautiful elegy (II Sam. 1:19–27) pays final tribute to the beloved Jonathan and the tragic, but heroic Saul.

> Thy glory, O Israel, is slain upon thy
>   high places!
> How are the mighty fallen!
>
> Saul and Jonathan, beloved and
>   lovely!
> In life and in death they were not
>   divided;
> They were swifter than eagles,
>   they were stronger than lions.

The men of Jabesh-gilead, not soon to forget Saul's courageous delivery of their once oppressed city, risk their lives to remove his exposed body from the wall of Beth-shan and give it a proper burial (I Sam. 31:11–13).

DAVID (c. 1000–961 B.C.). The latter half of the book of I Samuel records the overlapping period in the careers of Saul and David. Three stories introduce David into the narrative. First, we are told of Samuel's carefully concealed mission to Bethlehem (16:1–13), where from the eight sons of Jesse, the ruddy shepherd lad is chosen. Samuel anoints him on the spot as Israel's future king. The highly theologized account has an unmistakable message to declare, namely, that Yahweh had plans for David even from his childhood. As the older brothers pass in review, likely candidates all, Samuel the king-maker is reminded:

> Do not look on his appearance or on the height of his stature . . . for the Lord sees not as man sees; man looks on the outward appearance, but the Lord looks on the heart.
>
> 16:7

A second story (16:14–23) explains how the secretly anointed youth is introduced into Saul's court at Gibeah as a consequence of his reputation as a musician. Whenever Saul was beset with the evil spirit from God, we are told, David's skillful playing of the lyre would soothe the king and exorcise the malignant spirit. He soon becomes a favorite of Saul and is appointed as the king's personal armor-bearer. The story is a plausible one; David's reputation as a musician and poet is fixed firmly within Hebrew tradition (cf. Amos 6:5), and his later successes in battle presuppose early military training that the role of armor-bearer would have provided.

Yet another account (17:1–18:5) explains David's rise to prominence as a result of his famous slingshot victory over the Philistine giant, Goliath. The incident itself is not beyond belief, indeed, such an heroic exploit would help explain David's early popularity as a military champion (18:6–7). The account, however, is beset with several problems. It takes no cognizance of the fact that David is elsewhere introduced into the narrative (cf. 16:1–13 and 17:12–16) or that he is already familiar to Saul. Thus the king has to inquire of Abner as to the young hero's identity (17:55–58). The notation that David took the slain Philistine's head to Jerusalem (17:54) is anachronistic as the city was not yet in Israelite hands. Most perplexing of all is the fact that the slaying of Goliath is elsewhere attributed to a certain Elhanan of Bethlehem (II Sam. 21:19).[39] It would be easy enough to conceive of David's having gotten the credit for an otherwise obscure soldier's heroic feat. Quite possibly, however, it is only a matter of the name of Elhanan's victim having been transferred to an anonymous Philistine killed by David.[40]

David's favor with Saul could not survive the growing popularity which accompanied the young hero's military successes. Even in his saner moments the king might with good reason have heard a threat in the song of the Israelite women.

Saul has slain his thousands, and David his ten thousands.

18:7

Unsuccessful in his schemes to do away with David quietly and unable to divert the affections of Jonathan and Michal from their winsome companion and husband, Saul declares openly his intentions to slay David. Jonathan, concerned only for David's personal safety and not at all for securing his own succession to the throne, warns David of the threat, whereupon he flees Gibeah. The hunted man eventually is forced into the one area where Saul could not reach him—Philistia and its outlying regions. Here David makes the best of a bad situation. After surrounding himself with a stalwart group of devoted followers, he wins the confidence of Achish, the Philistine king of Gath, receives the village of Ziklag as a gift, and makes his way by raiding Amalekite villages in southern Palestine and the Negeb. Though little more than an outlaw band, he and his men grow in favor with the Philistines, who are led to believe that his battles are against the Israelites. At the same time, his popularity increases with his own people of Judah who welcome the relief he brings from the hated Amalekites. When Saul

---

[39] I Chron. 20:5 is an attempt to harmonize the two traditions.

[40] George B. Caird, following A. R. S. Kennedy, explains this position in "The First and Second Books of Samuel," *IB*, Vol. 2, pp. 971ff. Yet another theory is that Elhanan is David's preregnal name. There is evidence of changes in names upon assumption of kingship in Israel (as in Egypt); see Roland de Vaux, *Ancient Israel*, pp. 107–108.

and Jonathan fall before the Philistines at Gilboa, Judah, acting independently, declares David its king.

King of Judah. For a period of two years David ruled Judah from Hebron
while Saul's surviving son, Ishbaal,[41] ruled as king over the rest of the nation. A weakling who depended completely upon his father's general,
Abner, Ishbaal was poorly equipped to offer any resistance to the Philistine
menace. It was apparently in an effort to get beyond the aggressor's reach
that the capital was removed to Mahanaim in Transjordan. David on the
other hand, was content to rule Judah as a Philistine vassal until such time
as he could take control of all Israel and mobilize the nation's defenses.
Owing to a rapid succession of politically inspired blood lettings, that time
was not long in coming.

To assume that David secretly engineered the events which propelled
him to the kingship over all Israel is to go beyond the evidence (II Sam.
1–4). It is enough to recognize the rare diplomatic skill by which he turned
each eventuality to his best political advantage. His lament over Saul and
Jonathan was doubtless an expression of genuine sorrow which was given
added emphasis by his execution of Saul's self-proclaimed slayer (II Sam.
1). At the same time, it served to demonstrate David's magnanimous spirit
of forgiveness and to enhance his stature in the eyes of those who revered
the memory of the late king. When a feud developed between Abner and
David's strong-willed nephew and general, Joab, leading eventually to
Joab's murder of Abner, David did not become involved. Rather, Abner's
death became the occasion for mourning and fasting. David's reaction did
not go unnoticed in the north.

> And all the people took notice of it, and it pleased them; as everything that
> the king did pleased all the people. So all the people and all Israel under-
> stood that day that it had not been the king's will to slay Abner the son of
> Ner.
>
> 3:36–37

Finally, when Ishbaal was assassinated by two of his captains, clearing the
way for David to take the Israelite throne, the assassins were denied their
expected reward. Instead, David once again showed his respect for the
house of Saul and sentenced the murderers to death. Confident of David's
qualifications to rule, the northern tribes came to Hebron and together
with Judah anointed him king of all Israel.

King of All Israel. The first and most crucial challenge facing the new
king was the Philistine problem. In two decisive engagements in the Valley
of Rephaim, west of Jerusalem (II Sam. 5:17–25), David's army drove the
invaders out of central Palestine, back to their old territory on the southern
plain. Henceforth they were to continue as a neighboring people, occasionally making further trouble for Israel but never again becoming a

---

[41] On the names Ishbaal and Ishbosheth, see above, p. 21.

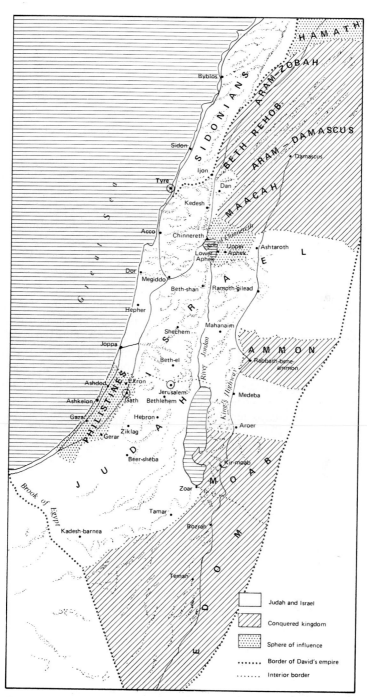

The kingdom of David, c. 1000–961 B.C. (Adapted with permission of Macmillan Publishing Co., Inc., from Macmillan Bible Atlas by Y. Aharoni and Michael Avi-Yonah. Copyright © 1968 Carta, Jerusalem. © Copyright 1964 by Carta, Jerusalem. © Copyright 1966 by Carta, Jerusalem.)

major threat. David's victories over this long-time enemy have been cited as "the most lasting successes of a life that was rich in success."[42] Now free from all foreign intervention, he could turn his attention to building the nation. Further military campaigns against the Moabites, Edomites, Ammonites, and Syrians, along with the conquest of the remaining Canaanite city-states in Palestine, gave David command of a small empire extending from southern Syria to the Gulf of Aqabah. Israel's golden age had arrived.

David's success is to be credited not only to his military skill, but also to his effective organization of Israel's administrative machinery. Well aware of the sectional tensions between north and south, he judiciously chose Jerusalem, situated almost directly between the two, as the site of the new capital. The city had only recently been taken from the Jebusites and consisted at the time of a heavily fortified hill (Ophel) surrounded by three valleys, the most formidable of which were the Hinnom and the Kidron on the southwestern and eastern sides, respectively. Here David built his palace (5:11–12) and conducted affairs of state for the remainder of his forty-year reign.[43] The Ark of the Covenant was brought up from Kiriath-jearim, where it had lain neglected since the Philistines returned it to Israel a generation earlier (I Sam. 5:1–7:2). Installed by David in a tent shrine in Jerusalem, it established the city as the religious center of the realm and doubtless did more to unite the people than any other single act performed by the brilliant administrator. There is no reason to doubt the tradition that David purchased a site north of the palace grounds for the erection of a temple, but on the basis of wise counsel left the actual fulfillment of the plans to Solomon (II Sam. 7). Israel was slow in adapting to the idea of permanent houses of worship, and David was unwilling to risk alienating those who would have seen in such a move a paganizing innovation and an insult to Yahweh, who "tents" among his people.

Archaeological excavations on the Ophel Hill and the slopes of the Kidron Valley have added considerably to our comprehension of David's Jerusalem.[44] A small area, probably no more than eleven acres in extent, the city was supplied with an excellent water source in the Gihon spring, located on the lower slopes of the Kidron. The city's walls, built by the Jebusites, encompassed a shaft connecting with the spring, the entrance to which was thus protected from enemy attack. This protective measure,

---

[42] Martin Noth, *The History of Israel*, p. 189.

[43] The entirety of David's reign from Hebron is cited as seven and one half years (II Sam. 5:5). Thus for five years after becoming king of all Israel, he continued to reign from Hebron.

[44] See Kathleen Kenyon, *Digging Up Jerusalem* (London: Ernest Benn Limited, 1974), pp. 76–106; Benjamin Mazar, *The Mountain of the Lord* (Garden City, NY: Doubleday & Company, Inc., 1975), pp. 153–174; idem, "Jerusalem in the Biblical Period," *Jerusalem Revealed,* Yigael Yadin, ed. (Jerusalem: Israel Exploration Society, 1975), pp. 1–8; Hershel Shanks, *The City of David: A Guide to Biblical Jerusalem* (Washington, D.C.: The Biblical Archaeology Society, 1975), pp. 15–37; Yigal Shiloh, "City of David Excavation 1978," *BA*, 42 (1979), pp. 165–171; idem, "Digging in the City of David," *BAR*, V, 4 (July/August 1979), pp. 36–49.

The Ophel Hill. South of Jerusalem's Old City walls and the Dome of the Rock
(upper left), is the small hill of Ophel, which was the original Jerusalem—the
Jebusite city captured by David. Bounded by the Kidron Valley on the east (center
of the picture), the Tyropoeon on the west (left edge of picture), and the Hinnom
on the south (bottom), the Davidic city's defenses included a stone wall, a small
portion of which has been excavated on the lower slopes of the Kidron.
(Courtesy of Werner Braun.)

237

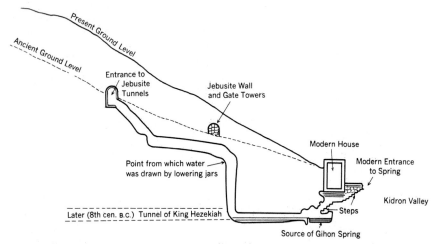

Jebusite wall and water system in David's day, shown in relation to the later channel of Hezekiah.

however, may not have prevented David's men from discovering another entrance to the spring from outside the walls and, with some difficulty, gaining entry into the city through the vertical shaft.[45] The excavations of Kathleen Kenyon during the 1960s uncovered a small part of the original Jebusite wall, some 8 feet thick, consisting of rough stones, and located about two thirds of the way down the Kidron's slope. Miss Kenyon theorized that this piece of wall formed part of an eastern gate to the city which was flanked by two large towers. It appears that it was this wall that David repaired and maintained (II Sam. 5:9) as Jerusalem's defenses throughout his reign from the city.

Following perhaps Egyptian governmental models,[46] David chose a cabinet consisting of a military chief of staff (Joab), a commander of foreign mercenaries (Benaiah), two chief priests (Zadok and Abiathar), a public

[45] Cf. II Sam. 5:6–9 and I Chron. 11:4–7. Interpretations of the Samuel passage, and hence the manner of Jerusalem's capture, vary widely. The debate concerns, in part, the meaning of the Hebrew word *tsinnar*, usually translated "water shaft" but rendered "grappling hooks" in the New English Bible. Cf. Benjamin Mazar, *The Mountain of the Lord*, pp. 168–169, and Hershel Shanks, ibid., pp. 31–37.

[46] B. D. Redford argues for Canaanite rather than Egyptian influence on David's court and disputes the genuineness of the list of officials recorded in II Sam. 8:15–18 and 20:23–26 ("Studies in Relations between Palestine and Egypt during the First Millennium B.C.," *Studies on the Ancient Palestinian World*, J. W. Wevers and D. B. Redford, eds., *TSTS*, Vol. 2 [1972], pp. 141–156). Compare, however, J. Alberto Soggin's defense of the reliability of the Davidic officials lists and his contention that Egypt's influence had been sufficiently dominant in Phoenicia and Canaan to assure its effect on David's administration, even if at secondhand ("The Davidic-Solomonic Kingdom," *Israelite and Judaean History*, John H. Hayes and J. Maxwell Miller, eds., pp. 356–359). See also John Bright, "The Organization and Administration of the Israelite Empire," *Magnalia Dei: The Mighty Acts of God*, Frank Cross et al., eds. (Garden City, NY: Doubleday & Company, Inc., 1976), pp. 193–197.

Excavations on the Ophel Hill. Modern excavations on the eastern crest of the Ophel have revealed a monumental stone structure (upper center of the picture) and Israelite houses dated to the Iron Age—including the period of David and Solomon (tenth century B.C.). Further down the slope (bottom, center), below modern terrace walls, are portions of the Jebusite wall of David's day and the later wall of Hezekiah (eighth century B.C.). Modern steps (seen diagonally on the lower left) lead down to the Gihon spring, a few yards up from the bottom of the Kidron Valley. (Photo by the author.)

relations secretary (Jehoshaphat), and a secretary of state.[47] There is also mention of an overseer of forced labor (II Sam. 20:24)—a certain Adoram— which suggests that the labor corvée described in the Solomon accounts was actually instituted during David's administration. Although we are told of no systematic taxation or military conscription, it appears more than likely that David laid the groundwork for both. The taking of the census (II Sam. 24), which brought criticism from Israel's prophetic circles, may reflect the initial establishment of administrative districts such as we hear about in Solomon's day.

David's most serious problems and shortcomings appear to have been those affecting his personal and domestic affairs. We possess in the so-called Court History of David or Succession Narrative (II Sam. 9–20; I Kings 1–2) an especially well-informed and ancient source for the study of these more intimate details of the king's career. These chapters read like a first-hand account of court life and are hardly to be dated later than Solomon's day. Their unknown author, writing some five centuries before

---

[47] II Sam. 8:15–18; 20:23–26.

years, then turns to the other kingdom and traces its history up to and beyond that point, then returns to the former, and so on. Each monarch is accordingly dated by the regnal years of his royal counterpart in the sister kingdom. Stereotyped opening and closing formulas mark the descriptions of each reign. The opening formula includes (1) the date of the king's accession as synchronized with the reign of the rival monarch, (2) the duration of his administration, and (3) the historian's judgment on his reign. For the southern kings there are additional notations regarding (4) the king's age at his accession and (5) the identification of the queen mother. The closing formula consists of (1) a reference to further sources of information about the king, (2) a notice of his death and burial, and (3) the name of his successor.

Each king—north and south—is judged by a strict Deuteronomic standard of faithfulness and accordingly condemned or praised. The result is much condemnation and only very slight praise. Without exception, each of the northern kings is censured for his failure to correct the evils instituted by Jeroboam, the first king of the north. Jeroboam's most heinous offense, by Deuteronomic reckoning, was his creation of shrines outside Jerusalem. The standard of the one altar also figures in the evaluation of the southern kings, each of whom is subjected to a comparison with "David, his father." The latter receive a decidedly more favorable report than the northerners, but only two—Hezekiah and Josiah—can be given wholehearted approval, since they are the only ones who made serious efforts to remove the outlying high places.

Some of the older sources utilized by the compiler of I–II Kings are acknowledged by name as "The Book of the Acts of Solomon" (I Kings 11:41), "The Book of the Chronicles of the Kings of Israel" (I Kings 14:19), and "The Book of the Chronicles of the Kings of Judah" (I Kings 14:29). Since we possess no extant copies of these works (they are not to be identified with the canonical books of Chronicles), it cannot be determined how much of the Kings history derived from them. Other unnamed sources have supplied some of the material, among them the Davidic Court History (I Kings 1–2); separate cycles of stories concerning King Ahab (portions of I Kings 16:29–22:40) and outstanding ninth- and eighth-century prophets, such as Elijah (portions of I Kings 17–II Kings 2), Elisha (portions of II Kings 2–9, 13), and Isaiah (II Kings 19–20); and, perhaps, a history of the Jerusalem Temple (I Kings 5–8).

Solomon (c. 961–922 B.C.)

Solomon's accession to the throne came in a manner quite different from that of either Saul or David. Qualified by Davidic lineage rather than personal charisma, he nevertheless had first to prevail over his elder brother Adonijah, who was not only ambitious for the throne but enjoyed the support of Joab and Abiathar. The strong backing of Nathan, Zadok, and Ben-

*Interior o
tibule, H
eastern F.*

palace com
was small l
and was bu
must be rei
the building
Israel worsh
the sacrifice

Numerou
Phoenician
that of a Sy
sisted of thr
between tw
This opened

Megiddo Stable
the Twentieth C
is disputed by Y
Frank M. Cross
1976], pp. 18–2
Hazor, Megiddo
building activiti
187–231.

56 See P. L.
Yigael Yadin, *H*

aiah, together with his father's favor, gave Solomon the needed edge in the power struggle. Even as Adonijah was having himself acclaimed king at a spring to the south of Jerusalem, David, near death, authorized the anointment of Solomon. At the sacred spring of Gihon on the western slopes of the Kidron, he was anointed by Zadok and acclaimed by the crowd as David's successor.

Upon the death of his father, Solomon moved quickly to eliminate his political opponents and consolidate his power. Adonijah was summarily executed when he betrayed his lingering designs for the kingship by petitioning for David's former concubine, Abishag; Joab, ostensibly on David's orders, was likewise put to death; and Abiathar was banished to his home village of Anathoth, outside Jerusalem. Solomon's supporters in the contest with Adonijah were given vital cabinet posts; Benaiah was put in charge of the army and Zadok became chief priest.

The kingdom inherited by Solomon was relatively free from external menace. Egypt's once prestigious role in Near Eastern affairs was long since a thing of the past,[52] and Assyria's advance westward had not yet begun. Israel's command of the corridor between Egypt and Mesopotamia, with its vital international trade routes, placed it in an excellent position to become the major political and commercial power of the Near East. Solomon set out to exploit these potentialities to the fullest.

Through a program of judicious alliances with the surrounding states, typically sealed by marriages to daughters of the foreign rulers, Solomon established agreements important for peace and commericial exchange. Within his harem, reputed to consist of seven hundred wives and three hundred concubines (I Kings 11:3), there was no less a noblewoman than the daughter of the Pharaoh. None of his treaties proved to be of greater significance, however, than that with Hiram, king of Tyre (Phoenicia). A major maritime power, Tyre provided Solomon with the trained seamen with whom he manned his own fleet of ships. The lack of natural harbors on the Palestinian coast posed no insurmountable problem for the enterprising monarch. Ezion-geber, on the Gulf of Aqabah, became the major seaport from which his ships sailed on regular trading voyages to southern Arabia and Africa.[53] Israelite grain and olive oil were exchanged for such exotic products as gold, silver, jewels, ivory, rare woods, spices, incense, and even monkeys. For the same exports, Hiram supplied Solomon with cyprus and cedar timber, as well as the architects and artisans for his ambitious

52 Cf. the affront offered the Egyptian ambassador by the king of Byblos as recorded in the *Tale of Wen-Amon* (*ANET*, pp. 25–29; *ANE*, pp. 16–24).

53 The site of Solomon's seaport (i.e., Ezion-geber), once identified with Tell el-Kheleifeh near Eilat, is now associated by Beno Rothenberg with the small offshore island Jezirat Fara'un ("Island of the Pharoahs"), popularly known as Coral Island. See Beno Rothenberg, *Timna: Valley of the Biblical Copper Mines* (London: Thomas and Hudson, 1972), also published as *Were These King Solomon's Mines: Excavations in the Timna Valley* (New York: Stein and Day, Publishers, 1972).

buildin
the kin
and Cil

Anci
Aqabah
mon's I
has sho
ianites,
turies b
betweer
credited
(refiner
refer to

The Ho
the grea
basis of
side of
entrance
Atlanta.)

SOLOMC
Solomon's
operations
ies were fc

54 Beno Rc
55 Excavati
capable of sh
dence points
Megiddo," B/
tention that

exercised a final control over temple affairs. The temple, as Israel's national shrine, was an indispensable symbol of corporate unity. After surviving a number of serious crises, it was finally destroyed in the Babylonian capture of Jerusalem in 587 B.C. Rebuilt after the Exile (520–515 B.C.), the second temple stood until A.D. 70, when with the Roman conquest it fell, never to rise again.

THE ROAD TO SCHISM. The Deuteronomist's praise of Solomon's great wisdom, no matter if embellished with popular legends, is not without warrant. The king's exploitation of Israel's commercial potential was nothing short of brilliant, and no other Israelite monarch matched his record for building. Though heir to a peaceful age, he did not neglect the nation's military defenses, but developed an army of chariots equal to or superior to those of surrounding states. His reign, furthermore, was one that brought cultural advance, nurtured particularly by broad international contacts. There is no reason to doubt Solomon's reputed role as a patron of wisdom—the collection and teaching of proverbs and wise sayings—even though later literary productions were attributed to him which he did not write.[59] The works produced (by unknown authors) during his time apparently include the Court History of David and the Yahwist's epic, both unsurpassed works of literature. It is also from this period that we possess one of the oldest Hebrew inscriptions so far discovered in Palestine: a schoolboy's tablet from Gezer containing a mnemonic ditty on the twelve months of the agricultural year—from early autumn through late summer.

> His two months are (olive) harvest,
> His two months are planting (grain),
> His two months are late planting,
> His month is hoeing up of flax,
> His month is harvest of barley,
> His month is harvest and feasting,
> His two months are vine-tending,
> His month is summer fruit.[60]

Israel had entered upon a classical age of artistic creativity and learning.

Unfortunately, Solomon's illustrious accomplishments were purchased at a heavy cost. As the resources required for his lavish buildings and governmental bureaucracy increased, he was forced to resort to harsh measures to meet the financial strain. He reorganized Israel into twelve administrative

59 Cf. below, p. 399, R. B. Y. Scott correctly questions the antiquity and reliability of the more extravagant accounts of Solomon's wisdom and wealth ("Solomon and the Beginnings of Wisdom in Israel," Wisdom in Israel and the Ancient Near East, VTS [Leiden, Netherlands: E. J. Brill, 1955]); and Siegfried Herrmann perceives the cultural "enlightenment" of the Solomonic period as confined primarily to court circles (A History of Israel in Old Testament Times, p. 182).
60 ANET, p. 320 (ANE, p. 209).

Interior of the Howland-Garber model of the Jerusalem temple, showing the vestibule, Holy Place, and Holy of Holies. (Courtesy of Paul L. Garber and Southeastern Films, Atlanta.)

palace complex was thirteen years under construction. Solomon's temple was small by modern standards, only 90 by 30 feet and 45 feet in height, and was built in only one half the time required to construct the palace. It must be remembered, however, that—unlike modern houses of worship—the building itself was entered by no one other than the priests. The rest of Israel worshiped in the open-air courts outside, before the high altar where the sacrifices were offered.

Numerous details of the temple's architecture reflect the Canaanite-Phoenician patterns after which it was modeled.[56] Its basic floor plan, like that of a Syrian temple at Tell Tainat (ninth or eighth century B.C.), consisted of three parts. From the entrance, which faced the east, one passed between two bronze, free-standing pillars into a small vestibule (*ulam*). This opened upon the central and largest chamber, the Holy Place (*hekal*),

Megiddo Stables—A Reassessment" in James A. Sanders, ed., *Near Eastern Archaeology in the Twentieth Century* [Garden City, NY: Doubleday & Company, Inc., 1970], pp. 268–276) is disputed by Yadin ("The Megiddo Stables," *Magnalia Dei: The Mighty Acts of God*, ed. by Frank M. Cross et al, pp. 249–252; "In Defense of the Stables at Megiddo," *BAR*, II, 3 [Sept. 1976], pp. 18–22). Yadin dates to Solomon's time a unique 6-chambered city gateway found at Hazor, Megiddo, and Gezer—all three cities mentioned in I Kings 9:15 as sites of Solomon's building activities. Cf. Yadin, *Hazor: The Rediscovery of a Great Citadel of the Bible*, pp. 187–231.

[56] See P. L. Garber, "Reconstructing Solomon's Temple," *BA*, XIV (1951), pp. 2–24; Yigael Yadin, *Hazor: The Rediscovery of a Great Citadel of the Bible*, pp. 79–119.

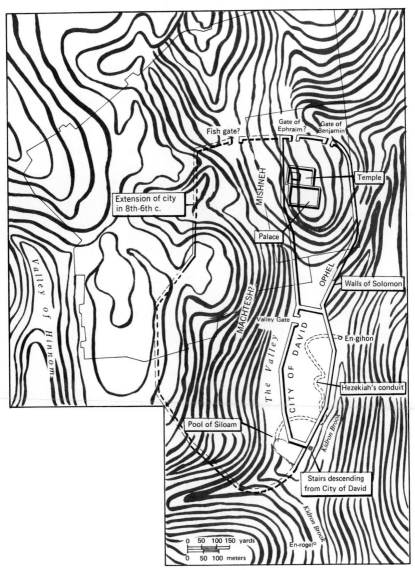

Jerusalem in the period of the Monarchy. (Adapted with permission of Macmillan Publishing Co., Inc. from The Macmillan Bible Atlas, Revised Edition, *by Y. Aharoni and Michael Avi-Yonah. Copyright © 1968, 1977 Carta, Ltd. Copyright © 1964 by Carta, Jerusalem. Copyright © 1966 by Carta, Jerusalem.)*

Great bronze "sea" mounted on the backs of twelve bullocks (Howland-Garber model). The four triads of beasts formed the four points of the compass. (Courtesy of Paul L. Garber and Southeastern Films, Atlanta.)

a room about 60 feet long containing an incense altar, a table of shew bread, and ten golden lampstands. The *hekal* was lighted by small windows just beneath the roof, and its walls were decorated with Canaanite art motifs: pomegranates, lilies, and palms. The third room, the Holy of Holies (*debir*), was a perfect cube, 30 feet square, and presumably was approached by stairs. Without windows of any sort, it housed the Ark of the Covenant, on either side of which stood guardian cherubim. Here Yahweh was believed to be invisibly present, enthroned over the ark. A three-story complex of rooms built along the side and back walls of the temple probably served for storage.

The recent discovery of an Israelite sanctuary at Arad, in the extreme south of Palestine, has revealed much the same floor plan as that of the Jerusalem temple: an inner court (vestibule), a large room, and a holy of holies, with an eastern entrance opening upon a large court.[57] The propor-

[57] Yohanan Aharoni, "The Israelite Sanctuary at Arad," *New Directions in Biblical Archaeology*, D. N. Freedman and J. C. Greenfield, eds. (Garden City, NY: Doubleday & Company, Inc., 1969), pp. 25–39; idem, "Arad: Its Inscriptions and Temple," *BA*, XXXI (1968), pp. 2–32.

The Holy of Holies of the temple at Arad. The only Israelite temple so far discovered by archaeologists, the Arad sanctuary included the same three divisions as the Jerusalem temple: vestibule, Holy Place, and Holy of Holies. The vestibule was part of a large courtyard; and two free-standing pillars (cf. Jachin and Boaz in the Jerusalem temple) stood at the entrance to the Holy Place. Shown here are the three steps leading into the Holy of Holies, two small altars, and a massebah (sacred stone). (Courtesy of the Consulate General of Israel in New York.)

Large altar of burnt offerings at Arad. Standing in a corner of the temple court-yard, the altar is crowned by a large flint slab with plaster gutters for the blood of animal sacrifices. (Courtesy of the Consulate General of Israel in New York.)

tions of the original (tenth century) Arad temple are the same as those of the Jerusalem temple; but a second (ninth century) phase of the sanctuary is larger, possibly reflecting a deliberate change from the short cubit to the royal or long cubit between the tenth and ninth centuries B.C. A major difference is that, unlike the entrance to Solomon's temple, the entrance to the *hekal* at Arad is on its broad rather than its narrow side and is situated off-center. The bases of two stone pillars were found at the entrance to the Arad *hekal*, leading some to conclude that the free-standing pillars of Solomon's temple may have been so situated, rather than at the entrance to the vestibule as generally supposed.[58] Other interesting features of the Arad sanctuary were two small, beautifully carved altars, found at the entrance to the Holy of Holies, a high altar constructed of unhewn stones (cf. Ex. 20:25), and a cultic stone pillar (*maṣṣebah*), the first such that can be definitely associated with Israelite worship.

The close connection between king and temple was to continue throughout the period of the monarchy. As the primary patron of the cult, he appointed the chief priest, contributed to the temple treasury, and in general

[58] Yohanan Aharoni, "The Israelite Sanctuary at Arad," pp. 34–35.

exercised a final control over temple affairs. The temple, as Israel's national shrine, was an indispensable symbol of corporate unity. After surviving a number of serious crises, it was finally destroyed in the Babylonian capture of Jerusalem in 587 B.C. Rebuilt after the Exile (520–515 B.C.), the second temple stood until A.D. 70, when with the Roman conquest it fell, never to rise again.

THE ROAD TO SCHISM. The Deuteronomist's praise of Solomon's great wisdom, no matter if embellished with popular legends, is not without warrant. The king's exploitation of Israel's commercial potential was nothing short of brilliant, and no other Israelite monarch matched his record for building. Though heir to a peaceful age, he did not neglect the nation's military defenses, but developed an army of chariots equal to or superior to those of surrounding states. His reign, furthermore, was one that brought cultural advance, nurtured particularly by broad international contacts. There is no reason to doubt Solomon's reputed role as a patron of wisdom—the collection and teaching of proverbs and wise sayings—even though later literary productions were attributed to him which he did not write.[59] The works produced (by unknown authors) during his time apparently include the Court History of David and the Yahwist's epic, both unsurpassed works of literature. It is also from this period that we possess one of the oldest Hebrew inscriptions so far discovered in Palestine: a schoolboy's tablet from Gezer containing a mnemonic ditty on the twelve months of the agricultural year—from early autumn through late summer.

> His two months are (olive) harvest,
> His two months are planting (grain),
> His two months are late planting,
> His month is hoeing up of flax,
> His month is harvest of barley,
> His month is harvest and feasting,
> His two months are vine-tending,
> His month is summer fruit.[60]

Israel had entered upon a classical age of artistic creativity and learning.

Unfortunately, Solomon's illustrious accomplishments were purchased at a heavy cost. As the resources required for his lavish buildings and governmental bureaucracy increased, he was forced to resort to harsh measures to meet the financial strain. He reorganized Israel into twelve administrative

---

[59] Cf. below, p. 399, R. B. Y. Scott correctly questions the antiquity and reliability of the more extravagant accounts of Solomon's wisdom and wealth ("Solomon and the Beginnings of Wisdom in Israel," *Wisdom in Israel and the Ancient Near East*, VTS [Leiden, Netherlands: E. J. Brill, 1955]); and Siegfried Herrmann perceives the cultural "enlightenment" of the Solomonic period as confined primarily to court circles (*A History of Israel in Old Testament Times*, p. 182).

[60] *ANET*, p. 320 (*ANE*, p. 209).

Jezirat Fara'un ("Coral Island") lies just off the Israel coast in the Red Sea Gulf of Eilat. The natural lagoon, on the western side of the island, could have made it a haven for ships, thus leading to speculation that it possibly served as Solomon's seaport. (Courtesy of the State of Israel, Government Press Office.)

districts, each under a governor responsible to the crown, and required that each provide the necessary governmental revenues and provisions for one month out of the year. Although the levies were evidently exorbitant (cf. I Kings 4:22–23), taxation alone was not sufficient and a policy of forced labor (corvée) was instituted. Native Israelites were assigned to labor crews and put to work alongside state slaves in the forests of Lebanon and the Palestinian rock quarries. So deeply indebted did the nation become under Solomon's policies that a number of Galilean towns were ceded to Hiram of Tyre in return for cash payments or loans (9:10–14).

The Deuteronomist reserves his critical appraisal of Solomon for the concluding years of his reign (ch. 11). Having applauded the king's devotion to the temple, he attributes his weaknesses to senility and the foreign wives in his harem who "turned away his heart" after their pagan gods. As evidence of God's disfavor, he points to revolts in Edom, Damascus, and northern Israel. Well before the king's death, the kingdom was slipping out of his control.

Israel's most serious losses under Solomon were those affecting individual and tribal rights, as guaranteed by the Sinai Covenant. The further centralization of power in the hands of the king called into question the older tribal ideals and the relevancy of much of the covenant law. The absorption of the Canaanite population, the rapid pace of urbanization, and the reorganization of the land along nontribal lines abetted the process. The Ark of the Covenant, chief symbol of Yahweh's sovereign rule over his people, now rested in the king's temple, attended by priests who were them-

251

selves subject to the king's bidding. Owing chiefly to the preservation of covenant principles and the vigilance of the prophets, kingship in Israel was not to assume as its typical expression the absolutist extremes that marked the pagan monarchies of the ancient world. The king was not God; nor did he have the right to assume divine prerogatives.[61] Solomon, however, by his oppressive policies made many in Israel aware of monarchy's implicit dangers. It was his reign that provided the Deuteronomist with the prime examples of what a king should not do:

> Only he must not multiply horses for himself, or cause the people to return to Egypt in order to multiply horses. . . . And he shall not multiply wives for himself, lest his heart turn away; nor shall he greatly multiply for himself silver and gold.
>
> Deut. 17:16–17

The Dual Monarchies (922–722 B.C.)

Resentment toward Solomon's highhanded policies, felt most acutely by Israelites in the north, came quickly to the surface at the king's death. Rehoboam, Solomon's son, took the throne in Jerusalem without opposition. The principle of dynastic succession was by now well-established in Judah. The new king found it necessary, however, to go to Shechem for acceptance by the former northern tribes, a fact that witnesses to the lingering identities of north and south. Facing the irate northerners' demands for reforms, particularly for the abolition of the labor corvée, the inexperienced Rehoboam turned for counsel to equally inept advisors. When he harshly and unwisely rejected the demands and promised tougher policies for the future, the northerners responded with an immediate withdrawal from the united kingdom. They elected as their king Jeroboam, an Ephraimite and former officer of Solomon who had plotted an unsuccessful revolt in Solomon's day and had only recently returned from exile in Egypt. Thus, sparked by just grievances, long-standing sectional tensions, and the urging of northern prophets (e.g., Ahijah, I Kings 11:26–40) for a return to tribal ideals, the schism was both thorough and lasting. For the next two centuries the covenant people were to exist as the divided kingdoms of Judah and Israel.

Jeroboam's kingdom (922–901 B.C.) consisted of all the former northern tribes except Benjamin. The latter, purportedly under Judah's control (I Kings 12:21; II Chron. 11:12), served as a buffer zone between north and south and was for a time the scene of sporadic border skirmishes. Rehoboam (922–915 B.C.) lacked either the strength or the inclination to force the north back into the realm. Neither kingdom was of very great size,

---

[61] Cf., however, J. Alberto Soggin's comments on the royal-state cult in "The Davidic-Solomonic Kingdom," *Israelite and Judaean History*, John H. Hayes and J. Maxwell Miller, eds., pp. 370–373, and the bibliography cited there.

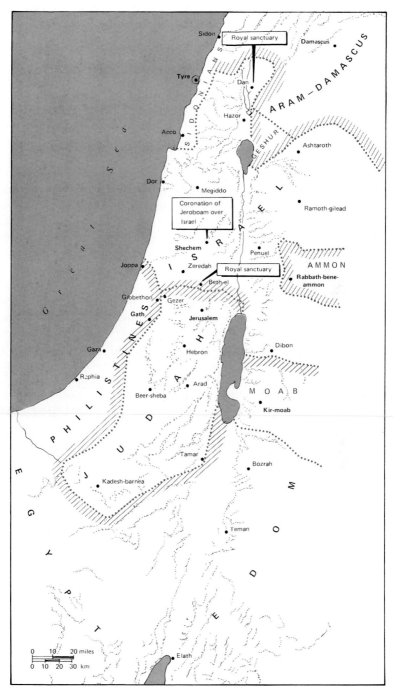

The division of the kingdom, 922 B.C. (*Adapted with permission of Macmillan Publishing Co., Inc., from* Macmillan Bible Atlas *by Y. Aharoni and Michael Avi-Yonah. Copyright © 1968 Carta, Jerusalem. © Copyright 1964 by Carta, Jerusalem. © Copyright 1966 by Carta, Jerusalem.*)

since the schism resulted in the loss of most of the border territories conquered by David. An invasion by Pharaoh Shishak (Sheshonk I) in Rehoboam's fifth year dealt a devastating blow to both kingdoms, as revealed in
archaeological evidence and Shishak's inscriptions at Karnak.[62]

Though the northern kingdom lacked the stabilizing influence of the
Davidic dynasty, it was the stronger of the two states, in both population
and economic resources. Less isolated than Judah, it was considerably
more embroiled in the international affairs of the ninth and early eighth
centuries. Under Jeroboam, the capital was placed first at Shechem, then
at Tirzah. To offset the influence of Jerusalem, the ancient cult centers of
Dan and Bethel were established as the official northern shrines. There
Jeroboam set up golden calves for which he received the severe criticism of
the Deuteronomist. Though the calves were probably no more than pedes-
tals for the invisible Yahweh, their association with the fertility cults made
them a symbol of idolatry in the Deuteronomist's eyes.

Hostilities continued between Israel and Judah and the northern kingdom entered a period of bitter internal strife until the appearance of Omri
(876–869 B.C.). One of the most able of the northern kings, Omri not only
brought peace to the two kingdoms, but cultivated close relations with
Tyre by marrying his son Ahab to the Tyrian princess Jezebel, regained the
Transjordan territories lost to Aram and Moab, and established a dynasty
that included four successive kings of Israel (876–842 B.C.). Ironically, his
reign is accorded only six verses in the Deuteronomic history (I Kings
6:23–38), whereas in extrabiblical records he is mentioned prominently.
Mesha, king of Moab, wrote of him on the Moabite Stone:

> As for Omri, king of Israel, he humbled Moab many years (lit., days), for
> Chemosh was angry at his land.[63]

Assyrian records continued to refer to Israel as "the land of the house of
Omri" long after his descendants had ceased to rule. After reigning from
Tirzah for six years, he purchased the strong hill of Samaria, fortified it,
and made it his capital. So well chosen was the site for defensive purposes,
that the Assyrian army had to besiege it for more than two years before taking it in 722 B.C. (II Kings 17:1–6).

If Omri has received only slight mention in the biblical record, his son
Ahab (869–850 B.C.) has captured a lion's share of attention (I Kings
16:29–22:53). Although an important figure in his own right, Ahab owes his
place in tradition to a fascination with his illustrious and diabolical wife,
Jezebel, and his equally colorful and staunch prophetic critic, Elijah. The
most serious international crisis of his reign goes unmentioned in the Old
Testament. Assyria, long the major power in Mesopotamia, under Ashur-

---

[62] *ANET*, pp. 263–264 (*ANE*, p. 187).
[63] *ANET*, p. 320 (*ANE*, p. 209).

Moabite stone of Mesha, recognizing Omri as one who "oppressed Moab many days." (© ARCH. PHOTO., Paris/S.P.A.D.E.M./V.A.G.A., 1981.)

nasirpal II (883–859 B.C.) and Shalmaneser III (859–824 B.C.) began to encroach upon the smaller states to the west.[64] Ahab and Hadadezer (Ben-hadad) of Damascus patched up their quarrels long enough to join with Hamath and other western states in a coalition aimed at stopping Shalmaneser. The crucial engagement came in 853 B.C. at Qarqar on the Orontes River in Syria. Shalmaneser recorded in his annals that Ahab came

[64] *ANET*, pp. 275ff. (*ANE*, pp. 188ff.).

equipped with 2,000 chariots and 10,000 foot soldiers, almost twice as many chariots as were supplied by any other member of the coalition.[65] One can scarcely take Shalmaneser's boasts of a smashing victory with greater seriousness than his claims to have spanned the Orontes with the bodies of the enemy dead.[66] Had he done so, it is a practical certainty that an Assyrian occupation of the conquered territories would have followed. It would appear, rather, that the allies succeeded in halting for the time being the Assyrian advance.

The interest of the Deuteronomist centers on Israel's internal crisis as exposed in the struggle between Yahwism and Baalism and their respective advocates, Elijah and Jezebel. Jezebel's passion for her Tyrian Baal-Melqart faith came to symbolize all that was wrong with the Omri dynasty. The crisis, however, went beyond the mere patronage which Ahab accorded the Baal cult. At issue, as well, was Jezebel's Phoenician concept of kingship, with its tradition of the unlimited privileges of the sovereign, vis-à-vis Yahwism's insistence on the rights and responsibilities assured to all equally by covenant guarantees. It was the problem of Solomon all over again! Covenant law protected the small Israelite landholder against the very abuse which the king, at Jezebel's urging, committed against Naboth (I Kings 21). That the king was capable of such a highhanded act of injustice suggests the likelihood of a widespread mistreatment of the poor throughout the society.[67]

Reaction to Ahab's policies came after his death, during the reign of the second of his sons, Jehoram (849–842 B.C.). Israel's wars with Aram (Damascus), which had occupied Ahab during much of his reign, finally claimed his life on the battlefield at Ramoth-gilead as he tried vainly to eject the enemy from northern Transjordan. Several years later (842 B.C.), as Jehoram's armies engaged Hazael's forces at the same place (8:28ff.), Jehoram's general, Jehu, with the backing of Elisha and the prophetic party, began a *coup d'état* that swept the Omrides from power in a bath of blood. Jehu's wholesale slaughter took the lives of both Hebrew kings (Ahaziah of Judah was also a descendant of the Omrides through his mother, Athaliah), as well as those of Jezebel and the northern Baal party. It was a thorough job of housecleaning, from which Baalism was not soon to recover. Its undue bloodletting, however, was to be a bitter burden on the Israelite conscience for years to come (cf. Hos. 1:4).

Jehu's dynasty lasted five generations (842–745 B.C.), longer than any other royal house in northern history. His own reign (842–815 B.C.), however, was far from illustrious. Both Judah and Tyre were alienated as a result of his violence, and Hazael took advantage of his lack of allies to oc-

---

[65] *ANET*, pp. 278–279 (*ANE*, p. 190).
[66] *ANET*, p. 279 (*ANE*, pp. 190–191).
[67] John Bright, *A History of Israel*, p. 225.

The black obelisk of Shalmaneser III, Assyrian king (859–824 B.C), showing kings of various lands bringing tribute. (Courtesy of the Trustees of the British Museum.)

257

The "Jehu panel" of the black obelisk, showing Jehu, king of Israel (842–815 B.C.), kneeling before Shalmaneser in the presence of Assyrian attendants. (Courtesy of the Trustees of the British Museum.)

cupy Transjordan. Shalmaneser III, furthermore, having recuperated from the Battle of Qarqar, began once again to put pressure on the west. On his famous Black Obelisk the Assyrian king pictures Jehu kneeling before him, together with a group of Israelites bearing tribute. An inscription records the "tribute of Jehu, son of Omri."[68]

By the end of Jehu's reign, the two Hebrew kingdoms were weaker than at any time since the schism, with both largely at the mercy of Damascus.

[68] *ANET*, p. 280 (*ANE*, p. 192).

Resurgence came in the eighth century. Under the strong kings Jehoash (801–786 B.C.) and Jeroboam II (789–746 B.C.), Israel recovered all her lost territories, while Judah increased under Uzziah's rule (783–742 B.C.). This was, however, the last, brief manifestation of Israelite strength. The most crucial phase of Assyrian expansion coincided with a period of political anarchy in the northern kingdom (746–732 B.C.), and within a generation after Jeroboam II (722 B.C.), Samaria collapsed before Assyrian armies.

Judah Alone (722–587 B.C.)

Throughout the better part of the period of the dual monarchies, Israel had maintained its ascendancy over Judah. Under the Omrides the southern kings had been little more than vassals of Samaria. Judah, nevertheless, possessed the stability of the unchanging Davidic house. Whereas the northern kingdom produced no fewer than nineteen kings and nine dynasties during its two centuries of existence, Judah, for the same period, was governed by only eleven monarchs—all of them (except for the brief usurpation of Athaliah) descendants of David. For another century and a half after the fall of Samaria, Judah weathered the successive crises brought on by the Assyrians and Babylonians. Eight more successors of David were to rule in Jerusalem before Babylon finally destroyed the city (587 B.C.) and instituted the period of Babylonian captivity.

Political events alone fail to represent the complex patterns of life in Israel and Judah throughout the years of the monarchies. The Deuteronomic History, with its running theological commentary and the inclusion of prophetic traditions, bears witness to this fact. It is only as we consider the internal life of the two societies as reflected in the books of the Latter Prophets, however, that we begin to understand the spirit of the time.

SELECTED READINGS

Joshua and the Occupation of Canaan

Alt, Albrecht, "The Settlement of the Israelites in Palestine," *Essays on Old Testament History and Religion*, R. A. Wilson, trans. (Garden City, NY: Doubleday & Company, Inc., 1967), pp. 173–221. The original statement of the immigration model of the occupation of Canaan.

Bright, John, "Introduction and Exegesis to the Book of Joshua," *IB*, Vol II.

Gottwald, Norman K., *The Tribes of Yahweh* (Maryknoll, NY: Orbis Books, 1979), pp. 191–219. An important study that analyzes different theories of Israel's settlement in Canaan and offers a provocative defense of the revolt model.

Kaufmann, Yehezkel, *The Biblical Account of the Conquest of Palestine*, M. Dagut, trans. (Jerusalem: Magnes Press, 1955).

Kenyon, Kathleen, *Digging Up Jericho* (New York: Praeger Publishers, Inc., 1957). Details the archaeological findings at Jericho and their bearing on Israelite history.

Mendenhall, George E., "The Hebrew Conquest of Palestine," *BA*, XXV (1962), pp. 66–87, reprinted in *BA Reader*, 3, pp. 100–120. The original and path-finding proposal that Israel's settlement in Canaan resulted from internal revolt.

Noth, Martin, *Das Buch Josua*, Handbuch zum Alten Testament, I, 7, 2nd ed. (Tübingen, West Germany: Mohr, 1953). Takes a view different from that of Bright (see above) on many questions concerning the historicity of the Joshua accounts. A summary of Noth's positions appears in his *History of Israel* (see below).

——, *The History of Israel*, S. Godman, trans., rev. by P. R. Ackroyd, 2nd ed. (New York: Harper & Row, Publishers, 1960), pp. 53–109. Reconstructs the settlement of Canaan according to the immigration model.

Pritchard, James B., *Gibeon Where the Sun Stood Still* (Princeton, NJ: Princeton University Press, 1962).

Soggin, J. Alberto, *Joshua: A Commentary*, R. A. Wilson, trans. (Philadelphia: The Westminster Press, 1972).

Weippert, Manfred, *The Settlement of the Israelite Tribes in Palestine*, James D. Martin, trans., Studies in Biblical Theology, series 2, no. 21 (Naperville, IL: Alec R. Allenson, 1971). Surveys theories of the settlement in Canaan and defends the Alt-Noth immigration model.

Wright, G. Ernest, *Biblical Archaeology*, 2nd ed. (Philadelphia: The Westminster Press, 1962), pp. 69–85. Utilizes archaeological data to present the settlement in Canaan as a military invasion.

——, *Shechem: The Biography of a Biblical City* (New York: McGraw-Hill Book Company, 1965).

Cultures and Religions of Canaan

Albrektson, Berril, *History and the Gods* (Lund, Sweden: CWK Gleerup, 1967), An essay on the idea of historical events as divine manifestations in the ancient Near East and in Israel.

Albright, William F., *Yahweh and the Gods of Canaan* (Garden City, NY: Doubleday Anchor, 1969). Paperback.

Coogan, Michael David, ed., *Stories from Ancient Canaan* (Philadelphia: The Westminster Press, 1978). Paperback.

Cross, Frank Moore, *Canaanite Myth and Hebrew Epic* (Cambridge, MA: Harvard University Press, 1973).

Driver, G. R., *Canaanite Myths and Legends* (Edinburgh: T. and T. Clark, 1956).

Ginsburg, H. L., "Ugaritic Studies and the Bible," *BA*, VIII, (1945), pp. 41–58. Reprinted in *BA Reader*, 2, pp. 34–50.

Gray, John, *The Legacy of Canaan*, 2nd ed. (Leiden, Netherlands: E. J. Brill, 1965).

Harrelson, Walter, *From Fertility Cult to Worship* (Missoula, MT: Scholars Press, 1980).

Hindson, Edward E., *The Philistines and the Old Testament*, Baker Studies in Biblical Archaeology (Grand Rapids, MI: Baker Book House, 1971).

Van Zyl, A. H., *The Moabites*, Pretoria Oriental Series, III (Leiden, Netherlands: E. J. Brill, 1960).

Wright, G. Ernest. "Philistine Coffins and Mercenaries," *BA*, XXII (1959), pp. 54–66. Reprinted in *BA Reader*, 2, pp. 59–68.

————, "Fresh Evidence for the Philistine Story," *BA*, XXIX (1966), pp. 70–86.

Judges and the Tribal League

Anderson, George W., "Israel: Amphictyony: 'Am; Kāhāl; 'Edâh," *Translating and Understanding the Old Testament*, Harry Thomas Frank and William L. Reed, eds., (Nashville, TN: Abingdon Press, 1970), pp. 135–151. Argues against Noth's view that the tribes of Israel were organized as an "amphictyony."

Boling, Robert G., *Judges*, The Anchor Bible (Garden City, NY: Doubleday & Company, Inc.,1975).

McKenzie, John L., *The World of the Judges* (Englewood Cliffs, NJ: Prentice-Hall, Inc., 1966).

Myers, Jacob M., "Introduction and Exegesis to Judges," *IB*, Vol. II.

Noth, Martin, *Das System der Zwölf Stämme Israels*, *BWANT*, IV–1 (Stuttgart, West Germany: Kohlhammer, 1930). Sets forth the author's classic theory of an Israelite tribal league modeled after the Graeco-Roman amphictyonies.

Orlinsky, Harry M., "The Tribal System of Israel and Related Groups in the Period of the Judges," *Studies and Essays in Honor of Abraham A. Neuman*, Meir Ben-Horin et al., eds. (Leiden, Netherlands: E. J. Brill, 1962), pp. 375–387. Opposes the theory of an Israelite "amphictyony."

Smend, Rudolph, *Yahweh War and Tribal Confederation*, Max Gray Rogers, trans. (Nashville, TN: Abingdon Press, 1970).

Samuel-Kings: The Hebrew Monarchy

Caird, George B., "Introduction and Exegesis to I–II Samuel," *IB*, Vol. II.

Gray, John, *I and II Kings*, Old Testament Library (Philadelphia: The Westminster Press, 1963).

Hertzberg, Hans W., *I and II Samuel: A Commentary*, Old Testament Library, J. S. Bowden, trans. (Philadelphia: The Westminster Press, 1964).

Kenyon, Kathleen M., *Digging Up Jerusalem* (London: Ernest Benn, Ltd., 1974). Describes the author's important archaeological discoveries in the Davidic city.

Maly, Eugene H., *The World of David and Solomon* (Englewood Cliffs, NJ: Prentice-Hall, Inc., 1966).

Montgomery, James A., and Henry S. Gehman, *The Books of Kings*, International Critical Commentary (New York: Charles Scribner's Sons, 1951).

Mazar, Benjamin, *The Mountain of the Lord* (Garden City, NY: Doubleday & Company, Inc., 1975). A description of modern excavations in Jerusalem, lavishly illustrated.

Rost, Leonhard, *Die Überlieferung von der Thronnachfolge Davids*, *BWANT*, 42 (Stuttgart, West Germany: Kohlhammer, 1926). An analysis of II Samuel 9–20; I Kings 1–2 as a throne succession document. Rost's findings are summarized in the work of Whybray.

Snaith, Norman H., "Introduction and Exegesis to I–II Kings," *IB*, Vol. III.

Whybray, Roger Norman, *The Succession Narrative: A Study of II Samuel 9–20; I Kings 1 and 2* (London: S.C.M. Press, 1968). A challenge to the Davidic Court History's reliability as a historical source (see Rost above).

Yadin, Yigael, *Hazor: The Rediscovery of a Great Citadel of the Bible* (New York: Random House, Inc., 1975). Details the latest finds from Hazor, Megiddo, and Gezer pertaining to Solomon's period.

Temple

Aharoni, Yohanan, "The Israelite Sanctuary at Arad," *New Directions in Biblical Archaeology*, D. N. Freedman and J. C. Greenfield, eds. (Garden City, NY: Doubleday & Company, Inc., 1969). A report on the Israelite temple unearthed at Arad and its bearing on our understanding of Solomon's temple.

Wright, G. Ernest, et al., "The Significance of the Temple in the Ancient Near East," *BA Reader*, 1, pp. 145–200. Paperback.

4

---•◦•---

samaRia shall BeaR
heR guilt

Samaria shall bear her guilt, because she has rebelled against her
God.
—Hosea 13:16

The books of the Former Prophets, as we have seen, contain narrative
accounts of Israel's early (pre-eighth century) prophets, notably Samuel,
Nathan, Gad, Micaiah, Elijah, and Elisha. None of their oracles have survived, however, in the form of independent collections, such as we have
for prophets of the eighth century and following in the books of the Latter
Prophets, hence the somewhat presumptuous distinction between the so-
called "nonwriting prophets" (pre-eighth century) and "writing prophets"
(Amos and his successors). Perhaps the pattern of recording prophetic utterances simply did not develop so early, though it seems more likely that
such records once existed, only to be lost before the Latter Prophets were
finally compiled.[1] Interestingly enough, the only figure mentioned in the
Former Prophets (II Kings 18–20) for whom we possess a separate collection of his words is Isaiah of Jerusalem.[2]

In turning to the books of the Latter Prophets, one enters the great clas-

---

[1] The Chronicler refers to a "Book of Nathan" (II Chron. 9:29), "The Chronicles of Gad, the
Seer" (I Chron. 29:29), "The Chronicles of Samuel the Seer" (I Chron. 29:29), and "The
Chronicles of Shemaiah the Prophet and of Iddo the Seer" (II Chron. 12:15).

[2] The prophet Jonah, who is mentioned in II Kings 14:25, is not the author of the book that
bears his name. See below, pp. 430–432.

sical age of Hebrew prophecy. Beginning with Amos in the mid-eighth century and continuing through the so-called Deutero-Isaiah of the Exile, a period of roughly two centuries, a succession of brilliant and spiritually sensitive spokesmen not only kept Hebrew faith alive during their own generations, but in large part determined its direction for all time to come. Although they were themselves the inheritors and guardians of earlier Yahwistic tradition and its incipient ethical monotheism, under their influence the broader implications of the older faith were brought to light and its high ethical standards applied to every conceivable facet of human existence. Alongside the influence of the Mosaic and Davidic traditions, the impact of their witness is to be seen throughout the entire Bible, Old and New Testaments alike. Post-Exilic prophecy did not attain the creative heights of the earlier prophecy, but for at least another century following Deutero-Isaiah influential spokesmen continued to appear who, for the most part, were worthy representatives of prophetic religion.

In our treatment of the books of the Latter Prophets we shall depart from the sequence of the Jewish Canon (Isaiah, Jeremiah, Ezekiel, and the Twelve) in order to set each prophet in historical context and expose such developmental patterns as may be justifiably traced through the prophetic collection as a whole. By way of depicting the prophets' backgrounds, the present chapter and the three to follow trace the Hebrew history from the period of Jeroboam II through the days of Nehemiah and Ezra, thus carrying forward the beginnings which were made in the earlier chapters. The division of the prophets into four groups follows the pattern suggested by the prophetic books themselves, in which the dominant concerns cluster around four major historical crises: (a) the decline and fall of the northern kingdom, (b) the decline and fall of the southern kingdom, (c) the Exile, and (d) the restoration. The chart on the following page indicates the location of the individual prophets according to this arrangement, as well as the other relevant labels by which they are often identified.

1. THUS SAYS THE LORD: PROPHECY IN ISRAEL

Before proceeding to the books of the Latter Prophets, it is well to consider the phenomenon of prophecy itself: its definition, origins, and literary character. Broad definitions are useful but unfortunately none too helpful in the effort to distinguish prophecy from other Old Testament forms, such as law, history, apocalyptic, and psalmody. This would have to be remarked of an otherwise insightful definition proposed by Davie Napier as "that understanding of history which accepts meaning only in terms of

THE LATTER PROPHETS

	THE DECLINE AND FALL OF SAMARIA				
750	Amos c. 750 B.C. ⎫ Prophets to		Eighth-		
	Hosea c. 745–735 ⎭ the north		century	Prophets	
	Isaiah c. 742–701 ⎫ Prophets to		prophets	of the	
700	Micah c. 730–701 ⎭ the south			Assyrian	Pre-Exilic
650	THE DECLINE AND FALL OF JUDAH			Period	prophets
	Pre-Exilic				
	Zephaniah	c. 630–627 B.C.	Seventh-		
	Nahum	c. 612	century		
	Habakkuk	c. 627–598	prophets		
600	Jeremiah	c. 627–587		Prophets of the	
	THE EXILE			Babylonian	Exilic
	Ezekiel	c. 592–570 B.C.		Period	prophets
	Deutero-Isaiah c. 540		Sixth-		
550			century		
	THE RESTORATION		prophets		
	Haggai	c. 520 B.C.			
	Zechariah	c. 520–518		Prophets	
500				of the	Post-Exilic
450	Malachi	c. 450 B.C.	Fifth-	Persian	prophets
	Trito-Isaiah	?	century	Period	
	Obadiah	? Prophets of	prophets		
	Joel	? indefinite	(or later)		
	Jonah	? date			

divine concern, divine purpose, divine participation."[3] By such a broad criterion the greater part of the biblical record would have to be regarded as the work of the prophets or their disciples and the prophetic movement itself traced all the way back to the Bible's beginnings, perhaps to Moses himself. The description, as such, is an accurate one, however, and witnesses both to the broad consistency of perspective which binds together most of the Old Testament books and the powerful impact of the prophets themselves, under whose influence the entire corpus of scripture reached its final form. It is also noteworthy that Moses and other early figures, namely, Abraham, Aaron, Miriam, and Deborah, are on occasion referred to as "prophet" or "prophetess,"[4] though the title is probably to be understood in these instances as one of respect for great, inspired leaders of the past.

Historically defined, Old Testament prophecy is best restricted to that succession of spokesmen from Samuel onward and their collective influence

[3] "Prophet, Prophetism," *IDB*, K–Q, p. 896.
[4] Gen. 20:7; Exod. 7:1; 15:20; Judg. 4:4; Deut. 18:18; 34:10; Num. 11:26–29; 12:5–8.

within Hebrew history. Information concerning the earliest prophets is far from complete, however, and in common usage the label "classical prophecy" is reserved for the great prophets of the eighth century and following, by which time it is generally agreed that Hebrew prophecy reached its definitive form.

The Nature of Prophecy

The difficulty of arriving at a definition of the Hebrew prophet is due in no small part to the diversity of persons who are called by that name in the Old Testament and the equally diverse patterns associated with them. Under the same categorical label we find such contrasting personalities as the ecstatic dervish and the counselor of kings; the clairvoyant seer and the moral spokesman; Amos the shepherd and Ezekiel the priest; the rough-hewn Eliah and the sophisticated Isaiah; the iconoclastic Jeremiah and the domestically inclined Hosea. More often than not a multiplicity of such traits is found in a single prophet; and in no case save one—the "true" as distinguished from the "false" prophets—are they regarded as mutually exclusive.[5]

Our English word "prophet" derives from the Greek *prophetes* (found, for example, in the Septuagint), "one who speaks for another." The Hebrew term for prophet, *nabi'* (plural, *nebi'im*), used more than three hundred times in the Old Testament, is etymologically vague. That it can be connected with an Akkadian root meaning "to call" is generally conceded, but whether in the active sense of "one who calls or proclaims" (thus, a spokesman) or in the passive sense of "one who is called" (selected by the deity) is uncertain. Even the revealing use of the word in the reference to Aaron as Moses' *nabi'* (Exod. 7:1; cf. 4:16), that is, as a representative of his brother in the capacity of a spokesman, does not entirely settle the matter. Nevertheless, the *nabi'* as one who is chosen to declare a message given to him, and who speaks with the authority of the one who sends him, is consistent with the descriptions of the Old Testament prophets. The prophet is, above all else, one who speaks as the messenger of God.[6]

The *nabi'* is in certain instances referred to as "seer" (*ro'eh* or *ḥozeh*)[7]; by one explanation (I Sam. 9:9), "seer" was the commonly employed name for the prophet in an early phase of Israel's history. Perhaps the implication

---

[5] Even in the case of "true" and "false" prophecy the criteria for distinguishing the one from the other are none too exact. See James L. Crenshaw, *Prophetic Conflict: Its Effect Upon Israelite Religion*.

[6] Although the prophets seldom referred to themselves as "messengers," some form-critical scholars find the formal elements of messenger speech in their oracles. See the discussion of form-critical analyses of prophecy in "Literary Features of Hebrew Prophecy," below. Cf. also James F. Ross, "The Prophet as Yahweh's Messenger," *Israel's Prophetic Heritage*, Bernhard W. Anderson and Walter Harrelson, eds. (New York: Harper & Row Publishers, 1962), pp. 98–107.

[7] Cf. II Sam. 24:11; II Kings 17:13; Isa. 29:10; 30:9–10; Mic. 3:7; Amos 7:12.

is that Hebrew prophecy developed out of the art of foretelling or the exercise of clairvoyant talents. Samuel, who in some fashion not easily defined stands at the beginning stages of prophecy in Israel, had a reputation as a seer, according to the promonarchical source in I Samuel, and is credited with directing Saul to his strayed asses (I Sam. 10). Foresight, moreover, remained a distinctive feature of Old Testament prophecy, even after it had attained its classical form. Isaiah purportedly prophesied the date of King Hezekiah's death (II Kings 20:1ff.) and Jeremiah the manner of King Jehoiakim's (Jer. 22:19). In a less spectacular fashion, perhaps, all of Israel's great prophets strove to create in their hearers a vivid awareness of the impingement of future events—notably the Day of Yahweh—upon the present. Though far more than simply a technique of persuasion, it was nevertheless an ever-present reality as they pushed for decision on crucial contemporary issues. Consequently, their oracles are filled with warnings of national catastrophe as well as promises of deliverance and restoration.

To characterize the prophets simply or primarily as prognosticators of the future, however, would be a grave error. No matter what prophecy's earliest beginnings were like, once classical prophecy had achieved its full stature in Israel, the *nabi'* was above all else the spokesman of Yahweh's message to his generation. If he functioned as a true prophet he declared whatever word Yahweh directed him to declare, whether directly involved with the future or not. As such, the prophet's function was basically twofold: (1) to proclaim the word (*dabar*) of Yahweh in order (2) to bring its impact to bear upon the society in a redemptive manner.

The word of Yahweh according to Hebrew psychology was more than simply the ideas or teachings—or for that matter even a mystic revelation—of the prophet. It was nothing less than a vital force let loose within the society; a word that not simply foretold what would happen, but a power that made things happen.[8] Thus, when the prophet pronounced Yahweh's judgment upon the people's crimes, more than simply warning of impending danger, he was actually putting into motion the wheels of retribution which even then began to grind out their bitter consequences. Only, the process was conceived in no mechanistic fashion, but was totally at Yahweh's command. In such a role, the prophet disavowed any pretense of speaking on his own authority; he spoke rather as one commanded, indeed compelled, by Yahweh. Thus his word was characteristically prefaced with, "Thus says Yahweh."

Since the divine word was, in the first place, a force rather than a rational preachment, it could take the form of symbolic enactment as well as verbalized pronouncements. Thus, the prophet often "acted out" his message, not simply for dramatic effect, we may assume, but in order to bring the totality of his personality and faculties into the service of his commis-

---

[8] Cf. Johannes Pedersen, *Israel*, pp. 99–181.

sion to declare Yahweh's word. It is this sort of behavior that frequently gives to the prophet the appearance of a strange, ecstatic—even abnormal—personality. That some of the most powerful examples of the prophetic witness, nevertheless, come out of such dramatic enactments as Hosea's pursuit of his wayward wife (Hos. 3) or Ezekiel's simulation of the siege of Jerusalem (Ezek. 4) is evident enough.

The divine compulsion to declare Yahweh's word is one of the characteristic features of the prophetic personality. Unlike the office of the priest or that of any other official in Israel, the prophetic role was not, in the first instance, at the disposal of either heredity or appointment. This is not to deny that there were both cultic and court prophets who were almost certainly subject to royal or priestly appointment; it is even possible, though not very probable, that some of the "sons of the prophets" were so by reason of physical descent. It is furthermore undeniable that some, if not most, of the canonical prophets functioned within the broader context of the cult and court, though it is far from certain that any of them were in the direct employ of either.[9] But, whatever their relationship to Israelite institutions, the classical figures of Hebrew prophecy—to judge from their express words—were placed in their roles by divine compulsion. It was of the very nature of God's word that it chose its agent, rather than vice versa. Thus we find the experience of the prophet's call figuring prominently in the books of the three Major Prophets.[10] Typically, the prophet displays a reluctance to presume to declare Yahweh's word. But, also characteristically, the word carries with it its own compelling urgency and cannot be put off; thus the prophet becomes captive to his mission. Jeremiah gave to the experience its classical description:

[9] Nathan, Gad, and Micaiah were court prophets, in some sense; and some of the later figures, notably Isaiah, functioned as counselors of the kings. The prophets' frequent and stringent criticism of royal policies, however, caution against drawing too close a connection between prophet and court. The same point applies in respect to the cult. Recent studies have stressed the relationship between prophet and cult, both within Israelite circles (cf. especially Aubrey Johnson, *The Cultic Prophet in Ancient Israel*, 2nd ed. [Cardiff: University of Wales, 1962]; H. H. Rowley, "Ritual and the Hebrew Prophets," *Myth, Ritual, and Kingship*, S. H. Hooke, ed. [New York: Oxford University Press, Inc., 1958], pp. 237–260) and in the Near East at large (cf. A. Haldar, *Associations of Cult Prophets Among the Ancient Semites* [Uppsala, Sweden: Almquist ad Wiksells boktryckeri ab, 1945]). The protest against cultic abuses, however, is a dominant feature of classical Hebrew prophecy (cf. Richard Hentshke, *Die Stellung der vorexilischen Schriftpropheten zum Kultus, Beiheft zur ZAW*, 75 [Berlin: A. Töpelmann, 1957]; and J. Philip Hyatt, "The Prophetic Criticism of Israelite Worship," *Interpreting the Prophetic Tradition*, Harry M. Orlinsky, ed., The Library of Biblical Studies [Cincinnati, OH: The Hebrew Union College Press, 1969], pp. 201–224). See also the necessary distinction drawn by Georg Fohrer between a prophet's utilization of a cultic form, on the one hand, and his official relationship to the cult and the content he gives to the form, on the other ("Remarks on Modern Interpretation of the Prophets," *JBL*, LXXX [1961], pp. 309–319).

[10] Isa. 6; Jer. 1; Ezek. 1–3. Even where there is no call account, as such, there may be the assumption of such an experience in expressions such as, "The word of the Lord came to_____."

> If I say, "I will not mention him,
>   or speak any more in his name,"
> there is in my heart as it were a burning fire
>   shut up in my bones,
> and I am weary with holding it in,
>   and I cannot.
>
>   Jer. 20:9

Since Yahweh's word so often threatened disaster, the stereotype of the prophet as a vengeful preacher of doom serves for many as a persistent barrier to a full appreciation of the prophetic message. This is the point at which the second function of the prophet must be recognized, namely, as the one who bore some degree of responsibility for the effect of his words upon the society. For the prophet was not only spokesman of the divine word, which was ultimately addressed to the whole covenant society, he was, as well, the agent who confronted the sources of power in the community in order to assure the greatest impact of Yahweh's word upon those who held pivotal policy-making responsibilities—especially the king. The prophet, that is to say, was more than one who simply made his people aware of what was going to happen; rather, he was compelled to bring his witness to bear precisely at those points where it might serve to avert disaster.

Not all of the prophets' pronouncements, perhaps, carried this note of contingency. For example, when Amos prophesied Samaria's fall and Ezekiel pronounced Jerusalem's doom, one receives the impression that neither prophet entertained the slightest hope that these cities would escape their judgment. In such instances, hope could lie only on the other side of catastrophe. But, in either case, the oracles of doom were delivered not because their spokesmen desired to see them fulfilled, but, quite the contrary, because they wished to bring Israel to repentance. How otherwise are we to explain the indomitable persistence with which the prophets confronted hostile kings, a callous citizenry, imprisonment, rejection of friends and family, and in some instances even death?

Prophecy in the Ancient Near East

As Kurt Kuhl has remarked, "the prehistory of Israelite prophecy is shrouded in the mists of antiquity."[11] Prophecy, as such, is not a uniquely Israelite phenomenon, but neither from the Bible nor any other ancient source can we trace its precise origins. Its broad antecedents lie, perhaps, among the variety of divining techniques practiced throughout the ancient world. In early Mesopotamia, for example, communication with the gods was most generally sought through the expertise of *baru* priests, trained in the art of divining omens in the configurations of animal livers (hepatos-

---

[11] *The Prophets of Israel* (Atlanta, GA: John Knox Press, 1960), p. 8.

copy), patterns in bird flights, designs created by oil in water, and the like. In the Old Testament itself such practices as the casting of lots, dream interpretation, spreading the fleece, cup divining, and incubation rites are abundantly attested.[12]

From recently published texts discovered at ancient Mari,[13] we are now informed about a class of persons who functioned in a manner somewhat akin to that of the Old Testament prophets and are earlier by almost a millennium than Elijah and Elisha.[14] The wider range of prophecy that flourished in and around Mari included different categories of cultic and noncultic seers, who delivered solicited and unsolicited oracles of a varied character. Some of the oracles reported in the texts enjoin the king to rule justly; others warn of plots against his life or promise the protection of the god; yet others solicit his support for building a temple or sacrificing to a dead king. In a fashion similar to the Hebrew prophets, the Mari prophets claimed to speak under the compulsion of the god or goddess and prefaced their oracles with such formulas of divine commission as, "This is what Shamash has said," or "Dagan has sent me." The new evidence clearly shows the technical divination rites to have been the more authoritative and normative means of revelation in Mari culture, however, since in certain instances validation of a prophet's oracle with divination results was deemed necessary.[15]

The significance of ecstatic prophecy for Canaanite culture has long been recognized and until the Mari discoveries was assumed to have provided the immediate backgrounds of Hebrew prophecy.[16] The Old Testament reports the activities of Baal and Asherah prophets, as in the memorable account of Elijah's contest with a contingent of such ecstatics at Mount Carmel (I Kings 18:19f.). In the latter episode their most distinguishing feature is a dervish dance, performed in an induced state of collective seizure which releases uncontrolled emotions and leads to a sustained raving and gashing of the flesh with swords and lances. The ecstatic element is also present in the actions of a Phoenician youth described in the eleventh cen-

---

[12] As examples, see Josh. 7:14; I Sam. 14:42; Gen. 40:8f.; Dan. 4; Judg. 6:36–40; Gen. 44:4–5; I Sam. 1:9–11.

[13] ANET, pp. 623–625, 629–632 (ANE, Vol. II, pp. 174–186).

[14] A description and evaluation of the relevant data in the Mari tablets appear in Herbert B. Huffmon, "Prophecy in the Mari Letters," BA, XXXI (Dec. 1968), pp. 101–124; William L. Moran, "New Evidence from Mari on the History of Prophecy," Biblica, 50 (1969), pp. 15–56; and John F. Craghan, "Mari and its Prophets," BTB, V (1975), pp. 32–55.

[15] Herbert B. Huffmon, "Prophecy in the Mari Letters," p. 109.

[16] Huffmon (ibid., p. 123) tentatively questions the theory of Canaanite influence in light of the closer parallels from Mari; Rolf Rendtorff ("Reflections on the Early History of Prophecy in Israel," JTC, 4 [1967], p. 15) and John F. Craghan (ibid., pp. 52–55) theorize a merging within Israelite prophecy of both Cananite and Mari-type elements. Yet another attempt at connecting Syrian, Mari, and Hebrew prophecy is set forth in James F. Ross, "Prophecy in Hamath, Israel, and Mari," HTR, 63 (1970), pp. 1–28.

tury Egyptian *Tale of Wen Amon*.[17] While in a state of cataleptic seizure ascribed to the action of a god, the youth advises the king of Byblos to receive Wen Amon, the Egyptian ambassador.

Whatever the foreign elements back of Hebrew prophecy, of one thing we may be sure, namely, that once adapted to Israel's own peculiar Yahweh faith, they underwent radical transformation. The Mari and Canaanite parallels so far adduced prove to be similarities of form and delivery rather than content or message. Thus, the newer evidence in no sense nullifies the claim long made for Hebrew prophecy as "a phenomenon to which the history of religion affords no real parallel."[18] This is to be seen specifically in the manner whereby the classical prophets combined in the prophetic role the highest ethical and moral insights with a vivid sense of divine immediacy and inspiration. In no other contemporaneous literature do we read of such spokesmen addressing themselves to the conscience of an entire people, exhorting them to faithfulness to common covenant vows, and threatening utter extinction as the consequence of disloyalty. The essential contrast between Mari and Hebrew prophecy is poignantly summarized by Martin Noth:

> At Mari the message deals with cult and political matters of very limited and ephemeral importance. Any comparison with the content of the prophetical books is out of the question. The prophetic literature deals with guilt and punishment, reality and unreality, present and future of the Israelite people as chosen by God for a special and unique service, the declaration of the great and moving contemporary events in the world as part of a process which, together with the future issue of that process, is willed by God.[19]

Early Prophecy in Israel

The earliest examples of Israelite prophecy for which we have any evidence belong to the period of the monarchy's beginnings. Separate strands of tradition within I Samuel associate both Samuel and Saul with bands of ecstatic prophets after the order of the Canaanite dervishes. According to the promonarchical source (I Sam. 10), Samuel foretells Saul's encounter with such a group, coming down from the high place of Gibeah. Saul joins in their ecstatic prophesying, in this instance induced by music and characterized by temporary personality transformation, whereby he is "turned into another man." In an independent story identifiable with neither the promonarchical nor the antimonarchical source (I Sam. 19:18–24), Saul participates with an identical group at Ramah, over which Samuel stands as head. So contagious is their activity that three groups of Saul's messengers

---

[17] *ANET*, pp. 25–29 (*ANE*, pp. 16–24).

[18] John Skinner, *Prophecy and Religion* (Cambridge University Press, 1963), p. 1.

[19] "History and the Word of God in the Old Testament," *BJRL*, XXXII (1950), pp. 200ff.

succumb before Saul himself strips off his clothes and lies overnight in a cataleptic stupor.

Both these accounts purport to explain the proverb, "Is Saul also among the prophets?" In so doing, they suggest something of the still unfamiliar and foreign character of such dervish activity within Israelite circles. That it was a phenomenon as yet only partially integrated into normative Hebrew faith and practice explains the onlookers' astonishment at Saul's ravings and their puzzled inquiry, "What has come over the son of Kish?" (10:11). As late as the Elohist's day it was felt necessary to produce evidence of the legitimacy of the practice by so interpreting a story from the Mosaic period regarding the ecstatic behavior of a certain Eldad and Medad (Num. 11:26–30). Moses himself is cited as approving such performances when provoked by Yahweh's spirit: "Would that all the Lord's people were prophets, that the Lord would put his spirit upon them." That the words here are those of the later tradition and not Moses' own seems assured by the fact that no further instances of this sort are reported prior to the period of the monarchy.

Israel's earliest prophecy, then, was probably indistinguishable in form from the group ecstasy practiced in Canaanite circles; and both ecstasy and group associations were to continue as aspects of Israelite prophecy right on through its classical period. Elisha prophesied under the inspiration of music (II Kings 3:15), and one of his fellow prophets was referred to as a "mad fellow" (II Kings 9:11). Trances, visions, and a variety of supranormal actions are a characteristic mark of even the most rational of the classical prophets. Were we but able to trace the lines of prophecy's development more precisely, however, we should doubtless see its evolvement away from the more orgiastic expression toward more moderate forms. Lindblom has distinguished the "concentration ecstasy" which predominates in Old Testament prophecy from the "absorption ecstasy" of the dervish sects. Whereas the latter is an artificially induced state in which the personality loses itself totally in a mystic fusion with God or the universe, the ecstasy typical of the Hebrew prophets entails an intense concentration upon a single feeling or notion, resulting in a total but brief suspension of normal sense perception.[20] The brief and powerful pronouncement of judgment characteristic of the classical prophets—in the terms of form criticism, the prophetic *Drohwort*—was presumably the product of such phases of concentration ecstasy.

The prophetic groups about which we read in the Elijah and Elisha stories (I Kings 17–II Kings 13) appear to have functioned on the whole as orderly, well-organized, and peaceful communities. At the head of each group was a master or "father" (I Sam. 10:12; II Kings 2:12; 6:21; 13:14), ac-

---

[20] Johannes Lindblom, *Prophecy in Ancient Israel* (Philadelphia: Fortress Press, 1962), pp. 4–6 and passim.

cepted as a holy "man of God" (I Kings 17:18–24; II Kings 1:10–13; 4:7, 9), about whom there collected "sons of the prophets"—disciples who were eager to share in his charisma. Elijah was such a "father" to Elisha; and Elisha, in turn, was a master to groups who functioned in such scattered localities as Bethel (II Kings 2:2–3), Jericho (II Kings 2:5, 15), and Gilgal (II Kings 4:38). Judging from Elijah's and Elisha's ubiquitous patterns, such groups were probably committed to broad freedom of movement; they nevertheless built for themselves settlements (II Kings 6:1ff.), where they lived, worked, and ate together as a prophetic colony. Marked by their peculiar dress—the hair mantle and perhaps other distinctive marks—they were doubtless easily recognized as mantic personalities. They might on occasion be jeered (II Kings 2:23), ridiculed (II Kings 9:11), or even shunned by polite society (I Kings 21:20); but they were at the same time widely sought out for their peculiar powers (II Kings 4:1f; 5:1f.; 8:7f.) and were not lacking patrons who contributed to their support (II Kings 4:8, 42). King Ahab both sought out Elijah and avoided him like the plague.

Prophets were brought into the court as early as the reign of David, though Gad and Nathan are the only ones mentioned in connection with his administration, and Nathan's designation as "the prophet" (II Sam. 12:25) may indicate the singularity of the office at that stage. By Ahab's day there were purportedly no fewer than four hundred prophets kept on ready standby for counseling the king (I Kings 22:6). They were consulted on such strategic military matters as the potential for victory in battle (I Kings 22), chances for sustaining a siege (II Kings 6:24–7:2), and even maneuvers on the field (I Kings 20:13–14; II Kings 3:9ff.). Loyalty to the national welfare was expected and received, but to a surprising degree criticism of the administration was tolerated.

From its very beginnings, Hebrew prophecy appears to have maintained close associations with the cult and, perhaps, as some contend, had its origins in cultic circles.[21] Samuel is associated with both priestly and prophetic functions, and Elijah at Mount Carmel set out the sacrifice for Yahweh after the manner of a priest (I Kings 18:23, 30ff.). Most of the places with which the sons of the prophets were associated, moreover, were sites of well-known shrines. The early band of prophets encountered by Saul (I Sam. 10) were connected with the shrine at Gibeah. Indeed, some of Israel's prophets may have continued to function as cult personnel until some time prior to the work of the Chronicler (fourth or third century B.C.), when they were no longer distinguishable from the temple singers.[22]

Some scholars seek the background of at least some of Israel's prophets in a hypothetical office within the early Israelite cult, namely, that of a cov-

---

[21] Alfred Haldar, *Associations of Cult Prophets Among the Ancient Semites;* Theophile J. Meek, *Hebrew Origins,* pp. 148ff.

[22] Aubrey Johnson, *The Cultic Prophet in Ancient Israel,* pp. 60–75; Sigmund Mowinckel, *The Psalms in Israel's Worship,* Vol. II, pp. 54–55.

enant mediator or law-proclaimer, modeled after the prototype of Moses.[23] The key Old Testament passage cited in support of such an office is the declaration of Moses in Deuteronomy 18:15:

> The Lord your God will raise up for you a prophet like me from among you, from your brethren—him you shall heed.

At annual festivals of covenant renewal, it is theorized, the role of Moses was assumed by a succession of prophets, who proclaimed, interpreted, and applied covenant law to the Israelite community and pronounced judgments in the form of covenant lawsuits. Accordingly, a variety of legal and liturgical forms which appear within the oracle collections of the Old Testament prophets are thought to have originated in such a setting.[24] The most that can be said of this theory is that it offers one possible explanation of prophecy's relation to the Israelite cult and the covenant authority on which the prophets may have based their appeal. Lacking more explicit evidence, however, such an interpretation remains highly conjectural. An entirely different meaning is given the pivotal passage in Deuteronomy 18:15 by Ronald E. Clements, who believes that "it represents a Deuteronomic interpretation of the work of certain prophets in Israel, rather than a historical recollection or reinterpretation of an office of covenant mediator."[25] This is not to deny that the prophets found in the charisma and initiative of Moses a model for their own prophetic role.[26]

Precursors of Classical Prophecy

Notwithstanding the influence of the classical prophets upon our accounts of pre-eighth-century prophecy, it is unthinkable that the staunch moral courage and social-political-religious stature ascribed to such figures as Samuel, Nathan, Micaiah, Elijah, and Elisha can be written off as simply the idealizations provoked by prophecy's later image. A more debatable

---

[23] Cf. James Muilenburg, "The 'Office' of the Prophet in Ancient Israel," *The Bible in Modern Scholarship*, J. Philip Hyatt, ed. (Nashville, TN: Abingdon Press, 1965), pp. 74–97; R. V. Bergren, *The Prophets and the Law* (Cincinnati, OH: Hebrew Union College/Jewish Institute of Religion, 1974). The hypothesis developed largely from Albrecht Alt's and Martin Noth's claim that the minor judges functioned as covenant mediators in the tribal "amphictyony" (see above, p. 221); cf. Hans Joachim Kraus, *Die prophetische Verkündigung des Rechts in Israel*, Theological Studies, 51 (Zurich: Zollikon, 1957), pp. 11ff., and H. Graf Reventlow, "Prophetenamt und Mittleramt?" *ZThK*, 58 (1961), pp. 269–284. A useful description and critique of the hypothesis is provided by Ronald E. Clements, *Prophecy and Tradition* (Atlanta, GA: John Knox Press, 1975), pp. 8–23, 88.

[24] Cf. G. Ernest Wright, "The Lawsuit of God: A Form-Critical Study of Deuteronomy 32," *Israel's Prophetic Heritage*, W. Anderson and Walter Harrelson, eds. (New York: Harper & Row, Publishers, 1962), pp. 26–67; Herbert B. Huffmon, "The Covenant Lawsuit in the Prophets, *JBL*, LXXVIII (1959), pp. 285–295; and D. R. Hillers, *Treaty Curses and the Old Testament Prophets*, Biblica et Orientalia, no. 16 (Rome: Pontifical Biblical Institute, 1964).

[25] *Prophecy and Tradition*, p. 14.

[26] Cf. Herbert B. Huffmon, "The Origins of Prophecy," *Magnalia Dei; The Mighty Acts of God* (Garden City, NY: Doubleday & Company, Ind., 1976), p. 179.

question is whether or not some of these men—particularly Samuel and Elijah—were known as prophets in their own generations. It would have been easy enough, certainly, for later writers to have applied the prophetic label in cases where it was not originally used, as almost certainly occurred with Abraham, Moses, Aaron, Miriam, and Deborah.[27] The fact that groups of *nebi'im* were a reality within Israelite society by the eleventh century, however, lends a higher degree of credibility to the use of the name for Samuel and his successors. That they stood apart as unique and uncompromising spokesmen for the Yahweh faith, and that in so doing they helped set the pattern for the classic prophetic personality, appears to be beyond doubt.

SAMUEL. Samuel is unique in being associated with several vital roles: seer, judge, priest, and king-maker, as well as prophet.[28] He is referred to as *nabi'* only in the antimonarchical tradition (I Sam. 3:20); in the promonarchical passages in I Samuel he is called a "seer" and "man of God" (9:6, 8, 11). As we have seen, the one tradition ascribes to him an antimonarchical bias which possibly overstates the case for whatever misgivings he entertained toward the kingship. It is not at all unlikely, however, that we possess in that source something of the authentic spirit of Samuel, as for example in the rebuke addressed to Saul at Gilgal:

> Has the Lord as great delight in burnt offerings and sacrifices,
>   as in obeying the voice of the Lord?
> Behold to obey is better than sacrifice,
>   and to hearken than the fat of rams
>   I Sam. 15:22

In the Samuel-Saul relationship we are allowed our first view of the close association which prophecy would continue to maintain with the monarchy. Significantly, the most vital phase of prophecy's history coincides closely with the history of the monarchy. It is as if the passing of the leadership from charismatic leaders (the judges) to those who ruled by hereditary privilege (the kings) necessitated the presence of a man of charisma and conscience who would assure the king's exposure to Yahweh's word.[29]

---

[27] See footnote 4, above.

[28] For different evaluations of the role of Samuel, cf. Gerhard von Rad (*Old Testament Theology*, Vol. I, p. 33; Vol. II, p. 7), who regards him as a preacher of the law; W. F. Albright ("Samuel and the Beginnings of the Prophetic Movement," *Interpreting the Prophetic Tradition*, Harry M. Orlinsky, ed., pp. 151–176), who connects him with the ecstatic prophets; and Herbert B. Huffmon ("The Origins of Prophecy," pp. 176–180), who finds no one title adequate for him.

[29] Cf. the view of Herbert Huffmon that with the monarchy's formation the role of judge (*shophet*) was "redistributed into the roles of the *nabi'*, the charismatic messenger, and the *melek* (king), the permanent war leader" ("The Origins of Prophecy," p. 178).

NATHAN. The encounter between David and Nathan following the Bath-sheba affair and Uriah's murder (II Sam. 12) reads like a paradigm of the most momentous prophet-king confrontations to come. Without recourse to any of the techniques of ecstatic prophecy, but only through the reasoned persuasion of the ewe lamb parable and the terrible words of indictment, "You are the man," Nathan exposes the king's violations to the absolute principle of the covenant ethic—applicable alike to monarch and subject. Lest we be too quick to assign the famous episode to the fertile imagination of a later age, we do well to note similar instances from the Mari texts whereby an unbidden prophet confronts the monarch with remonstrances and commands of the deity. In one such text a prophetic mouthpiece of the weather god Hadad reminds the king that the god by whose good pleasure he was placed on the throne can revoke the appointment at will: "What I gave, I shall take away."[30] The unique feature in the Hebrew account is, of course, the peculiar covenant ethic which stands back of the prophet's words, holding the king accountable for his critically significant role in Israel's mission as the people of Yahweh.

MICAIAH. The Micaiah episode (I Kings 22) is most revealing as an indication of the conflict between individual prophets within Israel—the "true" as over against the "false" prophet.[31] Opposing the promise of victory assured King Ahab by four hundred prophets of the court, Micaiah assumes the role of a lone dissenter. So unlikely are his chances of prevailing against the assurances of the majority—particularly after one of their number, a certain Zedekiah, simulates an Israelite victory by donning horned headgear and with fine prophetic mimicry charging the imaginary Syrians off the field—that he initially mocks the request for his counsel by adding his own favorable word to that of the four hundred "yes-men." Ahab, however, aware of the ruse, presses him for the truth and receives the fatal answer: the king shall meet sure defeat and death. As telling evidence of the power of Yahweh's word to effect its ends, neither the wary king's disguise nor the effort to use his ally Jehoshaphat to draw the enemy's missiles away from himself succeeds in averting one fateful arrow's finding the small chink in his armor.

Zedekiah's demand of Micaiah that he show proof to defend his claim to a revelation that contradicts the counsel of the court prophets is no slight challenge. How does one distinguish "true" from "false" prophecy? We assume perhaps that one could detect the evident eagerness of the four hundred to please their patron with a favorable report; but this is not necessarily the case. The Deuteronomist was to wrestle with the question, and

[30] Gerhard von Rad, *Old Testament Theology*, Vol. II, pp. 10–11.
[31] A detailed analysis of the Micaiah narrative and its implications for the phenomenon of prophetic conflict is provided by Simon John DeVries, *Prophet Against Prophet* (Grand Rapids, MI: Eerdmans Publishing Company, 1978).

Model of Megiddo. The model shows features belonging to the periods of Solomon (cut-out section, foreground) and Ahab (most of model). To Ahab's day belonged the offset-inset city wall, a palace complex (top of picture), buildings with long, narrow chambers, a water tunnel (the circular entrance to which is seen at the upper right), and a well-protected city gate (foreground). (Courtesy of the State of Israel, Government Press Office.)

even to suggest two basic criteria for true prophecy, namely, (1) its correspondence with the established claims of Yahweh faith (Deut. 13:1–5) and (2) its consistency with empirical facts (Deut. 18:21–22). Demonstrated success in foretelling future events was obviously a significant test; but, according to the Deuteronomist, even if the prophet was able to forecast events with a favorable "batting average," but enticed his hearers to "go after other gods," he was no true prophet. Micaiah's credentials were likewise of a similar twofold character: He claims to have stood in Yahweh's council (where, indeed, he learns that Yahweh "inspires" false prophecy as well as true); and, in this case, he is willing to stake his life on the fulfillment of the word which he declares.[32]

[32] For the complexity of the problem of distinguishing "false" from "true" prophecy, see James L. Crenshaw, *Prophetic Conflict: Its Effect Upon Israelite Religion*. The "false prophets" have been variously portrayed as ecstatics, professional guild or cult figures, pro-establishment propagandists, superpatriots, etc. The provocative proposal of James A. Sanders perceives as the missing element of "false prophecy" the classical prophets' affirmation of God as the creator of all peoples and a consequent participation in the canonical monotheizing process ("Hermeneutics in True and False Prophecy," *Canon and Authority*, George W. Coats and Burke O. Long, eds. [Philadelphia: Fortress Press, 1977], pp. 21–41).

The remains of buildings at Megiddo, once thought to date from Solomon's time, more recently have been assigned to Ahab's administration. (Courtesy of the Oriental Institute, University of Chicago.)

ELIJAH. The prophet Elijah is the subject of an entire cycle of stories which includes some of the most familiar episodes in biblical literature (I Kings 17–19; 21; II Kings 1–2). As we have seen, Ahab's administration would scarcely have received the share of attention which it occupies in the Deuteronomic History but for the inclusion of the Elijah material. The stories are of a diversified character, ranging from popular wonder tales to the sensitive description of the Horeb theophany (19:8–18), all of which were brought together and made to yield their corporate impression by the Deuteronomist. They display a vividness of detail which testifies to both the historicity of the charismatic personality whom they describe and the antiquity of the traditions themselves. Since the historian selected only those episodes from the current folklore which suited his purposes, linking them together with vague phrases such as "after this," or the like, there can be no certainty as to chronological sequence. Biographical details concerning the prophet are few; we are informed only that he was from Tishbe in central Transjordan (Gilead) and that he wandered at will throughout the countryside, stopping occasionally to visit a patron (17:8ff.) and appearing unannounced before Ahab in moments of crisis.

Elijah appears to have been the first prophetic champion for Yahweh faith against its pagan rivals, in this case Baalism. The earlier Ahijah's

A model of the Megiddo buildings. The exact function of these buildings—whether they were stables, storehouses, or something else—is uncertain.
(Courtesy of the Oriental Institute, University of Chicago.)

remonstrances against Jeroboam's idolatry (14:7–16) are dubious, as they
are written in the style of the Deuteronomist and may even reflect the influence of Elijah's oracle against Ahab (cf. I Kings 14:11 and 21:17–19, 24).
That the faith crisis of the ninth century, provoked by Jezebel and the in-
cursion of fertility religion into Israelite worship, was ever recognized as
such is to be credited to the uncompromising Elijah. Reared in Transjordan, which was little affected by Canaanite influences felt in the rest of Palestine, he was spokesman for a pristine Mosaic faith that declared Yahweh's
total and unqualified claims upon Israel's religious loyalties. Ironically,
Baalism played its most significant role in religious history by confronting
Yahwism with the crucial either-or through which the latter faith was to
gain a fuller understanding of its incipient monotheism. Although it remained for prophets of future generations to explicate its principles, the
credit for first exposing that challenge in face-to-face encounter with king
and people must go to Elijah.

The contest with the Baal prophets at Mount Carmel (I Kings 18:20–46)
stands as the classic portrayal of the impotency of pagan gods before the
might of Yahweh. It comes at the time of a severe drought which the
prophet has already announced as the work of Yahweh (I Kings 17). The extant form of the story appears to fuse two older versions, in one of which
the issue of the contest was the lifting of the drought (vss. 33–35; 41–46)
and in the other the sending down of fire from heaven (vs. 38).[33] In either

[33] For a full discussion of the literary complexities of the account, cf. John Gray, *I and II
Kings: A Commentary*, 2nd ed., The Old Testament Library (Philadelphia: The Westminster
Press, 1970), pp. 383–405. For a vivid description of the episode on Mount Carmel, see H.
H. Rowley, "Elijah on Mount Carmel," *BJRL* XLII (1960), pp. 190–219.

event, the control of the forces of nature is at stake. Choosing a site at which the Baal cult flourished and where Yahweh's altar has fallen into ruins, Elijah challenges his opponents, four hundred and fifty strong, to prove Baal's alleged lordship by prevailing upon the deity to consume their exposed offering. The contrast between the frenzied and unavailing dance of the Baal prophets and the quiet, assured demeanor of Elijah suggests how far one phase of Hebrew prophecy had moved beyond its early dervish beginnings.

Other than the mimetic ritual of pouring water upon his sacrifice (a simulation of the rain which Yahweh was about to send—a feature of the drought-breaking version of the story), Elijah's only effort at persuading Yahweh to act is his simple but profound prayer (18:36–37). The ingenious effort to rationalize the account by alleging that the prophet poured inflammable naptha rather than water on the sacrifice is not only gratuitous but completely misses the point of the story. When Yahweh's fire breaks forth, consuming the oblation, the people respond with a shout reminiscent of the prophet's name (Elijah means "Yahweh is my God"), "Yahweh, he is God!" (18:39). In obedience to an old but largely forgotten law which imposed the death penalty for sacrificing to other gods (Exod. 22:19; cf. Deut. 13:7–12),[34] the prophets of Baal are put to the sword. Then as final proof of his rule of the heavens Yahweh sends down rain. Elijah, ecstatic with joy, runs before Ahab's chariot all the way to Jezreel—some seventeen miles. This is the one ecstatic action attested of him.

The Mount Carmel account serves as a fine example of the theological tone of the entire Elijah cycle of stories. From beginning to end, it is Yahweh, much more than the prophet himself, who is subject of the action. As von Rad observes, "the world in which Elijah lived was chock-full of miracles, yet he himself never works a single one."[35] The mighty works are Yahweh's alone. That the prophet invokes the faith of the patriarchs in his prayer before the altar is no fortuitous choice of words (18:36); the providential trust with which the names of Abraham, Isaac, and Jacob are associated is the faith for which he stands. We have reached that point in prophecy's development where the potency of Yahweh's word supports that which the prophet says and does in his name, and it is invoked as such throughout these accounts.[36] It both brings on and breaks the drought (17:2; 18:36), indicts all those in Israel who "go limping with two different opinions" (18:36), dispels the prophet's fear before Jezebel's threat on his life (19:9), stands in judgment upon Ahab for his crime against Naboth (21:17), and assures the death of Ahaziah (II Kings 1:17).

The victory over the Baal prophets was Elijah's supreme blow against the threat of fertility syncretism. Each of the episodes that follows this account

[34] Gerhard von Rad, *Old Testament Theology*, Vol. II, p. 18.
[35] Ibid., p. 24.
[36] B. Davie Napier, "Prophet, Prophetism," IDB, K–Q, p. 910.

has its own additional truth to disclose. The theophany at Horeb (19:1–18), with the "still small voice," brings Yahweh's assurance that the prophet does not stand alone against the forces of paganism; there are yet some seven thousand faithful persons who shall stand with him as ones who "have not bowed the knee to Baal" (19:18). The confrontation with Ahab following the murder of Naboth (21:20–24) calls forth a rebuke comparable to Nathan's words to David. The king is subject to Yahweh's law, just as any other person within Israel; and by his treachery he has forfeited his right to rule over Yahweh's people. Interestingly enough, in this encounter the prophet's words of accusation are scarcely needed. His very appearance is enough to provoke the king's despondent and guilty confession: "Have you found me, O my enemy?"

Elijah's departure in a whirlwind was legend's manner of finding a fitting exit for a remarkable figure whose career had been one of abrupt appearances, as if out of nowhere, and disappearances which were just as sudden and mysterious. Of greater significance, his commanding role as a man of God[37] reserved for him an honor in Hebrew tradition accorded few other figures: Like Enoch (Gen. 5:24) and Ezra (II Esdras 8:19; 14:9, 48), he did not die as other mortal men but was miraculously translated to heaven.[38] As such, he was still a subject of interest centuries later, when in the book of Malachi he was identified as the future messenger of the Day of Yahweh (Mal. 4:5) and in the New Testament as the messianic herald (Matt. 11:14).

ELISHA. In a number of respects the stories concerning Elijah's disciple and successor, Elisha, read like a continuation of the career of the master himself. Just as the Ahab era is portrayed by the Deuteronomist through the framework of the Elijah traditions, even so the Elisha cycle provides most of our information about Jehoram and notable episodes from the reigns of Jehu and Jehoash. Elisha's charisma, it was assumed, derived from his inheritance of Elijah's spirit (II Kings 2:15). As a result, the same feats performed by the master tended to be ascribed to the disciple: parting the Jordan with the wonder-working mantle (II Kings 2:8, 14), replenishing the pantry of a poor widow (I Kings 17:8–16; II Kings 4:1–7), raising a dead child (I Kings 17:17–24; II Kings 4:8–37), and announcing a drought (I Kings 17:1; II Kings 8:1). Both shared the same honorific title, "the chariots of Israel and its horsemen" (II Kings 2:12; 13:14); and even their names are similar (Elisha means "God is salvation").

Significant differences mark the accounts, as well, and leave little doubt but that Elisha was an individual in his own right. Whereas Elijah acted alone, Elisha is depicted as the head of a prophetic guild whose members look to him for instruction and are quick to do his bidding (II Kings 6:1f.;

[37] "Man of God" is used of Elijah more than of any other prophet, some six times.
[38] On the death and assumption of Moses cf. R. H. Charles, ed., *The Apocrypha and Pseudepigrapha of the Old Testament*, Vol. II (Oxford: Clarendon Press, 1913), pp. 407–409.

The water shaft at Megiddo, over 80 feet deep, appears to have been constructed during the Israelite period—perhaps in the reign of Ahab. (Courtesy of the Consulate General of Israel in New York.)

9:1f.). That he was no impoverished itinerant is attested by his sacrifice of twelve oxen at the time of his call and his ownership of the slave Gehazi. He appears to have enjoyed more cordial relations with the court than did Elijah; in more than one instance he offers the king counsel favorable to his cause in the struggle against the Syrians. In the most significant political action of his career, and his only direct involvement in the struggle with Baalism which had occupied Elijah—the appointment of Jehu to his bloody task of destroying the house of Ahab—his deed is credited to the explicit instructions that Yahweh had earlier given Elijah (I Kings 19:16).

The Elijah stories are so centered in the acts of Yahweh that, in spite of their variety, they reflect a unity which the Elisha cycle fails to appropriate. Not only is Elisha the subject of a greater number of disconnected wonder works, but they are most often recounted in such a manner as to enhance the extraordinary powers of the man himself. It would be difficult to find a deeper significance for such stories as making bitter water sweet (II Kings 2:19–22), the destruction of forty-two boys by she-bears

(2:23–24), or the recovery of a sunken axe head (6:1–7). A comparison of the doublet of the dead child's resuscitation (I Kings 17:17–24; II Kings 4:8–37) reveals a heightening of the miraculous and magical elements in the Elisha version.

The story of Naaman's healing (ch. 5) is the highlight of the Elisha cycle of tradition and, of all its original episodes, the one that most truly resembles the spirit of the Elijah stories. The wonder that is performed for the leprous Syrian is clearly the work of Yahweh, as demonstrated by the cured man's vow henceforth to worship no other god. The manner in which Naaman humbles himself to the obedience demanded by Yahweh's prophet and the willingness of Elisha to assist a leader of the armies of an enemy people made the episode an apt illustration for Luke's teachings on the universality of the Gospel (Luke 4:25–27).

Literary Features of Hebrew Prophecy

The basic literary unit of Hebrew prophecy is the oracle—in its most primitive and characteristic form, a brief, poetic declaration, preceded or followed by the formula that establishes it as a message from God, "Thus says Yahweh." The books of the Latter Prophets are, in large part, collections of such poetic utterances, as distinctly marked by the rhythmic meter and parallelism of Hebrew poetry as are the Psalms or Proverbs. Only five of these books (Obadiah, Micah, Nahum, Habakkuk, and Zephaniah), however, are cast entirely in the poetic form. The remainder contain some amount of prose material: prose discourses, autobiographical or biographical narratives, and historical excursus. The book of Jeremiah, for example, consists roughly of an equal amount of poetry and prose; Ezekiel's oracles are contained chiefly in autobiographical narratives; and the books of Haggai and Malachi are cast entirely in their own peculiar prose forms.

Modern readers interested in the personal lives of the prophets are quick to discover that biography, as such, was of little concern in the formation of the prophetic books. Even in those works containing significant amounts of biographical or autobiographical narrative, it is not biography for its own sake that is offered. It is rather the prophet's message—which, after all, is Yahweh's word—that is uppermost; and in some instances we are told no more about the man who speaks it than his name. Typically, however, there is a superscription supplied by the compiler of the book, which indicates the prophet's family connections and the kings who reigned at the time the oracles were delivered.

Prophecy consisted in the first instance of oral speech delivered by the prophet in face-to-face encounter with his hearers. The varied settings in which the oracle was proclaimed, ranging from the court of the temple (Jer. 7:1–2; 19:14) or some lesser shrine (Amos 7:13) to a public highway (Isa. 7:3), a city gate (Jer. 17:19; 19:2), or even a prison (Jer. 32:2f.), suggest the spontaneous and *ad hoc* character of much of Israel's prophecy.

The question of how such spoken oracles finally reached their written form in the books as we have them is not easily answered. We cannot be certain, for example, whether or not the prophets themselves characteristically recorded their own words. In Jeremiah's case, we are informed that he dictated oracles declared over a long period of his career to his scribe Baruch (36:1–2, 18, 28); and Isaiah is commanded by God to "bind up the testimony" (8:16) and "write before them as on a tablet, and inscribe it in a book" (30:8)—though these latter may be no more than figurative expressions. Some of the prophetic materials, such as the autobiographical narratives, almost surely originated as the personal, written records of the prophets themselves.

The evidence adduced in recent years, however, showing the important role of oral tradition in early Hebrew culture leaves little doubt but that some prophetic oracles were in their originally brief and poetic form stored in the memory and transmitted for a time from mouth to ear before finally being written down. That some of this activity is to be attributed to disciples of the prophets seems a reasonable assumption. It is apparent that Isaiah, for example, had such a following who attended his words during his lifetime (8:16) and compiled and enlarged them after his death. Thus, we must conjecture the transmission of both oral and written materials, in some instances for several centuries, before the final compilation of the four prophetic scrolls: Isaiah, Jeremiah, Ezekiel, and the Twelve.

The principles that guided the compilation of the prophetic books were varied and in some cases are altogether beyond our ability to comprehend. There are abundant instances in which words of threat and promise, oracles delivered in widely separated periods, and otherwise totally different materials stand side by side. Except for a few books, notably Ezekiel, Haggai, and Zechariah, chronology played a relatively insignificant role. Even when oracles are dated to the regnal year of the king, they are not always arranged in strict chronological sequence (e.g., Jer. 21ff.). Subject matter was more frequently a factor, particularly in the broad groupings evident in the Major Prophets and Zephaniah, whereby (1) oracles of judgment against Israel, (2) oracles against foreign nations, and (3) oracles of promise tended to be placed together. In chapters 4 and 5 of Ezekiel a number of accounts involving the prophet's symbolic actions appear as a collection; and Amos 7–9 is organized around five visions. Also, one may expect to find brief series of oracles that share the same opening or concluding formulas, such as a group of woes (Amos 5:18–6:7; Isa. 5:8–24), or even those joined by the catchword principle. In Isaiah 1:9 and 10, for example, the sequence has been determined by nothing more than the catchword "Sodom" and in Isaiah 8:5–9 and 8:9–10, "Immanuel." We have to reckon, moreover, with separate collections which were presumably incorporated into the books intact, such as Baruch's memoirs (Jer. 26–45). Finally, such a practical consideration as the length of the separate scrolls doubtless influenced the inclusion or exclusion of some materials. Where space permitted, oracles other than those of the prophet under whose name they appear might be attached with no indication of separate authorship, as in the instance of the additions to Isaiah (chs. 40–66).

The prophetic books, then, are in large part collections of collections, brought together in stages by editors or disciples who often worked with the most heterogeneous sorts of materials. The fact that a prophet's original words were often modified or expanded in the process should not be misunderstood as an indication of irreverence or dishonesty on the editors' part. On the contrary, such expansions resulted from the conviction that the prophetic word was ever new and adaptable to changing circumstances. Once uttered, it was destined to be fulfilled, not only in the prophet's own day but for each new generation.[39]

Form criticism, the study and classification of the individual literary units in an effort to determine early oral and written forms, was first applied on a broad scale to the prophetic books by Hermann Gunkel.[40] Recognizing that the prophets were originally speakers rather than authors, Gunkel identified the oldest style of address as brief, poetic oracles, oriented toward the future and consisting of two primary types: oracles of threat and oracles of promise. Received by the prophet in moments of inspiration or ecstatic concentration, these terse messages typically bear a secretive, mysterious, and indefinite quality. By the time of the classical prophets, Gunkel concluded, the primary oracle was expanded to include not only the announcement of what was in store, but the reasons to explain why it should be so and the exhortations provoked by its reality. Thus, the divine word of threat or judgment was accompanied by a reproach, consisting of the prophet's reflection on the disaster and his indictment of the guilty party, as follows:

> Reproach: "They do not know how to do
> right," says the Lord,
> "those who store up violence and
> robbery in their strongholds."
> Threat: Therefore thus says the Lord God:
> "An adversary shall surround the
> land,
> and bring down your defenses
> from you,
> and your strongholds shall be
> plundered."
> Amos 3:10–11

[39] Gerhard von Rad, *Old Testament Theology*, Vol. II, pp. 45–49.

[40] "The Israelite Prophecy from the Time of Amos," *Twentieth Century Theology in the Making*, J. Peliken, ed. (New York: Harper & Row, Publishers, 1969), pp. 48–75; idem, "The Secret Experiences of the Prophets," *Expositor*, IX 1 (1924), pp. 356–366, 427–435; 2 (1924), pp. 23–32.

The reproach often appears as a prelude to the threat, as in the above example, in which case the latter is introduced by "therefore." In other instances the threat precedes the reproach, which begins with "because" (e.g., Amos 1:3ff.). Exhortations or calls to repentance may accompany words of promise or judgment, respectively, and consist of the prophet's appeal for a response appropriate to the relevation of Yahweh's action (e.g., Hosea 10:12; Amos 5:23–24).

Although Gunkel's identifications of patterns of threat and reproach have proved basic in modern analyses of the prophetic oracle, recent critics have modified his classifications. Claus Westermann,[41] for example, outlines the basic judgment speech (addressed to individuals) as follows:

Accusation:	You say, "Do not prophesy against Israel,
	and do not preach against the house of Isaac."
Messenger formula:	Therefore thus says the Lord:
Announcement of judgment:	"Your wife shall be a harlot in the city,
	and your sons and your daughters shall fall by the sword, . . ."
	Amos 7:16–17

Thus, Westermann replaces Gunkel's "threat" and "reproach" terminology, which he regards as too weak to express either the seriousness of the charges brought against the accused or the finality of the approaching doom. By specifying the messenger formula, "Thus says the Lord," Westermann emphasizes the role of the prophet as Yahweh's messenger, sent after the manner of a king's courier, bearing the official word of the sovereign. In this, Westermann is opposed by Klaus Koch and W. Eugene March, who find no pure messenger-speech form in the prophetic oracles.[42] Referring to the judgment speech as a "prediction of disaster," Koch and March perceive it as typically accompanied by a statement of the situation calling for remedy, and concluded with a description of either the sender or the recipients of the prophecy.

---

[41] *Basic Forms of Prophetic Speech*, Hugh C. White, trans. (Philadelphia: The Westminster Press, 1967).

[42] Klaus Koch, *The Growth of the Biblical Tradition: The Form-Critical Method*, S. M. Cupitt, trans. (New York: Charles Scribner's Sons, 1969), pp. 183–220; and W. Eugene March, "Prophecy," *Old Testament Form Criticism*, John H. Hayes, ed., pp. 141–177.

Indication of situation:	And Jeremiah the prophet said to the prophet Hananiah, "Listen Hananiah, the Lord has not sent you, and you have made this people trust in a lie.
Prediction of disaster:	Therefore thus says the Lord: 'Behold, I will remove you from the face of the earth. This very year you shall die,
Concluding characterization:	because you have uttered rebellion against the Lord.' "
	Jer. 28:15–16

According to the latter analysis, the prediction of disaster has its counterpart in the "prophecy of salvation," which typically includes the same structure but conveys a positive rather than a negative word (e.g., Jer. 28:1–4).

These primary forms of prophetic address, whether as formulated by Gunkel, Westermann, or Koch and March, undoubtedly point to elements which are central to the prophets' messages. That they by no means apply to all, or even a majority, of the oracles in the Old Testament, however, will be evident to anyone who reads the prophetic books with a view toward applying the structural models. Thus, form criticism recognizes a vast and complex variety of patterns in the prophetic oracles, representing both expansions of the primary forms and additional secondary forms, i.e., speech types found in nonprophetic as well as prophetic settings. Among the more notable of these are the woe oracle, the trial speech, and the disputation. The woe oracle typically begins with "Woe!" or "Alas!" (e.g., Amos 5:18–20; 6:1–7) and has affinities with the cultic curse, wisdom saying, and funeral rite. The trial (or judicial) speech, which derived from the legal sphere of Israel's life, pictures the violaters of Yahweh's law as defendants before their accuser and is replete with summons, trial, and sentencing (e.g., Mic. 6:1–8).[43] In the disputation speech a response is made to implied or expressed charges against God or his prophet (e.g., Mic. 2:6–11).

In recent years a spirited debate has centered around the question of the extent and nature of wisdom forms and vocabulary in the prophetic books and their implications for the prophets' backgrounds.[44] Greatest attention

---

[43] Some scholars contend for a more specific legal form called the *rib* ("controversy," "trial"), based on the suzerainty treaty form and reflective of a covenant pattern, i.e., God's lawsuit against his people who have broken their covenant treaty. Cf. Herbert H. Huffmon, "The Covenant Lawsuit in the Prophets," *JBL*, LXXVII (1959), pp. 285–295, and G. Ernest Wright, "The Lawsuit of God: A Form-Critical Study of Deuteronomy 32," *Israel's Prophetic Heritage*, Bernhard W. Anderson and Walter Harrelson, eds., pp. 26–67.

[44] See below, pp. 292–294, 322, 450–452.

has centered on the books of Amos[45] and Isaiah,[46] where such formal elements as parables, woe cries, didactic questions, numerical sequences, proverbs, and riddles have been attributed to a wisdom influence on these prophets. That the prophetic and wisdom books share such common features is not to be denied, but that they represent formal genres belonging to an exclusive wisdom school in Israel is open to question. If wisdom literature was produced not solely by a group of professional sages in Israel, but flourished within clan and family circles from an early stage of Hebrew history, then prophecy might be expected to share with wisdom some of the patterns of this common cultural heritage. It thus appears unnecessary to posit a direct influence of wisdom schools on specific Old Testament prophets.[47]

2. FOR THREE TRANSGRESSIONS OF ISRAEL: AMOS

The earliest of Israel's prophets for whom we have a book of oracles bearing his name is Amos of Tekoa. Though the biographical data concerning him is slight (1:1; 7:10–15), it is clear that he prophesied in the mid-eighth century, during the reigns of Jeroboam II of Israel (786–746 B.C.) and Uzziah of Judah (783–742 B.C.). He was remembered by those who preserved his oracles as having spoken out two years before a memorable earthquake (Amos 1:1).[48] There is no indication of the duration of his prophetic career; most likely it was brief. An approximate date of 750 B.C. fits the circumstances of the book.

In Amos' day many of the losses which the northern kingdom had suffered under Jehu and his immediate successors were recovered under Jeroboam.[49] The northern Transjordan lands, formerly held by Israel but most recently under the control of Damascus, were regained; and the

---

[45] Cf. Hans Walter Wolff, *Amos the Prophet: The Man and His Background* Foster R. McCurley, trans. (Philadelphia: Fortress Press, 1973) or idem, *Joel and Amos*, Waldermar Janzen, et al., trans. (Philadelphia: Fortress Press, 1977), pp. 89ff.; Samuel Terrien, "Amos and Wisdom," *Israel's Prophetic Heritage*, Bernhard W. Anderson and Walter Harrelson, eds., pp. 108–115.

[46] Cf. J. William Whedbee, *Isaiah and Wisdom* (Nashville, TN: Abingdon Press, 1971).

[47] Cf. James L. Crenshaw, "The Influence of the Wise Upon Amos," *ZAW*, 79 (1967), pp. 42–52; Ronald E. Clements, *Prophecy and Tradition* (Atlanta, GA: John Knox Press, 1975), pp. 73–83. William McKane (*Prophets and Wise Men*, Studies in Biblical Theology, no. 44 [Naperville, IL: Alec R. Allenson, 1965]), by connecting Israelite wisdom primarily with the secular and worldly interests of the royal court, posits too sharp a contrast between prophets and wisdom.

[48] Cf. Zech. 14:5.

[49] Cf. II Kings 14:23–29; 15:1–7; II Chron. 26.

period of Syrian encroachment came to an end. Assyria was occupied with problems closer to home and offered no immediate threat. Uzziah, until stricken with leprosy, maintained an aggressive administration in the south. Judah controlled the Negeb and southern desert, all the way to Ezion-geber, including Edom and the important southern trade routes.

Freedom from foreign intervention and peaceful relations between Israel and Judah were accompanied by a domestic prosperity unknown since the days of Solomon. Particularly for the "new rich" of the north, the period was marked by a steady advance in foreign trade and business (Amos 8:4–6), the development of large landed estates (5:11), and the construction of luxurious winter and summer houses, filled with costly ivory-decorated furnishings (3:15; 4:4). A newly discovered leisure encouraged the pursuit of music and the arts (6:4–6), as well as the scrupulous discharge of perfunctory religious duties (4:4–5; 6:21–24). The shrines at Bethel and Gilgal received the hearty patronage of both the king, who kept them properly staffed with cult personnel, and the affluent devout, who brought their "sacrifices every morning and tithes every three days" (4:4).

Prosperity, peace, and religious activity, notwithstanding, we are shown through the eyes of Amos a society whose internal health was in rapid decline. The heightened pace of urbanization and shifting class structures, together with the land-grabbing by which the peasantry was dispossessed of its holdings, brought on a disintegration of the covenant ethic which had assured justice and fair treatment for all members of the society—without regard to economic or social status. A flourishing cult was but a façade for rampant cheating in business (8:5), bribery of judges (5:12), sexual license (2:7), and gross mistreatment of the poor and powerless (2:6–7; 5:11–12; 8:4–6).

So accurate are Amos' warnings concerning impending invasion and exile (3:11; 6:7–8, 14; 9:4) that some scholars would extend the date of his prophetic ministry into the period of Tiglath-pileser III (745–727 B.C.), the king who renewed Assyria's policy of aggression in the west. It is unlikely that any of the original oracles are that late, however, since they reflect no awareness of the political upheavals that followed the reign of Jeroboam II. Nor is there any indication that Amos' fears were shared by his contemporaries. It was, rather, the prophet's insight that Israel's unchecked moral decline was a sure disaster course that caused him to prophesy its doom. As one interpreter comments, "the prophet's ability to read the signs of the times was one of the characteristics that distinguished him from his generation."[50] Assyria, though for the time quiescent, was the only nation with the potential for emerging as the agent of such devastating judgment as Amos describes.

[50] Hughell E. W. Fosbroke, "The Book of Amos," *IB*, Vol. 6, p. 766.

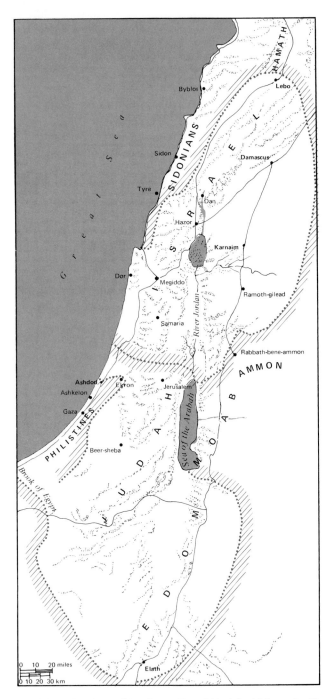

Israel and Judah in the days of Jeroboam II and Uzziah. (Adapted with permission of Macmillan Publishing Co., Inc., from Macmillan Bible Atlas *by Y. Aharoni and Michael Avi-Yonah. Copyright © 1968 Carta, Jerusalem. © Copyright 1964 by Carta, Jerusalem. © Copyright 1966 by Carta, Jerusalem.)*

2. FOR THREE TRANSGRESSIONS OF ISRAEL: AMOS

Go, Prophesy to My People Israel

The prophet's home village, Tekoa, was situated some twelve miles south of Jerusalem in the bleak, rock-bound, southern hill country. Here he pursued the, apparently itinerant, life of a shepherd and "dresser" of sycamore trees (piercing the figlike fruit to allow it to ripen properly [1:1; 7:14]). Although his roots were in the rural south, his prophetic message was directed particularly to the urban centers of the north. According to the one narrative episode in the book (7:10–15), he appeared at the northern shrine of Bethel and delivered oracles there against the house of Jeroboam. In the words of Amaziah, Jeroboam's priest at Bethel who accused Amos of preaching treason and demanded that he go back to Judah, Amos had proclaimed:

> Jeroboam shall die by the sword, and Israel must go into exile away from his land.
>
> 7:11

Amos' reply to Amaziah was, literally translated, "Not a prophet I. . . ." If taken in the past tense, the words simply prepare the way for his claim to speak as one called of God: "I *was* no prophet . . . but the Lord took me . . ." (KJV). If however, the present tense is intended ("I *am* no prophet . . ." [RSV]), as would be the more natural rendering, Amos seems to have disclaimed for himself a professional prophetic role.[51] Possibly he felt himself commissioned to declare a specific word to Israel—this, and nothing more. Since nowhere in his oracles is there an attack on the prophetic guilds, it does not necessarily follow that he shrank from any association with them.[52] As Hans Walter Wolff has noted, the intent of Amos' response to Amaziah is to deny that either his right to function as a prophet or to earn his living as a seer is pertinent to the discussion. "The sole issue is rather Yahweh's precise commission."[53] Amaziah had spoken only of Amos' personal qualifications and his conflict with the king. Amos thus sets the matter straight by shifting attention away from himself to the God who summoned him. That the shepherd of Tekoa was a *nabi'* in the best sense of the word is beyond all doubt.

[51] For different views on this passage cf. H. H. Rowley, "Was Amos a Nabi?" *Festschrift Otto Eissfeldt*, J. Fück, ed. (Halle, East Germany: Niemeyer, 1947), pp. 191ff.; J. Lindblom, *Prophecy in Ancient Israel*, pp. 183ff.; Hans Walter Wolff, *Joel and Amos*, pp. 305–316; H. N. Richardson, "A Critical Note on Amos 7:14," *JBL*, LXXXV (1966), p. 89, and the sources he cites.

[52] The positive estimate of the prophetic role affirmed in 3:7 unfortunately cannot settle this issue, as the verse probably derives from a later redaction of Amos' oracles. Cf. Hans Walter Wolff, ibid., p. 187 and James Luther Mays, *Amos: A Commentary*, The Old Testament Library (Philadelphia: The Westminster Press, 1969), pp. 61–62, both of whom attribute the verse to Deuteronomic editors. Mays points to 2:11, however, as indicating that "Amos knew of prophets with whom he would not deny identification" (pp. 137–138).

[53] Hans Walter Wolff, *Joel and Amos*, p. 311.

. . . and the Lord said to me, "Go, prophesy to my people Israel." Now therefore hear the word of the Lord.

7:15–16

Efforts to determine the precise religious and intellectual milieu in which Amos functioned have opened in recent years a provocative new chapter in Amos studies. One significant result is an increased awareness of the influence of the cult, as evidenced by an extensive use of cultic vocabulary and liturgical forms in Amos' oracles.[54] It by no means follows, however, that the prophet was an official cult functionary, as some scholars contend.[55] In fact, it appears that he has often reversed the import of the cultic materials employed or even turned the liturgical traditions against his hearers for noncultic ends.[56] Another approach stresses the influence of the wisdom tradition upon the prophet's theology and literary style.[57] Without doubt, certain of the speech forms and terminology commonly associated with wisdom literature were natural to the style of Amos. A good match for the wise man in the use of proverbs and riddles, he nevertheless brought to the forms a genuine prophetic message:

> Do two walk together
>   unless they have made an appointment?
> Does a lion roar in the forest,
>   when he has no prey?
>
> 3:3–4a

> Does evil befall a city,
>   unless Yahweh has done it?
>
> 3:6b

> Do horses run upon rocks?
>   Does one plow the sea with oxen?
> But you have turned righteousness into wormwood.
>
> 6:12

His facility with the graduated-numbers sayings, which are characteristic of proverbial wisdom (cf. Prov. 30:15ff.), heightens the dynamic element in some of his most powerful oracles:

[54] A. S. Kapelrud, *Central Ideas in Amos* (Oslo Skrifter utgitt av Det Norske Videnskaps-Akademi i Osol, 1961); "New Ideas in Amos," *VTS*, XV (1966); Aage Bentzen, "The Ritual Background of Amos 1.2–II.16," *Oudtestamentische Studien* VIII (1950), pp. 85–99; G. Farr, "The Language of Amos, Popular or Cultic?" *VT*, 16 (1966), pp. 312–324; E. Würthwein, "Amos-Studien," *ZAW*, LXII (1949–50), pp. 10–51.

[55] H. Graf Reventlow, *Das Amt des Propheten bei Amos*, Forschungen zur Religion und Literatur des Alten und Neuen Testaments, 80 (Göttingen, West Germany: Vandenhoeck und Ruprecht, 1962); W. Brueggemann, "Amos IV. 4–13 and Israel's Covenant Worship," *VT*, XV (1965), pp. 1–15; J. D. W. Watts, *Vision and Prophecy in Amos* (Grand Rapids, MI: W. B. Eerdmans, 1958).

[56] J. L. Crenshaw, "Amos and the Theophanic Tradition," *ZAW*, LXXX (1968), pp. 203–215.

[57] See footnote 45, this chapter.

Winged man-headed lion from a doorway in the palace of Ashurnasirpal, king of Assyria (883–859 B.C.). (Courtesy of the Trustees of the British Museum.)

For three transgressions of Damascus,
and for four, I will not revoke the punishment.
1:3

It does not follow, however, that Amos belonged to a professional circle within Israelite society to which modern interpreters give the name "wisdom." It is enough to note that he drew from a common experience shared alike by family, court, scribes, and even prophets.[58] The evidence thus adduced for Amos's background in either cultic or wisdom circles is sufficient to demonstrate that the prophet was no unlearned backwoodsman, isolated from society and its institutions.

The Words . . . Which He Saw

The Book of Amos consists almost entirely of prophetic oracles, the original sequence and setting of which can only be guessed for the most part. The oracle units are better preserved and more clearly marked than in some of the other prophetic collections; and the book separates most naturally into three major units. The two sections most easily distinguished are (1) chapters 1 and 2, where the oracles take the form of eight judgments against nations, and (3) chapters 7 through 9, consisting of five visions of doom, with interpolations. These units, in turn, set apart (2) the intervening oracles (chs. 3–6), which lack the formal unity of (1) and (3) but share the common theme of the judgment awaiting Israel.

1. Oracles against nations: chs. 1–2
   a. Damascus: 1:3–5
   b. Philistia: 1:6–8
   c. Phoenicia: 1:9–10
   d. Edom: 1:11–12
   e. Ammon: 1:13–15
   f. Moab: 2:1–3
   g. Judah: 2:4–5
   h. Israel: 2:6–16
2. Oracles against Israel: chs. 3–6
3. Visions of doom: chs. 7–9
   a. Locusts: 7:1–3
   b. Fire: 7:4–6
   c. Plumb line: 7:7–9
      (Amos at Bethel: 7:10–17)
   d. Summer fruit: 8:1–3
      (An indictment of Israel: 8:4–14)

---

[58] See footnote 47, this chapter. The study of Crenshaw, cited there, concerns Amos's theological milieu as a theophanic mode of thought—a tradition built on appearances of God to men and the earth's response to the divine presence.

e. Altar theophany: 9:1–4
(A doxology [9:5–6]; prophecies of judgment [9:7–10] and restoration [9:11–15])

Although there is general agreement that the prophet's own words constitute most of the book, clearly others were responsible for putting the collected oracles into their final form. Probably some of this work fell to Amos's disciples shortly after the prophet's death. If this took place in Judah, following the fall of the northern kingdom in 722 B.C., it could explain some of the evident editorial touches which point to a connection with the south. For example, Uzziah, King of Judah, is named in the superscription before his northern counterpart, Jeroboam II (1:1). On the basis of the concluding verses of the book (9:11–15), which presuppose the fall of the Davidic state, we may conclude that the editorial process was not finally complete until the period of Exile or later. Hans Walter Wolff distinguishes some six stages of composition in the book's formation, the first three attributed to Amos himself and his contemporaries and the last three resulting in the addition of material composed after the prophet's death. The oldest levels of the book are thought to be the oracles against Israel in Chapters 3–6 and the visions of doom in 7–9. The later additions include the hymnic doxologies of 4:13, 5:8f., and 9:5f.; a Deuteronomic redaction, which contributed the oracles against Judah (2:4–5), Phoenicia (1:9–10), and Edom (1:11–12); as well as other materials designed to show that Judah and Jerusalem stood under the judgment of Yahweh; and the post-Exilic addition of promise in 9:11–15.[59]

Oracles Against Nations

The universal tone of Amos' message is established from the very beginning in a series of oracles addressed to the small states surrounding Israel and Judah: Damascus (1:3–5), Philistia (1:6–8), Phoenicia (1:9–10), Edom (1:11–12), Ammon (1:13–15), and Moab (2:1–3). The series concludes with oracles against Judah (2:4–5) and Israel (2:6–16) themselves. The eight oracles consist of indictments for national crimes and proclamations of coming judgment and are cast in a stereotyped pattern which, in its full form, includes the following elements:

Messenger formula: "Thus says the Lord . . ."
Indictment formula: "For three transgressions of _____ and for four, I will not revoke the punishment."
Specification of crime: "Because they have . . ."
Judgment formula: "So I will send a fire upon _____ and it shall devour the strongholds of _____."

[59] *Joel and Amos*, pp. 106–113 and passim.

Specification of judgment: "I will cut off the inhabitants from _____
and him that holds the scepter from _____" (people and king).
Concluding formula: ". . . says the Lord."

The indictment formula, "for three transgressions and for four," must be taken to mean "for multiplied transgressions." In other contexts such phrasing corresponds to the specific number of items named,[60] but here— except in Israel's case—each people is charged with a single crime. The foreign atrocities are drawn from the history of international relations among Israel's neighbors and, significantly, do not involve solely those hostile acts committed against Israel herself. Damascus and Ammon are reproached for earlier ravishings of Gilead—which was by Amos' day safely once more within Israel's control. Philistia and Phoenicia are identified with slave-raiding, or perhaps the sale of prisoners of war—of what peoples it is not said. Edom, located on the major southern trade routes and a ready market for slaves to labor in its mining operations east of the Arabah, is named as the buyer. The "covenant of brotherhood" which Phoenicia is accused of having broken may refer to treaties involving her pledge to abstain from such traffic.

The Phoenician oracle, because of its similarity to the Philistine oracle and its shorter form, has been held by some to be a later addition to the collection. Both the specification of judgment and the concluding formula are missing. Likewise, Edom's crime, the pursuit of "his brother" (Judah) with a sword, is frequently taken as secondary (note here also the abbreviated form) and as reflecting that people's exploitation of Judah's destruction by Babylon in the sixth century. If genuine, the reference would of necessity extend far back into the history of Israelite-Edomite relations, perhaps even to the events recorded in Numbers.[61]

The atrocity ascribed to Moab is at once the most obscure and the most noteworthy of the foreign oracles. The event, the desecration of the bones of an Edomite king, is otherwise unknown. Significant is the fact that a foreign people is condemned for an inhumane action against other non-Israelites—indeed against a traditional Israelite enemy.

The Judah oracle, like those against Phoenicia and Edom, lacks the last two parts of the standard form; and its Deuteronomic phrasing ("because they have rejected the Torah of Yahweh, and have not kept his statutes . . . after which their fathers walked") makes it particularly suspect as a later interpolation. It is doubtful, furthermore, that Amos intended the final oracle (2:2–16) solely for northern Israel, exclusive of Judah. The northern kingdom doubtless provided the more specific examples of the crimes which he denounces; but the recital of salvation history (vss. 9–11),

---

[60] Cf. Job 33:14; Prov. 6:16; 30:15, 18. In late wisdom texts, however, only the last item in such a series is important.
[61] Cf. Num. 20:14–21.

which has the effect of intensifying the favored people's guilt, includes the whole of the covenant people—north and south.

The oracle against Israel brings the series to its shocking climax. It is fitting that the form in which it is cast begins with the same stereotyped formula of the foreign oracles: Israel, shameless in her evil, is not unlike the foreign nations and is no more to be exempt from her deserved punishment than are they. Indeed, she bears a greater responsibility owing to the more complete revelation which she has received and the covenant to which she is a party (3:1–2). Thus, the prophet proceeds to indict Israel on multiple charges of internal corruption: for capitalizing on the afflictions of the poor, stripping bare and enslaving debtors, freely satisfying gross sexual lusts, abusing holy men, and silencing the prophets. Likewise, her punishment is developed in greater detail. There shall be no escape for Israel in the day of Yahweh's judgment. Neither swiftness of movement, physical strength, skill with weapons, nor stout courage will avail for anything "in that day" when Yahweh holds her to an accounting for the broken covenant vows.

Drawing upon the analogy of execration (cursing) texts from Egypt, wherein curses against foreign enemies and native evil-doers were pronounced in cultic rites, it has been proposed that the formal structure of these oracles derives from the Hebrew cult.[62] It is possible, though not at all certain,[63] that the foreign oracles of 1:1–2:3 were drawn from longer cultic denunciations of Israel's enemies which the prophet revised to suit his own unique message. If the words had a familiar ring to the ears of his hearers, who had chanted them at the shrines, how much more startling would have been the new twist which Amos gave them. Israel had become like the peoples whom she denounced; and, whereas the crimes of each pagan nation could be reduced to a single atrocity, Israel's sins were manifold.

Oracles Against Israel

Some of the principles by which the collection of oracles in chapters 3–6 was brought together may be seen in certain catchwords and refrains: "Hear this word!" (3:1; 4:1; 5:1), "Seek" (5:4, 6, 14), "Woe" (5:18; 6:1, 4). One series (4:6–11) consists of oracles beginning, "I gave," "I withheld," "I smote," "I sent," "I overthrew," each one concluding with the refrain, "yet you did not return to me, says Yahweh." Two of three doxologies in the book (4:13; 5:8–9; 9:5–6) are located here, and, whether from Amos or later editors, reinforce a central theme of the prophet's message: God's sovereign command over the affairs and destiny of the world.

[62] Cf. Aage Bentzen, "The Ritual Background of Amos I.2–II.16," *OTS*, 8 (1950), pp. 85–99.

[63] For the case against the analogy of the Egyptian texts, see Hans Walter Wolff, *Joel and Amos*, pp. 144–147.

Casemate walls at Samaria, possibly erected by Omri (ninth century B.C.). Such dual walls were partitioned into casemates or rooms which were filled with earth or stones or used for storage. They provided a strong fortification and were characteristic of Israelite cities. (Courtesy of Dr. Richard Schiemann.)

Frequent references to the northern kingdom ("Joseph"; "house of Joseph"; "house of Israel") and its towns (Samaria, Bethel, Gilgal) make it practically certain that these oracles were delivered in the north and attacked specific evils there. Judah, nevertheless, is not ignored as a party to the same covenant infidelities (3:1); lethargic Zion (Jerusalem) is a match for smug Samaria (6:1).

Luxurious self-indulgence and vain piety provoked the most caustic of Amos' vivid figures of speech. The pampered wives of rich Israelite merchants and landlords are compared to the sleek, fat cattle of Bashan (4:1). They and their husbands lie upon beds of ivory, drink wine from bowls, and anoint themselves with the finest oils, "but are not grieved over the ruin of Joseph" (6:4–6). They shall be among the first of those taken away piecemeal into exile.

> The Lord God has sworn by his holiness
>> that, behold, the days are coming upon you,
> when they shall take you away with hooks,
>> even the last of you with fishhooks.
>
> 4:2

The hypocritical worship is not merely without meaning; it is blasphemy.

> I hate, I despise your feasts,
>> and I take no delight in your solemn assemblies.
>
> . . .
>
> Take away from me the noise of your songs,
>> and the melody of your harps to which I will not listen,
> in order that deliverance (*mishpaṭ*) may roll down
>> like waters,
> and salvation (*tsedaḳah*) like an ever-flowing stream.
>
> 5:21–24[64]

It was Israel's inability to seek God sincerely that cut her off from the saving benefits which he alone could bestow. Lacking a spirit of true resolve to correct the evils of the corrupt society, the noise of the assemblies served only to praise the clever machinations of those who benefited from injustice and unrighteousness. With biting satire, the prophet invites Israel to compound her sin by bringing more and more vain offerings (4:4–5).

It is possible that the "day of Yahweh," in which the people took such delight (5:18–20), was Israel's new year's festival—the day of cultic renewal of the nation's life.[65] If so, it was viewed as the guarantee of continued peace and prosperity. The prophet's words shattered that naïve hope.

> Woe to you who desire the day of the Lord!
> Why would you have the day of the Lord?
> It is darkness, and not light.
>
> 5:18

That Yahweh could be appeased by the mere keeping of feast days was to Amos unthinkable. Had not the wilderness generation responded to God's leadership without benefit of sacrifice or cult (5:25)? On the coming day of

---

[64] The translation and the interpretation that follow are those of J. Philip Hyatt, "The Translation and Meaning of Amos 5:23–24," ZAW, LXVIII (1956), 17–24. The verb at the beginning of vs. 24, *weyiggal*, is an imperfect with simple *waw* used to express purpose. The terms here translated "salvation" and "deliverance" are generally rendered "justice" and "righteousness" and are commonly interpreted to mean social righteousness. For examples of their usage in the sense suggested here (i.e., deliverance), cf. Judg. 5:11; Isa. 45:8; 46:13; 51:5, 6; 56:1; Mic. 6:5; and the Dead Sea Scrolls (e.g., IQS 11:2ff.).

[65] This interpretation is proposed by Sigmund Mowinckel, *He That Cometh*, G. W. Anderson, trans. (Nashville, TN: Abingdon Press, 1956), pp. 132–133.

reckoning Israel's shrines would provide no refuge. Along with the nation's defenses and the fine houses of the rich, the altars too were destined to fall (5:5–6; 9:1ff.).

The same shattering message would apply if the "day of Yahweh" had reference to an expected day of Yahweh's vengeance on Israel's enemies.[66] The day of Yahweh, far from being a day of comfort and deliverance, would be Yahweh's day of dread reckoning with his faithless people. Thus, to flee from present ills by placing hope in the day of Yahweh would be to go from the frying pan to the fire. Israel was forced to confront the gigantic rift which separated the corrupt nation from the righteous God whom she claimed to serve—a gap which could not be breached by a magical or superstitious misuse of cultic ritual.

Occasionally there surfaces in Amos's oracles a glimmer of hope—the summons to "seek the Lord and live" (5:6; cf. 5:4, 14–15, 24). Israel's present condition held out little possibility, however, that such a change was forthcoming. Yahweh had offered repeated warnings (4:6–11) to no avail. Israel had not turned.

> I gave you cleanness of teeth in all your cities,
>   and lack of bread in all your places,
> yet you did not return to me, says the Lord.
>   4:6

Repentance, in the biblical sense, is always more than simply contrition—a Godly sorrow for past sins. As brought out here, the term *shub* ("to turn," "return," or "repent," according to context) describes a total change of direction. The prophet saw no signs of such a move on Israel's part.

The nation's fate was as good as sealed. Hence a funeral elegy was in order. Employing the *kinah* (lament) metrical form—a 3/2, 3/2 meter—a formal dirge was sung over the doomed house of Israel.

> Fállen no móre to ríse
>   is the vírgin Ísrael;
> forsáken (she líes) on her lánd,
>   with nóne to raíse her.
>   5:2

Visions of Doom

Possibly at the time of his call, the prophet beheld the coming doom in the form of the five visions of chapters 7–9: (1) locusts (7:1–3), (2) fire (7:4–6), (3) plumb line (7:7–9), (4) summer fruit (8:1–3), and (5) Yahweh

---

[66] This is the view of Gerhard von Rad (*Old Testament Theology,* Vol II, pp. 119–125), who explores the sixteen appearances of the expression "day of Yahweh" in the Latter Prophets and concludes that it was not, as such, an eschatological concept but a notion based in Israel's tradition of holy war, wherein Yahweh had given historical proof of his readiness to save his people. As such, "Amos's contemporaries cherished the expectation of such an uprising to war and victory on the part of Yahweh" (p. 124).

standing beside an altar (9:1–4). Recorded in the first person, the formal structure of the visions reveals two pairs (1 and 2; 3 and 4), with the final vision differing significantly from the others. In the first four the formula of introduction is "Yahweh God (or He) showed me. . . ." Then the subject of the vision is described ("behold . . ."). In visions (1) and (2) the revelation of the terror is followed by the prophet's intercession for his people: "O Lord God, forgive (cease), I beseech thee!" And in both cases God relents, withdrawing the threatened judgment.

The form changes in (3) and (4). The prophet is asked, "What do you see?" and replies by naming a commonplace object: first, a plumb line; then, a basket of late summer fruit. Then follows the interpretation of the vision by Yahweh himself. The plumb becomes the measure by which the society's wickedness is exposed; and the (overripe?) fruit (*kayits*) becomes a reminder of the impending end (*kets*). The meaning is in both cases the same: Israel will not be excused (bypassed) for its sins; destruction and death will befall people, cult, and king. The prophet perceives the futility of interceding for an unrepentant people.

The fifth vision is a dreadful scene which draws on the imagery of earthquake phenomena, mythology, warfare, and exile. It begins simply, "I saw. . . ." This time it is Yahweh himself standing at the altar, on the very spot where his holiness has been defiled by the mockery of half-hearted ritual. Having been thus shut out as Israel's savior, his coming can only bring devastating retribution from which there shall be no escape or hiding place.

Within the material which has been combined with the visions is the clearest expression of universalism to be found in the Amos collection (9:7).

> "Are you not like the Ethiopians to me,
>   O people of Israel?" says the Lord.
> "Did I not bring up Israel from the land of Egypt,
>   and the Philistines from Caphtor and the Syrians from Kir?"

This passage proceeds a step beyond the internationalism implicit in the foreign oracles (chs. 1–2) and the summons to the nations to come up to view Israel's guilt (3:9–10). Israel had for too long assumed that her unique role carried preferential status and privilege. But, says the prophet, God has plans as well for such peoples as Philistines and Syrians. It was a stiff reminder to Israel that she did not exist to serve herself. When God's judgment falls, Israel shall feel the blow, just as the other nations.

The two oracles with which the collection concludes (9:11–12, 13–15) are usually taken as later additions, appended after the Exile to stimulate hope in a restoration of Zion ("the booth of David that is fallen") and a renewal of life throughout the devastated land. They reflect a hope which the prophet apparently was prevented from declaring to his own stubborn generation. They are hardly inconsistent, however, with his confidence that Yahweh intervenes redemptively on behalf of a repentant and chastened people. The unhappy fulfilment of Amos' prophecies of doom effected that which his warnings alone could not do. Only his ability to perceive the saving element in Yahweh's judgment can account for his compulsion to pronounce Israel's ruin.

The Old and the New in Amos

Scholars of the last century tended to depict Amos and his successors as radical innovators and lonely iconoclasts who set themselves against Israel's traditional institutions and gave birth to a totally new ethic of individual and social responsibility. The oversimplification of this approach to the prophets is today generally acknowledged.[67] It gave too little attention either to the ethical content of Hebrew religion prior to Amos or to the reformatory stance of the prophets, who worked largely within the context of Israel's institutions.

Even in his most critical attacks upon the religious and political institutions of his day, Amos called for neither the abandonment of the cult nor the overthrow of the monarchy—even though Yahweh's own actions would accomplish just that. Rather, his plea for justice and righteousness called Israel back to her earliest religious commitments. It was these that she had broken and, consequently, by them she would be judged. Law, cult, and kingship, as well as popular wisdom, provided the framework within which both the religious life of Israel and the prophet's own sensitive conscience functioned. His protests against monarchy and priesthood are not so much against the institutions *per se* as against the corruption of the purposes which they were designed to serve. Within Israel's early legal traditions appear prohibitions of the very sins against which the prophet inveighed. The cult not only supplied some of his most effective oracular formulas, but the shrines provided the most likely setting in which to proclaim them. His prophecies of Israel's demise as a kingdom stop short of a denunciation of monarchy as such, so much so that later tradition saw no inconsistency in ascribing to him the anticipated national restoration (9:11f.).

The new element which Amos brought to Israelite life and faith was a fresh sense of Yahweh's presence in all that was happening in national and international affairs.[68] It is this that makes the prophet and his successors

---

[67] Cf. E. Würthwein, "Amos-Studien," ZAW, LXII (1949–1950), pp. 10–15; Gerhard von Rad, *Old Testament Theology*, Vol. II, pp. 3–5 and passim.

[68] Other assessments of the new element in Amos' message include a shift in the object of prophetic address away from the king to the people of Israel as a whole (John S. Holladay, "Assyrian Statecraft and the Prophets of Israel," *HTR*, 63 [1970], pp. 29–51); the sense of Yahweh as the God of the nations and the end of Israel's privileged position within the older salvation history (Hans Walter Wolff, *Joel and Amos*, pp. 106, passim); and a denial of the equation of prosperity and righteousness through the identification of the oppressed poor as the truly righteous element in Israel (Arvid S. Kapelrud, "New Ideas in Amos," *VTS*, XV [1965], pp. 193–206).

more than mere defenders of tradition—perhaps more than reformers. Georg Fohrer thus describes the prophetic experience:

> What is decisive is, on the one hand, the individual experience of the terrifying and merciful presence of God in those moments of secret experiences (*geheimer Erfahrungen*) in which the spirit or the word of God came upon them; and, on the other hand, the living impress of the belief of the Mosaic age, which lived anew in them in a more refined and expanded form.[69]

This comes to expression in Amos' startling message of doom for the whole covenant people, without exception or qualification. Such preaching had not been heard before in Israel. It denied that a faithless people had any longer a claim to Yahweh's protection and favor. In a new sense, Israel was now but one among the nations of earth and was forced to acknowledge Yahweh's purpose at work outside her own borders. At the same time, such a message reveals a radical appraisal of the consequences of social and personal evil. A society in which the cause of weak and dependent members was offered no defense against the neglect and oppression of powerful and corrupt institutions and groups had forfeited its right to exist. The prophet thus intensified the older covenant demand for social justice by insisting that the true measure of the just society is never simply a matter of legal guarantees or broad economic prosperity, but includes, first of all, the actual conditions which prevail among its weakest elements.

It thus fell to the lot of Amos to explore at greater length than any of his predecessors had done, the relationship between ethical performance and religious ceremony. He stands firmly on the principles of Yahwistic faith in his declarations of the intrinsic dependence of the one upon the other. Quick to connect the practices in the marketplace with the motives at the shrines, Amos had a word respecting the interior and exterior dimensions of religious experience. He was by no means the first to insist on the necessary consistency between Israel's covenant demands and the spirit that prompted their performance; but his is the strongest denunciation to that day of the intolerable hypocrisy of divorcing the one from the other.

3. HOW CAN I GIVE YOU UP, O EPHRAIM? HOSEA

The death of Jeroboam II (746 B.C.) corresponds with the reappearance in Near Eastern history of a strong and ambitious Assyria.[70] Tiglath-pileser III (745–727 B.C.) brought to an end the long half century of Assyrian slumber by securing his control over Babylonia, where he reigned under the throne name of "Pulu" (hence his Old Testament name, "Pul"), while

---

[69] "Remarks on Modern Interpretation of the Prophets," *JBL*, LXXX (1961), p. 316.
[70] For the historical background to Hosea's period, see II Kings 15–17; II Chron. 26–28.

Campaigns of Tiglath-pileser III, king of Assyria (745–727 B.C.). Evacuation of a captured city, Assyrian scribes taking account of the spoil. (Courtesy of the Trustees of the British Museum.)

extending his conquests to the east and west. Syria and Palestine, with their minerals, timber, and strategic location for commerce and military defense, became immediate targets of his expansionist policy.

Political unrest in Israel aided Assyrian ambitions. The years following Jeroboam's reign brought a series of regicides and *coup d'états* in the northern kingdom that resulted in a state of near anarchy and civil war. Within the fifteen years from Jeroboam's death to Hoshea's enthronement there were four such bloody assassinations and the throne changed hands six times. Zechariah, the son of Jeroboam, had reigned only six months when Shallum struck him down; and after only one month the usurper, in turn, became the victim of Menahem of Tirzah. Although Menahem held the throne for several years (745–738 B.C.), he was able to do so only through capitulation to Assyria. With Tiglath-pileser pressing in upon him and desperate to hold the throne against rival claimants, Menahem paid the Assyrian king a thousand talents of silver "that he might help him to

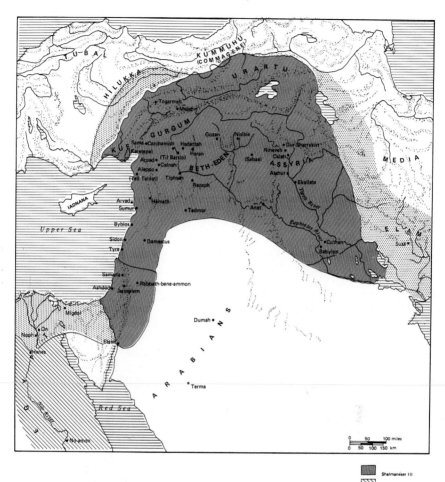

The Assyrian Empire, ninth to seventh centuries B.C. (Adapted with permission of Macmillan Publishing Co., Inc., from Macmillan Bible Atlas *by Y. Aharoni and Michael Avi-Yonah. Copyright © 1968 Carta, Jerusalem. © Copyright 1964 by Carta, Jerusalem. © Copyright 1966 by Carta, Jerusalem.)*

confirm his hold of the royal power" (II Kings 15:19). The transaction is confirmed by Tiglath-pileser's own annals, where "Menahem of Samaria" is named in a list of kings from whom he claims to have received tribute.[71] In order to pay, Menahem levied a head tax of fifty shekels on all the landlords in Israel.

Anti-Assyrian nationalists were doubtless responsible for the next bloody coup, which came two years after Menahem's death, when his son Peka-

---

[71] *ANET*, p. 283 (*ANE*, p. 193).

Sargon II, king of Assyria (722–705 B.C.), credited with the conquest of Samaria in 722 B.C. (Courtesy of Alinari/Editorial Photocolor Archives.)

hiah (739–737 B.C.) was murdered by his army commander, Pekah (737–732 B.C.).[72] The new king switched policies toward Assyria. While Tiglath-pileser's energies were diverted elsewhere, he joined an alliance with Rezin of Damascus against their common overlord. Other western states, including Philistia and Edom, joined the coalition; but Ahaz of Judah refused to participate. When Rezin and Pekah attempted to force the southern king, Ahaz, in desperation, called upon Tiglath-pileser for help.

The Assyrian king took full advantage of the situation. He chose to strike

---

[72] The involvement of Gileadites in the conspiracy suggests that Pekah reigned in Gilead as a rival claimant to the throne during Menahem's administration. Such a possibility helps explain the record of a twenty-year reign for Pekah (II Kings 15:27), otherwise much too long a period to fit the royal chronology.

first at Israel and the southern states, thereby isolating the stronger Damascus. In 734 B.C. his armies drove down the Palestinian coast, subduing the Philistine cities and cutting off all possible aid from Egypt. He then swept through Galilee, Esdraelon, the Plain of Sharon, and Gilead, taking most of the northern kingdom except the mountainous heartland around Samaria and incorporating it into the Assyrian empire. The characteristic and hated Assyrian policy of deporting captive peoples away from their land and settling foreigners in the conquered territory was invoked. The occupied territory was divided into three provinces: Gilead (northern Transjordan), Megiddo (including Galilee), and Dor (the coastal plain). Tiglath-pileser then (732 B.C.) turned to Damascus, captured and ravaged it, put Rezin to death, and parceled out the land into more Assyrian provinces.

The murder of Pekah at this point may have saved Israel further reprisals. Hoshea (732–724 B.C.), the assassin, became immediately an Assyrian vassal and was allowed to reign over what was left of the northern kingdom. His loyalty, however, did not last. Shortly after the death of Tiglath-pileser and the accession of his son, Shalmaneser V (727–722 B.C.), Hoshea, depending upon Egypt for support, withheld tribute. Shalmaneser attacked Israel in 724 B.C. and Hoshea was taken prisoner. The whole land was occupied except the city of Samaria, which lay under siege for more than two years. Shalmaneser died during the course of the siege and was succeeded by Sargon II (722–705 B.C.). The city fell in 722 B.C. and, together with the surrounding countryside, became but another province ruled by an Assyrian governor.[73] According to Sargon's annals, 27,290 of its citizens were deported to Mesopotamia and replaced with foreigners from Aramaic-speaking lands. Thus, after two centuries of independent statehood, the northern kingdom was no more.

A Wife of Harlotry

The last known prophet of the northern kingdom was Hosea, son of Beeri, who belongs to the period just following Amos and barely before the collapse of Samaria. A study of his oracles reveals some to be as early as the reign of Jeroboam or Zechariah, the last kings of the Jehu dynasty (1:4), and others as late as the chaotic period from Shallum to Hoshea (745–737 B.C.).[74] Most recent interpreters of the book follow Albrecht Alt's contention that the background of 5:8–14 is the period of the Syro-Ephraimitic crisis and reflects a retaliatory invasion of Israel by Judah (735 B.C.).[75] We cannot be assured that any of the extant oracles are later than this, though

---

[73] *ANET*, pp. 284–287 (*ANE*, pp. 195–198).

[74] The superscription to the book (1:1) has obviously been edited. The original (1:1b) named only the northern king Jeroboam II, doubtless in reference to the *beginning* of the prophet's career (cf. Ezek. 1:1). A later southern editor added the names of the southern kings (Uzziah, Jotham, Ahaz, and Hezekiah), thus synchronizing Hosea's ministry with that of Isaiah (cf. Isa. 1:1).

[75] "Hosea 5:8–6:6," *Kleine Schriften zur Geschichte des Volkes Israel*, II, 143–187.

some scholars find the very last days of Hoshea and the fall of Samaria in passages such as 10:9–15.[76]

Hosea's personal life has received more attention in the surviving tradition than has the life of Amos. The interest, however, was hardly in biography for its own sake; the prophet's marriage was significant only because it served as an illuminating metaphor for God's relationship to Israel. Excluding the marriage account (chs. 1 and 3), whatever else may be determined about Hosea must be gleaned solely from his oracles. These make it clear that his message was addressed primarily to the northern kingdom, and for that reason it is generally assumed that he lived in the north. Of the exact location there can be no certainty. Neither is there any word as to his occupation—if indeed he, like Amos, was other than a professional prophet. The contention that his agricultural figures of speech show him to have been a farmer, or that his incisive attacks on the corruption within the cult point to priestly origins, is less than convincing.

The prophet's marriage to Gomer is beset with questions which have never been satisfactorily answered.[77] Basic to the problem is the ambiguous connection between chapters 1 and 3, where the story is recounted first in biographical, then in autobiographical terms. Chapter 3 is most frequently taken as the sequel to chapter 1, particularly in view of the command of Yahweh, "Go again . . ." (3:1).[78] It is possible, however, to read the two chapters as parallel accounts of the same event, or even to reverse the sequence so that chapter 3 becomes the prophet's personal version of what preceded the marriage, as such, which is related in chapter 1. The oracles of chapter 2 provoke further questions concerning the degree of correspondence between Israel's broken relationship with Yahweh—the actual subject of chapter 2—and the prophet's marriage to Gomer.

Among the many issues related to this classic problem, the following are the most debated. (1) Was the marriage a normal one, a fictional allegory, or a symbolic enactment of a prophetic sign? (2) Was Gomer a known harlot (perhaps a cult prostitute) before Hosea made her his wife or did she become unfaithful only after the marriage—if at all? (3) Was the prophet related to one or two women? As to the first of these: the emotional intensity of the marriage analogy, its inclusion in both biographical and autobiographical versions, and the absence of allegorical meanings in the specific details of the account (e.g., the name Gomer), all argue for a real flesh and blood marriage. The more difficult question is whether Hosea was actually

---

[76] Cf. James Ward, *Hosea: A Theological Commentary* (New York: Harper & Row, Publishers, 1966), pp. 186–187. The following passages should be studied carefully for their relevance to the dating of the book: 1:4–5; 4:1–3; 5:8–14; 7:1–7, 11; 8:4, 8–10; 9:6; 10:6–15; 11:5; 12:1; 13:9–16.

[77] For a review of the divergent approaches, see H. H Rowley, "The Marriage of Hosea," *BJRL*, 39 (1956–1957), pp. 200–233.

[78] Those who take a different view either regard the "again" as a gloss or else translate, "He said to me a second time, 'Go. . . .' "

enamored of Gomer and expected to find with her a happy home life, or whether the marriage was from the beginning intended as nothing more than a prophetic sign—a dramatic act designed to make the point that Israel had become like a harlot to Yahweh. Ethics and sentiment notwithstanding, symbolic enactments by the prophets sometimes took extreme turns as when Isaiah walked nude through the streets of Jerusalem or when Ezekiel refused to mourn for his dead wife.[79] By such patterns, for Hosea to have taken a practicing harlot as a wife would have been a startling, but by no means impossible, action.[80]

If the marriage was a normal one, however, such a union with a harlot might appear to contradict Hosea's own strictures against immorality. The only obstacle to assuming that Gomer's wantonness developed *after*, rather than before, the marriage is God's command to the prophet in chapter 1: "Go take to yourself a wife of harlotry . . ." (1:2), which is possibly a statement made in retrospect, based on the later knowledge of what Gomer in fact became after the marriage. Thus, some would find in the names of the three children a progressive discovery of Gomer's unfaithfulness. Only of the first child, Jezreel, is it specifically said that she "bore *him* (Hosea) a son"; whereas the name of the last, Loammi (not my people), would be particularly appropriate were he fathered by someone other than Hosea.

If the unnamed woman of chapter 3 is not Gomer, but some prostitute taken by the prophet at a later time, there would be grounds for the position that Gomer was at no time a professional harlot. In fact, by one interpretation—which understands the "harlotry" of 1:2 as a reference not to sexual fornication but to the general apostasy of the period—Gomer is defended against the charge of unfaithfulness of any sort.[81]

In spite of the paucity of evidence (it amounts to no more than eleven verses) and the endless variety of viable but unproven theories, some tentative conclusions may be ventured, based particularly on the effective use of the marriage as an analogy for Israel's covenant with Yahweh. The question of Gomer's premarriage morals and the possibility of a connection with the fertility cult must be left unanswered, as the evidence is neither clear nor crucial for the metaphor which the marriage provides. That Hosea loved his wife, however, is a necessary assumption if, as seems to be the case, his experience with her gave rise to his acute sense of Yahweh's boundless and persevering love. For the same reason, Gomer must have proved unfaithful within the marriage itself, betraying her husband— whether for newly found lovers or a former pattern of life. Presumably, the

[79] Isa. 20; Ezek. 24:15–18.

[80] Hans Walter Wolff believes that Gomer was not a professional prostitute, but that she participated in a Canaanite fertility rite whereby young virgins, prior to their nuptials and on a single occasion, surrendered themselves to strangers at a shrine (*Hosea*, Gary Stansell, trans. [Philadelphia: Fortress Press, 1974], pp. 12–16).

[81] Robert H. Pfeiffer, *Introduction to the Old Testament*, pp. 567ff.

prophet's first reaction was to repudiate her and cast her out (2:3). Finding, however, that her betrayal had not extinguished his love for her—"even as Yahweh loves the people of Israel, though they turn to other gods" (3:1)—the prophet pursued her and brought her back (cf. 2:14ff.). The auto-biographical account (ch. 3), then, appears to describe Hosea's purchase of his former wife from her new owner or husband (3:2) and the corrective punishment which she had to endure (3:3) before the relationship could be restored.

> For the children of Israel shall dwell many days without king or prince, without sacrifice or pillar, without ephod or teraphim.
> 3:4

The Book

Hosea's oracles lack the simplicity of organization and literary style that mark the book of Amos. The frequently corrupt and fragmentary state of the text and the absence of the usual introductory and concluding formulas make for difficulty in distinguishing the separate oracle units. The prophet's diction, moreover, is so abrupt and turbulent as to suggest the outpourings of an intense, passionate personality.

> His emotional and distraught nature is reflected in short sentences with frequent lack of syntactic connections. The classical cadences of Amos dis-solve into shrieks and sobs in Hosea. It is not easy to decide when the words of Hosea have been lost because of textual confusion and when they are before us exactly as disordered as the prophet's emotions.[82]

The broad outline of the book is, nevertheless, clear.

1. Israel, Yahweh's faithless but redeemed bride: chs. 1–3
   a. Hosea and Gomer: 1:2–9; 3:1–5
   b. Yahweh and Israel: 1:10–2:23
2. Oracles of judgment against faithless Israel: 4:1–9:9
3. A history of Israel's sins and Yahweh's faithfulness: 9:10–13:16
4. Israel's future hope: 14:1–9

Much scholarly discussion has centered on the relationship between the doomful and hopeful elements in the book. Efforts have been made to re-strict the prophet's message entirely to the words of doom; or, less radi-cally, some propose two stages in the development of his thought whereby the oracles of hope were composed at a time later in his career. Neither of these positions is required, however, if due attention is given the specific nature of the hope which the prophet holds out for the doomed nation. The restoration which he envisions is conditioned on the purging judgment

---

[82] Norman Gottwald, *A Light to the Nations*, p. 292.

which must come first. Therefore, to a greater degree than in Amos, Israel's doom is at the same time her redemption.

That the book passed through a process of literary redaction can be regarded as a certainty. An editorial hand is evident, for example, in passages in which an unfavorable word against Israel is followed immediately by a word of praise for Judah (e.g., 1:7; 4:15; 6:11). Perhaps the original collection of oracles, recorded by the prophet and his disciples in the north, were brought to Judah following the fall of the northern kingdom and reworked by southern editors. It was they, presumably, who not only contributed the peculiarly southern elements that appear in the book, but who also placed in juxtaposition some of the doomful and hopeful oracles which stand in such sharp contrast in their present contexts (e.g., 1:4–9, 10–11).

Yahweh's Faithless but Redeemed Bride

Chapter 1, far from offering simply an account of Hosea's marriage, serves as an indictment of Israel and a pronouncement of her doom. It includes at least three verses which, though probably from Hosea, are out of place in their present context: 7, 10, and 11.[83] Possibly 4c and 5 were also added later. With the removal of the interpolated material, the chapter separates into four sign events, each including (1) a divine command, beginning with the formula, "God (He) said . . ." and (2) a denunciation, as follows:

vs. 2: The marriage. Object of denunciation: the land of Israel
vs. 4: Birth of Jezreel. Object of denunciation: the dynasty of Jehu
vs. 6: Birth of Loruhamah (not pitied): Object of denunciation: the northern kingdom
vs. 9: Birth of Loammi (not my people). Object of denunciation: the people of God

Verses 2a, 3, 6a, and 8 provide brief, explanatory introductions for each of the four signs.

Chapter 2 sets the pattern for the entire book. The first half (vss. 2–13) is a judgment on Israel's apostasy and reflects the message of doom which dominates much of chapters 4–13; the second half (vss. 14–23) envisions reconciliation and compares with the other oracles of hope (3:5; 5:15–6:3; 11:8–12; 14; and the interpolations in ch. 1). The words with which the chapter begins may embody an ancient divorce formula: "she is not my wife and I am not her husband." In Nuzi custom divorce was accompanied by stripping off the clothes of the cast-off woman (cf. vs. 2). The meaning

---

[83] Our view of the literary structure in ch. 1 is dependent upon the analysis of James Ward, *Hosea: A Theological Commentary*, pp. 3–20.

here, at any rate, is allegorical. The exhortation is to the "children" of Israel whom the prophet is trying to awaken; and the "mother" is the nation itself. Israel had gone after the Baals, wrongly assuming that they offered delights which Yahweh did not. Bitterly, she would discover her error. Utterly bereft of Yahweh's life-giving favors, she would come at last to know her dependence upon him.

> Then she shall say, "I will go and return to my first husband, for it was better with me then than now."
>
> vs. 7b

Yahweh would not simply await the return of his faithless partner. He would pursue her and bring her back to the wilderness—the locale of their "honeymoon." Nothing short of Yahweh's relentless love and Israel's willing response could effect a renewal of the fresh, youthful relationship of the Mosaic era when Israel, so recently redeemed by Yahweh from Egyptian slavery, had first taken her covenant vows. The disastrous results of her subsequent rebellions found an apt symbol in the early apostasy of Achan and his annihilation in the Valley of Achor (vs. 15; cf. Josh. 7). Once again, Yahweh's people stood on the brink of tragedy. Achor would once more claim its guilty victims. This would not, however, be the full end of Israel. Yahweh would open out of Achor a door of hope.

> Therefore, behold I will allure her
>   and bring her into the wilderness,
>   and speak tenderly to her.
> And there I will give her her vineyards,
>   and make the Valley of Achor a door of hope.
> And there she shall answer as in the days of her youth,
>   as at the time when she came out of the land of Egypt.
>
> 2:14–15

The goal of the restoration is the society which Yahweh had desired for his people all along, one characterized by harmony within the natural and social spheres and oneness of purpose between man and God.

Samaria Shall Bear Her Guilt

Hosea's presentation of Yahweh's controversy with his people reflects the chaotic conditions of the northern kingdom's last years.

> There is no faithfulness or kindness,
>   and no knowledge of God in the land;
> there is swearing, lying, killing,
>   stealing, and committing adultery;
>   they break all bounds and murder follows murder.
>
> 4:1b–2

312

The usurpers who seized the throne by bloodshed are compared to heated ovens.

> All of them are hot as an oven,
>> and they devour their rulers.
> All their kings have fallen;
>> and none calls upon me.
>> 7:7

The people themselves are held accountable for the prevailing anarchy. The prophet rails against the fickle loyalties and misguided confidence with which they rally around each new power-hungry prince. As he disavows the involvement of Yahweh in such madness his words approach the antimonarchical speeches of Samuel.

> They made kings, but not through me.
>> 8:4a

> Where now is your king to save you;
>> where are all your princes to defend you—
> those of whom you said,
>> "Give me a king and princes"?
> I have given you kings in my anger,
>> and I have taken them away in my wrath.
>> 13:10–11

Hosea is specific in his charges against the national policies of both Israel and Judah. Having condemned the Jehu dynasty for its undue bloodletting (1:4), he upbraids Israel further for selling out to Assyria under Menahem's shortsighted leadership (5:13), and for Pekah's unprovoked attack upon Judah (5:9, 11). Pekah and Rezin had tried unsuccessfully to force Ahaz off his throne and replace him with an ally friendly to the anti-Assyrian alliance. It was while the two were preparing for a second military assault against the southern kingdom that Ahaz had called in Tiglath-pileser. Ahaz, furthermore, appears to have taken advantage of the interlude just preceding Assyria's invasion to carry out a retaliatory march into Pekah's territory (5:8–14). Hosea's condemnation falls upon both houses for the total disregard of their common covenant history, the resort to internecine warfare, and alliances with pagan powers.

> For they have gone up to Assyria,
> a wild ass wandering alone;
> Ephraim has hired lovers.
>> 8:9

Consequently, the prophet was assured that Israel and Judah would be devoured by the very ally whose costly favors they had courted.

313

An Assyrian king, probably Sargon, in conference with his commander-in-chief.
(Courtesy of the Trustees of the British Museum.)

Though they hire allies among the nations
I will soon gather them up.
8:10a

For behold they are going to Assyria;
Egypt shall gather them,
Memphis shall bury them.
9:6

314

For many northern Israelites, five centuries of covenant history was about to be undone. Exile in Assyria would be tantamount to the Egyptian slavery from which Yahweh had initially delivered them. Once more they should be a people destitute and homeless, precisely as Yahweh had first found them in Egypt.

Clearly, Hosea was at one with Amos in perceiving Israel's imminent end as Yahweh's decreed judgment. Like a wild beast robbed of her cubs (13:7, 8) or the death-dealing sirocco wind (13:15), Yahweh was about to fall upon his faithless people. No group, apparently, was free of guilt. Priests (4:4–10, 15–19; 5:1; 6:6, 9; 8:12; 9:4), prophets (9:7–9; 12:10–14), and kings—those most responsible for keeping Israel faithful to her covenant vows—were alike culpable.

Israel's harlotry is depicted as a pursuit of foreign lovers (alliances), but, more especially, as her idolatrous flirtations with the Baal cults. Infiltration of the shrines with idols and fertility practices had cut off any vital relationship between Israel and Yahweh. Activity at the cult centers still flourished; but, just as in the day of Amos, Israel "multiplied altars for sinning" (8:11). Hosea, like Amos, decried worship that was devoid of total commitment of the heart to Yahweh. Better no rites at all than those offered as substitutes for genuine religious faith.

> For I desire steadfast love and not sacrifice,
> the knowledge of God, rather than burnt offerings.
> 6:6

Steadfast love (*ḥeṣedh*) and knowledge (*da'ath*) of God represent the prophet's conception of true religion. "Knowledge of God," in this sense, stands for the closest possible relationship between God and man. Thus, Hosea's lament that there was "no knowledge of God in the land" (4:1) was the most severe indictment with which he could denounce his people; they had renounced all right to Yahweh's protective love and stood naked before the wrath which they had stored up for themselves.

As the Dew to Israel

Chapter 14 is an excellent conclusion and summary of the positive note in the prophet's message to Israel. It begins with a summons to return to Yahweh, not with more vain offerings or glib affectations of repentance, but with words of true confession and resolve (14:1–3); and it continues with Yahweh's promise to heal his broken people (vss. 4–8). Joined with the other hopeful passages in the book (esp. 1:7, 10–11; 2:14–23; 3:5; 5:15–6:3; 11:8–12), there emerges a picture of the restoration which Yahweh offers. It includes both Israel and Judah (1:11), gathered home (11:10–11), living together in a populous (1:10), peaceful (2:18), and fruitful land (2:15), purged of their rebellious spirit (2:16–17; 14:2–3), and once again betrothed to Yahweh in covenant faithfulness (2:19–20).

Hosea's Contribution to Hebrew Prophecy

The common element in the oracles of Amos and Hosea is considerable. Standing squarely in the tradition of Israel's covenant history, both prophets deplored the nation's failure to keep faith with Yahweh and, as a consequence, warned of inevitable catastrophe. At the same time, significant differences mark their respective messages. Of the two spokesmen, Amos exhibits a broader international perspective and a stronger sense of God's concern for non-Hebrews. Hosea, without denying foreign nations a place in God's economy, concerned himself exclusively with Israel's special covenant role and the internal problems which threatened it. In the metaphor of the marriage, Yahweh had but one "wife" and Hosea's concern was with that union and the consequences of those broken vows. Amos' sense of a universal moral law to which all peoples are accountable finds no expression in the oracles of Hosea. It is apparent, nevertheless, that Hosea, like Amos, perceived God's hand in the international developments of his day; Yahweh was using Assyria as the agent of his judgment. The small states addressed in Amos' foreign oracles, moreover, had become in Hosea's time either vassals or provinces of Assyria—a fact which doubtless precluded the latter prophet's directing further threats against them.

In respect to the diagnosis of Israel's sickness, Amos had inveighed most heavily against gross social inequities, particularly the oppression of the poor. For Hosea, the greater stress fell upon religious apostasy—idolatry and Baal worship. Amos' biting denunciations of the unscrupulous rich are replaced in the oracles of Hosea by sweeping declarations of a total loss of heartfelt devotion to Yahweh. From either perspective, true worship at the shrines was corrupted and deprived of its vital and reconciling function.

Both prophets foresaw the impending devastation of Israel and they were equally adamant in allowing the guilty nation no escape. Whereas Amos, however, left the cutting edge of his doomful oracles unqualified, Hosea spoke of what lay beyond, juxtaposing words of judgment and renewal. If Amos was the first to prophesy ruin for the entire covenant people, Hosea was first in warning of such an end and then going on to proclaim a new beginning which would emerge beyond the calamity. This remarkable faith was rooted in the initial action which Yahweh had taken on behalf of a helpless and dependent people in Egyptian slavery. The prophet's conception of a recapitulation of past covenant history—a new Exodus and a renewal of Israel's youthful response—presupposed a purging of the nation's self-sufficient and wanton spirit. To "go back to Egypt" was to return to a position which alone could give birth to a new Israel.

In view of the Canaanite fertility influences, Hosea's analogy of Yahweh as Israel's husband carried implicit dangers. No other aspect of the prophet's theology, however, is as revealing or so crucial to his concept of Hebrew faith. Nothing short of such a personal figure of speech could do justice to the love with which God loved Israel. Thus, in one of his most moving passages, the prophet uses the father-son metaphor for this relationship (11:1–4). His portrayal of the divine anguish, whereby God is moved in consistency with his very character to temper judgment with mercy, is unsurpassed as a basis of hope for errant mankind.

> How can I give you up, O Ephraim!
> How can I hand you over, O Israel!
>
> . . .
>
> for I am God and not man,
> the Holy One in your midst,
> and I will not come to destroy.
> 11:8–9

4. THE WATERS THAT FLOW GENTLY: ISAIAH

The southern kingdom, unlike Samaria, managed to escape annihilation at the hands of Assyria.[84] Ahaz's appeal for Assyrian aid in the Syro-Ephraimitic crisis, however, put him in Tiglath-pileser's debt and hastened Judah's inevitable servitude to the larger power. So ruinous were the Assyrian demands that Ahaz was forced to deplete the royal treasury and even strip the temple to meet them. Assyrian cult furnishings, moreover, were installed in the temple as a mark of Judah's complete subservience. For the next century the small state, reduced in size by the loss of Edom and the Negeb, remained a tribute-paying vassal. The one major effort at revolt ended in failure and only served to expose the nation to the merciless reprisals with which the Assyrians punished rebellious dependencies.

The biblical record credits Ahaz with neither political resistance to Assyrian demands nor religious reforms of the apostatized cult. Consumed by the fear of losing his throne, he was prepared to appease both the Assyrian master and the pagan gods—including those of the child sacrifice cult to whom he apparently offered one of his sons. When Hezekiah (715–687 B.C.) assumed the throne, he reversed the policies of his father, first through cautious religious reforms and fortification of Jerusalem and finally by open rebellion against Assyria. Quite possibly under his patronage old and uncorrupted covenant traditions, once preserved at the northern shrines, were brought to Jerusalem and made the basis for the limited reform movement he instituted. Some of the paganizing high places outside Jerusalem were abolished and, according to the Chronicler, the temple was cleansed of its idolatrous cult objects and the Passover observed

---

[84] For the historical background to Isaiah's period, see II Kings 15:32–20.21; II Chron. 27–32.

The Siloam tunnel, built by Hezekiah (715–687 B.C.) beneath the city of Jerusalem, is open to tourists today. (Courtesy of the Consulate General of Israel in New York.)

there with pilgrims from the north. In part, at least, Hezekiah's cleansing of the cult was a manifestation of his independent spirit and thus was politically motivated. That he was edging toward a showdown with Assyria may be seen in his efforts to fortify Jerusalem against attack. He not only rebuilt portions of the broken city wall,[85] but carried out the remarkable feat of

[85] II Chron. 32:5 attests that Hezekiah built another wall outside the broken wall. It is possible that it was a segment of this wall that was excavated in the Jewish Quarter of the Old City in 1970 by Nachman Avigad. Located on the eastern slopes of the western hill, the massive wall (some 23 feet thick) appears to have extended the city westward and thus doubled its size. Cf. Benjamin Mazar, "Jerusalem in the Biblical Period," *Jerusalem Revealed: Archaeology in the Holy City 1968–1974* (Jerusalem: The Israel Exploration Society, 1975), pp. 5, 7; idem, *The Mountain of the Lord*, pp. 176–180; Kathleen Kenyon, *Digging Up Jerusalem*, pp. 144–151, pl. 62, fig. 26.

cutting a 1,749-foot water tunnel through solid rock underneath the city. Up to that time, the reservoir ("the upper pool") connecting with the Gihon Spring was situated outside the city walls, where it was vulnerable to an enemy in time of siege. As a result of Hezekiah's ingenuity, the older reservoir was sealed and the Gihon waters channeled through the new aqueduct to the Pool of Siloam inside the city. Words inscribed on the tunnel wall relate how two groups of pickmen, working from either direction, performed the monumental job.[86]

Hezekiah apparently remained aloof from a revolt led by Ashdod and encouraged by Egypt in 713–711 B.C. When Egyptian military support failed to materialize, the Philistine towns involved were quickly overrun by Sargon's army and Ashdod became an Assyrian province. Hezekiah awaited the death of Sargon and the problems inherited by his son and successor, Sennacherib (705–681 B.C.), before making his major move. With Babylon in revolt and Egypt growing in strength, Hezekiah joined with several Phoenician and Philistine cities in withholding tribute. His active leadership in the movement is attested by the fact that King Padi of Ekron, an Assyrian loyalist, was held captive in Jerusalem.

The revolt did not succeed. By 701 B.C. Sennacherib had settled affairs with Babylon and was ready to move upon the rebels in the west. Tyre was

Tell ed-Duweir (ancient Lachish), one of the largest occupied sites in ancient Palestine, lies 30 miles southwest of Jerusalem. The tell measures about 22 acres on its summit and 39 acres at its base. Founded earlier than the Israelite period, Lachish was a target of Assyrian and Babylonian invaders of Judah in the late eighth and early sixth centuries B.C. (Courtesy of Dr. Richard Schiemann.)

[86] *ANET*, p. 321 (*ANE*, p. 212). Cf. Kathleen Kenyon, *Digging Up Jerusalem*, pp. 151–165, fig. 27, pls. 65–69; Benjamin Mazar, *The Mountain of the Lord*, pp. 56, 175–178.

Assyrian relief showing the siege of Lachish by Sennacherib's army. The Assyrian soldiers, with their siege engines, advance up battle ramps in the face of the defenders' arrows and missiles. Some inhabitants of the city escape through a door in a tower (center); three are caught and impaled on stakes (lower right). (Courtesy of the Trustees of the British Museum.)

Artist's sketch of Lachish, showing the double-wall fortifications and the palace-fort in the center. (Courtesy of the Wellcome Trust.)

the first to fall, after which other members of the coalition readily submitted. Only Ashkelon, Ekron, and Judah continued to resist. An Egyptian army appeared on the Philistine plain but failed to stop the powerful forces of Sennacherib, whereupon Philistia and Judah were left defenseless. In Sennacherib's record of his campaign, inscribed on a clay prism, he claims to have conquered 46 of Hezekiah's strong cities, besieging them with beaten-earth ramps and battering rams.[87] Detailed and revealing reliefs from the royal palace at Nineveh picture the fall of Lachish and its captives passing in review before Sennacherib.[88] Excavations at the latter site have borne further witness to its terrible destruction in the form of some 1,500 skeletons, buried along with the garbage left by the Assyrian army.

Jerusalem was besieged, as both the biblical records and Sennacherib's prism attest. Sennacherib boasted of Hezekiah's plight:

Himself (Hezekiah) I made a prisoner in Jerusalem, his royal residence, like a bird in a cage. I surrounded him with earthwork in order to molest those who were leaving his city's gate.[89]

For reasons that have long been a subject of debate, the siege was never carried through to completion and the city did not fall. The book of II

---

[87] ANET, pp. 287–288 (ANE, p. 200).
[88] Ibid.; p. 288, see ANE, illustration, 101.
[89] Ibid., p. 288.

321

Kings (18:14–16), in agreement with Sennacherib's claims, records Hezekiah's payment of enormous tribute in order to save the city. In a most confusing manner, however, the Kings account goes on to relate further threats directed by Sennacherib against Jerusalem which failed to materialize, due either to a "rumor" which reached the king (19:7)—perhaps telling of new trouble in Babylon—or to a devastating plague which crippled the Assyrian army (19:35). In any case, Jerusalem's deliverance was taken as a sign of Yahweh's miraculous intervention on behalf of the city in which he had "placed his name"; and it is from this perspective that the accounts in Isaiah and II Chronicles, as well as II Kings, are written.[90]

Whom Shall I Send?

The major southern prophet during the Jotham (742–735 B.C.), Ahaz (735–715 B.C.), and Hezekiah (715–687 B.C.) years was Isaiah of Jerusalem. The extent of his influence may be inferred not only from the length of the book which bears his name but from the attention he receives in the narratives of II Kings (chs. 18–20) and II Chronicles (ch. 32), as well. His prophetic career lasted at least forty years, beginning in the year of Uzziah's death (741 B.C.) and extending through the Sennacherib crisis (701 B.C.), perhaps longer.

Nothing is known about the prophet's life prior to his call. The speculation that he might have been a priest is based chiefly on the call vision (ch. 6) with its temple setting and priestly imagery. He appears to have been completely at home within Jerusalem, with easy access to kings Ahaz and Hezekiah. He was married and like Hosea gave his sons prophetic names: Shearjashub ("a remnant shall return") and Mahershalalhashbaz ("the spoil speeds, the prey hastes"). Although characterized in popular treatments as urbane and aristocratic, he was capable of the most rustic tendencies of his calling, as when he appeared naked and barefoot to warn of reprisals that would follow the futile revolt of Ashdod (ch. 20). Some interpreters are sufficiently impressed with the prophet's use of proverbial language and wisdom forms as to associate him with Israel's wisdom tradition.[91]

Such stories as survive concerning Isaiah, as well as the tone of his oracles, attest an urgent sense of personal destiny and a profound awareness of God's holiness and its ethical consequences, all of which assured for him a unique prophetic role. Perhaps his most outstanding personal mark was a quiet, steadying faith in Yahweh; no figure in the Old Testament appears as

---

[90] John Bright (*A History of Israel*, pp. 282ff.) posits two separate invasions by Sennacherib which have not been clearly distinguished in the biblical accounts. But see Brevard S. Childs' criticisms of this and other proposed solutions of the historical problem (*Isaiah and the Assyrian Crisis*, Studies in Biblical Theology, ser. 2. no. 3 [Naperville, IL: Alec R. Allenson, 1967]).

[91] See J. William Whedbee, *Isaiah and Wisdom* (Nashville, TN: Abingdon Press, 1971). Cf, also, Joseph Jensen, *The Use of Tôrâ by Isaiah; His Debate with the Wisdom Tradition* (Washington, D.C.: Catholic Biblical Association of America, 1973).

a cooler head in time of crisis. Even so, the prophet's trusting spirit can hardly be reduced to the smug assurance of one who "has all the answers" or views the future as a fixed dogma. Rather, as Th. C. Vriezen has remarked, his faith was characteristically open-ended.

> Isaiah watches with a fearful amazement for the signs of his time and looks for the manner in which God will fulfill his judgment . . . At every turn one gets the impression that Isaiah during the course of his life is faced with great surprises.[92]

Any analysis of the prophet's personality and message must see him in relationship to the historic events of his age. Two episodes in particular—the Syro-Ephraimitic crisis and the Sennacherib invasion—are pivotal. We can reconstruct with some confidence the broad eras in the prophet's career, as well as his positions on each of the major crises, even though the prophetic book itself bears only a rough approximation of chronological order.

Bind Up the Testimony

Only within the first 39 chapters of the book which bears Isaiah's name do we find the materials that derive from the prophet himself. There appears to have gathered around him a circle of disciples who, after their master's death, carried on his spirit, collected and preserved his words, and occasionally expanded them to cover new situations (8:16). Much later, in the Babylonian Exile, one such inspired follower wrote the moving poetry now contained in chapters 40–55. Still later, the prophet's spirit was reborn in the oracles with which the collection concludes, chapters 56–66. So distinct are the contrasts that set these sections of the book apart from the first 39 chapters that they have been named "Deutero-Isaiah" and "Trito-Isaiah," respectively.

Not all of chapters 1–39 come from the original Isaiah. Three sections in particular are later additions. (1) Chapters 24–27, "The Isaiah Apocalypse," represents a fully developed apocalyptic style which did not appear until the Exile and later. It should be noted, however, that Isaiah's own oracles are marked by certain features which the later apocalyptic school found compatible with its point of view, such as the dualistic contrast between light and darkness (cf. 9:1–7) and the prophet's quiet trust that God is sure to act on behalf of his people (cf. 7:3ff.). (2) Chapters 33–35 bear an exilic coloration; 34 and 35 are in the style of Deutero-Isaiah. (3) Chapters 36–39 are historical narratives nearly identical with II Kings 18:13–20:19, having been taken from the same source utilized by the Deuteronomist. Obviously they were attached to the Isaiah collection owing to their accounts of the prophet's involvement in the crisis of the Hezekiah period.

---

[92] Th. C. Vriezen, "Essentials of the Theology of Isaiah," *Israel's Prophetic Heritage*, B. W. Anderson and W. Harrelson, eds. (New York: Harper & Row, Publishers, 1962), p. 141.

The remaining material in chapters 1–39, most of which is from the prophet himself, consists of three collections:

1. Chapters 1–12: Oracles and narratives concerning Israel and Judah, chiefly from the years 742–732 B.C. Here at least three shorter collections have been combined: (a) chapter 1, a brief collection of oracles against Judah, probably from widely separated periods; (b) chapters 2–5 and 9:8–12:6, a second collection (note the superscription, 2:1), containing chiefly the prophet's early warnings addressed to Judah plus two prophecies of the future Zion (2:2–4) and her king (11:1–9); (c) chapters 6–9:7, sometimes called "The Testimony Book," containing the prophet's account of his call (ch. 6; appropriate to the beginning of yet another collection), his counsel to Ahaz during the Syro-Ephraimitic crisis, and another prophecy concerning the future king (9:2–7). That the Testimony Book was originally a separate unit, later inserted into its present context, is to be seen in the fact that it breaks the continuity of 5:8–30 and 9:8ff. (compare the common refrain in 5:25; 9:12, 17, 21; 10:4; and the sevenfold series of woes beginning at 5:8 and concluding with 10:1ff.). Composed chiefly of narrative, it was apparently written by the prophet himself just following the Syro-Ephraimitic crisis, and quite possibly was the original nucleus around which the Isaiah materials gathered.

2. Chapters 13–23: Oracles against foreign nations. Not all of these are from Isaiah. The setting for some of the material which can be assigned to the prophet belongs to the period of Sargon's campaigns (715–711 B.C.)

3. Chapters 28–32: Oracles concerning Israel and Judah, chiefly from the Sennacherib crisis (705–701 B.C.). In its original form this collection appears to have been brought together by the prophet himself, probably as a result of the commission related in 30:8.

My Eyes Have Seen the King

Isaiah's call narrative (ch. 6) is one of the most graphically descriptive and artistically pleasing accounts in prophetic literature. Written by the prophet about a decade after the experience, it records the youthful awakening which set in motion his long and faithful career as God's spokesman. In an ominous year, just prior to the death of good king Uzziah and the ascendency of his inept son Jotham, the young Isaiah stood in the presence of Israel's real and abiding king: Yahweh of Hosts.

The Jerusalem temple provided the physical setting and rich imagery for the vision. Standing perhaps in the narthex, looking through the smoke-filled Holy Place toward the Holy of Holies, Isaiah beheld its transformation into a heavenly throne room with the king of the universe "sitting upon a throne high and lifted up." Surrounding the throne were attendant beings whose resounding *Trisagion* (thrice holy) proclaimed the superlative holiness of Yahweh—as perceived in the awesome setting of Zion, so also throughout the entire earth.

> Holy, holy, holy is the Lord of hosts:
> the whole earth is full of his glory.

The holiness of God, conceived here as more than simply his distance from humankind, meant for Isaiah the difference between God's moral demands and the rebellion of his creatures. To behold the holy God was to know one's own guilt and to have no leg on which to stand. It was also to confess the sins of one's people.

> Woe is me! For I am lost; for I am a man of unclean lips,
> and I dwell in the midst of a people of unclean lips.

Amid the temple trappings, however, the sensitive youth perceived that God cleanses the man who forthrightly abandons all pretended status in favor of serving the King of Kings. Absolution of guilt and dedication to service were seen to be inseparable. When Yahweh asks, "Whom shall I send?," Isaiah responds,

> Here am I! Send me.

The temple vision has left its imprint on the whole of the prophet's message. Zion, kingship, and holiness—the central elements of the vision—are familiar themes in his oracles. Doubtless, the experience impressed upon the young Isaiah the illustrious heritage of Jerusalem as the seat of the unbroken Davidic dynasty and the place of Yahweh's choosing. Davidic covenant tradition with its promises for Zion's future appears to have exercised a greater influence upon the prophet than did the older Exodus covenant. His regard for Jerusalem not only exceeded that of any other prophet, but the promises of an exalted Zion and its future king of peace stand among the finest portions of the book. Any holiness that might be ascribed to Zion, nevertheless, was but a reflection of the holy and world-wide reign of Yahweh himself. "The Holy One of Israel" (Isaiah's favorite title for God), who was in no sense restricted to his temple, remained the sole source of the prophet's trust.

Early Prophecies

The temple vision concludes with the awesome commission given the young prophet (6:9).

> Go, and say again and again to this people, Hear ye!—but understand not if you will not. See! but perceive nothing since you choose to be blind.[93]

The burden of the message which hardened the hearts of its hearers appears in the early oracles of chapters 1–12 (especially 1–5) and takes the form of a reproof of God's rebellious sons (1:2) who had thrown off all instruction ("torah"; 1:10). In a manner reminiscent of Hosea, the prophet

---

[93] R. B. Y. Scott's paraphrase, "The Book of Isaiah," *IB*, Vol. 5, p. 211.

found no knowledge of God among his people (1:3; 5:13), but instead a "land filled with idols" (2:8). Comparing his generation to that of ancient Sodom and Gomorrah (1:10), the catalogue of Israel's and Judah's sins runs the gamut from rebellion and pride to all the social treachery earlier exposed by Amos: land-grabbing, oppression of orphans and widows, wasteful self-indulgence, bribery of officials, and broadspread injustice and bloodshed. Judah's guilt, if not so blatant as that of Israel, could run it a close match. Amos' parody on Samaria's "fat cows" finds a memorable counterpart in Isaiah's portrait of the haughty daughters of Jerusalem who

> . . . walk with outstretched necks,
> glancing wantonly with their eyes,
> mincing along as they go,
> tinkling with their feet . . .
> 3:16

For all the prophet's love of Zion, he saw in the vain rites prevailing at the temple no remedy for Judah's sickness.

> Bring no more vain offerings;
> incense is an abomination to me.
> New moon and sabbath and the
> calling of assemblies—
> I cannot endure iniquity and
> solemn assembly.
> 1:13

Perhaps the autumn feast of Tabernacles was the setting for the famous vineyard song (5:1–7), which begins much as one might expect of a poem composed to celebrate the joyful season of grape harvest.

> My beloved had a vineyard
> on a very fertile hill.

It tells of the infinite patience and care with which a plot of earth was cleared, planted with choice vines, and supplied with watchtower and winevat. Such a labor of love should naturally have assured an abundant harvest of choice grapes. But not so!

> When I looked for it to yield grapes
> why did it yield wild grapes?
> 5:4

What could be done with a vineyard that produced only worthless fruit but to pronounce it a failure and trample it down? Then comes the revelation that the song is allegory.

> For the vineyard of the Lord of
>   Hosts is the house of Israel,
> and the men of Judah
>   are his pleasant planting;
> and he looked for justice,
>   but behold bloodshed;
> for righteousness,
>   but behold a cry!
> 5:7

Yahweh had carefully prepared a people for himself; Israel was to have been his choice vineyard. But instead of the harvest of justice (*mishpaṭ*) for which he had looked, Israel had produced a history of bloodshed (*mispaḥ*); in place of righteousness (*tsedaḳah*), there was heard the cry (*tse'aḳah*) of the oppressed.

On the Day of Yahweh all Israel's false pride would be laid low.

> For the Lord of Hosts has a day
>   against all that is proud and lofty,
>   against all that is lifted up and high . . .
> 2:12

In bold metaphors the prophet warns of the imminent terror: Yahweh would whistle for Assyria (5:26–30), the "rod of his anger" (10:5), his "hired razor" with which he would shave Israel bare (7:20). Swiftly and efficiently her armies would execute Yahweh's judgment, until all that remained of the once promising vineyard would be a burnt-over stump (6:13).

The Syro-Ephraimitic Crisis

Isaiah's memoirs record a historic encounter between the prophet and King Ahaz (ch. 7) at the time of the Syro-Ephraimitic crisis. It came shortly after Pekah and Rezin's invasion of Judah, when the frightened king "shook as the trees of the forest shake before the wind" (7:2). Accompanied by the sign-child Shearjashub, Isaiah met Ahaz on the slopes of the Kidron, apparently as the king inspected his obsolete water system. In a supreme effort to calm the distraught king, discourage a deal with Assyria, and counsel the needful trust in Yahweh, Isaiah assured Ahaz that the Syro-Israelite coalition would not succeed. Reminding him that Pekah and Rezin were but small men with grandiose dreams—"two smoldering stumps of firebrands"—he counseled firm reliance upon Yahweh's thwarting of their futile scheme. Ahaz could do nothing better than to "take heed, be quiet, do not fear." "If you do not believe (*ta 'aminu*)," the prophet warned in a play on words, "you shall not be established (*te 'amenu*)."

In the prophet's view, Judah had nothing to gain and all to lose from a covenant with Assyria, more especially one that was hastily conceived and provoked by fear. Perhaps he reasoned that Tiglath-pileser would soon move in and crush the coalition anyway, making quite unnecessary the vassalage which was sure to accompany Ahaz's appeal for aid. Apart from sheer political strategy, however, the prophet saw the danger of such an alliance for Judah's total dependence upon her covenant with Yahweh. Neither practical politics nor utopian theology adequately accounts for Isaiah's position. Rather, we confront here a peculiarly prophetic logic described by Martin Buber as "theopolitics."

> the world of prophetic faith is in fact historic reality, seen in the bold and penetrating glance of the man who dares to believe. What here prevails is indeed a special kind of politics, theopolitics, which is concerned to establish a certain people in a certain historical situation under the divine sovereignty, so that this people is brought nearer the fulfillment of its task, to become the beginning of the kingdom of God. Men trust the Lord of this kingdom, that He will protect the congregation attached to Him; but at the same time they also trust in the inner strength and the influence of the congregation that ventures to realize righteousness in itself and towards its surroundings.[94]

In an effort to convince the king, Isaiah coupled his assurances with the offer of a sign—an event, not in itself miraculous, that should nevertheless authenticate the truth of his words. A young woman (7:14ff), even then pregnant and known to both men,[95] should soon bear a child; and by the time of the infant's weaning Pekah and Rezin's threat should have completely spent itself.[96] That the prophet envisioned the child as the future king, and thus a son of Ahaz, is possible; his name Immanuel ("God with us") is not unlike the names given the righteous king in 9:2–7. His most obvious and immediate significance as a sign-child, however, is identical with that of the prophet's second child, Mahershalalhashbaz (8:1–4); their births should signal the imminent collapse of Samaria and Damascus. Failing to arouse faith in the unresponsive Ahaz, Isaiah saw no reprieve from the same fate for the southern kingdom.

> Because this people have refused the waters of Shiloah that flow gently, and melt in fear before Rezin and the son of Remaliah; therefore, behold the Lord is bringing up against them the waters of the River, mighty and many, the king of Assyria and all his glory . . .
>
> 8:6–7

The Sennacherib Crisis

From 732 B.C. until the death of Ahaz (715), it would appear that Isaiah retreated from public affairs and devoted himself to instructing his inner

---

[94] Martin Buber, *The Prophetic Faith* (New York: Harper Torchbooks, 1960), p. 135.
[95] The text reads literally, *"the* young woman."
[96] Cf. G. B. Gray, *A Critical and Exegetical Commentary on the Book of Isaiah, I–XXXIX, ICC,* (New York: Charles Scribner's Sons, 1912), p. 131, where the choosing between good and evil is interpreted as the facility for selecting tasty food.

The pool of Siloam. This vast cistern was built to hold the water brought into Jerusalem by Hezekiah's tunnel from the Gihon spring outside the city's walls. (Courtesy of the Jordan Ministry of Information.)

circle of disciples (8:16–22). None of his oracles, at least, clearly dates from that period. Hezekiah's accession to the throne (715 B.C.) quite possibly raised the prophet's hopes, particularly so if the passages describing the future king of righteousness (9:1–7; 11:1–9) were composed in celebration of Hezekiah's coronation. The new king's religious reforms most likely met with the prophet's approval, though nowhere in the extant oracles is there a clear reference to them.

Isaiah's immediate role in the early Hezekiah years was to caution against futile revolts and ill-advised alliances. The growing demand in Judah and surrounding states for relief from the burdensome tribute paid to Assyria was encouraged by promises of aid from the new Ethiopian dynasty in Egypt and perhaps from Babylon as well. Mindful of the disasters

329

that had overtaken the now defunct northern kingdom and distrustful of Egypt and Babylon, the same prophet who had warned Ahaz against a covenant with Assyria now counseled Hezekiah against similar hasty efforts to align with the overlord's enemies. Isaiah had hardly switched to a pro-Assyrian position; rather, once again, his stance was thoroughly "theopolitical." To trust in Egypt—aptly described by Sargon's deputy as "that broken reed of a staff which will pierce the hand of any man who leans on it" (36:6)—was not only to take foolish risks with the nation's welfare, but, more to the point, it was to abandon her one sure source of strength.

> The Egyptians are men, and not God;
> and their horses are flesh, and not spirit.
> 31:3 [97]

Isaiah was convinced that Yahweh would deal in due time with Assyria. Having used the great devastator to perform his work of judgment, he would not overlook the arrogant manner in which she had plundered nations.

> When the Lord has finished all his work on Mount Zion and on Jerusalem he
> will punish the arrogant boasting of the king of Assyria and his haughty pride.
> 10:12

> And the Assyrian shall fall by a sword, not of man,
> and a sword, not of man, shall devour him . . .
> 31:8 [98]

The counsel offered Hezekiah was thus the same as that given Ahaz, to keep still and trust Yahweh.

> In returning and rest you shall be saved;
> in quietness and in trust shall be your strength.
> 30:15

So strong was the prophet's opposition to the Ashdod revolt (715–711 B.C.) that he walked naked and barefoot for three years as a sign of what it was certain to bring (ch. 20). His influence may well have been a factor in restraining Hezekiah's participation. Similar warnings availed for nothing, however, when with the death of Sargon II the time seemed right for resistance and Hezekiah withheld tribute. The prophet's worst fears were soon realized in Sennacherib's invasion and the devastation of all Judah except Jerusalem. The city, standing alone in the midst of the ruined land, was described by the prophet:

---

[97] Cf. chs. 18 and 19.
[98] Cf. 14:24–27.

Sennacherib receiving tribute from Lachish. (Courtesy of the Trustees of the British Museum.)

> And the daughter of Zion is left
> like a booth in a vineyard,
> like a lodge in a cucumber field,
> like a besieged city.
> 1:8

As we have seen, the historical narratives of the siege of Jerusalem (II Kings 18–19; Isa. 36–39) are less than clear and suggest different reasons for Sennacherib's failure to take the city. Some interpreters are likewise skeptical of the narratives' portrayal of Isaiah's position toward the crisis.[99] The prophet's optimistic word as reported there seems to them out of character with his oracles predicting Judah's doom.

---

[99] For a discussion of the complexity of the problem see Brevard Childs, *Isaiah and the Assyrian Crisis*.

For I will defend this city to save it, for my own sake and for the sake of my servant David.

37:35

Within the oracles, however, are similar words of hope for Jerusalem which there is no convincing reason for denying to the prophet himself. He speaks of how, with the city surrounded by the enemy,

> in an instant, suddenly, you will be visited by the Lord of Hosts.
>
> 29:5–6

Just as in the narratives, the deliverance of Jerusalem is attributed to Yahweh's defense.

> So the Lord of Hosts will come down
> to fight upon Mount Zion and upon its hill.
> Like birds hovering, so the Lord
> of hosts will protect Jerusalem;
> he will protect and deliver it,
> he will spare and rescue it.
>
> 31:4–5

There is no necessary contradiction in the prophet's opposition to revolt and his warnings of its dire consequences, on the one hand, and his confident assertion of Jerusalem's security, on the other. On each occasion, we may assume, he declared the word of Yahweh as viewed in the light of rapidly changing historical circumstances. We are left to surmise, nevertheless, the reasons for his sure conviction that Jerusalem would stand at the very time when its end appeared imminent. Already convinced of Zion's special place in the covenant society, the prophet perhaps viewed the taunts hurled by Sennacherib's deputy (II Kings 18–19; Isa. 18–19; Isa. 36–37) as too serious a challenge for Yahweh's endurance. Yahweh would save the city as a defense of his holy honor ("for my own sake"; Isa. 37:35). The narrative may be correct, moreover, in connecting the prophet's assurance with his firm reliance upon the Davidic covenant ("for the sake of my servant David"; Isa. 37:35). According to the tradition preserved in II Samuel 7, Yahweh had assured David through the words of the prophet Nathan that his house in Jerusalem would be established forever. Whereas Isaiah had much too realistic a view of Judah's sins and their consequences than to have taken the Davidic covenant as an unconditional guarantee of Zion's inviolability, he apparently found enough faith left among his people to convince him that God would not abandon them utterly—a remnant should remain. What more appropriate spot for a demonstration of Yahweh's faithfulness in preserving the remnant than the place of his own choosing, the city identified with his holy name!

332

The Future Zion and Its King

In the figure of the remnant Isaiah joined threat and promise. The name given his eldest child, Shearjashub, threatened such national calamity as "*only* a remnant" could survive. Perhaps this explains the child's presence at the confrontation with Ahaz, namely, as a reminder to the king of what should be the nation's fate should he turn to Assyria rather than to Yahweh. The name is clearly interpreted in this sense in a passage describing the coming doom.

> For though your people Israel be as the sand of the sea, only a remnant of them will return. Destruction is decreed, overflowing with righteousness.[100]
>
> 10:22

At the same time, the sign-name carried the promise that *at least* a remnant would remain. From the burnt-over stump there would sprout forth new life.

> In that day the remnant of Israel and the survivors of the house of Jacob will no more lean upon him that smote them, but will lean upon the Lord, the Holy One of Israel, in truth. A remnant will return, the remnant of Jacob to the mighty God.[101]
>
> 10:20, 21

Other passages, much debated as to date and authorship, envision an exalted Zion and a righteous king whose reign would institute an era of world-wide peace. The crucial passages are 2:2–4; 9:2–7; and 11:1–9. The first of these makes no mention of a king, as such, but anticipates the centrality of Jerusalem "in the latter days," when nations should abandon warfare and flock to Zion to be taught Yahweh's law. The universalism of the passage and its noble vision of peace in the new age make it one of prophecy's finest.

> He shall judge between the nations,
>   and shall decide for many peoples;
> and they shall beat their swords into plowshares,
>   and their spears into pruning hooks;
> nation shall not lift up sword against nation,
>   neither shall they learn war any more.

This passage is often treated as an addition of the later Isaiah editors especially because of its unlikely location among the early oracles of doom (chs. 1–6) and its reappearance in the Micah oracles (Mic. 4:1–4). Its universalistic tone, moreover, has been taken as most appropriate to the post-

---

[100] Other doomful passages in which the remnant figures are 1:8f.; 6:13; 17:5–; 30:17.

[101] The remnant connotes promise also in 37:32 and in some passages which appear to be from the prophet's later followers: 4:2ff.; 11:10–16; 28:5.

Exilic period. One theory is that we have here a floating oracle, composed by neither Isaiah nor Micah but popular within southern Zionist circles and treasured by disciples of both prophets. None of these objections is decisive, however, and the oracle would constitute a fitting summation of the hopeful element in the prophet's message.

The two other prophecies, both of which are directed toward the righteous king, likely come from Isaiah himself. Their style and perspective are not so different from Isaiah's as to suggest otherwise. If originally composed as enthronement liturgies, as some have claimed, their exalted promises might represent little more than the rhetoric appropriate to such occasions.[102] This, however, is a debatable interpretation, and one that is hardly applicable to the 11:1–9 passage, where the princely "shoot" is not simply another successor to the throne but one who "comes forth from the stump of Jesse." A temporary end of the Davidic lineage is anticipated ("stump"), and the king of Peace is envisioned as Yahweh's answer to the coming—or partially realized—destruction by the Assyrians.

The latter prophecies are traditionally labeled messianic, and that is legitimate so long as the term is properly defined. "Messiah" (Hebrew *mashiah*) means literally "anointed (one)" and generally has reference in Old Testament usage to the Hebrew king, who upon assuming the throne was anointed as a sign of the Godly favor with which his high office was endowed. It was not until the post-Old Testament period, however, that the name was used of the ideal and God-appointed king of the final age of world history. The figure developed various nuances of meaning within late Jewish circles according to the different eschatological schemes with which it was combined; and in Christian usage it assumed yet a further set of meanings.[103] In the Isaiah passages the term *mashiah* does not appear. The prophet seems to have given birth, nevertheless, to the basic concept of Messiah, namely, the expectation of an ideal Davidic prince endowed with God's spirit, who would restore the fortunes of Israel and effect righteousness and peace throughout the whole earth.

5. TELL IT NOT IN GATH: MICAH

A contemporary of Isaiah and one who shared much of his spirit was Micah of Moresheth. Though hardly so famous as the Jerusalem prophet, he proclaimed a vital prophetic message and his influence was still alive in the south fully a century after his time. That he began to prophesy prior to the fall of Samaria is apparent in oracles foretelling the northern kingdom's

---

[102] R. B. Y. Scott, *IB*, Vol. 5, p. 232.

[103] For a modern Jewish understanding of these passages cf. C. G. Montefiore, *The Synoptic Gospels*, 2nd ed., Vol. I (New York: KTAV Publishing House, 1968), pp. 13ff.

doom. The words for which he is best remembered, however, are those directed against Jerusalem during the reign of Hezekiah. His vivid descriptions of invading foreign armies are difficult to connect with more specific dates, especially 1:10–16, which has been variously ascribed to campaigns of Sargon in 720 or 711 B.C. or Sennacherib's invasion in 701 B.C.

Moresheth was a small village in the foothills of the Shephelah, about 25 miles southwest of Jerusalem. Situated in the very area which smouldered with revolt during the late eighth century and through which the ravaging armies of Sargon and Sennacherib marched, it provided the prophet a first-hand view of the Assyrian terror.

> Tell it not in Gath,
>   weep not at all;
> in Beth-le-aphrah
>   roll yourselves in the dust.
>
>   . . .
>
> because evil has come down from
>   the Lord
>   to the gate of Jerusalem.
>   1:10–12

Such a rural background, furthermore, quickened Micah's sensitivity to the needs of the lowly people of the land and aroused his suspicion of large cities. Samaria and Jerusalem he viewed as centers of powerful and corrupt cliques which epitomized the worst of Israel's and Judah's ills.

> What is the transgression of Jacob?
>   Is it not Samaria?
> And what is the sin of the house?
>   of Judah?
>   Is it not Jerusalem?
>   1:5

Whether his oracles were originally delivered in Jerusalem and whether he was personally acquainted with Isaiah, we have no way of knowing.[104] That the latter prophet was altogether unknown to him appears most unlikely, however, and certain of his oracles suggest Isaianic influence.[105]

No Old Testament prophet surpassed Micah in his caustic criticism of the professional prophets who shaped their words to the payment they received.

---

[104] Walter Beyerlin (Die Kulttraditionen Israels in der Verkündigung des Propheten Micha, Forschungen zur Religion und Literatur des Alten und Neuen Testaments, 54 [1959] contends that Micah's prophecies should be understood against the background of the autumn festival at Jerusalem. See also Norman W. Porteous, "The Prophets and the Problem of Continuity," Israel's Prophetic Heritage, Bernhard W. Anderson and Walter Harrelson, eds, pp. 11–25.

[105] Cp. Mic. 1:10–16 with Isa. 10:27ff.; 2:1–5 with Isa. 5:8ff.; Mic. 5:9–14 with Isa. 2:6ff.

> Thus says the Lord concerning the
> prophets
> who lead my people astray,
> who cry "peace"
> when they have something to eat,
> but declare war against him
> who puts nothing into their
> mouths.
> Therefore it shall be night to you,
> without vision
> and darkness to you, without
> divination.
>
> 3:5–6

He offered himself as an example of a different breed of prophet.

> But as for me, I am filled with
> power
> with the spirit of the Lord,
> and with justice and might,
> to declare to Jacob his transgression
> and to Israel his sin.
>
> 3:8

Both his stern oracles of judgment and his sensitive laments bear out the truth of this self-appraisal. That he was the first southern spokesman to detail Zion's collapse is not without significance, and the resulting personal grief and alienation from his fellows belie the courage and conviction which moved him to speak.

The Book

Micah's oracles exist in an edited collection in which chronological sequence appears to have played little or no part. The most obvious pattern is their arrangement in alternating sections of threat and promise, as follows: (1) oracles against Israel and Judah (chs. 1–3); (2) promises to Judah (chs. 4–5); (3) more oracles of judgment (6:1–7:7); and (4) words of confession and promise (7:8–20).

Since the studies of Bernhard Stade in the late nineteenth century,[106] it has been the position of most scholars that not all of the book comes from the prophet himself. Stade recognized only the first three chapters as Micah's, and almost all would agree that at least this much is genuine, excepting 2:12–13. There are no decisive reasons, however, for denying the authenticity of the remainder of the book, with the following exceptions: ch. 4; 5:5–9; and 7:8–20. As we have seen, 4:1–4 repeats the Isaiah 2:2–4

---

[106] "Bemerkungen über das Buch Micha," u.s.w., ZAW, I (1881), pp. 161–172; III (1883), pp. 1–16; IV (1884), pp. 291–297; VI (1886), pp. 122–123; XXIII (1903), pp. 163–171.

prophecy of Zion's exaltation; only here there is an additional verse (vs. 4) portraying the domestic tranquility of the coming era. The remainder of chapter 4, like 2:12–13, envisions the return of the remnant from Babylonian captivity and therefore presupposes the Exile. The remnant prophecy of 5:5–9, with its promise of deliverance through a coalition of princes, fits awkwardly with the preceding prophecy of the one deliverer—the famous shepherd king from Bethlehem (5:1–4). The latter passage is often assigned to the secondary additions, but it is no more subject to doubt than are the similar Isaiah oracles (Isa. 9:2–7; 11:1–9). The concluding hopeful section of the book (7:8–20) is cast in a liturgical form which suggests a late cultic background.

The final edition of the book of Micah was likely the work of the same circle of redactors who edited the oracles of Isaiah. The redactional element in both books reflects common editorial formulas and liturgical influences, as well as the same distinctive pattern of alternating oracles of judgment and salvation.[107] Such editorial activity undoubtedly took place at Jerusalem between the beginning of the seventh century B.C. and the early post-Exilic period. By one manner of reckoning, Micah's oracles were not simply edited and expanded, but were essentially reinterpreted within the context of the larger body of prophetic literature associated with Isaiah,[108] Thus, the prophecy of Zion's exaltation (Mic. 4:1–4; Isa. 2:2–4) serves as an example of redactional use of a common tradition, rather than an instance of the one prophet borrowing from the other.

What Is the Transgression of Jacob?

Micah's oracles provide a worthy summary of the major themes of eighth-century prophecy. Addressing himself to both houses in Israel, he made his chief concern the sure and swift judgment about to befall Samaria and Jerusalem.

> Therefore I will make Samaria a heap in the open country,
>   a place for planting vineyards;
> > 1:6

> . . . Zion shall be plowed as a field;
> Jerusalem shall become a heap of ruins,
>   and the mountain of the house a wooded height.
> > 3:12

The significance of these warnings, otherwise equally characteristic of Amos, Hosea, and Isaiah, is the unconditional pronouncement of Jerusalem's doom; none of the other prophets went quite so far in detailing the destruction of Zion itself. That the Zion prediction was most likely deliv-

---

[107] See Brevard Childs, *Introduction to the Old Testament as Scripture*, pp. 434–436.
[108] Ibid., pp. 434–439.

ered during the Sennacherib era, at the very time when Isaiah was moved to declare the city secure, makes the contrast all the more striking. Any attempt to explain the difference between the two southern prophets on this matter must look to their respective situations—the rural Micah's perspective on the collective social evils for which Jerusalem had become a symbol, and Isaiah's immediate presence in the beleagured city with the pagan invader's threats challenging Yahweh's power to act on behalf of his people. One cannot assume a lack of respect for the temple, as such, on Micah's part. The initial oracle in the collection (1:2–9) begins with the announcement of Yahweh's coming forth "from his holy temple" to tread the earth, which suggests that the prophet shared Isaiah's conception of a heavenly counterpart for the earthly temple.

If Micah himself incorporated within his oracles the prophecy of Zion's exaltation (4:1–4), then he, like Isaiah, envisioned the city's restoration. The prophecy of the Bethlehemite king (5:1–4), at any rate, implies a hope for Zion. Although the city is never mentioned, and it may appear that the prophet has chosen the small village rather than Jerusalem as a pointed rejection of the latter, the more likely interpretation is that the birthplace of the shepherd king is here being identified as the village of David's birth. Thus, the coming deliverer would be after the order of David and as such might be expected to reestablish Zion, the city of David. Indeed, if 5:1 served as the original introduction to the oracle, the prophecy appears to have been offered to inspire hope when Jerusalem was under Assyrian siege. In contrast with Isaiah, Micah offers no miraculous deliverance for the city; but he promises in due time a Davidic ruler.

> And he shall stand and feed his flock in the strength of the Lord,
> in the majesty of the name of the Lord his God.
> And they shall dwell secure, for now he shall be great
> to the ends of the earth.
>
> 5:4

At the very least, Micah was concerned with maintaining the purity of the cult and, like Hosea, he was incensed by its idolatrous corruptions. Zion would fall because priests and prophets, as well as rulers and officials, had become those

> who build Zion with blood
> and Jerusalem with wrong.
> 3:10

The naïve sense of security displayed by these Jerusalem cliques was sign enough of their hopeless estate.

> Is not the Lord in the midst of us?
> No evil shall come upon us.
> 3:11

After the manner of Amos, Micah perceived that no amount of trust in the external forms of the cult could benefit a people who allowed oppression, bribery, injustice, and corruption of sacred institutions to go unchecked.

What Does the Lord Require of You?

Micah utilized the form of the lawsuit in drawing up charges against his people. The 6:1–8 oracle can be easily separated into its component parts: (1) summons (vs. 1), (2) charge to witnesses (vs. 2), (3) plaintiff's case, (vss. 3–5), (4) defendant's response (vss. 6–7), and (5) judgment (vs. 8). The basic premise here is not the Zion tradition but the older Exodus faith; it is Yahweh's covenant claims that have been violated. Israel having failed in her response to Yahweh's saving acts, the prophet could conceive of nothing more that Yahweh could have done for her.

> O my people, what have I done to you?
> In what have I wearied you?
> 6:3

Guilty and utterly without a case to present, Israel would find that no amount of cultic ritual—not even the sacrifice of the first-born—could substitute for a genuine reaffirmation of Yahweh's salvation in the same spirit with which the nation had made its original covenant vows. The final judgment of the case is an apt statement of the substance of eighth-century prophecy: Amos' call for justice, Hosea's certainty of Yahweh's love, and Isaiah's summons to quiet faith.

> He has showed you, O man, what is
>   good;
>   and what does the Lord require
>   of you
> but to do justice, and to love
>   kindness,
>   and to walk humbly with your
>   God?
> 6:8

SELECTED READINGS

Prophecy

Anderson Bernhard W., and Walter Harrelson, eds., *Israel's Prophetic Heritage* (New York: Harper & Row, Publishers, 1962).

Buber, Martin, *The Prophetic Faith*, C. Witton-Davies, trans. (New York: Macmillan Publishing Co., Inc., 1949). Also in paperback (Harper Torchbooks, 1960).

Buss, Martin J., "Prophecy in Ancient Israel," *IDBS*, pp. 694–697.

Clements, R. E., *Prophecy and Covenant*, Studies in Biblical Theology, 43 (London: S.C.M. Press, 1965).

————, *Prophecy and Tradition* (Atlanta, GA: John Knox Press, 1975). Paperback. A good introduction to Israelite prophecy through an examination of the traditions and institutions which provided its context.

Crenshaw, James L., *Prophetic Conflict: Its Effect Upon Israelite Religion* (Berlin/New York: Walter de Gruyter, 1971). A fresh examination of the problem of "false prophecy" in ancient Israel.

DeVries, Simon John, *Prophet Against Prophet* (Grand Rapids, MI: William B. Eerdmans Publishing Company, 1978). A study of prophetic conflict or "false prophecy," centering on the Micaiah account (I Kings 22).

Fohrer, Georg, "Remarks on Modern Interpretation of the Prophets," *JBL*, LXXX (1961), pp. 309–319.

Fosbroke, Hughell E. W., "The Prophetic Literature," *IB*, Vol I, pp. 201–211.

Gerstenberger, Erhard, "The Woe Oracles of the Prophets," *JBL*, LXXXI (1962), pp. 249–263.

Gottwald, Norman K., *All the Kingdoms of the Earth: Israelite Prophecy and International Relations in the Ancient Near East* (New York: Harper & Row, Publishers, 1964).

Haldar, Alfred, *Associations of Cult Prophets Among the Ancient Semites*, H. S. Harvey, trans. (Uppsala, Sweden: Almquist and Wiksells, 1945).

Heaton, E. W., *The Old Testament Prophets* (Atlanta, GA: John Knox Press, 1977). Paperback. A revised edition of a standard handbook on the prophets.

Henshaw, Thomas, *The Latter Prophets* (London: Allen & George Unwin Ltd., 1958).

Heschel, Abraham J., *The Prophets* (New York: Harper & Row, Publishers, 1963). Also in paperback, 2 vols. (Harper Colophon Books, 1969).

Holladay, John S., Jr., "Assyrian Statecraft and the Prophets of Israel", *HTR*, 63 (1970), pp. 29–51.

Huffmon, Herbert B., "The Origins of Prophecy," *Magnalia Dei: The Mighty Acts of God*, Frank M. Cross, Werner E. Lemke, and Patrick D. Miller, Jr., eds. (Garden City, NY: Doubleday & Company, Inc., 1976), pp. 171–186.

————, "Prophecy in the Mari Letters," *BA*, XXXI (1968), pp. 101–124. A report on the references to prophecy in the Mari tablets and some tentative conclusions as to their significance for Hebrew prophecy.

Johnson, Aubrey R., *The Cultic Prophet in Ancient Israel* (Cardiff: University of Wales, 1961). Contends for a relationship between the early prophets and the cult.

Koch, Klaus, *The Growth of the Biblical Tradition*, S. M. Cupitt, trans. (New York: Charles Scribner's Sons, 1969), pp. 183–220. Paperback. A form-critical analysis of Old Testament prophecy.

Kuhl, Curt, *The Prophets of Israel* (London: Oliver & Boyd, 1960).

Lindblom, J., *Prophecy in Ancient Israel* (Oxford: Basil Blackwell, 1962). One of the best works on prophecy, treated topically.

McKane, William, *Prophets and Wise Men*, Studies in Biblical Theology, 44, (Napierville, IL: Alex R. Allenson, 1965).

March, W. Eugene, "Prophecy," *Old Testament Form Criticism*, John H. Hayes, ed. (San Antonio, TX: Trinity University Press, 1974), pp. 141–177. A useful summary of form-critical research on the prophetical books.

340

Moran, William L., "New Evidence from Mari on the History of Prophecy," *Biblica*, 50 (1969), pp. 15–56.

Napier, B. Davie, "Prophet, Prophetism," *IDB*, K-Q, pp. 896–919.

Noth, Martin, "History and Word of God in the Old Testament," *The Laws in the Pentateuch and Other Studies*, D. R. Ap-Thomas, trans. (Philadelphia: Fortress Press, 1967), pp. 179–193. A comparison of Mari and Hebrew prophecy.

Orlinsky, Harry M., ed., *Interpreting the Prophetic Tradition*, The Goldensen Lectures 1955–1966 (Cincinnati, OH: The Hebrew Union College Press, 1969).

Rad, Gerhard, von, *Old Testament Theology*, D. M. G. Stalker, trans. (New York: Harper & Row, Publishers, 1965), Vol. II. An important work which treats Old Testament prophecy topically and in terms of the separate prophetic figures. Available in an abridged paperback edition as *The Message of the Prophets* (Harper & Row, Publishers, 1967).

Scott, R. B. Y., *The Relevance of the Prophets*, rev. ed. (New York: Macmillan Publishing Co., Inc., 1976). Paperback. A revised edition of a standard hardback, first published in 1944.

Skinner, John, *Prophecy and Religion* (New York: Cambridge University Press, 1922). Also in paperback (Cambridge University Press, 1963).

Westermann, Claus, *Basic Forms of Prophetic Speech*, Hugh K. White, trans. (Philadelphia: The Westminster Press, 1967). A form-critical approach to Old Testament prophecy.

Winward, Stephen, *A Guide to the Prophets* (Atlanta, GA: John Knox Press, 1976). Paperback.

Amos

Bentzen, A., "The Ritual Background of Amos 1:1–2:16," *OTS*, VIII (Leiden, Netherlands: E. J. Brill, 1950), pp. 85–99.

Brueggemann, W., "Amos 4:4–13 and Israel's Covenant Worship," *VT*, XV (1965), pp. 1–15. Argues a cultic background for Amos.

Crenshaw, J. L., "Amos and the Theophanic Tradition," *ZAW*, LXXX (1968), pp. 203–215. Finds the background of Amos' prophecies in a theophanic tradition.

———, "The Influence of the Wise upon Amos," *ZAW*, LXXIX (1967), pp. 42–52.

Fosbroke, Hughell E. W., "Introduction and Exegesis to the Book of Amos," *IB*, Vol. VI pp. 763–853.

Kapelrud, Arvid S., *Central Ideas in Amos* (Oslo: Oslo University Press, 1961). Reprint of a work published in 1956.

———, "New Ideas in Amos," *VTS*, XV (1965), pp. 193–206.

Mays, James L., *Amos: A Commentary*, The Old Testament Library (Philadelphia: The Westminster Press, 1969).

Rowley, Harold H., "Was Amos a Nabi?" *Festschrift Otto Eissfeldt*, J. Fück, ed. (Halle, Belgium: Niemeyer, 1947), pp. 191–198.

Terrien, Samuel, "Amos and Wisdom," *Israel's Prophetic Heritage*, Bernhard W. Anderson and Walter Harrelson, eds. (New York: Harper & Row, Publishers, 1962), pp. 108–115. Attempts to show a close relationship between Amos and the wisdom tradition.

Ward, James M., *Amos and Isaiah: Prophets of the Word of God* (Nashville, TN: Abingdon Press, 1969).

Watts, John D., *Vision and Prophecy in Amos* (Grand Rapids, MI: W. B. Eerd-mans, 1958). Contends for a cultic background for Amos.

Wolff, Hans Walter, *Amos the Prophet: The Man and His Background,* Foster R. McCurley, trans., John Reumann, ed. (Philadelphia: Fortress Press, 1973). Paperback. A succinct and clearly written exposition of the author's theory that Amos' intellectual milieu was the wisdom tradition.

————, *Joel and Amos,* Waldemar Jargen et al., trans., S. Dean McBride, Jr., ed. (Philadelphia: Fortress Press, 1977). The English translation of an important German commentary.

Hosea

Brueggemann, Walter, *Tradition for Crisis: A Study in Hosea,* (Atlanta, GA: John Knox Press, 1968).

Buss, Martin J., *The Prophetic Word of Hosea: A Morphological Study,* BZAW, Vol. III (Berlin: A Topelmann, 1969).

Mauchline, John, "Introduction and Exegesis to the Book of Hosea," *IB*, Vol. VI pp. 553–725.

Robinson, H. Wheeler, *The Cross of Hosea,* Ernest A. Payne, ed. (Philadelphia: The Westminster Press, 1949).

Rowley, Harold H., "The Marriage of Hosea," *BJRL*, XXXIX (1956), pp. 200–233.

Ward, James M., *Hosea: A Theological Commentary* (New York: Harper & Row, Publishers, 1966).

Wolff, Hans Walter, *Hosea,* Gary Stansell, trans., Paul D. Hanson, ed. (Philadelphia: Fortress Press, 1974). The English translation of an outstanding German commentary.

Mays, James L., *Hosea: A Commentary* (Philadelphia: The Westminster Press, 1969).

Isaiah 1–39

Blank, Sheldon M., *Prophetic Faith in Isaiah* (New York: Harper & Row, Publishers, 1958). A provocative but debatable effort to restrict the oracles of the original Isaiah to a kernel of the book.

Childs, Brevard, *Isaiah and the Assyrian Crisis,* Studies in Biblical Theology, series 2, no. 3 (London: S.C.M. Press, 1967).

Gottwald, Norman K., "Immanuel as the Prophet's Son," *VT*, VIII (1958), pp. 36–47.

Kaiser, Otto, *Isaiah 1–12: A Commentary,* R. A. Wilson, trans. (Philadelphia: The Westminster Press, 1972).

————, *Isaiah 13–39: A Commentary,* R. A. Wilson, trans. The Old Testament Library (Philadelphia: The Westminster Press, 1974).

Kissane, Edward J., *The Book of Isaiah,* 2nd ed. 2 vols. (Dublin: Browne and Nolan, 1960).

Scott, R. B. Y., "Introduction and Exegesis to Isaiah 1–39," *IB*, Vol. V, pp. 151–381.

Vriezen, Th. C., "Essentials of the Theology of Isaiah," *Israel's Prophetic Heritage,* Bernhard W. Anderson and Walter Harrelson, eds. (New York: Harper & Row, Publishers, 1962), pp. 128–146.

Ward, James M., *Amos and Isaiah: Prophets of the Word of God* (Nashville, TN: Abingdon Press, 1969).

Whedbee, J. William, *Isaiah and Wisdom* (Nashville, TN: Abingdon Press, 1971). Argues for a strong influence of wisdom tradition on Isaiah.

Micah

Mays, James Luther, *Micah: A Commentary,* The Old Testament Library (Philadelphia: The Westminster Press, 1976).

Wolfe, Roland E., "Introduction and Exegesis to the Book of Micah," *IB*, Vol. VI, pp. 897–949.

5

—•‡•—

JeRusalem shall
Become a heap

**Therefore because of you Zion shall be plowed as a field; Jerusalem
shall become a heap of ruins, and the mountain of the house a
wooded height.**
                              —Micah 3:12; Jeremiah 26:18

The half century or more which separates the eighth-century prophets
from those of the late seventh and early sixth centuries (Zephaniah,
Nahum, Habakkuk, and Jeremiah) is a blank page insofar as prophecy is
concerned. If there was any major prophetic voice giving direction in those
uncertain years, it has escaped the notice of Hebrew tradition.[1] From the
histories of the Deuteronomist and the Chronicler one would infer as a
reason for the sterility of the period the long, oppressive reign of Hezekiah's son and successor Manasseh (687–642 B.C.).[2] Differing from his father as night from day, he was remembered as the darkest figure in Judah's
royal history. That he remained a loyal vassal of Assyria is hardly surprising
in view of the fact that Assyria's most acute problems in holding together
its empire did not develop until after Manasseh's time. Less forgivable was
his flagrant disregard for the basic principles of Yahweh faith, examples of
which are documented at length in the Old Testament records. Idolatry,
bloodshed, and even child sacrifice went unchecked; and legend has it that

---

[1] The references to prophets and seers in II Kings 21:10 and II Chron. 33:18 are vague.
[2] II Kings 21; II Chron. 33.

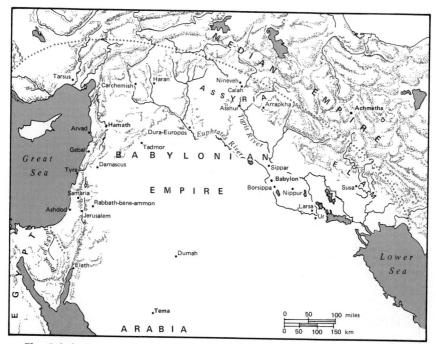

The Babylonian Empire, early sixth century B.C. (Adapted with permission of Macmillan Publishing Co., Inc., from Macmillan Bible Atlas by Y. Aharoni and Michael Avi-Yonah. Copyright© 1968 Carta, Jerusalem. © Copyright 1964 by Carta, Jerusalem. © Copyright 1966 by Carta, Jerusalem.

the aged Isaiah was martyred under his administration.[3] Only the Chronicler includes the story of the wicked king's subsequent captivity and repentance, a legendary embellishment which was extended yet further in the apocryphal Prayer of Manasseh.[4] Manasseh's son Amon (642–640 B.C.) was assassinated after a brief two-year reign and the latter's son Josiah (640–609 B.C.) was proclaimed king at only eight years of age.[5] Josiah's reign, praised by the Deuteronomist for its reformation of Judah's religious life, marks the revolutionary period in world history when Babylon replaced Assyria as master of the Near East.

With the murder of Sennacherib in 681 B.C., the sprawling and unstable Assyrian empire might have fallen apart but for the leadership of its last two strong kings, Esarhaddon (681–669 B.C.) and Ashurbanipal (669–633 B.C.). The territories brought under Assyrian hegemony were never welded into a solidly unified realm, and simmering revolts in the east

[3] Cf. the apocryphal work, *The Martyrdom of Isaiah* in R. H. Charles, *The Apocrypha and Pseudepigrapha of the Old Testament*, Vol. II (Oxford: Clarendon Press, 1913), pp. 155–162.

[4] R. H. Charles, *The Apocrypha and Pseudepigrapha of the Old Testament*, Vol. I, pp. 612–624.

[5] For Josiah's reign cf. II Kings 22:1–23:30; II Chron. 34–35.

posed a constant threat. In the middle of the seventh century Egypt was invaded and taken, making Assyria the largest empire in the history of the world to that time. The watershed had been reached, however, and the mighty empire was already on the brink of decline.

Assyrian control of Egypt lasted but a few years before Pharaoh Psammetichus I (663–609 B.C.) threw out the occupation forces and ushered in a brief period of Egyptian revival. Of greater consequence were developments in Mesopotamia, which was made a seething sphere of rebellion and restless movements by the Babylonians, Medes, and Scythians. Herodotus' report of a Scythian invasion down the Palestinian coast to Egypt, where Psammetichus allegedly turned them back by paying them off, is unattested in any other ancient source and must not be taken at face value.[6] Before the onslaughts of the Medes and Babylonians, however, first Asshur (614 B.C.), then Nineveh (612 B.C.) fell; and even with the support of Egypt, where the Babylonians were feared even more than the Assyrians, the tottering empire could no longer offer serious resistance. Retreating westward to Haran, the remnant of the Assyrian army was wiped out there in 609 B.C., and the once proud and feared Assyrian empire ceased to exist.

Josiah was killed at Megiddo (609 B.C.) in a futile effort to stop the Egyptian army of Pharaoh Necho (609–593 B.C.) as it marched up through Palestine to join forces with the Assyrians. For a brief period Palestine fell under the control of Egypt. Jehoiakim (609–598 B.C.), son of Josiah and hand-picked vassal of Necho, replaced his brother Jehoahaz on the throne of Judah after only three months of the latter's reign.[7] Events in the year 605 B.C., however, necessitated a switch of loyalties on Jehoiakim's part. In that year Nebuchadrezzar (605–562 B.C.) signally defeated the Egyptian army at Carchemish on the Orontes River and became king of the new Babylonian empire. From that time forth, until its very end, the kingdom of Judah was never to be free of Nebuchadrezzar's control.

1. I HAVE CUT OFF NATIONS: ZEPHANIAH

Late in the seventh century the long period of prophetic silence was broken by the preaching of Zephaniah, the great-great-grandson of Hezekiah, possibly the king of that name (Zeph. 1:1). The book of Zephaniah is much too brief and the evidence too slight to derive a very clear picture of the prophet's personal history; but his familiarity with Jerusalem and its precincts suggests that he was a citizen of that city, and the superscription

---

[6] Book I, chs. 104–106.

[7] For the period from Josiah's death to the fall of Jerusalem cf. II Kings 23:31–25:30; II Chron. 36.

to the book places him in Josiah's day. Since he inveighed most heavily against the very cultic corruptions which were the targets of Josiah's reformation in 622 B.C. and the years following, we can best place his prophecies in the early years of that king's administration, just prior to the reforms.

The collection of Zephaniah's oracles approximates the broad threefold pattern which appears in other prophetic collections: (1) oracles against Judah (1:1–2:3 and 3:1–7), (2) oracles against foreign nations (2:4–15), and (3) words of hope (3:8–13). Only the words of judgment against Jerusalem in 3:1–7 break the neat pattern. The one portion of the book clearly later than the seventh century is the concluding half of the hopeful section (3:14–20), with its promise of restoration to the Babylonian exiles.

The major theme of Zephaniah's preaching was the *Dies Irae*—the great and terrible Day of Yahweh, which was "near and hastening fast." In a manner reminiscent of Amos, he conceived the destined appointment between Yahweh and the nations as one foreboding darkness and devastation.

> The great day of the Lord is near,
> near and hastening fast;
> the sound of the day of the Lord is bitter,
> the mighty man cries aloud there.
> A day of wrath is that day,
> a day of distress and anguish,
> a day of ruin and devastation,
> a day of darkness and gloom,
> a day of clouds and thick darkness.
>
> 1:14–15

In one respect, at least, the horror depicted by Zephaniah exceeds that of his prophetic predecessors. He projects a picture of the feast which Yahweh has prepared for his guests, and for which a sacrifice is to be made; then comes the revelation that the sacrifice is to be none other than the guests themselves (1:7ff.).

Significantly the fate of the prophet's own people is identified with that of the nations at large; his warnings encompass "all the inhabitants of the earth" (1:18). Foremost attention, nevertheless, centers on Judah. In Jerusalem the first cry of alarm will be heard from the direction of the Fish Gate, signaling a foe approaching from the north (1:10). Whether the prophet foresaw a specific enemy such as the Scythians is not at all clear, since he never mentions the terror by name. Quite possibly he was able to determine no more than that the restless conditions in Mesopotamia were rushing toward a head and were sure to bring violent disruptions throughout the lands of the Near East. Furthermore, for so long a time had the major threats to Israel's life centered in Assyria that by Zephaniah's day

Hebrew prophecy was well on the way toward employing the far north as a symbol for national catastrophe.[8] When power changed hands from the Assyrians to the Babylonians, the geographical orientation remained unchanged.

As has already been remarked, the threats of Israel's prophets were conditioned not so much by political guesses as by theological convictions. So it is that Zephaniah's *Dies Irae* is premised chiefly on the corruption of Judah's inner life. His condemnations fall equally on cultic and ethical abuses, for both of which he offers Jerusalem as the prime example. The effects of Manasseh's adulteration of the temple cult were still to be seen; with the worship of Yahweh, the Jerusalem priesthood had joined a host of foreign deities, including the Canaanite Baal, Milcom of Ammon, and the Assyrian Queen of Heaven (1:4–5). The pagan superstition of leaping through doorways to avoid demonic spirits supposedly lurking under the thresholds is condemned in the same breath with the ethical evil of "those who fill their master's house with violence and fraud" (1:9).

Along with apostate prophets and priests, Jerusalem was defiled by its "roaring lions" and "evening wolves"—the oppressing officials and judges (3:3–4)—and its lethargic citizens who, like coagulated wine at the bottom of a vessel, could not be aroused to the approaching disaster.

> At that time I will search Jerusalem with lamps,
>   and I will punish the men
> who are thickening upon their lees,
>   those who say in their hearts,
> "The Lord will not do good, nor will he do ill."
>   1:12

The threats against Judah's immediate neighbors, Philistia (2:4–7), Moab, and Ammon (2:8–11), are colorless for want of more detail respecting their crimes; and even less revealing is the bare mention of the Ethiopians (2:12). Only a boastful scoffing against Judah on the part of the Transjordan people is cited, a fact which leads some interpreters to assign this section of the book to the post-Exilic period. The prophet's theme of a universal judgment, however, necessitates some such portrayal of the imminent international chaos, even if only in the generalized form we find here. The remnant of Judah is promised the possession of the surrounding lands as its future inheritance (2:9), which is a nationalistic emphasis considerably more prominent than that found in the foreign oracles of Amos.

The prophet reserved his most vivid imagery for the reproach against Assyria (2:13–15). Yahweh's annihilation of Nineveh would make it an object of derision, the desolate ruins of its once fine buildings now inhabited by vultures, porcupines, and hoot owls.

---

[8] Cf. Jer. 6:22; Ezek. 38:15.

1. I HAVE CUT OFF NATIONS: ZEPHANIAH

This is the exultant city
    that dwelt secure,
that said to herself,
    "I am and there is none else."
What a desolation she has become,
    a lair for wild beasts!
Every one who passes by her
    hisses and shakes his fist.
                    2:15

There is a summons to repentance in Zephaniah's oracles which lends support to his promises for the remnant of Judah. Even as his people have sinned within and without the cult, the prophet's appeal is for both a proper assembly at the temple and right conduct throughout the society.

Come together and hold assembly,
    O shameless nation,
before you are driven away
    like the drifting chaff . . .
Seek the Lord all you humble of the land
    who do his commands;
seek righteousness, seek humility;
    perhaps you may be hidden
    on the day of the wrath of the Lord.
                    2:2–3

To put away false pride and wait upon Yahweh, was the response sought by the prophet (3:8ff.). Yahweh himself, moreover, was still present within the city, and that should be basis enough for Judah's hopes.

The Lord within her is righteous,
    he does no wrong;
every morning he shows forth his justice,
    each dawn he does not fail . . .
                    3:5

In his concluding picture of the future remnant (3:8–13) none of the nationalistic note of the foreign oracles is apparent. The prophet ties the destiny of the chastened remnant to that of the nations at large. With the conversion of a myriad of foreign languages to one pure tongue, all peoples would call on Yahweh's name and serve him with one accord. Zion would no longer harbor a proud and boastful citizenry.

For I will leave in the midst of you
    a people humble and lowly.
                    3:12

No Old Testament prophet, other than those anonymous figures whose words are now embodied within the Isaiah collection, qualifies more read-

Jerusalem today. Looking eastward across the Old City from the direction of the Jaffa Gate (foreground), the Islamic Dome of the Rock is seen in the upper center and the Mount of Olives at the top of the picture. It is believed that the Israelite temple stood approximately on the site of the Dome of the Rock. (Courtesy of the Consulate General of Israel in New York.)

ily for a place among Isaiah's disciples than does Zephaniah. Among the more significant of their common elements are the portrayals of Assyria's evil and Yahweh's control over the pagan empire's destiny; the concentration on pride as the cardinal sin; the assurance that quietness, trust, and humility are the needful human graces; and the persistent hope for Zion and the remnant. Zephaniah's forceful oracles are proof enough that the

350

brilliant gains established by eighth century prophecy had survived without major loss the long period of prophetic quiescence.

2. NINEVEH IS LIKE A POOL: NAHUM

Assyria's reputation for ruthless aggression was unsurpassed among the conquering empires of the ancient world. The Assyrian annals themselves are replete with examples of the infamous scorched-earth tactics, displacements of conquered peoples, and brutal reprisals administered against rebellious vassals. It was inevitable, therefore, that events heralding the empire's collapse should have brought a malevolent satisfaction to many of its long-suffering victims. The fall of Nineveh in 612 B.C., following a three-month siege of Babylonian and Median armies, appeared to dramatize the grim justice of the violence that overtakes oppressors.

One of those who celebrated Nineveh's humiliation was Nahum of Elkosh. An otherwise obscure figure, his one contribution to Hebrew prophecy is the brilliant ode of triumph composed on the eve of the city's fall. Even those who regard him as unworthy of a place among the classical prophets do not fail to appreciate the high literary quality of his poetry.[9] Embodying vivid descriptions of a city under siege, well-chosen metaphors, and a keen sense of irony, it ranks easily alongside the finest of the Old Testament epic poems, such as the Song of Deborah (Judg. 5) and David's elegy over Saul and Jonathan (II Sam. 1:19–27).

The oracle against Nineveh is confined to chapters 2 and 3 of the book, where in a two-part poem Nahum first depicts the attack on the city, its frenzied and futile defense, collapse, and destruction (ch. 2), and follows with a taunt song detailing the irony of the great bloodletter's own bloody end (ch. 3). Most of chapter 1 (1:2–11, at least) is the fragment of an acrostic psalm which was at some point, by either the prophet or an editor, appended to the Nineveh oracle. The prophet could hardly have composed his famous ode much earlier than the last few months preceding the siege, so assured and emotionally charged are his descriptions of what is about to befall.

That Nahum's exultation in Assyria's ruin is unworthy of the prophetic ethic at its best is undeniable. Unlike the classical prophets we have considered thus far, he fails to balance his attack on the enemy with any word of judgment against his own people. If Nineveh's sorry plight evoked any sense of revulsion at Judah's less infamous but equally real crimes, the prophet has failed to draw the parallel. In the eyes of the modern critic, certainly, he missed an excellent opportunity to use the lesson of Nineveh as a plea for Judah's own repentance; and thereby he deserves his reputation as a greater poet and patriot than prophet. There are, nevertheless,

---

[9] Cf., for example, R. H. Pfeiffer, *Introduction to the Old Testament*, pp. 594–597.

two respects in which he speaks in true prophetic form: first, in his ascription of Nineveh's fate to Yahweh's controlling will; and, second, in the conviction that Yahweh does not let evil go unpunished.

Nahum's words read much like a literal fulfillment of Isaiah's earlier assurances that after Yahweh had used Assyria, his "hired razor," he would punish her for all her arrogant crimes. In the turn of events accompanying the shifts of power in the Near East, Nahum perceived that this at last was about to happen. The great devastator was about to be called to account, not simply as a result of historical circumstances, but because Yahweh had willed it so.

> Behold, I am against you,
> says the Lord of hosts, . . .
> 2:13; 3:5

Only against the background of Assyria's evil, furthermore, is the irony of Nineveh's bitter plight understandable. There is more than sheer vengeance in the prophet's portrayal of the city's collapse, its citizens running like water through the broken walls.

> Nineveh is like a pool
> whose waters run away.
> "Halt! halt!" they cry;
> but none turns back.
> 2:8

Nineveh's unlamented fate is offered as the assurance that those who live by the sword die thereby.

> Woe to the bloody city,
> all full of lies and booty—
> no end to the plunder!
> 3:1

> There is no assuaging your hurt,
> Your wound is grievous.
> All who hear the news of you
> clap their hands over you.
> For upon whom has not come
> your unceasing evil?
> 3:19

3. IT HASTENS TO THE END: HABAKKUK

Another voice raised alongside those of Zephaniah and Nahum, apparently only slightly removed in time and providing a commentary on the same events of the late seventh century, was that of Habakkuk. As in the case of Zephaniah, we are not even told the name of his home town, though presumably it was in the south. In the apocryphal story of Bel and the Dragon, which contains a colorful legend of Habakkuk's miraculous mission to Babylon to assist Daniel in the lion's den, his lineage is traced through the priestly tribe of Levi. Some scholars are persuaded from a study of the prophet's oracles, moreover, that he was a temple singer and liturgist, whose compositions were intended for cultic use.[10]

The superscription to the book of Habakkuk offers no date for his career, but the reference to the emerging Chaldean (Babylonian) empire (1:6) places his work at least as late as the final quarter of the seventh century.[11] Notwithstanding many theories to the contrary, there appears no definitive reason for denying either the fundamental unity of the book nor the authenticity of the present arrangement of its contents. Separate headings at the beginnings of chapters 1 ("The oracle of God which Habakkuk the prophet saw") and 3 ("A prayer of Habakkuk . . .") set apart two segments of the text; and the five woes of 2:6–20 are easily distinguished as yet a third unit. The outline of the book, then, becomes: (1) a dialogue between the prophet and Yahweh (1:1–2:5), (2) woes against an oppressive nation (2:6–20), and (3) Habakkuk's prayer (ch. 3).

The Dead Sea Scrolls include a late sectarian commentary on the book of Habakkuk which omits the prayer (ch. 3) altogether. This bit of evidence fits well with the theory of those who regard chapter 3 as a late and secondary addition to the original work, but it by no means proves the case.[12] The prayer (which is actually a theophanic psalm) differs from the first two chapters in its appended liturgical directions, indicating its use as a cultic hymn. An argument for its placement here by the prophet himself, however, is its close connection with the promised vision of 2:1–3.[13] Quite possibly it is itself the vision referred to.

Much of the problem of interpreting the book's message centers on the dialogue between the prophet and Yahweh (1:2–2:5). Without any rearrangement of the material, we find a two-cycle speech pattern consisting of the prophet's complaints and Yahweh's responses, as follows:

---

[10] Paul Humbert, *Problèmes du livre d'Habacuc* (Neuchâtel, Switzerland: Neuchâtel Université, 1944); E. A. Leslie, *The Prophets Tell Their Own Story* (Nashville, TN: Abingdon Press, 1936), pp. 204–226.

[11] The contention of Bernhard Duhm and C. C. Torrey that the "Chaldeans" of 1:6 should be emended to "Kittim" and identified with the armies of Alexander the Great (thus dating the book in 331 B.C.) has won few adherents. The Dead Sea Scroll commentary on Habakkuk supports the "Chaldeans" reading. Cf. Otto Eissfeldt, *The Old Testament, An Introduction*, pp. 419–420.

[12] Cf. Frank Cross, *The Ancient Library of Qumran and Modern Biblical Studies* (Garden City, NY: Doubleday Anchor, 1961), p. 168.

[13] Cf. especially 3:16 [b] ("I will quietly wait . . .").

1. The first cycle: 1:2–11
   a. The prophet's complaint: 1:2–4
   b. Yahweh's response: 1:5–11
2. The second cycle: 1:12–2:5
   a. The prophet's complaint: 1:12–2:1
   b. Yahweh's response: 2:2–5

The prophet's complaints concern the problem of theodicy, whereby the sovereignty and justice of God's claims upon history are challenged by the overriding presence of the world's evil. Habakkuk laments the prevalence of violence and injustice and seeks an answer to the question of why the righteous suffer and the wicked prevail.

Scholars are divided in their attempts at identifying the source of the injustice of which the prophet complains. Who are "the wicked who surround the righteous" (1:4), the "faithless men" who swallow up God's people (1:13)? The more viable proposals include the Assyrians, the Babylonians, King Jehoiakim and his party, or a combination of these. If we assume for the speeches a consecutive development of thought, as seems best, we must see in the prophet's second complaint (1:12–2:1) a reference to the Babylonians, who had already begun to replace the Assyrians as masters of the Near East (1:6). The object of the beginning complaint (1:2–4) is not so easily identified, however, since Yahweh points to Babylon as a corrective to the wickedness lamented there. Most probably, the long, hard years under Assyrian domination are in view; but, admittedly, the phrasing ("the law is slacked and justice never goes forth") allows for domestic injustices such as Jeremiah attributes to Jehoiakim's administration.

The dialogue may be reconstructed along these lines. Habakkuk regards the plight of the righteous Judeans suffering under oppression—whether of the Assyrian overlord or their own native despot—and laments the injustice of it all. Yahweh answers, assuring the prophet that he is even now raising up an agent of judgment in the "bitter and hasty" Babylonians, who will balance the scales of justice by subjecting the violent to their own brand of terror. To this point, the message is essentially that of Nahum. But the dialogue continues, setting forth Habakkuk's dissatisfaction with Yahweh's reply. Apparently unable to share Nahum's delight in the retribution accorded the wicked so long as the plight of the innocent remains unchanged, the prophet views Babylon as a part of the problem rather than its solution. One oppressor nation falls, only to be replaced by a new devastator; the suffering of the righteous continues unabated. He prepares himself, nevertheless, for a further word from Yahweh, much like one stationed on a watchtower awaiting a messenger. In Yahweh's second response, he is assured that a vision is forthcoming and is instructed to wait for it yet further. When it arrives, he is to write it down plainly upon tablets so that "he who runs may read it."

According to some interpretations, 2:4, the verse made famous by St. Paul, is "the climax of the book, the long-awaited answer."[14] This is unlikely, however, since the words follow immediately upon Yahweh's admission that the vision awaits its fulfillment and, by the prophet's timetable, will seem slow in coming. The words, moreover, do not constitute an answer to the problem of theodicy which troubles the prophet. They stand, nevertheless, at the heart of a theology of expectancy, which is Habakkuk's chief contribution to prophetic faith. Lacking the full answer which he seeks, the sensitive man is directed to a life of faithfulness, trusting in Yahweh's integrity to fulfill his promise.

> Behold, he whose soul is not
> upright in him shall fail,
> but the righteous shall live by
> his faith(fulness).

"Faithfulness" is the best rendering for the pivotal word in the text, since it (*emunah*) includes the total steadfastness of belief and action which should occupy the person who waits upon Yahweh.

4. TO BREAK DOWN AND TO BUILD: JEREMIAH

In the eighteenth year of his reign (622 B.C.)[15] Josiah began the sweeping reforms which, by Deuteronomic standards, were to make his administration the most illustrious in the history of the southern kingdom. The reformation, as Albright has remarked, was one response to the widespread uneasiness and antiquarian interests that pervaded the Near East during the Assyro-Babylonian period.[16] The book of law discovered in the temple in 622 B.C. and adopted as the program of the king's reforms represented ancient covenant tradition, purportedly derived from Moses himself. Though probably a deposit of legal norms developed under the auspices of a northern shrine and later made the core of the book of Deuteronomy, the prescriptions bore the authoritative ring of authentic covenant faith and lent themselves naturally to the ceremony of covenant renewal in which Josiah read them before the people assembled in Jerusalem.[17] Thus rediscovered and promoted as a return to Mosaic Torah, they offered an an-

---

[14] Charles L. Taylor, Jr., "The Book of Habakkuk," *IB*, Vol. VI, p. 988.

[15] The Chronicler's reference to reform measures as early as Josiah's twelfth year (629/628) is not to be discounted (cf. W. A. L. Elmslie, "I–II Chronicles," *IB*, Vol. III, pp. 537–539); but in all likelihood these did not reach widespread proportions until the discovery of the law book in 622.

[16] *From the Stone Age to Christianity*, pp. 314–319. Cf. also John Bright, *A History of Israel*, pp. 297–298.

[17] II Kings 23:1–3; II Chron. 34:29–32.

tidote for the insecurities of the age, even as they revived nationalistic hopes for a reunited and independent Israel.

The religious aspects of the reformation captured the major attention of the biblical historians.[18] Pagan altars and images admitted to the temple in the days of Ahaz and Manasseh were demolished; fertility priests, cult prostitutes, and astrologers were banished or put to death; and, in keeping with the law of the one altar, all the high places outside Jerusalem—both in Judah and northern Palestine—were shut down.[19] Priests at the local shrines either transferred to Jerusalem and became secondary members of the temple staff or else ceased functioning altogether. For many, apparently, the latter alternative proved the more feasible. The first Passover observed in accordance with the new law offered the occasion for an impressive cultic celebration of the reforms.[20]

Viewed from its political side, the reformation amounted to a virtual declaration of independence from foreign control. Like Hezekiah before him, Josiah sought through religious reforms the recovery of both a purified cult and a free nation. That his programs were more thorough and far-reaching than those of the earlier king was owing in no small part to the more favorable international conditions, namely the waning strength of Assyria and its near withdrawal from Palestinian affairs. Judah, in fact, achieved a brief independence during the Josiah years and came closer to restoring the former kingdom of David than at any time during the long, oppressive Assyro-Babylonian period. Not only were the rejection of pagan influences and the centralization of religious authority in Jerusalem designed, in part, to unify Judah politically and encourage national pride, but the bold assertion of jurisdiction over the religious affairs of the north initiated a program aimed at eventual reunification of north and south.[21]

Although certain of the reformation's principles were destined to endure in Judaic faith and practice, the reform as such was short-lived. That it was not lacking in theological deficiencies can be determined from a careful reading of the late oracles of Jeremiah. Its overly confident premise, for example, that faithfulness to the covenant assured the nation success, offered no explanation for Josiah's defeat and untimely death at Megiddo in 609 B.C.[22] Judah's failure to achieve lasting political freedom, however, resulted not so much from the ineffectiveness of the reforms as from the un-

---

[18] II Kings 22:3–23:25; II Chron. 34:1–35:19.

[19] The temple at Arad was apparently destroyed at this time. That sacrifice ceased there at an earlier date (perhaps during Hezekiah's reign) is attested by the absence of an altar during the last stage of the sanctuary's existence. See Yohanan Aharoni, "The Israelite Sanctuary at Arad," New Directions in Biblical Archaeology, D. N. Freedman and J. C. Greenfield, eds., pp. 25–39.

[20] II Chron. 35:1–19.

[21] II Kings 23:15–20; II Chron. 34:6–7, 9; 35:18.

[22] See Stanley B. Frost, "The Death of Josiah: A Conspiracy of Silence," JBL, LXXXVII (Dec. 1968), pp. 369–392.

avoidable turn of events in international history. Briefly Egypt (609–605 B.C.), then Babylon (605–539 B.C.), arose to take Assyria's former role as Judah's overlord.

Jehoiakim (609–598 B.C.) proved to be as lacking in his father's virtues as the earlier Manasseh had been unlike his father Hezekiah. Thoroughly despotic, he expended his energies on palace rebuilding and allowed the reforms to languish, if not lapse altogether.[23] Unable to resist Nebuchadrezzar's takeover of Syria and Palestine following the battle of Carchemish, he became an unwilling vassal of Babylon. When Nebuchadrezzar failed, however, in an effort to bring Egypt into his empire, Jehoiakim miscalculated Babylon's actual strength and withheld tribute. Before the Babylonian army reached Jerusalem to suppress the rebellion (Dec. 598 B.C.) Jehoiakim died, leaving his son Jehoiachin to bear the consequences.

After a three-month siege, Nebuchadrezzar's forces entered the city (Mar. 597 B.C.) and took captive the young king. Along with a contingent of his subjects,[24] Jehoiachin was taken into Babylonian exile, where he lived out the remainder of his life. Replaced on the throne by his uncle Zedekiah (597–587 B.C.), the last of Josiah's sons, the exiled king remained, nevertheless, in both Judah's and Babylon's eyes the true heir to the throne. His name appears in a Babylonian rations list (dated 592 B.C.) as "Yaukin (Jehoiachin), King of Judah," and on Palestinian jar handles from the same period as the rightful administrator of crown properties in Judah.[25] For many years, apparently, he was the object of wistful hopes of those Judeans who anticipated both his return to the throne and the restoration of Judah's independence.[26] Neither of these dreams, however, was to be realized.

Zedekiah, being little more than a regent for Jehoiachin and Babylon's puppet, could have best served his nation in just that role, namely, as a submissive vassal, securing for his people whatever advantages he could cajole from the empire which was far too powerful for his resistance. Apparently he would have followed such a course had he not been too weak to withstand the irrational surge of nationalism that swept Judah during his period. An inept and vacillating leader, he sought the sane counsel of Jeremiah but lacked the ability to implement it in the face of a strong court faction bent on rebellion. In 589 B.C., in expectation of Egyptian assistance, he joined Ammon and Tyre in open resistance to Babylon.

By January 588 B.C., Nebuchadrezzar's armies were once more on Palestinian soil, and Jerusalem was again placed under siege. While Jerusalem held on, one by one the surrounding towns fell before the Babylonians.

---

[23] Jer. 22:13–19.

[24] In II Kings 24:14 the number of those deported is cited as 10,000; in Jer. 52:28 it is 3,023.

[25] G. Ernest Wright, *Biblical Archaeology*, pp. 122–124; *ANET*, p. 308 (*ANE*, p. 205); *DOTT*, pp. 84–86.

[26] Jer. 28:4.

Ostracon from Lachish, one of the Lachish Letters, depicting conditions in Judah during the invasion of Nebuchadrezzar (588–587 B.C.) (Courtesy of the Trustees of the British Museum.)

Vivid evidence of the holocausts has been uncovered in the debris of such sites as Lachish and Debir.[27] Also, at Lachish were found twenty-one broken ostraca (inscribed potsherds), some of which were communications sent to the commander of the Judean forces there from a sentry located at a nearby outpost.[28] The latter, watching for the fire signals from the besieged towns, seems to have written just after the fall of Azekah, whose signals he could no longer make out, and shortly before the capture of Lachish itself. In one of the letters he writes:

> And let (my lord) know that we are watching for the signals of Lachish, according to all the indications which my lord hath given, for we cannot see Azekah.[29]

The arrival of an Egyptian army, sent by Pharaoh Hophra to relieve Jerusalem, resulted in a brief lifting of the siege. Remembering the miracu-

---

[27] Cf. G. Ernest Wright, *Biblical Archaeology*, pp. 121–126; "Judean Lachish," *BA*, XVIII (1955), pp. 9–17 (reprinted in *BA Reader*, 2, pp. 301–309); Kathleen Kenyon, *Archaeology in the Holy Land* (New York: Praeger Publishers, Inc., 1966), pp. 291–296.

[28] *DOTT*, pp. 212–217; *ANET*, pp. 321–322 (*ANE*, pp. 212–214).

[29] *ANET*, p. 32 (*ANE*, p. 213).

lous deliverance of the city in the days of Hezekiah, the hopes of Jerusalem's distraught citizens soared high. There was to be no repetition of the earlier event, however; the Egyptian forces were quickly driven back to their land and the siege of Jerusalem resumed. In July 587 B.C., with the city on the brink of starvation, Nebuchadrezzar's forces breached the walls. Zedekiah's soldiers slipped him out of the doomed city, but failed to make good his escape. Captured near Jericho, he was taken to Nebuchadrezzar's camp at Riblah, in Syria, where he was forced to witness the slaughter of his sons before having his own eyes gouged out. Thus blinded and in chains, the last of Judah's kings was taken away to Babylon.

Nebuchadrezzar, having lost all patience with Jerusalem, put the city to the torch. The palace, temple, and all significant buildings were burned and the city walls demolished. Once again, the best equipped of the survivors were taken to Babylon, leaving "the poorest of the land to be vinedressers and plowmen." [30] Judah, already reduced in size to a fraction of its former glory, became a Babylonian province administered by a native governor, Gedaliah (587–? B.C.). The son of a respected adviser to King Josiah, and experienced through service in Zedekiah's cabinet, Gedaliah advocated full cooperation with Babylon. He would doubtless have brought peace to the troubled land had he not become the early victim of an assassination plot led by Ishmael, a disgruntled member of the royal house. The date of the assassination, and thus the length of Gedaliah's administration, are not known. In 582 B.C., Babylon instituted reprisals, deporting yet a third group of Judeans and, apparently at that time, incorporating the land into the neighboring province of Samaria.

A Prophet to the Nations

Much of what is known about the last days of Judah, particularly in respect to the troubled events within Jerusalem, derives from the book of Jeremiah. Like no other personality of his generation, the so-called "weeping prophet" reflects both the mood of despair that accompanied Judah's end and the painful first efforts to plot a course for the covenant people's future. His was the difficult mission of exposing the false promises of those who refused to face the imminent disaster and, once it had befallen, arousing hope for a new era in the covenant history. This dual role was stressed in Yahweh's call which came to him as a youth.

> See, I have set you this day over nations and over kingdoms,
>   to pluck up and to break down,
>   to destroy and to overthrow,
>   to build and to plant.
>
> 1:10

---

[30] II Kings 25:12. The number of deportees is cited as 832 in Jer. 52:29.

We possess more biographical data on Jeremiah than on any other prophet. Included are a number of personal laments or "confessions" which allow us a view of the inner life of a prophet as do no other prophetic materials in the Old Testament. According to the superscription to the book, his career began in the thirteenth year of Josiah's reign (627 B.C.) and extended through the destruction of Jerusalem (587 B.C.), a total of forty years. Born into a priestly family of the village of Anathoth, just two miles northeast of Jerusalem, he was at home within the city itself and was imprisoned there during the Babylonian siege. Like Isaiah, he had intermittent and predominantly unhappy encounters with the reigning monarchs. A devoted follower and secretary named Baruch recorded his prophecies and, most probably, wrote his memoirs. Following a long, turbulent, and faithful career, the prophet was at last taken against his will into Egypt by a group of Judeans fleeing Nebuchadrezzar's reprisals for the assassination of Gedeliah.

The Book

As in our study of Isaiah, so too in approaching the lengthy and complex book of Jeremiah we must attempt to set the prophet's message within the historical sequence of events during his period. Such an effort involves no slight degree of conjecture on our part, since chronological interests have not consistently guided the development of the book's format, nor can we always determine the date of a passage from internal evidence alone. Most of the biographical narratives, nevertheless, are assigned to the reign of this or that king, and there is a rough approximation of chronological order in the first major collection of the prophet's words (chs. 1–25).

As noted long ago by Bernhard Duhm, the book consists of three types of materials: (1) poetic oracles, (2) biographical prose, and (3) prose discourses.[31] The materials of each type are not consistently grouped together, but appear throughout the various parts of the book. The first two types provide interpreters with fewer problems than does the third. There is broad agreement that the poetic oracles, cast in the first person, were largely composed by Jeremiah himself. Most of the exceptions are found in the foreign oracles of chapters 46–51, some of which are undeniably secondary. The biographical narratives represent the authentic memoirs of a biographer who stood in close relationship to the prophet, the most likely candidate being the secretary Baruch.

The prose discourses, cast in a stereotyped, wordy, and rhetorical style

---

[31] *Das Buch Jeremia* (Tübingen, West Germany: J. C. B. Mohr, 1901), pp. XI–XX. Sigmund Mowinckel popularized the designations A, B, and C for the three types, respectively (*Zur Komposition des Buches Jeremia* [Oslo: J. Dybwad, 1914]). Cf. John Bright, *Jeremiah*, Vol. 21, *The Anchor Bible* (Garden City, NY: Doubleday & Company, Inc., 1965), pp. LV–LXXXV, for an excellent survey of the literary structure of the book.

closely akin to that of Deuteronomy, comprise roughly a quarter of the total book.[32] Although some interpreters regard all material of this genre as the Exilic or post-Exilic additions of a school of Deuteronomists and discount its historical value, these are hardly necessary conclusions. Bright has pointed out the fine peculiarities of the style as distinguished from that of the Deuteronomists, and holds it to be a characteristic rhetorical prose of the seventh and sixth centuries.[33] The prose discourses are to be dated somewhat later than the poetic oracles, however, and as a rule represent the gist of the prophet's thought as remembered within the circle of his followers, rather than his verbatim words.

The book as we have it is a collection of collections, each one of which underwent expansions at the hands of the prophet's circle of followers. Its broad outline consists of the following units.

1. Prophecies against Jerusalem and Judah: chs. 1–25
   a. Largely from Josiah's period: chs. 1–6
   b. Largely from Jehoiakim's period: chs. 7–20
   c. Largely from Zedekiah's period: chs. 21–25
2. Biographical narratives (Baruch's memoirs): chs. 26–45
   (Including "The Book of Consolation," chs. 30–33)
3. Prophecies against foreign nations: chs. 46–51
4. Historical appendix (II Kings 24:18–25:30): ch. 52

From a revealing story in chapter 36, we learn that in 605 B.C. the prophet dictated his early oracles to Baruch, who recorded them on a scroll. When the oracles were read before King Jehoiakim, as he sat before the brazier in his winter palace, the haughty monarch expressed his displeasure by cutting up the scroll with his penknife and tossing it bit by bit into the fire. Thus was lost for a time the oracles of the prophet remembered from the first twenty-two years of his ministry. Not to be outdone, Jeremiah dictated another scroll, containing the words of the original scroll plus additional oracles. This second enlarged scroll became the nucleus of the book as we know it, and is found together with the expansions of later disciples in chapters 1–25 (1).[34] These chapters, it will be noted, consist of poetic oracles and prose discourses and are recorded, with few exceptions, in the first person. Their chronological arrangement as suggested in the above outline is at best a broad and partial one.

Chapters 26–45 (2) consist chiefly of biographical narratives in the third

[32] Cf. as typical examples chs. 7 and 11:1–17.

[33] John Bright, "The Date of the Prose Sermons of Jeremiah," *JBL*, LXX (1951), pp. 15–35. Cf. also W. L. Holladay, "Prototype and Copies: A New Approach to the Poetry-Prose Problem in the Book of Jeremiah," *JBL*, LXXIX (1960), pp. 351–367.

[34] Note especially 25:1–13, which appears to have concluded the prophet's original scroll.

person, although most of the accounts embody words attributed to the prophet himself and occasionally underlying autobiographical material may be detected. Chapters 30 and 31 constitute a separate oracle and discourse unit and, since together with chapters 32 and 33 they contain most of the hopeful message of Jeremiah, all four of the chapters have come to be known as "The Book of Consolation." In the Septuagint version the foreign oracles, chapters 46–51 (3), are inserted between units 1 (chs. 1–25) and 2 (chs. 26–45), which is good evidence that each of these three major portions of the book once circulated as an independent collection. The historical appendix (ch. 52), similar to the historical additions to "First" Isaiah, is largely a duplicate of the II Kings account of the fall of Jerusalem (II Kings 24:18–25:30).

In no Old Testament book do the Septuagint and Masoretic texts diverge more widely than in Jeremiah. These differences consist not so much in contradictory readings as in the arrangement and length of the material. The difference in arrangement extends both to the transposition of the broad units 2 and 3, as just noted, and to the sequence of the individual oracles within unit 3. The entire Septuagint text is shorter by about one eighth than the Masoretic text, the omissions consisting of single words, phrases, and passages here and there throughout the book. It is now clear from the Qumran discoveries, where examples of both the longer and shorter forms of the text have appeared, that the two textual traditions are to be traced back to early Hebrew recensions.[35]

In the Days of Josiah

If Jeremiah's call to prophesy came in the thirteenth year of Josiah's reign (627 B.C.), as the superscription to the book asserts, then no fewer than eighteen years of the prophet's career fell within the Josiah era. That this could have been the case is vigorously denied by some scholars, chiefly on the grounds that few if any of his oracles can be definitely shown to date from this period. Of particular concern is the lack of clear references to Josiah's reforms, so much so that the debate continues as to whether Jeremiah favored or opposed them. The common tendency to regard the prophet's early years as a "silent period" is less than convincing to those who feel that this is to picture him as an "inept and naïve person who took eighteen years to find himself but suddenly did so with startling self-assurance after Josiah's death."[36]

Gordon, Bardtke, and, more recently, Gottwald get past the problem by emending the superscription to read "twenty-third year of Josiah" rather

---

[35] Cf. Frank Cross, *The Ancient Library of Qumran and Modern Biblical Studies*, ch. IV, especially pp. 186–187.
[36] Norman K. Gottwald, *All the Kingdoms of the Earth* (New York: Harper & Row, Publishers, 1964), p. 241.

than "thirteenth year."[37] This moves the date of the prophet's call down to 617 B.C., long after the reformation had become established policy and consequently when there was no necessity for his taking a vocal position in respect to it. Hyatt would remove the adult prophet entirely from the Josiah period by taking the "thirteenth year" in reference to the prophet's birth rather than his call.[38] By this theory Jeremiah would have been barely old enough to have begun prophesying by the beginning of Jehoiakim's reign.

From our own perspective, the tradition that associates the prophet with Josiah's reign, whether in the early or later phase, appears too well established to be discounted altogether. Other passages in addition to the superscription attest that he prophesied that early (3:6; 25:3), and much of the material in chapters 1–6, though subjected to the prophet's own later revision, fits best into that period.[39]

JEREMIAH AND THE REFORMATION. For a number of reasons it is to be assumed that Jeremiah initially supported Josiah's reforms. In the first place, the reformation was directed against pagan abuses within the cult which Jeremiah and the classical prophets as a whole consistently opposed. The prophet's strong attack on idolatry in the early chapters of the book would suit the period just prior to the climactic phase of the reform (before 622 B.C.) and possibly even served to influence the king. Again, covenant and law—watchwords of the reformation—center prominently in Jeremiah's message, even when the necessary allowances have been made for the later Deuteronomic-like phrasing of the prose discourses.[40] His hope for the restoration of northern Israel, moreover, conceivably was encouraged by Josiah's intervention in northern affairs.

What is more, we know of Jeremiah's high appraisal of Josiah (22:15–16) and of the manner in which the prophet was befriended by the family of Shaphan, an official of Josiah's court.[41] Finally, if Jeremiah endorsed the reforms in any active manner whatsoever, that would provide a most logical explanation for the alienation of his priestly family at Anathoth (11:21; 12:6). As persons whose livelihood was threatened by Josiah's closing of the local shrine, they almost surely opposed the reformation and those connected with it.

[37] Ibid., pp. 241–242.
[38] J. Philip Hyatt, "Jeremiah," IB, Vol. V, pp. 779–780, 797–798.
[39] Not only does the location (ch. 7) of the prophet's sermon at the beginning of Jehoiakim's reign point in this direction, but cf. the reference to Assyria as a world power in 2:18. Some of the oracles in this section, nevertheless, have undergone later revision—most likely by the prophet himself (cf. 2:16, which alludes to Egypt's brief take-over of Judah in 609). See further Bright's commentary on these chapters (Jeremiah, Vol. 21, The Anchor Bible).
[40] Cf. especially 11:1–8, which is taken by some interpreters as dating from the period of the reformation and as representative of the prophet's appeal for its support.
[41] Jer. 26:24; 36:10; 39:14. Cf. II Kings 22:3ff; II Chron. 34:15ff.

Perhaps the most serious doubts regarding the prophet's approval of the reforms concern the less-than-hopeful tone of his early oracles and the distrustful view of external codes found in his later prophecy of the "new covenant." It is hardly necessary, however, to assume that his enthusiasm for Josiah's program was so unbounded as to have blinded him either to the severity of Judah's internal problems or to the limitations of externally imposed covenants. Just as the earlier prophets had joined appeals for reform with visions of doom, so too in the message of Jeremiah one should not be surprised to find, from the very beginning, oracles of judgment and threat. In due time, furthermore, such confidence as he had in the effectiveness of the reformation almost surely was dissipated in the face of its undeniable failure in bringing the necessary changes. Ultimately, therefore, his most telling witness was to the total inadequacy of any reformatory efforts save those that begin with the renewal of man's inner being.

THE FOE FROM THE NORTH. A further question related to the prophet's early preaching concerns the identity of the foe from the north. Apparently quite soon after his call, though not necessarily in conjunction with it, there came the visions of the almond tree and the boiling pot (1:11–16), the latter warning of an unnamed terror about to break forth out of the north. The early-blooming almond tree ("the watcher," *shaked*) served as a reminder that Yahweh was "watching" (*shoked*) over the world scene to assure the fulfillment of his word; and the boiling pot, whose scalding contents should inundate the lands to the south, betokened an invasion by some overwhelming northern power. Such warnings continue in ominous portrayals of the onslaught of armies; the raising of alarm signals, first from Dan, then Ephraim and Benjamin; and the siege and destruction of cities.[42] The prophet's vision of the devastated land approaches the wasteland imagery of apocalyptic:

> I looked, and lo, there was no man,
>   and all the birds of the air had fled.
> I looked, and lo, the fruitful land was a desert,
>   and all its cities were laid in ruins
>   before the Lord, before his fierce anger.
>   4:25–26

Only if these warnings are as late as the concluding years of Josiah's reign is it very probable that the prophet initially envisioned Babylon as the foe. Older scholars inclined toward the view that he spoke of the Scythians, who, if we follow Herodotus' report, swept down the Mediterranean coast to Egypt in the period 630–624 B.C. Scythian armies did not normally besiege cities, however, and the devastation portrayed by Jeremiah far

---

[42] Cf. 4:5–31; 5:14–17; 6:1–26; 8:16; 10:22.

exceeds the actual impact, if any, which those people made upon Palestine. The prophet need not have had a specific nation in view when he first issued the warnings; but in due time—certainly by the time of the first public reading of his scroll (605 B.C.)—it became evident that the threatening power was none other than Babylon.

JUDAH'S INFIDELITY. Jeremiah's northern background—Anathoth was located in the older tribal territory of Benjamin—may explain the dominant influence of Mosaic covenant tradition upon his thinking and the virtual absence of the Davidic-Zion theology popular within Jerusalem circles. His message from beginning to end builds upon the Exodus faith; and the manner of its expression is clearly dependent upon the northern prophet Hosea. The faithfulness of Yahweh in guiding his people out of Egypt and into the land of promise; the early devotion of Israel as Yahweh's bride; the subsequent harlotry of the people in turning from Yahweh and pursuing the Baals; Yahweh's divorce of the faithless bride, but without abandoning all hope for her restoration; in all these respects, together with an impressive amount of common phraseology, Jeremiah's prophecies resemble those of Hosea.[43]

Jeremiah created, as well, his own unique themes and vivid figures of speech. Yahweh, he announced, was a "fountain of living waters" for which his foolish people had substituted broken cisterns which could hold no water (2:13). Idolatrous Israel had become "a restive young camel" (2:23), "a wild ass . . . in her heat sniffing the wind" (2:24), an ox that had broken its yoke (2:20). Israel and Judah were like sister harlots (3:6–11). When Yahweh divorced Israel for her adultery, Judah should have learned her lesson, but she did not. Yahweh's verdict was:

Faithless Israel has shown herself less guilty than false Judah.
3:11

Along with the forebodings of coming judgment and the condemnation of the prevailing paganism, Jeremiah's proclamations struck deep into the heart of the ethical and moral life of his people. If Josiah's reforms checked for a time his warnings of invasion and reproof of cultic abuses, it does not necessarily follow that he withheld for a moment his demand for fair and just dealing among Judah's citizens nor his attack upon a worship based solely on externals. Cultic purification, he insisted in true prophetic form, is meaningless apart from repentance and cleansing of the heart.

Circumcise yourselves to the Lord,
remove the foreskin of your hearts,
O men of Judah and inhabitants of Jerusalem.
4:4

[43] Cf. especially chs. 2–3.

Such was the mission of the prophet. Yahweh had chosen him, indeed predestined him as an assayer of the religious life of his people (6:27–30). Against his own will, he knew himself delegated to test the faithfulness of Judah, after the manner of the metallurgist separating the alloy from the pure ore. He had been set apart as "a fortified city, an iron pillar, and bronze walls, against the whole land, against the kings of Judah, its princes, its priests, and the people of the land" (1:18). For such a formidable assignment, the young prophet had the assurance of Yahweh, "I am with you" (1:8).

In the Days of Jehoiakim

In view of Jeremiah's respect for Josiah, it is beyond question that the king's death at Megiddo brought him personal grief. In the prophet's only extant reference to the tragedy, however, he counsels tears not for the dead king, but for the unfortunate Jehoahaz (Shallum), who was immediately exiled by Necho (22:10–12). Jeremiah had only bitter words for Jehoahaz's replacement, Jehoiakim (22:13–19). Possibly Jehoiakim's ineptness had caused his own people to bypass him in favor of his younger brother. At any rate, he early proved himself to be a greedy tyrant by spending lavish sums on a new palace built with forced labor. His contempt for the prophetic message as declared by Jeremiah was noted in the story of the destruction of the prophet's scroll. Jeremiah minced no words in depicting the king's dishonest, despotic, and violent character, nor in predicting for him a shameful end and "the burial of an ass."

THE TEMPLE SERMON. Near the beginning of Jehoiakim's reign, Jeremiah delivered the famous Temple Sermon for which we have both the text in 7:1–15 and a narrative version in chapter 26. Standing in the temple court, the prophet issued a ringing summons:

> Thus says the Lord of hosts, the God of Israel, Amend your ways and your doings, and I will let you dwell in this place. Do not trust in these deceptive words: "This is the temple of the Lord, the temple of the Lord, the temple of the Lord."
>
> 7:3–4

He charges his hearers with both idolatry and violations of the moral law, which may reflect the new wave of apostasy ushered in with Jehoiakim. The more specific thrust of the prophet's attack, however, is directed against a naïve and hypocritical dependence upon the temple—a fault for which the despotic king can hardly share all the blame. The Deuteronomic reform's emphasis on the temple had doubtless heightened the popular belief in its inviolability. It had become for its most ardent supporters a veritable "robber's den," a hide-out to which violaters of Yahweh's law could retreat, persuaded by their perfunctory chants—"This is the temple of the Lord, the temple of the Lord, the temple of the Lord"—that inde-structible Zion would protect them from any accounting for their guilty deeds. The prophet's charges thus bespeak the bankruptcy of the reforma-tion and the deterioration of its deepest principles at the hands of those who looked only to its external demands and unconditional promises.

Jeremiah found in the example of Shiloh, the early Israelite shrine de-stroyed by the Philistines, the destiny awaiting Jerusalem.

> I will do to the house which is called by my name, and in which you trust, and to the place which I gave you and your fathers, as I did to Shiloh.
>
> 7:14

Such a frontal assault on the temple, and more particularly on the popular theology, could not be tolerated by the temple hierarchy. Hearing Jere-miah's words only as blasphemous untruths, they called upon the city of-ficials to decree his death as a false prophet. Only through the intervention of Ahikam, son of Shaphan, and a group of elders who recalled Micah's predictions of the temple's destruction, did the prophet escape with his life.

THE SPOILED VESSEL. At this point, apparently, Jeremiah gave up all hope of averting the coming disaster. Regarding his people as too hardened to hear his appeals, their conversion as unlikely as the changing of the leop-ard's spots (13:23), he ceased to pray any longer for their deliverance (7:16; 14:11). That the prophet was in no sense blind to man's capacity for change nor Yahweh's readiness to honor repentance is evident in the allegory of the potter (18:1–12). If only Israel would turn, Yahweh might abandon his plans for destruction and mold the nation into a useful and worthy vessel. But his people having become unwilling clay in the potter's hand, Yahweh had abandoned his good designs for them and was now shaping evil against them, instead.

To dramatize Judah's plight and set in motion its decreed doom, the prophet assembled a group of Jerusalem's citizens at the southwestern gate of the city and smashed a pottery flask, saying:

> So will I break this people and this city, as one breaks a potter's vessel, so that it can never be mended.
>
> 19:11

His performance so aroused a temple officer named Pashhur that he had Jeremiah beaten and placed in stocks overnight.

As the prophet's castigation of popular vices and threats of destruction mounted, so too did his unpopularity within court and temple circles, until he became something of an outcast among the populace at large. By the time of the scroll incident (605 B.C.) he was no longer allowed inside the temple courts (36:5); and, following that episode, he was forced into hiding to escape Jehoiakim's wrath (36:19).

THE "CONFESSIONS". It was most likely during the Jehoiakim years that the prophet poured out his inner loneliness and despair in the series of laments interspersed between chapters 11 and 22 and popularly known as "the Confessions of Jeremiah."[44] Although there can be no certainty about the specific dates and settings of the separate poems, we may agree with John Skinner that a "psychological continuity" unites them— "that they exhibit in different aspects one great spiritual conflict which is the key to Jeremiah's inner life."[45] We may be sure, furthermore, that only the prophet himself could have composed such personal and intimate reflections on his experiences.

Quite unlike anything else within the prophetic literature, and more akin to the individual laments of the Psalter or Job, the poems may yet unveil the anguish of soul experienced by other Old Testament prophets; for it is the tension of the prophet's calling that lies at the base of his complaints. In emotional and cathartic outbursts, he denies any personal satisfaction in his role as a preacher of doom. It was not as if he had taken delight in pronouncing the nation's downfall. But for that terrible mission he would not have been the rejected outcast that he was, run out of his native village by the hatred of family and former friends, unmarried and lonely, his life in jeopardy wherever he went, "a man of strife and contention to the whole land" (15:10).

But, having accepted the role Yahweh had given him as the "iron pillar and bronze walls" within the tottering and hostile society, he found himself utterly dependent upon Yahweh's support. Both his own integrity and that of Yahweh were at stake. His opponents, seemingly justified in their rejection of his warnings, taunted and persecuted him; and no harm befell them. The "Confessions" represent the prophet's cry for help and search for understanding. Similar to Habakkuk, but with greater emotional intensity and personal involvement, he questions why the wicked should be given free rein over their innocent victims (12:1–4, 18:20). In words approaching blasphemy, he likens Yahweh to a deceitful wadi (dry stream bed) that runs with no refreshing streams (15:18) and accuses him of failing to keep his promise, leaving the prophet exposed to his enemies as "a gentle lamb led to the slaughter" (11:19). It is in a vituperative and vengeful mood, that he petitions Yahweh to turn the tables on his persecutors and bring on the decreed destruction.[46]

---

[44] Although there are many brief utterances in the book which bear a confessional character, the passages most generally accorded the title "Confessions" are 11:18–12:6; 15:10–21; 17:14–18; 18:18–23; 20:7–13, 14–18. Sometimes 10:23–24 and 17:9–10 are included.

[45] *Prophecy and Religion*, p. 210.

[46] 11:20; 12:3; 15:15; 17:18; 18:21–23; 20:12.

Two of the laments take the form of a dialogue in which Yahweh responds to Jeremiah's complaints (11:18–12:6, 15:10–21). Here, as elsewhere in the poems, their dialectical character is evident, as the prophet juxtaposes doubt and faith. Yahweh promises no immediate relief, but reassures him that in good time he will deliver him from his oppressors. Jeremiah thus shows himself, in spite of his darkest doubts, capable of trusting Yahweh to perform his word. But, perhaps in an even more profound manner, he confesses that Yahweh's word has become such an integral part of his being that to fail to utter it would be unthinkable.

> If I say, "I will not mention him
>   or speak any more in his name,"
> there is in my heart as it were a burning fire
>   shut up in my bones,
> and I am weary with holding it in,
>   and I cannot.
>
> 20:9

Thus captive to God's word, he becomes as no other prophet the very incarnation of the elect people of Yahweh. Even in his resistance to his mission, he testifies mightily to the compelling claims of Yahweh upon his total existence; and, notwithstanding rejection by his own people and the human longing for vengeance, the nation's suffering becomes his own.

When Jehoiakim's folly precipitated the Babylonian invasion of 598/97 B.C., the last person to take delight in Judah's plight was Jeremiah. In an oracle (10:17–22) presumably from that year, he exposes his personal grief at Jerusalem's siege—as real for the prophet as bodily pain:

> Woe is me because of my hurt!
> My wound is grievous.
>
> 10:19

Moved to tears by the sight of young Jehoiachin being led away captive to Babylon (15:18ff.), Jeremiah nevertheless rejected the naïve idealism that predicted his quick return to reclaim the throne. Neither Jehoiachin nor any of his descendants, said the prophet, would ever again reign from Jerusalem (22:24–30). And so it was.

In the Days of Zedekiah

Strangely enough, the failure of Jehoiakim's revolt did not silence for long the clamor for independence on the part of Judah's superpatriots. Perhaps Nebuchadrezzar's leniency with Jerusalem only strengthened their conviction that Yahweh would never allow the city's fall. At any rate, the weak Zedekiah was helpless before the pressure they exerted upon him; and Jeremiah, continuing to view Judah's internal condition as hopeless, turned his attention to the Hebrew exiles in Babylon. In the prophet's

Babylonian tablet containing the account of the conquest of Jerusalem by Nebuchadrezzar in 597 B.C. (Courtesy of the Trustees of the British Museum.)

eyes, it was this group that held the promise of Israel's future in their hands. Selected by Nebuchadrezzar for their superior training and skills, they included among them stalwart pillars of faith capable of a positive response to the demands of the times. Jeremiah likened them to "good figs" in contrast to the worthless culls—the "bad figs"—left in the land (ch. 24).

In a letter to the exiles (29:1–23), the prophet encouraged them to "build houses and live in them: plant gardens and eat their produce," and to "take wives and have sons and daughters," always seeking the welfare of the new land which was now their home. Thus would they assure both their own survival and that of the Israel of the future. The prophet entertained the hope that in seventy years a return would be possible.

> For I know the plans I have for you, says the Lord, plans for welfare and not for evil, to give you a future and a hope.
> 29:11

THE FALL OF JERUSALEM. Early in Zedekiah's reign new conspiracies began among Babylon's vassals. Convinced of the hopelessness of such revolts, and equally certain that Yahweh was presently using Babylon as an agent to effect his purposes, Jeremiah's consistent counsel to Zedekiah and the rulers of neighboring states was this:

> Bring your necks under the yoke of the king of Babylon, and serve him and his people, and live.
>
> 27:12

To symbolize this message, he fashioned a wooden yoke and wore it on his neck (ch. 27). When the yoke was removed and broken to pieces by a prophet named Hananiah, the latter predicting total restoration of Jehoiachin and the exiles within two years, Jeremiah replaced the wooden yoke with a yoke of iron (ch. 28).

Jeremiah was neither pro-Babylonian in his sympathies nor a Babylonian collaborator, as his prophecies of Babylon's ultimate ruin clearly show.[47] To his contemporaries, however, he appeared as nothing less than a traitor. When Zedekiah's participation in the revolt of 589 B.C. brought in the army of Nebuchadrezzar, followed by the one and one-half year siege of Jerusalem, the all-out war effort by the citizens of the besieged city received no support from Jeremiah. His counsel remained unchanged: surrender to the superior force of Babylon.[48] As a result, there was no more hated figure in Jerusalem; and the wonder is that he escaped with his life.

When the approach of Hophra's army brought a temporary lifting of the siege, Jeremiah was quick to squelch the unwarranted enthusiasm that reigned in the city (37:6–10). In but a little while, he warned, the Babylonians would return. He likewise berated the "foxhole" religious tactics of slaveowners who, having previously released their Hebrew slaves in a feverish effort to comply with covenant law, took them back again once the threat to the city appeared less ominous (34:8–22).

At the time of the lifting of the siege the prophet attempted to leave the city on business—to settle a land transaction at Anathoth (37:11ff.). Interpreting his action as a treasonous desertion, a group within the court persuaded Zedekiah to imprison the prophet so that he might no longer "weaken the hands" of the war effort. Though confined in the court of the guard and placed for a time in a miry cistern, the prophet's voice was never completely stilled. He continued to offer his counsel to any who would hear and especially to Zedekiah, who sought privately the word of deliverance that never came.

When the city finally fell, Jeremiah refused Nebuchadrezzar's offer to go

---

[47] 25:12–14, 26; 27:10. The oracles against Babylon in chs. 50–51 may contain some of Jeremiah's own words, but in their present form represent the expression of the later circle of the prophet's followers. The narrative describing the scroll of judgments dispatched to Babylon (51:59–64), however, may be authentic. Norman Gottwald discusses the details of the prophet's attitude toward Babylon in *All the Kingdoms of the Earth*, pp. 239–302.

[48] 21:1–10; 32:1–5; 33:1–5; 34:1–22; 37:16–38:28.

to Babylon, choosing instead to remain with Gedeliah and his remnant administration at Mizpah.[49] Gedeliah, perhaps under Jeremiah's influence, advised his people to "dwell in the land, and serve the king of Babylon, and it will be well with you" (40:9). But, in spite of everything, a small group of hotheads refused to submit. When Ishmael and his band of conspirators assassinated the governor and his entourage and escaped across the Jordan to Ammon, the people remaining in the land, fearful of being held responsible for the deed, sought Jeremiah's counsel. The prophet, after ten days, received a word from Yahweh advising them to stand their ground and not to flee the land. In open contempt of the prophet's advice, they fled instead to Egypt, taking the captive prophet with them. The final picture we have of the aged Jeremiah depicts him still active among the refugees at Tapahanes, prophesying Egypt's invasion by Babylon and the doom of the Jewish colony there.

The "Book of Consolation"

Surely there is no more tragic figure among the Hebrew prophets than Jeremiah. The trying times in which he lived, his sensitive and uncompromising character, the divine compulsion to speak out, and his almost total rejection by his people—such were the circumstances which coalesced to produce his anguished career. The "weeping prophet" label, nevertheless, is at best a caricature. For Jeremiah's labor "to build and to plant" is as authentic and intrinsic an element of his ministry as the spate of threats and laments which fill his book. We have already noted the optimism reflected in his letter to the first group of exiles.

Most of the prophet's hopeful words are contained in the so-called "Book of Consolation" (chs. 30–33). Introduced with a superscription promising Yahweh's restoration of Israel and Judah, these chapters consist of oracles, discourses, and narratives, representing both early and late phases of the prophet's career. There is evidence of considerable editing, presumably by the prophet himself as well as later followers. Words of promise directed to the northern kingdom in Josiah's day are joined with the later reassurances offered Judah's exiles; and some original oracles of doom have been converted into words of hope (cf. 30:12–17).

Notably absent from Jeremiah's promises, except in passages of disputed authorship,[50] are the messianic and Zion themes featured so prominently in Isaiah's future prophecies. The greater preoccupation of Jeremiah's thinking centered on the problem of why Israel had failed so miserably in

---

[49] 39:11ff. The record of events from the fall of Jerusalem through the flight of the band of Judeans following Gedeliah's assassination is found in chs. 39–45.

[50] 3:15–18; 23:5–6; 30:9; 33:14–26. Gottwald judiciously concludes that "room must be allowed in Jeremiah's outlook for a civil leader of some authority, whether of the Davidic line or not" (*All the Kingdoms of the Earth*, p. 296), but proposes that a king of chastened and limited powers and aspirations (30:21) is the key to his expectations (ibid.).

her covenant obligations and what could be done for a people that showed themselves repeatedly incapable of a constant affection for Yahweh's good purposes. The difficulty, he had come to believe, was essentially one of the stubborn human will.

> The heart is deceitful above all things
> and desperately corrupt;
> who can understand it?
> 17:9

In the prophet's view, apparently, not even a righteous king and Zion's restoration could by themselves assure the faithfulness demanded by Yahweh of his people. He had witnessed the failure of the best of Judah's kings to stave off disaster and the inability of the cult to revitalize the nation's life. Nothing short of a renovation of heart could qualify Israel for a renewal of her covenant status; and this was what she had proved herself incapable of accomplishing. The only sufficient hope, Jeremiah concluded, was in a new act on Yahweh's part, whereby the stubborn will of man would be created anew by Yahweh himself. This, he affirmed, was what Yahweh would do. He would make a new covenant with his people which would depend, in the first instance, not upon external demands or codes, but upon an inner change of will. In effect, God's people would come to desire that which Yahweh himself desires.

> Behold the days are coming, says the Lord, when I will make a new covenant with the house of Israel and the house of Judah, not like the covenant which I made with the fathers. . . . But this is the covenant which I will make. . . . I will put my law within them, and I will write it upon their hearts. . . . And no longer shall each man teach his neighbor and each his brother saying, "Know the Lord," for they shall all know me, from the least of them to the greatest, says the Lord.
> 31:31–34

There is no finer statement of man's yearning for personal harmony of the human and divine wills than in this prophecy of the new covenant. Two words of caution are, however, needful. First, the prophet's stress on the personal dimension of religious faith does not conflict with the corporate and historical—the covenant—presuppositions of Hebrew religion. He envisions no restriction of religious experience to the individual in isolation from the group, but thinks throughout in terms of the new community of God's faithful. He speaks of the change which God will effect within the hearts of all his people. And, second, the prophet's vision is more than sheer poetic idealism. He looked for a literal return of the exiles, a rebuilding of the land, and a restoration of Israel and Judah. The hope he entertained was concrete to the degree that he could not only call upon his hearers to accept it, but was altogether willing to act upon it himself.

The latter point is made clear in an unforgettable transaction carried out

373

by the prophet during the siege of Jerusalem (ch. 32). With the city on the brink of collapse and the prophet himself imprisoned in the court of the guard, an unlikely and presumptuous offer was made by a relative named Hanamel to dispose of an ancestral estate at Anathoth. Fully aware of the imminent Babylonian take-over and, indeed, on the heels of a prophecy declaring its inevitability, Jeremiah nevertheless gathered the necessary witnesses and purchased the family property as a sign of his confidence in Judah's future.

> For thus says the Lord of Hosts, the God of Israel: Houses and fields and vineyards shall again be bought in this land.
>
> 32:15

5. ENDURING CONTRIBUTIONS OF PRE-EXILIC PROPHECY

The influence of the pre-Exilic prophets was in no small part responsible for the survival of the covenant faith through the critical period of the Exile. Having failed in their efforts to turn Israel back from its suicidal course, their witness nevertheless had prepared the nation for the worst. But for their unremitting warnings of judgment—to the point of proclaiming Zion's utter annihilation—the remnant of Judah would have hardly sustained the shock of the unprecedented collapse of every outward symbol of national and religious identity. Thus, years after their declaration, the bitter predictions of doom bore positive fruit. The shattered people could recall the unheeded oracles of Israel's finest spokesmen and assure themselves that what had befallen was no fortuitous work of fate, but Yahweh's very act of judgment upon a rebellious nation.

The prophetic insight that warned against absolutizing the traditional institutions of Hebrew life, including kingship and cult, likewise helped pave the way for a new style of life and worship that was forced to accommodate itself to the loss of the former structures. The prophets had consistently directed Israel to its ultimate commitment to Yahweh alone, had stressed his independence of human institutions—no matter how worthy—and had fervently counseled against the substitution of perfunctory ritual and chauvinistic nationalism for heart-felt religious faith and practice. Although it is doubtful that any pre-Exilic prophet went so far as to campaign for the abolition of either the cult or the monarchy, as such, these men of faith were able to perceive that Israel's religious life was dependent upon no formal institutions other than those provided by Yahweh himself. Israel had once gotten along without temple, kingship, or even a land to call her own.[51] If she did not abandon faith, she need not perish now.

[51] Amos 5:25; Jer. 7:21–23.

It was the prophets' insistence, moreover, that God acts in new and unprecedented ways, but always in keeping with his righteous character, that offered hope to Israel's defeated and scattered people. By the rules of covenant logic, Israel had broken her vows to Yahweh, and therefore could make no further claims to his promises. The fall of the nation left no doubt as to Israel's failure, particularly if one considered the repeated and fruitless warnings of the prophets. In their respective ways, nevertheless, the pre-Exilic prophets had made room for the totally new and unexpected act of Yahweh. Convinced that nothing but sheer grace had prompted his election of Israel in the first place, they found it possible to believe that he would not now abandon all his plans for them. As we have seen, they drew upon the past history of the covenant relationship and its institutions—the Exodus, kingship, temple, and law—to suggest a new and more permanent venture through which Yahweh would succeed in establishing his reign among men. Hosea's and Jeremiah's vision of a new Exodus: Isaiah's and Micah's magnificent portrayals of the righteous king, new Zion, and peaceful kingdom; Jeremiah's brilliant formulation of the new covenant; in all these ways the prophets had anticipated a future for God's people even before the fall of the nation. In the context of Exile such promises were no longer so susceptible to the misinterpretations of those seeking false assurances of security. They were available, rather, as the nucleus of hope for a chastened and repentant people.

SELECTED READINGS

Jeremiah

Berridge, John M., *Prophet, People, and the Word of Yahweh: An Examination of Form and Content in the Proclamation of the Prophet Jeremiah* (Zurich: EVZ Verlag, 1970).

Bright, John, *Jeremiah*, Anchor Bible (New York: Doubleday & Company, Inc., 1965).

Habel, Norman, *Concordia Commentary: Jeremiah, Lamentations* (St. Louis, MO: Concordia Publishing House, 1968).

Holladay, William L., *Jeremiah: Spokesman Out of Time* (Philadelphia: United Church Press, 1974). Paperback.

———, "Jeremiah the Prophet," *IDBS*, pp. 470–472.

Hyatt, J. Philip, "Introduction and Exegesis to the Book of Jeremiah," *IB*, Vol. V, pp. 777–1142.

———, *Jeremiah: Prophet of Courage and Honor* (Nashville, TN: Abingdon Press, 1958).

Leslie, Elmer A., *Jeremiah* (Nashville, TN: Abingdon Press, 1954). Also in paperback (Apex).

Nicholson, E. W., *Preaching to the Exiles: A Study of the Prose Tradition in the Book of Jeremiah* (Oxford: Basil Blackwell, 1970). Interprets the prose sermons of the book of Jeremiah as Deuteronomic compositions, dating from the Exile.

Overholt, Thomas W., *The Threat of Falsehood: A Study in the Theology of the Book of Jeremiah*, Studies in Biblical Theology, 2nd series, no. 16 (London: S.C.M. Press, 1970). Paperback.

Rowley, H. H., "The Prophet Jeremiah and the Book of Deuteronomy," *Studies in Old Testament Prophecy* (Edinburgh: T. and T. Clark, 1950).

Skinner, John, *Prophecy and Religion* (New York: Cambridge University Press, 1922). Available in paperback (Cambridge University Press, 1963).

Welch, Adam C., *Jeremiah, His Time and His Work* (Oxford: Basil Blackwell, 1951).

Zephaniah

Taylor, Charles L., Jr., "Introduction and Exegesis to the Book of Zephaniah," *IB*, Vol. VI, pp. 1007–1034.

Nahum

Haldar, A. O., *Studies in the Book of Nahum* (Uppsala, Sweden: Lundequistska Bokhandeln, 1947).

Taylor, Charles L., Jr., "Introduction and Exegesis to the Book of Nahum," *IB*, Vol. VI, pp. 953–969.

Habakkuk

Albright, William F., "The Psalm of Habakkuk," *Studies in Old Testament Prophecy*, H. H. Rowley, ed. (Edinburgh: T. and T. Clark, 1950).

Brownlee, William H., *The Text of Habakkuk in the Ancient Commentary from Qumran* (Philadelphia: Society of Biblical Literature and Exegesis, 1959).

Gowan, Donald E., *The Triumph of Faith in Habakkuk* (Atlanta, GA: John Knox Press, 1976).

Sanders, James A., "Habakkuk in Qumran, Paul, and the Old Testament, *JR*, XXXIX (1959), pp. 232–244.

Taylor, Charles L., Jr., "Introduction and Exegesis to the Book of Habakkuk," *IB*, Vol. VI, pp. 973–1003.

6

the plans i have for you

For I know the plans I have for you, says the Lord, plans for welfare and not for evil, to give you a future and a hope.
—Jeremiah 29:11

The collapse of Judah was hardly an epochal event in world history. Babylonian annals make no mention of it.[1] In the history of the covenant people, however, it marks a decisive turning point, the significance of which can scarcely be exaggerated. After roughly half a millennium as a political entity, the Hebrew nation was extinct. The fall of Samaria in the eighth century and the long period of Assyro-Babylonian domination notwithstanding, so long as Judah maintained its statehood under the Davidic dynasty and Zion stood as the impregnable symbol of Yahweh's presence with his people, dreams for the restoration of Israel's former glory refused to die. The Exile had the immediate effect of dashing those hopes and confronting Hebrew faith with the most crucial test of its long and turbulent history.[2]

---

[1] The seizure of Jerusalem in 597, however, is noted in Nebuchadrezzar's records (*ANET*, pp. 306 *ANE*, p. 203).
[2] Cf. Martin Noth's discussion of this point (*The History of Israel*, pp. 289ff.).

1. THE PERIOD OF EXILE

Our knowledge of conditions within Palestine during the half-century of the Exile (587–538 B.C.) is slight,[3] but such evidence as we have suggests a miserable and precarious existence for those who were left there. The former territories of Israel and Judah, and presumably at some point the neighboring lands as well, were parceled out as Babylonian provinces and placed under the administration of officials of the empire. Excavations at Debir, Lachish, and Beth-shemesh reveal the enormity of the devastation wrought by the Babylonian armies[4]; and, though towns in the north (e.g., Samaria) apparently went unharmed, it is doubtful if there remained in the south a single fortified town that escaped total or partial destruction. Judah's neighbors, moreover, especially Edom and Ammon, took advantage of her plight to confiscate such leftovers as were to be had.[5]

Numbers of Judah's stalwarts had died in her defense; others had perished of starvation; the most able of her leaders had been deported to Babylon; and yet others had fled the land to live as refugees in Transjordan, Egypt, and elsewhere. In contrast with Assyrian practice, the Babylonians brought in no foreigners with whom to resettle the depopulated land. Thus, according to rough estimates, from a population which had numbered perhaps a quarter of a million in the eighth century, there remained scarcely more than 20,000, even after the return of the first exiles.[6]

The misery that prevailed among Palestinian Jews[7] during these years is poignantly described in the series of poems that make up the book of Lamentations. Attributed traditionally but erroneously to Jeremiah because of their profound tone of personal grief, these laments were written shortly after the fall of Jerusalem and compare the city to a widow, sitting alone and mourning her dead.

> How lonely sits the city that was full of people!
> How like a widow has she become,
> she that was great among the nations!
> Lam. 1:1

---

[3] The biblical data consist chiefly of indirect references in the books of Jeremiah and Ezekiel, such conditions as carried over into the post-Exilic period and are thus mentioned in the post-Exilic prophets and Ezra-Nehemiah, and the poetical descriptions in Lamentations.

[4] Cf. G. Ernest Wright, *Biblical Archaeology*, pp. 121, 126.

[5] Ps. 137:7; Ezek. 25:1ff.; 25:12ff.; 35:5; Obad. 11ff.

[6] John Bright, *A History of Israel*, p. 324.

[7] The name "Jew" (Hebrew, *Yehudi*) came into wide usage after the Exile for the descendants of the former citizens of Judah.

[8] 1:4; 2:6–7, 20; 4:1–2. Jer. 41:5 has been interpreted to mean that pilgrims continued to come up to worship at the burnt-over ruins of the temple site.

A major source of concern centers on the fallen temple and the festivals that go unobserved.[8] Hunger and peril are depicted as the common lot of the citizenry, as widows and children forage for food and fear for their lives and honor in a land bereft of any semblance of order. Everywhere there is a mood of despair.

> The old men have quit the city gate,
> the young men their music.
> The joy of our hearts has ceased;
> our dancing has been turned to mourning.
> Lam. 5:14–15

Along with a sense of puzzled disbelief and queries as to whether Yahweh has utterly rejected his people (5:22), there appears the repeated confession that Judah's sufferings are the direct result of her transgressions.[9]

BY THE WATERS OF BABYLON. The number of Jews taken to Babylon was not impressively large. According to figures cited in Jeremiah 52, the three deportations of 597, 587, and 582 B.C. totaled 4,600, though this figure may include only the adult males.[10] As compared with conditions in Palestine, the exiles fared none too badly. Although captives of the empire, they were permitted to live in agricultural settlements, possess houses, assemble together, and marry and raise families.[11] Apparently they were not long in entering into the commercial life of Babylon, as well, since by the time for the first return (538 B.C.) some of their number were able to make significant monetary contributions for rebuilding the temple.[12] Ample evidence of the prosperity of fifth-century Jews is revealed in a large number of business tablets discovered at the site of ancient Nippur, south of Babylon.[13] These were records of a banking house by the name of Murashu and contain the names of a considerable number of Jewish investors, representing descendants of the earlier deportees who had chosen to remain in Babylon.

These facts should not blind us, however, to the inevitable homesickness and despair of heart suffered by the exiles. Though Nebuchadrezzar had made Babylon one of the most beautiful cities in the world and the culture of the realm must have dazzled the eyes of the bands of displaced Jews, the new land surely represented for most of them a threat to all the values they treasured most. The first group of exiles was characterized by a restless and unrealistic expectation of a speedy return. A small-scale rebellion appears to have been sparked by some of their prophets in 595 or 594 B.C., but was

[9] 1:5, 8–9, 14, 18–20; 2:14; 3:39–42; 4:13; 5:16.
[10] II Kings 24:14 records a total of 10,000 deported in 597 alone.
[11] Jer. 29:5–6; Ezek. 3:15; 8:1; 14:1; 33:30ff.; Ezra 2:39; 8:17.
[12] Ezra 2:68–69.
[13] *ANET*, pp. 221ff.

quickly put down by the Babylonian authorities.[14] Such futile uprisings subsided more quickly than did the deep-seated fears and disillusionment which gripped even the most devout of the exiled Jews once Jerusalem had fallen. Theirs was basically a twofold theological problem: Had Yahweh been defeated by the more powerful gods of Babylon? Or, barring that, had he forever cast off his people? Israel was eventually to find answers for her questions, but for the time being her despair at the loss of Zion and the land of promise was uppermost. The mood is reflected in Psalm 137.

> By the waters of Babylon
> > there we sat down and wept,
> > when we remembered Zion.
> On the willows there we hung up our lyres.
> . . .
> How shall we sing the Lord's song in a foreign land?

According to Deuteronomic law there could be no temple or official cult outside Jerusalem. Only among heterodox Jews, such as those who inhabited a military outpost on the island of Elephantine in Upper Egypt, was there deviation in this regard.[15] From the Elephantine Papyri we know that at some time prior to the late fifth century B.C. this colony of syncretistic-minded Jews built and maintained their own temple, which was finally destroyed by a rival religious group in 410 B.C. This, of course, did not happen with the more orthodox Jews in Babylon. As a result, they were forced to utilize means others than burnt offerings by which to worship God and keep faith alive. Such practices as Sabbath observance and circumcision, both of which predate the Exile, began to receive greater attention.[16] It is also more than likely that the synagogue developed in the Exile, and as a substitute of sorts for the former temple. Probably from simple gatherings of the exiles in private homes, such as we hear about in Ezekiel,[17] the formal synagogue of later times had its beginnings. Unlike the temple, the synagogue was not equipped with an altar for sacrifices; but other rites of worship were conducted there, much as they are today: prayers, recitation and singing of psalms, oral readings, and study of Torah.

As has so often proved to be the case in comparable situations, the trials of the Exile ultimately served as a strengthening and renewing influence upon Hebrew religious faith. This is not to imply that all the developments in faith and practice provoked by the Exile were altogether positive. But no period in Hebrew history, short of the Mosaic era, was more creative and productive; and it was during these years that the foundations of the later Judaism were laid. It was in Babylon that the collection and commit-

---

[14] Jer. 29; cf. vss. 7–9, 21–23.
[15] Cf. G. Ernest Wright, *Biblical Archaeology*, pp. 132–135; *ANET*, pp. 491–492 (*ANE*, 278–282). In respect to the Arad temple, see above, p. 356 fn. 19.
[16] Ezek. 20:12ff.; 22:8, 26; 23:38; Gen. 2:3 (P); 17:11 (P).
[17] 8:1; 14:1; 33:30–33.

An artist's reconstruction of Nebuchadrezzar's Babylon, showing the ziggurat Etemenanki. The Euphrates River, shown in the foreground, separated the two parts of Babylon. (Courtesy of the Oriental Institute, University of Chicago.)

ment to writing of much oral and partially written Hebrew tradition took place. As we have seen,[18] the several strands of Pentateuchal tradition were woven together there under the auspices of a priestly minded circle. Likewise, collections of prophetic materials were compiled and, in some cases, updated with messages for the new day—frequently words of hope for the exiles themselves. If, then, the initial step toward making Israel a "people of the book" was Josiah's earlier promulgation of the Deuteronomic law, the major impetus toward expanding that principle to encompass all authoritative Hebrew tradition was the production of written documents in the Exile. The centrality of the Torah and Prophets in later Judaism was the direct result of these developments.

[18] See above, ch. 1.

The vexing problems accompanying the Exile were responsible, in part, for arousing and revitalizing significant theological issues which were to occupy Hebrew thought for the next several centuries. The scattering of the covenant people and the loss of the tangible symbols of corporate unity introduced a whole gamut of questions involving the individual Jew, his relationship to covenant history, his responsibility, and his destiny. At the same time, exposure to the larger world of the Near East had for some Jews the effect of expanding horizons and recalling Israel to her universal world mission. The Exile produced its prophetic voices who not only gave expression to the moods of their times but turned them to the purpose of bold and creative reappraisals of the older covenant faith.

2. CAN THESE BONES LIVE? EZEKIEL

Ezekiel was among the exiles taken to Babylon in the first deportation (597 B.C.). The beginning of his prophetic career is dated in the fifth year of his exile, thus 593 or 592 B.C. (Ezek. 1:2); and the last of the dated oracles in his book (29:17) is from 571 or 570 B.C. At the very least, then, his ministry lasted more than twenty years. His period overlaps the career of Jeremiah and includes the fall of Jerusalem and the two further deportations. Along with the slightly later Deutero-Isaiah, he is one of the two known prophets of the Exile.

By the River Chebar

Ezekiel is the first prophet expressly said to have been a priest (1:3); the son of a certain Buzi, he was quite possibly of Zadokite lineage. Following his deportation to Babylon, he lived with his wife in a house by the Chebar canal. Tel-abib, the name of the Jewish settlement, means "mound of the flood," doubtless reflecting a tradition that the site had been inundated in the primeval deluge.

The fall of Jerusalem was the pivotal event in the prophet's career and had the effect of separating his ministry into two distinct phases. Prior to 587 B.C., he devoted himself exclusively to proclamations of Judah's doom; after that date his words ring with promises of restoration and healing. The fact that the doom oracles are addressed to Judah and claim precise knowledge of events there during the decade prior to the temple's fall has given rise to numerous theories either challenging or defending the Babylonian setting. The positions may be summarized as follows.[19]

---

[19] Cf. H. G. May, "Ezekiel" *IB*, Vol. 6, pp. 41–56; Otto Eissfeldt, "The Prophetic Literature," *The Old Testament and Modern Study*, H. H. Rowley, ed., pp. 153–158. See also Walther Zimmerli, *Ezekiel I*, Ronald E. Clements, trans. (Philadelphia: Fortress Press, 1979); Walther Eichrodt, *Ezekiel*, Crosslett Quin, trans. (Philadelphia: The Westminister Press, 1975).

2. CAN THESE BONES LIVE? EZEKIEL

1. An exclusively Palestinian ministry. John Harford, I. G. Matthews, Volkmar Herntrich and others have maintained that all the authentic oracles in the book are addressed to Judah, the alleged locale of the prophet's ministry, and that the Babylonian setting was added to the tradition at a later time. C. C. Torrey's view that there never was an Ezekiel, but only a fictitious character of that name, has few adherents.

2. A double ministry divided between Palestine and Babylon. Alfred Bertholet, H. W. Robinson, Robert Pfeiffer, and Herbert May are among those who account for the problem in this way. In the view of some, the transfer to Babylon is marked by the switch in the prophet's message from condemnation to hope. Others contend for an initial ministry among the exiles, broken by a trip to Jerusalem, then a return to Babylon.

3. An exclusively Babylonian ministry. This is the traditional view and has the advantage of accepting as authentic the claims of the book as it stands. A significant number of contemporary scholars take this approach, differing chiefly in the explanations offered for the Palestinian elements. Some assume clairvoyance on the prophet's part; others postulate close lines of communication between Palestinian and Babylonian Jews.[20]

The last of these positions seems best and enables us to interpret the message of the prophet without undue recourse to elaborate and highly conjectural reconstructions of the geographical circumstances.

Because of his propensity for visions, dramatized signs, and cataleptic trance-states—perhaps even clairvoyance—the prophet's personality is a major item in Ezekiel studies. He is associated with more symbolic actions than any other Old Testament prophet. Most of these enacted parables are dated from the period before Jerusalem's fall and are contained within chapters 4, 5, and 12. The visions are on occasion couched in stories of angelic translation and include bizarre symbolism, doubtless borrowed from Babylonian art and mythology as well as from Hebrew tradition. The total effect is to lend a mystic and ecstatic character to his person and a surrealist and Kafkaesque quality to his message. Perhaps such extremes were necessary in order to attract and convince his hearers in the difficult period in which he lived.

The Book

Just as there are different schools of thought on the question of the locale of Ezekiel's ministry, so too there is broad disagreement concerning the

---

[20] Cf. G. A. Cooke, *The Book of Ezekiel* (Edinburgh: T. and T. Clark, 1960), pp. xx-xxvii and commentary; G. Howie, *The Date and Composition of Ezekiel* (Philadelphia: Society of Biblical Literature, 1950), pp. 5–26.

unity of the book. In the early days of Ezekiel scholarship, the book's complete authenticity was assumed. On the surface, at least, the oracles appear to be less disordered than those of Isaiah or Jeremiah. Thirteen of the oracles are assigned precise dates, and there is a general consistency of historical background and literary style. Furthermore, the prophet's many-sided personality (e.g., prophet and priest) has been assumed to account for the variety of interests manifest in the book. By the early decades of this century, however, the unity of the book had become highly suspect. Apart from the problem of the setting, one can perceive abrupt transitions in the text,[21] some doublets or redundancies,[22] and some units which stand apart from the rest of the book (e.g., the apocalyptic section, chs. 38–39). There can be no doubting the fact that the book has been edited. The superscription, for example, shows quite clearly the work of two hands, one that of the prophet (vs. 1, written autobiographically) and another that of an editor (vss. 2 and 3, written in the third person); as a result it is impossible to determine the precise meaning of "the thirtieth year."

Some scholars have established such stringent criteria for authenticity that they are compelled to regard major portions of the book as secondary. Holscher and Irwin, for example, admit as authentic only the poetical portions. Irwin assigns only 250 verses to Ezekiel; and Holscher strips the book of all but 170 verses. May allows about one half of the book to the prophet.[23] More conservative approaches, however, do not go nearly so far, reserving the most serious questions for the latter chapters of the book, 38–48. The position taken here is that the book is basically the work of Ezekiel, but that its extant format is largely the result of editing (perhaps a century or more later), whereby the authentic Ezekiel materials were collected according to a topical and chronological arrangement with minor editorial additions.

As to the topical organization of the book, we observe once again the characteristic threefold pattern: (1) oracles of doom against Judah, (2) oracles against foreign nations, and (3) oracles of hope. These divisions also mark out the major periods in the prophet's career; the oracles against foreign nations (chs. 25–32) belong chiefly to the middle phase (587–585 B.C.)[24] and serve to separate the oracles of judgment dating before Jerusalem's fall (1–24) from the oracles of hope delivered after that date (33–48). The following is a summary outline of the book, with indications of some of the more significant subunits.

1. Ezekiel's call: chs. 1–3
2. Oracles of doom against Judah: chs.

---

[21] E.g., compare the contexts of the following: 11:14–21; 12:8–16; chs. 38–39.
[22] E.g., compare chs. 1 and 10; 3:16–21, ch. 18, and ch. 33.
[23] H. G. May, "Ezekiel," *IB*, Vol. 6, pp. 45–51.
[24] A notable exception is 29:17–21, dated 571 B.C.

Wheels Within Wheels

The magnificent theophany with which the book of Ezekiel opens is fully as significant for understanding the prophet's mission and message as are the call visions of Isaiah and Jeremiah for their respective prophetic roles. The greater abundance of symbolic detail and surrealist imagery in Ezekiel's account is altogether typical of his more pronounced visionary and mystic nature. The account is replete with such strange and grotesque figures that the ancient rabbis forbade its reading by anyone under thirty years of age. The prophet beholds Yahweh's throne chariot coming on a great storm cloud out of the north, the conveyance surrounded by composite animal, fowl, and human creatures and supported on omnidirectional wheels affixed with eyes. Seated above its platform on a throne resembling sapphire and encompassed by the brightness of fire is Yahweh himself.

Bizarre though the vision may be, its association of the deity with storm phenomena and fire is in no sense alien to Hebrew thought[25]; nor are the throne chariot and its guardian cherubim other than an extension of temple symbolism—the ark and its winged attendants in the Holy of Holies. One can but be impressed, moreover, with the powerful and sensitive manner in which the grotesque imagery is made to depict "the majestic transcendence, cosmic power, and unapproachable holiness of the deity."[26] So aware is the prophet of the ineffable mystery of God that he punctuates his account repeatedly with a variety of similes and such qualifying terms as "the likeness of," "the appearance of," and the like. Without violating Yahweh's holiness, he succeeds in conveying an overwhelming impression of his arrival to be with his people in Babylon; and this, indeed, is the point of the vision.

Unlike the call experiences of the other prophets, Ezekiel's account

---

[25] Cf. Exod. 3:2; 19:16–19; Ps. 18:7–15; 29:3–8.
[26] R. H. Pfeiffer, *Introduction to the Old Testament*, p. 535.

makes no mention of the message which Yahweh commissions him to declare. Rather, he is given a scroll containing God's words and is commanded to eat it.

> And he said to me, "Son of man, eat this scroll that I give you and fill your
> stomach with it." Then I ate it; and it was in my mouth as sweet as honey.
>
> 3:3

This strange symbolism speaks tellingly of the prophet's endowment with Yahweh's spirit and message. Henceforth he shall be the very embodiment of the word which Yahweh would have his exiles hear; as such, the prophet's overt actions are fully as significant as his spoken oracles. He humbly acknowledges his status as a "son of man," a title which occurs 93 times in the book of Ezekiel in the non-messianic sense of man's finite dependence and lowliness in the presence of God's infinite power and glory.

Ezekiel thus offers himself as a living symbol of what he has beheld in the awesome vision of the throne chariot. Although a thousand miles removed from Yahweh's temple and surrounded by the strange gods of Babylon, the exiles are not beyond the reach of Yahweh's presence and dominion. In this sense, the separated people are one with those who remain in Palestine; and it is apparently the intent of the prophet to address them collectively as "the house of Israel."

They Will Know That I Am Yahweh

The first six years of Ezekiel's ministry were spent discouraging unfounded hopes for a reversal of Judah's political fortunes. Regardless of whether or not he had come under Jeremiah's influence, the message of the two prophets in this respect was essentially the same. Judging from the unrest among the first group of exiles,[27] moreover, such warnings were as needful in Babylon as in Judah.

Beginning with a cataleptic stupor of seven days' duration,[28] Ezekiel dramatically enacted one sign after another until his compatriots were forced to acknowledge the presence of a prophet in their midst. Employing a clay brick made up to resemble Jerusalem, he simulated the imminent siege of the city.[29] He lay for 150 days on his right side and 40 days on his left to indicate the duration of Israel's and Judah's exile, all the while eating the skimpy and defiled rations of a starving people.[30] Cutting off his hair and dividing it into separate lots, he disposed of it in such manner as to demonstrate the fate awaiting Jerusalem's citizens.

[27] See above, pp. 379–380.
[28] 3:22–27.
[29] 4:1–3.
[30] 4:4–17.

A third part of you shall die of pestilence and be consumed with famine in the midst of you; a third part shall fall by the sword round about you; and a third part I will scatter to all the winds. . . .

5:12

Again, he knocked a hole in the wall of his mud-brick house and through it pulled out his belongings in anticipation of the next group of deportees soon to be leaving the doomed city.[31] When his wife died in the year of Jerusalem's siege, the prophet maintained a mute silence until the city's final collapse, apparently repressing his tears as a rebuke to the latter-day mourners who had earlier failed to lament Judah's waywardness.[32]

In a series of temple visions (chs. 8–11) Ezekiel displays such detailed knowledge of events in Jerusalem as to suggest open channels of communication between the prophet-priest and Jerusalem's temple circles. He speaks of being transported ("in visions"; 8:3) miraculously by God's spirit, who takes him hither and thither by a lock of his hair. Allowed a view of the innermost temple precincts—perhaps reflecting information available to him as a priest—he is alarmed at the abundance of idolatry there: pagan mystery rites, lamentations for Tammuz, and worship of the sun.[33] He witnesses Yahweh's departure from his defiled sanctuary—in the same dazzling multiwheeled chariot, and accompanied by the same cherubic retinue, described in the call vision.

Employing the familiar allegories of Hosea and Jeremiah, the prophet depicts the "harlotry" of his people. Israel and Judah are like twin harlots; and the latter failed to learn her lesson from the former's ruin. Unlike the two earlier prophets, however, there is no suggestion of a halcyon wilderness "honeymoon" in Israel's past. Rather, he traces her rebellion back to her very origins—to peoples known for wantonness.

Your father was an Amorite, and your mother a Hittite.

16:3

Her entire history has been one of unfaithfulness; and now her defilement has caused Yahweh to withdraw his glory from the land.

From the prophet's perspective, it is God's holiness, which abides neither cultic impurity nor ethical unrighteousness, that assures the doom of the rebellious covenant people. Convinced that Israel's unfaithfulness has impugned God's name among the nations, he sees no alternative but that Yahweh act in defense of his honor and holiness. Again and again, he ends

---

[31] 12:1–16. The original account has been reworked from a later perspective (cf. esp. vs. 8–16) so as to include Zedekiah's attempt to escape the city (II Kings 25:4; Jer. 39:4).

[32] Ch. 24.

[33] The fact that Jeremiah did not inveigh so heavily against pagan influences in the temple should not cause us to discount the evidence here, as does Yehezkel Kaufmann (*The Religion of Israel*, pp. 426–436). Ezekiel's account has the ring of sober reality and is regarded by some as "one of the most genuinely historical parts of the book" (R. H. Pfeiffer, *Introduction to the Old Testament*, p. 538).

an oracle with the refrain, "Then they (you) will know that I am Yahweh." So assured is Judah's doom that not even the presence of the greatest of her departed saints could now avail to save her.

> even if these three men, Noah, Daniel, and Job were in it, they would deliver but their own lives by their righteousness, says the Lord God.
>
> 14:14

The Soul That Sins Shall Die

Ezekiel is concerned to make the point that it is contemporary Israel that bears the burden of guilt for her disasters, and not merely the faithless generations of the past. Altogether too facile was the popular proverbial explanation for the exile:

> The fathers have eaten sour grapes, and the children's teeth are set on edge.
>
> 18:2

The saying, of course, had its truth, and particularly so for a people whose thinking was grounded in the principle of corporate and historic solidarity.[34] Israel's collapse indeed had been long in coming, and her moral—if not political—demise must be attributed to the compounded errors of more than a single generation. The prophet has, however, two points to make in respect to it (ch. 18): (1) A people or an individual is not accountable for another's sins; but (2) they are responsible for their own guilty deeds.

> As I live, says the Lord God, this proverb shall no more be used by you in Israel. Behold, all souls are mine; the soul of the father as well as the soul of the son is mine; the soul that sins shall die.[35]
>
> 18:3–4

Ezekiel's words have frequently been understood as the beginning of a new attitude toward corporate responsibility in Hebrew thinking, and the elevation of the individual to his rightful place within the broader context of community involvement. Undeniably the Exile provoked new thinking of this sort. It is likely, nevertheless, that Ezekiel's major concern here is not so much with the individual versus the group as with present versus past. What he denies in his illustration of the three generations (18:5ff.)—a righteous grandfather, a wicked father, and a righteous son—is the logic which falls back upon the past either to depend upon a storehouse of merits, on the one hand, or, on the other, to blame the sins of a past day for inactivity in the present. He is thus saying to his contemporaries: "Israel deserved its punishment; but today is the day for action—there is something we can do." This latter point, of course, awaited the fall of Jerusalem for its full explication.

---

[34] Cf. Exod. 20:5.

[35] "Soul" (nephesh) is used here of an individual—the whole person—not in the Greek sense of the nonbodily component of a person.

I Will Bring You Home

To some interpreters Ezekiel appears to take unwarranted delight in pronouncing his people's doom. He has been described as "the first fanatic in the Bible . . . a stern zealot with a forehead hard as a diamond."[36] If his early oracles are unrelieved by expressions of sympathy for the victims whose judgment they foretell, they nevertheless ring true to the prophet's understanding of his commission. He knew himself to be appointed as God's watchman for the house of Israel; and the role of the watchman is clearly to warn of impending danger.

> So you, son of man, I have made a watchman for the house of Israel; whenever you hear a word from my mouth you shall give them warning from me. If I say to the wicked, O wicked man, you shall surely die, and you do not speak to warn the wicked to turn from his way, that wicked man shall die in his iniquity, but his blood I will require at your hand.
>
> 33:7–8

So long as Jerusalem stood, persistent to the very end in her false sense of security, the only word the prophet could declare to her was warning. The more startling the threat, the more likely its chances of taking effect. As for his own sympathies, they could hardly have been other than Yahweh's express desires for humankind.

> As I live, says the Lord God, I have no pleasure in the death of the wicked, but that the wicked turn from his way and live.
>
> 33:11

The best evidence that Ezekiel was not lacking a sense of personal grief over Judah's ruin is the abrupt change which takes hold of his message once Jerusalem has fallen. No longer obligated to warn of danger now that the worst had happened, he was free to offer encouragement for the future. His first assurances, it would appear, come in the form of pronouncements against those nations which had either ignored or profited from Israel's plight, particularly Tyre and Egypt (chs. 25–32). Just as Yahweh had defended his honor in punishing his own rebellious subjects, now he would show his power in bringing low the proud and lofty nations among whom his name was profaned. It is difficult to decide whether the apocalyptic-like Gog of Magog oracles (chs. 38–39) belong with the other foreign oracles and represent a veiled prophecy of Babylon's end. If so, this special treatment was perhaps accorded Babylon because of that nation's peculiar role in Israel's humiliation. The obscure foe has been taken by some as a mythological figure for all the forces, past and present, that set themselves against God. Moreover, serious doubts respecting the authenticity of these

[36] R. H. Pfeiffer, *Introduction to the Old Testament*, p. 543.

chapters cannot be ignored.[37] In any event, the prophet looked for an end to Babylon's mastery over the Near East, as his prophecies of Israel's restoration certainly imply.

THE GOOD SHEPHERD. Israel's "shepherds"—her kings and officials—having failed her, Yahweh himself was preparing to search out the scattered sheep of Israel, heal their injuries, and "feed them on the mountains of Israel" (ch. 34).

> I will seek out the lost, and I will bring back the strayed, and I will bind up the crippled, and I will strengthen the weak, and the fat and the strong I will watch over; I will feed them in justice.
>
> 34:16

He would keep them in safety and, in place of the greedy kings who had formerly fed upon the flock, appoint as their leader a Davidic prince (*nasi'*) of his own choosing.[38] The picture here is reminiscent of Isaiah's peaceful kingdom, but with less significance assigned to the king. In designating him a prince, rather than a king, the prophet emphasizes his subordination to the sovereign reign of Yahweh over his people. Yahweh alone is the author of Israel's salvation; he is the Good Shepherd. The figure was to have a significant influence upon Christian conceptions of Christ.

THE VALLEY OF DRY BONES. None of Ezekiel's restoration imagery is quite so memorable as that of the revivified dry bones (ch. 37). Seeing in a vision the valley of lifeless bones, the prophet is instructed to pronounce over them Yahweh's powerful word.

> So I prophesied as I was commanded; and as I prophesied, there was a noise, and behold, a rattling; and the bones came together, bone to bone.
>
> 37:7

Bones, sinews, and flesh are joined and lack only the regenerative life force itself in order to become living beings. Again, the prophet is commanded to prophesy; and from the wind (*ruah*) the bodies are infused with breath (or spirit: also *ruah*) and rise up and take their leave.

Though the description here bears a surface resemblance to the later doctrine of the resurrection of individuals from the grave, it in fact means something quite different. The dead bones symbolize the collective body of exiles in Babylon, those whose former presumptuous plots have now given way to pessimism and despair.

> Our bones are dried up, and our hope is lost; we are clean cut off.
>
> 37:11

---

[37] Cf. 38:17, which may imply the perspective of a later generation.
[38] 34:23–24; cf. 37:24–25, 17:22–24.

It is this corpse of a people into whom God will breathe new life. Enlivened with his spirit, Israel will be resurrected as a nation and once more placed in possession of her land.

> Behold, I will open your graves, and raise you from your graves, O my people; and I will bring you home into the land of Israel. . . . And I will put my spirit within you, and you shall live, and I will place you in your own land; then you shall know that I, the Lord, have spoken, and I have done it, says the Lord.
>
> 37:12, 14

The prophet's refrain, "You (they) shall know that I am the Lord," is now seen in a new light. Yahweh's cause is vindicated, his honor defended, as effectively in restoration as in judgment. Indeed, it is in regeneration, and not death, that Yahweh desires to be known (cf. 33:11).

THE RESTORED COMMUNITY. Notwithstanding the differences, particularly of personality and temperament, that distinguish Ezekiel from his older contemporary Jeremiah, the two prophets shared a common conviction respecting Israel's chances for survival. They were equally convinced that hope turned not so much upon a strong new leader as upon a fresh infusion of God's spirit. Ezekiel's prophecy of the "new heart" is a close counterpart to Jeremiah's "new covenant":

> A new heart I will give you, and a new spirit I will put within you; and I will take out of your flesh the heart of stone and give you a heart of flesh. And I will put my spirit within you, and cause you to walk in my statutes and be careful to observe my ordinances.
>
> 36:26–27

Ezekiel went beyond Jeremiah, however, in drawing up a blueprint for the restored community of the future. The plans are unveiled in chapters 40–48, in a vision replete with a miraculous trip to Jerusalem and an angel's guided tour of the Zion-to-be.[39] Drawn from a background in the Jerusalem temple and reflecting close contact with the circles which produced the Priestly Code, the prophet's conception of the restored Israel is that of an idealized priestly theocracy. Yahweh is beheld returning to Jerusalem, approaching through the same east gate through which he had earlier departed (43:1–9). From henceforth the city will be known as "Yahweh is there" (48:35). A regenerated and purified people will live perpetually in the presence of God's glory, though great care is taken to distinguish between sacred and profane functions and precincts.

The boundaries of the land extend from Syria to the southern Negeb and from the Mediterranean to the Jordan (47:15–20). Each of the former

---

[39] The substance of these chapters is in all likelihood from Ezekiel himself, though a later editor may be responsible for their present form.

twelve tribes is allotted an equal strip of territory, but the geographical boundaries that obtained in the tribal era are ignored (ch. 48). In the center of the land, between seven tribal territories to the north and five to the south, is a special holy district, roughly eight miles square. In the midst of this portion—in the half of it reserved for officiating priests— stands the restored temple. Just to the south of the holy precincts, in an area only one quarter its size, is located the city itself. The city and lands to the west and east are administered by a prince (*nasi'*).

Much of the prophet's attention centers on the temple and its priesthood. In a manner closely akin to the priestly legislation in the Pentateuch (P), he distinguishes two classes of priests: the "sons of Zadok," the officiating priests; and the "Levites," those who do the menial temple chores.[40] Apparently the Zadokite priests are conceived as those who could trace their lineage back through the Jerusalem priesthood (and hence to Zadok, Solomon's chief priest); whereas the Levites represent descendants of the rural priests whose shrines had been closed in Josiah's reformation. Only the Zadokites can function at the altar, judge cases, and enter the inner courts of the temple. The Levites' quarters are located within the holy district but outside the Zadokite precincts.

The centrality of the temple and priesthood has the effect of subordinating the political state to the religious community. Considering the utopian character of the vision, Israel's territorial possessions are modest, no claim being made to land east of the Jordan. The prince and his successors are clearly neither conquering warriors nor absolute monarchs.

> And my princes shall no more oppress my people; but they shall let the house of Israel have the land according to their tribes.
> 45:8

They are charged, rather, with the responsibilities of executing justice, establishing fair standards of weights and measures, and collecting the offerings for the temple. Indicative of the distinction between priestly and political authority is the description of the royal palace as no longer adjoining the temple area.

Eager to portray Yahweh as the source of life and well-being for his people, the prophet adds a feature drawn from the ancient mythology of the Garden of God and its rivers. From beneath the threshold of the temple emerges a life-giving stream which flows eastward through the wilderness and empties into the Dead Sea. The effect is to bring lush vegetation and fruit-bearing trees to the desert and an abundance of fish to the once stagnant Dead Sea waters. In a land where Yahweh sets his glory, everything must be fruitful!

---

[40] In the P source, however, the distinction is between "sons of Aaron" and "Levites."

392

"The Father of Judaism"

Ezekiel has with good reason been dubbed "the father of Judaism." He perceived, as did Jeremiah, that Israel's future lay with the exiles, and his efforts to influence their thinking pointed the way toward certain of the most characterstic features of the post-Exilic era. His preoccupation with cult, priesthood, and temple proved to be more than antiquarian musings, as the second temple was destined to achieve an even more central role in Jewish life than its Solomonic counterpart. His priestly concern for purity and separation from defiling influences is reminiscent of later Judaism's scrupulous attention to such matters; and his exclusion of non-Israelites from the restoration community smacks of the exclusivism practiced by post-Exilic Judaism. It is hardly defensible to portray him as the champion of a new individualism, though his principle of the responsibility of each person for his own actions was to provide the starting point for many later questions concerning individual values and personal destiny. Again, he was no thorough-going apocalypticist; but his bizarre symbols, angelic interpreters, cataclysmic battle with Gog, and vision of the New Jerusalem were to find their way into much of the later apocalyptic literature.[41]

3. AND SET MY EXILES FREE: DEUTERO-ISAIAH

As long as Nebuchadrezzar lived (d. 562 B.C.) Babylon's empire remained intact. He wisely counterbalanced the growing strength of Media to the north by securing his control of the Fertile Crescent. At his death there followed a rapid succession of weak kings; within a period of seven years the throne changed hands three times. Finally power was seized by the usurper Nabonidus (556–539 B.C.), who was destined to be the last king of the Babylonian empire.

Nabonidus fell into disfavor with his subjects, particularly concerning religious matters. A devotee of the moon god Sin, he favored the Sin cult over the strong Marduk party, and even allowed the long-established New Year's festival to lapse. For reasons that are obscure, he spent the last eight years of his reign at the Arabian oasis of Teima, leaving his son Belshazzar in charge of affairs in Babylon.

Early in his reign Nabonidus lent support to the young prince Cyrus of Anshan (in Persia), seeing in him a useful ally in his efforts to offset Media. By 550 B.C., however, the complexion of matters changed altogether when

---

[41] Whether or not Ezekiel deserves the title "father of apocalyptic" hinges largely on the authenticity and interpretation of the "Gog" prophecy, chs. 38–39.

The Cyrus Cylinder, containing the record of Cyrus' conquest of Babylon (539 B.C.). (Courtesy of the Trustees of the British Museum.)

Cyrus succeeded in overthrowing the Median empire, thus making himself master of a sprawling territory and a major threat to Babylon. Nabonidus quickly entered into defensive alliances with Amasis of Egypt and Croesus of Lydia, but to no avail. When Cyrus surprised Croesus in his winter palace at Sardis (546 B.C.) and speedily brought Lydia into his kingdom, Egypt refused to take up the challenge. Babylon, surrounded by Cyrus, could only await the inevitable.

In the summer of 539 B.C. the Babylonian army was crushed by the Persians at Opis on the Tigris; and in October of that year the city of Babylon was taken without a struggle. Cyrus recorded on a clay cylinder the acclaim with which he was received by his new subjects and, in a display of tolerance rare for ancient monarchs, attributed his victory to the Babylonian Marduk.

> Marduk, the great lord, a protector of his people/worshippers, beheld with pleasure his [i.e., Cyrus'] good deeds and his upright mind [lit. heart] [and therefore] ordered him to march against his city Babylon [Ká. dingir. ra]. He made him set out on the road to Babylon [DIN. TIR^{ki}] going at his side like a real friend.[42]

Behold, a New Thing

An interpretation of these events, differing significantly from that offered by Cyrus, comes from the anonymous prophet-poet responsible for chapters 40–55 of the book of Isaiah. Deutero-Isaiah, as he is known to modern scholarship, lived as an exile in Babylon during the very years when Cyrus rose to power. Separated from Isaiah of Jerusalem by a cen-

[42] *ANET*, pp. 315–316 (*ANE*, pp. 206–207).

tury and a half, he is the brilliant and unsurpassed spokesman for Israel's mission in the new era that dawned with the release of the first exiles.

Easily recognized differences of historical background, language, literary style, and theological perspective leave no doubt that these chapters are the work of someone other than Isaiah of Jerusalem. The Assyrian threat of Isaiah's day has long since passed and Babylon's empire is fast collapsing. Cyrus has already appeared as the next world conquerer and is twice mentioned by name (44:28; 45:1). The typically terse and restrained prophetic rhetoric of chapters 1–39 gives way here to a flowing and lyric poetry that is unmistakable in its difference. A characteristic vocabulary, rich in such terms as "comfort," "way (in the wilderness)," "servant," "chosen," and a variety of creation and salvation figures are to be seen.[43] Isaiah's warnings and prophetic invective, prompted by the crises of the eighth century, are replaced in these chapters by words of comfort and promise from one who looks for new beginnings and restoration under the Persians. The reader confronts the new note at the very beginning of the work: "Comfort, comfort my people" (40:1).

To recognize these distinctions is not to overlook basic elements the two prophets shared in common. It was hardly sheer accident that Deutero-Isaiah's poems were attached to the Isaiah collection rather than to some other prophetic work of the past. The original Isaiah, for example, had held out hope for a remnant and a future kingdom established upon righteous principles. This hopeful note is expanded and deepened in the oracles of Deutero-Isaiah. As Kittel put it, "the spirit of the old Isaiah in fact celebrates its resurrection in him."[44] So powerful and enduring was the influence of the great eighth-century prophet, that we must allow for a succession of his disciples through the period of Exile and beyond.[45] The greatest of these, surely, was the one we know as Deutero-Isaiah.

Comfort, Comfort My People

Deutero-Isaiah's poems resist the sort of literary analysis which attempts to find in them a structured sequence and logical progression of thought. Some would distinguish between (1) chapters 40–48, where Cyrus and the deliverance from Exile are especially prominent, and (2) 49–55, where the redemption wrought through Yahweh's servant is uppermost. But the work shows throughout the unfettered enthusiasm of a master poet committed to no formal stratagems save those dictated by the compelling truths to which he gives utterance. Pfeiffer compares his work to "a succession of ecstatic shouts," his thoughts "poured out glowing and fluid, like molten metal

[43] Cf. James Muilenburg, "Isaiah 40–66," *IB*, Vol. 5, pp. 386–393.
[44] Rudolph Kittel, *Geschichte des Volkes Israel* (Gotha, East Germany: Leopold Klotz, 1929), III, p. 203. Cited by James Muilenburg, "Isaiah 40–66," *IB*, Vol. 5, p. 383.
[45] Cf. Martin Buber, *The Prophetic Faith*, pp. 202ff.

before it has hardened into a definite shape."[46] The poems, however, share a thematic unity not unlike that of a symphonic composition. Again and again, the prophet's major themes break through in an exhilarating rhapsody of words. Reduced to prosaic theological formulations, they are (1) Israel's restoration, (2) Yahweh's creation of the world and sovereign lordship of history, and (3) the redemption of the nations through the vicarious suffering of Yahweh's servant.

The startling announcement of deliverance with which the first of the poems begins sets the mood for the whole work.

> Comfort, comfort my people,
>   says your God.
> Speak tenderly to Jerusalem,
>   and cry to her
> that her warfare is ended,
>   that her iniquity is pardoned,
> that she has received from the Lord's hand
>   double for all her sins.
>   40:1–2

As Muilenburg observes, "the primary matrix of all the poems is eschatological."[47] That is to say, the prophet regards the decisive divine event toward which the earlier prophets looked as now taking place in his own age. Repeatedly he speaks of the "new thing" which is happening,[48] and summons his people to celebrate with him the wondrous new era which Yahweh has inaugurated.

> Israel's time of service has come to an end; the old age is passing away and a new age is about to dawn. The new age will be ushered in by new events, and the new events are greeted with eschatological singing.[49]

No imagery is too bold to express this eschatological transformation of nature: highways suddenly appearing in the desert, mountains effortlessly brushed aside, valleys snapped into place to make way for Yahweh's arrival for deliverance. In an interesting parallel to the Babylonian New Year procession, Yahweh leads his people in a triumphant return to their land (49:8–13). Primarily, however, it is the Exodus tradition, with its familiar details of Yahweh's provisions for food and water in the wilderness, that furnishes the imagery here. The prophet speaks of a new Exodus.

> They shall feed along the ways,
>   on all bare heights shall be their pasture;
> they shall not hunger or thirst
>
>   . . .

---

[46] R. H. Pfeiffer, *Introduction to the Old Testament*, p. 465.
[47] James Muilenburg, "Isaiah 40–66," *IB*, Vol. 5, p. 399.
[48] 42:9; 43:19; 48:6.
[49] James Muilenburg, "Isaiah 40–66," *IB*, Vol. 5, p. 399.

> for he who has pity on them will lead them,
> and by springs of water will guide them.
> 49:9–10

The new thing that Yahweh is doing is wholly consistent with his initial action on Israel's behalf. Once revealed as the redeemer of his people, who marshaled the forces of nature for their deliverance, it follows that he is both sovereign Lord of history and sole creator of the world and all that it contains. The poems are alive with creation figures: from Yahweh's initial spreading of the heavens "like a curtain" (40:22) to the latter-day "rivers in the desert" (41:18; 43:19). We meet with the same tripartite universe (waters-heavens-earth) of Priestly cosmology (Gen. 1).

> Who has measured the waters in the hollow of his hand
> and marked off the heavens with a span,
> enclosed the dust of the earth in a measure
> and weighed the mountains in scales
> and the hills in a balance?
> 40:12

The prophet is familiar with the ancient mythology of the primeval battle with the dragon of chaos[50]; but it interests him chiefly as a figure by which he can relate God's command of the waters in creation to his delivery of Israel at the Sea of Reeds. In one magnificent passage he ties together the themes of creation, exodus, and restoration.

> Awake, awake, put on strength,
>   O arm of the Lord;
> awake, as in days of old,
>   the generations of long ago.
> Was it not thou that didst cut Rahab in pieces,
>   that didst pierce the dragon?
> Was it not thou that didst dry up the sea,
>   the waters of the great deep;
> that didst make the depths of the sea a way
>   for the redeemed to pass over?
> And the ransomed of the Lord shall return,
>   and come to Zion with singing;
> everlasting joy shall be upon their heads;
>   they shall obtain joy and gladness,
>   and sorrow and sighing shall flee away.
> 51:9–11

The restoration is at once both New Exodus and New Creation. The land of promise will be refurbished; Zion will become like Eden (51:3).

What was implicit in the faith of Moses, the Yahwist, and Amos, be-

---

[50] 27:1; 30:7; 51:9–10.

comes for the first time an explicit article of faith for Deutero-Isaiah: Yahweh is the one God beside whom there is no other.[51]

> Thus says the Lord, the King of Israel
>   and his Redeemer, the Lord of hosts:
> "I am the first and I am the last;
>   besides me there is no god."
> 44:6

The other gods do not exist. They are as lifeless as the wood and metal from which their images are fashioned. Repeatedly, the prophet heaps his bitterest satire upon the idol worshiper. The same tree, he observes, supplies him with fuel for his fire and the image to which he bows down (45:5). Pity the poor Bel (Marduk) worshiper, his beasts immobilized by the excess baggage of his images (46:1–2)! How different is Yahweh, who bears his people on eagles' wings (40:31). That such idols were properly regarded as no more than the earthly representations of the gods was surely a subtle distinction that escaped most of their devotees. For the prophet, at any rate, it would have been a moot point. Since there was but one God who controlled heaven and earth, and who was represented by no man-made image, the idols' significance did not extend beyond themselves alone.

Listen, O Coastlands

It follows as a logical consequence of the prophet's strict monotheism that Yahweh's lordship extends to all peoples of earth. The nations are but a "drop from a bucket" before him and are powerless to thwart his purposes (40:15). Yahweh nevertheless has plans for them, just as for Israel. Earlier prophets had depicted pagan conquerors as instruments of Yahweh's judgment, but never before had such claims been made for a gentile ruler as Deutero-Isaiah makes for Cyrus. Though an unbeliever, he is God's "anointed," his "shepherd," raised up as an agent of deliverance (44:28–45:7). Ironically akin to Cyrus' own claims to Marduk's patronage, Yahweh is said to have grasped the Persian's hand, enabling him to subdue nations and open doors that will lead to Jerusalem's rebuilding.

Israel's elect status, to be sure, has not been abrogated by exile. Yahweh's rejection has been temporary and for a purpose.

> For the Lord has called you
>   like a wife forsaken and grieved in spirit,
> like a wife of youth when she is cast off,
>   says your God.
> For a brief moment I forsook you,
>   but with great compassion I will gather you.
> 54:6–7

---

[51] 44:9–20; cf. 40:18–20; 41:6–7.

Israel's dreams of national restoration and glorification are due for fulfilment; and in some of the poems the gentile nations are accordingly mocked or depicted as Israel's future subjects.[52] Gottwald has observed, however, that where such imagery is employed, it is used to exalt Israel's faith in the power of God, even as elsewhere the nations are summoned to accept Yahweh's dominion and Israel is directed to go to them in acknowledgment of his universal lordship.

> Depending on whether the prophet seeks to deepen the exiles' faith in God or to move them to a wider view of their task, he stresses respectively the impotence of the nations before God or the preciousness of the nations to God.[53]

What the lifeless idols cannot offer their devotees, Yahweh provides. The incipient universalism of the Yahwist and Amos is here articulated in terms of a world-wide mission for Israel. Her whole history is a *praeparatio evangelica* for the salvation of the nations. The prophet thus manages to combine the finest sense of Yahweh's love for the elect people—the insights of Hosea and Jeremiah—with the clearest summons in the Old Testament to the whole race of men to come forward and accept their salvation.

> Turn to me and be saved,
> all the ends of the earth!
> For I am God, and there is no other.
> 45:22

The Suffering Servant

The one exegetical challenge that surpasses all others in Deutero-Isaiah scholarship concerns the interpretation of the Suffering Servant Songs. For many years it has been generally acknowledged that certain poems in the collection stand apart from the others in depicting a servant of the Lord who suffers redemptively for the peoples of earth. Although opinions differ as to how many such poems there are and where some of the units begin or end,[54] there is broad agreement on four: (1) 42:1–4, (2) 49:1–6, (3) 50:4–9, and (4) 52:13–53:12. There are, to be sure, other poems that mention a servant, in all of which the reference is to the nation Israel.[55] In these four, however, the servant is a more highly individualized and idealized figure, one whose submission to Yahweh's will is unmatched by anything else in the Old Testament.

Efforts to remove the Suffering Servant poems altogether from the Deutero-Isaiah work—to prove an independent origin—have been as un-

---

[52] 40:15–17, 22–24; 41:15–16; 45:14; 49:7, 22–23; 54:3.
[53] Norman Gottwald, *All the Kingdoms of the Earth*, p. 330.
[54] The extent of the second poem (49:1–6) is especially a point of dispute, some contending for the inclusion of verses 7, 7–9, or 7–13.
[55] 41:8; 42:19; 43:10; 44:1, 2, 21, 26.

successful as attempts to disprove their unique character. It is hardly conceivable that another author would have employed so much of Deutero-Isaiah's characteristic vocabulary and theological perspective.[56] More defensible, but by no means certain, is the possibility that the Suffering Servant represents a later development of the prophet's thinking, and thus a subsequent addition to the rest of the poems. The four poems must find their meaning as an integral part of the context in which they stand, even as one analyzes them for their unique message. Their chief features may be summarized.

1. 42:1–4. Yahweh speaks. He describes the servant as his chosen agent for bringing justice to the nations. Emphasis falls on his complete submission to the role Yahweh has given him.

2. 49:1–6. The servant speaks. His words are reminiscent of Jeremiah: he was foreordained to his mission even prior to birth; he laments the futility of his efforts, but rests his case with Yahweh. The universal note of the first poem is struck once more: the servant addresses himself to peoples afar off and announces his mission as one which will be for their benefit, as well as Israel's. He will be their light and salvation. The difficulty of the problem of the servant's identity becomes apparent here. He will serve to bring Israel back to God (vs. 5); but Israel itself is also named as a servant (vs. 3). If the servant is simply the nation, how is he to become the agent of his own deliverance?

3. 50:4–9. The servant speaks. Again in the tone of Jeremiah's laments, the servant affirms his devotion to his mission; he endures shame, knowing that God will vindicate him.

4. 52:13–
   53:12. Yahweh and the nations speak. Yahweh foretells the future exaltation of the lowly servant. The astonished nations look on the unseemly "man of sorrows," who is now recognized as one who has suffered on their behalf. He has borne the iniquity of the nations, becoming an offering for their sins. Though guilty of no violence or deceit of his own, he has made no protest against his role.

The mission of the servant, and thus Yahweh's designs for the world, are in principle clear. One could not wish for a more profound symbol of God's

---

[56] Cf. James Muilenburg, "Isaiah 40–66," *IB*, Vol. 5, pp. 406–408; and below, pp. 402–403.

encompassing love for mankind nor the redemptive role of vicarious suffering than that set forth in the figure of the servant. The perspective extends significantly beyond the Deuteronomic interpretation of suffering as the necessary consequence of guilt. Although Deutero-Isaiah is indebted to earlier thought, he, for the first time in the Old Testament, affirms clearly and unmistakably the principle of righteous suffering as a positive good— not simply for the benefit of the sufferer, but of one person for another. The principle of the sacrificial offering associated with the cult is extended to the moral choice of a free person acting on behalf of other persons.

> Surely he has borne our griefs
>   and carried our sorrows;
> yet we esteemed him stricken,
>   smitten by God, and afflicted.
> But he was wounded for our transgressions,
>   he was bruised for our iniquities;
> upon him was the chastisement that made us whole,
>   and with his stripes we are healed.
>   53:4–5

Yahweh's message and worship is offered to the gentile nations and his saving work exists for their healing, just as surely as for Israel's.

> It is too light a thing that you should be my servant
>   to raise up the tribes of Jacob
>   and to restore the preserved of Israel;
> I will give you as a light to the nations,
>   that my salvation may reach to the end of the earth.
>   49:6

Though the servant's mission is clear, the question of his identity admits of no easy solution. As early as the first century it puzzled the Nubian ambassador who inquired of the Apostle Philip,

> About who, pray, does the prophet say this, about himself or about some one else?
>   Acts 8:34

Scholars have proposed every conceivable possibility, but, in the opinion of Rowley, "it seems probable that no view will ever command general agreement."[57] The primary issue turns on whether the servant is interpreted as (1) an individual, (2) a collective personification of the nation or its faithful remnant, or (3) in some sense, both together.

---

[57] H. H. Rowley, *The Growth of the Old Testament* (New York: Harper Torchbooks, 1963), p. 97. For a full review of the theories, cf. C. R. North, *The Suffering Servant in Deutero-Isaiah*, 2nd ed. (New York: Oxford University Press, Inc., 1956), and H. H. Rowley, *The Servant of the Lord*, 2nd ed. (Oxford: Blackwell 1965), pp. 3–60.

401

The Servant as an Individual

Together with Philip's questioner, many have seen the individual and personal characteristics of the servant as decisive. There is not lacking a host of proposed candidates who in one way or another fulfill striking aspects of the servant's role. These range from known historical figures such as Moses, Jeremiah, Jehoiachin, or Cyrus to anonymous contemporaries of Deutero-Isaiah, or even the prophet-poet himself. Of a slightly different sort, but nevertheless individual in approach, are the efforts to apply the mythology of the dying and rising god (as in the Tammuz cult) or the ideal future king (Messiah).

The basic fallacy of this group of theories is the illegitimate isolation of the Suffering Servant poems from the rest of Deutero-Isaiah, with its references to Israel as Yahweh's servant. Likewise unconvincing are the efforts at explaining away the identification of the servant with the nation in the second servant song (49:3). Aspects of the various theories, nevertheless, have real merit. One finds it altogether convincing, for example, that figures from Israel's past like Moses and, more especially, Jeremiah had a profound influence upon the thought of Deutero-Isaiah. And, though the prophet's themes are basically Hebraic, the Babylonian environment may well have contributed to his storehouse of ritual concepts. The messianic interpretation of the servant's role, on the other hand, is hardly a viable one, as the servant is described with none of the trappings of kingship, and suffering is not for normative Judaic tradition a messianic function. This does not, however, preclude the faith-conviction of Christian interpreters that Jesus of Nazareth appropriated unto himself both roles—becoming at once Messiah and Suffering Servant.

The Servant as Israel

The evidence for a collective interpretation of the servant, a personification of Israel or the ideal remnant, is considerable. As we have seen, the unity of chapters 40–55 argues for it. Not only the crucial designation "servant," but other descriptive phrases and concepts applied to the Suffering Servant appear outside the four servant songs with reference to the nation. Both are chosen and upheld by God,[58] elected from the womb,[59] hidden away for future service,[60] endowed with God's spirit,[61] despised,[62] and exalted.[63] Each is an agent of Yahweh's righteousness, law, and salvation,[64] a

---

[58] 41:8–10; 44:1–2; 45:4 (42:1).
[59] 44:24; 46:3 (49:1).
[60] 51:16 (49:2).
[61] 42:5; 44:3; 48:16 (42:1).
[62] 49:7 (53:3ff.).
[63] 49:7 (52:13ff.).
[64] 42:21, 24; 45:8; 51:4–5; 54:14 (42:3–4; 49:4–6).

witness to the coastlands,[65] and a light to the nations.[66] In the second servant song, moreover, the servant is explicitly identified with Israel.

> And he said to me, "You are my servant,
> Israel, in whom I will be glorified."
> 49:3

That Israel's humiliation through exile could have called forth her personification as a suffering servant, and that the hard lesson thus learned could redound to her own and others' benefit is hardly difficult to conceive.

The major objection to the collective identification is the failure of the national history to fit the descriptions of the innocent suffering so willingly borne by the servant.

> The Lord God has opened my ear,
> and I was not rebellious,
> I turned not backward.
> I gave my back to the smiters,
> and my cheeks to those who pulled out the beard;
> I hid not my face
> from shame and spitting.
> 50:5–6

> He was oppressed, and he was afflicted,
> yet he opened not his mouth;
> like a lamb that is led to the slaughter,
> and like a sheep that before its shearers is dumb,
> so he opened not his mouth.
> 53:7

Only by totally disregarding the witness of the earlier prophets could Deutero-Isaiah have absolved the nation of her guilty involvement in the fate that befell her; and the prophetic influence upon his thinking makes that all but impossible. Outside the servant songs, Israel, for all her suffering, is anything but willing and uncomplaining in accepting her lot; even as a servant, she is deaf and blind to Yahweh's will.[67] In the second servant song the work of the servant is required to bring Israel back to Yahweh.

> And now the Lord says,
> who formed me from the womb to be his servant,
> to bring Jacob back to him,
> and that Israel might be gathered to him,
> 49:5

---

[65] 41:1, 5; 51:5 (42:4; 49:1).
[66] 42:6; 50:10; 51:4 (49:6). Note also the figure of the "wick," 43:17 (42:3).
[67] 42:19; 43:22–28; 48:1–8.

Finally, the concrete, personal description of the servant, especially as "the man of sorrows" in the fourth poem, seems more fitting for an individual than a people.

The Servant as Individual and Nation

Yet another approach to the problem begins with the well-known capacity of Hebrew thought to encompass individual and corporate realities within a single figure. We have seen numerous examples of the so-called "corporate personality" in the Old Testament: Abraham is Israel, so too Moses; or, to turn the figure, Israel is Yahweh's bride, or, at her worst, a harlot. Deutero-Isaiah clearly thinks in such patterns:

> Look to Abraham your father
> and to Sarah who bore you;
> for when he was but one I called him,
> and blessed him and made him many.
> 51:2

Such an approach probably best accounts for the otherwise irreconcilable corporate and individual features of the Suffering Servant. In a manner unnatural to western thought, the prophet's figure is a fluid one and oscillates from group to individual without marked transitions. The servant is the nation, the called people of God; also the faithful remnant, purged by the suffering of exile; but, again, an individual representing and embodying the nation. The servant, therefore, is Israel, but at the same time Israel as fulfilled in one personality which truly carries out the mission to which Israel is called by Yahweh.

That the Suffering Servant poems have called forth such widely divergent interpretations in no way discredits the profound truths they embody. Indeed, the appeal of the poems to persons of all theological persuasions only testifies to the basic and abiding validity of their approach to religious truth. Their author sums up the deepest insights of the centuries' old religious tradition which he represents and interprets its basic mission in such a brilliant and spiritually sensitive manner as to put all religions forever in his debt.

SELECTED READINGS

The Exile

Ackroyd, Peter R., *Exile and Restoration: A Study of Hebrew Thought of the Sixth Century B.C.*, The Old Testament Library (Philadelphia: The Westminster Press, 1968).

——, *Israel Under Babylon and Persia*, New Clarendon Bible (New York: Oxford University Press, Inc., 1970).

Klein, Ralph W., *Israel in Exile: A Theological Interpretation,* Overtures to Biblical Theology (Philadelphia: Fortress Press, 1979).

Raitt, Thomas M., *A Theology of Exile* (Philadelphia: Fortress Press, 1977).

Ezekiel

Broome, E. C., "Ezekiel's Abnormal Personality," *JBL,* LXV (1946), pp. 277–296.

Eichrodt, Walther, *Ezekiel: A Commentary,* Cosslett Quin, trans., Old Testament Library (Philadelphia: The Westminster Press, 1970).

Howie, Carl G., *The Date and Composition of Ezekiel, JBL* Monograph Series, Vol. 4 (Philadelphia: Society of Biblical Literature, 1950). Paperback.

May, Herbert G., "Introduction and Exegesis to the Book of Ezekiel," IB, Vol. VI, pp. 41–338.

Rowley, Harold H., *The Book of Ezekiel in Modern Study* (Manchester: Manchester University Press and John Rylands Library, 1953).

Torrey, C. C., *Pseudo-Ezekiel and the Original Prophecy* (New Haven, CT: Yale University Press, 1930).

Zimmerli, Walther, "Ezekiel," *IDBS,* pp. 314–317.

———, *Ezekiel I,* Ronald E. Clements, trans., Hermeneia (Philadelphia: Fortress Press, 1979). The English translation of a major commentary on Ezekiel 1–24, first published in German in 1969. The remainder of the commentary is currently available only in the German edition: *Ezechiel,* Biblischer Kommentar (Neukirchen, West Germany: Neukirchener Verlag, 1959).

Deutero-Isaiah

Anderson, Bernhard W., "Exodus Typology in Second Isaiah," *Israel's Prophetic Heritage,* Bernhard W. Anderson and Walter Harrelson, eds. (New York: Harper & Row, Publishers, 1962).

Knight, George A. F., *Deutero-Isaiah* (Nashville, TN: Abingdon Press, 1965).

McKenzie, John L., *Second Isaiah: Introduction, Translation, and Notes, The Anchor Bible,* Vol. 20 (Garden City, NY: Doubleday & Company, Inc., 1968).

Muilenburg, James, "Introduction and Exegesis to Isaiah 40–66," *IB,* Vol. V, pp. 381–773. An exceptionally fine work.

North, Christopher R., *The Suffering Servant in Deutero-Isaiah, an Historical and Critical Study* (New York: Oxford University Press, Inc., 1964).

Radday, Y. T., "Two Computerized Statistical-Linguistic Tests Concerning the Unity of Isaiah," *JBL,* 89 (1970), pp. 319–324. The application of computer techniques to the question of the authorship of the book of Isaiah.

Rowley, Harold H., *The Servant of the Lord and Other Essays on the Old Testament* (London: Lutterworth Press, 1952).

Smart, James D., *History and Theology in Second Isaiah: A Commentary on Isaiah 35, 40–66* (Philadelphia: The Westminster Press, 1965).

Torrey, Charles C., *The Second Isaiah: A New Interpretation* (New York: Charles Scribner's Sons, 1928).

Westermann, Claus, *Isaiah 40–66,* David M. G. Stalker, trans., The Old Testament Library (Philadelphia: The Westminster Press, 1969).

Zimmerli, Walther, and J. Jeremias, *The Servant of God,* Studies in Biblical Theology, No. 20 (Naperville, IL: Alex R. Allenson, 1959).

7

I WILL RETURN TO ZION

Thus says the Lord: I will return to Zion, and I will dwell in the midst of Jerusalem.

—Zechariah 8:3

With Cyrus' conquest of Babylon in 539 B.C., all the former Babylonian territories, including Syria and Palestine, came under Persian control. From his capital in Ecbatana, Cyrus ruled (539–530 B.C.) virtually all the Near East except Egypt. Even by modern standards his reign appears as an unusually enlightened one. Not only did he reject the Assyrian and Babylonian policies of brutal subjugation and displacement of conquered populations, but he actually encouraged cultural autonomy among the separate peoples of the realm. On the same clay cylinder which extols his conquest of Babylon, Cyrus cites his restoration of uprooted peoples to their homelands and the rebuilding of fallen shrines.

> I returned to [those] sacred cities on the other side of the Tigris, the sanctuaries of which have been in ruins for a long time, the images which [used] to live therein and established for them permanent sanctuaries. I [also] gathered all their [former] inhabitants and returned [to them] their habitations.[1]

1. THE PERIOD OF RESTORATION

In this light, the decree issued by Cyrus in 538 B.C. permitting the Jewish exiles to return home comes as no surprise. There is no reference to the

---

[1] *ANET*, p. 316 (*ANE*, p. 208).

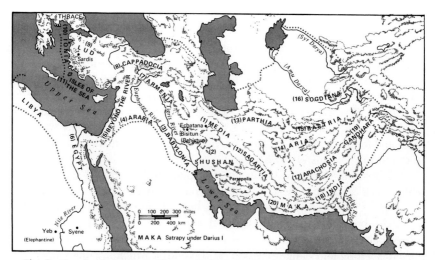

The Persian Empire, 539 to 332 B.C. (Adapted with permission of Macmillan Publishing Co., Inc., from Macmillan Bible Atlas by Y. Aharoni and Michael Avi-Yonah. Copyright © 1968 Carta, Jerusalem. © Copyright 1964 by Carta, Jerusalem. © Copyright 1966 by Carta, Jerusalem.)

edict as such in extant Persian records, but in the book of Ezra it is found in two versions: one in Hebrew (1:2–4) and the other in Aramaic (6:3–5). The latter report is from a collection of Aramaic documents utilized by the Chronicler (Ezra 4:8–6:18), the authenticity of which is highly regarded. The Aramaic language was by this time the *lingua franca* of international relations, used alike in Persia and Palestine; and apparently Ezra 6:3–5 preserves the king's official memorandum. The edict calls for restoration of the temple, prescribes its broad dimensions, and provides for defraying the cost of materials from the royal treasury. The temple vessels taken by Nebuchadrezzar, moreover, were to be returned to Jerusalem. The Hebrew report (1:2–4), which may preserve a royal proclamation made to the Jews throughout the empire, likewise records the king's directive for rebuilding the temple and provides further that the exiles shall be free to return to Jerusalem for that purpose or otherwise to assist the efforts financially. That Cyrus acted as a devotee of Yahweh, as assumed in the Hebrew account, is unsupported by any other available evidence. As we have seen, however, the king says virtually the same things in his cylinder inscription about Marduk as he is reported to say here about Yahweh.

Restoration: The Early Years

For the history of the restoration we are dependent upon the concluding portion of the Chronicler's work (Ezra–Nehemiah), supplemented by the Deuterocanonical (Apocryphal) book of I Esdras and the historical allusions in the books of the post-Exilic prophets. Problems abound, owing in no small degree to the disarranged text of Ezra-Nehemiah and the tendency of the Chronicler to telescope portions of the history.[2] We can determine, nevertheless, that the efforts to restore Judah lasted for more than a century and included four major stages: (1) the first return under Sheshbazzar's leadership, presumably in 538 B.C., and the initial efforts at laying the foundations of the temple; (2) a second return under Zerubbabel, bringing a renewal of work on the temple (520 B.C.) and its completion in 515 B.C.; (3) Nehemiah's governorship and the rebuilding of Jerusalem's walls (445 B.C. and following); and (4) Ezra's arrival with more returnees in 428 or 399 B.C and his reforms of Jewish life.

Sheshbazzar, a prince of Davidic lineage and possibly a son of Jehoiachin,[3] was chosen to lead the first group of exiles back to Judah. The number of the volunteers is unknown; but, in view of their meager efforts toward rebuilding, one would judge that they were few.[4] The reluctance of many Babylonian Jews to join the venture is scarcely surprising. The journey was a long and dangerous one, at the end of which lay many uncertainties. Since the arrival of the exiles in Babylon, moreover, a whole new generation had grown up who had never seen Jerusalem. Many, no doubt, had interests in Babylon which they could ill afford to abandon, and for that reason found it more practical to support the restoration efforts with monetary contributions. The first-century Jewish historian Josephus offers the succinct explanation: "Many abode in Babylon because they did not wish to leave their possessions."[5]

The conditions that confronted the repatriated Jews were extremely discouraging. The remnant territory of Judah was confined to a small area, roughly twenty-five miles square; and both Jerusalem and the surrounding countryside had recovered but little from the Babylonian devastation. Tensions were quick to develop between the returned exiles and Palestinian Jews who had not gone to Babylon, on the one hand, and the mixed population of northern Palestine (the Samaritans) and the inhabitants of Judah, on the other. The impoverished conditions were such that each man was kept busy securing his own basic needs and consequently had little time to give to the rebuilding efforts. All in all, the picture of things could hardly have contrasted more with the glowing promises of Ezekiel and Deutero-Isaiah.

The Chronicler has so conflated the work of Sheshbazzar with that of Zerubbabel that it is impossible to determine the full contribution of the former. It appears that, like Zerubbabel, Sheshbazzar was appointed gover-

---

[2] Cf. below, pp. 484–487.

[3] Cf. the "Shenazzar" of I Chron. 3:18.

[4] The figure of almost 50,000 cited in Ezra 2:64–65 and Neh. 7:66–67 represents the total of a later census list. Cf. W. F. Albright, *The Biblical Period from Abraham to Ezra*, pp. 110–111.

[5] *Antiquities of the Jews*, XI, 1.3.

nor over Judah, and that under his leadership the foundations of the temple were laid. Although it is not recorded of him, we would assume that the altar was rebuilt and the official cult resumed. Apparently very little else was accomplished, however, as the work had to begin all over again under Zerubbabel almost two decades later. We are not told what finally happened to Sheshbazzar; if he was Jehoiachin's son, and therefore a man of some years, perhaps he died shortly after the return.

Sometime before 522 B.C., Zerubbabel, a grandson of Jehoiachin, arrived with a second band of exiles.[6] Within the party was Joshua ben Jehozadak, a priest of Zadokite lineage who was elevated to the position of "high priest." The Jewish community now had two leaders: the governer Zerubbabel, appointee of the Persian king, and the high priest Joshua, director of spiritual affairs. Chiefly because of their efforts and the morale-building support provided by the prophets Haggai and Zechariah, the work on the temple commenced again in the autumn of 520 B.C.

Political developments within the Persian empire most likely played a part in reviving the languishing spirits of the Jews. Cyrus was succeeded by his son Cambyses (530–522 B.C.), who in 525 B.C. invaded Egypt and brought it into the empire. At the latter's death, Darius I (522–486 B.C.) was faced with the rival claims of a pretender to the crown and far-flung revolts which had to be settled before he could secure control of the realm. He celebrated his victories over the rebels in the famous relief carved high on the Behistun Rock. In the second year of his reign, however, he was still occupied with revolts in Babylon. In this upheaval some Jews saw signs of Yahweh's imminent intervention—an approaching downfall of Persia and the rise of a new Jewish state under Zerubbabel's messianic rule.[7] Needless to say, these hopes did not materialize; but because of them a new zeal for raising the temple was discovered.

From the beginning, the builders faced the twin problems of meager resources and outside intervention. When the Samaritans, who occupied central Palestine, were rebuffed in their offer of assistance,[8] they proceeded to frustrate the efforts at every opportunity. Their complaints, it would appear, led to an investigation by Tattenai, a satrap of Abar-nahara ("Beyond the River," or the Fifth Satrapy,[9] which included all Palestine and Syria). His inquiry addressed to Darius concerning the Jews and their rebuilding program led to the discovery of Cyrus's earlier edict and consequently the king's confirmation and renewal of support.[10] Given this

---

[6] Cf. John Bright, A History of Israel, pp. 348–349, for a discussion of the problem of the date.

[7] Cf. Haggai and Zechariah, esp. Hag. 2:20–23; Zech. 3.8; 4:1–6, 10–14; 6:9–15 (substitute "Zerubbabel" for "Joshua").

[8] Ezra 4:1–5.

[9] Herodotus, iii, 89f.

[10] Ezra 5:3–6:15.

The gate of Xerxes at Persepolis, the site to which Darius moved the main Persian capital from Pasargadae. (Courtesy of the Oriental Institute, University of Chicago.)

needed boost, the work proceeded and the temple was completed in March 515 B.C.

The new edifice was not so splendid as the former temple of Solomon, as evidenced by the Jewish elders' tears of disappointment.[11] It was a mighty achievement for the Jewish community, nevertheless, and was destined to become the center and bulwark of its life in the post-Exilic era. Priestly leadership, in fact, once established in the high priest Joshua, was from this time onward the dominant internal force in Judah. That the Persians recognized ecclesiastical rule in the provinces is shown by the fact that the priests of Hierapolis in northern Syria were able to levy their own taxes and strike their own coins.[12] From the end of Zerubbabel's administration until the appointment of Nehemiah, Judah apparently existed as a part of the larger province of Samaria, but under the local authority of Joshua and his successors.

The fate of Zerubbabel remains one of the unsolved mysteries of post-Exilic history. Having become the object of messianic prophecies, he possibly was removed by the Persians to prevent his leading a Jewish insurrection. Had he been guilty of any overt act of disloyalty to the empire, how-

[11] Ezra 3:12–13.
[12] W. F. Albright, *The Biblical Period from Abraham to Ezra*, pp. 95–96.

ever, it is inconceivable that Darius would have lent him support at the time of Tattenai's inquiry. There may be significance in the fact that Zerubbabel is the last known member of the Davidic family to hold political office.

Restoration: The Later Years

Our sources of information for the next seventy years of Jewish history are limited to a brief passage in the book of Ezra (4:6–23, misplaced as to context) and the commentary on social and moral conditions reflected in the books of Malachi, Obadiah, and Nehemiah. This evidence is enough to show, however, that the restoration of the temple did not effect the immediate changes that its builders had anticipated. The morale of the Jews continued to suffer from impoverished conditions and the harassment of hostile neighbors. Not only did the rift with the Samaritans grow ever wider, but Edomites, pressured out of their former territory by Arab tribesmen, now became a menace in southern Palestine.[13] It was doubtless for these reasons that an abortive effort to rebuild the broken walls of Jerusalem, and thus fortify the city, was attempted early in the reign of Artaxerxes I (465–424 B.C.). The misplaced Ezra passage (4:6–23) accounts for the thwarting of the plans by local officials (probably Samaritans), who managed to convince Artaxerxes that the Jews were plotting revolt.

If the restored temple failed to attract huge numbers of Diaspora (i.e., dispersed) Jews back to Judah, the population nevertheless steadily increased until by the middle of the fifth century it totaled roughly 50,000.[14] Unfortunately, religious zeal did not increase proportionately. The prophet Malachi decried his people's lack of support for the temple, the unpaid tithes, and the profane sacrifices. The Levites were so poorly supported that they were forced to take work in the fields,[15] and peasants cut grain on the Sabbath while hucksters in the marketplace did business as usual.[16] The hard times, worsened by poor crop years, called forth the base and selfish interests of men.[17] It was a bitter time for indigent members of the community, as neither bonds of blood nor covenant were taken very seriously by merciless moneylenders who foreclosed on their helpless victims, forcing entire families into slavery.[18] If any further proof were needed of the people's failing sense of covenant identity, it was evident in the increasing rate of divorce among Jews and the growing number of Jewish-gentile marriages.[19] Nothing less than a fresh, vital leadership,

[13] Cf. Obad. 1:1ff.
[14] Cf. footnote 4, above.
[15] Neh. 13:10.
[16] Neh. 13:15–22.
[17] Implications of such hardships are to be seen in the Book of Malachi (cf. Mal. 3:11). Also the locust plague and drought described by Joel belong probably to this period.
[18] Neh. 5:1–5.
[19] Mal. 2:11f.; Neh. 13:23–27.

forceful enough to rally the disheartened and apathetic populace around a common cause, could suffice to recover the spirit of the restoration. The two men fitted to fill such a role were Nehemiah and Ezra, both raised in the strict traditions of Babylonian Judaism.

THE EZRA–NEHEMIAH PROBLEM. The question of the relationship of Ezra to Nehemiah—the sequence of their careers and their respective dates—is a much debated problem. Once again, it is the disarranged and sometimes obscure text of Ezra–Nehemiah that gives rise to the confusion. One receives the impression that Ezra's mission preceded that of Nehemiah; it is said (Ezra 7:7) that he was sent to Judah in the seventh year of Artaxerxes, whereas Nehemiah arrived for the first time in the twentieth year of Artaxerxes (Neh. 2:1) and, following a brief return to Persia, was sent back once more in the thirty-second year of the same king (13:6–7). We are also given to believe (Neh. 8:9; 12:36) that the work of the two leaders overlapped at some point. Were our sources taken at face value, then, it would appear that Ezra arrived in 458 B.C. (the seventh year of Artaxerxes I) and was still active as a reform leader when Nehemiah began his administration as governor in 445 B.C. (the twentieth year of Artaxerxes I).

Most scholars are convinced, however, that these impressions are partially incorrect, and that Nehemiah's career, in fact, preceded that of Ezra. A full presentation of the evidence would take us into greater detail than we can develop here[20]; but, in large part, it concerns the conditions in Judah as described in the Ezra accounts which presuppose Nehemiah's work, and conversely the circumstances of Nehemiah's day which are scarcely conceivable were Ezra's reforms already accomplished. When Ezra arrived in Jerusalem, for example, it appears more than probable that the walls were already rebuilt (Ezra 9:9) and the city largely repopulated (Ezra 10:11), both the results of Nehemiah's efforts. Nehemiah, furthermore, was contemporary with the high priest Eliashib (Neh. 3:1), and Ezra with Eliashib's grandson Johanan (Ezra 10:6; Neh. 12:10–11, 22), apparently after the latter had succeeded to the high priestly office. A telling point, finally, is the difficulty of believing that Ezra's reforms were the failure that we should have to assume them to have been had they come prior to Nehemiah's administration.[21] The abuses deplored by Nehemiah were in fact attacked head on by Ezra and the latter's effectiveness as a reformer is attested by the lasting mark he left on the later Judaism.

As for Nehemiah's dates, there is little doubt that he was sent by Artax-

---

[20] A thorough review of the evidence, together with a proposed solution which has been adopted here, is offered in John Bright, *A History of Israel*, pp. 362–386. For a recent proposal which argues for the traditional Ezra–Nehemiah sequence, see Frank M. Cross, "A Reconstruction of the Judean Restoration," *JBL*, 94 (1975), pp. 4–18.

[21] Cf. John Bright, *A History of Israel*, pp. 377–378.

Aramaic papyrus from the Jewish colony at Elephantine, in Egypt; fifth century B.C. The text is a legal document, the deed of a house from a father to his daughter. (Courtesy of the Brooklyn Museum.)

erxes I in 445 B.C. and then after a twelve-year administration returned to Persia and received reappointment for a second term (c. 433 B.C.). The more difficult question concerns the dates for Ezra. It is entirely possible that "the seventh year of Artaxerxes" should be taken in reference not to Artaxerxes I but to Artaxerxes II (404–360 B.C.), in which case Ezra would have arrived in Jerusalem in 398 B.C. If so, however, we should have to discount those passages which make Ezra and Nehemiah contemporaries, since by no stretch of the imagination could the latter's second term have lasted so long.[22] There are other and perhaps more serious objections as well. The Elephantine correspondence (i.e., the Passover Papyrus), for example, reveals that by 419 B.C. the Persian authorities were dispatching directives via Jeruslem which regulated the cultic life of Egyptian Jews in accordance with Pentateuchal law. That this could have happened prior to Ezra's reforms, which established Torah in Jerusalem itself, is difficult to conceive. For such reasons, an alternate position which accepts the year 428 B.C. for the beginning of Ezra's mission appears to be growing in acceptance among scholars and provides the most plausible theory yet proposed.[23] This date is premised on the likelihood of a scribal omission of a single letter in Ezra 7:7 (a case of haplography due to the consecutive occurrence of three words with the same initial letter) so that the "seventh

[22] More to the point, we know from the Elephantine Papyri that in 408 Bagoas, a native of Persia, was serving as governor of Judah. Cf. *ANET*, pp. 491–492 (*ANE*, pp. 279–281).

[23] Cf. John Bright, *A History of Israel*, pp. 385–386; W. F. Albright, *The Biblical Period from Abraham to Ezra*, p. 93 and footnote 193; Martin Noth, *The History of Israel*, pp. 315–335.

year of Artaxerxes" initially read "thirty-seventh year" (428 B.C.). Supposing this hypothesis to be correct, the following reconstruction of the two leaders' careers may be sketched.

NEHEMIAH. The memoirs of Nehemiah[24] present a vivid picture of the man and his devotion to Israel's mission as the people of Yahweh. Hearing of the intolerable conditions in Jerusalem while serving as cupbearer to Artaxerxes, he requested the king's permission to go there to help with its restoration. His petition was not only granted, but the zealous Jew received the king's appointment for a term as Judah's governor, as well. It was at this point, presumably, that Judah was established as a province apart from Samaria.

Nehemiah's major achievement was the rebuilding of Jerusalem's broken walls. With such enthusiasm did he recruit the necessary workers, organize their labor, and spur their energies, that within 52 days the walls, in some form, were erect (Neh. 6:15).[25] All the more to his credit was the effective manner in which he offset the opposition of neighboring peoples—some of them Yahweh worshipers—who attempted to prevent the completion of the work: Sanballat, governor of Samaria; Tobiah, an Ammonite; and Geshem, an Arabian (6:1f.).[26] With one hand on their weapons and half their number standing guard, the builders withstood every effort of their opponents to shatter their morale. Eventually there was held an impressive ceremony of dedication, with a procession around the new walls, a sacrifice of thank offerings, and the singing of psalms (Neh. 12:27–43).

With the city of Jerusalem thus fortified and repopulated with one tenth of Judah's citizenry (Neh. 11:1f.), Nehemiah turned his attention to problems yet unsolved: an improvement of the community's economic and moral standards and a restoration of Jewish identity. A blunt and tactless man, he did what he could to put a stop to the exploitation of the poor by prohibiting usury and demanding immediate restitution of all unjustly acquired properties. Sabbath observance and tithing were enjoined and marriages to foreigners prohibited. Clearly, Nehemiah was convinced that Judah's survival as a unique people depended upon her separation from "the people of the land," that is to say, from all foreigners and syncretistic-minded Jews who did not share the strict faith of the repatriated exiles. Consequently, the walls which he was hopeful of erecting about his people consisted of more than fortifications of stone.

[24] Neh. 1:1–7:73; 11:1–2; 12:27–43; 13:4–31.
[25] Bright judiciously interprets the notation of Josephus (Antiquities of the Jews, XI, V, 8) that the work took two years and four months to mean that the full completion of the task—battlements, gates, revetments—took that long (A History of Israel, p. 365).
[26] Tobiah's name and those of both his and Sanballat's sons are Yahweh names.

EZRA. We have no way of determining the duration of Nehemiah's second term[27]; but, if our theory is correct, a few years after his return to Judah from Persia (c. 433 B.C.), Ezra arrived (428 B.C.) with his own letter of appointment from the Persian king (Ezra 7:12–26). The presence of the two leaders in Jerusalem at the same time poses no problem, as their roles were not identical. Nehemiah, as governor, was a political administrator, whereas Ezra was commissioned as a spiritual leader and religious reformer. Once again, it is interesting to observe that the Persians continued to encourage the indigenous religions of the provinces. Jews still in Babylon and Persia were invited to join Ezra's party, and funds from the royal and provincial treasuries were allocated for the support of the temple cult.

Ezra is described as a priest and a "scribe skilled in the law of Moses" (Ezra 7:6, 11). His appointment, however, made him an official agent of the king, a "Commissioner for Jewish Affairs," as it were. He was duly authorized to investigate religious conditions in Jerusalem and Judah, apportion subsidies and gifts for the temple, and install judges in accordance with Jewish religious law. His jurisdiction extended, moreover, to practicing Jews throughout the entire Fifth Satrapy. Not only was he the recognized authority in religious affairs, but his decisions in this sphere were tantamount to royal law (Ezra 7:26). He was thus delegated to carry through in a more systematic manner than Nehemiah had been able to do the regulation and reform of Jewish religious life. Nehemiah had prepared the way for Ezra, however, and so close was their understanding of the community's needs that we can well imagine that when Nehemiah was in Persia in 433 B.C. he petitioned the king to appoint Ezra.[28]

Ezra seems to have wasted no time in beginning his work; perhaps his basic aims were accomplished within the course of a single year. He had brought with him from Babylonia the "book of the law of Moses" (Neh. 8:1)—possibly the Pentateuch or at least the Priestly Code[29]—and this provided the program for his reforms. Within two months after his arrival, at the autumn Feast of Booths, he assembled the Jewish community in one of the city squares and read to them from the Torah. The scene is a memorable one. Standing on a high wooden platform built for the purpose, he read from early morning until midday as the Levites stood alongside and translated the Hebrew into the spoken Aramaic of the day. The people were moved to tears by what they heard, and on the following day began

[27] Though we know that Bagoas was serving as governor of Judah in 408 (cf. footnote 22 above), we have no information as to the date when his term began.

[28] Some have theorized a rivalry between the two men on the basis of the failure of Ezra's memoirs to mention Nehemiah and the slight references to Ezra in Nehemiah's reports. If this is to be taken seriously, it should have to be assumed that their differences were of a personal rather than a doctrinal nature.

[29] Note the discovery (Neh. 8:14) of the Levitical prescription for the Feast of Booths (Lev. 23:33–43; P).

the celebration of the week-long Feast of Booths in the manner prescribed by Torah.

In making Torah the authoritative guide for the community's life, Ezra had established a secure base for the rest of his work. He turned next to the disturbing problem of mixed marriages. Two months after the Feast of Booths, during the rainy winter season, once more he addressed the people as they huddled in a driving rain (Ezra 10:9f.). Charging them with trespassing the Law by their foreign marriages, he called upon them to separate once for all from the people of the land and immediately dissolve all such illegal unions.[30] This they agreed to do, and judges were appointed to oversee the matter. Within three months the order was carried out in respect to every mixed marriage in Judah. Then followed yet another assembly of the community (Neh. 9–10) in which the people affirmed their faith in Yahweh's covenant and pledged themselves to conform their lives to his Torah. They should henceforth refrain from all marriages with foreigners, keep the Sabbath and the Sabbatical Year, render their tithes and offerings, and support the maintenance of the temple with an annual tax.

Ezra's final years are as obscure as those of the other restoration leaders. Perhaps he died in Jerusalem a few years after instituting his reforms, as Josephus claims.[31] His lasting contribution to Judaic religion, however, is quite clear. Many would say that he, more than Ezekiel, deserves the title "Father of Judaism"; for it was he, above all others, who made Judaism a religion of "the Book." The importance of this can scarcely be exaggerated. With Jewish statehood no longer possible of achievement and with large numbers of Jews scattered throughout distant lands, Judaism was forced to find a new focal point if it were to survive. The temple's restoration was a step in this direction; it symbolized God's presence with his people, even for Diaspora Jews who visited Jerusalem but rarely if at all. It was not sufficient, however, to recover the sense of corporate solidarity which had made Israel a vigorous force in the past, or to provide the needed instruction in Hebrew tradition upon which the life of faith depended. This the Torah was best suited to do; and the synagogue provided the institutional setting in which it could be studied and taught. Thus it was Ezra who introduced into Palestinian Judaism the model of the Babylonian community gatherings (cf. Neh. 8–9: the reading and expounding of Torah before the assembled people; its translation into the spoken Aramaic; the prayers and psalms) that were soon to be found wherever Jews lived.

There were serious dangers, of course, inherent in Ezra's methods. To exalt the written law to such pivotal status was to run the risk of an undue stress on externals—a perennial problem which the prophets had warned against and one which would plague Judaism to an even greater degree in

[30] Cf. Deut. 7:1–4.
[31] *Antiquities of the Jews*, XI, V, 5.

the years ahead. Likewise, the spirit of separatism which he and Nehemiah promoted with such passion falls miserably short of the depth of perception with which Deutero-Isaiah called upon his people to go to the nations. Indeed, the thought of Jewish fathers sending away their gentile wives and children in compliance with Ezra's enforced dissolution of mixed marriages is for most readers of the Old Testament one of the low points of its history. Were the action motivated simply by racial animosity, it would be altogether beyond defense. But in point of fact the provocation was more akin to the state of affairs in Elijah's day when Canaanite syncretism threatened to obliterate Hebrew faith. Much of the Yahweh worship found by the exiles upon their return to Palestine was doubtless of such a syncretistic sort, and its fruits were all too evident in the community ills we have noted. Ezra's aims were not directed toward racial isolation so much as toward religious reform; he conceived it to be his task to restore to a deteriorating religious community the dignity and holiness without which it could not continue to exist. In this, his efforts proved most successful.

2. THE LATTER SPLENDOR OF THIS HOUSE: HAGGAI, ZECHARIAH, AND MALACHI

Though the quality of Hebrew prophecy reached its watershed with Deutero-Isaiah, the prophetic influence upon contemporary affairs in Judah was never greater than during the restoration period. Three prophets in particular spoke to the immediate, practical necessity of restoring the cult: Haggai, Zechariah, and Malachi. The first two are credited by the Chronicler (Ezra 5:1; 6:14) with a role in the rebuilding of the temple, and their oracles show them to have been the moving spirit behind Zerubbabel. Malachi belongs to the later period after the temple's restoration, but, like Haggai and Zechariah, his consuming passion was for Yahweh's house and the proper support of its worship.

Haggai

Personal details concerning the prophet Haggai are limited strictly to his role in the temple rebuilding of Zerubbabel's day. Inferences to the effect that he was an old man (on the basis of Hag. 2:3) and perhaps a priest (2:10–14) are gratuitous. His small book consists of four (possibly five) oracles, each one precisely dated and all belonging to the autumn of the year 520 B.C.

    1. The summons to rebuild the temple: 1:1–15a
       (Aug.–Sept., 520 B.C.)

417

2. The future splendor of the temple: 1:15b–2:9
   (Sept.–Oct., 520 B.C.)
3. Holiness and uncleanness: 2:10–19
   (Nov.–Dec., 520 B.C.)
4. God's word to Zerubbabel: 2:20–23
   (Nov.–Dec., 520 B.C.)

Some scholars, following J. W. Rothstein, regard 2:15–17 as a separate and misplaced oracle which originally followed 1:15a.[32] Such a transposition is plausible (thus changing the "ninth month" in 2:18 to read "the sixth month"), but it does not so readily clarify the obscure meaning of 2:10–14 (taken to refer to the unclean Samaritans) as its supporters claim. The chronicle-like format of the book and the consistent third-person references to the prophet incline some to believe that we have here excerpts from a temple work report rather than Haggai's own personal accounts. It is doubtful, however, that the style is all that different from the first-person reports in the other prophetic books.[33]

If ever a prophet's work was marked by singleness of purpose, it is Haggai's. We have no way of knowing the full scope of his prophetic career; but for so long as the temple remained a heap of ruins, it was his declared mission to expend his total energies toward seeing it rebuilt. In the early autumn of 520 B.C., therefore, he took his stand alongside Zerubbabel and Joshua (interestingly, neither he nor his colleague Zechariah ever mentions the other) and exhorted his fellow Jews to fall in behind their efforts to restore Yahweh's house.

In no sense blind to the prevailing poverty as a factor in his people's apathy, he takes pains to describe their sorry plight.

> You have sown much and harvested little. You eat but you never have enough . . . and he who earns wages earns wages to put them into a bag with holes.
>
> 1:6

In looking only to their bare physical needs, the prophet says, the people have found no satisfaction. The hard times go on; there is drought and there are no returns from the soil. He therefore recalls the old Deuteronomic logic; when things go bad, it should call one back to God. The reason in this case is plain to see.

> Because of my house that lies in ruins . . .
>
> 1:9

Behind his words is the threat of further poverty and starvation so long as this insult to Yahweh is allowed to continue.

---

[32] Cf. D. Winton Thomas, "Haggai," *IB*, Vol. 6, pp. 1043–1044.
[33] Cf. Otto Eissfeldt, *The Old Testament, An Introduction*, p. 428.

As we have seen, conditions were propitious for such a challenge as he issues. Thus, after eighteen years in which each man had busied himself with his own house to the neglect of the temple, the work began again. It then became the prophet's task to inspire the builders' confidence by assuring them of Yahweh's support. When in less than a month the work began to lag because of the modest results of their labor (2:1–4), he promised a splendor for the new temple that would surpass the first one and a bounty from the land that would replace the prevailing poverty. There are obscure references to an apocalyptic-like shaking of the cosmic order and the overthrow of kingdoms, events which should avail to fill the temple with the treasures of the nations and establish Zerubbabel as Messiah (2:6–7, 20–23).

The final oracle (2:20–23) is sometimes regarded as secondary since it is dated on the very same day as the preceding oracle and repeats 2:6. It is doubtful, however, if these are ample grounds for denying it to Haggai. His description of Zerubbabel as God's "chosen" and his "signet ring" envision him as the long-awaited Davidic ruler. As the signet ring bears the unique seal of its owner's personal authority, so is Zerubbabel's relationship with Yahweh as his chosen agent. Harrelson comments on the dangerous precedent of fixing the eschatological hope upon a living political figure, but praises the prophet's restrained language and consistent emphasis on Yahweh himself as the sovereign Lord of Israel's affairs.[34]

The most serious charge popularly leveled against Haggai, and Zechariah and Malachi as well, is the alleged loss of the spiritual and moral thrust of the older prophecy. Strong denunciations of sin and corruption, it is said, have given way to the pragmatic concerns of a prophecy now submerged in the service of the cult. Although none could debate the point that post-Exilic prophecy is not the equal of the earlier prophecy at its best, the total disparagement of these later figures fails to do justice either to the peculiar demands of their times or to the prophetic verve with which they responded to them. Prophecy in the old sense was on the way out, but its exit was not so rapid as sometimes conceived. Haggai and his colleagues, convinced that Hebrew faith could survive only if it recaptured its vital center, gave themselves unstintingly to the task of restoring its broken structures. If there is a basic difference between the pre-Exilic and post-Exilic prophets in this respect, then Rowley has stated it succinctly:

> The pre-exilic prophets declared that the forms of religion without the substance were meaningless, since it was the substance that gave meaning to the forms, while the post-exilic prophets rather urged that where there was the substance of religion it must express itself in the forms.[35]

[34] Walter Harrelson, *Interpreting the Old Testament*, p. 389.
[35] H. H. Rowley, *The Growth of the Old Testament*, pp. 120–121.

Given this change of emphasis, and allowing its justification on the basis of a new set of needs, the post-Exilic prophets were as truly the conscience of their age as the earlier prophets had been of theirs. Indeed, the observation of one of Haggai's detractors that "the prophet seems to have included stone and timber amongst the essentials of his spiritual and religious ideal"[36] may be cited as an unwitting tribute.

Zechariah

Like Ezekiel, whose influence he reflects, Zechariah appears to have been both prophet and priest (cf. Neh. 12:16).[37] The initial oracle in his book is dated October–November 520 B.C., two months after Zerubbabel's beginning on the temple and a month prior to Haggai's last oracle. Whether this means that he was later than Haggai in throwing his support behind the rebuilding program or even a younger protégé of the former prophet, we have no way of knowing. The length of his career is equally as obscure as Haggai's; his final oracle is dated November–December 518 B.C.

It is generally agreed that only the first eight chapters of the book of Zechariah can with certainty be ascribed to the prophet himself. Unlike the book of Haggai, the oracles here are recorded in the first person, excepting the dated headings which introduce the three main divisions of the work (1:1; 1:7; 7:1).[38]

1. A summons to repentance: 1:1–6
   (Oct.–Nov. 520 B.C.)
2. Eight visions: 1:7–6:15
   (Jan.–Feb. 519 B.C.)
3. Oracles on fasting and Yahweh's return to Zion: chs. 7–8
   (Nov.–Dec. 518 B.C.)

Not nearly so prosaic as Haggai's oracles, much of Zechariah's message is couched in visions replete with the baroque figures and symbols reminiscent of an Ezekiel: night riders that patrol the earth on horses of different colors (1:8–17), oppressive nations symbolized as horns (1:18–21), a flying scroll (5:1–4), wickedness personified as a woman in a basket (5:5–11), and the like. Together with his Exilic predecessor, Zechariah must be reckoned as a forerunner of the later apocalyptic school. Typical of the style, the prophet is instructed concerning the future by angels with direct access to

[36] T. H. Robinson, *Prophecy and the Prophets in Ancient Israel* (New York: Charles Scribner's Sons, 1923), p. 177.

[37] A scribal confusion of Zechariah the prophet with Zechariah son of Berechiah (Isa. 8:2) accounts for the error in the superscription (1:1). That Zechariah the prophet was the son of Iddo the priest seems beyond doubt (Ezra. 5:1; 6:14; Neh. 12:16).

[38] The verse 7:8, a third-person heading without a date, breaks the connection between verses 7 and 9 and is best deleted.

the heavenly councils. Consequently, he does not so much deliver oracles in Yahweh's name as report the revelations vouchsafed to him through angelic mediation. This contrast with the older prophecy, though ever so subtle, is indicative of the movement away from prophecy in its traditional form. The direct, though sporadic, illumination of the spokesman of the divine word is giving way, however gradually, to the assured but once-removed revelations of the apocalyptist, as well as to the legal interpretations of the scribe.

Likewise anticipatory of such changes is Zechariah's appeal to the witness of past prophecy (1:1–6; cf. 7:7). For the first time, we have a prophetic summons to repentance issued under the invoked authority of "the former prophets." If his own stature as an authoritative spokesman of Yahweh is not thereby enhanced, he nevertheless proves himself an authentic representative of the prophetic tradition. "Return to me and I will return to you" are Yahweh's only terms for Judah. That warnings of Israel's earlier prophets overtook the fathers, he declares, is acknowledged fact; his people should not make the same mistake again. When a delegation inquires of the prophet whether with the new temple there is any need to continue the fast commemorating the destruction of the first temple (ch. 7), Zechariah's reply turns them toward the indispensable elements that precede all true fasts. It is no narrow cultist, insensitive to human values and the moral imperative, who more than once enjoins his compatriots:

> Thus says the Lords of hosts, Render true judgments, show kindness and mercy each to his brother, do not oppress the widow, the fatherless, the sojourner, or the poor; and let none of you devise evil against his brother in your heart.
>
> 7:9–10

The original burst of energy that moved the temple builders to rally behind Zerubbabel had by Zechariah's day largely spent itself. As Darius proved himself equal to his challenges and secured his control of the realm, the dream of national restoration suffered a corresponding reversal in Judah. But for the morale-building efforts of Haggai, the enterprise might once more have stopped short. When Zechariah joined his support to the project it was a time for restoring confidence and hope. Consequently, his series of visions (1:7–6:15) are directed toward that end. The horsemen who patrol the earth (1:7–17) find all at rest, but it is only the calm that precedes the storm. Yahweh is preparing to shake the nations that his people might be restored in their land.

> I have returned to Jerusalem with compassion; my house shall be built in it, says the Lord of hosts. . . . My cities shall again overflow with prosperity, and the Lord will again comfort Zion and again choose Jerusalem.
>
> 1:16–17

The oppressor nations shall be scattered like horns before the blows of Yahweh's smiths (1:18–21). When a man with a measuring line makes ready to determine Jerusalem's dimensions, he is counseled to desist, since the city is to be inhabited with such a multitude as to resist any encompassing wall. As in the Eden mythology, God himself will serve as walls to his people.

Zechariah, nevertheless, did not succumb to the narrow nationalism which looked for Judah's subjugation of the nations. He envisioned the oppressor's defeat, but apparently entertained no further dreams of conquest. The influence of Isaiah can be seen in his finest description of the coming kingdom, wherein the nations willingly join themselves to Yahweh's people and both alike dwell in his presence.

> And many nations shall join themselves to the Lord in that day, and shall be my people; and I will dwell in the midst of you.
> 2:11

For those who "despised the day of small things"—the slow and painstaking work of rebuilding—Zechariah offered the encouragement of changes soon to take place. In even less mistakable terms than Haggai's he depicts Zerubbabel as the Davidic prince chosen by Yahweh to lead Judah to her destined glory. Addressing the great pile of rubble and stone awaiting its place in the temple's construction, he confidently promises: "Before Zerubbabel you shall become a plain." As the messianic "Branch,"[39] he will not only rebuild the temple, but will bear royal honor and be duly crowned and enthroned.[40] Reflecting a more complex set of expectations than is apparent in Haggai, Zechariah's portrayal of the high priest Joshua has him share a significant role alongside Zerubbabel. He is first mentioned in the vision of Yahweh's heavenly council (3:1–10), where he is charged with some unnamed guilt by the accusing angel, "the satan" ("the accuser"; not yet the demonic, tempting power he was to become for later Hebrew thought). But Yahweh himself acts as Joshua's defender, invests him with the garments of purity, and charges him with the administration of his house. He and Zerubbabel are depicted as two olive trees flanking a gold lampstand, for which they serve as a constant supply of oil. The lampstand is Yahweh, with Zerubbabel and Joshua, his princely and priestly servants. This conception of a prince and a high priest allied in the cause of building God's kingdom anticipates the later Qumran messianism with its royal and

---

[39] In Isaiah (11:1) and Jeremiah (23:5; 33:15) the figure of the branch is used in reference to the coming king.

[40] The reference to Joshua as the one who is crowned (6:11) represents either (1) a later scribal substitution of the name Joshua for that of Zerubbabel or (2) a dual crowning, whereby the crown is placed first upon the head of Joshua, who in turn confers it upon Zerubbabel.

priestly Messiahs.[41] There is, nevertheless, no mistaking the fact that for Zechariah Yahweh himself is the sole source of Judah's hope.

Not by might, nor by power, but by my spirit, says the Lord of hosts.
4:6

DEUTERO-ZECHARIAH. The reasons for denying Zechariah's authorship of chapters 9–14 of the book are well founded. The Persian background of the earlier chapters is nowhere evident; the peaceful conditions of Zerubbabel's day have given way to a time of international upheaval; and at one point, Greece, the next world conqueror, is called by name (9:13). Nowhere is there mention of Zerubbabel or Joshua; rather, unnamed "shepherds" appear as the leaders of the community. Neither does the theological perspective nor the literary style set well with Zechariah's oracles. The apocalyptic element is more pronounced in these chapters and the viewpoint more narrowly nationalistic—sometimes unjustifiably offensive (cf. 9:15; 14:12).

Often referred to as "Deutero-Zechariah," as if ascribed to one author, the work in fact may come from two or more of the prophet's disciples who possibly lived at different times. Many scholars are inclined to view chapters 9–11 and 12–14 as separate units and from different hands, though the obscurity of the material makes all such distinctions somewhat tenuous. Although a pre-Exilic date has never been conclusively ruled out for some of the oracles (cf. the references to Assyria, Egypt, and the northern kingdom), in their present form the chapters fit best within the Greek period and therefore are to be dated as late as the fourth century B.C., following Alexander's conquests (possibly the subject of 9:1–8). The historical allusions and the advanced apocalyptic style argue for such a position. Interestingly enough, prophecy is assumed to have ceased (ch. 13), presumably because all that the prophets had foretold is now felt to be on the brink of fulfillment.

Notwithstanding the objectionable passages depicting the victorious Judah lording it over her defeated enemies, there appears here as well the memorable portrayal of the triumphant king who comes to his kingdom riding on an ass—the symbol of peace (9:9–10). The influence of Isaiah (Isa., ch. 9) and Micah (Mic., ch. 5) is unmistakable. Likewise, the obscure shepherd oracle (11:4–17) and the references to one who is pierced in 12:10 would appear to pick up the Suffering Servant theme of Deutero-Isaiah. The influence of these passages upon the formation of the New Testament Gospel tradition was considerable.

[41] Cf. Helmer Ringgren, *The Faith of Qumran* (Philadelphia: Fortress Press, 1963), pp. 167ff.; Millar Burrows, *More Light on the Dead Sea Scrolls* (New York: The Viking Press, Inc., 1958), pp. 297–311.

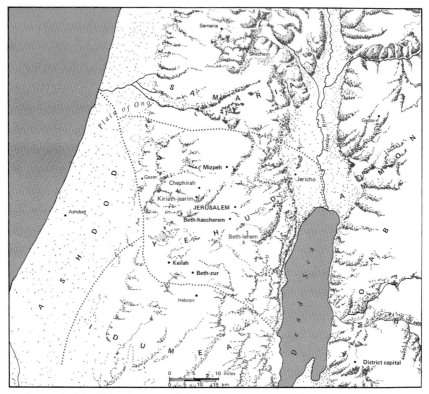

The land of Judah in the days of the return, c. 440 B.C. (Adapted with permission of Macmillan Publishing Co., Inc., from Macmillan Bible Atlas by Y. Aharoni and Michael Avi-Yonah. Copyright © 1968 Carta, Jerusalem. © Copyright 1964 by Carta, Jerusalem. © Copyright 1966 by Carta, Jerusalem.)

Malachi

The book of Malachi concludes the collection of the Twelve Prophets in the Jewish Canon. Neither the prophet's ancestry nor any other personal datum concerning him is given; even his name, which means "my messenger," may be no more than a label appended by an editor on the basis of 3:1, "Behold I send my messenger." Since the initial word, *massa'* ("oracle" or "burden") appears also as the headings for Zechariah 9–11 and 12–14, it has been theorized that the oracles here once stood with the latter collections as an anonymous tripartite appendix to the Minor Prophets.[42] Such considerations, however, in no way challenge either the unity or independent authorship of these four chapters. Whatever the prophet's name, he is to be associated with a specific period and a distinctive style and message.

On the basis of the circumstances depicted in the book, its date can be

---

[42] Cf. Robert Dentan, "Zechariah 9–14;" "Malachi," *IB*, Vol. 6, pp. 1089, 1117.

determined with reasonable certainty as sometime during the first half or middle of the fifth century. The temple is standing (1:10; 3:1, 10) and Judah is under a governor (1:8); therefore it is later than 515 B.C.. The condemnation of mixed marriages (2:10–16), however, is a sure indication that Ezra's reforms have not yet been instituted; and the failure to distinguish between priests and Levites (2:4–9; 3:3) shows that the Priestly Code has yet to be introduced. All told, a date of about 450 B.C. is likely.

The book takes the form of dialogues between God or the prophet, on the one hand, and the people and priests (the ones being addressed), on the other. There is a resemblance to other Old Testament books wherein concentration on theodicy leads to the dialectical question and answer style (e.g., Habakkuk, Job), but the intensity with which the technique is applied places the work in a class by itself. It is as if each affirmation provokes a question and each question its rejoinder, with the latter more often than not itself couched in the form of a rhetorical question. In contrast to the older prophecy and its "thus says the Lord," the appeal here is basically to logic and reason, after the manner of the wisdom literature. To some degree, surely, the prophet's style was patterned after the character of the times. As Dentan remarks, "there was a spirit of rationalism in the air which required a logical and reasoned argument."[43] A careful reading of the oracles, nevertheless, shows them to rest upon the basic covenant demands for repentance and ethical obedience to Yahweh's revealed truths.

The chief concern of the prophet is with the mood of depression and spiritual apathy which had settled upon the Jewish community in his day. As the passing years failed to bring the desired changes in Judah's political and economic status, every additional hardship—a drought year, a locust plague, or the like—added to the prevailing cynicism. The protests against righteous suffering and divine injustice raised by Habakkuk and Jeremiah in years past were now the stock complaints of persons less well equipped than they to hold them within the broader perspective of faith (2:17–18); 3:13–15). Such doubts, moreover, became manifest in a careless indifference to traditional attitudes respecting marriage and divorce (2:10–16), but had their most devastating effects in the loss of respect for the temple. Pledges taken for its support were either ignored altogether or fulfilled through deals with dishonest priests who accepted lame and sickly animals as worthy sacrifices for Yahweh's altar (1:6–2:9; 3:3–4, 8–10). It was this, above all else, that drew the prophet's bitter attack. It were better, he said, to leave the doors of the temple closed and bank the altar fires. Or, again:

Will man rob God? Yet you are robbing me. But you say, "How are we robbing thee?" In your tithes and offerings.
3:8

[43] Robert C. Dentan, "Malachi," *IB*, Vol. 6, p. 1119.

Finding it necessary to defend so basic a tenet as Yahweh's love for his remnant people, the prophet points to the current plight of the Edomites as the historical verification of Yahweh's intention of keeping his promise to the sons of Jacob (1:2–5). For God's choice of Israel through the ancestral father, Jacob, carried with it the rejection of Esau, prototype of Edom. True to the promise, so the prophet reasons, Edom is even now being driven from its land by the Nabataean Arabs. No amount of striving on its part, he asserts (quite correctly, as it turned out), could possibly effect its recovery. By analogy, no sincere effort of Judah's can fail. God's promise is not abrogated; Judah's survival is as sure as Edom's ruin.

Much like Haggai, and true to a Deuteronomic logic, Malachi views the conditions about which his generation complains as the effects of their own covenant unfaithfulness. Yahweh has been like a father to his people, but they have failed to honor him in return (1:6). By breaking faith with Yahweh they have shut out the source of strength they needed so badly. When issued in the form of a positive appeal, this comes out altogether too much like a bargain struck with God, and—equally objectionable—one that makes divine favor contingent upon external duties.

> Bring the full tithes into the storehouse, that there may be food in my house; and thereby put me to the test, says the Lord of hosts, if I will not open the windows of heaven for you and pour down for you an overflowing blessing.
>
> 3:10

To do justice to the prophet's position, however, it must be observed that his appeal presupposes the repentance ("return"; 3:7) of his hearers. He was convinced, furthermore, that Judah's unwillingness to meet her pledges demonstrated a loss of faith which would not be recovered without high resolve and self-sacrifice. The deeper theological and empirical problems which his words entail would be left to Judaism's more analytical minds.

Malachi's ultimate word of encouragement (and judgment) concerns the coming Day of the Lord (3:1–2, 17; 4:1), a notable development of which is his conception of one who shall prepare the way for Yahweh's return to his temple (3:1). This "messenger" was likely conceived by the prophet as an angel,[44] but the editor who attached the book's concluding verses (4:5–6) explains it in reference to Elijah. The great prophet of the past, purportedly taken up to heaven in a fiery chariot, would prepare the hearts of men for Yahweh's "great and terrible day."

---

[44] The Hebrew *mal'akhi* may be translated either as "my messenger" or "my angel."

3. OF WHAT PEOPLE ARE YOU?
TRITO-ISAIAH, OBADIAH, JOEL, AND JONAH

The remaining books of the Latter Prophets, though of a heterogeneous character, share in common (1) an origin in the post-Exilic Jewish community, but (2) an otherwise obscure background which makes their precise dates all but impossible to determine. To a considerable degree, the concerns manifest in Haggai, Zechariah, and Malachi are present in these books as well, but without the distinguishable references to known historical persons and events. The variety of viewpoints represented by their respective messages, moreover, warns against the facile stereotypes with which post-Exilic Judaism is all too often depicted.

Trito-Isaiah

Since Duhm first popularized the view at the end of the last century,[45] chapters 56–66 of the book of Isaiah have been widely acknowledged as the product of the post-Exilic period and thus distinguishable from chapters 40–55 as "Trito-Isaiah." Some of the oracles, to be sure, bear a strong resemblance to the poems of Deutero-Isaiah; possibly chapters 60–62 and 57:14–21 even belong with that work. For the most part, however, a contrast with the Exilic prophet's Babylonian milieu, matchless poetic style, and broad theological vistas is evident. The excited anticipation of Cyrus' edict of liberation and the dawning of a new era in Israel's world mission has given way to the sober realities of life in post-Exilic Judah. Preoccupation with such practical concerns as sabbath observance, fasts, cultic purity, separation from evildoers, prayer, and keeping the law "ushers us into the living faith of an emerging Judaism."[46]

From some of the oracles the impression is received that both the temple and Jerusalem's walls still lie in ruins (60:10; 63:18; 64:10); elsewhere, however, the cult appears to be functioning (56:5ff.; 60:7; cf. also 62:6). This, together with the fact that no substantial unity of literary style or singleness of theme exists in these chapters, suggests that the work should be attributed to more than a single writer. Doubtless, disciples of Deutero-Isaiah, committed to a reinterpretation of the great prophet's hopes in their new and different setting, are responsible for these additions to his work. Although they did not match their master's brilliance of insight and poetic expression, in a number of respects they deserve to share with him the original Isaiah's famous name.

Deutero-Isaiah's lofty conception of deity is far from lost in these chap-

---

[45] *Das Buch Jesaja* (Gottingen, West Germany: Vandenhoeck and Ruprecht, 1892; "Göttinger Handkommentar zum Alten Testament").
[46] James Muilenburg, "Isaiah 40–66," *IB*, Vol. 5, p. 414.

ters. Yahweh, in some respects, is farther removed from man: he is petitioned to "look down from heaven," his "holy and glorious habitation" (65:15f.; cf. 64:1); and a special point is made of the fact that he, as creator and Lord of heaven and earth, cannot be contained in any house that one might build for him (66:1f.). But, in the true prophetic vein, it is affirmed that nothing other than human wickedness causes Yahweh's withdrawal so that he does not hear (59:1f.). Picking up the note of the Exilic prophet, the poems extol God's very righteousness as the source of his people's hope (59:9f.). This, in essence, balances and brings into clearer perspective the stress on pious duties and cultic obligations that appears throughout these chapters.

Not only are cultic exercises and moral duties linked together (cf. 56:1–2), but there are, in fact, explicit interpretations of the deeper aspects of the cultic act itself. Similar to the situation reflected in Zechariah (7:1–7; 8:18–19), a vital concern with fasting in the post-Exilic community is apparent here (58:1–14). Queries about the ineffectiveness of the fasts (their failure to bring desired rewards) provide the prophet with the occasion for his striking words on the spirit of the true fast:

> Is not this the fast that I choose;
>> to loose the bonds of wickedness,
>> to undo the thongs of the yoke,
> to let the oppressed go free,
>> and to break every yoke?
> Is it not to share your bread with the hungry,
>> and bring the homeless poor into your house;
> when you see the naked, to cover him,
>> and not to hide yourself from your own flesh?
>> 58:6–7

Clearly, the eschatological passages in the collection depend upon Deutero-Isaiah's glorious promises, notwithstanding significant deviations from his consistently lofty perspective. The most serious difference concerns the absence of the Suffering Servant motif (unless 61:1–3—if not assigned to Deutero-Isaiah himself—is so interpreted). Not only does Israel's suffering on the nations' behalf go without mention, but a note of exclusivistic nationalism occasionally appears. According to some passages, Israel's coming day of redemption will find her enjoying the wealth of the nations (60:5f.; 61:6; 66:12); and in the oracle against Edom (63:1–6), a spirit of vengeance breaks forth that is a match for Obadiah's bitter poem against that people. Also, in certain instances the eschatology is more akin to apocalyptic, with its "new heaven and new earth" (65:17f.), cosmic upheaval (64:1f.), and separation of the righteous from the wicked (63:1–6; 65:12f.; 66:16–17). At its best, however, the hope includes all peoples. Yahweh will gather all nations and tongues to see his glory (66:18f.) and share in a world-wide peace which encompasses even the wild beasts (65:25). Foreigners and eunuchs will serve in Yahweh's temple (56:3f.; 66:21), which will be a "house of prayer for all people" (56:7).

Obadiah and Joel

The oracles of Obadiah and Joel, though not anonymous, are from otherwise obscure figures whose common names add little distinction to their short books.[47] The dates suggested for them vary widely, ranging from the pre-Exilic to the Hellenistic eras; but the post-Exilic period satisfies most of the inferences and enjoys the widest support. The two prophets share the prevailing mood of separatism manifest within Palestinian Judaism during the fifth century and later; both see in the current events signs of the coming Day of Yahweh, which receives in each case a decidedly nationalistic interpretation.

Obadiah's brief work, a mere twenty-one verses, is almost in its entirety a venting of the spleen against the Edomites, the first half (vss. 1–14) containing an indictment and denunciation of that people's offenses, and the second half (vss. 15–21) foretelling their destruction on the Day of Yahweh. Arab encroachment upon the former Edomite holdings is viewed with more than casual interest ("How Esau has been pillaged"; "All your allies have deceived you"), and as the harbinger of worse things to come. Though reproached for her once smug pride (vss. 3–4), Edom's chief undoing is traced to her crimes against Judah ("the violence done to your brother Jacob") at the time of the Babylonian conquest: refusing assistance and rejoicing in her neighbor's plight, looting her goods and handing over her refugees to the enemy (vss. 11–14). The bitter memories, renewed no doubt by the recent Edomite occupation of former Judean lands to the south, convince the prophet that Yahweh's day of judgment on wickedness will restore all the former territories of Israel and Judah to their rightful owners.

The occasion of the book of Joel is an unusually severe locust plague, accompanied perhaps by a drought. The dramatic and picturesque description of the locusts and their removal through Yahweh's intervention (1:1–2:27) is followed by promises of Israel's restoration and the judgment of the nations (2:28–3:21). Though Joel's locusts are sometimes taken allegorically as invading armies of the past or symbolically as the supernatural creatures of apocalyptic, neither of these interpretations accounts convincingly for either the choice of the figure or the vividness of detail with which it is applied.[48] The prophet does, however, see in the calamity the proportions of a national crisis and test of faith, and accordingly summons his people to repent of their sins, declare a fast, and petition Yahweh's de-

---

[47] Each of the names, Obadiah ("Servant of Yahweh") and Joel ("Yahweh is God"), is used of twelve different Old Testament figures.

[48] Cf. J. A. Thompson, "Joel," *IB*, Vol. 6, pp. 733–734.

liverance. The cultic element in the book is pronounced: the blowing of the shophar, solemn assembly at the temple, invoking of the fast, and frequent mention of priests and sacrifices; some even regard the oracles themselves as a collection of temple liturgies. The penitential element in true worship has found no finer expression than in the oft-quoted summons:

> "Yet even now," says the Lord,
>> "return to me with all your heart,
> with fasting, with weeping, and with mourning;
>> and rend your hearts and not your garments."
>>> 2:12–13

The devastation wrought by the locusts apparently suggested to the prophet the coming Day of Yahweh (2:28–3:31) after the manner of Amos' vision (Amos 7:1–3). The first in a series of such forewarnings, it will be followed by an outpouring of God's spirit until persons of all ages and classes will "see visions and dream dreams" (2:28). Signs in the sky will portend the final climactic battle and judgment of the nations in "the Valley of Jehoshaphat" ("Valley of Yahweh's Judgment"). In preparation for the engagement, the idyllic picture of Isaiah 2:4 and Micah 4:3 is reversed; the tools of peace are beaten into weapons of war (3:10). But the actual battle is Yahweh's. In apocalyptic fashion, his coming is accompanied with cosmic upheaval.

> Multitudes, multitudes,
>> in the valley of decision!
> The sun and the moon are darkened,
>> and the stars withdraw their shining.
>>> 3:14–15

The pagan nations—Phoenicia, Philistia, Egypt, and Edom—will be once for all judged for their cruelties to God's people. Yahweh will take up his residence in Zion; the land will enjoy abundant fertility; and strangers shall never again pass through Jerusalem.

Jonah

The delightful little book of Jonah is unique among the books of the Latter Prophets in consisting not of a collection of prophetic utterances but of a single prose narrative concerning an otherwise obscure eighth-century prophet (II Kings 14:25) of that name. That the book itself is not nearly so early, and therefore the work of someone other than the prophet himself, is the view of most scholars.[49] Nineveh is for the writer a city of the distant past, its size greatly magnified (3:3), and its history romanticized (3:5–10).

---

[49] Cf., however, Yehezkel Kaufmann, *The Religion of Israel*, pp. 282–286, where the eighth-century date is defended.

The influence of Deutero-Isaiah, moreover, has most probably made its impact upon him.

The narrative separates rather easily into two episodes: (1) the prophet's flight from God's initial commission to preach to Nineveh, the storm at sea, and the three days in the great fish (chs. 1–2); and (2) the second commission, Nineveh's repentance, and the prophet's remorse (chs. 3–4). Except for the poem (2:2–9), which did not belong to the original work, the story is told with a consummate skill that avoids undue details and theologizing and entertains the reader from beginning to end.[50] That the poem, which is actually a psalm of thanksgiving, is a later interpolation is evidenced by its total lack of connection with the context; it is inappropriate to the prophet's condition, since he had not yet been delivered from his plight, and is otherwise out of keeping with his mood as developed in the narrative.[51]

Notwithstanding the theological storms that have raged about it, the episode involving the great fish (not a whale!) occupies only three verses of the narrative and is equally as incidental to the story's meaning. Once it is recognized that the account is in no sense literal history (observe the lack of historical names and events, the unlikely title "King of Nineveh," and the overnight repentance of the pagan empire), the question of the writer's purpose turns on the total effect of all his figures—whether they are allegory or parable—and the nature of the problem which prompted him to write. It is likely that his material derived from popular legends for which he supplied the deeper theological message. That he imposed upon them a detailed allegorical scheme is not very probable, though ingenious interpretations are at once suggested by such an approach: that the prophet stands for Israel, the great fish the Exile, and the deliverance from the fish's belly the return from Babylon. It has even been proposed that the gourd plant that withers overnight (4:6–11) represents the short-lived hopes inspired by Zerubbabel. Upon closer scrutiny, however, the fish is seen to be no figure of judgment (i.e., Exile) but rather the source of the prophet's deliverance.

It is much more likely that our unknown writer intended for his account a message most closely akin to that of a parable. As such, it speaks forcefully of Yahweh's unrestricted desire to bring persons into accord with his best interests for them, to forgive their iniquities and honor their conversion of will. Whether this lesson in God's mercy concerns primarily the Jews themselves, however, or especially the nations to whom they were called

---

[50] The redundancy of two accounts of Nineveh's fast (3:5; 3:6–9) and other minor inconsistencies (cf. 3:10 and 4:5; 4:5 and 4:6) are not surprising in a tale of this sort.

[51] Brevard Childs (*Introduction to the Old Testament as Scripture*, pp. 417–427) assigns a pivotal redactional role to the psalm as providing a contrasting parallel to ch. 4 and thus shifting the original intention of the story from a concern with unfulfilled prophecy to the extension of God's salvation to all peoples.

to minister, is no moot point.[52] As we have seen, Judah itself sorely needed such reassurances in the period of Exile and beyond. If God can forgive bloody Nineveh, perhaps the writer is saying, how much more will he save his own people! But in view of the fact that the story has its own explicit truth to declare (to this degree unlike a parable with its veiled truth), namely, that God desires the Assyrians' repentance, it appears doubtful that the lesson can be so restricted. Standing under the influence of Deutero-Isaiah, it would seem, the writer calls his people back to the broad interpretation of Yahweh's universal purpose and Israel's mission to the nations. As such, his voice is a highly significant one in the post-Exilic period when Judah's chief concerns were directed inwardly in the interests of self-preservation. Even if he was not himself a prophet, according to the usual definition, the writer's simple but profound message is prophetic in the finest sense of the word.

SELECTED READINGS

The Restoration

Ackroyd, Peter R., *Exile and Restoration* (Philadelphia: The Westminster Press, 1968).

———, *Israel Under Babylon and Persia*, New Clarendon Bible (New York: Oxford University Press, Inc., 1970).

Haggai, Zechariah, Malachi, Obadiah, Joel, Jonah, and Trito-Isaiah

Ahlström, G. W., *Joel and the Temple Cult of Jerusalem*, VTS (Leiden, Netherlands: E. J. Brill, 1971).

Dentan, Robert C., "Introduction and Exegesis to Malachi," *IB*, Vol. VI, pp. 1117–1144.

———, "Introduction and Exegesis to Zechariah 9–14," *IB*, Vol. VI, pp. 1089–1114.

Fretheim, Terence E., *The Message of Jonah: A Theological Commentary* (Minneapolis: Augsburg Publishing House, 1977). A clearly written and provocative analysis of the literary structure and theology of the book of Jonah.

Hanson, Paul D., "Zechariah, Book of," *IDBS*, pp. 982–983.

Kapelrud, Arvid S., *Joel Studies* (Uppsala, Sweden: Almquist and Wiksells, 1948).

Muilenburg, James, "Introduction and Exegesis to Isaiah 40–66," *IB*, Vol. V, pp. 381–773.

North, F. S., "Critical Analysis of the Book of Haggai," *ZAW*, LXVII (1956), pp. 25–46.

---

[52] Yehezkel Kaufmann (*The Religion of Israel*, pp. 282–286) finds no universalism in Jonah, but solely the message of the efficacy of repentance. Walter Harrelson (*Interpreting the Old Testament*, pp. 359–361) agrees with this approach but conceives the book as written to bring hope and confidence to Jewish exiles between 586 and 538 B.C. Terence E. Fretheim similarly contends that the book displays no direct concern with Jewish/gentile distinctions but has as its central theological focus the issue of the divine justice; i.e., the mercy extended to the guilty (*The Message of Jonah: a Theological Commentary* [Minneapolis MN: Augsburg Publishing House, 1977], pp. 22ff.).

Thomas, D. Winton, "Introduction and Exegesis to Haggai," *IB*, Vol. VI, pp. 1037–1049.

———, "Introduction and Exegesis to Zechariah 1–8," *IB*, Vol. VI, pp. 1053–1088.

Thompson, John A., "Introduction and Exegesis to Joel," *IB*, Vol. VI, pp. 729–760,

———, "Introduction and Exegesis to Obadiah," *IB*, Vol. VI, pp. 857–867.

Trible, Phyllis, *Studies in the Book of Jonah* (Thesis, Columbia University, 1963; Ann Arbor, MI: University Microfilms, 1970).

Watts, John D. W., *Obadiah: A Critical Exegetical Commentary* (Grand Rapids, MI: Eerdmans, 1969).

Westermann, Claus, *Isaish 40–66: A Commentary*, David M. G. Stalker, trans., The Old Testament Library (Philadelphia: The Westminster Press, 1969).

III

the other books of our fathers

My grandfather Jesus, after devoting himself especially to the reading of the law and the prophets and the other books of our fathers. . .

—Ecclesiasticus, Prologue

8

——◦•◦——

where is the
place of
understanding?

But where shall wisdom be found? And where is the place of understanding? . . . God understands the way to it, and he knows its place.

—Job 28:12, 23

The third division of the Hebrew Bible known as the Kethubim, Hagiographa, or Writings, consists of a miscellaneous collection of eleven books grouped traditionally as follows:

1. Poetical books: Psalms, Job, Proverbs
2. Festal scrolls (Megilloth): Song of Songs, Ruth, Lamentations, Ecclesiastes, and Esther
3. Apocalyptic: Daniel
4. History: Ezra–Nehemiah and Chronicles

There are, to be sure, other methods of classifying these works, but no single arrangement does justice to their mixed literary genre. It is common practice among modern scholars to disregard the categories of poetical books and festal scrolls, in favor of a wisdom classification consisting of Proverbs, Job, and Ecclesiastes. Poetry, as such, is not a feature unique to the first three works, as a glance at the Song of Songs, Lamentations, and the proverbial portions of Ecclesiastes reveals. But neither is wisdom exclusive to Proverbs, Job, and Ecclesiastes, as some of the Psalms afford excellent examples of Hebrew wisdom. Just as little is to be gained by a rearrangement of the books according to a supposed chronological sequence. Except for Ecclesiastes and Daniel, specific dates are out of the question; and in Psalms and Proverbs we have collections assembled over a period of several centuries. In their final editions, at least, all the writings appear to belong to the post-Exilic period. In our treatment we shall follow the Hebrew canonical order, giving due attention to the literary and theological features of poetry, wisdom, and apocalyptic as they appear.

1. BLESSED IS THE MAN: PSALMS, JOB, AND PROVERBS

Psalms, Job, and Proverbs are the three longest books in the canon that consist entirely (except for the brief prologue and epilogue of Job) of poetry. As we have seen, however, some of the oldest Hebrew poems appear in the Torah and Former Prophets, and the oracles of the Latter Prophets are chiefly poetical in form. Altogether, roughly one third of the Old Testament is written in poetry.

The formal characteristics of Old Testament poetry are, by and large, typical of the poetry of the ancient Near East, particularly that revealed in the Canaanitic tablets from Ras Shamra. Unlike modern verse, Semitic poetry depends neither on rhyme nor on a fixed meter of long and short syllables. Its distinguishing features, rather, are rhythm and parallelism. Rhythm is based on an elusive system of stressed syllables which follows the thought structure of the poetic line. The line or verse is the basic unit and consists often of a couplet of half lines (stichs or cola), marked by three beats to each stich (3/3), thus:

Verse $\begin{cases} \text{Stich 1: O Lórd} \quad \text{how-mány-are} \quad \text{my-fóes!} \\ \text{Stich 2: Mány} \quad \text{are-rising} \quad \text{against-me!} \end{cases}$

There may be, however, three or four stichs to a single line; and a variety of rhythmic patterns is possible. Other than the 3/3 meter the second most common pattern is the so-called *ḳinah* (lament) meter, three beats followed by two beats (3/2).[1]

The major key to understanding Hebrew poetry has long been recognized as a parallelism of thought whereby the ideas expressed in one part of

---

[1] See above p. 300.

a verse or stanza are echoed or extended in another part.[2] This most frequently takes the form of *synonymous* parallelism, a repetition of the thought expressed in slightly different words, as seen in the line quoted above. A common variation is *antithetical* parallelism, wherein the second of two members of a line or stanza presents the same idea as the first member, but in contrasting fashion, thus:

> The Lord knows the way of the righteous,
> but the way of the wicked will perish.
> Ps. 1:6

Yet a third form is seen in the so-called *synthetic* parallelism, in which the second member either balances the first by completing its thought or partially repeats the thought of the first and expands it, sometimes in "staircase" fashion.

> I have set my king
> on Zion, my holy hill.
> Ps. 2:6

> Lift up your heads, O gates!
> and be lifted up, O ancient doors!
> that the King of Glory may come in.
> Ps. 24:9

The fluidity of Hebrew poetry allowed for innumerable variations on these basic patterns.

Psalms

It is doubtful that any other book has enjoyed so wide an appeal or found as practical a role in man's worship as has the Book of Psalms (Psalter). Known in Jewish tradition as the *Tehillim* or "Praises," it consists of 150 poems depicting the private and corporate religious experiences of ancient Israel's most sensitive poets. The present form of the book is but the end product of a long and complex literary history and reflects its use in the worship rites of the post-Exilic temple. The division into five collections or "books" (1–41; 42–72; 73–89; 90–106; 107–150) is doubtless patterned after the fivefold division of the Torah. The first psalm introduces the collection as a whole and psalm 150 serves as its doxology. In addition, each of the

---

[2] The earliest explication of the principle of parallel members (*parallelismus membrorum*) is credited to Bishop Robert Lowth in a work published in 1753. For further discussion of this and other aspects of Hebrew poetry cf. G. B. Gray. *The Forms of Hebrew Poetry* (London: Hodder & Stoughton Ltd., 1915); Theodore H. Robinson, *The Poetry of the Old Testament* (London: Gerald Duckworth Co. Ltd., 1952); S. Gevirtz, *Patterns in the Early Poetry of Israel* (Chicago: University of Chicago Press, 1963); and Mitchell J. Dahood, "Poetry, Hebrew," *IDBS*, pp. 669–672.

first four books concludes with a doxology of its own (41:13; 72:18–19; 89:52; 106:48).[3]

Something of the age and complexity of the Psalter is evident in the varied patterns that cut across its present divisions. In several instances two originally separate psalms have been combined into one (e.g., Ps. 19, vss. 1–6 and 7–14), and in other cases a single poem has been divided into two (Pss.9 and 10). Several psalms appear in duplicate versions (14=53; 40:13–17=70; 108=57:7–11 and 60:6–12), wherein the major differences consist in the preference for one or the other of the divine names, Yahweh (14; 40:13–17) or Elohim (53; 70). In Psalms 42–83, moreover, Elohim is the preferred name, having been employed even in contexts in which the personal name Yahweh would seem the more natural usage. Apparently there existed in some phase of the Psalter's history an independent Elohistic collection in which the name Yahweh was changed to Elohim.

Other earlier collections are possibly reflected in groups of psalms assigned by their headings to David,[4] Asaph,[5] and the Sons of Korah,[6] as well as those designed specifically for festivals and pilgrimages—the so-called Hallelujah Psalms[7] and Songs of Ascent.[8] Once again, the Psalter's piecemeal growth may be seen in the editorial colophon at the end of Book II, which purports to conclude the "prayers of David," but is in fact followed by yet other Davidic psalms. Altogether, 73 psalms are prefixed with David's name, though there is some question as to whether the Davidic headings were originally intended to attribute authorship to him. "Psalm of David" might as easily be translated "in David's style" or "dedicated to David." That the great king and reputed patron of psalmody could not himself have written all the psalms attributed to him is shown in the fact that some of them clearly presuppose the existence of the temple.[9] All the psalm headings, moreover, are the work of later editors and in no instance belong to the original compositions.

DATE AND OCCASION OF THE PSALMS. Study of the Psalter has undergone significant changes during the present century, not the least of which is an altogether different approach to the question of the date and occasion of individual psalms. In years past interest centered on efforts to

---

[3] Ancient testimony to the fivefold partition of the Psalter is now to be seen in a liturgical fragment from Qumran, dating to the turn of the Christian era. Cf. Mitchell Dahood, *Psalms, I*, Vol. 16 of the Anchor Bible (Garden City, NY: Doubleday & Company, Inc., 1966), p. xxxi, and references cited.

[4] David's name is affixed to all the psalms in Book I except Pss. 1, 2, 10, and 33 (10, however, was originally a part of 9); in Book II, Pss. 51–65 and 68–70; and beyond Book II, Pss. 86, 101, 103, 108–110, 122, 124, 131, 138–145.

[5] Pss. 50; 73–83.

[6] Pss. 42–49; 84–85; 87–88.

[7] Pss. 111–114; 116–118; 135–136; 146–150.

[8] Pss. 120–135.

[9] Pss. 5, 27, 28, 63, 69, 101, 138. Cf. also the title of ps. 30.

determine the specific occasion for which each psalm was composed, and the prevailing tendency was toward late dating. Most, if not all, psalms were assigned to the post-Exilic period, and it was not uncommon to date some as late as the Hasmonean era (second and first centuries B.C.). The present trend is toward earlier dating, allowing for a considerable number of pre-Exilic psalms, but with a reluctance to fix precise dates.[10] It now appears that there are few, if any, psalms for which the specific historical occasion is beyond doubt. Following the path-finding studies of Hermann Gunkel, the major aim of psalms scholarship has become the discovery of the peculiar functions served by the psalms in their separate settings (*Sitzen im Leben*).[11] As the Psalter found its primary use in cultic worship, this approach (form criticism) is concerned especially with liturgical forms.

PSALTER AND CULT. Gunkel distinguished several basic categories (*Gattungen*) of psalms, most of which originally served a specific function within temple ritual. Although some psalms were later reshaped and adapted to individual use, they continued to reflect the patterns of the cult. Gunkel listed five major categories: (1) hymns (psalms of praise), (2) communal laments, (3) royal psalms, (4) individual laments, and (5) individual thanksgiving psalms. He also distinguished several lesser types, including communal thanksgiving psalms, pilgrimage psalms, and wisdom psalms.

Sigmund Mowinckel, whose influence in modern psalms study has been second only to that of Gunkel, treats all psalms as cultic poems, written specifically for ritual accompaniment.[12] In his view, the psalm headings indicate the particular rituals with which they were associated. Other notations, including the enigmatic "selah," are commonly regarded as instructions for the temple musicians, indicating the musical accompaniment or tunes to which the psalms were to be sung.

As has already been remarked,[13] the psalms should be read in conjunction with the book of Leviticus. For it is only when the prayers and hymns of the Psalter are brought together with the rites of worship—processions to the temple, offerings and sacrifices before the altar, and the taking of vows—that either can be properly understood. A few biblical passages preserve the unity of ritual and song, for example, the Chronicler's account

---

[10] A second-century B.C. copy of the canonical Psalter from Qumran, though fragmentary, indicates that the collection of canonical psalms was already fixed by Maccabean times. The noncanonical Qumran hymns (of Hasmonean date), moreover, contrast with the canonical hymnody in respect to language and poetical structure. Cf. Frank Cross, *The Ancient Library of Qumran*, pp. 165–166.

[11] Gunkel's monumental work on the Psalms, *Die Psalmen*, appeared in 1926, and his *Einleitung in die Psalmen* (with Joachim Begrich) was published posthumously in 1932. A succinct synopsis of these studies is available in Hermann Gunkel, *The Psalms*, Thomas M. Horner, trans. (Philadelphia: Fortress Press, 1967).

[12] Mowinckel's work is available in English translation as *The Psalms in Israel's Worship*, D. R. Ap-Thomas, trans., Vols. I–II (Nashville, TN: Abingdon Press, 1962).

[13] See above, p. 189.

of David's bringing the ark to Jerusalem (I Chron. 16:7–36). Here the rite is accompanied by instrumental music and songs (portions of Pss. 105, 96, and 106) of the Levitical choir, together with the appropriate responses of the worshipers. The psalms themselves, moreover, bear witness to the color and excitement of temple worship:

> These things I remember, . . .
> how I went with the throng
>   and led them in procession to the house of God,
> with glad shouts and songs of thanksgiving,
>   a multitude keeping festival.
>   Ps. 42:4

> The singers in front, the minstrels last,
>   between them maidens playing timbrels.
>   Ps. 68:25

Not infrequently the very structure of a psalm suggests its liturgical character, as in Psalm 136 where each sentence of the hymn is followed by the antiphonal response of the congregation.

> Sentence: O give thanks to the Lord, for he is good,
> Response: for his steadfast love endures forever.

HYMNS (PSALMS OF PRAISE). The object of some psalms is simply to offer praise to God.[14] Such hymns typically begin with a call to worship, proceed to develop motives for praise, and often conclude with a renewed summons to worship. The invitation may be addressed to Israel, the nations at large, the world of nature, the angelic hosts, or even the psalmist himself ("Bless the Lord, O my soul"). The motives for praise often include God's manifest glory in the created order. There is accordingly a resemblance to the hymnody of the larger Near East, in which the natural elements are hailed as manifestations of the gods. Psalm 104 seems to depend on the Egyptian Hymn to Aton[15]; and Psalm 68 depicts Yahweh as a "rider of the clouds," after the manner of the descriptions of Baal in the Ras Shamra tablets.[16]

> O Lord, how manifold are they works!
>   . . . the earth is full of thy creatures.
>   104:24

> Thou hast made the moon to mark the seasons;
>   the sun knows its time for setting.
>   104:19

---

[14] The following psalms, though in some instances encompassing more than a single psalm type, may be classified as hymns: 8, 19, 29, 33, 46–48, 65, 68, 76, 78, 84, 87, 93, 95–100, 103–106, 113, 114, 117, 135, 136, 145–150.

[15] *ANET*, pp. 369–371 (*ANE*, pp. 226–230).

[16] *ANET*, pp. 129–142 (*ANE*, pp. 92–118).

Blowing the shophar (ram's horn), a summons to worship. (Courtesy of Israel Government Tourist Office.)

lift up a song to him who rides upon the clouds.

68:4

The mythological element common to pagan hymnody is, however, restricted here to passing allusions[17] and is thoroughly historicized through the praise offered Yahweh's election of Israel[18] and his work among the na-

[17] E.g., 74:13–14; 77:16–19; 89:9–10.
[18] E.g., 105; 114.

tions.[19] His creation and direction of the natural elements are viewed as expressions of his providential care for man's needs, and not infrequently are celebrated in the same breath with his past deliverance in the Exodus, his gift of Canaan, and his instruction in the Torah. Chief among God's attributes praised by the psalmists are his steadfast love (*ḥesedh*), faithfulness, justice, and forgiveness. No experience of his goodness is too trivial for mention, not even the naming of the stars (147:4) or the feeding of the young ravens (147:9).

Two special categories of hymns are the so-called "Songs of Zion"[20] and "Enthronment Psalms,"[21] both closely connected with Yahweh's saving work. The Zion psalms extol Jerusalem as the place of his choosing, his holy habitation and "resting place for ever" (132:14). The Enthronement Psalms acclaim God's kingship over the earth in terms analogous to the coronation and reign of Israel's earthly king. A subject of much debate is the question of whether Israel observed an annual New Year's festival after the order of the ceremony of ancient Babylon, in which the god was enthroned anew over his people year by year. Mowincklel argues for such a tradition, tracing its beginnings to the pre-Exilic monarchy and supposing its observance to have fallen each year on the Feast of Booths (Tabernacles).[22] The ceremony, if observed in Israel, could not have implied that Yahweh ever ceased reigning over his creation, but presumably would have served as a reaffirmation of his covenant with the nation as well as with David and the Jerusalem dynasty. As such, these psalms, with their festal shout, "Yahweh reigns!," would find their proper liturgical setting. Perhaps, as some contend, the ceremony included a reenactment of David's rite of bringing the ark up to Jerusalem. Psalm 24 possibly records the climactic moment when the procession reached the temple gates:

> Lift up your heads, O gates!
>   and be lifted up, O ancient doors!
>   that the King of glory may come in.
> Who is this King of glory?
>   The Lord of hosts,
>   he is the King of glory.
>   24:9–10

LAMENTS. Roughly a third of the Psalter consists of laments in which the psalmists brought before God the deep-seated fears, doubts, and longings of both themselves and the worshiping community. In the individual lament several parts can be distinguished: (1) invocation, (2) complaint, (3)

---

[19] E.g., 135.
[20] Pss. 46, 48, 76, 84, 87, 122, and 132.
[21] Pss. 24, 47, 93, 95–99.
[22] Cf. Zech. 14:16. See above p. 77.

supplication, (4) expression of confidence, and (5) vow.[23] The invocation is an urgent cry for help addressed directly to God: "Help Lord" (12:1); "How long, O Lord?" (13:1); "Hear a just cause, O Lord" (17:1); "My God, my God, why hast thou forsaken me?" (22:1). The complaint is couched in traditional and stereotyped phrases which obscure the actual threat from which the psalmist seeks deliverance. Typically, however, there is mention of either personal enemies who persecute him or physical illness foreboding of death, or both.

Mowinckel identifies the enemies in the Psalms with workers of magic, to whose curses the illnesses and other calamities suffered by the worshiper were supposedly traced. Although this may explain the setting of some laments, the more obvious fact is that the beleaguered psalmist seeks from Yahweh both the reason for his predicament and his release from it. Doubtless the enemies often became the psalmist's accusers, interpreting his adversity as a sure sign of guilt. The lament provided the worshiper the needful opportunity to defend himself to Yahweh, to protest his innocence, and to vent his anger against undeserved suffering. Such a mood could produce vehement and vindictive outbursts against the enemies, an otherwise indefensible and embarrassing deviation from the Psalter's profoundly religious tone. Not in every case, however, does the sufferer protest his innocence. In certain instances, including those psalms known in Christian tradition as the Penitential Psalms,[24] he readily confesses his sin against God and views his adversity as deserved punishment:

> For I know my transgressions,
>   and my sin is ever before me.
> Against thee, thee only, have I sinned, . . .
> So that thou art justified in thy sentence.
>
> 51:4

The worshiper's supplication typically leads to an expression of confidence that Yahweh will hear and answer his prayer. There is a possibility that such confessions sometimes followed words of assurance pronounced by a priest or prophet at the temple. Occasionally the mood of confidence is so pronounced as to obscure the note of lamentation altogether.[25] Though the suppliant's concluding vow must have frequently accompanied a sacrificial offering, several of the psalms acknowledge that sacrifice is no substitute for repentance.

---

[23] The following psalms are in their entirety or in large part individual laments: 3–7, 12, 13, 17, 22, 25–28, 31, 35, 38, 39, 42, 43, 51, 52, 54–59, 61, 63, 64, 69, 70, 71, 86, 88, 94, 102, 109, 120, 130, 139–143.

[24] Pss. 6, 32, 38, 51, 102, 130, and 143. All but one (32) belong to the category of individual lament.

[25] These so-called psalms of confidence are 4, 11, 16, 23, 27:1–6, 62, 131.

The sacrifice acceptable to God is a broken spirit;
a broken and contrite heart, O God, thou wilt not despise.
51:17 [26]

The communal lament is similar in form to the individual lament, except that the prayer is offered on behalf of the whole community and omits such personal elements as the concluding vow. [27] Usually the two types can be distinguished simply by the speaker's choice of singular or plural pronouns; but occasionally the "I" is used in a corporate sense, as shown by the alternation of "I" and "we" in some psalms. [28] Such national disasters as military defeat, drought, or locust plague prompted the community's appeals for Yahweh's deliverance as demonstrated so mightily in the past. A penitential note might be struck here, even as in the individual lament:

Both we and our fathers have sinned;
we have committed iniquity, we have done wickedly.
106:6

ADDITIONAL PSALM TYPES. Some psalms are difficult to categorize in one or the other of Gunkel's classifications because they share the characteristics of more than a single psalm type. This is particularly true once we move beyond the two major categories of hymns and laments. The thanksgiving psalms, for example, share the affirmations of faith characteristic of the laments and the element of praise found in the hymn. There are, nevertheless, a number of psalms in which the supplications of the individual or the community have found their answers, and the response is primarily one of gratitude for favors granted. [29] As with the laments, the thanksgivings are both individual and communal and relate to deliverance from such adversities as illness and attack by personal and national enemies. Royal psalms [30] and wisdom psalms [31] are distinguished primarily on the basis of content rather than form. [32] The royal psalm is one written about or by the king; in some instances the specific occasion may have been the king's coronation. Embodying the ideals of Davidic kingship, they in time came to be interpreted messianically. The wisdom psalms typically contrast the blessings which accompany the way of the godly with the sad and futile lot

---

[26] Cf. 40:6–8; 50:8–13; 69:30–31.

[27] The communal laments are 14, 44, 58, 60, 74, 77, 79, 80, 83, 85, 90, 106, 123, 125, 126, 129, 137.

[28] Cf. 44:1, 4, 5, 6, 7, 15, 17; 74:1, 12; 123:1, 2.

[29] Pss. 9, 18, 21, 30, 32, 34, 41, 92, 116, 118, and 138 are individual thanksgivings; Pss. 67, 107, and 124 are communal thanksgiving psalms.

[30] Pss. 2, 18, 20, 21, 45, 72, 89, 101, 110, and 132.

[31] Pss. 1, 37, 49, 73, 78, 91, 111, 112, 119, 127, 128, and 133.

[32] Wisdom psalms, however, share some of the formal characteristics of proverbs, particularly in their address to the individual in need of enlightenment. See R. B. Y. Scott, *The Way of Wisdom in the Old Testament* (New York: Macmillan Publishing Co., Inc., 1971), pp. 197–201.

Ancient musicians and musical instruments.

of the wicked. The assurance that righteousness does not go unrewarded is a dictum of faith.

> I have been young, and now am old;
>> yet I have not seen the righteous forsaken
>> or his children begging bread.
>> 37:25

When the problem of God's justice does arise in respect to innocent suffering or the prosperity of the wicked, an answer is not long in coming:

> For the wicked shall be cut off;
>> but those who wait for the Lord shall possess the land.
>> 37:9

Such a ready answer, however, was not available to a sufferer like Job.

Hebrew Wisdom

The books of Proverbs, Job, and Ecclesiastes in the Hebrew Bible, as well as Ben Sirach and Wisdom of Solomon in the Deuterocanon, are known as the Old Testament wisdom books. The name is derived from the Hebrew term *hokmāh* (wisdom), which appears more frequently in these books than elsewhere in the Old Testament. As a collective label, however, wisdom is a modern scholarly designation since, as we have observed, none of the canonical divisions within the Hebrew Bible were so named. An analogous literature, though not an exact counterpart, existed in other ancient Near Eastern cultures, notably in Egypt and Babylonia, and at some points appears to have influenced Israel's own wisdom developments.[33] Efforts to isolate the definitive character of this literature and thereby mea-

---

[33] For a survey of the relevant Mesopotamian and Egyptian texts see R. B. Y. Scott, *The Way of Wisdom in the Old Testament*, pp. 23–47; William McKane, *Proverbs: A New Approach*, The Old Testament Library (Philadelphia: The Westminster Press, 1970), pp. 51–208; and Roger J. Williams, "Wisdom in the Ancient Near East," *IDBS*, pp. 949–952. The imprecision of "wisdom" as a literary genre for the Egyptian and Babylonian texts is maintained by W. G. Lambert, *Babylonian Wisdom Literature* (New York: Oxford University Press, Inc., 1960), p. 1, and H. Brunner, "Die Weisheitsliteratur," *Handbuch der Orientalistik*, (1952), pp. 90–110.

sure wisdom's impact on other parts of the Old Testament have proved unusually elusive.[34] The complexity is reflected in the following summary of representative definitions:

> Wisdom is the art of succeeding in life; practical knowledge of laws governing the world, based on experience; the totality of experience transmitted by a father to his son as a spiritual testament; ability to cope; the right deed or word for the moment; an intellectual tradition.[35]

Both within and outside Israel, wisdom took two different forms, the one practical and utilitarian, the other speculative, critical, and sometimes pessimistic.

Practical wisdom appears chiefly in the form of wise sayings or proverbs which advocate all such prudential habits, skills, and virtues as will assure one's fullest happiness, success, and well-being. The oldest example of Egyptian wisdom consists of such a collection of wise sayings bearing the name of Ptah-hotep, a vizier to the Pharaoh who lived some fifteen hundred years before Solomon, Israel's traditional patron of wisdom. Looking back on a long and successful life in the king's service, the sage reminds his son that "there is no one born wise,"[36] and counsels strict discipline, hard work, and good manners as the route to material success. Justice, too, is commended, since experience teaches that "wrongdoing has never brought its undertaking into port."[37] Stressing the basic human values of personal responsibility and fair-dealing, such instruction obviously contributed toward the maintenance of a stable social and political order, hence its popularity within courtly circles. Israel, whose covenant ethic was grounded in a corporate consciousness of responsibility to Yahweh that moved beyond motives of material well-being and personal success, nevertheless found a place for practical wisdom. The Book of Proverbs affords its best example in the Hebrew Old Testament. Ben Sirach and Wisdom of Solomon are its representatives in the Deuterocanon.

Speculative wisdom differs from its utilitarian counterpart in delving into the deeper and more vexing issues confronting man. It tended to look with skepticism upon the very virtues taken for granted by the prudential ethic and thereby served as a corrective to its more superficial features.[38] Once again, the literature of the larger Near East offers examples. The troubled period in Egypt following the end of the Old Kingdom (late third millen-

---

[34] The problem of defining wisdom is discussed by Roger N. Whybray, *The Intellectual Tradition in the Old Testament* (Berlin/New York: Walter de Gruyter, 1974), esp. pp. 1–5, and James L. Crenshaw, "Prolegomenon," idem., ed., *Studies in Ancient Israelite Wisdom* (New York: KTAV Publishing House, 1976), pp. 1–45, and idem, "Wisdom in the Old Testament", *IDBS*, pp. 952–956.

[35] James L. Crenshaw, "Wisdom in the Old Testament," *IDBS*, p. 952.

[36] *ANET*, p. 412.

[37] Ibid.

[38] Cf. Gerhard von Rad, *Old Testament Theology*, Vol. 1, pp. 421ff.

nium) brought a widespread questioning of the instructions for material success, as witnessed by such popular but pessimistic writings as the Dispute over Suicide and the Song of the Harper.[39] In the so-called "Babylonian Job," extant copies of which date from the seventh century B.C., an early poet laments the injustice of innocent suffering and one's insecurity before the inevitability of death.[40] It is a similar skeptical wisdom that finds expression in the books of Job and Ecclesiastes.

WISDOM'S SETTING. Israel's wisdom tradition has most often been attributed to a professional circle of sages or wise men who functioned under the patronage of the Jerusalem court.[41] King Solomon's legendary reputation as the wisest of men and Israel's sage (ḥakām) par excellence clearly associates him with wisdom:

> He [Solomon] also uttered three thousand proverbs; and his songs were a thousand and five. He spoke of trees, from the cedar that is in Lebanon to the hyssop that grows out of the wall; he spoke also of beasts, and of birds, and of reptiles, and of fish.
>
> I Kings 4:32–33

It is conjectured that, as a part of the administration of his empire, Solomon established a school of sages, who had the responsibilities of offering counsel to the king and training young men for governmental office. Such a group could have served, as well, to collect, record, and preserve the practical instruction contributed by wise men of the past. Court scribes of King Hezekiah's day are mentioned in the superscription to a collection of maxims in Proverbs 25:1: "These also are proverbs of Solomon which the men of Hezekiah king of Judah copied." That similar wisdom texts were produced by the royal courts of ancient Egypt and Mesopotamia is offered in support of such a professional circle in Israel. If such was the case, then the wise man occupied a role in respect to wisdom that paralleled the priest's guardianship of the Torah and the prophet's pronouncement of the revelatory word.

> for the law shall not perish from the priest, nor counsel from the wise [ḥakām], nor the word from the prophet.
>
> Jer. 18:18

Although it appears undeniable that wisdom enjoyed the encouragement of the court and expressed many of its values, how little can be said with certainty about a professional circle of Israelite sages has become increasingly evident. Some scholars go so far as to deny their existence al-

---

[39] *ANET*, pp. 406–407; 467.

[40] *ANET*, 438–440; *DOTT*, pp. 97–103. Note the comparison with Job in Samuel Terrien, "The Book of Job," *IB*, Vol. 3, pp. 880–883.

[41] Gerhard von Rad, *Wisdom in Israel* (Nashville, TN: Abingdon Press, 1972), pp. 15–23.

together.[42] Questions that have not been satisfactorily answered are whether scribal and teaching functions were normally combined in the same wise men or whether court sages were distinct from popular wisdom spokesmen who addressed gatherings at the city gate or otherwise gave instruction outside the confines of the court.[43] Certainly it would be too narrow a view to limit all wisdom to the setting of the court. It seems more likely that Israel's earliest wisdom originated in family and clan circles, where the parent offered practical moral advice, bearing the characteristic form of address, "my son" (e.g., Prov. 1:8ff). Counsel respecting home life and family relationships, ranging from respect for parents to the performance of simple domestic duties, is one of the more typical features of proverbial wisdom. Thus firmly based in the larger Israelite society, wisdom was the perquisite of no one social or professional class, but reflected basic goals and values to which all could aspire. In the real sense, wisdom's "sage" was any person who made such goals and values effective in his life.

WHERE IS WISDOM TO BE PLACED?[44] One of the most vexing problems in recent Old Testament studies concerns the place of wisdom within the broader scope of the books and theological patterns of the Old Testament. Precisely where does wisdom fit within the larger canonical context? We have noted in our examination of the separate Old Testament books that some interpreters seek to extend wisdom's influence to include additional books or literary units omitted by the broadly accepted wisdom grouping of Proverbs, Job, Ecclesiastes, Wisdom of Solomon, and Ecclesiasticus.[45] The proposed inclusions encompass a variety of otherwise contrasting literary categories: primeval narrative (Gen. 1–11), patriarchal saga (Gen. 37–50), law (Deut.), history (II Sam. 9–20; I Kings 1–2), prophecy (Amos, Isa., Hab., Jon.), psalmody ("wisdom psalms"), didactic stories (Esther), and apocalyptic (Dan.). The reasoning on which these judgments are based varies from case to case, and each must be judged on its own merits.

In only one of the proposed literary units, i.e., the wisdom psalms, is the resemblance to proverbial wisdom so striking as to leave virtually no doubt as to the correctness of the wisdom identification. In the other instances we are presented with certain themes, forms, or vocabulary which are common to wisdom literature, but which do not so cohere within the units in question as to make a conclusive case. The problem is one of methodology, in that the precise controls of a technical wisdom vocabulary or set of themes exclusive to the wisdom literature are lacking. Wisdom's origins

---

[42] Roger N. Whybray, *The Intellectual Tradition in the Old Testament*, pp. 6–54. See especially his interpretation of Jer. 18:18 (pp. 24–31).

[43] Cf. Job 29:7, 21–25; Prov. 8:3; 24:7; 31:23, 26, 31.

[44] This apt phrasing appeared as the title of a perceptive exploratory article by John F. Priest, *JBR*, XXI (1963), pp. 275–282.

[45] See above, pp. 139–140, 240, 292–294, 322.

in Israel, as we have seen, were likely in a popular clan setting; and its vehicles of expression were shared with Israelite life and culture as a whole. Many of the concerns of wisdom, moreover, were those involving the universality of the human situation and, as such, were the inescapable preoccupations of all thinking persons. Some scholars have recently broadened the definition of wisdom so as to encompass Israel's entire "intellectual tradition," which but attests the difficulty of the problem.[46] As James L. Crenshaw has shown, the unavoidable dilemma is one of a circular reasoning, whereby the selection of books with which one begins (itself a subjective selection) furnishes one's definition of wisdom and thereby excludes any other texts that differ from that normative corpus.[47]

If the search for wisdom outside the commonly accepted wisdom books has largely failed to prove its case, it has nevertheless heightened our awareness of the breadth and complexity of Old Testament literature and theology. The discovery of common dimensions of thought and feeling that join wisdom and the rest of the Old Testament indeed comes as a partial answer to the dilemma of trying to find a place for wisdom. In years past, we were most concerned with the manifest distinctions that set wisdom apart from common Old Testament patterns of corporate and national identity—of covenant, cult, and saving history. Wisdom's emphases on universal and timeless realities, humanistic values, worldly affairs, rationality, individual experience, and pragmatic methods caused some scholars to view the wisdom literature as an alien presence in the Old Testament, standing in stark and irreconcilable contrast with the rest of the books.[48] Although these differences are real, it is important to remember that wisdom in Israel was treasured by the same people who also found Yahweh as Israel's covenant partner, historic deliverer, and object of praise. Nothing short of the all-encompassing faith in Yahweh himself, as the Lord of both creation and history, holds together the diverse facets of Israelite faith. Wisdom's sensitivity to an established world order which invites the wise to seek out its dimensions and apply its principles to daily living shares, at least broadly, some common features of the creation faith celebrated in the Genesis accounts.[49] The sage's sense of a divine logic woven into the fabric of human

[46] Roger N. Whybray, *The Intellectual Tradition of the Old Testament.*

[47] "Prolegomenon," *Studies in Ancient Israelite Wisdom*, pp. 9–13; "Wisdom in the Old Testament", *IDBS*, pp. 952–953.

[48] Compare the contrasting perspectives on this matter as expressed in G. Ernest Wright, *God Who Acts*, Studies in Biblical Theology, no. 8 (London: S.C.M. Press, 1952), p. 104; idem, *The Old Testament and Theology*, pp. 39–69; James Barr, "Revelation Through History in the Old Testament and in Modern Theology," *Int.*, XVII (1963), pp. 193–205; idem, *Old and New in Interpretation; A Study of the Two Testaments* (New York: Harper & Row, Publishers, 1966), pp. 15–102.

[49] Cf. H. H. Schmid, *Gerechtigkeit als Weltordnung*, BhTh, 40 (Tübingen, West Germany: 1968), pp. 15–77, passim; James L. Crenshaw, "Popular Questioning of the Justice of God in Ancient Israel," *ZAW*, 82 (1970), pp. 380–395, reprinted in idem, ed., *Studies in Ancient Israelite Wisdom*, pp. 289–304; and idem, "Prolegomenon," Ibid., pp. 22–35.

society is not totally different from the operation of grace and retribution reflected in the stories of Joseph, David, and Esther. And even the revelatory insights of the prophets could find expression in some of the same devices of reasoned discourse, i.e., proverbs, parables, riddles, and the like, utilized by Israel's wise men.

Proverbs

The book most nearly representative of ancient Near Eastern wisdom tradition is Proverbs. Here the fundamental literary unit is the *mashal,* typically a pithy aphoristic saying based on practical experience and universal in its application.[50] The form is familiar to most cultures, ancient and modern, suited by its brevity, concreteness, and rhythm to retention in the oral mind for millennia. The Hebrew proverb abounds in metaphors drawn from everyday life and exhibits the poetic parallelism—synonymous, antithetical, and synthetic—characteristic of Old Testament verse.

> A good name is to be chosen
> rather than great riches,
> and favor is better than silver or
> gold.
> 22:1

> The mouth of the righteous is a
> fountain of life,
> but the mouth of the wicked
> conceals violence.
> 10:11

> Like a gold ring in a swine's snout
> is a beautiful woman without discretion.
> 11:22

Although the Book of Proverbs is largely an anthology of such one-line maxims, the *mashal* also takes the form of longer compositions such as the personifications of wisdom in the first section of the book[51] and the poem on the ideal housewife at the end (31:10–31).

The "telescoping" tendency of Israelite tradition, which attributed the entire Torah to Moses and most of the Psalms to David, is evident once again in the ascription of Hebrew proverbial wisdom to Solomon (1:1–6).[52] There is no reason to doubt that some proverbs go back to Solomon's court, but clearly he is not the author of the book as it stands. Not only are certain

[50] Somewhat broader in meaning than our word "proverb," *mashal* can also designate a parable (Ps. 78:2), allegory (Ezek. 17:2), riddle (Prov. 1:6), taunt (Isa. 14:4), or oracle (Num. 23:18).
[51] 1:20–33; 8:1–36; 9:1–6.
[52] In addition to Proverbs, tradition ascribed to Solomon the books of Ecclesiastes, Wisdom of Solomon, Psalms of Solomon, and Odes of Solomon.

of its parts explicitly credited to others (cf. 24:23, 30:1, 31:1), but the broad range of subject matter and interests witnesses the contributions of numerous Israelite sages. Similar to the Psalter, Proverbs is a collection of collections which developed by stages over the centuries, achieving its completed form not earlier than the fourth century B.C. Separate headings and other distinguishing features set apart the following units:

1. Introduction to the collection: chs. 1–9
2. "The proverbs of Solomon": 10:1–22:16
3. "The words of the wise": 22:17–24:22
4. More "sayings of the wise": 24:23–34
5. "Proverbs of Solomon which the men of Hezekiah of Judah copied": chs. 25–29
6. "The words of Agur": 30:1–14
7. Numerical proverbs: 30:15–33
8. "The words of Lemuel": 31:1–9
9. Poem in praise of the good wife: 31:10–31

A different order of these divisions in the Septuagint provides further evidence that they once existed as independent collections.[53] The presence of doublets and the lack of coherent sequence within the longer divisions, moreover, attest the complexity of the separate collections themselves.

The bulk of the Book of Proverbs is contained within the four longer collections (1, 2, 3, and 5), to which the five short units serve as appendices. At the heart of the book are the two Solomonic collections (2 and 5), consisting of terse, disconnected, and largely "secular" sayings generally associated with the early stage of Israel's wisdom. The first of the two (2) is widely regarded as the oldest portion of the book and of pre-Exilic date. There is nothing in the other collection (5) that refutes its ascription to the days of Hezekiah. The first part of section 3 closely resembles the Egyptian wisdom text, *The Teaching of Amenemope,* which has been assigned to various dates between the tenth and sixth centuries B.C. Among the close verbal parallels is the reference to "thirty sayings" in 22:20 and the "thirty chapters" in Amenemope's collection. By one accounting there are precisely thirty proverbs in section c, about a third of which appear to be adaptations from the Egyptian work.

Section (1) appears to be the latest of the collections. It consists of a series of short wisdom poems, is marked by a strong moral and religious tone, and includes personifications of wisdom as a prophetess (1:20–33; 8:1–36) and gracious hostess (9:1–6). The latter passages resemble the hypostatizations of wisdom in the late Deuterocanonical wisdom books.[54]

[53] The Septuagint order is 1–9; 10:1–22:16; 22:17–24:22; 30:1–14; 24:23–34; 30:15–33; 31:1–9; 25–29; 31:10–31.
[54] Ecclesiasticus 24; Wisdom of Solomon 7.

Taken together, these features suggest a date for the collection in the fourth or third century B.C.

THE FEAR OF THE LORD IS THE BEGINNING OF WISDOM. Many of the proverbs, taken by themselves, appear to offer little more than a "worldly wisdom." One is warned against laziness, thoughtless speech, relations with harlots, drunkenness, ill manners, and the like, all of which defeat the ends of a full and satisfying life. The way to true happiness is through the common-sense virtues of hard work, prudent speech, good manners, and discipline in all things. Much emphasis is placed on the family: the father's role as firm but compassionate disciplinarian, the mother's wise example and teaching, the diligent son's attentiveness to the instruction of his elders. In all these respects, Hebrew wisdom is not noticeably different from the wisdom of the larger Near East. The values are utilitarian; and the appeal is to the lessons of experience rather than the great revelatory events of covenant history. Of the temple and cult, we hear scarcely anything at all.

In its broader context, however, the wisdom of Proverbs is distinctly religious. No small number of proverbs are explicitly concerned with morals—with service to God and one's fellow man. All the principles of the Decalogue, save the prohibition of idols and the law of the Sabbath, are to be found here. So, too, are some of the familiar prophetic themes. Corruption in business (11:1; 20:10, 23), perversion of justice (15:27; 17:15, 23; etc.), and mistreatment of the poor (22:22ff.; 31:5) are denounced as loathsome to Yahweh; whereas to do what is right and just is declared better than sacrifice (21:3). Compassion and kindness are the marks of the righteous man (11:17; 14:22; 16:6; 24:10ff.; etc.) who refuses to rejoice in another's misfortune (17:5) or to return evil for evil (20:22; 24:29).

The morality of Proverbs, to be sure, is not lacking a utilitarian character of its own. Right living is taken as the assurance of personal good fortune.

> The Lord does not let the righteous go hungry
> but he thwarts the craving of the wicked.
> 10:3 [55]

"A man who is kind," we are told, "benefits himself" (11:17). Likewise, befriending an enemy effects a twofold satisfaction,

> For you will heap coals of fire
> upon his head,
> and the Lord will reward you.
> 25:21–22

The deeper problem with which Job wrestled is nowhere in view. According to the express theme of the wisdom poems in chapters 1–9, however,

---

[55] Cf. 3:9–10; 11:8.

"the fear of the Lord," and not the hedonistic principle, is the moving force behind the wise man's style of life.[56] Even granting different levels and stages in the development of Israel's wisdom, one can agree that there is a "Godward thought"[57] at the back of the mind of the Hebrew sage that gives religious meaning even to those aspects of wisdom that we would call "secular." All of life is under God; thus no insight which assists in improving the quality of life can be labeled "profane."

One of the most interesting developments in the late stages of the wisdom movement was the personification and hypostatization of wisdom. In the intertestamental wisdom books, Ecclesiasticus and Wisdom of Solomon, wisdom is depicted as a divine being created by God, his associate in fashioning and governing the world, a guide and instructor provided for his people. The personifications of wisdom in Proverbs (cf. 1:20–33; 8:1–35; 9:1–6) have not yet reached so developed a level but stand at some point between wisdom's poetic objectification as an attribute of God in Job 28 and the later portrayals of the intertestamental books.[58] As a prophetess, wisdom cries out in public places, urging the simple to learn prudence (8:1ff.); as a hostess, she invites her guests to partake of the food of insight (9:1–6). The first of God's creatures, she represents the rational principle set within the world from creation (8:22ff.). Far from a polytheistic notion, however, wisdom here is little more than God himself in action. According to one recent study, such characterizations represent an effort to bridge the gap between the wisdom tradition and the rest of Israelite religious tradition by emphasizing that all wisdom comes from God.[59]

Job

Among the poetic works produced by the Israelite community, none ranks above the Book of Job. Artur Weiser thus assesses its place within world literature:

> Not only its value as a work of art, displayed by the power of its language, by the depth of its feeling, by the grandeur of its structure, but also the subject with which it deals, the daring titanic struggle with the immemorial, yet ever new, questioning of mankind concerning the meaning of suffering, places this composition as regards its general significance beside Dante's *Divina Commedia* and Goethe's *Faust*.[60]

Superficially, the book has the form of a drama and has undergone adaptation for the modern stage in Archibald MacLeish's *J.B.* That it was not in-

---

[56] 1:7, 29; 2:5; 8:13; 9:10.

[57] W. O. E. Oesterley, *The Book of Proverbs* (New York: E. P. Dutton & Co., Inc., 1929), p. lvii.

[58] See Helmer Ringgren, *Word and Wisdom; Studies in the Hypostatization of Divine Qualities and Functions in the Ancient Near East* (Lund, Sweden: H. Ohlssons boktr., 1947).

[59] R. N. Whybray, *Wisdom in Proverbs*, Studies in Biblical Theology, (Naperville, IL: Alec R. Allenson, 1965).

[60] *The Old Testament: Its Formation and Development*, p. 288.

tended for dramatic presentation, however, is evident from the great length of its monologues. Rather, as a production of Israel's wisdom tradition, it was written to be read and pondered for its insights respecting one's proper response to the human situation in which he exists.

The Book consists of two distinct parts. The bulk of the work, and by far its more significant element, is the long poem in which Job, his friends, and eventually Yahweh himself engage in extended dialogue concerning the implications of Job's suffering (3:1–42:6). Providing the framework for the poem (prologue, chs. 1–2; epilogue, 42:7–17) is a brief prose narrative which relates the legend of the righteous man's adversities, their beginnings in the heavenly councils, and their happy issue in the sufferer's restoration.

The prose account is written in an archaic style which bears all the marks of an ancient and popular folk tale. That its hero is a virtuous Edomite[61] is good evidence that it predates the Exile, when Jewish distrust of Edomites was most intense. The poem, by contrast, reflects the influence of Jeremiah[62] and the speculative mood of the Exilic or post-Exilic period. If the poet influenced the thought and vocabulary of Deutero-Isaiah, as seems likely,[63] his work could not be dated later than the middle of the sixth century B.C. Notwithstanding the contrasts between the poem and its narrative setting—most especially the patience of the legendary hero as compared with the impatient subject of the poetry—the poem would be unintelligible apart from the story. Having utilized the legend as the basis for his work, the poet himself, presumably, affixed it to the poem as prologue and epilogue.

The book is easily outlined, as follows:

A. Prologue: chs. 1–2
B. Poetic dialogues: 3:1–42:6
   1. Job's lament: ch. 3
   2. Dialogues between Job and his friends: chs. 4–27
      a. First dialogue cycle: 4–14
      b. Second dialogue cycle: 15–21
      c. Third dialogue cycle: 22–27
   3. Poem in praise of wisdom: ch. 28
   4. Job's further laments: chs. 29–31
   5. Elihu's speeches: chs. 32–37

[61] Cf. Uz, 1:1.

[62] Compare Job's curse of his birth in ch. 3 with Jeremiah's curse in Jer. 20: 14–18; and see further the analysis offered by Samuel Terrien, *IB*, Vol. 3, p. 889.

[63] Cf. S. R. Driver and G. B. Gray, *A Critical and Exegetical Commentary on the Book of Job*, ICC, Vol. I (New York: Charles Scribner's Sons, 1921), lxvff.; Robert H. Pfeiffer, *Introduction to the Old Testament*, pp. 675–78; Samuel Terrien, *IB*, Vol. 3, pp. 889–890.

6. Yahweh's speeches: chs. 38–41
7. Job's repentance: 42:1–6
C. Epilogue: 42:7–17

In the dialogue cycles between Job and his friends (chs. 4–27) the speech of each friend is followed by Job's response, according to a strict sequence: Eliphaz–Job–Bildad–Job–Zophar–Job. The omission of a Zophar speech in the third cycle is due to the disarranged order of the text; a fragment of his words is probably embedded within the third reply of Job (27:13–23).

Three units within the book are best regarded as later interpolations: (1) the Elihu speeches (32–37), (2) the wisdom poem (28), and (3) a portion of the second Yahweh speech (40:6–41:34). Elihu is mentioned nowhere in the prose or poetry outside of chapters 32–37; nor is there any response to his speeches in accord with the dialogue pattern established in the rest of the book. His words contribute nothing of substance to the discussion but only delay unduly Yahweh's response (ch. 38) to Job's final challenge (ch. 31). The wisdom poem might have been written by the author of Job, but it is out of place in its present context. The second Yahweh speech, with its lengthy descriptions of the hippopotamus and crocodile, contrasts with the more effectively composed first Yahweh speech; and by further rebuking Job after his initial submission, it comes "perilously near nagging."[64]

The Story of Job. The Job of the prose account can hardly be other than the legendary prototype of righteousness mentioned by the prophet Ezekiel as a counterpart to Noah and Daniel (Ezek. 14:14, 20). His exemplary piety and material prosperity make him the object of a test instigated by the satan, a cynical angel whose role is to search out men's failings and accuse them before God.[65] God permits the satan to afflict the blameless man with loss of goods, family, and health in order to settle the issue of whether Job serves God simply for the love of God rather than for purely selfish ends.

The satan's cynicism is tellingly disproved by Job's unyielding faithfulness in the face of overwhelming adversity. Not for one moment does the afflicted man rail out against Yahweh as the author of his suffering—not even when exhorted by his wife to curse God that he might be stricken dead and thus delivered out of his misery. Job's capacity for trusting Yahweh's goodness makes him an unsurpassed model of Godly patience:

---

[64] A. S. Peake, quoted in Harold H. Rowley, *The Growth of the Old Testament*, p. 144.

[65] Cf. Zech. 3:1–10 and p. 422 above. The satan is not yet depicted in the role of a tempter of men such as underlies the Chronicler's reference in I Chron. 21:1, but is more akin to Zechariah's accusing angel. Cf. Rivkah Schärf Kluger, *Satan in the Old Testament*, Hildegard Nagel, trans. (Evanston, IL: Northwestern University Press, 1967); T. H. Gaster, "Satan," *IDB*, R–Z, pp. 224–228.

Shall we receive good at the hand of God, and shall we not receive evil?

2:10

The three friends occupy an obscure role in the extant version of the folk tale. They are described in the prologue as comforters of the stricken Job; but the reason for God's harsh words for them in the epilogue is less than clear, and even within the context of the poem they are unexpectedly severe. Presumably, the original version of the story included more detail regarding them, which was omitted in order to make way for the poetic dialogues. Job's intercession for the friends, at any rate, is followed by a two-fold restitution of all his losses, plus the further blessing of a full and fruitful life. The happy ending vindicates God's justice, but without contradicting the truth established by the experiment, namely that Job's goodness was not prompted by selfish motives.[66]

The Poem: The Problem of Righteous Suffering. The problem of innocent suffering is not, as such, at issue in the folk tale. Other than the implication that God can allow suffering as a test, it offers no reasons for the afflictions to which good men are subjected. In a peculiar sense, however, the problem was a major concern of the poet. He undoubtedly knew suffering first-hand and had experienced for himself "the dark night of the soul" whereby the reason searches for answers that faith is reluctant to supply. He, in effect, becomes Job, the righteous sufferer. As a result, the legendary hero's unquestioning acceptance of his fate gives way to the impatient and anguished protest of flesh and blood experience. The test that confronted the man of superlative holiness becomes the crisis of any man who seeks to maintain faith in the face of overwhelming odds.

In the speeches of the three friends, the poet exposes the inadequacy of the orthodox approach to the problem that prevailed in his day. This was essentially the Deuteronomic philosophy of rewards and punishment applied at the individual level. Just as Israel's obedience could be trusted to bring national prosperity and her disobedience adversity, so also it was assumed that the same principle applies in the sphere of personal morality. One could reason, moreover, from effect to cause; suffering implies divine disfavor and, therefore, the guilt of the sufferer.

Think now, who that was innocent ever perished?

Or where was the upright cut off?

4:7

Without recourse to a doctrine of rewards and retribution in the afterlife—a view which had not yet developed in Israelite religious faith—there appeared to be no other means of defending God's justice (cf. 7:7–10). It is for

[66] See Carl G. Jung, *Answer to Job*, R. F. C. Hull, trans. (London: Routledge and Paul, 1954).

this reason that Eliphaz, Bildad, and Zophar are adamant in urging Job to confess his sins and await God's forgiveness. Persuaded by the necessity of their logic, they find it possible to conform personal experience to theological dogma. They can reason, for example, that no man is without sin and thus wholly undeserving of God's reproof (4:17). Nor do they overlook the truth that adversity can serve a positive role in discipline and teaching (5:17–27). Only when Job resists their efforts at friendly persuasion do they resort to open accusation and passionate rebuke.

The friends speak as the defenders of a rational and moralistic system and consequently view the problem from an external perspective. Job, however, knows "the inner infinity of the suffering soul"[67] and can only reject the facile answers of his orthodox counselors. His position is not that he is without sin, but that he can find no wrong sufficiently great to justify such thoroughgoing rejection at God's hands. Thus the friends' logic of just recompense provides no real defense of God's justice.

Job's speeches display a pattern of vacillating moods, from an utter despair in which he flings accusations at God and yearns for death, to fervent appeals for a hearing and even fleeting glimpses of hope. In one badly preserved passage (19:25–27) he appears confident that after his death a vindicator (go'el)—perhaps his next of kin, or possibly even God himself—will establish his innocence.[68] In truth, Job can abandon neither his belief in God, on the one hand, nor his sense of justice, on the other.[69] Behind his bitter complaints is the indomitable hope that by some divine logic the two can be joined. In his present extremity, however, he experiences God as the altogether inscrutable One before whom it is impossible either to be just (9:2) or to receive justice. He deplores a God who pursues with affliction (7:19) but remains hidden from human need (9:11). At the height of his anguish, he cries out for a mediator who will judge between God and man.

> For he is not a man, as I am, that I
>   might answer him,
> that we should come to trial
>   together.
> There is no umpire between us,
>   who might lay his hand upon us
>   both.
>
> 9:32–33

The Voice from the Whirlwind. The climax of the poem is reached in the speeches of God. Here Job at last confronts the object of all his appeals, accusations, and veiled hopes. Only, God comes not as object, but as subject,

---

[67] Martin Buber, *The Prophetic Faith*, p. 191.

[68] The corrupt Hebrew of verse 26 is sometimes taken as an expression of belief in an afterlife. Not only is the meaning of the verse uncertain, however, but any hope of life beyond the grave is explicitly denied elsewhere in the Job speeches.

[69] Martin Buber, *The Prophetic Faith*, pp. 191–192.

The Book of Job, Plate XIII: Then the Lord answered Job out of the Whirlwind, engraved by William Blake, British, 1757–1827. (Courtesy of the National Gallery of Art, Washington, D.C.)

choosing his own time, place, and manner of appearance—the whirlwind. In neither of God's speeches does he offer the sufferer the facile logic of the friends. No rationally constructed formula can suffice for the sort of questions Job has raised. Thus God's reproof of the friends in the epilogue appears to speak the mind of the poet: "You have not spoken of me what is right, as my servant Job has" (42:7). For all his impatient complaints and near blasphemy, Job has come nearer the truth than have the friends. In choosing no answer at all in preference to the wrong answer, he has left an opening for God.

To be sure, God's discourses are not lacking a rebuke for Job. God asks,

> Who is this that darkens counsel by words without knowledge?
> 38:2

The role of interrogator and respondent, moreover, must be reversed,

> I will question you, and you shall
> declare to me.
> 38:3

With heavy irony, God questions Job as to his comprehension of the un-fathomed mysteries of the universe, from the measurements of the earth to the "fearful symmetry" of the wild beast. Job is thus shown to have shared in the error of the friends insofar as he has held God accountable to a human and fallible scheme of justice. In impugning God's motives he has pursued a presumptuous course:

> Will you even put me in the wrong?
> Will you condemn me that you may
> be justified?
> 40:8

The effect of God's questions is not lost on Job. It is a chastened and wiser man that replies to the divine interrogator,

> Therefore I have uttered what I did not
> understand,
> things too wonderful for me, which
> I did not know.
> 42:3

God's intent, however, is not to shut Job's mouth, but to direct him toward a more profound understanding of the human situation. In essence, God offers himself as an answer.[70] He comes to Job as the author of the mysterious and wonderful designs written into the fabric of existence which both include and exceed the norms of human justice. More than simply a device to overwhelm Job, the illustrations drawn from the natural order reveal "the incomprehensibly wonderful Creator God, who cannot be caught in a system of reasonable purposes, but escapes all human calcula-tions."[71] The most revealing fact is simply that God comes to the sufferer, bidding him to "gird up his loins like a man" for dialogue and affirming his

---

[70] Ibid., p. 195.
[71] Walther Eichrodt, *Man in the Old Testament* (Chicago: Henry Regnery Company, 1951), p. 59.

good intentions for the world and man. The end result for Job is an eman-
cipation from his obsession with his own righteousness and just deserts and
a vision of God as he actually is.

> I had heard of thee by the hearing of the ear
> but now my eye sees thee.
> 42:5

The poem is consequently to be understood as an expansion on the theme
of the folk tale, "Does Job serve God for naught?" Not only, declares the
poet, is selfless righteousness possible for Job, but for any person willing
to acknowledge God's designs in his life.

2. FOR SUCH A TIME AS THIS: SONG OF SONGS, RUTH, LAMENTATIONS, ECCLESIASTES, AND ESTHER

The five writings known as the *Megilloth* ("scrolls") or festal scrolls have
been grouped together since Talmudic times when it became customary to
read each of them publicly at one of the annual religious festivals. Their appearance in Hebrew Bibles usually follows the order of the cultic calendar:

Song of Songs	Passover	(Mar.–Apr.)
Ruth	Pentecost	(May–June)
Lamentations	9th of Ab	(July–Aug.)
Ecclesiastes	Feast of Tabernacles	(Sept.–Oct.)
Esther	Purim	(Feb.–Mar.)

Aside from their role in the liturgy, the books share few common characteristics. The Song of Songs and Lamentations consist entirely of poetry, and
Ruth and Esther relate the stories of their respective heroines; but a
sharper contrast in the moods and purposes of the former and latter pairs
could scarcely be conceived. As for Ecclesiastes, it is a unique example of
Hebrew wisdom, marked by a pessimism exceeding that of any other writing in the canon.

Song of Songs

Though the title which ascribes the Song of Songs to Solomon (1:1) is a
late addition to the book, it is easily explained on the basis of Solomon's
reputation as a writer of songs (I Kings 4:32) and the occurrence of his
name in the text of the book (1:5; 3:7ff.; 8:1ff.). It is chiefly the late vocabulary of the poems—the frequent Aramaisms and the Persian and Greek
loan words—that argues otherwise. The present form of the book is as late

as the Hellenistic era (third century B.C.), though the poems themselves may derive from a much earlier period.

The chief problem respecting the Song of Songs concerns its proper interpretation. Briefly stated, there are five approaches, each of which takes different forms: (1) allegory, (2) cult myth, (3) drama, (4) a single love poem, or (5) an anthology of poems. From a very early time, an allegorical interpretation provided theological meaning to an otherwise thoroughly erotic and secular poetry. The expressions of love were taken by Judaism as representing Yahweh's relation to Israel, and later by Christians as Christ's love for the church. Arguing the allegorical theory at Jamnia, Rabbi Akiba declared that "no day outweighed in glory the one on which Israel received the Song of Solomon." Aside from its arbitrariness, such an approach is altogether incompatible with the sensuous, earthy character of the poems. A similar objection must be raised against the more recent theory of a connection with the Near Eastern fertility cults. To find in the poems the sacred marriage of god (or king) and goddess is to substitute allegorization of another sort and necessitates the gratuitous assumption that eventually "the early connections of the book were forgotten."[72]

Once it is determined that the poems speak simply—but beautifully—of an altogether human and romantic love of man for maid,[72a] the chief questions revolve about their unity and function. Efforts to uncover a sustained dramatic plot involving Solomon and his bride, or Solomon, the bride, and her shepherd lover, founder on the absence of clear divisions into acts and scenes, not to speak of the frequent uncertainty as to the identity of the speakers. The episodic character of the book, in fact, is the chief objection to regarding it as a single lyric poem. It seems best to accept the book as a collection of songs, joined only by the common theme of human love and perhaps sung at the ceremonies and festivals of Jewish weddings. Parallels have been adduced from modern Syrian wedding celebrations, in which the bride and bridegroom are enthroned as "king" and "queen." Notwithstanding the misconceptions by which the book found its way into the canon, it is surely no discredit to a religious faith which recognizes sexual love as a sacred and indispensable feature in God's designs for man and woman.[72b]

---

[72] Theophile J. Meek, "The Song of Songs," *IB*, Vol. 5, pp. 95.

[72a] Phyllis Trible refers to the book as "a symphony of love," and declares that "love for the sake of love is its message" (*God and the Rhetoric of Sexuality* [Philadelphia Fortress Press, 1978], pp. 161–192). See also Brevard S. Childs, *Biblical Theology in Crisis*, pp. 192ff., and Gillis Gerleman, *Ruth—Das Hohelied*, Biblischer Kommentar: Altes Testament, 18 (Neukirchen-Vluyn: Neukirchener Verlag, 1965), pp. 72–75, 83–85.

[72b] An interpretation of the Song of Songs that focuses on its canonical role is that of Brevard Childs, *Introduction to the Old Testament as Scripture*, pp. 569–579. Childs regards as decisive the appended title (1:1) which ascribes the book to Solomon. This, he contends, lends a wisdom function to the poems and results in an exploration of the mysteries of human love expressed in the marriage festival.

463

Ruth

The much beloved story of Ruth is told with a consummate skill that most likely reflects a long process of polishing through repeated retellings. Though the events described are set in the period of the Judges, the form of the story as we have it can hardly be earlier than the post-Exilic era. The opening verse shows a familiarity with the Deuteronomic edition of the Book of Judges; and the custom described in 4:7–12 is explained as belonging to "former times."

The sheer beauty of the story and the magnanimity of its characters appear to some sufficient reason for its preservation. One can almost agree with the judgment that "the worst service one can do the story is to comment on it."[73] The work would likely not have survived, however, had it not served some purpose other than simply the readers' enjoyment. In its present form, primary interest appears to lie in the record it provides of King David's ancestry. The son born to Ruth and Boaz is identified as Obed, father of Jesse, grandfather of David. Although the genealogical note that concludes the book (4:17b–22) appears to be a late appendage (cf. I Chron. 2:4ff.), it is improbable that a Moabite ancestry for David would have been invented in the post-Exilic period.[74]

Surely the impressive truths that modern readers find in the story were not missed by ancient Israel. Ruth's words to the bereft Naomi stand as a supreme example of the devotion that exceeds the demands of conventional duty.

> Where you go I will go, and where you lodge I will lodge; your people shall be my people, and your God my God.
>
> 2:16

Also exemplary is the willingness of Boaz to perform the responsibility of the Levirate marriage for his deceased kinsman, and his initial kindnesses to Ruth, the gleaner. Perhaps of greatest significance, particularly for the post-Exilic Jewish community in which marriages to foreigners were prohibited under Ezra and Nehemiah, was the appearance of a Moabitess in such a favorable role—beloved of Naomi and Boaz, model of devotion, ancestress of David!

---

[73] Richard Moulton, quoted by D. Harvey in the article on Ruth, *IDB*, R–Z, p. 133. See, however, the sensitive handling of the story by Phyllis Trible in "Two Women in a Man's World: a Reading of the Book of Ruth," *Soundings* 59 (1976), pp. 251–279 (reprinted in idem, *God and the Rhetoric of Sexuality*, Chap. 6).

[74] Gillis Gerleman has contended (*Ruth*, Biblicher Kommentar, Altes Testament, XVIII [Neukirchen Kreis Moers: Neukirchener Verlag, 1960], pp. 5–11) that David actually was of Moabite descent (cf. I Sam. 22:3–4) and that the Book of Ruth is directed toward explaining that relationship.

Lamentations

The Book of Lamentations consists of five poems (corresponding to its five chapters), detailing Israel's grief over the fall of Jerusalem in 587 B.C.[75] The first four poems are alphabetic acrostics in which the initial word of each verse begins with the corresponding letter of the Hebrew alphabet—running the full gamut of the twenty-two letters, *aleph* to *tau*.[76] The fifth poem, though not an acrostic, consists of exactly twenty-two verses. Perhaps more than simply a mnemonic device, the alphabetic form was chosen to express the completeness of Israel's grief, penitence, and hope.[77]

Whether or not the five poems are the work of a single author is unclear. Different literary forms are evident—funeral dirge (most of chs. 1, 2, and 4), individual lament (1:11c ff.; 3:1–39, 52–66), and communal lament (3:48ff.; 4:17ff.; ch. 5)—but are so blended together within the separate compositions as to constitute no adequate criterion of authorship. A more significant difference may involve the confessional character of some passages (e.g., 1:5ff.; 3:22ff.) as compared with the mood of protest in others (e.g., ch. 5). The Psalter, nevertheless, provides examples of similar fluctuation within a single psalm. The tradition (Septuagint) which ascribes the poems to Jeremiah has little to support it. The language and style are unlike those of the prophet; so too are the attitudes manifested toward Babylon (1:21ff.; 3:59–66), Egypt (4:17), King Zedekiah (4:20), and the reason for Judah's fall (5:7).

Ecclesiastes

In Ecclesiastes we confront another work attributed by tradition to Solomon. One Rabbinic source declares that "he wrote the Song of Songs, with its accent on love, in his youth; Proverbs, with its emphasis on practical problems, in his maturity; and Ecclesiastes, with its melancholy reflections on the vanity of life, in old age."[78] As with Song of Songs, the Solomonic tradition was the chief factor in winning the disputed book a place in the canon; and, once again, the notion was incorrect. The book's title (1:1), ascribing it to "the son of David, king in Jerusalem," was doubtless suggested by a single passage in which the author speaks as "king over Israel in Jerusalem" (1:12–2:20). That this instance represents no actual evidence of Solomonic authorship but only an innocent device used by the sage to give substance to his argument is shown by the mention of "all who were over

---

[75] See above, pp. 378–379.

[76] In poem 3 the verses are in triplicate; thus each letter appears three times.

[77] Norman K. Gottwald, *A Light to the Nations*, p. 375. Cf. also by the same author, *Studies in the Book of Lamentations*, Studies in Biblical Theology, 14 (London: S.C.M. Press, 1954).

[78] Robert Gordis, *Koheleth—The Man and His World* (New York: Schocken Books, Inc., 1968), p. 39; cf. Midrash *Shir Hashirim Rabba* 1:1, sec. 10.

Jerusalem before me" (1:16; 2:9). Solomon's only predecessor on the Jerusalem throne, of course, was his father David. In any case, the title is best regarded as editorial. Far from actually having been a king, the author frequently writes from the perspective of a subject condemning the administration (3:16; 4:1; 10:20) and counseling loyalty as a calculated necessity rather than a virtue (8:1–9). The language of the book, with its numerous Aramaisms, familiarity with popular Greek patterns of thought, and spirit of individualism, points to a date as late as the early Greek period (fourth or third centuries B.C.). That the work is older than the second century B.C., however, is attested by its influence upon Ben Sira (c. 180 B.C.) and its appearance among the manuscripts from Qumran.

The name Ecclesiastes derives from the Septuagint, where it translates the author's pen name, Koheleth. The English rendering, "Preacher," is unfortunate as it conveys an image quite different from the one intended. The name comes from the same Hebrew root as Kahal, [79] "a gathering, assembly, or congregation," and seems to mean "the one who assembles a company or congregation." The content and form of the book make it clear that Koheleth was a wisdom teacher who addressed gatherings of students or disciples (cf. 12:9). Writing no doubt late in life (12:1ff.), he speaks as one thoroughly schooled in the conventional, orthodox Hebrew wisdom. But, more significantly, he voices an unconventional, skeptical view of life which runs counter at many points to the accepted principles of pragmatic wisdom. Perhaps he belonged to Jerusalem's well-to-do [80] and had ample leisure to think long and hard about the deeper problems ignored by less sensitive colleagues.

The book takes the form of a series of personal reflections, expressed in the popular maxims of the day and in longer poems and discourses composed by the author. It begins and ends (1:2, 12:8) with the skeptical declaration: "Vanity of vanities, says Koheleth, all is vanity"—or, perhaps better, "Futility of futilities . . . all is futility." This theme is expounded throughout and underlies the broad range of topics touched upon. Otherwise, the work lacks a formal structure and is more akin to a sage's notebook of random observations on life.

Much of the debate about the book's meaning turns upon the question of its unity. Not a few interpreters have labeled as interpolations or glosses those passages that are judged to be more orthodox than Koheleth's prevailing pessimism. [81] Most recently, however, there has been broader agreement on the basic integrity of the book, save for the concluding "epi-

---

[79] Kahal is translated by the Greek ekklesia, which appears in the New Testament as the word for "church."

[80] This is the view of Robert Gordis, whose Koheleth—The Man and His World includes a provocative theory of Koheleth's personality and background.

[81] E.g., 2:26; 3:17; 4:5; 6:7; 7:6, 26b; 8:11–13; 9:17–10:3; 10:8–14a; 11:9b. Cf. O. S. Rankin, "The Book of Ecclesiastes," IB, Vol. 5, pp. 7ff.

logue" (12:9–14), which almost all regard as editorial.[82] The uniformity of language throughout argues for this position. Also Koheleth's unconventional use of religious vocabulary and his frequent citation of popular proverbs[83] to serve his own special purposes help account for the alleged inconsistencies.

For all his skepticism, Koheleth denies neither the reality of God nor a meaningful role for man and the world. Rather, like the author of Job, he knows the frustration that accompanies man's quest for ultimate answers. Life's weary and monotonous patterns, the inevitability of injustice and death, the innumerable uncertainties that threaten every human enterprise—these are the mysteries that will not yield to Koheleth's keen and educated mind. His descriptions of nature's changeless cycles have been compared to the view of historical process held in certain of the Greek schools. For example,

> What has been is what will be,
> and what has been done is what
> will be done;
> and there is nothing new under the sun.
>
> 1:9

Though evidently familiar with Greek ideas, the sage remains consistently within the broad framework of Hebrew thought and the wisdom circles in which he was trained. It is no abstract problem of history with which he wrestles, but the wearisome round of human events themselves.

> For everything there is a season,
> and a time for every matter under
> heaven:
> a time to be born, and a time to die;
> a time to plant, and a time to pluck
> up what is planted . . .
>
> 3:1–2

Any realization of truth at the level of ideals has eluded Koheleth. The justice he conceives with his mind finds no counterpart in reality. He knows that a man can as soon get into trouble through his goodness as through his evil (7:15–18), and many a wicked man outlives and outprospers his righteous neighbor (7:15). Then, of course, there is the inevitability of death which ends all (2:14–15; 3:19–21). Even such practical goals as knowledge (1:12–18), wealth (5:10–17), and pleasure (2:1–11) can leave one empty. Koheleth knows of what he speaks; he has tested them all. The one indisputable truth that God has given man to know, Koheleth

---

[82] Cf., however, the view of Walter Harrelson (*Interpreting the Old Testament*, pp. 441–444), who accepts the last chapter as the work of the author himself.
[83] Cf. Robert Gordis, *Koheleth—The Man and His World*, ch. XII.

concludes, is the desirability of fulfilling such capacities for wisdom, creativity, and joy as God has placed within him.

> There is nothing better for a man that that he should eat and drink, and find enjoyment in his toil. This also, I saw, is from the hand of God; for apart from him who can eat or who can have enjoyment? For to the man who pleases him God gives wisdom and knowledge and joy . . .
> 2:24–26[84]

The course envisioned here is a sort of "golden mean," whereby one resigns himself to his humanity, avoids extremes, and seeks joy in all he does. It is precisely at this point that Koheleth can invoke the principles of conventional wisdom. He has abandoned none of its practical counsel, apparently, but only the idealism upon which it is based. Some readers doubtless find this to be the one "saving element" in an otherwise objectionable work. To others, Koheleth's chief contribution to religious faith lies in the skepticism itself—in his rejection of all glib and imperfect answers to life's mysteries. The vitality of the sage's protests suggests that the quest was not yet finished; the full weight of the old man's words were now released upon a new generation of younger protégés; the test of their truth must go on. Perhaps it was one such who attached the memorable words of the epilogue:

> Fear God and keep his commandments;
> for this is the whole duty of man.
> 12:13

Esther

Esther is the only book in the canon written specifically to explain the origin of a religious festival. The late winter feast of Purim is interpreted in this fictional work as the celebration commemorating the deliverance of Jews in Persia during the reign of Xerxes (485–465 B.C.; here called "Ahasuerus"). The combined courage of the Jewess Esther and her cousin and guardian, Mordecai, is shown to have been effective in thwarting the evil Agagite Haman and his plot to massacre the Jews on the thirteenth of Adar. The reversal of the scheme brings the slaughter of the enemies of the Jews instead—on the very same day; thus the fourteenth and fifteenth of Adar become days of rejoicing.[85] The name Purim is explained by reference to the lots (*purim*) by which Haman fixed the date for the pogrom (9:23ff.).

Whether or not this entertaining story rests upon some historical incident is impossible to say. The account as such is manifestly fictional and its knowledge of Persian affairs sufficiently remote to make unlikely a date

---

[84] Cf. also 3:12–13; 5:18–20.

[85] Purim was observed on the fourteenth of Adar in the provinces and the fifteenth of Adar in Susa. The author of Esther reconciles these divergent customs by recounting a two-day victory and celebration.

for the work earlier than the Greek period. Several considerations argue for a second-century date. No reference to either the story or the feast of Purim appears elsewhere in Jewish literature before the first century B.C.[86]; and the Qumran discoveries have thus far failed to produce a single fragment of the book. Had it circulated prior to the second century, moreover, the absence of the names of Esther and Mordecai from the exhaustive list of heroes in Ecclesiasticus (c. 180 B.C.)[87] would be difficult to explain.

The book's nationalistic spirit and its failure to mention even once the name of God are often remarked. It is no more a religious work, in the strict sense, than is the Song of Songs; indeed, for many readers its story of the slaughter of the enemy (upward of 75,000 [9:16]) is far more objectionable than are the pleasant love poems of the latter work.[88] It should not be overlooked, however, that the mood of Purim is no sword-rattling chauvinism, but the celebration of deliverance by a people faced time and again with the threat of extinction. Similar to the stories of Daniel and other Jewish works produced under Greek persecution, the Book of Esther provided both the model of selfless courage (". . . if I perish, I perish"; 4:16) and the trust in a providential destiny for God's people (". . . relief and deliverance will rise for the Jews . . ."; 4:14) that have sustained Judaism from its beginnings to the present day.

3. THE VISION IS FOR THE TIME OF THE END: DANIEL

The last phase of Old Testament history takes us beyond the written accounts of the Deuteronomist and Chronicler into the period of Hellenistic rule inaugurated by Alexander the Great (334–323 B.C.). Alexander's far-flung conquests are familiar to every student of world history: the crossing of the Hellespont and the sweep through Asia Minor in 334 B.C.; the victorious march down the Mediterranean coast, bringing Phoenicia, Palestine, and Egypt under his control (333–332 B.C.); the campaign eastward across Mesopotamia, which saw the crushing defeat of the Persian army at Gaugamela (331 B.C.), the capitulation of Babylon, Susa, and Persepolis, and the end of all active resistance to the invincible Greeks. Only after reaching the Indus Valley (326 B.C.), where legend has it that he wept for want of more worlds to conquer, did Alexander finally turn again westward. His premature death in Babylon at thirty-three years of age (323 B.C.) cut short his illustrious and unparalleled career.

[86] There is a reference to Mordecai's Day in II Macc. 15:36, a work to be dated no earlier than the first century B.C.

[87] Ecclus. chs. 44–49.

[88] The additions to the book that appear in the Septuagint manuscripts (107 verses) were incorporated chiefly to supply the missing religious element.

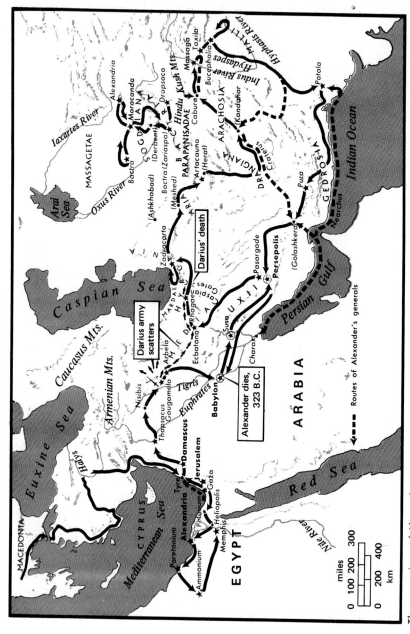

The campaigns of Alexander, 334 to 323 B.C. (Adapted with permission of Macmillan Publishing Co., Inc., from Macmillan Bible Atlas by Y. Aharoni and Michael Avi-Yonah. Copyright © 1968 Carta, Jerusalem. © Copyright 1964 by Carta, Jerusalem. © Copyright 1966 by Carta, Jerusalem.)

Silver tatradrachma of Alexander the Great. Obverse, head of the God Hercules; reverse, Zeus on his throne. This was one of the coins minted for the new Hellenistic world following the conquests of Alexander. (Courtesy of the Money Museum, National Bank of Detroit.)

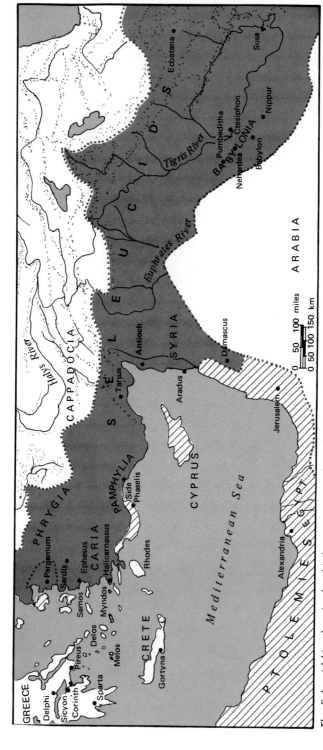

The Seleucid kingdom in the third century B.C. (Adapted with permission of Macmillan Publishing Co., Inc., from Macmillan Bible Atlas by Y. Aharoni and Michael Avi-Yonah. Copyright © 1968 Carta, Jerusalem. © Copyright 1964 by Carta, Jerusalem. © Copyright 1966 by Carta, Jerusalem.)

So great was Alexander's devotion to Greek culture that each new territory he entered became at once a ripe field for Hellenization—the dissemination of Greek ideals, learning, dress, and customs. Greek festivals and athletic contests became common, and the Greek language was made the *lingua franca* of the realm. The Egyptian city of Alexandria, in particular, was founded as a showplace of Hellenistic learning and culture. There many Jews during the next several centuries would be introduced to Hellenistic ideas and develop a Hellenized form of Judaism; there, too, the Greek-speaking Jewish community would produce the Greek version of the Old Testament (Septuagint).

At Alexander's death, his empire was divided among his several generals, including the two whose dynasties were to have lasting importance for Palestinian affairs, Ptolemy Lagi and Seleucus I. The Ptolemaic dynasty, centered in Egypt with Alexandria as its capital, held a firm grip on the coveted Palestinian corridor for a full century, from 301 to 198 B.C. Seleucid control extended initially over Syria, Asia Minor, and Mesopotamia, with Antioch as capital. Our knowledge of Jewish fortunes under Ptolemaic rule is extremely limited, but such evidence as there is suggests few changes from the conditions that prevailed throughout the Persian period.[89] Hellenization doubtless continued in Palestine, as elsewhere throughout the Near East, but apparently there was little interference in Jewish affairs other than the monetary exactions and loyalty to the crown required of a subject people.

It was under Seleucid rule that Jewish fortunes took a distinct turn for the worse. This did not happen, however, in the days of Antiochus III (223–187 B.C.), the strong Seleucid king whose victory over Ptolemy V in 198 B.C. gave the Seleucids control of Palestine. The crisis came rather in the reign of his younger son, Antiochus IV (175–163 B.C.), who assumed the name "Epiphanes" ("the manifest [God]"). Antiochus Epiphanes is depicted in Jewish writings[90] as the most infamous tyrant ever to rule over the Jewish people. Whether or not one accepts that verdict at face value, there can be no doubt that he displayed an utter lack of feeling for the Jewish religion and made inevitable the Jewish revolt of 166 B.C. and succeeding years.

Eager to unify his unsteady realm and thereby offset the growing threat posed by Rome, Antiochus surpassed Alexander in his zeal for cultural solidarity—based, of course, on Greek models. Among those Jews for whom Greek culture held a strong attraction, his Hellenizing policies initially met with little or no resistance. Within these circles the gymnasium and Greek dress were popular; some Jewish males even submitted to surgery to disguise their circumcision and thus avoid embarrassment when partici-

---

[89] John Bright, *A History of Israel*, pp. 397–399.
[90] I and II Macc., and Josephus, *Antiquities of the Jews*, Book XII, chs. 5–9.

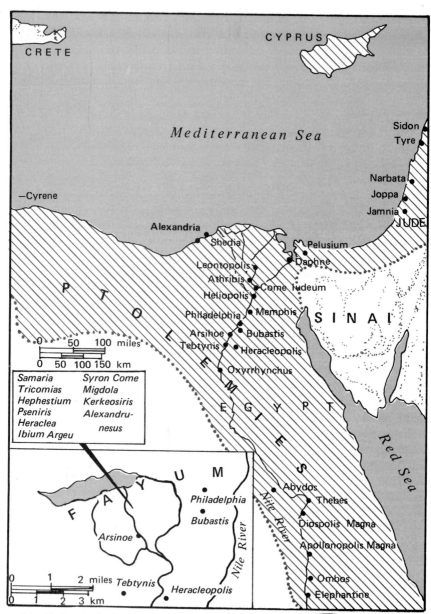

The Ptolemaic kingdom in the third century B.C. (Adapted with permission of Macmillan Publishing Co., Inc., from Macmillan Bible Atlas by Y. Aharoni and Michael Avi-Yonah. Copyright © 1968 Carta, Jerusalem. © Copyright 1964 by Carta, Jerusalem. © Copyright 1966 by Carta, Jerusalem.)

474

pating in sports in the nude.[91] Membership in the gymnasium, moreover, involved a recognition of the Greek gods who were its patrons.[92] When Antiochus replaced the legitimate high priest, Onias, with the latter's Hellenizing brother, Jason, he gained an active supporter for his policies. After three years, however, Jason was supplanted by yet another Hellenizer named Menelaus, who was able to outbid Jason for the office. Antiochus, hard-pressed for funds, had the cooperation of Menelaus in his act of looting the temple.

Jews faithful to the ways of their fathers found these practices appalling, and with good reason. In all fairness to Antiochus, however, he probably failed to understand the uncompromising character of Jewish monotheism, its inability to pay allegiance to other gods or to a king who claimed divine honors. Thus, as Jewish resistance to his policies stiffened, sterner measures were enacted. The final break came in 167 B.C., shortly after Antiochus' humiliating withdrawal from Egypt on Roman orders. Treating Jerusalem as an enemy city, he loosed his army upon it, resulting in widespread death, looting, and destruction. A citadel, called the Acra, was erected there and garrisoned with Syrian troops. Soon after, an edict was issued forbidding the practice of Judaism in all its traditional forms: temple sacrifices, circumcision, sabbath observance, kosher restrictions, and possession of sacred books. Jews were compelled to eat foods forbidden by the Torah and to sacrifice at pagan altars erected throughout the land. Failure to comply with any of these demands carried the death penalty. The crowning affront came in December, 167 B.C., when an altar to Zeus was set up in the temple and swine's flesh sacrificed upon it. This act of desecration became known in Jewish circles as the "abomination of desolation."[93]

Open rebellion broke out in 166 B.C. at the village of Modein near Jerusalem. Mattathias, a local priest of the family known later as the Hasmoneans, flatly refused the order to sacrifice to the Greek gods and struck down the king's officer sent to enforce it. Together with his five stalwart sons, foremost among whom was Judas, Mattathias summoned all who were zealous for the faith to join in a war of resistance to Antiochus. Support came quickly from the group known as the Hasidim ("the pious" or "loyal ones"; from the same verb root as ḥesedh, "steadfast love"), the probable forerunners of the later Pharisees and Essenes. Although Mattathias died shortly after the incident at Modein, leadership was ably borne by Judas, whose nickname "Maccabeus" (probably "Hammerer") became synonymous with the revolt. Pressing their skill in guerrilla tactics and abetted by Antiochus' occupation with affairs in the east, the Maccabeans administered successive defeats to the forces dispatched by the king. In

[91] I Macc. 1:14–15.
[92] John Bright, *A History of Israel*, p. 404.
[93] Dan. 9:27; 11:31; 12:11; I Macc. 1:54.

475

One of the series of great round gate-towers from Hellenistic Samaria, measuring from 42 to 48 feet in diameter. These towers have been described as the "finest monuments of the Hellenistic age in Palestine." (Courtesy of Dr. Richard Schiemann.)

December 164 B.C., three years to the month after the temple's profanation, Judas entered Jerusalem, fortified and garrisoned the city, and cleansed and rededicated the temple—the event celebrated ever since in the Feast of Hanukkah.

The Emergence of Apocalyptic

The same persecutions that provoked the Maccabean uprising also stimulated the development within Jewish circles of a new literary and theological form known as the apocalypse. The name itself (Greek *apokalypsis*) means "revelation" or "unveiling," in reference to the revealed truths which such writings purport to convey. The book of Daniel, which comes from this period, is the only true apocalypse in the Old Testament, though some portions of other books share close affinities with its style (Isa. 24–27; Ezek. 38–39; Zech. 1:7–6:8; Joel 2:1–11; 4:1–21). Between the second century B.C. and the end of the first century A.D., other books of this genre, both Jewish and Christian, became popular; the Revelation of John in the New Testament is one of its best-known representatives.[94] The char-

---

[94] Cf. II Esdras in the Deuterocanon; Enoch, Testaments of the Twelve Patriarchs, The Assumption of Moses, and The Apocalypse of Baruch in the Pseudepigrapha; and The War of the Sons of Light Against the Sons of Darkness from the Dead Sea Scrolls.

Coin of Antiochus IV (Epiphanes). (Courtesy of the American Numismatic Society.)

acteristic theology of the apocalypse is an eschatological dualism which depicts the present age of world history as about to give way to God's final age—a climactic intervention by God himself for judgment and deliverance. This message is couched in a literary form marked by visions, bizarre imagery, cryptic numbers, and angelic interpreters. Authorship is generally pseudonymous, the work being ascribed to some authoritative figure of the distant past, such as Enoch, Moses, Daniel, or Ezra.

Although the apocalypse shares some of the characteristics of wisdom literature,[95] its closest affinities are with Hebrew prophecy.[96] Like the prophet, the apocalyptist sees God as Lord of history, foretells the future, relates visions of judgment and hope, and exhorts to faithfulness. There are significant differences, nevertheless, between prophecy and apocalyptic. The prophets addressed their hearers in face-to-face encounter with words purporting to come directly from Yahweh. The hearers, moreover, were typically charged with disloyalty to the faith and made to stand under the judgment of the prophetic word. The apocalyptists were writers, not spokesmen, whose authority depended largely upon the reputation of the ancient worthies under whose names they wrote. Their message was for the faithful, to whom they offered encouragement and hope in perilous times; judgment was reserved for the enemies of God, the oppressors under whom the righteous presently endured persecution. Whereas the prophets were ever attentive to the future, especially the Day of Yahweh, the prophetic word was directed chiefly to the present, this-worldly sphere of things. The prophets challenged their respective generations to turn from wickedness and work for the implementation of justice and righteousness here and now, hopeful that with God's aid society could be changed for the better. By contrast, the difficult times which gave birth to the apocalypse offered little encouragement to such hopes; the present age was too much under the sway of evil to be greatly affected by anything short of the dramatic intervention of God himself. Thus, apocalyptic hopes centered in the New Age, which was already prepared and ready to be set in motion by God.

Great mystery though it were, a manner of viewing the panorama of history—past, present, and future—is offered in the coded visions of apocalyptic. Under the figures of grotesque beasts, idols, or the like, the great world empires are made to pass in review, until one can see in perspective his own age within the grand scheme and understand that the time of

---

[95] Gerhard von Rad, *Old Testament Theology*, Vol. II, pp. 301–315; idem, *Wisdom in Israel*, pp. 263–283.

[96] Cf. D. S. Russell, *The Method and Message of Jewish Apocalyptic* (Philadelphia: The Westminster Press, 1964); Harold H. Rowley, *The Relevance of Apocalyptic*, rev. ed. (New York: Harper & Row, Publishers, 1955). Paul D. Hanson (*The Dawn of Apocalyptic* [Philadelphia: Fortress Press, 1975]; "Apocalypticism," *IDBS*, pp. 27–34) traces the development of apocalyptic from pre-Exilic prophetic eschatology, the transformation of which resulted from historical crises and an increasing use of cosmic and mythical motifs.

3. THE VISION IS FOR THE TIME OF THE END: DANIEL

God's appearing grows short. By assuming the guise of one living centuries earlier, the apocalyptist can write with the assured knowledge of past history until, of course, he reaches his own point in time; then his prophecies become predictive in the real sense and thus subject to the contingencies of foretelling. It is this very feature within Daniel's visions that enables us to date the book with such precision.

The appeal of the apocalypse lies in what it offers the persecuted generation for which it is written: the assurance of lasting victory for all the faithful who do not abandon hope. The more intolerable grows the pagan oppression, the shorter the time until deliverance will break forth. For, according to the logic of apocalyptic, great persecution, turbulence, and warfare must precede the end time. The cosmic scope of the later apocalyptic, with its shaking of the heavens and earth, falling stars, and binding of Satan, is overwhelming. The conception of a cosmic order of evil—Satan and his angels—which must once-for-all be put to rout is a post-Old Testament development that reflects the influence of Persian theology. For the writer of Daniel, the warfare and ultimate triumph are restricted to the earth though directed from above.

The Book of the Hasidim

The book of Daniel, though set within the period of Babylonian Exile, clearly comes from the days of Antiochus Epiphanes and reflects the spirit of the faithful Hasidim who suffered under his rule. The author's numerous discrepancies concerning the Babylonian and Persian eras, unless intentionally inserted as clues to the book's fictional character, display an altogether hazy knowledge of Exilic times. Among the more glaring inaccuracies are the dating of Jerusalem's fall in the third year of Jehoiakim (1:1), the identification of Belshazzar as "king" of Babylon (5:1) and son of Nebuchadrezzar (5:2ff.),[97] the notion that Media followed Babylon as a ruling world empire (5:28, 31), and the utter confusion concerning Darius, who is wrongly represented as a Median (5:31), successor of Belshazzar (6:1), son of Xerxes (9:1), and predecessor of Cyrus (6:29).[98] Once the author turns to the ostensibly predictive visions of the Greek period (11:2ff.), the record becomes more accurate and detailed. Any reader familiar with the period of Alexander and his successors, the Ptolemies ("kings of the south") and the Seleucids ("kings of the north"), has little trouble decoding the thinly disguised history. Antiochus Epiphanes appears as "a contemptible person" (11:20ff.) and his desecration of the temple in 167 as "the abomination that makes desolate" (11:31). Most likely the beginning of the Maccabean revolt is reflected in the cryptic reference to "a little help" that is promised the faithful (11:34). It is only when the apocalyptist reaches the

[97] See above, pp. 393–94.
[98] The actual historical sequence of the Persian kings was Cyrus, Cambyses, Darius, and Xerxes.

latter half of the reign of Antiochus, in 11:40 and following, that notable inaccuracies reappear—an indication that here current history leaves off and prediction begins.[99] It is with relative assurance, then, that the book can be dated between 167 and 164 B.C., after the temple's desecration and most probably after the beginning of Mattathias' rebellion—but prior to Judas' victories and temple cleansing, of which the writer knows nothing at all.

Other factors consistent with this dating are the absence of Daniel's name from the record of famous men in Ecclesiasticus 44–50, the book's omission from the prophetic portion of the canon, and its peculiar linguistic characteristics. The bilingual character of the book (2:4a–7:28 is in Aramaic; the remainder in Hebrew) poses a problem that has never been satisfactorily answered.[100] It offers no proof of composite authorship, for the linguistic divisions fail to correspond with meaningful subject matter divisions, and common ideas and motifs link the Hebrew and Aramaic portions. Possibly the author switched to Aramaic in 2:4a to record the Chaldeans' speech, continued in that language to the end of Daniel's first vision (ch. 7) because of the frequent speeches, then, after a lapse of time, added the concluding chapters in Hebrew.

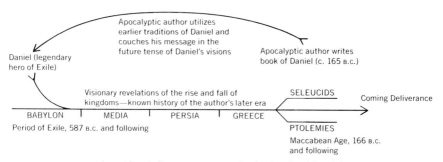

Apocalyptic literary structure in the book of Daniel.

Whether or not there is any connection between the hero of the book and the "Daniel" mentioned in Ezekiel (14:14, 20; 28:3) and the Ras Shamra texts[101] is impossible to say. In each instance we have to do with a man of superlative righteousness; but the subjects of the latter sources belong to pre-Exilic times and the name is spelled differently. The Exilic hero reappears in the Additions to Daniel in the Deuterocanon, the stories of Susanna and Bel and the Dragon.

The book of Daniel divides naturally into two halves: (1) chapters 1–6, inspirational stories of Daniel and his friends in exile, and (2) chapters

---

[99] The predictions of further warfare between Ptolemy and Antiochus, Antiochus' conquest of Libya and Ethiopia, and his subsequent death in Palestine did not transpire.

[100] Cf. Otto Eissfeldt, *The Old Testament: An Introduction*, p. 516.

[101] *ANET*, pp. 149–155 (*ANE*, pp. 118–132).

7–12, Daniel's apocalyptic visions. The shorter units are rather easily isolated, as follows:

1. Inspirational stories: chs. 1–6
   a. Faithfulness to dietary laws: ch. 1
   b. Nebuchadrezzar's dream: ch. 2
   c. The fiery furnace: ch. 3
   d. Nebuchadrezzar's madness: ch. 4
   e. Belshazzar's feast: ch. 5
   f. The den of lions: ch. 6
2. The visions of Daniel: chs. 7–12
   a. The four beasts: ch. 7
   b. The ram and he-goat: ch. 8
   c. The seventy years: ch. 9
   d. The last days: chs. 10–12

INSPIRATIONAL STORIES. The marked unity of spirit and purpose displayed by the Book of Daniel argues forcefully for unitary authorship. Only the concluding verses, 12:11–12, exhibit clear evidence of later interpolation.[102] In chapters 1–6, however, the apocalyptist appears to have worked with older stories that once circulated independently of each other. The chronological sequence of the first and second stories is confused (1:1, 5; 2:1); and Daniel puts in no appearance at all in the third story. Had the author simply created his material, one would expect a closer correspondence between his portrayals of the foreign rulers and the ruthless and tyrannical Antiochus. Even in their present setting, the stories bear a closer resemblance to the wisdom tradition or the edifying tales of the Deuterocanon than to apocalyptic as such.

All six stories have one fundamental message to declare to the Hasidim of the author's day, namely, that God will not abandon those who persist in trust and faithfulness to his Law. Daniel and his friends, already familiar perhaps as the heroes of older folk tales, are offered as examples. The point of the first story would not likely have escaped a generation of Jews under pressure from Antiochus to eat forbidden food. The four young exiles put loyalty to God before life and health; yet they do not perish for want of nourishment. Daniel's interpretation of Nebuchadrezzar's dream (ch. 2) introduces the epochs of world history which are explored at greater length in the visions of chapters 7–12. After four successive kingdoms—Babylon,

---

[102] These verses are generally regarded as two efforts at extending the time of the final consummation beyond the 1,150 days (three and a half years), first to 1,290 days (vs. 11), then to 1,335 days (vs. 12). Other approaches view them as "marking successive stages in the events leading up to the final climax" (Norman W. Porteous, *Daniel*, The Old Testament Library [Philadelphia: The Westminster Press, 1965], p. 172) or as modifications reflecting different calendar systems (H. Burgmann, "Die vier Endzeittermine in Danielbuch," *ZAW* 86 [1974], 542ff.).

Media, Persia, and Greece—have filled their allotted periods of world rule, God will replace them with the indestructible kingdom of his loyal followers. The reader is doubly assured: "The dream is certain, and its interpretation sure" (2:45). Not even the flames of Nebuchadrezzar's oven avail against Hananiah (Shadrach), Mishael (Meshach), and Azariah (Abednego) when they refuse to bow down to the king's image (ch. 3). Mighty Nebuchadrezzar, by contrast, can be debased in a moment to the level of a mindless beast (ch. 4), and the great kingdom of Babylon can fall in a night (ch. 5). Daniel, fearless in his religious duties although under threat of death, escapes the hungry lions and increases in the king's respect (ch. 6).

The stories, however utopian, cannot be lightly dismissed. Underneath their confident and simplistic tone lies the deeper realization that God is under no obligation to rescue his followers from the persecutor, that real courage involves always the willingness to die. This is brought out in the response of the three young men:

> O Nebuchadnezzar, we have no need to answer you in this matter. If it be so, our God whom we serve is able to deliver us from the burning fiery furnace; and he will deliver us out of your hand, O king. But, if not, be it known to you, O king, that we will not serve your gods or worship the golden image which you have set up.
>
> 3:16–18

This, says the writer of Daniel, was the courage of Jews in days past. Could the Hasidim afford to do less?

VISIONS OF DELIVERANCE. The latter half of the Book of Daniel (chs. 7–12) is a true apocalypse. Daniel having been introduced in the foregoing stories as an unequaled interpreter of God's mysteries, the apocalyptist now ascribes to the wise man and his angelic interpreters four visions detailing the course of history from Nebuchadrezzar to Antiochus. The overriding message is not unlike that of the stories: the victory belongs to God's faithful. The means of assurance, however, is no longer inspiring examples of individual deliverance, but the revelation of a pattern implicit in history which assures the collapse of all human empires and the establishment of God's everlasting kingdom.

The first of Daniel's visions (ch. 7) repeats substantially the dream of Nebuchadrezzar in chapter 2. The same four empires symbolized there as the component parts of a great image are depicted here as grotesque beasts which emerge from the sea. Behind both schemes lies a theory of world epochs that circulated in a variety of forms throughout the ancient world.[103] In the portrayals here the pagan kingdoms grow progressively

---

[103] The metallic symbols of gold, silver, brass, and iron are employed for the four world epochs in Hesiod's *Works and Days* (109–201); cf. Ovid, *Metamorphoses*, I, 89–150. For the schema of four kingdoms without the metal imagery, which appears in sources from the

IMAGE (CH. 2)	BEASTS (CH. 7)	IDENTIFICATION
Head of gold	Lion	Babylon
Torso of silver	Bear	Media
Belly and thighs of bronze	Leopard	Persia
Legs of iron	Indescribable beast	Greece
(Feet of iron and clay)		(Ptolemies and Seleucids)
	(Ten horns)	(Alexander's immediate successors)
	(Little horn)	(Antiochus Epiphanes)

worse, reaching their climax in the Greek epoch and specifically in the arrogant "little horn," Antiochus. The "saints of the most high" are destined to suffer under Antiochus for "a time, two times, and a half time" (7:25)—apparently, three and one half years. Relief comes only when God himself intervenes, sits in judgment upon the nations, and gives dominion to his people, the latter depicted as the "stone unhewn by human hand" that topples the image in chapter 2, and the "one like a son of man" who appears before the "Ancient of Days" (God) and receives the kingdom in chapter 7.[104]

The remainder of the book is chiefly an elaboration on the scheme of chapter 7. The second vision (ch. 8) describes once again the fall of Medo-Persia (the ram) before Alexander (the he-goat) and the rulers (horns) who succeed him. The angel Gabriel interprets the cryptic figures for the seer, after which he is instructed to "seal up the vision, for it pertains to many days hence" (8:26). Chapter 9 contains a lengthy speculation on the meaning of Jeremiah's prophecy of a seventy-year exile (Jer. 25:11–12; 29:10). The seventy years are taken as "seventy weeks of years" (490 years), which will conclude with the "half week" (three and one half years) of Antiochus' desecration of the temple. Obviously any literal application of the scheme is impossible, since 490 years reckoned from the beginning of Exile extends well beyond the period of Antiochus. Whether the apocalyptist followed some confused dating system or whether he deliberately obscured his chronology is not apparent.

The last three chapters (10–12) offer a detailed outline of the history of the Seleucid period, extending through the writer's own day and into the immediate future. His dismissal of the Maccabean uprising as "a little

Hellenistic age and later, see J. W. Swain, "The Theory of the Four Monarchies: Opposition History under the Roman Empire," *Classical Philology*, 35 (1940), pp. 1–21, and David Flusser, "The Four Empires in the Fourth Sibyl and in the Book of Daniel," *Israel Oriental Studies*, II (1972), pp. 148–175.

[104] Unlike some of the later apocalyptic writings (IV Ezra and Enoch) in which the "son of man" is an otherworldly figure who comes on the clouds of heaven and defeats the enemies of God, here God himself subdues the enemies, and the "son of man," i.e., his people, rules over a peaceful kingdom.

help"—if that is its meaning—may imply a rejection of armed resistance in favor of awaiting God's imminent deliverance. That apocalyptic hopes and resort to arms are not necessarily incompatible, however, is shown clearly enough by the great apocalyptic battles depicted in the War Scroll from Qumran. The remarkable fact is the total absence of the scenes of carnage associated with God's victory in the later apocalyptic writings. Chapter 12 simply records the coming of "a time of trouble, such as never has been since there was a nation" (12:1). Chief emphasis falls on deliverance: the arrival of Michael, patron angel of the Jews, and the liberation of those whose names are recorded in God's ledger. In one further note—and in a most unpretentious form—there appears here for the first time in any extant Jewish text a clear expression of belief in the resurrection of the dead, coupled with further rewards and punishments.

> And many of those who sleep in the dust of the earth shall awake, some to everlasting life, and some to shame and everlasting contempt.
>
> 12:2

Born out of reflection upon the fate of heroic martyrs and offered here for the comfort and assurance of the Hasidim, the significance of this development for later Jewish and Christian theology, particularly as related to the problem of theodicy, was far-reaching and lasting.

4. WE ARE YOURS, O DAVID: I AND II CHRONICLES; EZRA AND NEHEMIAH

The Hebrew Canon concludes with the books of Ezra-Nehemiah and Chronicles, arranged in that order and accounted as two books. The fourfold division familiar to readers of the English Bible derives from the later Greek and Latin versions. Our concern in the preceding pages with the history which these books record has already given us some perspective on their contents.[105] It remains now to consider them as a literary and theological source.

As we have seen, the books are but parts of a single work, for convenience referred to as the Chronicler's History. A uniformity of language, style, and outlook is evident throughout, and the concluding verses of II Chronicles (36:22–23) are repeated verbatim as the opening verses of Ezra (1:1–3). The division apparently resulted from the admission of the latter portion of the work (Ezra–Nehemiah) into the canon prior to the acceptance of the first part (Chronicles). Ezra–Nehemiah was admitted first because it records a phase of Hebrew history provided by none of the other

---

[105] See above, pp. 406–417.

canonical books, whereas Chronicles repeats in large part the history contained in the older works. When at a later time Chronicles became a part of the canon, Ezra–Nehemiah retained its prior position. It remained for the Greek version to restore the proper sequence as we find it in our English Bibles.

The broad plan of the work may be outlined as follows:

1. Genealogy of Israel from Adam to the restoration: I Chron. 1:1–9:34
2. Genealogy of Saul and Saul's death: I Chron. 9:35–10:14
3. Reign of David: I Chron. 11–29
4. Reign of Solomon: II Chron. 1–9
5. Kingdom of Judah from Rehoboam to Zedekiah: II Chron. 10:1–36:21
6. Edict of Cyrus: II Chron. 36:22–23
7. Return from Exile and restoration of the temple: Ezra 1–6
8. Reforms of Ezra: Ezra 7–10
9. Rebuilding of Jerusalem's walls; the work of Nehemiah: Neh. 1–7
10. Further reforms of Ezra and Nehemiah: Neh. 8–13

Some modern scholars, including W. F. Albright, agree with the Jewish tradition that identifies Ezra as the Chronicler.[106] Chief support for this position rests on affinities of style and outlook between the Chronicler's work and the Ezra Memoirs (Ezra 7:1–10; 7:27–10:44; Neh. 7:73b–9:38), one of the Chronicler's important sources.[107] Others would see in the author's pronounced concern with the Levites and cultic musicians evidence that he was himself one of the Levitical temple singers. On the subject of the date of the work, there is more to be said. Obviously, in its final form it cannot be earlier than Ezra, whose career it records; and this, as we have seen, was either the late fifth or early fourth century B.C.[108] The last Persian king mentioned is Darius II (423–405 B.C.); and the Davidic genealogy in I Chronicles 3:10–24 is brought down to the sixth generation after Zerubbabel. Language considerations point to the late Persian period and include similarities between the Aramaic portion of the work (Ezra 4:8–6:18) and the vocabulary, idioms, and spelling forms of the Elephantine Papyri (late fifth century B.C.). All told, a date for the book in the first half of the fourth century B.C. seems best.

The Chronicler had at his disposal a considerable number of historical sources, some of which he mentions by name. A variety of titles represent-

[106] W. F. Albright, *The Biblical Period from Abraham to Ezra*, p. 95.
[107] C. C. Torrey was the first to make this point (*Ezra Studies* [Chicago: University of Chicago Press, 1910], pp. 238ff.).
[108] See above, pp. 412–417.

ing royal histories and prophetic records are cited.[109] In addition, one can detect the use of the personal memoirs of Nehemiah and Ezra, plus numerous lists, letters, and other official documents, most probably from the temple archives. The basic framework for I and II Chronicles, however, was provided by the Pentateuch and the Deuteronomic History, more especially the books of Samuel and Kings. Large blocks of material have simply been lifted verbatim from the latter books; yet much recorded there has been omitted, and some segments modified or completely rewritten. The availability of two parallel works of this sort—the Deuteronomist's and the Chronicler's—provides the Old Testament scholar with unique opportunities for comparative literary and historical analyses. Most revealing of all is the picture that emerges of the Chronicler's own peculiar interests and outlook, as gauged by the manner in which he used his source material.

Evaluation of the Chronicler's work hinges largely on a determination of the purpose for which he wrote. As a historian, he has to be relegated to a position inferior to that of the Deuteronomist. This, not simply because he depended so heavily upon the latter's work—the Deuteronomist himself no doubt relied just as heavily upon his own sources—nor because his chronology of the Nehemiah–Ezra era is so hopelessly confusing (and, apparently, confused). The judgment concerns, rather, the transparent techniques by which he rewrote Hebrew history to suit his own theological bias. Of all that transpired prior to David's reign, he found it necessary to show—chiefly through genealogical lists (chs. 1–9)—only how the divine purpose had centered first on Israel, then on the pivotal tribes of Judah and Levi. His overriding interest in the Jerusalem temple, especially the Levitical priests and their functions, prompted him to omit crucially significant phases of the Davidic history itself in favor of long, legendary accounts attributing the entire plan of the temple cult to David. So close was David's relationship to Jerusalem that, even though he did not himself erect the temple, in the Chronicler's eyes he became the idealized patron of worship and the supreme symbol of Israel's role as God's holy priesthood. It was this, rather than simply the desire to "whitewash" David, that led the Chronicler to omit most of the uncomplimentary stories about him recorded in the Deuteronomic history (and especially the Court History): the bloody intrigues which gave him the kingship, the Bathsheba and Uriah affair, and the turbulence that marked the latter years of his reign. By comparison, Saul, who had no connection with Jerusalem or Davidic lineage, is given a light and negative treatment, consisting of a genealogy, an obit-

---

[109] Cf. the "book of the kings of Israel and Judah," "book of the kings of Judah and Israel," "book of the kings of Israel," "words of the kings of Israel," and "commentary of the book of the kings"—all of which may, however, be a single royal history referred to under a variety of titles. Prophetic works of Samuel, Nathan, Gad, Shemaiah, Iddo, Jehu, Ahijah, and Isaiah are mentioned.

uary, and the notation that he was unfaithful to Yahweh. His anointing as king is omitted, as if to say that kingship actually began with David. Solomon, however, shares the aura of his father and receives a favorable report. From Solomon and onward, the northern kingdom is all but ignored, as the Chronicler records the successive reigns of the kings in Jerusalem, the fall of the city, and the story of its restoration.

If the Chronicler cannot be commended as a historian, he has received nevertheless high praise as a theologian. Judged in such a light, Chronicles is described by one writer as "one of the most stimulating books in the Bible, courageous and practical . . . the only instance of Hebraic philosophy of history presented on an immense scale."[110] It has been argued, moreover, that the author never intended his work as a history at all, but as a midrash or interpretation of the inner meaning of the older histories.[111] Although some such approach doubtless takes us close to the Chronicler's purpose, two key points should not be overlooked. One is the point made in earlier chapters that any record of past events inevitably involves a point of view—an interpretation whereby the events are selected, arranged, and perhaps subjected to explicit analysis and commentary. In the technical sense, the Chronicler can hardly be denied his rightful role as historian. The other point is that Chronicles–Ezra–Nehemiah is unquestionably an indispensable source for our knowledge of Hebrew history. For many aspects of restoration history, it is our one and only source; but, in respect to the history of the monarchy, also, recent years have seen a new and growing appreciation of the Chronicler's worth. In a considerable number of instances—notably involving aspects of the reigns of kings Jehoshaphat, Joash, Uzziah, Hezekiah, and Josiah—he preserves a more revealing tradition than that supplied by the Deuteronomist.[112]

SELECTED READINGS

Hebrew Poetry

Dahood, Mitchell, "Poetry, Hebrew," *IDBS*, pp. 669–672.

Gevirtz, S., *Patterns in the Early Poetry of Israel* (Chicago: University of Chicago Press, 1963). Paperback.

Gray, G. B., *The Forms of Hebrew Poetry* (London: Hodder & Stoughton Ltd., 1915).

Robinson, Theodore H., *The Poetry of the Old Testament* (London: Gerald Duckworth & Co. Ltd., 1952).

---

[110] W. A. L. Elmslie, "The First and Second Books of Chronicles," *IB*, Vol. 3, p. 341.

[111] J. M. Myers, *I Chronicles*, The Anchor Bible (Garden City, NY: Doubleday & Company, Inc., 1965), p. xviii.

[112] Cf. John Bright, *A History of Israel*, pp. 185, 209–210, 238, 240, 266, 296.

Psalms

Anderson, Bernhard W., *Out of the Depths: The Psalms Speak to Us Today* (Philadelphia: The Westminster Press, 1974). Paperback. An introduction to the Psalms, written for contemporary life and worship.

Barth, Christopher, *Introduction to the Psalms* (New York: Charles Scribner's Sons, 1966). Paperback. A concise, well-written introduction to the Psalms.

Cohen, A., *The Psalms, Hebrew Text, English Translation and Commentary*, The Soncino Books of the Bible (London: The Soncino Press, 1945).

Dahood, Mitchell, *The Psalms*, 3 vols., Anchor Bible (New York: Doubleday & Company, Inc., 1966, 1968, 1970). A thorough, technical work that makes wide and sometimes controversial use of the Syrian Ugaritic literature.

Drijvers, Pius, *The Psalms, Their Structure and Meaning* (New York: Herder and Herder, 1965). A concise work by a Roman Catholic scholar.

Engnell, Ivan, "The Book of Psalms," idem, *A Rigid Scrutiny: Critical Essays on the Old Testament*, John T. Willis, trans. (Nashville, TN: Vanderbilt University Press, 1969).

Gunkel, Hermann, *Die Psalmen* (Göttingen, West Germany: Vandenhoeck und Ruprecht, 1926). A work by the pioneer of form-critical studies in the Psalms.

————, *The Psalms*, Thomas M. Horner, trans. (Philadelphia: Fortress Press, 1967). Paperback. A synopsis of Gunkel's monumental studies in the Psalms.

Guthrie, H. H., *Israel's Sacred Songs* (New York: The Seabury Press, 1966). A helpful introduction to the worship element in the Psalms.

Hayes, John H., *Understanding the Psalms* (Valley Forge, PA: Judson Press, 1976). Paperback. A concise introduction to psalm forms.

Johnson, A., "The Psalms," *The Old Testament and Modern Study*, H. H. Rowley, ed. (New York: Oxford University Press, Inc., 1951).

Kraus, Hans Joachim, *Psalmen*, Biblischer Kommentar, 2nd ed. (Neukirchen Kreis Moers, West Germany: Neukirchener Verlag, 1961). A major critical work on the Psalter.

Leslie, Elmer A., *The Psalms, Translated and Interpreted in the Light of Hebrew Life and Worship* (Nashville, TN: Abingdon Press, 1949). Also in paperback. A clear treatment, based on Gunkel's form-critical approach.

McCullough, W. S., "Introduction and Exegesis to the Book of Psalms," *IB*, Vol. IV, pp. 3–763.

Mowinckel, Sigmund, *The Psalms in Israel's Worship*, D. R. Ap-Thomas, trans., 2 vols. (Oxford: Basil Blackwell, 1962). Ranks with Gunkel's work as a landmark in Psalms study.

Ringgren, Helmer, *The Faith of the Psalmists* (Philadelphia: Fortress Press, 1963). A good introduction to both the forms and the theology of the Psalms.

Sabourin, Leopold, *The Psalms: Their Origin and Meaning*, enlarged ed. (New York: Alba House, 1970). Paperback. A solid and comprehensive work by a Jesuit scholar, which includes analysis and commentary on the separate psalms.

Weiser, Artur, *The Psalms: A Commentary*, The Old Testament Library (Philadelphia: The Westminster Press, 1962). An important work which conceives the setting of many of the psalms in a covenant-renewal ceremony.

Westermann, Claus, *The Praise of God in the Psalms*, Keith R. Crim, trans. (Atlanta, GA: John Knox Press, 1965). A significant form-critical work.

Wisdom

Brueggemann, Walter A., *In Man We Trust: The Neglected Side of Biblical Faith* (Atlanta, GA: John Knox Press, 1972). Relates Old Testament wisdom—premised on a broad interpretation—to contemporary life.

Crenshaw, James L., "Method in Determining Wisdom Influence upon 'Historical' Literature," *JBL*, 88 (1969), pp. 129–142. Reprinted in Crenshaw, *Studies in Ancient Israelite Wisdom* (below). Advocates precise methodological controls in determining wisdom and its influence on Old Testament literature.

―――, ed., *Studies in Ancient Israelite Wisdom*, The Library of Biblical Studies (New York: KTAV Publishing House, 1976.) A collection of influential essays by leading wisdom scholars. See especially the Prolegomenon, pp. 1–45, which provides an excellent introduction to the issues in modern wisdom studies.

―――, "Wisdom," *Old Testament Form Criticism*, John H. Hayes, ed. (San Antonio, TX: Trinity University Press, 1974), pp. 225–264. Evaluates the results of form-critical studies of wisdom.

―――, "Wisdom in the Old Testament," *IDBS*, pp. 952–956.

McKane, William, *Prophets and Wise Men*, Studies in Biblical Theology, 44 (London: S.C.M. Press, 1965).

Murphy, Roland E., "A Consideration of the Classification 'Wisdom Psalms'," VTS, Vol. 9 (1962); (Leiden, Netherlands: E. J. Brill, 1963), pp. 156–167.

―――, "Form Criticism and Wisdom Literature," *CBQ*, XXI (1969), pp. 475–483.

Noth, Martin, and D. Winton Thomas, eds., *Wisdom in Israel and the Ancient Near East*, VTS, Vol. 3 (Leiden, Netherlands: E. J. Brill, 1955).

Rad, Gerhard von, *Wisdom in Israel*, James D. Martin, trans., (Nashville, TN: Abingdon Press, 1972). Highly recommended as a comprehensive and definitive work.

Rankin, O. S., *Israel's Wisdom Literature* (Edinburgh: T. and T. Clark, 1936). Also in paperback (New York: Schocken Books, Inc., 1969). Although old, this work is useful in evaluating the theological role of wisdom in Israelite religion.

Scott, R. B. Y., *The Way of Wisdom in the Old Testament* (New York: Macmillan Publishing Co., Inc., 1971). Paperback. A useful, up-to-date introduction to Israelite wisdom and the individual wisdom books.

Whybray, Roger N., *The Intellectual Tradition in the Old Testament*, BZAW, 135 (Berlin/New York: Walter de Gruyter, 1974). A provocative analysis of alleged wisdom vocabulary and themes in the Old Testament, for which Whybray prefers the name "intellectual tradition."

Proverbs

Fritsch, Charles T., "Introduction and Exegesis to the Book of Proverbs," *IB*, Vol. IV, pp. 767–957.

McKane, William, *Proverbs: A New Approach*, The Old Testament Library (Philadelphia: The Westminster Press, 1970). In addition to commentary on Proverbs, includes a comprehensive review of Egyptian, Babylonian, and Assyrian wisdom texts.

Scott, R. B. Y., *Proverbs and Ecclesiastes*, The Anchor Bible (Garden City, N.Y.: Doubleday & Company, Inc., 1965).

Whybray, R. N., *Wisdom in Proverbs: The Concept of Wisdom in Proverbs 1–9*, Studies in Biblical Theology, 45 (London: S.C.M. Press, 1965).

Job

The Book of Job, Illustrated by William Blake (New York: Paddington Press, 1976). Paperback. Large-page reproductions of Blake's famous Job etchings, with an introductory interpretive article by Michael Marqusee.

Crook, Margaret B., *The Cruel God: Job's Search for the Meaning of Suffering* (Boston: Beacon Press, 1959). A literary analysis of the book.

Glatzer, Nahum N., ed., *The Dimensions of Job: A Study and Selected Readings* (New York: Schocken Books, Inc., 1969). Paperback. A collection of valuable essays on Job, representing Judaic, Christian, and humanist perspectives.

Gordis, Robert, *The Book of Job: Commentary, New Translation, and Special Studies*, Moreshet Series, Vol. II (New York: The Jewish Theological Seminary of America, 1978). An important technical work by an outstanding Jewish scholar.

————, *The Book of God and Man: A Study of Job* (Chicago: University of Chicago Press, 1965). An excellent, sensitive study.

————, "The Temptation of Job: Tradition Versus Experience," *Judaism*, IV (1955), pp. 63–76.

Hone, Ralph E., ed., *The Voice Out of the Whirlwind: The Book of Job* (San Francisco: Chandler Publishing Company, 1960). Paperback. A useful collection of articles selected as research materials.

Jung, C. G., *Answer to Job*, R. F. C. Hull, trans. (London: Routledge and Kegan Paul, 1954).

Polzin, Robert M., *Biblical Structuralism, Method and Subjectivity in the Study of Ancient Texts*, Semeia Supplements (Philadelphia: Fortress Press, 1977), pp. 54–125. An analysis of the book of Job according to the methodology of structuralism.

Pope, Marvin H., *Job*, The Anchor Bible (Garden City, NY: Doubleday & Company, Inc., 1965).

Robinson, H. Wheeler, *The Cross in the Old Testament* (Philadelphia: The Westminster Press, 1955).

Rowley, Harold H., "The Book of Job and Its Meaning", *BJRL*, XLI (1958), 167–207.

Terrien, Samuel, "Introduction and Exegesis to the Book of Job," *IB*, Vol. III, pp. 877–1198.

The Festal Scrolls

Beth-Berg, Sarah, *The Book of Esther: Motifs, Themes, and Structure*, SBL Dissertation Series (Missoula, MT: Scholars Press, 1979).

Campbell, Edward F., Jr., *Ruth*, The Anchor Bible (Garden City, NY: Doubleday & Company, Inc., 1975).

Gerleman, Gillis, *Ruth*—Das Hohelied, Biblischer Kommentar, Altes Testament, 18 (Neukirchen-Vluyn: Neukirchener Verlag, 1965).

Gordis, Robert, *Koheleth*—The Man and His World (New York: Jewish Theological Seminary Press, 1951). Also available in paperback (Schocken Books, Inc., 1968). Translation, critical notes, and interpretation. One of the best studies of Ecclesiastes.

————, *The Song of Songs and Lamentations*, rev. (New York: *KTAV* Publishing House, 1974). Includes translations, technical notes, and commentary.

Hillers, Delbert R., *Lamentations*, The Anchor Bible (Garden City, NY: Doubleday & Company, Inc. 1972).

Loader, J. A., *Polar Structures in the Book of Qohelet* (Berlin/New York: Walter de Gruyter, 1979). An interpretation of Ecclesiastes as a delicate and complex literary production built upon patterns of tension.

Meek, T. J., "The Song of Songs and the Fertility Cult," *The Song of Songs, A Symposium*, W. F. Schoff, ed. (Philadelphia: The Commercial Museum, 1924), pp. 48–69.

Moore, Carey A., *Esther*, The Anchor Bible (Garden City, NY: Doubleday & Company, Inc., 1971).

Pope, Marvin H., *The Song of Songs*, The Anchor Bible (Garden City. NY: Doubleday & Company, Inc., 1977). One of the most comprehensive studies of Song of Songs available. Includes translation, notes, and commentary.

Rowley, Harold H., "The Interpretation of the Song of Songs," *The Servant of the Lord and Other Essays on the Old Testament*, 2nd ed. (Oxford, England: Basil Blackwell, 1965), pp. 195–245.

Sasson, Jack M., *Ruth, A New Translation with a Philological Commentary and a Formalist-Folklorist Interpretation* (Baltimore: Johns Hopkins University Press, 1979).

The Interpreter's Bible Vols. II, III, V, VI.

Trible, Phyllis, "Two Women in a Man's World; A Reading of the Book of Ruth," *Soundings*, 59 (1976), pp. 251–279. Reprinted in idem, *God and the Rhetoric of Sexuality*, Chap. 6.

Apocalyptic and Daniel

Charles, R. H., *Eschatology: The Doctrine of a Future Life in Israel, Judaism, and Christianity* (New York: Schocken Books, Inc., 1963). Paperback. A classic study, delivered as the first Jowett Lectures in 1898–1899.

Frost, S. B., *Old Testament Apocalyptic* (London: Epworth Press, 1952).

————, "Apocalyptic and History," *The Bible in Modern Scholarship*, J. Philip Hyatt, ed. (Nashville, TN: Abingdon Press, 1965), pp. 98–113.

Funk, Robert W., ed., *Apocalypticism* (New York: Herder and Herder, 1969). Paperback. Significant articles by outstanding scholars in the field of apocalypticism.

Hanson, Paul D., *The Dawn of Apocalyptic* (Philadelphia: Fortress Press, 1975). A fresh approach that traces an unbroken development of apocalyptic from pre-Exilic and Exilic prophecy.

Hartman, Louis F., and Alexander A. Di Lella, *The Book of Daniel*, The Anchor Bible (Garden City, NY: Doubleday & Company, Inc., 1978).

Jeffrey, Arthur, "Introduction and Exegesis to Daniel," *IB*, Vol. VI, pp. 341–549.

Klausner, Joseph, *The Messianic Idea in Israel from its Beginning to the Completion of the Mishnah* (New York: Macmillan Publishing Co., Inc., 1955).

Koch, Klaus, *The Rediscovery of Apocalyptic*, Margaret Kohl, trans., Studies in Biblical Theology, 2nd series, no. 22 (London: S.C.M. Press, 1972). Paperback. A reappraisal of apocalyptic and its relevance for the Old and New Testaments and contemporary theology.

Mowinckel, Sigmund, *He That Cometh*, G. W. Anderson, trans. (Nashville, TN: Abingdon Press, 1956). Traces eschatology and messianism through the Old Testament.

Noth, Martin, "The Understanding of History in Old Testament Apocalyptic," Idem., *The Laws in the Pentateuch and Other Studies*, D. R. Ap-Thomas, trans. (London: Oliver & Boyd, 1966).

Porteous, Norman W., *Daniel*, Old Testament Library (Philadelphia: The Westminster Press, 1965).

Rowley, H. H., *The Relevance of Apocalyptic*, 2nd ed. (London: Lutterworth Press, 1947).

Russell, D. S., *The Method and Message of Jewish Apocalyptic*, Old Testament Library (Philadelphia: The Westminster Press, 1964). One of the best studies of apocalyptic literature available.

Schmithals, Walter, *The Apocalyptic Movement: Introduction and Interpretation*, John E. Steely, trans. (Nashville, TN: Abingdon Press, 1975). Although concerned chiefly with New Testament apocalyptic, Schmithals traces its history from Old Testament times.

The Chronicler

Bickerman, Elias, *From Ezra to the Last of the Maccabees* (New York: Schocken Books, Inc., 1962). Paperback.

Bowman, R. A., "Introduction and Exegesis to Ezra and Nehemiah," *IB*, Vol. III, pp. 551–819.

Bright, John, "The Date of Ezra's Mission to Jerusalem," *Yehezkel Kaufmann Jubilee Volume* (Jerusalem: Magnes Press, 1960), pp. 70–87. Also see his *History of Israel* (General Bibliography).

Myers, Jacob M., *Chronicles I and II*, 2 vols., The Anchor Bible (Garden City, NY: Doubleday & Company, Inc., 1965).

————, *Ezra-Nehemiah*, The Anchor Bible (Garden City, NY: Doubleday & Company, Inc. 1965).

North, R., "Theology of the Chronicler," *JBL*, LXXXII (1963), pp. 369–381.

Torrey, C. C., *Ezra Studies* (Chicago: University of Chicago Press, 1910).

————, *The Chronicler's History of Israel: Chronicles-Ezra-Nehemiah Restored to Its Original Form* (New Haven, CT: Yale University Press, 1954).

9

to write
something also

My grandfather Jesus, after devoting himself especially to the reading of the law and the prophets and the other books of our fathers,
and after acquiring considerable proficiency in them, was himself
also led to write something pertaining to instruction and wisdom, in
order that, by becoming conversant with this also, those who love
learning should make even greater progress in living according to
the law.

—Prologue to Ecclesiasticus

Thus far we have been concerned with those books which comprise the
Hebrew Bible. But, as we have seen, the Old Testament of many Christians—notably those of Roman Catholic and Orthodox faiths—includes an
additional group of writings known either as the Deuterocanon or the
Apocrypha. This collection, as found in the Latin Vulgate, includes books
of two types: (1) those that are additions or supplements to books in the
Hebrew canon: Additions to Esther, Baruch, the Letter of Jeremiah, The
Prayer of Azariah, The Song of the Three Young Men, Susanna, Bel and
the Dragon, and The Prayer of Manasseh; and (2) several kinds of independent writings: (a) books of Wisdom: Wisdom of Solomon and Ecclesiasticus,
(b) edifying stories: Tobit and Judith, (c) historical works: I Esdras and I
and II Maccabees, and (d) apocalyptic: II Esdras. This Vulgate list corresponds approximately to the earliest known collection of Deuterocanonical
books, namely that of the Septuagint. The exceptions are that II Esdras is

not found in any known Septuagint text, and the Psalms of Solomon (some fourteen additions to the Psalter) and III and IV Maccabees, which appear in the LXX, have been omitted by the Vulgate.

Protestantism followed Jerome in designating these books of the larger canon as the Apocrypha, whereas the Roman Catholic Church chose the term Deuterocanon and consequently designated the Hebrew books as the Protocanon. In truth, neither term is entirely inappropriate. Probably R. H. Charles is correct in regarding the word apocrypha (a Greek word meaning to conceal or hide away) as an attempt to translate the Hebrew word *ganaz*, which means to "store away" something that is of value.[1] The term, therefore, originally bore no negative connotations, but could, in fact, be used of scripture generally. In the later Rabbinic period, in which the apocalypses, which were commonly called apocrypha, began to fall into disfavor, the term came to take on a negative meaning until it virtually became the Greek equivalent of the Hebrew term *hisonim*, meaning "outside." When in Protestantism "Apocrypha" was adopted as a name for the books of the larger canon which they rejected, the awkward and unsatisfactory term Pseudepigrapha (literally, "false writings") was adopted to replace the word Apocrypha for such documents of Judaism as the apocalypses, most of which were outside the LXX.

As it was originally intended, the name Deuterocanon simply indicated the books whose canonicity was decided at a later period. From the modern use of the word "deutero" attached to several biblical documents to indicate their relationships to adjacent materials (e.g., Deutero-Isaiah), the word Deuterocanon bears a significantly larger meaning. Inevitably it recalls the original Judaic concept of scripture with Torah at the center surrounded by the Prophets and Writings as ever larger circles of interpretation. The term Deuterocanon not only avoids the opprobrium which still clings to the use of the word Apocrypha with reference to these books, but also allows the latter to be returned to its original meaning in place of the unfortunate word Pseudepigrapha.[2]

1. THE HISTORICAL BACKGROUND

Since the books of the Deuterocanon were written over a period extending from the second century B.C. through the first century A.D., it will be useful for us, before surveying their content, to review briefly the history of the Near East during that period. Two of these books, I and II Maccabees, are important sources for the first part of the history.[3]

---

[1] *The Apocrypha and Pseudepigrapha of the Old Testament* (Oxford: Clarendon Press, 1913), p. vii.

[2] Cf. C. T. Fritsch, "Apocrypha," *IDB*, A–D, p. 163.

[3] For a remarkably full and useful history of the period see Morton Scott Enslin, *Christian Beginnings* (New York: Harper & Row, Publishers, 1938), pp. 3–77.

1. THE HISTORICAL BACKGROUND

The Maccabean Revolt

Antiochus Epiphanes failed in his efforts to destroy Judaism, as we have seen, owing to the effective opposition offered by Judas Maccabeus and the zealous Hasidim. With the rededication of the temple and the death of Antiochus, however, much of the support for the Maccabees among the Hasidim began to melt away. About this time, furthermore, the Hasidim themselves, by name at least, disappear from history. So while the danger of Syrian interference remained, the sons of Mattathias found themselves continuing the campaign with only a fraction of their original army (I Macc. 9:5). With the death of Judas at Elasa (160 B.C.), the original phase of the revolt was over. The contest between Judea and Syria which had raged for seven years had reached a standoff. The elusive troops of the Maccabees, at home among the wadies of the Judean hills, were impossible to crush; the detested citadel hard by the temple and the ring of fortified cities set up by the Syrians (I Macc. 9:50–53), on the other hand, stood between Judea and her coveted independence. In the meantime, Judas had taken one action which forebode the end of the Jewish independence for which he fought. Shortly before the fatal battle at Elasa he had sent a delegation to Rome to conclude a treaty with this burgeoning power in the West (I Macc. 8:17–32). He could not know that before a century had passed Rome would succeed where Syria had failed and bring Judea under subjugation and to its eventual destruction.

The Hasmonean Dynasty

In the subsequent developments, three important factors were at work: (1) From the death of Antiochus IV the Seleucid throne was constantly under dispute by rival pretenders, and consequently the once formidable power of the Syrian kingdom declined until it, along with Judea, lost its independence altogether, and its territory was annexed as a Roman province. (2) The Hellenism which had been largely responsible for the conflict with Syria from the outset, emerging once more in the person of the high priest Alcimus, showed itself to be a force to be reckoned with in Israel. (3) The Maccabean leaders themselves began to find the fresh taste of power to their liking, and their interests began to shift from the struggle for freedom to the establishment of what became known from Hasmon, Mattathias' ancestral name, as the Hasmonean dynasty.

The first of these factors, the instability of the Syrian government, allowed the Jewish forces under Jonathan, Judas' younger brother, to survive the defeat in which Judas had been killed, and later under Simon, the last surviving son of Mattathias after the treacherous elimination of Jonathan (I Macc. 12:39–13:24), to overthrow the remaining Syrian fortifications and proclaim at last (143–142 B.C.) the long-coveted Jewish independence (I Macc. 13:41–53). Because of the second factor, Jonathan had found it nec-

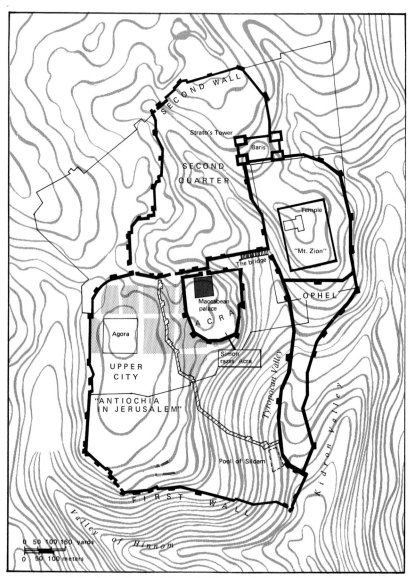

Jerusalem of the Maccabees. (Adapted with permission of Macmillan Publishing Co., Inc., from Macmillan Bible Atlas by Y. Aharoni and Michael Avi-Yonah. Copyright © 1968 Carta, Jerusalem. © Copyright 1964 by Carta, Jerusalem. © Copyright 1966 by Carta, Jerusalem.)

essary to assume the vestments of the high priest, ironically under the authority of a pagan contender for the Syrian throne (I Macc. 10:1–21), and thus had established the Hasmonean high priesthood, which subsequently served as an effective basis for the power of that dynasty. An early result of the third factor was the intrigue which accomplished the death of Simon and all his sons except John Hyrcanus (usually known as Hyrcanus I to distinguish him from the later high priest) at the hands of his ambitious son-in-law, Ptolemy (I Macc. 16:11–24). John, who fortunately had been occupied elsewhere at the time, once warned by the news of the treachery, entered Jerusalem and assumed his father's leadership.

Although, according to Josephus, the accoutrements of royalty did not appear until the reign of his son, Aristobulus, John Hyrcanus became for all practical purposes the first king to reign in Jerusalem since the fall of Zedekiah in 587 B.C.[4] There is no need to recite here in detail the checkered history of the Hasmonean kings, in whom the noble patriotism and valor of Judas Maccabeus degenerated into political ambition and murderous intrigue. Three items of importance, however, should be noted concerning this period (143–63 B.C.). First, John Hyrcanus I deepened Israel's fateful involvement with Rome by renewing the treaty which Judas Maccabeus had made with the Roman Senate.[5] Second, he began a program of expansion which, by the destruction of the temple on Mount Gerizim in the course of his Samaritan campaign, intensified the age-old hostilities between the Jews and the Samaritans and, by the forcible proselyting of the Idumeans during his southern campaign, set the stage for the rise of Antipater and the Herodian kings. Third, it is during his rule, in connection with his transfer of loyalties from the Pharisees to the Sadducees, that we first hear of the Pharisees and, except for the contention between the earlier Hellenizers and the loyal Hasidim, the appearance of competing parties within Judaism.

THE PHARISEES. Quite possibly the Pharisees, whose name apparently derives from the Hebrew word *perisha*, meaning "separate" or "separated one," developed as a movement from the Hasidim, who withdrew from Judas Maccabeus after the restoration of the temple. Because of their influence in shaping the Rabbinic Judaism which survived the fall of Jerusalem in A.D. 70, the appearance of the Pharisees at this point is important to the later history. On the premise that God's providential care and therefore Israel's fate were conditioned upon faithful obedience to his Torah, the Pharisees came to be the leading exponents of its study. They believed that Torah contained all knowledge necessary to right living and therefore required only a correct exegesis to discover the appropriate rule for every occasion. As a result, their interpretations developed into an extensive body of extrabiblical "oral Torah," which took its place alongside the written scripture. Although they would insist that they were only making explicit what was already implicit in Torah, this concern to interpret and

---

[4] *Antiquities of the Jews*, XIII, 11, 1.
[5] Josephus, *Ant.*, XIII, 9, 2.

reapply the Torah to the changing needs of their people made them the progressive party of Judaism. As opposed to the conservative Sadducees, for example, they taught a doctrine of a general resurrection and a corresponding system of rewards and punishments in "the age to come," which links them in several ways with the apocalyptists. Their belief in angels and demons also may reflect the persistence among them of the earlier Persian influence from the post-Exilic period. Although the strained exegesis sometimes required to extract an applicable rule for a new situation and the meticulous legalism for which they were noted sometimes exposed them to ridicule, they took their religious responsibilities very seriously. In spite of the unfortunate prejudice which has made their name a synonym for hypocrisy, they wielded the most significant religious influence of their time. Their utter reliance on divine providence gave their political views a passive turn which distinguished them to a considerable degree from the apocalyptists and the Qumran community, and which may help to explain their uneasy relationship to the Hasmonean dynasty. As the pious interpreters of Torah they represented and enjoyed the sympathy of the large, pious middle class of Judaism. John Hyrcanus' renunciation of the Pharisees in favor of the Sadducees, therefore, probably reflects more than his displeasure with one of their number who had made an unfortunate comment on his ancestry.[6]

THE SADDUCEES. This group, whose name probably derived from Zadok, Solomon's high priest, represented the wealthy minority of the landed gentry who controlled the temple priesthood. Basically conservative, they had little interest in adding interpretations to Torah. Hence they rejected the growing tradition of "oral Torah." They rejected also all belief in angelic beings and the resurrection. Divine retribution was for them confined to this life. Although they enjoyed little support among the common people and were forced by popular opinion to follow the direction of the Pharisees in performance of the temple rituals, their position gave them considerable power. In the later Roman period, as we shall see, this power placed them in an advantageous position with respect to the Roman government—a position which was to increase popular animosity toward them. In embracing the Sadducees, Hyrcanus was turning his back on the popular support to which the earlier Maccabean movement had owed so much for its success. What had begun as a popular movement among the pious common people had now become the ruling aristocracy.

Hyrcanus' change of loyalties had serious consequences. After the brief and insignificant reign of his oldest son, Aristobulus, a younger son, Alexander Jannaeus, came to the throne to continue his father's policies. His

[6] See Josephus, *Ant.*, XIII, 10.

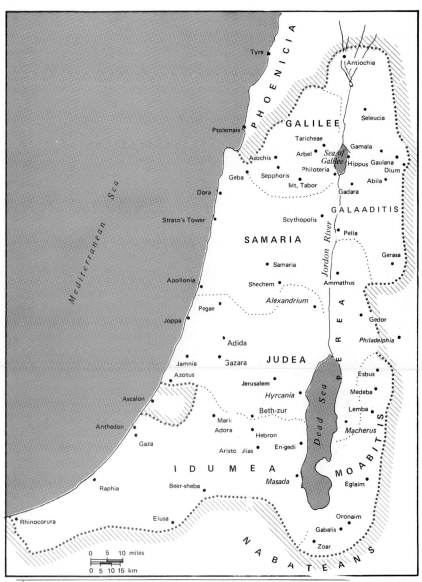

The kingdom of Alexander Janneus, 103 to 76 B.C. (Adapted with permission of Macmillan Publishing Co., Inc., from Macmillan Bible Atlas by Y. Aharoni and Michael Avi-Yonah. © 1968 Carta, Jerusalem. © Copyright 1964 by Carta, Jerusalem. © Copyright 1966 by Carta, Jerusalem.)

Khirbet Qumran as seen from the air. Built on a plateau northwest of the Dead Sea, this complex of buildings and courts served the Qumran sect as a center of community activity. (Courtesy of the Israel Department of Antiquities and Museums.)

unpopularity led to his being pelted with citrus fruit while presiding at the altar and a subsequent revolt that nearly succeeded, both of which were instigated by the disaffected Pharisees. In retaliation, he crucified some eight hundred of his opponents after mutilating their wives and children before their eyes.[7] The mounting pressure against him became so great that on his deathbed he willed his kingdom to his wife, Alexandra, with the advice that she make peace with the Pharisees lest they become her downfall. It is possible that at this time, as some scholars believe, a group of pious Jews, usually identified with the Essenes,[8] withdrew to Qumran above the shores of the Dead Sea to form a monastic community whose

[7] Josephus, *Ant.*, XIII, 13–14.
[8] Josephus, *Wars*, I, 5; *Ant.*, XIII, 5, 9; 10, 6; 15, 5; XVII, 2, 4; *Life*, 2; 38; 39.

library was the subject of the dramatic discoveries of 1947 and succeeding years. Although a few scholars still question this identification of the Qumran community with the Essene sect known to us from Josephus, Philo, and a brief mention in Pliny's *Natural History*, its probabilities are sufficient to warrant a brief sketch here of the sect and its literature.

THE QUMRAN SECT. The Dead Sea Scrolls, as the Qumran library has come to be known, provide vivid evidence of the radical eschatology that flourished within some Jewish groups of this period.[9] From the sect's beginnings until the destruction of its desert headquarters by Vespasian's armies in A.D. 68, its members lived in daily expectation of the great apocalyptic battle described in detail in one of their writings, The War of the Sons of Light Against the Sons of Darkness.[10] Believing themselves to be God's righteous volunteers, living under instructions laid down by their "teacher of righteousness" and set forth in a Manual of Discipline, they were assured that through their efforts an atonement was being made for the apostate land and a ready army kept on stand-by for God's awaited signal.

In contrast to the militaristic groups that arose during the Roman period, the Qumran Essenes instigated no nationalistic uprisings. Rather, consistent with their eschatological convictions, the warfare for which they prepared awaited that precise and predestined moment when God himself and his hosts of angels would intervene decisively on behalf of the righteous cause. Until then, the group's preparedness consisted of a constant study of Torah, the copying and maintenance of their sacred books, and a strict regimen of purificatory baths, ritual meals, and prayers. Demanding perfection of conduct, enforced by rigorously defined penalities for offenses, the community's ethical stringency appears to have outdistanced that of the Pharisees.

The sect's prolific literary activity produced a collection of commentaries on Old Testament books, one of which—The Habakkuk Commentary—describes in cryptic terms the hostilities which led to the group's separation from Jerusalem Jewry. Unfortunately, the veiled language and the poorly preserved state of the text prevents certainty concerning the identification of such intriguing figures as the teacher of righteousness, who is

---

[9] Cf. Krister Stendahl's Introduction to *The Scrolls and the New Testament* (New York: Harper & Row, Publishers, 1957), and Frank M. Cross, Jr., *The Ancient Library of Qumran*, ch. 5.

[10] English translations of the best-known Scroll texts are available in Millar Burrows, *The Dead Sea Scrolls* (New York: The Viking Press, Inc., 1955) and *More Light on the Dead Sea Scrolls* (New York: The Viking Press, Inc., 1958); Geza Vermes, *The Dead Sea Scrolls in English* (New York: Penguin Books, 1962); A. Dupont-Sommer, *The Essene Writings from Qumran* (Oxford: Basil Blackwell, 1961; New York: World [Meridian], 1962); Theodor H. Gaster, *The Dead Sea Scriptures*, 3rd. ed. (Garden City, NY: Doubleday Anchor, 1976); and Yigael Yadin, ed., *The Temple Scroll* (Jerusalem: Israel Exploration Society, 1977).

Qumran Cave IV. Located high in the cliffs above Wadi Qumran and to the south of Khirbet Qumran, this cave contained thousands of manuscript fragments. (Courtesy of the Jordan Ministry of Information.)

persecuted by a "wicked priest" and his followers. Hyrcanus, Aristobulus, Jannaeus, and a host of other historical persons have been cast in the role of the wicked priest by the flood of conflicting theories developed since the scroll discoveries. Particularly vexing is the question of whether the teacher—himself a priest and presumably the sect's founder—died as a martyr and thereby became a redeemer figure for the group. Theories that appeared shortly after the publication of the scrolls so characterizing the teacher and identifying him as Qumran's messiah have long since been revealed as hasty and inconclusive, based as they were on conjectured reconstructions of crucial textual lacunae. It is apparent, however, that the sectarians' eschatology included the expectation of a messiah—in fact, two messiahs, one priestly and the other a prince, who would officiate at the community's eschatological banquet.

Some of the Qumran literature may represent the work of the teacher himself, though this, too, is open to question. The Manual of Discipline speaks authoritatively not only in the sphere of community regulations, but

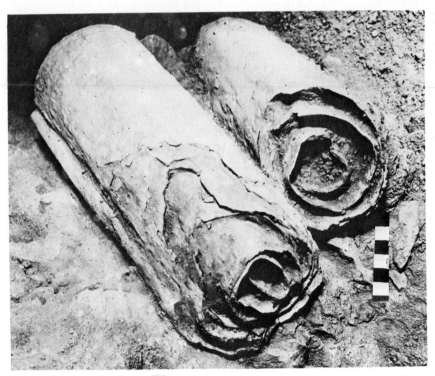

The copper scrolls. Most of the Dea Sea Scrolls were written on leather parchment. The two copper scrolls shown here contain fanciful descriptions of tons of hidden treasure. (Courtesy of the Israel Department of Antiquities and Museums.)

respecting the theological dogmas to which the sect subscribed. These included a metaphysical dualism, involving an Angel of Light and a Prince of Darkness, reminiscent of the patterns familiar in Iranian religions. A collection of Thanksgiving Psalms (Hodayoth), similar to the Old Testament Psalter, though scarcely its equal, bears the stamp of a sensitive poet (or poets), acutely conscious of man's natural perversity and his corresponding dependence upon God's righteousness and forgiveness. Employing phrases strikingly like those of Paul, the Qumran Hymns attest the coexistence within this stream of Intertestamental Judaism of a radical eschatological ethic and a clear-cut theology of grace.

Under Roman Occupation

With Alexandra's death the Hasmonean throne became the object of contention between her two sons, John Hyrcanus II and Aristobulus. In this struggle two new figures emerged. The first was the native governor of Idumea, Antipater, whose ancestry had been forcibly proselyted to Judaism. By placing his influence behind John Hyrcanus, the weaker and more pliable of the brothers, he proceeded to gain for himself the real control of Palestine. As a result of his influence, Hyrcanus, with assistance from the Arabian king Aretas, began to make progress against Aristobulus. At this point, both brothers appealed to the Roman commander Pompey, who at the time was in the process of organizing the newly subdued kingdom of Syria into a Roman province. Pompey, deciding in favor of Hyrcanus, marched to Judea, took Jerusalem, and left him in charge as high priest and "ethnarch" (roughly equivalent to "prince"); while Antipater, recognized as Hyrcanus' advisor, was thereby enabled to cultivate invaluable influence with Rome. Judea's brief period of independence was over. Finally freed from Greek (Syrian) domination in 143 B.C., this unhappy land was now, in 63 B.C., under the control of the burgeoning Empire of Rome.

By the time of the assassination of Antipater in 44 B.C., vast changes had taken place in the Mediterranean world. Only a few months earlier the assassination of Julius Caesar had ended the famous First Triumvirate, which itself had marked the end of the old senatorial republic, and the kaleidoscopic series of events was now in full motion toward the new Augustan Age. Herod, Antipater's famous son who had been serving under his father as governor of Galilee, managed by an incredible series of political juggling acts—a talent he inherited from his father—to stay on the side of the winner until he had obtained an appointment from Anthony and Octavian (later Augustus Caesar) as "King of the Jews." After two unsuccessful attempts, he managed to re-enter Judea, from which he had been driven by Antigonus, the son of Aristobulus, who was bent on avenging his father's loss to John Hyrcanus. After a bloody siege which nearly ruined his capital, Herod found himself established on the throne in Jerusalem in 37 B.C. An-

The rock fortress of Masada, built by Herod the Great on the southwest side of the Dead Sea, where Jewish zealots made their last stand before the Roman armies and perished by their own hands in A.D. 73. (Courtesy of the Israel Government Tourist Office.)

tigonus was beheaded and Hyrcanus, having been mutilated in order to render him ineligible to continue as the high priest, was finally mercilessly executed. With the defeat of Anthony at Actium and his reconfirmation by Augustus, Herod's power and position were secure.

In spite of the stability Herod brought to Palestine and his strenuous efforts to ingratiate himself with his subjects, the faithful of Judaism continued hostile to him to the end. Even though he was a product of the proselyting campaign of John Hyrcanus I, they regarded him as still an Edomite and therefore far from the scion of David for whom pious expectations had taught them to wait. More serious was the fact that he was a client king whose reign, however effective, represented the subjugation of Israel to a pagan foreign power. Finally, of course, Herod's vast building program, including pagan temples and Hellenistic gymnasia, clearly placed him among the hated Hellenizers who had played so malevolent a role in Israel's troubles during the preceding century. It is not surprising, therefore, that his one great contribution to Judaism, the rebuilding of the temple, should have been received with such mixed feelings.

More splendid and costly even than the original temple built by Solomon, and designed with the utmost attention to the scruples of Jewish law, Herod's temple was nevertheless rejected completely by the Qumran sect and regarded with such half-hearted devotion by the Pharisees that it helped pave the way for the survival after its destruction of the Rabbinic Judaism of the synagogue. It is a tragic irony that within a decade after the last construction on the temple precincts was complete, this splendid gift of a Roman client king was destroyed by the Roman legions.

THE FOURTH PHILOSOPHY. The animosity toward Herod stimulated the growth of a movement which after his death became a factor of fatal importance in the history of Palestine. With the dream of restoring the Davidic monarchy rekindled by the Maccabean victories and fanned into flame by Herod's reign, some Jews came to believe that by throwing off the Roman yoke and placing on Herod's throne the true messianic scion of David they could realize the golden age, Israel's destiny of ancient promise. Josephus regarded this zealous group, whom he calls the "fourth philosophy," as basically akin to the Pharisees in belief and practice; but their real interests seem to have been much more political and mundane.[11] Because of their increasingly violent, revolutionary activities, they came later to be known as Zealots or sicarii (dagger men).[12] The series of revolutions they fomented brought on the contest with Roman might that ended in the fall of Jerusalem in A.D. 70.

Following Herod's death in 4 B.C., and as a result of his will, his territory

[11] For a good study of the development of this party see W. R. Farmer, *Maccabees, Zealots and Josephus* (New York: Columbia University Press, 1956), esp. ch. VIII, pp. 175–204.

[12] See Josephus, *Wars*, II, 8, 1; IV, 3, 9.

Bronze coin minted by the Jewish revolutionaries c. A.D. 67–68. The obverse bears the date and an amphora; the reverse contains the vine branch and leaf. (Courtesy of the Money Museum, National Bank of Detroit.)

was divided among his three sons, who ruled, in consequence, as tetrarchs (Greek: *tetrarches*, lit., ruler of a fourth of a country, hence a minor prince). Philip was given a heterogeneous region northeast of the Sea of Galilee which became known as the territory of Caesarea Philippi, its capital city; Herod Antipas was given Galilee and Perea; and Archelaus re-

Coin of Vespasian, bearing his likeness and celebrating the capture of Judea by Titus in A.D. *70. (Courtesy of the Money Museum, National Bank of Detroit.)*

ceived Samaria, Judea, and Idumea. Ten years later, constant agitation and complaints, together with his frantic misrule, accomplished Archelaus' downfall. His territory was placed in the hands of procurators, i.e., Roman military governors of equestrian rank (knights). In connection with the accession of Coponius, the first of these, Quirinius, the governor of Syria—the "eyes and ears of the Emperor" in the East—was ordered to take a census of the territory. The ancient Hebrew aversion to "numbering the people" (cf. II Sam. 24), along with rising indignation over this reminder of Roman occupation and taxation, combined to trigger a rebellion led by a Galilean patriot named Judas. His revolt was soon crushed but his cause was far from forgotten.[13]

Some years later, Antipas' brother-in-law Agrippa contrived by a piece of chicanery to unseat Antipas and, with the assistance of Claudius, to regain the territory and title of king once held by Herod the Great (A.D. 41–44). Although more successful than Herod in gaining the favor of the Jews, Agrippa managed to arouse such suspicion in his Roman overlords that, but for his unexpected death after only three years of rule, he might well have followed Antipas into banishment. Following his death, Judea was returned to the supervision of procurators, and eventually, under Nero, his son Agrippa II became ruler of parts of Galilee and Perea.

The appearance, shortly after Agrippa's death, of two more rebels with messianic pretentions indicates something of the deteriorating political situation in Jerusalem.[14] Consequently, the great revolt (A.D. 66–70) which was brought on by the egregious misrule of Florus, the last of the procurators, and aggravated by no fewer than three rival rebel leaders, was virtually inevitable. As the war raged beyond the control of local Roman authorities, Nero dispatched his star commander, Vespasian, to end it. Shortly thereafter, when he was proclaimed Emperor to succeed Nero (following, of course, the three unsuccessful pretenders in the "year of four Emperors"), he left the battle in the hands of his son, Titus. In a little more than a year Titus was victorious; Jerusalem was demolished, the Temple destroyed, and he was on his way back to Rome, where the memorial of his victory celebration the following year is still preserved on his Triumphal Arch.[15]

In the course of the siege of Jerusalem, Rabbi Johanan ben Zakkai contrived to escape the city by having himself carried through the gate in a coffin. Having obtained permission from Titus, he established a Sanhedrin (council) at Jamnia, which in time established Phariseeism as the norm for Judaism. Deliberations within this Sanhedrin led eventually to the canonization of the Hebrew scriptures. The Mishnah, the Talmuds, and the entire production of the Tannaitic rabbis, furthermore, bore the influence of Johanan's community of scholars.

In the meantime, the turbulent political fortunes of Palestine under the Roman overlords stimulated the revival of apocalyptic literature. Just as such writings as Daniel and Enoch appeared in the time of the Seleucid tyrants, so now works like the Assumption of Moses, only part of which is still extant, IV Esdras, and the Apocalypse of Baruch began to appear. At the same time, the more militant messianism of the rebel leaders con-

---

[13] Josephus, *Ant.*, XVIII, 1, 1.
[14] Josephus, *Ant.*, XX, 5 and 8; *Wars*, II, 13.
[15] The whole tragic story is the subject of Josephus' work, *The Wars of the Jews.*

Scene on the Arch of Titus depicting Roman soldiers carrying away the holy objects, including the menorah or seven-branched lampstand, from the temple. This triumphal arch was erected in the Roman Forum to celebrate Titus' victory over Jerusalem. (Courtesy of Alinari/Editorial Photocolor Archives.)

tinued to smoulder beneath the surface until, in response to Roman strictures against circumcision and Hadrian's decision to rebuild Jerusalem as a pagan city named Aelia Capitolina, it burst into flame once more in the futile rebellion of Bar Cochba (Bar Kozibah) in A.D. 132–135. When the final defeat of his armies and his treacherous assassination brought the rebellion to an end, the land of Israel, now ironically renamed Palestine after the ancient Philistines, was in the hands of gentiles; and the Jews scattered throughout the world became a people without a homeland save "the Fatherland of the Torah."

2. THE LITERATURE

Since in this study we have chosen to follow the general order of the Hebrew canon, which reflects the history and relationships of the various groups of literature involved, in surveying the writings of the Deuterocanon we cannot follow the order in which they appear in the Vulgate. We shall, therefore, follow instead the two-part division suggested earlier

Petra, capital of the Nabatean kingdom (ancient Edom). An immensely high and narrow gorge is the only entrance to Petra, a city carved out of rock which fell to the Romans in A.D. 106. (Courtesy of the Jordan Ministry of Tourism and Antiquity.)

in this chapter, considering first those materials that are attached or related to works in the Hebrew Canon, and then the independent books arranged according to their literary types.

Additions and Supplements

There are three books in the Hebrew Canon (Protocanon) for which there are additions or supplements in the Deuterocanon: Jeremiah, Esther, and Daniel. To Jeremiah belongs as a supplement the Book of Baruch, including chapter 6, the Letter of Jeremiah, which in the LXX is a separate document. Additions to the Hebrew Esther occur in six places in the larger text. Along with some poetic material, which occurs in the story of the fiery furnace, three supplemental stories, Susanna, Bel, and the Dragon (the latter two combined as a single document), are attached to Daniel.

MAKE YOUR CONFESSION—TAKE COURAGE (BARUCH 1–5). The faithful, unassuming amanuensis of Jeremiah (cf. Jer. 36:32, passim) inspired several books published in his name of which this may be oldest.[16] According to the Introduction, 1:1–14, Baruch is writing from Babylon some five years after the fall of Jerusalem (i.e., 581 B.C.). Having read the book to the captive king Jehoiachin, he is forwarding it to those who remain in Jerusalem, along with the captured holy vessels and money, with the request that they pray for the health of the king Nebuchadrezzar and his son Belshazzar, and for the exiles. Several items prevent us from taking this claim of authorship literally.[17] Aside from the internal contradiction over whether the temple is standing or destroyed, which strongly suggests an actual post-Exilic point-of-view (cf. 1:2, 8; 2:26 with 1:7, 10, 14), it is virtually impossible to locate Baruch in Babylon (cf. Jer. 43), and the repetition in 1:11–12 of the error from Daniel 5:2–18, which places Belshazzar as the son of Nebuchadrezzar, would not have been possible for Jeremiah's scribe.

There is some evidence that the work actually comes from at least three authors. The most obvious division occurs between the prose of 1:1–3:8 and the poetry in 3:9–5:9, but there appear also to be two distinct poems in this latter section: a celebration of wisdom in 3:9–4:4 and a promise of Jerusalem's restoration in 4:5–5:9. The changes in style and the striking difference in the names for God ("Lord," "Lord God," "Lord Almighty, God of Israel" in 1:1–3:8; and "God," "the Holy One," "the Everlasting," "Everlasting Savior" in 3:9–5:9), along with subtle changes in point-of-view, make the separate authorship of these two parts fairly certain.[18] Between the two poems, moreover, there is reflected a difference in circumstance and interest which suggests that the poem on wisdom, 3:9–4:4, may have been interpolated at a later time. Although the prose section, especially 1:14–3:8, shows considerable dependence on Jeremiah, the final poem of encouragement, 4:5–5:9, is highly reminiscent of Deutero-Isaiah. There is little to go on in attempting to fix a date for any of the material

[16] See R. H. Charles, *The Apocrypha and Pseudepigrapha of the Old Testament*, Vol. II, pp. 470–471.

[17] See R. H. Pfeiffer, *History of New Testament Times* (New York: Harper & Row, Publishers, 1949), pp. 413–417.

[18] See Bruce M. Metzger, *Introduction to the Apocrypha* (New York: Oxford University Press, Inc., 1957), pp. 89–90.

in this work. It could have been written in any of several periods and possibly as late as the first Christian century.

As the book now stands it is a liturgical confession of sin and prayer for mercy and deliverance based on the Deuteronomic premise that the calamities which have befallen Israel were God's punishments for Israel's sins, followed by an apostrophe to the divine wisdom, which Israel in her sinfulness had forsaken, and a promise that God will restore the nation and the holy city, Jerusalem.

IN BABYLON YOU WILL SEE GODS (BARUCH 6, THE LETTER OF JERE-MIAH). Probably the inscription for this short tract was the letter preserved in Jeremiah 29:1–23, which Jeremiah had sent to the exiles in Babylon. Because of its association with Jeremiah it is included in the Vulgate as chapter 6 in the book of Baruch. It is, nevertheless, a separate work having no real connection with the latter and is so placed in the LXX. Although it opens with an announcement that God will end the Exile in the "seventh generation" (6:3; cf. Jer. 29:10–14), the writing is concerned with the apostasy of idol worship. It may be that, as R. H. Pfeiffer suggests,[19] the author is attempting to correct what he regards as the dangerous implications in Jeremiah's advice that the exiles make themselves at home in Babylon (cf. Jer. 29:5–7). Following the lead in Deutero-Isaiah's satire on idols (Isa. 44:9–20), he cautions in the name of Jeremiah against the danger that while making their home in Babylon the exiles may take up the worship of the lifeless, powerless, useless creations of human hands. Later readers of Jeremiah are thus protected from the erroneous conclusion that his letter may have given tacit approval to the Babylonian religions, and, at the same time, the author has had his say about the vanity of all other worship than that addressed to Israel's God.

THESE THINGS HAVE COME FROM GOD (ESTHER 10:4–16:24). As has already been observed, the Hebrew version of Esther contains no reference to God. It was virtually inevitable, therefore, that such an intolerable oversight in what was rapidly becoming one of the most popular Jewish writings should be corrected. Whether any or all of the additions found in the Greek version were translated from Hebrew or Aramaic, or were inserted directly into the Greek text,[20] they supply in abundance the piety lacking in the Protocanonical version. Of the five sections of this material, only the first edict of Artaxerxes—that against the Jews—omits (for obvious reasons) pious references to God.

Because Jerome simply tacked the Greek additions onto the end of his

---

[19] *History of New Testament Times*, pp. 427–428.

[20] On this question and that of the two recensions, as well as the variations of the longer version, see R. H. Pfeiffer, *History of New Testament Times*, pp. 304–312.

translation of the Hebrew version, they are in complete disarray. The following table will assist the reader in recovering the correct order as found in the LXX:

GREEK	HEBREW
1. 11:2–12:6	
	2. 1:1–3:13
3. 13:1–7	
	4. 3:14–4:17
5. 13:8–15:16	
	6. 5:3–8:12*
7. 16:1–24	
	8. 8:13–10:3
9. 10:4–11:1	

* 15:1–16 replaces the shorter Hebrew account in 5:1–2.

There are six items contained in these five sections. (1) 11:2–12:6 prefaces the story with a dream in which Mordecai receives a premonition of the events that are to follow and gives a variant of the story of the plot against the king discovered by Mordecai, which is related in 2:21–23 and alluded to in 6:2. (2) In 13:1–7 the text of the decree drafted by Haman in the king's name is supplied. (3) 13:8–18 and 14:1–19 supply appropriate prayers offered by Mordecai and Esther as she prepares to enter the presence of the king to intercede for the Jews. In Mordecai's prayer is a pious explanation for his refusal to bow to Haman; Esther's prayer ends with the striking petition, "And save me from my fear!" (4) 15:1–16 is a much more elaborate account of Esther's preparation, entrance, and reception by the king than the brief statement in 5:1–2 which it replaces. (5) 16:1–24 supplies the royal decree nullifying the original one against the Jews and making provisions for their self-defense. Here we learn the surprising fact that Haman is not a Persian but a Macedonian (16:10). The edict also provides the explicit connection of this letter with the Feast of Purim (cf. the colophon 11:1). (6) As the Greek Esther opens with an account of Mordecai's dream, so it closes with its interpretation and a note as to how it had been fulfilled. The appended colophon credits the Greek translation to one Lysimachus of Jerusalem. Several discrepancies between the Greek and the Hebrew texts make it appear likely that the additions were made at a later time in order to clarify and "correct" the older version (cf. 12:2 with 2:21–23; 12:5 with 6:3; 12:6 with 3:2–6; 16:10 with 3:1; 16:22–23 with 9:20–28).

IN THE MIDST OF THE FLAMES (THE PRAYER OF AZARIAH AND THE SONG OF THE THREE YOUNG MEN. DANIEL 3:24–90). In the familiar story of Shadrach, Meshach, and Abednego, who were thrown into the fiery furnace for their refusal to worship Nebuchadrezzar's golden image (Dan. 3), the Greek text supplies, between verses 23 and 24 of the Hebrew version, a prayer and a hymn. The prayer offered by Azariah (Abednego, cf. Dan. 1:7), apparently a spokesman on behalf of all three, has nothing to do with the immediate situation of the young men except insofar as their plight, according to the setting of the story in Daniel, was occasioned by the Babylonian captivity, which was in turn caused by Israel's sins. There is therefore a parallel in function as well as content between this prayer and Baruch 1:15–38 (cf. Dan. 9:4–19). Since the real background of Daniel is the pogroms of Antiochus Epiphanes, inserting this prayer has the effect of interpreting Israel's troubles under the Hellenistic-Syrian overlords, in line with Deuteronomic theology, as a punishment for her sins. Although the prayer was likely originally composed in Hebrew or Aramaic, it was interpolated into Daniel at a later time.

As the angel appears to dispel the deadly flames the three young men burst into song with what are, as the change in the form of address and responsory indicates, actually two canticles. Verses 52–56, *Benedictus es, Domine*, are addressed as a blessing directly to God; verses 57–90, *Benedicite, omnia opera*, call upon all the works of nature to bless the Lord. These canticles, except for verse 88, which was undoubtedly added to adapt the canticle to its present use, are general hymns of praise and have no more connection with their context in Daniel than does the Prayer of Azariah. This suggests that they, along with the Prayer, came from an otherwise unknown collection of psalms. From ancient times these canticles have been a part of the psalmnody of the Church. In the Roman Breviary the *Benedictus es, Domine*, with the addition of the first verse (vs. 57) of the second canticle, is used as the fourth psalm in the Sunday Office, Lauds II (for Lent); and in Lauds I (for the remaining Sundays of the year) the fourth psalm consists in a condensed form of the *Benedicite, omnia opera*, substituting a blessing of the Trinity and the last verse (vs. 56) of the first canticle for verses 88b–90, and omitting most of the responsories. The *Benedicite* also occurs as the celebrant's private thanksgiving after Mass in the Roman Rite (cf. the *Book of Common Prayer*, pp. 11–13). It is very similar in structure to Psalm 136 and in theme and content to Psalm 148 (cf. Ps. 150). R. H. Pfeiffer suggests that these hymns involving the works of creation may have been inspired by Ecclesiasticus 43 (cf. Ps. 19; Job 38; Ps. 104; Gen. 1:1–2:4).[21] This theme reappears in St. Francis' well-known *Laudes creaturarum*.

DANIEL HAD A GREAT REPUTATION (DANIEL 13–14). In the two chapters which the Greek text adds to the end of the Hebrew and Aramaic

---

[21] *History of New Testament Times*, p. 448.

Daniel, three deservedly famous detective stories occur. These stories were included in Daniel not only to extol virtue and a pious trust in God, but also, as 13:64 indicates, to enhance the figure of Daniel in a way reminiscent of the story of Solomon's judgment in I Kings 3:16–28. Because in the story of Susanna Daniel is pictured as a "young lad" (13:45), some texts have placed it at the beginning of Daniel rather than as chapter 13. The two puns on the Greek names of the trees in 13:54–55 and 58–59 have convinced a number of scholars that this story, at least, was composed in Greek. Considering the ease with which a translator might introduce such word plays, however, they can hardly outweigh the contrary evidence of a Semitic original. The presence of these additions in the LXX version of Daniel, which probably goes back to the end of the second century B.C., suggests a date for them not later than 100 B.C.[22]

Learning the Facts (The Story of Susanna). This story is a literary masterpiece. Although the two recensions in the LXX and Theodotian differ in some details, the essence of the story in both versions concerns Susanna, the young wife of Joakim, whose remarkable beauty incites the lustful passion of two elders appointed as judges for the Jewish community in Babylon. Having accidentally disclosed to each other their common passion, they plot to seduce Susanna. When they surprise her alone in her garden she refuses to yield to them, whereupon, in a development similar to the story of Potiphar's wife in Genesis 39:6b–20, they accuse her of committing adultery with a young man who has escaped unrecognized. Being the judges, they condemn her to death on their own testimony. As Susanna is being led to execution, however, Daniel is inspired to intervene. Insisting that they have not learned the facts, he asks each of the judges under what kind of tree the alleged affair took place. Since their stories do not agree they are exposed and executed, Susanna's life and honor are spared, and Daniel earns "a great reputation among the people" (13:64).

An Idol Called Bel (14:1–22). The second story is a satire on pagan divinities in the vein of Isaiah 44:9–20 and the Letter of Jeremiah (Baruch 6). In a discussion with King Cyrus of Babylon as to why he does not worship Cyrus' idol called Bel, Daniel denies the king's claim that Bel eats the food offered to him daily. When Bel's priests are challenged to prove it, they allow the king to place the food in the temple and seal the door. In the meantime Daniel has ashes sifted over the floor. The next day Daniel and the king find the food gone but the floor is covered with footprints. Discovering the secret doors by which he has been deceived, Cyrus is enraged and orders the execution of the priests and their families, while Daniel is permitted to destroy the temple and the idol.

Also a Great Dragon (14:23–42). In the companion story the same mo-

[22] On these questions and the complex problems surrounding the Church's preference for Theodotion's Greek text for Daniel over the LXX, see R. H. Pfeiffer, *History of New Testament Times*, pp. 433–456.

tive of lampooning pagan deities is apparent. The issue is approached, however, from the opposite angle. Whereas Bel is nothing more than a manmade statue, a fact which is eaily demonstrated by its inability to eat, the dragon is manifestly a living creature and does eat. To prove that the dragon also is no god, therefore, Daniel must somehow show that merely being alive and able to eat is not sufficient evidence to establish divinity. This he does by offering to perform the apparently impossible feat of slaying the dragon "without sword or club" (14:26). The king's acceptance of Daniel's challenge is a tacit admission of the premise that if Daniel succeeds the dragon is no god. Having concocted some cakes of pitch, fat, and hair, he feeds them to the witless beast which promptly explodes.

Whether Hermann Gunkel is correct in associating this story with Marduk's slaying of Tiamat, it is an instance of a widespread and ancient motif that finds expression as late as the Christian story of St. George and the dragon.[23] The unexpressed premise underlying both of these satires is that to discredit the pagan deities is to establish Israel's God as the one and only true God. This premise comes near the surface in the doublet (14:31–42) on the story of Daniel in the lion's den in the Hebrew text (ch. 6), which functions here as a sequel to both stories. Exactly what the author intended by having Habakkuk transported to Daniel's assistance is uncertain, but its effect is to establish a connection between Daniel and the Latter Prophets in the Hebrew canon.

The Independent Works

There remain six books in the Deuterocanon which may be classified according to types in three groups: (1) edifying stories: Tobit and Judith; (2) books of wisdom: The Wisdom of Solomon and Ecclesiasticus; (3) historical writings: I and II Maccabees. Not only because of the indispensable history in the books of Maccabees, but also because of the incidental glimpses of the life and piety of Judaism provided by the stories, and the more profound thought contained in the wisdom writings, these books are invaluable sources for our knowledge of late, pre-Christian Judaism.

HOW RIGHTEOUSNESS DELIVERS (TOBIT). This comparatively complex story is actually a combination of two themes: Tobit's blindness and Sarah's misfortunes at the hand of the demon Asmodeus. The marriage of Sarah and Tobias, Tobit's son, brings the two themes together and gives the book its unity. Along with the references to Ahikar (1:21; 2:10; 11:48; 14:10), the historical errors in the history of the Assyrian and Babylonian kings, and the numerous recensions which have survived, the two motifs have stimulated considerable discussion of the provenance and sources for this book. In view of the general Oriental disdain for dogs, the reference to the boy's

---

[23] See R. H. Pfeiffer, *History of New Testament Times*, pp. 455–456.

pet (the references vary, 5:16 or 17; or 6:1 and 11:4) further complicates the picture. The questions are too complex and the findings too inconclusive for discussion here, except to note that Tobit is probably related in some way to two widely known popular motifs: the grateful dead and the dangerous bride.[24] The first has to do with unexpected rewards accruing to one who had given a neglected corpse proper burial; the second concerns a maiden who because of some malevolence such as a curse, or a demonic presence of some sort, inadvertently causes on her wedding night the death of her bridegroom. If these are sources for Tobit, as is quite possible, the author has modified them thoroughly to fit his own purposes. The prominence of the angel Raphael and the demon Asmodeus is of interest for the light it sheds on the development of angelology in late Judaism.

The purpose of the work is clearly expressed in Tobit's farewell exhortations to his son in 14:3–11. Along with predictions of the restoration of Israel and the destruction of Nineveh, he exhorts Tobias to "keep the law and commandments and be merciful and just," as well as to "consider what almsgiving accomplishes and how righteousness delivers." The story abounds in examples of a homely Jewish piety nourished by Israel's scriptures, which reinforce the point that although God may allow misfortune to befall his people, if they continue in faithful dependence upon him, they will be delivered and amply rewarded for their trust in him. The absence of any apparent knowledge of the Syrian persecutions or the Maccabean revolt, on the one hand, and the literary affinities with works such as Ecclesiasticus, on the other, suggest that Tobit was written sometime between 200 and 170 B.C. The lovely story of the marriage of Tobias and Sarah has long been treasured as a model for Christian marriages. In the Roman Rite, the Introit for the Nuptial Mass still recalls their story with the words, "May he who had mercy on two only children abide with you."

The story in brief tells how the faithful Tobit, who has been taken to Nineveh by the victorious Assyrians, continues there amid varying fortunes his charitable acts and faithful obedience to the Law, especially giving proper burial to the bodies of fellow Israelites. While in the service of the Assyrian king he has amassed a modest fortune, which he deposits in Rages, a city in Media. Later, because of his preoccupation with giving proper burial to his fellow Israelites, he has to flee Nineveh, leaving his property to be confiscated; and he is able to return only through the good offices of his nephew Ahikar, who stands high in the government. Once, at the Feast of Pentecost, Tobias is sent out to bring in the poor of Israel to share the feast, but instead he finds the body of a murdered Israelite,

---

[24] For a full discussion of the question of sources, including these motifs, as well as the various recensions of Tobit, see R. H. Pfeiffer, *History of New Testament Times*, pp. 258–260, 264–273. For the story of Ahikar see R. H. Charles, *Apocrypha and Pseudepigrapha of the Old Testament*, Vol. II, pp. 715–784.

which Tobit promptly buries. While spending the night in his garden, because of the ritual impurity resulting from his charitable act, he is blinded by droppings of sparrows. Now reduced to poverty and supported by his wife's meager earnings, he prays for God to let him die.

Meanwhile, at Ecbatana in Media, Sarah, a young Israelite woman and daughter of Raguel of the same family, is praying for death. Because of the machinations of the demon Asmodeus each of seven husbands whom she married died on his wedding night, and now her maids have accused her of murdering them. Both prayers are heard and given an unexpected answer.

Recalling the money he left at Rages, Tobit sends his son Tobias to recover it. While he is looking for a traveling companion for Tobias, the angel Raphael appears to him under the guise of a relative and is employed. Raphael leads Tobias to Ecbatana, and on the way, after a frightening encounter with a great fish, instructs Tobias to preserve the fish's gall, heart, and liver. Once arrived at Ecbatana, Raphael instructs Tobias to marry Sarah. Tobias, hesitating because of the fate of the other seven bridegrooms, is told that burning the fish's heart and liver in incense will dispel the demon Asmodeus. While Raphael goes on to Rages to recover Tobit's money, Tobias and Sarah are married and, after a joyful celebration, return to Nineveh, where Tobit is cured of his blindness by the fish's gall. Raphael then reveals his true identity and ascends from their presence. Tobit grows old in peace and, after the traditional farewell exhorations (cf. Gen. 48–49), dies and is given "a magnificent burial." Tobias and Sarah return to Ecbatana for the remainder of their lives.

By THE HAND OF A WOMAN (JUDITH). In a very different mood from the celebration of the homely virtues of Tobit and his family, the story of Judith, telling of how God rewards his people's faith and piety by providentially delivering them from their enemies, transpires on a level of international conflict. Whatever may be the historical nucleus around which it was built, the story involves in its present form incredible historical impossibilities that alert the reader not to take it literally. Circumstances, persons, and events of the fateful years before the fall of Nineveh and the captivity of Judah are combined with those of the post-Exilic period in a manner that allows the story to gather up a whole segment of Israel's history into its affirmation of faith and trust in God. Among the more glaring errors and anachronisms are the placing of Nebuchadrezzar (605–562 B.C.) as the Assyrian king of Nineveh, and the Assyrian campaign against Persia at a time after Nineveh has fallen (612 B.C); yet, at the same time, the Jews are pictured as having already returned from the Exile (538 B.C.) and rebuilt the temple (515 B.C.)

Perhaps the suggestion that, as in Daniel, Nebuchadrezzar and his campaigns here actually represent the wars and persecutions of Antiochus Epiphanes provides not only a clue to the story's meaning but also to the date of its composition, which would therefore fall sometime after 167 B.C.[25] Other elements of the book tend to support such an impression. The name Judith itself actually means "Jewess"; and Judith's city, Bethulia, is not only otherwise unknown, but is placed in the geographically and historically impossible position of being a Judean fortress in the Valley of Esdraelon in the period immediately after the Exile (4:1–7).[26] Similarly, such names as the commander Holofernes and the high priest Joakim are as impossible to harmonize chronologically as Holofernes' incredible march of three hundred miles in three days is to take seriously.

The story has affinities with several other documents in Hebrew literature. The role of a woman in saving Israel recalls the stirring ballad of Deborah and Jael in Judges 5, and, of course, the story of Esther, which may have been inspired in part by Judith. Some interpreters believe the ode in 16:2–17 to be older than the book and perhaps its essential source in much the same way that Deborah's ode was the source of the prose story in Judges 4.[27] Bringing home Holofernes' head as a trophy recalls the scene in II Samuel 20:14–22, in which a woman of Bethmaacah had Sheba's head delivered to Joab. There are echoes, too, of the heroic exploits of Ehud (Judg. 3:12–30) and David's slaying of Goliath (I Sam. 17). In this composite form the story of Judith, while lampooning the enemy, brings from out of Israel's past the much needed encouragement for facing the harassments of the Syrian rulers.

Although elaborated with lengthy speeches and prayers, the story is quite simple. Nebuchadrezzar, angered by the refusal of the peoples in the West to assist him in his successful campaign against Media, sends his commander Holofernes to punish them and subdue the whole region. With frightful success, Holofernes arrives at the pass into the Judean hills guarded by the city of Bethulia (the Hebrew word means "virgin"), where he learns to his astonishment that the Jews, unlike the nations he has encountered, intend to resist. An Ammonite leader named Achior—as much for the reader's benefit as for Holofernes'—recites the story of the people Israel to explain their reason for resisting the Assyrian forces, for so long as they are faithful and obedient to their God he will defend them. Holofernes, unmoved by Achior's warning, proceeds to lay siege to Bethulia.

At this point Judith, a widow of considerable wealth whose beauty was only equaled by her great piety, after appropriate prayer and fasting, conceives a plan for the defeat of Holofernes. Accompanied by her personal maid and dressed in her most attractive manner, she escapes to his camp on the pretext of fleeing the inevitable fall of the city. Her extraordinary

[25] See R. H. Pfeiffer, *History of New Testament Times,* pp. 291–297.
[26] On the post-Exilic Judean territory see above p. 424.
[27] See R. H. Pfeiffer, *History of New Testament Times,* pp. 297–298. Also above, pp. 223–225.

beauty captivates Holofernes and she is invited to dine at his table. At length he contrives to be alone with her, but makes one fatal mistake. In his anticipation he drinks too much wine and falls into a drunken stupor, whereupon Judith beheads him with his own sword and escapes to her people in Bethulia. Heartened by the sight of their enemy's head, which Judith brings with her, the men of the city, along with all Israel, fall upon the Assyrian camp, put to rout its leaderless troops, plunder their goods, and end Nebuchadrezzar's threat. Judith continues her pious widowhood until her death at the age of one hundred and five years.

WISDOM IS A KINDLY SPIRIT (THE WISDOM OF SOLOMON). We have already examined the genre known as wisdom literature which forms so important a part of the third division of the Hebrew canon.[28] This book is the first of two such works in the Deuterocanon. Although the title in the Greek text, "The Wisdom of Solomon," can be supported from the stance of the speaker in the book itself—in such passages as 9:7–8, for example, where the speaker identifies himself as the king of God's people who built the temple—Jerome's title, preserved in the Vulgate, "The Book of Wisdom," is obviously more accurate. Although the book stands in the Judaic wisdom tradition, it belongs at the end of it, being nearer than the others to Hellenistic thought. Only in the broadest possible sense, that Solomon was the patron of wisdom, can this book be associated with his name.

No book in this collection has been the subject of more widely divergent opinions. Since the problems of authorship, integrity, original language, provenance, and the like are far from settled and highly complex, we must be content with a summary of what appear to be the prevailing opinions.[29] Whereas some scholars are inclined to think that all or parts of chapters 1–10 may have been translated from a Hebrew original, perhaps by the author of the last half of the book, most of them would agree with Jerome's ancient judgment that the entire work is so thoroughly in the style of Greek oratory that it must have been written in Greek. Its use, moreover, of Greek philosophical ideas and terminology, in the tradition of Philo, along with the characteristics of popular Greek literature, suggest that it was written by an Alexandrian Jew (cf. the *sorites* in 6:17–20 and the twenty-one attributes of wisdom in 7:22). That the author's quotations of biblical material reflect the LXX rather than the Hebrew requires a date for the work some time after 200 B.C.[30] Although a few scholars have suggested a date as late as A.D. 40, most prefer the period between 100 and 50 B.C.

[28] Above, pp. 447–452.

[29] For a discussion of these questions and a bibliography see R. H. Pfeiffer, *History of New Testament Times*, pp. 319–329.

[30] See R. H. Charles, *Apocrypha and Pseudepigrapha of the Old Testament*, Vol. I, pp. 524–527.

Since wisdom literature characteristically ranges over a wide spectrum of topics, it is notoriously difficult to outline or summarize. It is not surprising, therefore, to find little agreement on the outline of this book. Although there are junctures in which clear changes of topics appear, these are usually anticipated earlier and contain also repetitions and restatements of earlier topics. The over-all scheme of the book, which is only superficially related to its content, consists of two parts: (1) Solomon addresses his fellow monarchs, chapters 1–8 (cf. 1:1; 6:1, passim); (2) Solomon recounts to them his prayer for wisdom, chapters 9–19 (cf. I Kings 3:9–12. Noteworthy is the direct address to God throughout these chapters, e.g., 9:1; 10:20; 11:26; 14.3; 15:1; 16:12; 17:1; 18:1, 13; 19:9, 22; but the author lapses occasionally into indirect reference, e.g., 12:26–13:9; 14:8–31; 15:19; 16:18; 19:1). Under the guise of Solomon addressing the kings of earth, the author speaks to the secular, cynical Jew who has abandoned his religion, and holds before him the example of the righteous, who in contrast to him are immortal (1:16–5:23); using the legendary wisdom of Solomon as an example, he commends and defines wisdom to gentile rulers (chs. 6–9); to those under duress he appeals to the example of the history of Israel under the protection of God's wisdom (chs. 10–12); to the ignorant pagans he addresses a tirade against idol worship (chs. 13–15). In the final section (chs. 16–19) he summarizes the wisdom of righteousness and obedience to God's law by contrasting—with fantastic exaggerations in places—God's treatment of Israel and Egypt in the Exodus. Curiously, although his descriptions enable the reader to identify the episodes and persons in his recitals of history, he avoids identifying them by name.

Among the characteristics of wisdom, two are of particular interest. First, the afterlife is described in terms of the Hellenistic dualism which debases matter in contrast to the immortality of the soul, rather than the Judaic concept of the resurrection of the body (cf. the remarkably beautiful passage in 3:1–9, also such vss. as 8:13). Second, the personification of wisdom, introduced, for example, in Proverbs 1–9, is here carried much further than in any parallel Judaic literature. In Proverbs the personification is symbolic, but in this book wisdom is described in terms intended to be taken quite seriously as: "a kindly spirit" (1:6); "radiant and unfading" (6:12); "the fashioner of all things," whose twenty-one attributes include intelligence, holiness, mobility, omnipotence, interpenetration, and the like (7:22); "breath of the power of God, and a pure emanation of the glory of the Almighty" (7:25); "spotless mirror of the working of God, and an image of his goodness" (7:26; cf. 10:1, 5, 6, 9; 11:1; 12:1). These descriptions of wisdom, especially the crucial passage in 7:22–8:21, reflect the increasing emphasis on the transcendence of God characteristic of later Judaism, combined with an unmistakable influence from Hellenism. To what degree the author conceived of wisdom as an intermediary between God and the world is impossible to say. Viewing his words from the perspective of

Greek thought, it would probably be easy to read too much into them. Whether consciously or not, he nevertheless spoke a language that during the next two centuries and later was to play a profound role in religious development

ALL WISDOM COMES FROM THE LORD (ECCLESIASTICUS). By far the longest book, comprising almost one third of the Deuterocanon, Ecclesiasticus, or by its Greek title, the Wisdom of Jesus (from the Hebrew, Joshua), the Son of Sirach, provides the reader with the unusual advantage of a translator's preface. The author himself, moreover, has obliged the reader with his signature along with a blessing upon those who concern themselves with wisdom (50:27–29). From these passages, therefore, we learn that the book was composed in Hebrew in Judea by an ardent collector of gnomic sayings whose Hebrew name was Joshua ben Sira, and was brought to the Jewish community in Alexandria by his grandson and translated into Greek. In his reference to "the thirty-eighth year of the reign of Euergetes," furthermore, the grandson provides us with a clue to the date. How long after his arrival in Egypt he made the translation we are not told, but his arrival can be dated quite precisely as 132 B.C. If, as is usually assumed, the high priest Simon, celebrated in 50:1–21, is the Simon mentioned by Josephus in *Antiquities* XII, 4, 10 (c. 200 B.C.), the original composition of the book can be fixed somewhere between 190 and 170 B.C.[31]

Ecclesiasticus is so characteristic an example of the Judaic wisdom literature that it has been said that if Ben Sira had not insisted on attaching his own name to it, but had been content, like the author of Wisdom, to write under the name of an ancient worthy, his work would probably have been retained in the Hebrew canon. Ben Sira makes no claims to originality; "all wisdom comes from the Lord," and he has been content to collect it from every source available to him and record it for posterity. Like the book of Proverbs, which apparently was his model, Ben Sira's work is concerned with prudential wisdom and is a loosely connected chain of proverbs, gnomic poems, allegories, and the like. The thought may be regarded as typical of Palestinian Judaism prior to the Maccabean period. To attempt to identify the work with any one of the later parties in Judaism, such as the Sadducees or Pharisees, would, of course, be anachronistic. There are, in fact, traits of both in the work. His interest in the temple cultus, so eloquently expressed in the praise of Simon (50:1–2), Aaron, and the Levites (45:6–26), would fit the later Sadducean attitude, as would his emphasis on the present life rather than speculation about life after death. His emphasis on the importance of keeping the precepts of Torah, on the other hand, would suit well the Pharisees. He appears to have been an urbane,

---

[31] See R. H. Pfeiffer, *History of New Testament Times,* pp. 364–367. Also Box and Oesterley in R. H. Charles, *Apocrypha and Pseudepigrapha of the Old Testament,* Vol. I, pp. 293–294.

self-confident teacher, with a low opinion of women and a great confidence in the ability of true piety balanced with sufficient prudence to produce a rewarding and satisfying life.

As is generally true of gnomic literature, the very nature of Ecclesiasticus makes any summary or outline of its content difficult and of questionable value; it has to be read to be appreciated. Ben Sira has provided a comprehensive compendium of sage advice on every conceivable subject from the most profoundly religious to the purely secular, from the solemn ceremonies at the temple to instructions for speakers and toastmasters at banquets. A few general observations here will suffice. R. H. Pfeiffer cites the allegory in 24:30–34 depicting wisdom as a stream which became a sea as evidence that the book was written in two parts: chapters 1–23, which was Ben Sira's original project "to water his garden"; and chapters 24–51, which was the larger project into which his collection grew as time went on. Ben Sira was not the last author, certainly, to find his project mushrooming into proportions beyond his original intent. These two parts are introduced by the longest poems in the book celebrating wisdom (1:1–20 and 24:1–34).[32] Like Proverbs—and perhaps in deliberate imitation of Proverbs—Ecclesiasticus closes with a summation in the form of an acrostic poem (51:13–22). Among the noteworthy passages in the book, perhaps the best known is that entitled "Let Us Now Praise Famous Men" (44:1–50:21), which concludes with the picture of the high priest Simon at the altar.

MACCABEUS TOOK COMMAND (I MACCABEES). We have already surveyed the history which is related in the two historical works in the Deuterocanon. It remains now for us only to deal briefly with the introductory matters concerning them. I Maccabees, most scholars agree, was written in Hebrew by a pious Palestinian Jew. Not only the statements of Origen and Jerome, but the characteristics of "translation Greek" attest to the original language, whereas the author's obvious familiarity with Palestinian geography and vagueness about the world beyond, locate him within the land about which he is writing. That he ends his story with John Hyrcanus I (cf. 14:23–24) suggests that he was writing either near the end or shortly after the reign of Hyrcanus (135–104 B.C.), in other words, approximately 100 B.C.

After a brief preface summarizing Alexander's conquests, death, and successors, the author begins his story with Antiochus Epiphanes' invasion of Egypt and subsequent desecration of the temple, and traces the story of the Maccabean revolt, the death of Antiochus, the defeat of Nicanor, and Simon's achievement of independence, his death, and the accession of John

---

[32] *History of New Testment Times*, pp. 353–354. For an excellent characterization of the author and his thought, see pp. 364–408.

Hyrcanus I. The story is told in the idiom of the Former Prophets and Chronicles (cf. 9:22 and 16:23 with I Kings 11:41 passim) and is concerned principally with the war itself and the providential victories of the Jews. So similar is the form, in fact, that Pfeiffer conjectures that the author may have planned his work as a sequel to Chronicles-Ezra-Nehemiah.[33] The large place he gives to the exploits of Judas Maccabeus leaves no doubt that Judas is the author's hero, and that the book was written to show how God used him to bring deliverance once more to Israel. As with most ancient historians, the author provided appropriate speeches and prayers to help interpret the story, accent its important turns, characterize the heroes, and the like. At several points he presents copies of official documents affecting the course of his history. Whether these are authentic materials is a matter of dispute among scholars. Probably they represent a knowledge of the existence of such documents, and perhaps also at least a general knowledge of their content. Although in II Maccabees we have an alternate source for a considerable part of this history, this work is so basic to our knowledge of the period as to be indispensable. Not without reason, Josephus took it over as his main source for the period in his *Antiquities of the Jews* (XII, 5 to XIII, 7).

INTO A SINGLE BOOK (II MACCABEES). The differences between this work and I Maccabees are well represented in the opening section, 1:1–2:18, which consists of two letters (or three?) written by the author to the Jews in Egypt. The first of these consists of an exhortation to piety and especially to keep the Feast of Booths; the second is in two parts, the first of which anticipates the content of the work as a whole by announcing the Maccabean victory and the death of Antiochus and urges the Egyptian Jews to join them in rededication of the temple. In the second part of this letter several items having to do with the temple are recalled: the hiding of the fire from the altar by pious priests at the time of the Babylonian Exile (587 B.C.), which miraculously was converted to naphtha and reignited in the time of Nehemiah; Jeremiah's provisions for preserving the holy vessels; the heavenly fire which appeared at Solomon's dedication of the temple; and Nehemiah's collection of books about "kings and prophets."

From these letters, the author's interests are clear. He is primarily concerned with the temple cultus. His work is written, therefore, to show how God, through the valor of such warriors as Judas Maccabeus and by miraculous means (cf. 3:22–40; 10:29–31; and Antiochus' monstrous punishment and deathbed repentance in 9:5–29), "has kept his own place undefiled" (15:34b). Consequently, rededication of the temple and, therefore, the establishing of the Feast of Dedication occupy a pivotal position in the book (10:1–8). For the same reason, the author emphasizes the role of corrupt

---

[33] *History of New Testament Times*, pp. 485–486.

and Hellenizing priests and temple officials in bringing about the disaster of Antiochus' desecration of the temple (chs. 3–5). In contrast to such perfidy, the author relates in some of the most moving stories in the book the heroism of pious Jews who chose death rather than give up the institutions of their religion, such as circumcision, the sabbath, and kosher laws (6:10–7:42). The remainder of the work (chs. 8–15) carries the story of the Maccabean revolt from its beginning to the defeat of Nicanor (167–161 B.C.) and parallels I Maccabees 3–7.[34]

In the author's own preface, 2:19–32, he tells us that his work is an epitome, condensing "into a single book" a five-volume history of Judas Maccabeus and his brothers written by Jason of Cyrene. His description of the toils, difficulties, and responsibilities of the epitomizer is a classic (2:26–31). Since Jason's work has been lost, how faithfully the epitomizer has represented the scope and character of his work, and how much, if anything, has been imported into the present work from other sources, are moot questions into which we need not enter. The epitomizer has also assumed responsibility for making his work pleasant reading (2:25), and to that end employed the devices and style of popular Greek rhetoric. If the mention of "Mordecai's day," in 15:36, comes from Jason's work, the original from which the epitome of II Maccabees was made must have been written some time after Esther, not earlier than the last part of the second century B.C. The epitomizer, therefore, can hardly have written earlier than 100 B.C. Some scholars date his work as late as A.D. 50.

Three Extracanonical Works

There remain three documents which, because they appeared in some manuscripts of the Latin Bible, were placed, following the Council of Trent, as an appendix at the end of the Vulgate.[35] Although, as we have seen, they have not been included in any of the canonical lists of either Judaism or Christianity, their presence in the Latin Bible and consequent inclusion among the Apocrypha in the Protestant Bibles require us to notice them briefly.

That the first two of these documents bear the name of Ezra has resulted in considerable confusion. In the ancient Hebrew texts Ezra and Nehemiah were one book and were so treated in the older texts of the LXX. With the addition of the "Greek Ezra," however, the original Hebrew Ezra–Nehemiah was placed second, hence I Ezra equals the "Greek Ezra" and II Ezra equals Ezra-Nehemiah. When in the later Greek texts the latter was separated into two books, Nehemiah became III Ezra (IV Ezra, of course, does not appear in the LXX). In the Vulgate a fourth book appears and, because only two of these are included among the canonical books, their

---

[34] For a detailed comparison of the two accounts see R. H. Pfeiffer, *History of New Testament Times*, pp. 472–483. On the literary problems of II Maccabees, see pp. 506–522.

[35] See above, pp. 493–494.

numbering is reversed. The "Greek Ezra" becomes III Esdras, and the Apocalypse becomes IV Esdras. The English Bibles, on the other hand, have returned in part to the late LXX numbering. The following chart will help identify them:

	LXX	VULGATE	ENGLISH
"The Greek Ezra"	I Ezra	III Esdras	I Esdras
Canonical Ezra	II Ezra (early texts include Nehemiah)	I Esdras	Ezra
Canonical Nehemiah	III Ezra (in later texts)	II Esdras	Nehemiah
Apocalypse	—	IV Esdras[36]	II Esdras

THIS IS WHAT TOOK PLACE (THE GREEK EZRA, OR [I] III ESDRAS). With the exception of one section, this book appears to be nothing more than a parallel version of the history which begins with the Passover of Josiah (622 B.C.) described in II Chronicles 35:1 and continues through Ezra (except 4:6), including Nehemiah 7:73–8:12a and stopping abruptly with the story of Ezra's reading of the Law (c. 400 B.C.). Differences in detail as well as order, however, show that it is not a re-edited version of this material in the LXX, but a translation of a Hebrew text, of whose relationship to these books in the Hebrew Canon we cannot be certain. In some respects both the order and styles are superior to the parallel history contained in the LXX version of the canonical books.

The most interesting aspect of this book is a delightful story in 3:1–5:6, which attributes Darius' permission to rebuild the temple in Jerusalem to a reward granted Zerubbabel. In a debate among three of his young bodyguards over which is stronger, wine, the king, or women, Zerubbabel has contended for women, but added that "truth is victor over all things." His argument is so persuasive that the king promises to grant whatever he asks, whereupon Zerubbabel asks him to fulfill his promise to rebuild Jerusalem and the temple.

I, EZRA SAW ON MOUNT ZION (THE APOCALYPSE, OR [II] IV ESDRAS). Written probably near the end of the first century A.D., the original apocalypse, consisting of chapters 3–14 of the present text, is in the form of seven visions dealing with questions of theodicy, signs of the end-time, the fate of the dead, the number of the elect, and the program of history to the end of time.

Probably the most noteworthy and interesting part of the work is the final section, in chapter 14, having to do with the restoration of the sacred books. Although God had revealed his truth to Moses on Mount Sinai,

---

[36] In older Latin manuscripts the matter is more complex. IV Esdras is found in three separate documents numbered II, IV, and V Esdras. See R. H. Charles, *Apocrypha and Pseudepigrapha of the Old Testament*, Vol. II, pp. 542–543.

including the Law, published openly, and secrets of the times which were not to be revealed, the Law had been burned and, of course, the secrets lost. So at God's command Ezra assembles five scribes to whom he dictates as God gives him "the lamp of understanding" (14:25) for forty days, during which time he writes ninety-four books. Twenty-four (the Hebrew canon) are to be made public; the remaining seventy are to be stored (as apocrypha) for "the wise among your people" (14:46). Two points of interest appear in this section: (1) The picture of Ezra dictating the Hebrew scriptures by inspiration exemplifies a model for theories concerning the authority and inspiration of the Bible. (2) The esoteric works include, probably mostly, the growing number of apocalypses; and their treatment here illustrates the meaning of the term "apocrypha" which properly belongs to them.

IV Esdras was probably written in Aramaic and translated into a Greek version (both of which are now lost, except for a few Greek fragments) from which the extant Latin and Oriental versions were translated. Sometime during the next two centuries the Christian additions of chapters 1 and 2 and 15 and 16 were made.[37]

I BEND THE KNEE OF MY HEART (THE PRAYER OF MANASSEH). In II Chronicles 33:10–20 we are given an account of how the wicked king Manasseh, after being taken captive to Babylon by the Assyrians, repented and was restored to his kingdom, where he proceeded to undo much of the mischief he had done in his apostate days.[38] Special mention is made in verses 18 and 19 of Manasseh's prayer. As the prayer was not recorded by the Chronicler, an unknown writer of uncommon skill and piety has undertaken to supply the lack by means of this prayer.

The prayer cannot be traced beyond the third century A.D., and little can be said of its origins. The earliest references to it are in ancient Christian documents, but it probably was written by a Jew in Hebrew or Aramaic. Whether it ever stood in the story of Manasseh in any text of II Chronicles is a matter of dispute. As to its date there is scarcely a clue. Perhaps the author, who may not have expected the association of his work with the ancient king of Judah to be taken literally, found in the story of Manasseh an understanding of his own plight and voiced in this prayer the cry of his own soul. Certainly many faithful after him have discovered in it a profoundly meaningful vehicle for their own confessions.

---

[37] For the interesting story of the rediscovery of the lost verses in ch. 7, see Bruce M. Metzger, *Introduction to the Apocrypha*, pp. 23–24.

[38] See above, pp. 344–345. The version of Manasseh's story in II Kings 21, of course, knows nothing of his repentance.

SELECTED READINGS

The Intertestamental Period

Bickermann, E., *From Ezra to the Last of the Maccabees* (New York: Schocken Books, Inc., 1962).

Farmer, W. R., *Maccabees, Zealots, and Josephus* (New York: Columbia University Press, 1956).

Finkelstein, Louis, *The Pharisees, the Sociological Background of Their Faith*, Morris Loeb Series (Philadelphia: Jewish Publication Society of America, 1961).

Foerster, Werner, *From the Exile to Christ: A Historical Introduction to Palestinian Judaism*, Gordon E. Harris, trans. (Philadelphia: Fortress Press, 1964).

Herford, R. T., *The Pharisees* (New York: Macmillan Publishing Co., Inc., 1924).

Pfeiffer, Robert H., *History of New Testament Times, With an Introduction to the Apocrypha* (New York: Harper & Row, Publishers, 1949).

———, "The Literature and Religion of the Apocrypha," *IB*, Vol. I, pp. 391–419.

Rost, Leonhard, *Judaism Outside the Hebrew Canon: An Introduction to the Documents*, David E. Green, trans. (Nashville, TN: Abingdon Press, 1976). Paperback. A useful and up-to-date handbook providing basic facts about the Apocrypha (Deuterocanon), Pseudepigrapha, and Dead Sea Scrolls.

Russell, D. S., *Between the Testaments* (London: S.C.M. Press, 1960).

Sloan, W. W., *A Survey Between the Testaments* (Paterson, NJ: Littlefield, Adams Company, 1964). Paperback.

The Old Testament Apocrypha (Deuterocanon)

Charles, R. H., ed., *The Apocrypha and Pseudepigrapha of the Old Testament*, 2 vols. (Oxford: Clarendon Press, 1913, 1963). An old but standard translation and commentary on the apocryphal literature.

Dentan, Robert C., *The Apocrypha, Bridge of the Testaments* (New York: Seabury Press, Inc., 1964). Paperback.

Goldstein, Jonathan A., *I. Maccabees*, The Anchor Bible (Garden City, NY: Doubleday & Company, Inc., 1976).

Jewish Apocryphal Literature (New York: Harper & Row, Publishers). A series of volumes by different authors on the separate books of the Apocrypha.

Metzger, Bruce M., *An Introduction to the Apocrypha* (New York: Oxford University Press, 1957).

Milik, Josef T., *Ten Years of Discovery in the Wilderness of Judaea*, John Strugnell, trans., Studies in Biblical Theology, no. 26 (London: S.C.M. Press, 1959). Paperback.

Moore, Carey A., *Daniel, Esther, and Jeremiah, the Additions*, The Anchor Bible (Garden City, NY: Doubleday & Company, Inc., 1977).

Myers, Jacob M., *I. and II Esdras*, The Anchor Bible (Garden City, NY: Doubleday & Company, Inc., 1974).

Pfeiffer, Robert H., *History of New Testament Times, With an Introduction to the Apocrypha* (New York: Harper & Row, Publishers, 1940).

———, "The Literature and Religion of the Apocrypha," *IB*, Vol. I, pp. 391–419.

Winston, David, *Wisdom of Solomon*, The Anchor Bible (Garden City, NY: Doubleday & Company, Inc., 1979).

Qumran and the Dead Sea Scrolls

Burrows, Millar, *The Dead Sea Scrolls* (New York: The Viking Press, Inc., 1955).
———, *More Light on the Dead Sea Scrolls* (New York: The Viking Press, Inc., 1958).
Cross, Frank M., Jr., *The Ancient Library of Qumran and Modern Biblical Studies*, rev. ed. (Garden City, NY: Doubleday & Company, Inc., 1961). Also available in paperback (Doubleday Anchor, 1961).
Dupont-Sommer, A., *The Essene Writings from Qumran* (New York: Meridian, 1961). Paperback.
Murphy-O'Connor, J., "The Essenes in Palestine," *BA*, 40 (1977), pp. 100–124.
Ringgren, Helmer, *The Faith of Qumran* (Philadelphia: Fortress Press, 1961).
Sanders, James A., "The Dead Sea Scrolls—A Quarter Century of Study," *BA*, 36 (1973), pp. 110–148.
Vermès, Géza, *Dead Sea Scrolls in English* (New York: Penguin Books, 1962). Includes an introduction to the Scrolls and English translations of the separate texts. Paperback.
Yadin, Yigael, ed., *The Temple Scroll* (Jerusalem: Israel Exploration Society, 1977).

GLOSSARY

Acra (Greek: "citadel," "fortress") A citadel erected in Jerusalem by the Seleucid Greeks during the Maccabean era. A symbol of Seleucid oppression, it was captured by the Jewish leader Simon (c. 142 B.C.).

Adonai (Hebrew: "Lord") A title of honor and majesty, used within Judaism since the late post-Exilic period as a substitute for the sacred name Yahweh.

Aetiology See Etiology.

Akkadians An early Semitic people who, under Sargon the Great, subdued Sumer and all Mesopotamia and founded one of the first true empires in world history (2360–2180 B.C.).

Allegory A more or less elaborate story in which the various elements have symbolic meanings and often are included solely for the sake of such meanings.

Amalekites A nomadic tribe that occupied the desert south and southeast of Canaan. Biblical tradition traces their ancestry from Esau.

Amarna Letters A collection of cuneiform tablets found at Tell el Amarna, Egypt, many of which were written to Pharaohs Amenhotep III and Amenhotep IV (Akhenaton) from Canaanite and Phoenician princes, depicting the chaotic conditions in those lands during the first half of the fourteenth century B.C.

Amarna Age The period of Pharaoh Amenhotep IV (Akhenaton) whose capital was located at Tell el Amarna (or Akhetaton).

Ammonites A Semitic people who occupied the eastern edge of the Transjordan Plateau, between the Jabbok and Arnon rivers.

Amorites (Babylonian: "Westerners"; Hebrew: "Highlanders") Semitic peoples who infiltrated the Fertile Crescent in the late third and early second millennia, founders of the kingdoms of Mari (Zimri-Lim) and Babylon (Hammurabi). In biblical usage the name for a Canaanite tribe or the pre-Israelite population of Palestine in general.

Amphictyony The Greek name for an association of tribes or city-states which participated in the cult of a common deity at a central shrine.

Anath A fertility goddess in Canaanite mythology; sister-consort of the storm god Baal.

Anthropomorphism The ascription of human or manlike characteristics to that which is not human, especially in reference to deity.

Aphorism A concise, apt statement of a general principle or truth. A maxim.

Apiru Egyptian equivalent of Habiru. *See* Habiru.

Apocalypse A revelation or disclosure of a previously hidden truth. Specifically, a prophetic description of the events which lead up to and involve the cataclysmic end of history and the perfect New Age to follow. The system of beliefs fostered by such writings.

Apocrypha Literally, "hidden writings," regarded either as spurious or as too esoteric for general use. Protestants usually apply the term to the fourteen books of the Septuagint (Latin) Old Testament which are not in the Hebrew Canon. It is also used of the extracanonical books paralleling both the Old and New Testaments. *See* Deuterocanon.

Apodictic Law Law in the form of absolutes, "Thou shalt" or "Thou shalt not," as in the stipulations of the Decalogue.

Apostasy The act of defecting from and ceasing to practice one's religious faith.

Aqabah (Gulf of) The Northeastern arm of the Red Sea and southern extension of the Jordan rift, which separates the Sinai Peninsula from Midian and Arabia.

Arabah The earth depression which extends from the Sea of Galilee to the Gulf of Aqabah; a part of the larger fault which begins in Syria and ends in Africa.

Aramaic A Semitic language closely akin to Hebrew, employed as the Near Eastern language of diplomacy and commerce from about 1000 B.C. It replaced Hebrew as the spoken tongue in Palestine after the Exile. Portions of the books of Ezra and Daniel are written in Aramaic.

Arameans A Semitic people of the Syrian region whose early kinship ties with the Hebrew patriarchs are attested, but with whom the Israelites later struggled for control of northern Transjordan.

Ark (1) The houseboat in which Noah escaped the great flood. (2) In the KJV, the basket of rushes in which Moses was placed as an infant. (3) The portable chest or shrine containing the tablets of Mosaic law. Traced in biblical tradition from the period of wilderness wanderings, it accompanied the Hebrews in battle and finally was placed in the Holy of Holies of the Jerusalem Temple.

Asherah The Old Testament name for the Canaanite fertility goddess Ashirat; El's consort and mother of the gods, symbolized by a wooden pole.

Assyria (1) An extensive region centered along the upper Tigris River in Mesopotamia, including the important sites of Asshur and Nineveh. (2)

The dominant empire in the Near East from the eleventh through the seventh centuries B.C.

Aton The sun disk and sole god of Pharaoh Akhenaton (fourteenth century B.C.).

Atonement, Day of The most solemn of all Hebrew fasts, culminating ten days of penitence at the beginning of the autumn New Year.

Baal The most active deity of the Canaanite pantheon; god of the storm and male fertility symbol.

Babylon The city on the middle Euphrates which served as capital of the Old and Neo-Babylonian empires.

Babylonia (1) The central (and sometimes southern) region of Mesopotamia. (2) The empires founded by Hammurabi (c. 1728–1551 B.C.) and Nebuchadrezzar (612–538 B.C.).

Booths, Feast of Israel's autumn harvest festival, so named from the practice of erecting booths of branches, reminiscent of the wilderness journey from Egypt. Also known as Tabernacles, or Sukkoth.

Canaan, Canaanites The biblical name for the land of Palestine west of the Jordan prior to the Israelite conquest. The pre-Israelite inhabitants of that land.

Canon A standard or measure, hence those books that have been judged worthy to be included among the holy scriptures.

Canonical Criticism An interpretative method that gives primary attention to the Bible's origins, history, and continuing function as canon, i.e., as literature accepted as normative by the community of faith.

Casuistic law Law built on precedents and hence formulated in conditional terms, "if (the crime) . . . then (the penalty). . . ."

Chaldeans (1) Founders of the Neo-Babylonian empire (612–538 B.C.), thus Babylonians. (2) Astrologers or soothsayers such as were associated with the Babylonians.

Charismatic Of or pertaining to one who possesses the gift of God's spirit, made manifest in physical strength or religious zeal together with the ability to lead and inspire others.

Chemosh The national deity of Moab.

Cherubim Composite animal-fowl-human creatures derived from mythology and regarded as guardians of deity, as in the two figures that flanked the ark in the Holy of Holies.

Covenant An agreement or compact between individuals, groups, or, frequently in the Old Testament, between man and God.

Covenant Code The collection of Hebrew law found in Exodus 20:23–23:33. Much, though not all, of this collection is casuistic in form and dates from the period following the Israelite settlement.

Cult, Cultus The organized religious worship of a people, especially its public rites and ceremonies.

Cuneiform Wedge-shaped, applied especially to writing that developed in

the Sumerian culture of Mesopotamia as early as the third millennium
B.C.

Cyrus cylinder The barrel-shaped clay cylinder on which the Persian king
Cyrus the Great (550–530 B.C.) recorded his conquest of Babylon.

D The abbreviation for the Pentateuchal source found in the Book of Deuteronomy; one of the four sources identified by the Documentary Hypothesis and dated c. 650 B.C.

Dead Sea Scrolls Documents recovered in a remarkable series of discoveries beginning in 1947 in the cliffs along the western side of the Dead
Sea; the library of a Jewish monastic community living in the area during the period of late Judaism. *See* Essenes; Qumran.

Decalogue (Greek: "ten word [s]") The Ten Commandments, ascribed by
tradition to Moses, and found in two versions: Exodus 20 and Deuteronomy 5. Sometimes designated the "Ethical Decalogue." *See* Ritual
Decalogue.

Demythologization The removal or reinterpretation of the mythological elements in a tradition so as to make its truth claims consistent with a non-
mythological perspective.

Deuterocanon The fourteen books of the Vulgate not included in the Hebrew Bible. All but one are found in the Septuagint. *See* Apocrypha.

Deutero-Isaiah ("Second Isaiah") The name given the anonymous prophet-
poet who wrote chapters 40–55 (according to some 40–66) of the Book
of Isaiah. Also the name used for the work itself.

Deuteronomic History The books of the Former Prophets (Joshua,
Judges, Samuel, Kings), as created from older traditions by an author influenced by the Book of Deuteronomy. According to one view, Deuteronomy belongs to the larger work and provides its introduction. It is
dated slightly before or after the fall of Jerusalem in 587 B.C.

Deuteronomic reformation The name used by modern scholars for King
Josiah's reforms in Judah during the last quarter of the seventh century
B.C. The name reflects the conviction that Josiah's law book is to be
identified with the Deuteronomic Code (Deut. 12–26). One conspicuous
aim of the reformation was the centralization of sacrifice at the one altar
in Jerusalem.

Deuteronomist (1) The author or traditioner responsible for the present
form of the Book of Deuteronomy. According to one view, he added
some or all of the prefaces (chs. 1–11) and appendices (chs. 27–34) to the
original Deuteronomic Code (chs. 12–26). (2) The author or traditioner
responsible for the entire Deuteronomic History in something like its
present form. *See* Deuteronomic History.

Diachronic (Greek: "through time") In respect to methods of biblical interpretation, pertaining to a concern with the developmental stages in
the life of a text. Used in contrast with "synchronic."

Documentary hypothesis The theory of Pentateuchal composition, associated particularly with the name of Julius Wellhausen, that views the Pentateuch as the redaction of four literary sources, J, E, D, and P.

Doublet Two versions, from different sources, of the same account.

E The abbreviation for the Pentateuchal source identified by the Documentary Hypothesis as the second oldest literary stratum in the Pentateuch (c. 750 B.C.).

Ebla A city in northern Syria (modern Tell Mardikh) which served as the center of a major cultural, commercial, and political empire between c. 2250 and 2400 B.C.

El A Semitic word for divinity; in the Canaanite pantheon, the name of the high father god; in the Old Testament, both the generic name for deity and one of the names for Israel's own God. When used of the Israelite God, El most often appears in apposition with another word, such as El Shaddai ("God Almighty"), El Bethel ("God of Bethel"), El 'Olam ("Everlasting God"), etc. See Elohim.

Elder (1) In the pre-Exilic period, a clan or tribe leader who might serve in the administration of justice in the community. (2) In the post-Exilic period, an officer in the synagogue.

Elohim One of the two most prominent names for God used throughout the Old Testament. The longer (and plural) form of El. See El.

Elohist A designation for the anonymous traditioner responsible for the E source in the Pentateuch; so named because of his preference for the divine name Elohim. See E.

Enuna Elish The Babylonian creation account, which takes its name from the opening words, "When above."

Ephraim (1) Most prominent of the northern Israelite tribes, hence a poetic designation for the northern kingdom (Israel). (2) A Son of Joseph and the eponymous ancestor of the tribe of Ephraim.

Eponym The person from whom a tribe or a people is supposed to have taken its name.

Eschatology (Greek: "doctrine of last things") A set of beliefs or an attitude concerning the end of the present epoch of world history. In the biblical sense, a conception of God's ultimate plans for man and history.

Essenes An ascetic (or semiascetic) sect within late Judaism, described by Josephus, Philo, and Pliny the Elder. Most scholars believe the community at Qumran which produced the Dead Sea Scrolls belonged to this sect.

Etiology Literally, an inquiry into causes, hence a story told to explain, often in mythical terms, the origin and significance of a custom, ritual, institution, place, and the like.

Execration texts Egyptian pottery fragments dating from the nineteenth and twentieth centuries B.C. and inscribed with the names of actual or potential enemies. The pottery was smashed in magical ceremonies as a curse against the enemies.

Exegesis The technical analysis of a passage of scripture to discover its meaning as precisely and fully as possible.

Exile, the The separation of Jews from Palestine which resulted from the Babylonian deportations of 597 B.C., 587 B.C., and later. In 538 B.C., following Persia's conquest of Babylon, groups of Babylonian Jews were allowed to return home.

Exodus (Greek: "a going out") The escape of the Hebrew slaves from Egyptian bondage under Moses' leadership. Viewed in Israelite faith as Yahweh's mighty act of deliverance and the formative event in the nation's history.

Fertile Crescent The name coined by James Breasted for the crescent-shaped territory that extends from the Persian Gulf on the southeast to Egypt on the southwest, including Mesopotamia, Syria, and Palestine.

First Fruits, Feast of One of the three major feasts in early Israel, observed at the beginning of wheat harvest (in early summer), fifty days or seven weeks after the first day of Unleavened Bread. Also known as the Feast of Harvest, Weeks, and Pentecost.

Form Criticism The English designation for the school of biblical criticism that arose in Germany, where it is known as *Formsgeschichte*. Form criticism attempts to identify the preliterary (oral) units behind the written text of the Bible, classify their forms, reconstruct the life situation (*Sitz-im-Leben*) in which they arose, and trace the processes by which they passed from their original state to their present form.

Gilead A geographical region in central Transjordan, located between the Yarmuk and Arnon rivers.

Gilgamesh The hero of the ancient Babylonian Epic of Gilgamesh, who seeks from Utnapishtim, survivor of the great flood, the secret of immortality.

Habiru A vagrant class of Semites mentioned in texts from the late third and second millennia B.C. Their presence is attested throughout the Near East, but particularly in Palestine during the Amarna period (fourteenth century), where they raided towns and pestered the settled population.

Hanukkah, Feast of (Hebrew: "dedication") The eight-day festival commemorating the successes of Judas Maccabeus against the armies of Antiochus Epiphanes in freeing Jerusalem and cleansing the temple, which was rededicated on the twenty-fifth of Kislev (December), 164 B.C.

Hasidim (Hebrew: the "pious" or "loyal ones") Those Jews who expressed their loyalty to the covenant in the period of Seleucid persecution by resisting the efforts of Antiochus Epiphanes to modify or destroy Judaism.

Hasmoneans The independent Jewish dynasty founded by the Maccabees and named for Hasmon, great grandfather of Mattathias. The succession of Hasmonean rulers ended with the Roman conquest of Palestine in 63 B.C.

Hebrew The Semitic people traced in biblical tradition to Eber, great grandson of Shem, who comprised the nation Israel and in post-Exilic times came to be called Jews. Also the Semitic tongue spoken by those people.

Hellenism The presence and influence of Greek language, culture, and thought, particularly as disseminated by Alexander the Great and his successors.

Hexateuch (Greek: "six scrolls") The six books of Genesis through Joshua, so designated by those who find common elements in the Pentateuch and Joshua.

Holiness Code The code of laws found in Leviticus 17–26, dating in its present form from the Exile, and so named because of its emphasis on holiness of conduct.

Israel (1) The name given the patriarch Jacob, thus designating him the eponym of the Israelite nation. (2) The northern kingdom as distinct from the southern kingdom (Judah) during the period of the divided monarchies (922–722 B.C.). (3) The whole covenant people whose origins as a nation are traced to Moses and the ceremonies at Sinai.

J The abbreviation for the oldest literary stratum in the Pentateuch as identified by the Documentary Hypothesis. It contains southern traditions which reached their present form by the time of Solomon (c. 950 B.C.), and is the only Pentateuchal source in which the divine name Yahweh is attributed to the generations preceding Moses.

Jehovah A hybrid name formed of the consonants of Yahweh, Y (J), H, W (V), H, plus the vowels of "Adonai," the Hebrew word for "Lord."

Jews (1) A name that came into usage after the Exile to describe the people formerly known as Hebrews or Israelites; or, more precisely defined, the residents of Judea (formerly Judah) or their descendants. (2) As sometimes used, the name for those who profess the religious faith inherited from ancient Israel.

Judah (1) One of Jacob's twelve sons. (2) The Hebrew tribe whose ancestry was traced from the patriarch Judah. (3) The southern kingdom, as distinct from the northern kingdom (Israel), during the period of the divided monarchies. (4) In the post-Exilic period, the region around Jerusalem—the remains of the former kingdom of Judah.

Judaism (1) The religion of the Jews in its post-Exilic form, traced from the days of Ezra, but especially as developed under the great Rabbinic teachers (c. 100 B.C.–A.D. 200). (2) According to a broader definition, the Israelite religion from its very beginnings.

Judea The Graeco-Roman name for the Judah of post-Exilic times.

Judges (1) Charismatic figures who delivered Israel from enemy threat during the period of the tribal confederacy (c. 1200–1000 B.C.). (2) The Old Testament book in which the exploits of these heroes and heroines are recorded.

Kenite hypothesis The theory that Yahweh was originally the tribal god of the Kenite clan, from whom Moses and the Hebrews derived the faith.

Kenites The Midianite clan of Jethro, father-in-law of Moses.

Kethubim The Writings; third division of the Hebrew Canon, containing all the Old Testament books not found among the Law and Prophets.

Law See Torah.

Legend An unverifiable story or collection of stories about persons or places of the past, typically transmitted in the popular oral tradition of a people.

Levites (1) The priestly tribe whose ancestry was traced to Levi, son of Jacob. (2) The temple servants or priests of secondary rank in the post-Exilic priestly hierarchy.

Lights, Festival of See Hanukkah, Feast of.

LXX The abbreviation for Septuagint. See Septuagint.

MT The abbreviation for Masoretic Text. See Masoretic Text.

Maccabees The five sons of Mattathias and their followers, who led the attack against the Seleucid persecutors of the Jews; so named for Judas Maccabeus ("hammerer"), foremost among the brothers.

Manuscript In textual criticism, an early copy of one or more biblical books or a fragment of a book, written in the original language.

Mari texts Tablets found at the site of ancient Mari on the upper Euphrates River that date from the latter half of the eighteenth century B.C.

Masoretes Medieval Jewish scholars who copied, annotated, and added vowels to the text of the Hebrew Bible, produced by the medieval Masoretes.

Megilloth (Hebrew: "scrolls"). The five Old Testament books, Song of Songs, Ruth, Lamentations, Ecclesiastes, and Esther, each of which was read publicly at one of Israel's annual religious festivals.

Mesopotamia The land area bounded by the Tigris and Euphrates rivers.

Messiah (Hebrew: "anointed") One set apart for a divinely endowed office, such as priest or king, by a rite of anointment with oil. In time, the name came to be used of the future deliverer king.

Moabites The Transjordanian people who occupied the territory between the Arnon River and the Zered Brook.

Molech The national deity of the Ammonites, sometimes worshiped in rites of human sacrifice.

Monotheism Belief in the existence of one God.

Myth (1) A statement in human language of beliefs that lie outside the range of scientific, historical inquiry. (2) Stories of gods and goddesses in their relationships with each other. (3) A conception of a primeval event that determines present reality through continuous reenactment in cultic rites.

Nabi' (Hebrew: "prophet") A spokesman capable of delivering divinely inspired messages. Israel's classical prophets addressed king and people on crucial issues of the day, calling for decisions consistent with God's character and covenant.

Nazirite A person consecrated by sacred vows to a life of special sanctity, which included abstaining from strong drink and cutting the hair.

Negeb The dry steppe that extends from Palestine's southern extremity into the northern sector of the Sinai desert, roughly from Beersheba to Kadesh-barnea.

Nuzi texts Clay tablets found at the site of ancient Nuzi on the upper Tigris River, reflecting Hurrian customs and laws of the mid-second millennium B.C.

Omrids The dynasty founded by the Israelite king Omri, which lasted from 876 to 842 B.C.

Ophel The southern extremity of Jerusalem's eastern hill; the site of David's city.

Oracle A prophetic declaration or a single literary unit of prophecy.

Ostraca Inscribed potsherds.

P The latest of the literary sources in the Pentateuch according to the Documentary Hypothesis. So named because of its Priestly interests, it reflects a southern provenance and reached its present form no earlier than the post-Exilic period.

Palestine The land known in the early phase of the biblical period as Canaan, bordered on the north and south by Syria and the Sinai peninsula and on the east and west by the Mediterranean Sea and the Arabian Desert.

Passover Annual feast commemorating Israel's deliverance from Egypt. Specifically, it is a meal on the fourteenth day of Nisan (March–April), which includes roast lamb, unleavened bread, and bitter herbs, and begins the eight-day Feast of Unleavened Bread.

Pentateuch (Greek: "five scrolls") The first five books of the Hebrew canon; the Torah.

Peshitta The Syrian version of the Old Testament.

Philistines The "sea people" who migrated from the Aegean islands and settled on the southern coast of Palestine in the twelfth century B.C.

Phoenicia The coastal region north of Palestine, including the seaport cities Tyre and Sidon.

Polytheism The belief in multiple gods.

Priestly source See P.

Prophets The second division of the Hebrew canon. See *Nabi'*.

Pseudepigrapha (Greek: "falsely ascribed") (1) Literally, books fictiously ascribed to venerable biblical personalities. (2) A collection of intertestamental writings included in some Eastern Orthodox Canons, but excluded by Jews, Roman Catholics, and Protestants. In Roman Catholicism these books are known by the title "Apocrypha."

Ptolemies The Greek dynasty founded by Alexander's general, Ptolemy Lagi. Centered in Egypt, with Alexandria as capital, the Ptolemies ruled Palestine from 301 to 198 B.C.

Purim, Feast of A Jewish festival observed on the fourteenth and fifteenth of Adar (Feb.–Mar.), based on the events related in the Book of Esther.

Qumran The site on the northwest side of the Dead Sea where the sect that produced the Dead Sea Scrolls maintained its headquarters (c. 150–30 B.C.; A.D. 6–68).

Redaction, redactor The work of editing or composing a piece of literature, working from older written or oral sources; or the product of such work. The composer or editor is known as a redactor.

Redaction criticism A method of biblical criticism which seeks to expose the theological perspectives of a writer through a study of the compositional techniques and interpretations employed in shaping older traditions into the finished literary work.

Rhetorical criticism A refinement of the method of Form Criticism so as to place greater emphasis on the unique and personal aspects of the structural patterns employed in the fashioning of a literary unit.

Ritual Decalogue A set of cultic laws in Exodus, chapter 34, interpreted by some as a primitive decalogue.

Samaria (1) The city in central Palestine that served as capital of the northern kingdom from the reign of Omri (876–869 B.C.) until its fall to Assyria in 722 B.C. (2) The central region of Palestine between Galilee and Judah, made a province under Assyrian and Persian rule.

Samaritan Pentateuch An ancient pre-Masoretic textual tradition of the Pentateuch which derives from the sect of the Samaritans. For the Samaritans these five books constituted the entirety of the Bible.

Samaritans Inhabitants of the region of Samaria who broke away from the rest of Judaism during the Hellenistic period and built a temple on Mount Gerizim.

Satan (Hebrew: "adversary") Throughout most of the Old Testament, a common noun used in reference to an adversary or accuser. In some late Old Testament books, a cynical angel in Yahweh's heavenly courts; and, eventually (I Chron. 21:1), an evil agent tempting man to wickedness.

Seleucids The Greek dynasty founded by Alexander's general, Seleucus, which centered in Syria, with Antioch as capital. From 198 to 165 B.C. the Seleucids controlled Palestine.

Semites (1) According to Old Testament usage (Gen. 10), the descendants of Shem, son of Noah, identified with the peoples of Arabia, Mesopotamia, Elam, and southern Asia Minor; the strain from which Israel derived. (2) According to modern usage, ancient Near Eastern peoples or their descendants who used one of a common family of inflectional languages, such as Akkadian, Aramaic, Hebrew, and the like.

Septuagint The Greek version of the Old Testament, traditionally ascribed to seventy (or seventy-two) scholars; but actually a work completed over a long period of time, from c. 250 B.C. to the first century A.D.

Shema (Hebrew: "hear") Israel's confession of faith based on the words of Deuteronomy 6:4–9, beginning, "Hear, O Israel . . ."

Sheol The pit in the earth to which the shades of the dead were thought to descend, as mentioned throughout the Old Testament.

Shephelah The region of foothills and valleys situated between Philistia and the hills of southern Judah.

Sopherim Jewish scribes, from the time of Ezra and following, who copied and preserved the Hebrew manuscripts of the Old Testament.

Stele A pillar bearing an inscription, such as those used by ancient kings to record their victories.

Structuralism (1) As a method of biblical interpretation, the search for the underlying structure, i.e., "deep structures" of the mind, which are believed to be coded into the surface structures of a text. The method arises from the contention of structuralist philosophy that appearances do not constitute reality. (2) Apart from philosophical presuppositions, the method of identifying basic and unifying structures in a literary work.

Sukkoth. Feast of *See* Booths, Feast of.

Suffering Servant The subject of several poems in Deutero-Isaiah (Isa. 40–55), described as one who suffers vicariously for the nations of earth.

Synagogue An assembly consisting of not fewer than ten adult male Jews organized for worship, instruction of children, and regulation of the affairs of the local Jewish community. Probably originating during the Babylonian Exile as a surrogate for the temple, it became the effective center of Jewish life which enabled it to survive the temple's destruction. Its worship consisted of lessons from Torah and the Prophets (Haftarah), a homily, the Shema, Psalms, and eighteen prayers.

Synchronic (Greek: "with time") In respect to methods of biblical interpretation, a concern with the final stage in the life of a text, i.e., the text as it stands, rather than the evolutionary stages through which it developed. Used in contrast with "diachronic."

Syria (1) The region extending from the upper Euphrates River to northern Palestine. (2) The kingdom of Aram, with its capital at Damascus.

Tabernacle The movable tent shrine described in the accounts of the wilderness wanderings (Exod.-Num.), from which the Jerusalem temple was supposedly designed.

Tabernacles, Feast of *See* Booths, Feast of.

Targum The Aramaic version of the Old Testament.

Testament (Latin: "covenant") The name used for the two parts of the Christian Canon—Old and New Testaments (Covenants).

Theophany (Greek: "appearance of God") An appearance of a god to a man.

Torah The first five books of the Hebrew Canon, and the first of the three canonical divisions, Torah, Nebi'im, and Kethubim. Although traditionally translated into English as Law, the word Torah derives from a Hebrew verb meaning "to point the way" and is more accurately rendered as "guidance" or "instruction."

Transhumance pastoralism The seasonal migration of herdsmen who move with their livestock between summer and winter pastures, especially between lowlands and adjacent mountains. Recent studies reveal the coexistence of pastoralism and agriculture within the same tribal societies.

Transjordan The plateau east of the Jordan Valley and bordering the great Arabian Desert.

Twelve, Book of the The twelve books of the Minor Prophets, Hosea–Malachi, once written on a single scroll.

Version In respect to textual criticism, an early edition of the Bible or a portion of the Bible, translated into a language other than the original Hebrew (Old Testament) or Greek (New Testament).

Vulgate The Latin version of the Old Testament, translated by Jerome in the fourth century A.D.

Weeks, Feast of *See* Kethubim.

Yahweh The personal name for God in the Old Testament, translated "Lord" in the RSV, "Jehovah" in ASV and ERV. In Judaism the name is not pronounced; the surrogate Adonai is used instead.

Yahwist The anonymous author or traditioner responsible for the final form of the J source in the Pentateuch. *See* J.

Ziggurat The great tiered-earth towers associated with temple complexes in ancient Mesopotamia. The Tower of Babel story (Gen. 11) presupposes such a structure.

Zion (1) The eastern hill of Jerusalem on which the temple was built. (2) The entire city of Jerusalem. (3) After the fourth century A.D., the name associated erroneously with Jerusalem's western hill.

General Bibliography

The following books and articles, although by no means an exhaustive listing, are recommended as basic English works in the broad categories indicated. For bibliographies covering specific Old Testament books and topics, consult the lists at the end of each chapter.

Titles of journals and reference works indicated here in abbreviated form are cited in full in the table of abbreviations placed after the table of contents.

Recent Translations

The Anchor Bible (Garden City, NY: Doubleday & Company, Inc.). Original translations with notes and commentary by individual scholars of different faiths. Still in process.

The Good News Bible; The Bible in Today's English Version (New York: American Bible Society, 1976). A popular translation in the modern idiom; includes brief notes.

The Jerusalem Bible, Alexander Jones, ed. (Garden City, NY: Doubleday & Company, Inc., 1966). A first-rate translation with notes, produced by the Dominican biblical school in Jerusalem. Also available in a paperback edition, with abridged notes.

The New American Bible (New York: P. J. Kenedy & Sons, 1970). Paperback. A fine translation with notes, by members of the Catholic Biblical Association of America.

The New English Bible with the Apocrypha (New York: Oxford University Press, Inc., 1970). A fresh translation in the contemporary idiom.

The Oxford Annotated Bible with the Apocrypha, Revised Standard Version, Herbert G. May and Bruce M. Metzger (New York: Oxford University Press, Inc., 1965). The best student Bible available.

The Torah: The Five Books of Moses (Philadelphia: Jewish Publication Society of America, 1963). The first volume of The New Jewish Bible, prepared by a committee of eminent Jewish scholars.

Bible Dictionaries

Buttrick, George, et al., eds., *The Interpreter's Dictionary of the Bible*, 5 vols. (Nashville, TN: Abingdon Press, 1962 and 1976). The most comprehensive and up-to-date dictionary of the Bible available in English. An invaluable tool.

Hartman, Louis F., ed. and trans., *Encyclopedic Dictionary of the Bible* (New York: McGraw-Hill Book Company, 1963).

Hasting, James, ed., *Dictionary of the Bible*, rev. by F. C. Grant and H. H. Rowley (New York: Charles Scribner's Sons, 1963).

McKenzie, John L., *Dictionary of the Bible* (Milwaukee, WI: Bruce Publishing Co., 1965). Paperback.

Miller, Madeline S., J. Lane Miller, et al., *Harper's Bible Dictionary* (New York: Harper & Row, Publishers, 1952). The best one-volume dictionary of the Bible.

One-Volume Commentaries

Black, Matthew, and H. H. Rowley, eds., *Peake's Commentary on the Bible*, rev. (New York: Thomas Nelson Inc., 1962). A standard reference work, first published in 1919, completely revised in 1962.

Brown, Raymond E., Joseph A. Fitzmyer, and Roland E. Murphy, eds., *The Jerome Biblical Commentary* (Englewood Cliffs, NJ: Prentice-Hall, Inc., 1968). An excellent commentary by Roman Catholic scholars; detailed and up-to-date, with introductory articles.

Laymon, Charles M., ed., *The Interpreter's One-Volume Commentary on the Bible* (Nashville, TN: Abingdon Press, 1971). A comprehensive and up-to-date commentary by leading Jewish, Catholic, and Protestant scholars; also contains general articles.

Neil, William, *Harper's Bible Commentary* (New York: Harper & Row, Publishers, 1963).

Multivolume Commentaries and Series

Ackroyd, P. R., et al., eds., *The Cambridge Bible Commentary* (Cambridge, England: Cambridge University Press). A nontechnical commentary that includes the text of the NEB version.

Albright, William F., and David N. Freedman, eds., *The Anchor Bible* (Garden City, NY: Doubleday & Company, Inc., 1964–). A work still in process by scholars of different faiths, containing original translations.

Brueggemann, Walter, and John R. Donahue, eds., *Overtures to Biblical Theology* (Philadelphia: Fortress Press). Paperback.

Buttrick, George A., et al., eds., *The Interpreter's Bible* (Nashville, TN: Abingdon Press, 1952–57), 12 vols. A widely used commentary, both popular and technical in its approach. Vol. I contains valuable articles of a general nature on the Old Testament.

Cohen, Abraham, ed., *Soncino Books of the Bible* (London: Soncino Press, 1945–1952). A Jewish series with the Hebrew text; commentary from an orthodox perspective.

Cross, Frank M., et al., *Hermeneia: A Critical and Historical Commentary* (Philadelphia: Fortress Press, 1974–). A major technical commentary, including translations of distinguished works written in other languages.

Growing Points in Theology (Atlanta, GA: John Knox Press, 1972–). Paperback.

Kelly, Balmer H., ed., *The Layman's Bible Commentary* (Atlanta, GA: John Knox Press, 1959–64), 25 vols.

Manson, T. W., et al., eds. *Studies in Biblical Theology* (London: S.C.M. Press Ltd.). Monographs on special topics.

Marsh, John, and C. A. Richardson, eds., *Torch Bible Commentaries* (London: S.C.M. Press Ltd., 1952 onwards). A series designed primarily for the general reader.

Plummer, Alfred, et al., eds., *The International Critical Commentary* (New York: Charles Scribner's Sons 1895–1951). In production for over half a century, this series continues to provide a valuable tool for technical study.

Wright, G. Ernest, et al., eds., *The Old Testament Library* (Philadelphia: The Westminster Press). Contributors to this series are scholars of international standing, and their work incorporates knowledge hitherto accessible only in foreign languages or in technical articles and monographs.

Atlases

Aharoni, Yohanan, and Michael Avi-Yonah, *The Macmillan Bible Atlas*, rev. ed. (New York: Macmillan Publishing Co., Inc., 1977). One of the most detailed atlases available.

Atlas of the Bible Lands (Maplewood, NJ: Hammond Incorporated, 1959). Available in an inexpensive paperback edition.

Grollenberg, L. H., *Atlas of the Bible*, Joyce M. H. Reid and H. H. Rowley, trans. and eds. (New York: Thomas Nelson Inc., 1956).

Kraeling, Emil G., *Rand McNally Bible Atlas* (New York: Rand McNally & Company, 1956).

May, Herbert G., *Oxford Bible Atlas*, rev. ed. (New York: Oxford University Press, Inc., 1974). Paperback. A good student atlas, containing concise historical and archaeological data.

Wright, G. Ernest, and Floyd V. Filson, eds., *The Westminster Historical Atlas to the Bible*, rev. ed. (Philadelphia: The Westminster Press, 1956). An older, standard work; still valuable.

Ancient Extrabiblical Sources

Beyerlin, Walter, ed., *Near Eastern Religious Texts Relating to the Old Testament*, John Bowden, trans. (Philadelphia: The Westminster Press, 1978). Contains selections, some recently discovered, from writings of ancient nonbiblical religions.

Pritchard, James B., ed., *The Ancient Near East: An Anthology of Texts and Pictures* (Princeton, NJ: Princeton University Press, 1965), paperback, and *The Ancient Near East, Volume II: A New Anthology of Texts and Pictures* (Princeton, NJ: Princeton University Press, 1975). Paperback. These two volumes contain selections from the two following works and provide handy student sourcebooks for ancient texts and artifacts relating to the Old Testament.

———, ed., *The Ancient Near East in Pictures Relating to the Old Testament*, 2nd ed. (Princeton, NJ: Princeton University Press, 1969). Pictures of important artifacts relating to the Old Testament.

———, ed., *Ancient Near Eastern Texts Relating to the Old Testament*, 3rd ed. (Princeton, NJ: Princeton University Press, 1969). The most complete collection of extrabiblical texts relating to the Old Testament. An indispensable source for Old Testament study.

Thomas, D. Winton, ed., *Documents from Old Testament Times* (New York: Thomas Nelson, Inc., 1958). Paperback: Harper and Row Torchbooks, 1961.

Though containing fewer texts and pictures than the Pritchard volumes, this work includes useful editorial notes.

Journals

The Bible Today. A Catholic periodical designed for general readers. Six issues annually.

Biblica. A technical journal on the Bible published quarterly by the Pontifical Biblical Institute of Rome.

The Biblical Archaeologist. Published quarterly by the American Schools of Oriental Research to keep the general reader abreast of archaeological discoveries relating to the Bible.

The Biblical Archaeology Review. A quarterly publication featuring articles and news items for the nonprofessional.

Bulletin of the American Schools of Oriental Research. Published quarterly, this bulletin treats the more technical aspects of biblical archaeology.

Bulletin of the Israel Exploration Society. Reports on current archaeological excavations in Israel.

The Catholic Biblical Quarterly. A leading biblical journal, generally technical; not restricted to Catholic contributors.

The Expository Times. A Scottish journal which includes a limited number of nontechnical articles on biblical topics.

Hebrew Union College Annual. Contains technical and nontechnical articles.

Interpretation: A Journal of Bible and Theology. Scholarly, but generally nontechnical, articles on the Bible and biblical theology. Published quarterly.

Israel Exploration Journal. An important Israeli journal, containing articles in Hebrew and English on archaeological research in Israel.

Journal of the American Academy of Religion. A leading journal devoted to the study of religion in general. Contains some articles on the Bible.

Journal for the Study of the Old Testament. A British journal published quarterly, designed to facilitate scholarly communication among those engaged in Old Testament research and teaching.

Journal of Biblical Literature. The quarterly publication of the Society of Biblical Literature. The leading technical journal in biblical studies published in America.

Journal of Near Eastern Studies. A technical journal devoted to Near Eastern archaeology, history, religion, linguistics, and art.

Palestine Exploration Quarterly. A journal devoted to Palestinian archaeology.

Revue biblique. A leading French journal which publishes a few articles in English.

Revue de Qumran. Publishes articles in various languages on the Qumran Scrolls and related concerns.

Vetus Testamentum. Publishes articles in German, French, and English, both technical and general, on Old Testament subjects. Issued quarterly.

Zeitschrift für die Alttestamentliche Wissenschaft. A leading technical journal, the articles of which are chiefly in German.

Archaeology and Near Eastern Backgrounds

Albright, William F., *Archaeology and the Religion of Israel*, 2nd ed. (Baltimore, MD: The Johns Hopkins University Press, 1946). Paperback: Doubleday Anchor, 1969. A work by the renowned founder of "the Albright school" of archaeological interpretation.

————, *The Archaeology of Palestine*, rev. ed. (New York: Penguin Books, 1961). Paperback. A standard work of the recent past that still has value.

Amiran, Ruth, *Ancient Pottery of the Holy Land* (New Brunswick, NJ: Rutgers University Press, 1970). A survey of Palestinian pottery styles from the Neolithic through the Iron ages.

Archaeology (Jerusalem: Keter Publishing House, 1974). Paperback. Succinct descriptions of Palestinian sites; originally published in the *Encyclopaedia Judaica*. A convenient handbook for the student.

Cornfeld, Gaalyah, *Archaeology of the Bible: Book by Book* (New York: Harper & Row, Publishers, 1976). A clearly written survey that relates archaeological data to each book of the Bible. Illustrated.

Finegan, Jack, *Light from the Ancient Past*. 2nd ed. (Princeton, NJ: Princeton University Press, 1960). A well-written work, which retains its usefulness even if dated in some areas.

Frank, Harry T., *Bible, Archaeology, and Faith* (Nashville, TN: Abingdon Press, 1971). A clear survey of archaeological data arranged according to the biblical history.

————, *Discovering the Biblical World* (New York: Harper & Row, Publishers, 1975). A popularly written account of biblical history, illustrated with archaeological data and lavish color photos and maps.

Freedman, David Noel, and Edward F. Campbell, Jr. *The Biblical Archaeologist Reader*, 2 and 3 (Garden City, NY: Doubleday Anchor, 1964 and 1970). Paperback. Valuable articles selected from issues of the *Biblical Archaeologist*. See Wright, below, for first volume in the series.

————, and Jonas C. Greenfield, eds., *New Directions in Biblical Archaeology* (Garden City, NY: Doubleday & Company, Inc., 1969). Also in paperback (Doubleday Anchor, 1971).

Glueck, Nelson, *Rivers in the Desert: A History of the Negeb* (New York: Farrar, Straus & Giroux, Inc., 1959). Also in paperback (Grove Press, Inc., 1960).

Gray, John, *Archaeology and the Old Testament World* (New York: Thomas Nelson Inc., 1962). Paperback: Harper Torchbooks, 1965.

Harrison, R. K., *The Archaeology of the Old Testament* (London: The English Universities Press, 1963). Paperback: Harper Chapel Books, 1966.

Jerusalem Revealed (Jerusalem: The Israel Exploration Society, 1975). Succinct descriptions and illustrations of archaeological discoveries in Jerusalem between 1968 and 1974.

Kenyon, Kathleen, *Archaeology in the Holy Land*, 3rd ed. (New York: Praeger Publishers Inc., 1970). Paperback. An important basic survey of Palestinian archaeology (including prehistorical phases) by an eminent British archaeologist.

————, *The Bible and Recent Archaeology* (London: Colonnade Books, 1978). A concise summary of recent archaeological findings relating to biblical history, written shortly before the author's death. Also in paperback (Atlanta, GA: John Knox Press, 1978).

————, *Digging Up Jerusalem* (London: Ernest Benn Limited, 1974). A record of the history and results of excavations in Jerusalem with emphasis on the author's own work there in the 1960s. Retraces and supplements the material in *Jerusalem: Excavating 3000 Years of History*. Available in paperback.

————, *Jerusalem: Excavating 3000 Years of History* (New York: McGraw-Hill Book Company, 1967). A popularly written and well illustrated description of archaeological finds in Jerusalem through the mid-1960s.

————, *Royal Cities of the Old Testament* (New York: Schocken Books, Inc., 1971). Paperback. A summary description of finds at Jerusalem, Samaria, Megiddo, Hazor, and Gezer, as related to social, political, and cultural backgrounds.

Landay, Jerry M., *Silent Cities, Sacred Stones* (London: Weidenfeld and Nicolson, 1971). A concise, attractively written and illustrated survey of Palestinian archaeology, including the pre-Israelite era.

Lapp, Paul W., *Biblical Archaeology and History* (New York: William Collins & World Publishing Co., Inc., 1969). Evaluates the role of archaeology in interpreting biblical history.

Magnusson, Magnus, *Archaeology of the Bible* (New York: Simon & Schuster, Inc., 1977). An interestingly written work, up-to-date and attractively illustrated.

Mazar, Benjamin, *The Mountain of the Lord* (Garden City, NY: Doubleday & Company, Inc., 1975). Describes and illustrates with lavish photos the archaeological history of the Temple Mount. Written by the Israeli director of recent excavations at the site.

Noth, Martin, *The Old Testament World*, Victor I. Gruhn, trans. (Philadelphia: Fortress Press, 1966).

Pfeiffer, Charles F., ed., *The Biblical World* (Grand Rapids, MI: Baker Book House, 1966). A useful dictionary of Biblical Archaeology.

Pritchard, James B., *Archaeology and the Old Testament* (Princeton, NJ: Princeton University Press, 1958). Contains highly interesting accounts of the major episodes in the history of biblical archaeology.

————, *Gibeon, Where the Sun Stood Still* (Princeton, NJ: Princeton University Press, 1962). Paperback. The story of the excavation of Gibeon (el-Jib), interestingly related and illustrated by the excavator.

Sanders, James A., ed., *Near Eastern Archaeology in the Twentieth Century* (Garden City, NY: Doubleday & Company, Inc., 1970). Essays, chiefly technical, on aspects of biblical archaeology.

Schoville, Keith N., *Biblical Archaeology in Focus* (Grand Rapids, MI: Baker Book House, 1978). A clearly written introduction to the field, organized according to topics and sites.

Shanks, Hershel, *The City of David* (Washington, DC: The Biblical Archaeology Society, 1973). Paperback. A clear, succinct presentation of archaeological finds in Jerusalem relating to the Old Testament period.

Thomas, D. Winton, ed., *Archaeology and Old Testament Study* (Oxford: Clarendon Press, 1967). The Jubilee Volume of the Society for Old Testament Study. A comprehensive work, containing survey descriptions of twenty-five sites in the Near East, contributed by European, American, and Israeli scholars.

Williams, Walter G., *Archaeology in Biblical Research* (Nashville, TN: Abingdon Press, 1965). Contains clear descriptions of methodology.

Wright, G. Ernest, ed., *The Bible and the Ancient Near East* (Garden City, NY: Doubleday & Company, Inc., 1961). A valuable collection of essays evaluating the impact of recent archaeological findings upon biblical study. Paperbacks: Doubleday Anchor, 1965.

Wright, G. Ernest, *Biblical Archaeology,* 2nd ed. (Philadelphia: The Westminster Press, 1962). Also in abridged paperback (Westminster, 1960). Although in need of up-dating, one of the best works in the field by a leading American scholar of the Albright school.

———, and David N. Freedman, eds., *The Biblical Archaeologist Reader* (Garden City, NY: Doubleday Anchor, 1961). Paperback. The first in a series. See Freedman and Campbell, above.

Ancient Israel's Cultural and Religious Setting

Eliade, Mircea, *Cosmos and History: The Myth of the Eternal Return* (New York: Harper Torchbooks, 1954). Paperback. This and the following volume are significant comparative studies of ancient myth and ritual.

———, *The Sacred and the Profane: The Nature of Religion* (New York: Harper Torchbooks, 1961). Paperback.

Frankfurt, H., H. A. Frankfurt, et al., *The Intellectual Adventure of Ancient Man* (Chicago: University of Chicago Press, 1946). Also in paperback as *Before Philosophy* (Penguin Books, 1949). A classic study of ancient Mesopotamian and Egyptian thought patterns which both influenced and contrasted with Hebrew thought.

Gaster, Theodor H., *Myth, Legend, and Custom in the Old Testament* (New York: Harper & Row Publishers, 1969). Also in paperback (Harper Torchbooks, 1975). A valuable expansion of Sir James Frazer's earlier work, which relates extrabiblical folklore to common elements in the Old Testament.

———, *Thespis: Ritual, Myth, and Drama in the Ancient Near East* (New York: Abelard Schuman, 1950). Also in paperback (Harper Torchbooks, 1961).

Moscati, Sabatino, *The Face of the Ancient Orient* (Garden City, NY: Doubleday Anchor, 1962). Paperback.

Ringgren, Helmer, *Religions of the Ancient Near East,* John Sturdy, trans. (Philadelphia: The Westminster Press, 1973).

Van der Leeuw, G., *Religion in Essence and Manifestation,* J. E. Turner, trans. (London: George Allen & Unwin Ltd., 1938). Also in paperback (Harper Torchbooks, 1963).

The History of Israel

Albright, William F., *The Biblical Period from Abraham to Ezra* (Pittsburgh, PA: Biblical Colloquium, 1950). Also in paperback (Harper Torchbooks, 1965). A concise history of ancient Israel, written late in the career of the famous author.

Avi-Yonah, Michael, ed., *A History of the Holy Land* (New York: Macmillan Publishing Co., Inc., 1969). Lavishly illustrated and clearly written summary of life in Israel from prehistoric to modern times.

Bright, John, *A History of Israel,* 2nd ed. (Philadelphia: The Westminster Press, 1972). Shares with the work of Martin Noth in being one of the two most widely used histories of Israel available in English. Characterized by a clear, readable style and generally conservative positions, reflective of the Albright school.

549

Bruce, F. F., *Israel and the Nations: From the Exodus to the Fall of the Second Temple* (Grand Rapids, MI: Wm. B. Eerdmans, 1963). Paperback.

De Vaux, Roland, *The Early History of Israel*, David Smith, trans. (Philadelphia: The Westminster Press, 1978). A first-rate history of early Israel from its beginnings through the period of the Judges by an esteemed Dominican biblical scholar.

Ehrlich, Ernst Ludwig, *A Concise History of Israel*, James Barr, trans. (London: Darton, Longman and Todd, 1962). Also in paperback (Harper Torchbooks, 1965).

Gottwald, Norman K., *The Tribes of Yahweh; A Sociology of the Religion of Liberated Israel, 1250–1050* B.C.E. (Maryknoll, NY: Orbis Books, 1979). Also in paperback. A pioneering work which applies sociological methodology to the study of the premonarchical Israelite tribes. Interprets the occupation of Canaan as a peasants' revolt and corrects older conceptions of pastoral nomadism.

Hayes, John H., and J. Maxwell Miller, eds., *Israelite and Judaean History* (Philadelphia: The Westminster Press, 1977). A valuable work by leading scholars, assessing current interpretations of Israelite history during the Old Testament phases. Includes excellent bibliographies and summaries of scholarly positions.

Herrmann, Siegfried, *A History of Israel in Old Testament Times*, John Bowden, trans. (Philadelphia: Fortress Press, 1975). An English translation of a first-rate 1973 German work. Although not as detailed and comprehensive as the histories of Bright and Noth, it includes evaluations of some of the more recent data.

Mendenhall, George E., "Biblical History in Transition," *The Bible and the Ancient Near East*, G. Ernest Wright, ed. (New York: Doubleday Anchor, 1965), pp. 27–58.

Noth, Martin, *The History of Israel*, S. Godman, trans., rev. by P. R. Ackroyd, 2nd ed. (New York: Harper & Row Publishers, 1960). A major, original, and highly influential work by a leading German scholar.

Orlinsky, Harry M., *Ancient Israel*, 2nd ed. (Ithaca, NY: Cornell University Press, 1960). Paperback. A brief but useful summary of ancient Israel's history.

Biblical Criticism; Its Methodology and Recent History

Alonso-Schökel, Luis, S. J., *Understanding Biblical Research* (New York: Herder and Herder, 1963).

Anderson, G. W., "Some Aspects of the Uppsala School of Old Testament Study," *Harvard Theological Review*, XLIII (1950), pp. 239–256. A discussion of the so-called Scandinavian school of Old Testament study and its emphasis on the oral history of traditions.

———, ed., *Tradition and Interpretation* (Oxford: Clarendon Press, 1979). Essays by members of the Society for Old Testament Study, consisting primarily of British scholars.

Bright, John, *Early Israel in Recent History Writing* (London: S.C.M. Press, 1956). A discussion of method in the study of ancient Israelite history, delineating differences between the American Albright school and the German tradition-history approach of Martin Noth.

Childs, Brevard S., *Biblical Theology in Crisis* (Philadelphia: The Westminster Press, 1970). Includes the author's advocacy and explanation of canonical criticism as a method of biblical interpretation.

550

Clements, Ronald E., *A Century of Old Testament Study* (London: Lutterworth Press, 1976). Also in paperback: *One Hundred Years of Old Testament Interpretation* (Philadelphia: The Westminster Press, 1976).

Engnell, Ivan, *A Rigid Scrutiny: Critical Essays on the Old Testament*, John T. Willis, trans. and ed. (Nashville, TN: Vanderbilt University Press, 1969). Essays by a leading representative of the Scandinavian school.

Grant, Robert M., *A Short History of the Interpretation of the Bible*, rev. ed., (New York: Macmillan Publishing Co., Inc., 1963). A concise introduction to the methods used to interpret scripture.

Gunneweg, A.H.J., *Understanding the Old Testament*, The Old Testament Library (Philadelphia: The Westminster Press, 1978). An evaluation of the place of the Old Testament within the Christian canon of scriptures.

Habel, Norman, *Literary Criticism of the Old Testament*, Guides to Biblical Scholarship. (Philadelphia: Fortress Press, 1971). Paperback. A concise description of source criticism as a methodology in Old Testament interpretation.

Hahn, Herbert F., *The Old Testament in Modern Research*, with a recent bibliographical survey by Horace D. Hummel (Philadelphia: Fortress Press, 1966). Paperback. An enlightening survey of the several disciplines of modern criticism.

Hayes, John H., *An Introduction to Old Testament Study* (Nashville, TN: Abingdon Press, 1979). Paperback. An excellent introduction to the issues and methods of contemporary Old Testament study.

Hyatt, J. Philip, ed., *The Bible in Modern Scholarship* (Nashville, TN: Abingdon Press, 1965). Papers read at the 100th meeting of the Society of Biblical Literature.

Interpretation, XXVII, 4 (1973). Entire issue devoted to articles on form criticism.

Interpretation, XXVIII, 2 (1974). Entire issue devoted to structuralism as a method of biblical interpretation.

Jackson, Jared J., and Martin Kessler, eds., *Rhetorical Criticism: Essays in Honor of James Muilenburg*, Pittsburgh Theological Monograph Series I (Pittsburgh, PA: Pickwick Press, 1974). For a brief introduction to the method of rhetorical criticism, see especially the introductory essay by Bernhard W. Anderson, "The New Frontier of Rhetorical Criticism."

Klein, Ralph W., *Textual Criticism of the Old Testament: The Septuagint After Qumran*, Guides to Biblical Scholarship (Philadelphia: Fortress Press, 1974). Paperback.

Knight, Douglas A., *The Traditions of Israel*, S.B.L. Dissertation Series 9 (Missoula, MT: Society of Biblical Literature, 1973). Paperback. A study of the history of tradition-criticism in Old Testament research.

Koch, Klaus, *The Growth of the Biblical Tradition; the Form-Critical Method*, S. M. Cupitt, trans. (New York: Charles Scribner's Sons, 1969). An introduction to the broad field of form criticism.

Kraeling, Emil G., *The Old Testament Since the Reformation* (New York: Harper & Row, Publishers, 1955). Also in paperback (Schocken Books, Inc., 1969). A perceptive survey of Christian attitudes toward the Old Testament from Luther to the mid-twentieth century.

Krentz, Edgar, *The Historical-Critical Method*, Guides to Biblical scholarship (Philadelphia: Fortress Press, 1975). Paperback.

551

Levie, Jeann, S. J., *The Bible, Word of God in Words of Men* (New York: P. J. Kenedy & Sons, 1961).

Miller, J. Maxwell, *The Old Testament and the Historian*, Guides to Biblical Scholarship (Philadelphia: Fortress Press, 1976). Paperback. A concise discussion of methodology in interpreting the Old Testament as history.

Muilenburg, James, "Form Criticism and Beyond," *JBL*, LXXXVIII (1969), pp. 1–18. A description of rhetorical criticism by the "father" of the method.

Nielsen, Edward, *Oral Tradition*, Studies in Biblical Theology, No. 11 (Naperville, IL: Alec R. Allenson). Available in paperback. A classic statement of the role of oral tradition in Old Testament composition by a representative of the Scandinavian school.

Rast, Walter E., *Tradition History and the Old Testament*, Guides to Biblical Scholarship (Philadelphia: Fortress Press, 1972). Paperback.

Robertson, David, *The Old Testament and the Literary Critic*, Guides to Biblical Scholarship (Philadelphia: Fortress Press, 1977). Paperback.

Rowley, Harold H., ed., *The Old Testament and Modern Study* (New York: Oxford University Press, Inc., 1951). Highly useful articles contributed by leading scholars. Also in paperback (Oxford U.P., 1961).

Soulen, Richard N., *Handbook of Biblical Criticism* (Atlanta, GA: John Knox Press, 1976). Paperback. A handy reference work which defines technical terms, phrases, and names used in the field of biblical interpretation.

Terrien, Samuel, "History of the Interpretation of the Bible; Modern Period," *IB*, Vol. I (Nashville, TN: Abingdon Press, 1952), pp. 127–141.

Tucker, Gene M., *Form Criticism of the Old Testament*, Guides to Biblical Scholarship (Philadelphia: Fortress Press, 1971). Paperback. A concise introduction to the methods of form criticism.

Wright, G. Ernest, ed., *The Bible and the Ancient Near East* (Garden City, NY: Doubleday & Company, Inc., 1961). Also in paperback (Doubleday Anchor, 1965).

Introductions to the Old Testament

Anderson, Bernhard, *Understanding the Old Testament*, 3rd ed. (Englewood Cliffs, NJ: Prentice-Hall, Inc., 1975). A standard work that pioneered the approach to Old Testament literature and faith through the history of ancient Israel. Employs the Exodus event as the beginning point.

Bentzen, Aage, *Introduction to the Old Testament*, 2 vols. in 1 (Copenhagen: G. E. C. Gad, 1952). One of the leading technical introductions; emphasizes the role of oral tradition.

Childs, Brevard S., *Introduction to the Old Testament as Scripture* (Philadelphia: Fortress Press, 1979). A fresh and provocative approach, centering attention on the canonical process which shaped the Old Testament books into an authoritative collection.

Driver, S. R., *Introduction to the Literature of the Old Testament*, rev. ed. (New York: Charles Scribner's Sons, 1913). Available in paperback (Meridian Books, 1956). This technical work, though old, still has value, particularly as a record of source critical analysis earlier in the century.

Eissfeldt, Otto, *The Old Testament: An Introduction*, Peter R. Ackroyd, trans. (New York: Harper & Row, Publishers, 1965). A detailed and technical work organized according to a literary (canonical) arrangement. First written by Eissfeldt, a leading German scholar, in 1934, this introduction has taken its place in the forefront of Old Testament texts. The English translation is based on the third revision of the work.

Fohrer, Georg (initiated by Ernst Sellin), *Introduction to the Old Testament,* David E. Green, trans. (Nashville, TN: Abingdon Press, 1968). A thoroughly rewritten edition of Sellin's 1910 introduction. A technical and highly significant literary and form-critical work.

Gottwald, Norman, *A Light to the Nations* (New York: Harper & Row, Publishers, 1959). A basic, well-written, introduction that displays a fine appreciation for literary style; arranged according to historical sequence.

Harrelson, Walter, *Interpreting the Old Testament* (New York: Holt, Rinehart and Winston, 1964). A work that follows a strict canonical sequence; characterized by thorough and judicious interpretations of every Old Testament book.

Hayes, John H., *An Introduction to Old Testament Study* (Nashville, TN: Abingdon Press, 1979). Paperback. Not intended as an introduction to the full gamut of Old Testament concerns, this work offers perceptive descriptions of current scholarly methods and interpretative positions in the broad areas of the discipline.

Humphreys, W. Lee, *Crisis and Story: Introduction to the Old Testament* (Palo Alto, CA: Mayfield Publishing Company, 1979). Relates the formation of the Old Testament to the three events of David's empire-building, the Babylonian Exile, and the Roman conquest.

Kaiser, Otto, *Introduction to the Old Testament: A Presentation of its Results and Problems,* John Sturdy, trans. (Minneapolis, MN: Augsburg Publishing House, 1975). A major technical work, translated from the 1970 revised second edition of the German original, and incorporating further revisions by the author to 1973.

Kuntz, J. Kenneth, *The People of Ancient Israel* (New York: Harper & Row, Publishers, 1974). Paperback. A balanced treatment of Israelite history, literature, and religion, organized according to history.

Ohlsen, Woodrow, *Perspectives on Old Testament Literature* (New York: Harcourt Brace Jovanovich, Inc., 1978). Paperback. A collection of interpretative readings designed for the study of the Old Testament as literature.

Pfeiffer, Robert H., *Introduction to the Old Testament,* rev. ed. (New York: Harper & Row, Publishers, 1949). The most detailed literary-critical introduction produced by American scholarship; a classic in the field. Available in an abridged paperback edition.

Robert, André, and André Feuillet, eds. *Introduction to the Old Testament,* Patrick W. Skehan et al., trans., 2 vols. (Garden City, NY: Doubleday & Company Image Books, 1970). A significant technical work written by a group of distinguished Roman Catholic scholars. Paperback.

Rowley, Harold H., *The Growth of the Old Testament* (London: Hutchinson Publishing Group, 1950). A concise literary survey of the Old Testament by an outstanding British scholar. Also in paperback (Harper Torchbooks, 1963).

Sandmel, Samuel, *The Hebrew Scriptures: An Introduction to Their Literature and Religious Ideas* (New York: Alfred A. Knopf, Inc., 1963). An introduction for the general reader written by an eminent Jewish scholar.

————, *The Enjoyment of Scripture* (New York: Oxford University Press, Inc., 1972). Also in paperback (Oxford U.P., 1966). A book for the beginner, written in an appealing style.

Soggin, J. Alberto, *Introduction to the Old Testament*, John Bowden, trans. The Old Testament Library (Philadelphia: The Westminster Press, 1976). A significant and balanced technical work, clearly written. Translated from the revised second Italian edition of 1974.

Weiser, Artur, *The Old Testament: Its Formation and Development*, D. M. Barton, trans. (New York: Association Press, 1961). A fine technical introduction, presenting the balanced approach of an outstanding German scholar. Organized according to a canonical arrangement.

Old Testament Religion, Theology, and Culture

Albrektson, Bertil, *History and the Gods* (Lund, Sweden: C W K Gleerup, 1967). Challenges the view that Israel's conception of God acting in history was unique in ancient Near Eastern religion.

Albright, William F., *From the Stone Age to Christianity*, 2nd ed. (Baltimore, MD: The Johns Hopkins University Press, 1946). See entry under "The History of Israel" above.

Alt, Albrecht, *Essays on Old Testament History and Religion*, R. A. Wilson, trans. (New York: Doubleday & Company, Inc., 1967). Also in paperback (Doubleday Anchor, 1967).

Anderson, Bernhard W., ed., *The Old Testament and Christian Faith* (New York: Harper & Row, Publishers, 1963). An important collection of essays by outstanding scholars treating issues of theological significance in Old Testament interpretation.

Barr, James, *The Bible in the Modern World* (New York: Harper & Row, Publishers, 1973). Contains wide-ranging perspectives on methods of relating biblical meanings to modern life.

————, *Old and New in Interpretation* (New York: Harper & Row, Publishers, 1966). A provocative work which takes issue with some characteristic emphases in recent biblical theology, including "the acts of God in history."

————, *The Semantics of Biblical Language* (New York: Oxford University Press, Inc. 1961). Takes issue with the book by Boman (below) and the use of linguistic phenomena to contrast Greek and Hebrew thought.

Boman, Thorlief, *Hebrew Thought Compared with Greek*, Jules L. Moreau, trans. (Philadelphia: The Westminister Press, 1960).

Brueggemann, Walter, *The Land*, Overtures to Biblical Theology (Philadelphia: Fortress Press, 1977). Paperback. The study of an important biblical theme and symbol.

Childs, Brevard, *Biblical Theology in Crisis* (Philadelphia: The Westminster Press, 1970). Details the history and weaknesses of "the biblical theology movement" in America and proposes the alternative of "canonical criticism."

Crenshaw, James L., and John T. Willis, eds., *Essays in Old Testament Ethics* (New York: KTAV Publishing House, 1974).

Cross, Frank M., *Canaanite Myth and Hebrew Epic* (Cambridge, MA: Harvard University Press, 1973). Significant essays on the history of the religion of Israel.

Denton, Robert C., *The Knowledge of God in Ancient Israel* (New York: Seabury Press, Inc., 1968).

———, *Preface to Old Testament Theology*, rev. ed. (New York: Seabury Press, Inc., 1963). A succinct introduction to the history, nature, and method of Old Testament theology.

De Vaux, Roland, *Ancient Israel: Its Life and Institutions*, J. McHugh, trans. (New York: McGraw-Hill Book Company, 1961). A comprehensive survey of ancient Israel's social and religious institutions. An excellent and unparalleled work. Also in paperback (McGraw-Hill, 1965).

Eichrodt, Walther, *Theology of the Old Testament*, Vol. 1, J. A. Baker, trans., from the 6th German edition (Philadelphia: The Westminister Press, 1961); Vol. II (1967). One of the two most influencial Old Testament theologies of this century, the other being that of von Rad (below). Uses covenant as the organizing principle.

———, *Man in the Old Testament*, Studies in Biblical Theology, no. 4, K. and R. Gregor Smith, trans. (London: S.C.M. Press, 1956).

Fohrer, Georg, *History of Israelite Religion*, David E. Green, trans. (Nashville, TN: Abingdon Press, 1972). A comprehensive study of Israel's religion in its historical and cultural context.

Fromm, Erich, *You Shall Be as Gods* (Greenwich, CT: Fawcett Publications, 1966). Paperback. An appeal for a humanistic interpretation of the Old Testament.

Gaster, Theodor H., *Myth, Legend, and Custom in the Old Testament* (New York: Harper & Row, Publishers, 1969). Also in paperback. A wealth of comparative folklore and mythology applied to the interpretation of the Old Testament.

Gelin, Albert, *The Religion of Israel*, Twentieth Century Encyclopedia of Catholicism, J. R. Foster, trans. (New York: Hawthorn Books, Inc., 1959).

Harrleson, Walter, *From Fertility Cult to Worship* (Garden City, NY: Doubleday Anchor, 1970). A reassessment of the worship of ancient Israel.

Hasel, Gerhard F., *Old Testament Theology: Basic Issues in the Current Debate*, rev. ed. (Grand Rapids, MI: Wm. B. Eerdmans, 1975). Paperback. An excellent introduction to the current issues and trends in the discipline of Old Testament theology.

Hillers, Delbert R., *Covenant: The History of a Biblical Idea* (Baltimore, MD: The Johns Hopkins University Press, 1969). Paperback. Stresses the influence of ancient treaty forms and varying expressions of the covenant idea in the Old Testament.

Irwin, W. A., *The Old Testament: Keystone of Human Culture* (New York: Abelard-Schuman, 1952).

Jacob, Edmond, *Theology of the Old Testament*, A. W. Heathcote and P. J. Allcock, trans. (New York: Harper & Row, Publishers, 1958).

Johnson, Aubrey R., *The Vitality of the Individual in the Thought of Ancient Israel* (Cardiff: University of Wales Press, 1949). An essay on ancient Hebrew psychology.

———, *The One and the Many in the Israelite Conception of God*, 2nd ed. (Cardiff: University of Wales Press, 1961).

Kaufmann, Yehezkel, *The Religion of Israel*, Moshe Greenberg, trans., and abrd., (Chicago: University of Chicago Press, 1960). Also in paperback (Schocken

Books, Inc., 1972). A sensitive and provocative work by a highly original Jewish scholar, whose positions deviate at many points from majority opinion. Stresses the discontinuity between early Hebrew thought and other ancient religions.

Knight, George A. F., *A Christian Theology of the Old Testament* (London: S.C.M. Press, 1959).

Kohler, Ludwig, *Old Testament Theology*, A. S. Todd, trans. (Philadelphia: The Westminster Press, 1958).

Laurin, Robert B., ed., *Contemporary Old Testament Theologians* (Valley Forge, PA: Judson Press, 1970). Summary essays on the theologies of several important Old Testament theologians.

McCarthy, Dennis J., *Old Testament Covenant: A Survey of Current Opinions* (Oxford: Basil Blackwell, 1972). Also in paperback (John Knox Press, 1972). A clear, succinct examination of a pivotal Old Testament theme.

McKenzie, John L., *A Theology of the Old Testament* (Garden City, NY: Doubleday & Company, Inc., 1974). A clear presentation which avoids compressing Old Testament thought into an artificial system.

Mendenhall, George E., *Law and Covenant in Israel and the Ancient Near East* (Pittsburgh, PA: Biblical Colloquium, 1955). An important study proposing the relevance of ancient suzerainty treaties to patterns in early Israel's faith.

Morgenstern, Julian, *The Fire upon the Altar* (New York: Quadrangle/The New York Times Book Co., 1963).

Mowinckel, Sigmund, *He That Cometh*, G. W. Anderson, trans. (Nashville, TN: Abingdon Press, 1956). One of the most systematic studies available on Old Testament eschatology and messianism.

Muilenburg, James, "The History of the Religion of Israel," *IB*, Vol. I, pp. 292–348.

———, *The Way of Israel* (New York: Harper & Row, Publishers, 1961). Also in paperback (Harper Torchbooks, 1965).

Newman, Murray, *The People of the Covenant* (Nashville, TN: Abingdon Press, 1962).

Noth, Martin, *The Laws in the Pentateuch and Other Studies*, D. R. Ap-Thomas, trans. (Philadelphia: Fortress Press, 1967).

Otwell, John H., *And Sarah Laughed* (Philadelphia: The Westminster Press, 1977). A study of the status of women in the Old Testament which contends for the significance of their role.

Pedersen, Johannes, *Israel, Its Life and Culture* (New York: Oxford University Press, Inc.), Vols. I–II (1926); Vols III–IV (1940). The most detailed study of ancient Hebrew psychology.

Rad, Gerhard von, Vol. I: *The Theology of Israel's Historical Traditions*, D. M. G. Stalker, trans (New York: Harper & Row, Publishers, 1962); Vol. II: *The Theology of Israel's Prophetic Traditions* (1965). Shares with Eichrodt (above) the distinction of being one of the two most influential Old Testament theologies of this century. Regards sacred history as the definitive element in Israel's faith.

Renckens, Henry, *The Religion of Israel*, N. B. Smith, trans. (New York: Sheed & Ward, Inc., 1966).

Ringgren, Helmer, *Israelite Religion*, David E. Green, trans., (Philadelphia: Fortress Press, 1966). A descriptive account of ancient Israel's religion, arranged chronologically.

556

————, *The Messiah in the Old Testament*, Studies in Biblical Theology, no. 18 (Chicago: Alec R. Allenson, 1956).

Robinson, H. Wheeler, *Inspiration and Revelation in the Old Testament* (Oxford: Clarendon Press, 1946). Also in paperback (Oxford Paperbacks, 1962). An old but still valuable analysis of Hebrew thought by an outstanding British scholar.

Rowley, Harold H., *The Biblical Doctrine of Election* (London: Lutterworth Press, 1950).

————, *Worship in Ancient Israel: Its Forms and Meaning* (Philadelphia: Fortress Press, 1967).

Snaith, Norman, *Distinctive Ideas of the Old Testament* (London: Epworth Press, 1947). Also in paperback (Shocken Books, Inc., 1964).

Vriezen, Thomas, *An Outline of Old Testament Theology*, S. Neuijen, trans. (Oxford: Basil Blackwell, 1958).

Westermann, Claus, ed., *Essays on Old Testament Hermeneutics*, James Luther Mays, trans. and ed. (Richmond, VA: John Knox Press, 1963). This book and the one by Anderson (above) provide collections of some of the most important essays on Old Testament hermeneutics written in the 1950s and 60s.

Wolff, Hans Walter, *Anthropology of the Old Testament*, trans. by Margaret Kohl (Philadelphia: Fortress Press, 1974). An important study of Old Testament language and concepts concerning man and society.

Wright, G. Ernest, "The Faith of Israel," *IB*, Vol. I, pp. 349–389.

————, *God Who Acts*, Studies in Biblical Theology, no. 8 (London: S.C.M. Press, 1952). One of the early statements in English of the salvation-history approach to Old Testament religious faith.

————, *The Old Testament Against Its Environment*, Studies in Biblical Theology, no. 2 (London: S.C.M. Press, 1950).

————, *The Old Testament and Theology* (New York: Harper & Row, Publishers, 1969). The author's last major work; details some modifications in his later thought.

Young, Edward J., *The Study of Old Testament Theology Today* (Westwood, NH: Fleming H. Revell Company, 1959).

Zimmerli, Walther, *Man and His Hope in the Old Testament*. Studies in Biblical Theology, 2nd series (Naperville, IL: Alec R. Allenson, 1968). Paperback.

————, *Old Testament Theology in Outline*, David E. Green, trans. (Atlanta, GA: John Knox Press, 1978). An important work which, by employing the concept of Yahweh as its central focus, does justice to the multiplicity of Old Testament themes.

————, *The Old Testament and the World*, John J. Scullion, S.J., trans. (Atlanta, GA: John Knox Press, 1976). Translated from the German edition of 1971. A fresh consideration of the Old Testament perspective on "worldly" concerns.

appendix

A Chronological Chart of Hebrew History in the Biblical Period *

HEBREW HISTORY	PROPHETS	LARGER NEAR EAST
EARLY BRONZE AGE C. 3000–2200 B.C.		Classical Sumerian Age 2800–2360
		Egyptian Old Kingdom 2900–2300
		Empire of Akkad 2360–2180
MIDDLE BRONZE AGE C. 2200–1550 B.C.		Ur III 2060–1950
		Amorite infiltration of Fertile Crescent
		Hammurabi c. 1728–1686
The patriarchs (Gen. 12–50)?		"Mari Age" c. 1750–1697
		Mitanni (Hurrian Kingdom) c. 1500–1370
		Hyksos rule of Egypt c. 1720–1550
LATE BRONZE AGE C. 1550–1200 B.C.		Expulsion of Hyksos from Egypt c. 1550
		Amarna Period, fourteenth century
The enslavement in Egypt (Exod. 1–13)?		Amenhotep IV c. 1370–1353
		Egyptian Nineteenth Dynasty c. 1310–1200
		Seti I c. 1309–1290
The Exodus c. 13ᵗʰ. Cen. B.C. (Exod. 14-15)?		Rameses II 1290–1224
The wilderness era c. 1290–1250 (Exod. 16–Deut. 34)?		
The conquest and settlement of Canaan c. 1250–1200 (Josh.; Jud. 1)?		
EARLY IRON AGE C. 1200–900 B.C.		
The tribal league c. 1200–1020 (Judg.; I Sam. 1–12)		Philistines settle in Palestine, twelfth century
Fall of Shiloh (after 1050)	Samuel	
The united monarchy c. 1020–922 (I Sam. 13–I Kings 11; I Chron. 10–II Chron. 9)		
Saul c. 1020–1000	Nathan	
David c. 1000–961		
Solomon c. 961–922		
Schism 922		
MIDDLE IRON AGE C. 900–600 B.C.		
The divided monarchies 922–722/721 (I Kings 12–II Kings 17; II Chron. 10–28)		

560

Kings of Judah

†1. Rehoboam 922–915
2. Abijah 915–913
3. Asa 913–873

4. Jehoshaphat 873–849

5. Jehoram 849–842

6. Ahaziah 842
   (Athaliah 842–837)
7. Joash 837–800
8. Amaziah 800–783
9. Uzziah (Azariah) 783–742

10. Jotham 742–735

11. Ahaz 735–715
   Syro-Ephraimitic crisis 735–732

The Kingdom of Judah 722–587 (II Kings 18–25; II Chron. 29–36)
12. Hezekiah 715–687/686
   Sennacherib's invasion 701
13. Manasseh 687/686–642
14. Amon 642–640
15. Josiah 640–609

Kings of Israel

1. Jeroboam I 922–901

2. Nadab 901–900
1. Baasha 900–877
2. Elah 877–876
1. Zimri 876 (7 days)
1. Omri 876–869
2. Ahab 869–850
3. Ahaziah 850–849
4. Jehoram 849–842
   Jehu's rebellion 842
1. Jehu 842–815
2. Jehoahaz 815–801
3. Jehoash 801–786
4. Jeroboam II 786–746
5. Zechariah 746–745 (6 mo.)
1. Shallum 745 (1 mo.)
1. Menahem 745–738
2. Pekahiah 738–737
1. Pekah 737–732
1. Hoshea 732–724
   Samaria falls to Assyria 722/721

Prophets

Elijah
Micaiah
Elisha

Amos
Hosea

Isaiah
Micah

Zephaniah
Nahum

Events

Pharaoh Shishak invades Palestine c. 918

Assyria grows in strength

Shalmaneser III 859–824
Battle of Qarqar 853

Hazael (of Damascus) 842–806

Tiglath-pileser III 745–727

Israel begins paying tribute to Assyria

Shalmaneser V 727–722
Sargon II 722–705

Sennacherib 705–681

Fall of Nineveh 612

HEBREW HISTORY	PROPHETS	LARGER NEAR EAST
16. Jehoahaz 609 17. Jehoiakim 609–598 18. Jehoiachin 598/597 19. Zedekiah 597–587 First deportation of Jews 597 Fall of Jerusalem and second deportation of Jews 587 Third deportation of Jews c. 582	Habakkuk Jeremiah	Nebuchadrezzar 605/604–562 Babylon rules the Near East 605–539
LATE IRON (PERSIAN) AGE C. 600–300 B.C. The Babylonian exile 597 (587)–538		
Cyrus' edict of 538 allowing Jews to return	Ezekiel Deutero-Isaiah	Cyrus of Persia 550–530 Cyrus takes Babylon 539 Persia rules the Near East 539–300
The Restoration 538–(Ezra-Neh.) Sheshbazzar's return c. 538 Zerubbabel rebuilds the Temple 520–515	Haggai Zachariah Malachi	Cambyses conquers Egypt 525
Nehemiah 445– Ezra 428 (?)–		Artaxerxes I 465–424 Artaxerxes II 404–358 Egypt regains freedom 401 Artaxerxes III 358–338 Egypt reconquered by Persia 342
THE HELLENISTIC PERIOD C. 300–63 B.C. (I–II Macc.) The Jews under the Ptolemies 323–198		Alexander the Great 334–323 Alexander conquers the Near East Antiochus III (the Great) 223–187 Seleucid conquest of Palestine Antiochus IV (Epiphanes) 175–163
The Jews under the Seleucids 198–165 The Maccabean Revolt 166–135 Judas 166–160 Rededication of the Temple, Dec. 164 Jonathan 160–143 Simon 143–135 The Hasmoneans 135–63		

THE ROMAN PERIOD 63 B.C.–A.D. 323
Pompey takes Jerusalem 63 B.C.
Herod the Great (King of Judea) 37 B.C.–4 B.C.
Herod Antipas (Tetrarch of Galilee 4 B.C.–A.D. 39
Philip (Tetrarch of Iturea) 4 B.C.–A.D. 34
Archaelaus (Ethnarch of Judea) 4 B.C.–A.D. 6
Procurators of Judea A.D. 6–66
War with Rome A.D. 66–73
Jerusalem and Temple destroyed A.D. 70
Fall of Masada A.D. 73

Council of Jamnia c. A.D. 90
Jewish revolt led by Bar-Cochba A.D. 132–135

Augustus (Roman emperor) 30 B.C.–
                          A.D. 14

Vespasian A.D. 69–79

Titus A.D. 79–81

* The dating scheme followed here is largely that of W. F. Albright (cf. *Bulletin of the American Schools of Oriental Research*, No. 100 [Dec. 1945], pp. 16–22).
† The number associated with each king indicates his place within his respective dynasty. Except for the brief usurpation of Athaliah, Judah had only one dynasty.

SOURCE ANALYSIS OF THE PENTATEUCH

The Primeval History (Genesis 1–11)

YAHWISTIC SOURCE (J)	ELOHISTIC SOURCE (E)	DEUTERONOMIC SOURCE (D)	PRIESTLY SOURCE (P)
			Gen. 1:1–2:4a
Gen. 2:4b–4:26			
			5:1–28
5:29			
			5:30–32
6:1–8			
			6:9–22
7:1–5, 7–10, 12, 16b–17, 22–23			7:6, 11, 13–16a, 18–21, 24
8:2b, 3a, 6–12, 13b, 20–22			8:1, 2a, 3b–5, 13a, 14–19
9:18–27			9:1–17, 28–29
10:8–19, 21, 25–30			10:1–7, 20, 22–24, 31–32
11:1–9, 28–30			11:10–27, 31–32

The Patriarchal History (Genesis 12–50)

J	E	D	P
Gen. 12:1–4a, 6–20			Gen. 12:4b–5
13:1–5, 7–11a, 13–18			13:6, 11b–12
15:1–2, 3b–4, 6–12, 17–21	Gen. 15:3a, 5, 13–16		
16:1b–2, 4–14	16:1a, 3, 15–16		
			17:1–27
18:1–19:28			
19:30–38			19:29
20:1a	20:1b–18		
21:1a, 7	21:6, 8–21, 22–34		21:1b–5
22:20–24	22:1–19		23:1–20
24:1–67			
25:1–6, 11b, 21–26a, 27–34			25:7–11a, 12–18, 19–20, 25–26b
26:1–33			26:34–35
27:1–45			27:46–28:9
28:10, 13–16, 19	28:11–12, 17–18, 20–22		
29:1–35 (with E elements)			
30:4–5, 7–16, 20–21, 24–43	30:1–3, 6, 17–19, 22–23		
31:1, 3, 17, 19a, 20–23, 25b, 27, 30a, 31, 36a, 38–40, 46–49, 51–53a	31:19b, 24–25a, 26, 28–29, 30b, 32–35, 36b–37, 41–45, 50, 53b–55		31:18
32:3–13a, 22–32	32:1–2, 13b–21		

The Patriarchal History (Genesis 12–50)

J	E	D	P
33:1–3, 6–7, 12–17, 18b	33:4–5, 8–11, 19–20		33:18a
34:1–31 (with E elements)			
35:21–22a	35:1–5, 7–8, 14, 16–20		35:6, 9–13, 15, 22b–29
			36:1–43
37:3a, 4–21, 25–28	37:3b, 22–24, 29–36		37:1–2
38:1–30			
39:1–23			
40:1	40:2–23		
41:34a, 35b, 41–45, 46b, 49, 55–57	41:1–33, 34b, 35a, 36–40, 47–48, 50–54		41:46a
42:1b, 4–5, 8–11a, 12, 27–28a, 38	42:1a, 2–3, 6–7, 11b, 13–26, 28b–37		
43:1–34			
44:1–34			
45:1, 4–5a, 16–28	45:2–3, 5b–15		
46:5b, 28–47:5a	46:1–5a		46:6–27
47:6b, 13–26, 29–31	47:5b–6a, 7–12		47:27–28
	48:1–2, 7–22		48:3–6
49:2–28			49:1, 29–33
50:1–10a, 14	50:10b–11, 15–26		50:12–13

The Egyptian Oppression and The Exodus (Exodus 1–15)

J	E	D	P
Exod. 1:8–12, 22	Exod. 1:15–21		Exod. 1:1–7, 13–14
2:1–23a (with E elements)			2:23b–25
3:1–4a, 5–8, 16–17	3:4, 9–15, 18–22		
4:1–31 (with E elements)			
5:1–23			
6:1			6:2–30
7:14–18, 20b–21a, 23–25			7:1–13, 19–20a, 21b–22
8:1–4, 8–15, 20–32			8:5–7, 16–19
9:1–7, 13–35 (with E elements)			9:8–12
10:1–29 (with E elements)			
11:1–9			11:10
12:21–23, 29–39		Exod. 12: 24–27	12:1–20, 28, 40–51
13:20–22	13:17–19	13:1–16	
14:5–7, 10–14, 19b–20, 21b, 24–25, 27b, 30–31		14:1–4, 8–9, 15–18, 21ac, 22–23, 26–27a, 28–29	
15:1–21, 22b–25		15:25b–26	15:22a, 27

The Wilderness and Sinai Covenant Traditions (Exodus 16–Numbers 36)			
J	E	D	P
			Exod. 16:1–36
Exod.17:1b–16			17:1a
	Exod.18:1–27		
19:2b, 10–25 (with E elements)	19:3–9		19:1–2a
	20:1–26		
	21:1–36		
	22:1–31		
	23:1–33		
24:12–14	24:1–11		24:15–18
			25:1–31:18
32:1a, 4–6, 15–20, 25–35	32:1b–4a 21–24	Exod. 32:7–14	
33:1–23			
34:1–35			
			35:1–40:38
			Lev. 1:1–27:34
			Num. 1:1–10:28
Num.10:29–35			
11:1–35			
12:1–16			
13:17b–20, 22–24, 26–33			13:1–17a, 21, 25
14:1b, 4, 11–25, 39–45			14:1a, 2–3, 5–10, 26–38
			15:1–41
16:1–2, 12–15, 25–34			16:3–11, 16–24, 35–50
			17:1–19:22
20:14–21			20:1–13, 22–29
21:1–25			
22:1–24:25			
			25:1–36:13

The Deuteronomic Covenant Traditions (Deuteronomy)			
J	E	D	P
		Deut. 1:1–33:29	Deut.34:1a, 7–8
		34:1b–6, 9–12	

index

OF NAMES AND SUBJECTS

index
OF BIBLICAL REFERENCES

————◆————

(Entries in *italic* indicate the principal treatment of the passage indicated.)

OLD TESTAMENT

INDEX OF BIBLICAL REFERENCES

605

INDEX OF BIBLICAL REFERENCES